LET'S GO

www.letsgo.c

W9-AXG-228

FRANCE

researcher-writers
Ama Francis
Josh McTaggart
Ned Monahan
Taylor Nickel
Joe Tobias

staff writers
Taylor Nickel
Alexandra Perloff-Giles

research manager
Joseph B. Gaspard

editors
Teresa Cotsirilos

managing editor
Marykate Jasper

CONTENTS

DISCOVER FRANCE 1
when to go   2
what to do   2
suggested itineraries   6
how to use this book   11
PARIS 13
orientation   14
accommodations   21
sights   30
food   57
nightlife   68
arts and culture   79
shopping   81
essentials   84
excursions   88
LOIRE VALLEY 91
orléans   92
blois   102
tours   107
BRITTANY AND NORMANDY 121
rennes   122
rouen   130
mont st-michel   136
caen   139
bayeux   144
d-day beaches   146
STRASBOURG 151
orientation   152
accommodations   152

sights   154
food   154
nightlife   158
arts and culture   160
shopping   161
essentials   161
LYON AND RHONE-ALPES 163
lyon   164
grenoble   181
BORDEAUX AND WINE COUNTRY 191
bordeaux   192
saint-émilion   200
graves and médoc   204
biarritz   204
arcachon   210
TOULOUSE AND MONTPELLIER 213
toulouse   214
montpellier   223
PROVENCE 233
marseille   234
avignon   250
cassis   253
la ciotat   256
orange   259
arles   262
aix-en-provence   266
NICE AND MONACO 275
nice   276
monaco   293

villefranche sur mer	304
menton	307
CÔTE D'AZUR	**313**
antibes	314
cagnes-sur-mer	321
vence	323
îles des lérins	326
biot	327
juan-les-pins	330
cannes	335
grasse	343
st-raphaël	348
st-tropez	353
ESSENTIALS	**359**
planning your trip	360
money	362
safety and health	363
getting around	365

keeping in touch	367
climate	369
measurements	371
language	371
FRANCE 101	**373**
history	374
customs and etiquette	378
the arts	379
food and drink	381
BEYOND TOURISM	**383**
studying	384
volunteering	388
working	389
INDEX	**392**
map index	396
QUICK REFERENCE	**402**

RESEARCHER-WRITERS

AMA FRANCIS. Ama is from the lovely, but little known, island of Dominica. A Caribbean childhood in the Caribbean left Ama with fabulous French skills, a love for the beach, and a taste for mangoes. Her time in France was spent researching, drinking bottles of rose wine, and getting into a steady (or dependent) relationship with *pain au chocolat*.

JOSH MCTAGGART. Josh has a surprisingly good British accent. We promise, it has nothing to do with the fact that he grew up just outside Bristol, UK. Researching the Loire Valley as well as Brussels, Bruges, and parts of the Netherlands, Josh certainly got his fill of castles. He'd like to be a spy (channeling James Bond, much?), though he sampled wine, not martinis, throughout his travels.

NED MONAHAN. Born Edward Monahan III, Ned is truly Boston's boy. A hip-hop enthusiast with a habit of befriending strangers on the street, Ned once spent a summer working on a champagne vineyard in France. When he returned to France to work for Let's Go, he knew he'd be in for a whole new experience (and certainly one with a very different final product).

TAYLOR NICKEL. From the shores of SoCal to the French Riviera 20-year-old Taylor has already traveled to over 50 countries. When he wasn't researching the best hostels in Marseille, he was working the tables at a casino in Monte Carlo or riding a scooter from Saint-Tropez to Cannes. His winning smile and enviable tan make it hard for anybody, from hotel managers to customs officials, to say no to Taylor.

JOE TOBIAS. Hailing from the Great White North, Joe is a mountain man with a poet's soul. When he isn't writing sonnets, he can be found somewhere in the wilderness of the Northeastern US. His travels for Let's Go took him to Morocco and southwestern France, allowing him to master snake charming and wine tasting.

DISCOVER

FRANCE

Think of a famous idea. Any famous idea. Or for that matter any brushstroke, article of clothing, architectural style, camera technique, great thinker that should have been medicated, or hip reason to brew a Molotov cocktail. If that idea is Western, then it is probably French (or at least hotly contested and contributed to a French intellectual movement). Your first walk around Paris will be defined by a paralyzing level of excitement. Your first party in Monaco might result in a *Hangover*-esque situation. It's no secret that young Americans "backpack" through France to lose their virginity and construct their identity at a safe distance from their parents. The successes of James Baldwin, Gertrude Stein, and Ernest Hemingway suggest that we couldn't have chosen a better spot; there is a pervading sense in France that *everything* is here.

Students might go to France to be fashionably disaffected artists in boho-chic corner cafes, but this isn't the land of berets and baguettes anymore: it's the land of sustainable energy and the 35-hour work week of a (overly?) generous welfare state. As France wrestles with the economic and cultural ramifications of a globalized world, this is also, increasingly, the country of *parkour* and veil bans, sprawling Chinatowns and the Marie Leonie case of 2004. Nowhere is the cognitive dissonance of these cultural collisions more evident than in Marseille, whose burgeoning Little Algeria encroaches upon the city's Roman ruins. In the midst if these rapid transitions, the most sacred of French traditions remain gloriously preserved—you might eat a lot of kebabs while you're here, but you can still riot against The Man in the morning and commit adultery by noon.

when to go

If you're coming to France to bum, binge and go bi (we recommend it), hit France over spring break or in the summer, when hostels overflow with exhilarated students from around the world who are doing the exact same thing. These months can get desperately hot, and they're not the best time to assimilate into French culture. French business owners generally go on vacation in August and empty out of the cities to the coast, leaving only tourists and pickpockets behind. Still, folks flock to France in the summer for a reason. A series of quintessentially French events take place in June, including the French Open and the Paris Jazz Festival (see **Paris,** p.13), and the rollicking vibe of the French Riviera in summer is simply incomparable.

For those of you who wear unnecessary scarves, a trip to France in the off-season will yield fewer tourists hunting for photo ops and a more "authentic" cultural experience. Weather-wise, late spring and autumn are the best times to visit Paris, and many of the more intensive study-abroad opportunities are fall or spring semester programs (see **Beyond Tourism,** p. 383). It can get rainy and cold here in the winter, and France can't really deal with surprise snowfall. To cosmically compensate, these months also produce pristine skiing conditions in the Alps.

top 5 french affairs to remember

"A Frenchman's home is where another man's wife is." - Mark Twain

5. GERTRUDE STEIN AND ALICE B. TOKLAS. In an era when homosexuality was illegal in most of America, Gertrude and Alice were referred to by Hemingway as "husband and wife." Take that, Focus on the Family!

4. HÉLOÏSE AND ABELARD. It doesn't get racier than this. He was a 12th-century monk. She was his student. Their torrid love affair was discovered by Héloïse's uncle, who didn't take the news well and castrated Abelard in his sleep. Héloïse fled from her uncle to an abbey in Brittany, became a nun, and secretly had Abelard's child. Whom she named Astrolabius. Apple Martin's name has never seemed more OK.

3. JEAN-PAUL SARTRE AND SIMONE DE BEAUVOIR. The creators of existentialist thought and second-wave feminism maintained a famously open relationship, then shared the same underaged mistresses. Is it just us, or does this read like a bi-curious episode of *Big Love?*

2. CATHERINE BELLIER AND LOUIS XIV. Fearing that her son would be as inept in the bedroom as her husband, Queen Anne of Austria allegedly asked her handmaid, the hideous Bellier, to deflower her 16-year-old son Louis XIV. Bellier's husband was subsequently promoted to royal advisor. Best. Cougar. Ever.

1. MADAME BOVARY AND...EVERYONE. That went well.

what to do

THE ART OF FRENCH COOKING

Crème brulee. Merlot. Chocolate crêpes. Escargot. Personally, we think that France's famed kitchens should be named World Heritage Sites, and we cannot think of a better place to nourish your soul and regain the Freshman 15. Though French food is generally associated with white tablecloths and steep prices in the US, an appreciation of fine dining is evident throughout French society, right down to its discount markets and grocery stores. Our researchers report that it is both cheaper and more convenient to buy a loaf of baguette and a wheel of brie than it is to be a microwave dinner. Today, the country boasts a myriad of other culinary traditions, due to its extensive immigrant population. The Jewish delis in Paris's **Marais** neighborhood (p. 15) are unparalleled, and the North and West African cuisine of **Marseille** (p. 234) adds some additional spice.

- **LYON:** Once an innocuous suburban town, Lyon is now home to a series of traditional French restaurants that outshine the institutions of Paris (p. 164).

- **BORDEAUX:** Extend your knowledge of alcohol beyond those red solo cups at college parties (p. 192).

- **STRASBOURG:** Carnivores unite over this fusion of French and German cuisine (p. 151).

LOST IN THE LOUVRE

The Chuck Norris of revolutionary thought, France more creativity than the world knows what to do with. Spend as much time as humanly possible in the Louvre and the Pompidou, and be sure to visit the Sorbonne, Monet's gardens, and other famed sites of innovation. However, we encourage you to adopt a flexible view of what art is and dig a little deeper. France is home to a lot more than 20th century painting, and its apocalyptic medieval tapestries, ancient cave murals, and elite fashionistas yield a more panoramic view of its history.

- **THE LOUVRE:** Chances are this museum is the reason you came here. Spend as much time inside of it as possible (p. 34).

- **SAINTE-CHAPELLE:** Thanks to Victor Hugo, tourists come to Paris in search of the Notre Dame. In comparison to the breathtaking Sainte-Chapelle, we think it's overrated (p. 32).

- **MUSÉE MATISSE:** Observe the work of the master in his hometown of Nice (p. 283).

- **CHÂTEAU DE BLOIS:** Anything but blah, this small town's château housed no fewer than seven kings and ten queens of France (p. 104).

SEE THE REAL THING

Remember those famous paintings of sunflowers, lavender fields and water lilies you just saw in the Louvre? Paris may have the world-class art museums, but the most famous paintings in them are an homage to the French countryside, an area that student travelers tend to overlook. Get on a bus and go see what Monet, Cezanne, and Matisse were getting at. The lavender fields of **Provence** (p. 233) and Mediterranean beaches of **Nice** and **Monaco** (p. 275) are obviously must-sees, but we recommend some roads less traveled. The college town of **Grenoble** (p. 181) is ringed by the Rhône Alpes, which provide great ski slopes and breathtaking views.

- **ARLES:** Meander through the winding streets and surrounding countryside that inspired Van Gogh (p. 262).

- **GRENOBLE:** Refine your yodel in the Alps that surround the city (p. 181).

- **JUAN-LES-PINS:** Lounge topless on the city's pristine beaches, if you must (p. 330).

BEYOND TOURISM

If you're interested in more than a snapshot of the Eiffel Tower, we suggest that you enroll in a semester program and submerge yourself in French culture properly. Study-abroad programs in France really have their act together; the majority of them involve intensive language-immersion programs, place students with host families, and offer cross-enrollment in partner French institutions. Programs aimed at advanced speakers offer work placement and direct enrollment opportunities. Volunteer work in France is harder to come by for foreigners, but the country does boast several venerated outreach programs for those who get riled up about social justice. Work as au pairs or English teaching assistants is also readily available.

- **CENTER FOR UNIVERSITY PROGRAMS ABROAD (CUPA):** Study alongside Parisians in this intensive immersion program (p. 386).
- **WWOOF:** Revert to your secret dirty hippie and run away to an organic farm (p. 388).
- **AGENCY AU PAIR FLY:** Perfect your language skills with the aid of small children (p. 391).

student superlatives

- **BEST PLACE TO OVERHEAR A SUBVERSIVE POLITICAL ARGUMENT:** Anywhere in Paris, particularly the Marais and Butte-Aux-Cailles neighborhoods.
- **BEST PLACE TO INDULGE YOUR INNER DISNEY PRINCESS:** The Palace of Versailles and the Châteaux of Tours.
- **BEST GENDER-BENDING:** The venerated gay nightlife of Montpellier.
- **BEST PLACE TO DRINK UNTIL YOU CAN'T REMEMBER HAVING BEEN THERE:** The clubs of St-Tropez.
- **BEST PLACE TO GET TEAR-GASSED IN A RIOT:** Marseille after a soccer game. Or Paris during a workers' strike.

discover france

FROMAGERIE
NICOLE
BARTHELEMY

suggested itineraries

BEST OF FRANCE (2 WEEKS)

1. PARIS (4 DAYS): Immerse yourself in the epicenter of art, love, and revolution.

2. ORLÉANS (1 DAY): Channel your inner Joan of Arc in Orleans, and your inner Disney Princess in the nearby châteaus.

3. BORDEAUX (2 DAYS): Sample the local reds.

4. TOULOUSE (2 DAYS): Soak up the college-town vibes in the hometown of Thomas Aquinas.

5. ARLES (1 DAY): Hang on to your ears and indulge your inner Van Gogh in this artist's haven.

6. NICE (3 DAYS): Immerse yourself in other peoples' dreamscapes in the Cezanne, Matisse, and Picasso museums.

7. STRASBOURG (2 DAYS): Explore the crowning jewel of the historically contested Alsace-Lorraine region, which is now home to several of the European Parliament.

8. REIMS (1 DAY): Kick back and sip the best champagne in Champagne.

discover france

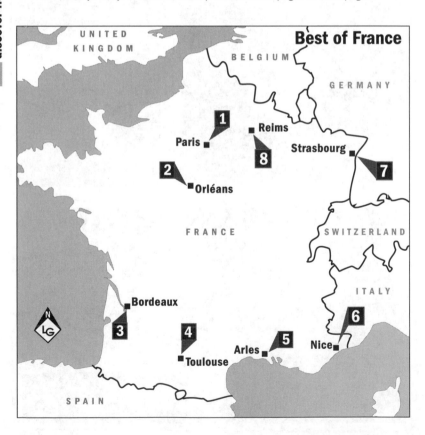

THE BACKPACKER (2 WEEKS)

1. PARIS (4 DAYS): In the spirit of cost-efficiency, we recommend that you stay in the Père Lachaise or Butte-Aux-Cailles neighborhoods.

2. MONTPELLIER (1 DAY): Club-hop through the vibrant gay clubs with hordes of college students.

3. MARSEILLE (2 DAYS): Use the chaotic city of Marseille as a home base to explore the picturesque fields of Provence.

4. NICE (3 DAYS): Couch surf on yachts with crown princes and celebutantes.

5. GRENOBLE (1 DAY): Hike through the day and drink through the night in this hip college town.

THE BEACH BUM (9 DAYS)

1. **PARIS (3 DAYS):** Shop til you drop for the perfect bathing suit.
2. **D-DAY BEACHES (1 DAY):** Less about tanning and more about remembering.
3. **CANNES (2 DAYS):** Storm the red carpet for autographs.
4. **ST-TROPEZ (1 DAY):** Think hip hop music videos. That's how rich this place is.
5. **ANTIBES (1 DAY):**   Lounge on hot beaches with hotter party-goers.
6. **MONACO (1 DAY):**   You can't afford to go here. Go anyway.

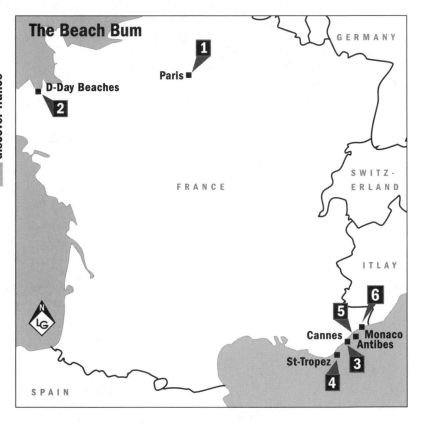

discover france

The Beach Bum

GERMANY

1

Paris ■

■ **D-Day Beaches**

2

FRANCE

SWITZ-
ERLAND

ITLAY

6

5

Cannes ■ **Monaco**
Antibes

St-Tropez **3**

4

SPAIN

THE NERD TOUR (2 WEEKS)

1. PARIS (4 DAYS): The hometown of all things surreal, existential, and (post)modern.

2. D-DAY BEACHES (1 DAY): Pay your respects to the Greatest Generation (p. 146).

3. MONT-ST-MICHEL (1 DAY): Meditate on the Church's excesses in this town's ornate monastery.

4. BLOIS (1 DAY): View the trap door in the local Château where Catherine de Medici hid her poisons.

5. AVIGNON (2 DAYS): When Popes throw hissy fits, apparently they camp out here.

6. AIX-EN-PROVENCE (1 DAY): Engineer your own social movement in this historic center of haloed thinkers.

7. NICE (3 DAYS): Picasso got down here. Need we say more?

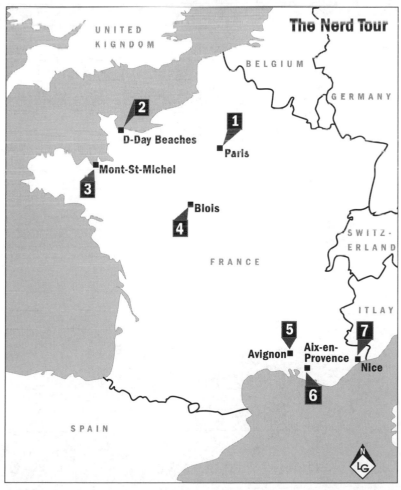

how to use this book

CHAPTERS

In the next few pages, the travel coverage chapters—the meat of any *Let's Go* book—begin with **Paris.** Your inner dork and pre-Madonna and will both go gaga as you move into the **Loire Valley** and **Brittany and Normandy** chapters; the regions host several of the most famous battlegrounds in history, as well as a collection of châteaux that make Warren Buffett look like a struggling entrepreneur. You'll find some of the best food in the country in **Strasbourg** and **Lyon and Rhône-Alpes**, though the aspiring winos among you might want to skip ahead to the **Bordeaux and Wine Country** chapter. Both **Toulouse and Montpellier** and **Provence** are characterized by a quintessentially French hodgepodge of provincial villages and immigrant enclaves; the historic haunts of famed thinkers are just blocks away from gay bars packed with tipsy college students. If you want to get a *Jersey Shore* tan with much classier people, schlep it to **Nice and Monaco** and the **Côte d'Azur,** where the rich and famous rub elbows with the young and topless along the Riviera's pristine beaches.

But that's not all, folks. We also have a few extra chapters for you to peruse:

CHAPTER	DESCRIPTION
Discover France	Discover tells you what to do, when to do it, and where to go for it. The absolute coolest things about any destination get highlighted in this chapter at the front of all *Let's Go* books.
Essentials	Essentials contains the practical info you need before, during, and after your trip—visas, regional transportation, health and safety, phrasebooks, and more.
France 101	France 101 is just what it sounds like—a crash course in where you're traveling. This short chapter on France's history and culture makes great reading on a long plane ride.
Beyond Tourism	As students ourselves, we at *Let's Go* encourage studying abroad, or going beyond tourism more generally, every chance we get. This chapter lists ideas for how to study, volunteer, or work abroad with other young travelers in France to get more out of your trip.

LISTINGS

Listings—a.k.a. reviews of individual establishments—constitute a majority of *Let's Go* coverage. Our Researcher-Writers list establishments in order from **best to worst value**—not necessarily quality. (Obviously a five star hotel is nicer than a hostel, but it would probably be ranked lower because it's not as good a value.) Listings pack in a lot of information, but it's easy to digest if you know how they're constructed:

ESTABLISHMENT NAME 💳💵♿🚫📶🍸❄⛅▼ type of establishment [1]
Address ☎phone number 🖥website
Editorial review goes here.
➡ Directions to the establishment. ℹ Other practical information about the establishment, like age restrictions at a club or whether breakfast is included at a hostel. [$] Prices for goods or services. ⏰ Hours or schedules.

ICONS

First things first: places and things that we absolutely love, sappily cherish, generally obsess over, and wholeheartedly endorse are denoted by the all-empowering 👍**Let's Go thumbs-up.** In addition, the icons scattered throughout a listing (as you saw in the sample above) can tell you a lot about an establishment. The following icons answer a series of yes-no questions about a place:

💳	Credit cards accepted	💵	Cash only	♿	Wheelchair-accessible
🚫	Not wheelchair-accessible	📶	Internet access available	🍸	Alcohol served
❄	Air-conditioned	⛅	Outdoor seating available	▼	GLBT or GLBT-friendly

The rest are visual cues to help you navigate each listing:

☎	Phone numbers	🖥	Websites	🪧	Directions
ℹ	Other hard info	$	Prices	⏰	Hours

OTHER USEFUL STUFF

Area codes for each destination appear opposite the name of the city and are denoted by the ☎ icon. Finally, in order to pack the book with as much information as possible, we have used a few **standard abbreviations.** Ave. for avenue, bld. for Boulevard, pl. for Place. *Entrées* mean appetizers in French, whereas *plats* are main dishes.

PRICE DIVERSITY

A final set of icons corresponds to what we call our "price diversity" scale, which approximates how much money you can expect to spend at a given establishment. For **accommodations,** we base our range on the cheapest price for which a single traveler can stay for one night. For **food,** we estimate the average amount one traveler will spend in one sitting. The table below tells you what you'll *typically* find in France at the corresponding price range, but keep in mind that no system can allow for the quirks of individual establishments.

ACCOMMODATIONS	RANGE	WHAT YOU'RE LIKELY TO FIND
[1]	under €25	Campgrounds and dorm rooms, both in hostels and actual universities. Expect bunk beds and a communal bath. You may have to provide or rent towels and sheets.
[2]	€25-40	Upper-end hostels or lower-end hotels. You may have a private bathroom, or there may be a sink in your room and a communal shower in the hall.
[3]	€40-60	A small room with a private bath. Should have decent amenities, such as phone and TV. Breakfast may be included.
[4]	€60-80	Should have bigger rooms than a [3], with more amenities or in a more convenient location. Breakfast probably included.
[5]	over €80	Large hotels or upscale chains. If it's a [5] and it doesn't have the perks you want (and more), you've paid too much.
FOOD	**RANGE**	**WHAT YOU'RE LIKELY TO FIND**
[1]	under €15	Probably street food or a fast-food joint, but also university cafeterias and bakeries (yum). Usually takeout, but you may have the option of sitting down.
[2]	€15-25	Sandwiches, pizza, appetizers at a bar, or low-priced entrees. Most ethnic eateries are a [2]. Either takeout or a sit-down meal, but only slightly more fashionable decor.
[3]	€25-35	Mid-priced entrees, seafood, and exotic pasta dishes. More upscale ethnic eateries. Since you'll have the luxury of a waiter, tip will set you back a little extra.
[4]	€35-45	A somewhat fancy restaurant. Entrees tend to be heartier or more elaborate, but you're really paying for decor and ambience. Few restaurants in this range have a dress code, but some may look down on T-shirts and sandals.
[5]	over €45	Your meal might cost more than your room, but there's a reason—it's something fabulous, famous, or both. Slacks and dress shirts may be expected. Offers foreign-sounding food and a decent wine list. Don't order a PB and J!

PARIS

From students who obsess over Derrida's *Of Grammatology* to tourists who wonder why the French don't pronounce half the consonants in each word, everyone enjoys the city where, by decree of law, buildings don't exceed six stories, *pour que tout le monde ait du soleil* (so that all have sunshine). Though Parisians may English you (speak in English when you speak in French), this city pulls through for those who let themselves indulge in the sensory snapshots around every corner—the aroma of a *boulangerie*, the gleam of bronze balconies, the buzz of a good €2 bottle of red, the jolt of the new fave metro line 14. For all its hyped-up snobbery (and yes, the waiters are judging you), Paris is open to those willing to wander. The truth is, this city will charm and bitchslap you with equal gusto, but don't get too le tired—by your third or fourth sincere attempt at *s'il vous plaît*, even the waiters soften up. Stick around long enough, and you'll be able to tell the *foux* from the *foux de fa fa*, the Lavazza from the Illy, and the meta hipster bars from the wanna-be meta hipster bars. *Et puis*, we'll see who's judging whom.

greatest hits

- **WHAT'S WITH THE MISSING EYEBROWS?** Throw some elbows for a good view of the Mona Lisa in **the Louvre** (p. 34).
- **"METAL ASPARAGUS" INDEED:** Lord knows the **Eiffel Tower** wasn't popular at first, but these days the number of people that visits the landmark annually is greater than the entire population of Montana (p. 42).
- **BIGGEST GAME OF CHUTES AND LADDERS EVER:** Wander through the endlessly eccentric exhibits of the **Pompidou** (p. 38).

Time for some real talk about how you're going to enjoy Paris. Your art history professor told you to go to **the Louvre**, and you should, but there is so much more to see in Paris than the Mona Lisa—and a lot of it is free. Not nearly as morbid as you might think, **Cimitière du Père Lachaise** is hauntingly beautiful, and the final resting place of Jim Morrison of The Doors. If you're staying in the "flavorful" Marais, try staying in **Maubuisson,** a convent-turned-hostel with 3 buildings and breakfast included. Penny-pinching? Try staying somewhere in Canal St-Martin, where prices tend to be a little lower (though you don't want to be traveling alone at night). We'll leave it to you to figure out how to ask for your snails on the side, but the best eats in Paris are most definitely in the 8ème. When the sun sets, you should know that Parisian clubs are all about how you look—if you don't fit the look, you won't be getting in.

orientation

In comparison to any sprawling post-war American cities, Paris is both dense and meticulously planned. The Seine river ("SEN") flows from east to west, and slices through the middle of Paris, dividing the city into two main sections: the Rive Gauche (Left Bank) to the north, and the Rive Droite (Right Bank) to the south. The two islands in the center of the Seine, the Île de la Cité and Île St-Louis, are both the geographical and historical heart of the city. The rest of Paris proper is divided into 20 arrondissements (districts), which spiral clockwise outwards from the center of the city, like a snail shell. Each arrondissement is usually referred to by an assigned number. For example, the Eiffel Tower is located in the seventh arrondissement of Paris; this district is simply referred to as le septième ("the seventh"), abbreviated 7ème. The city's first arrondissement is the only one that is not abbreviated by the grammatical form ème; it is known as the premier ("PREM-yay") and abbreviated 1er.

The city's organization may sound eminently reasonable, but Paris can be plenty hard to navigate in practice. Just to make things more difficult for travelers, Paris's most prominent neighborhoods regularly bleed into different arrondissements, and do not abide by their numerical divisions. The Marais, for example, spans both the 3ème and the 4ème. We have divided our coverage by both neighborhood and arrondissement, to keep our readers in the know. The most historic areas in Paris can devolve into a maze of narrowed cobbled streets, which can be poorly marked. The city is eminently walkable, however, so we recommend that newbies put away the map and just go with it. Getting lost in Paris is the reason you flew to France in the first place, isn't it?

ÎLE DE LA CITÉ AND ÎLE ST-LOUIS

Marooned in the middle of the Seine and tethered to the mainland by arched bridges, **Île de la Cité** is situated at the physical center of Paris. The island hosted Paris's first ramshackle settlement in 300 BCE, and became the seat of the French monarchy in the 6th century CE when Clovis crowned himself king of the Franks; it remained a hotbed of French political power until Charles V abandoned it in favor of the **Louvre** in the 14th century. The stunning **Notre Dame,** as well as the **Sainte-Chapelle** and the **Conciergerie,** ensured that the island would remain a center of Parisian religious,

paris

political, and cultural life; unsurprisingly, it is now a major center of tourism. All distances in France are measured from kilomètre zéro, a circular sundial in front of Notre Dame. As it often goes with twins, the neighboring Île St-Louis is less illustrious. Originally two small islands—**Île aux Vâches** (Cow Island) and **Île de Notre Dame**—Île St-Louis was considered a suitable location for duels, cows, and not much else throughout the Middle Ages. In 1267, the area was renamed for Louis IX after he departed for the Crusades. The two islands merged in the 17th century under the direction of architect Louis Le Vau, and Île St-Louis became a residential district. The island's *hôtels particuliers* (mansions, many of which were also designed by Le Vau) attracted a fair share of uppity citizenry including Voltaire, Mme. de Châtelet, Daumier, Ingres, Baudelaire, Balzac, Courbet, Sand, Delacroix, and Cézanne. In the 1930s, the idiosyncratic and artistic inhabitants declared the island an independent republic. The island retains a certain remoteness from the rest of Paris; older residents still say "Je vais à Paris" (I'm going to Paris) when they leave the neighborhood by one of the four bridges linking Île St Louis and the mainland. All in all, the island looks remarkably similar to its 17th-century self, and retains both its history and genteel tranquility.

CHÂTELET-LES HALLES (1ER, 2ÈME)

Paris's Châtelet-Les Halles is famous for turning Paris's pet vices into beloved institutions. Its most famous sight, the **Louvre**, was home to French kings for four centuries; absolute monarchy has since gone out of fashion, and the bedchambers and dining rooms of the *ancien régime* palace now house the world's finest art. The surrounding **Jardin des Tuileries** was redesigned in 1660 by Louis XIV's favorite architect, André Le Nôtre, but the Sun King's prized grounds are now a public park, host to crowds of strolling plebeians like ourselves that Louis probably wouldn't touch with a 10 ft. pole. Still, the arrondissement's legacy of excess is certainly alive and well; we suspect that toilet paper rolls are made of €1000 notes around the **Bourse de Valeurs**, and the world's oldest profession reigns supreme along the curbs of **rue St-Denis**. One of Paris's main tourist hubs, Châtelet-Les Halles is heavily frequented by travelers, locals, and lots of scam artists. Seeing somebody run after a pickpocket is not an uncommon occurence here, so move cautiously and confidently.

THE MARAIS (3ÈME, 4ÈME)

The Marais is the ultimate ugly duckling tale. Originally all bog—the name "Marais" literally translates to "swamp"—the area became remotely liveable in the 13th century, when monks drained the land to provide building space for the **Right Bank**. With Henry IV's construction of the glorious **place des Vosges** at the beginning of the 17th century, the area ironically became the city's center of fashionable living; **hôtels particuliers** built by leading architects and sculptors abounded, as did luxury and scandal. During the Revolution, former royal haunts gave way to slums and tenements, and the majority of the *hôtels* fell into ruin or disrepair. The Jewish population, a presence in the Marais since the 12th century, grew with influxes of immigrants from Russia and North Africa, but suffered tragic losses during the Holocaust. In the 1960s, the Marais was once again revived when it was declared a historic neighborhood. Since then, more than thirty years of gentrification, renovation, and fabulous-ization have restored the Marais to its pre-Revolutionary glory. Once-palatial mansions have become exquisite museums, and the tiny twisting streets are covered with hip bars, *avant-garde* galleries, and some of the city's most unique boutiques. **Rue des Rosiers**, in the heart of the *4ème*, is still the center of the city's Jewish population, though the steady influx of hyper-hip clothing stores threatens its existence. Superb kosher delicatessens neighbor Middle Eastern and Eastern European restaurants, and on Sundays, when much of the city is closed, the Marais remains lively. As if it didn't

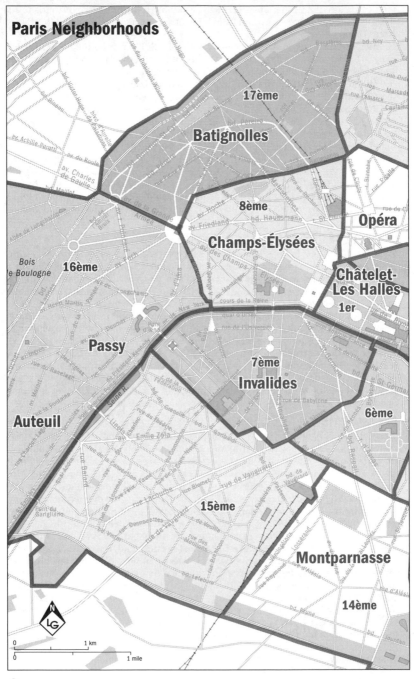

Paris Neighborhoods

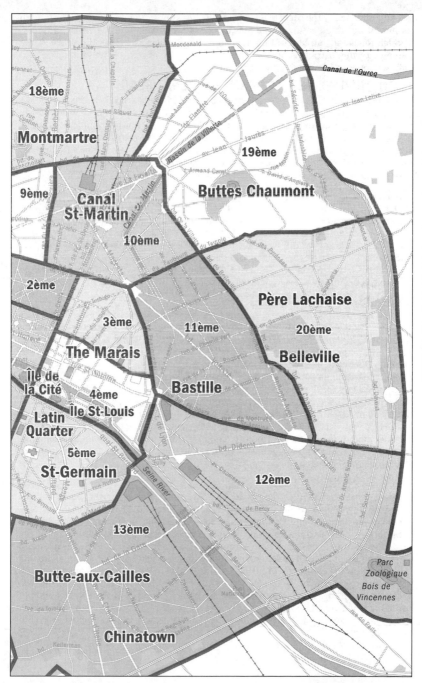

18ème

Montmartre

Canal de l'Ourcq

19ème

9ème

Canal St-Martin

Buttes Chaumont

10ème

2ème

Père Lachaise

3ème

11ème

20ème

The Marais

Belleville

Île de la Cité

4ème

Bastille

Île St-Louis

Latin Quarter

5ème

St-Germain

12ème

13ème

Parc Zoologique Bois de Vincennes

Butte-aux-Cailles

Chinatown

Seine River

already have it all, the Marais is also unquestionably the center of gay Paris, with its hub at the intersection of **rue Ste-Croix de la Bretonnerie** and **rue Vieille du Temple**. Though the steady stream of tourists has begun to wear away the Marais's eclectic personality, the district retains its signature charm: an accessible and fun mix of old and new, queer and straight, cheap and chic.

LATIN QUARTER AND ST-GERMAIN (5ÈME, 6ÈME)

The Latin Quarter and St-Germain tend to be two of Paris's primary tourist neighborhoods. From the hustle and bustle of the predatory cafes around **St-Michel** to the residential areas around **Cardinal Lemoine** and **Jussieu**, the schmoozy galleries of **Odéon** to the best museums Paris has to offer **(Musée de Cluny, Musée Delacroix)**, the fifth and sixth arrondissements truly have it all. They're also eminently walkable. Don't head underground during the day; you'll only encounter pickpockets, scammers, crowds, and—in the summertime—sweaty Metro rides.

INVALIDES (7ÈME)

With tourist attractions and museums at every corner, the 7ème bustles with activity, but could use some personality. French military prowess (stop laughing, that's not nice) is celebrated at **Invalides, Ecole Militaire,** and **Champ de Mars,** while the nation's artistic legacy is shown full force at the **Musée d'Orsay** and the **Quai Voltaire**. Formerly one of Paris's most elegant residential districts, the neighborhood is now home to many of the city's embassies. The **Tour Eiffel** appropriately towers over it all, securing the area as one of the most popular destinations.

CHAMPS-ÉLYSÉES (8ÈME)

If the Champs-Élysées were a supermodel, it would have been forced to retire for being well past its prime. The arrondissement was synonymous with fashion throughout the 19th century, and the boulevards here are still lined with the vast mansions, expensive shops, and grandiose monuments that keep the tourists coming. But the sense of sophistication and progress has since been dampened by charmless boutiques, office buildings, and car dealerships; these areas are comatose after dark. Only the **Champs** itself throbs late into the night, thanks to its unparalleled nightclubs and droves of tourists. A stroll along **avenue Montaigne, rue du Faubourg St-Honoré,** or around the **Madeleine** will give a taste of what life in Paris is like for the excessively rich. While low prices usually mean low quality here—particularly for accommodations—there are a few good restaurants and many great museums. The northern part of the neighborhood, near the **Parc Monceau,** is a lovely and less-touristed area for walking.

OPÉRA (9ÈME)

The 9th arrondissement is (surprise, surprise) best known for the **Opéra National Garnier,** a magnificent structure steeped in history that is difficult to top in terms of architectural triumph and OCD attention to detail. While the Opéra National is the 9ème's crown jewel, the area is more aptly characterized by a juxtaposition of opposing worlds. One of Paris's chic shopping districts on the Grands Boulevards and the anything-but-classy **Pigalle,** encompassing the red light district and a sickening amount of shops catering to tourists. A residential neighborhood is just a stone's throw away, with the St. Georges Metro at its center, as is the beautiful **Moreau Museum,** housed in the famous painter's former home. A couple days in the Opéra will probably leave you thinking that it's among the most bizarre city neighborhoods in the world. One comes to learn that the comfortable coexistence of opposing worlds is très French.

CANAL ST-MARTIN AND SURROUNDS (10ÈME)

The Canal Saint-Martin, i.e., the 10th arrondissment, is undeniably one of the sketchier neighborhoods in Paris. During the day as well as at night, you have to constantly watch your back for pickpockets, muggers, and swaying drunks. That being said, the neighborhood boasts some fantastic restaurants around the **Canal St. Martin,** and some great hotel deals around **Gare du Nord.** The Canal is kind of like a mini-Seine; it's smaller, less touristed, and has just as much trash in it. It becomes a more peaceful area on Sundays, when cars are barred from the streets that run alongside the water.

BASTILLE (11ÈME, 12ÈME)

As its name attests, the Bastille *(bah-steel)* area is most famous for hosting the Revolution's kick-off at its prison on July 14, 1789. Hundreds of years later, the French still storm this neighborhood nightly in search of the latest cocktail, culinary innovation, or up-and-coming artist. Five Metro lines converge at **République** and three at Bastille, making the Bastille district a transport hub and mammoth center of action—the hangout of the young and fun (and frequently drunk). The 1989 opening of the glassy **Opéra Bastille** on the bicentennial of the Revolution was supposed to breathe new cultural life into the area, but the party atmosphere has yet to give way to galleries and string quartets. Today, with numerous bars along **rue de Lappe,** manifold dining options on **rue de la Roquette** and **rue J.P. Timbaud,** and young designer boutiques, the Bastille is a great area for unwinding after a day at the museums.

BUTTE-AUX-CAILLES AND CHINATOWN (13ÈME)

The 13*ème* may have served as the setting of Victor Hugo's *Les Miserables*, but these days you're more likely to see a postmodern performance of *Les Miz* than any fashionably starving children. Though it was once one of Paris's poorest arrondissements, the arrival of the high-speed Metro line and the ZAC Paris Rive Gauche redevelopment project have since transformed the neighborhood into a dynamic community and colorful hub of food and culture. Butte Aux Cailles attracts a young, artsy crowd that lovingly tags the walls with graffiti. Across the way, Chinatown stretches across multiple Metro stops, and is defined by a unique cultural hybridization rarely seen among immigrant enclaves, in both Paris and beyond.

MONTPARNASSE (14ÈME, 15ÈME)

The Montparnasse area is home to two of Paris's most celebrated institutions, the **Catacombs** and the **Cité Universitaire,** and one of its most profitable tourist areas, **Montparnasse Bienvenue.** While the 14th arrondissement has historically been home to a trendy bohemian crowd (especially in the 1920s), the 15*ème* is generally residential and less exciting. Your key objective here is to avoid getting dragged into the touristy vortex of Montparnasse—you'll get fleeced by obnoxiously expensive restaurants and tourist outlets, and you'll think that Parisians are even snootier than they actually are (it's a behavioral conditioning thing; dealing with tourists all day, by definition, reinforces the satisfaction of being snooty).

One of Paris's more dynamic neighborhoods, the 14*ème* provides all the things any self-respecting arrondissement has to offer: a fairly diverse population, fantastic local restaurants, neighborhood specialty shops, leafy parks, mischievous children, and drunks. We recommend staying on the Metro's line 4 past Montparnasse and hopping off at Denfert, or, better yet, Mouton Duvernet. Check out the open-air markets on rue Daguerre, or stroll down **avenue René Coty,** and go strike up a conversation on the *grande pelouse* at the Cité Universitaire. The 15*ème* isn't that exciting after hours, and doesn't boast much excitement in terms of people watching, unless you enjoy seeing women struggle to carry the fruits of their daily labor (read: Cartier, Dior, and Kooples bags). But the area does boast some of Paris's best-priced fine dining (Le Troquet, Le Dix Vins) and a somewhat vibrant nighttime bar scene on **bld. Pasteur.** Stick a baguette in your bag, a cigarette in your mouth, a copy of *Le Monde* (or, if you're for Sarkozy, *Le Figaro*) under your arm, and hit the road.

PASSY AND AUTEUIL (16ÈME)

Perhaps one of the swankiest neighborhoods in Paris, the 16*ème* is home to the ladies who lunch, their beautiful children, and their overworked husbands. Its elegant, boutique-lined streets are calmer than surrounding areas and offer a glimpse into the lives of Parisian elites. Backlit by fabulous views of the Eiffel Tower, the neighborhood is home to a number of museums and attractions, and elderly local pedestrians are often swamped by mobs of eager sightseers. **Trocadero** witnesses the heaviest tourist traffic, with breakdancing street performers, sprawling gardens, and the best "I've been to Paris" photo opps.

BATIGNOLLES (17ÈME)

Far away from Paris's most touristed destinations, the 17*ème* offers a pleasant repite from the mobs of fellow tourists, and provides the chance to rub elbows (or other appendages, if you so choose) with the locals. A diverse group of Parisians are in residence here; varying widely block to block, bourgeois promenades with flowered trees are abruptly juxtaposed with working class areas and immigrant neighborhoods. The eastern and southern parts of the arrondissement share the bordering 8*ème* and 16*ème*'s aristocratic feel, while the quartier's western edge resembles the shoddier 18*ème* and **Pigatelle.** In the lively **Village Batignolles,** parents and their overly-earnest teenagers take leisurely strolls or sit in the many cafes. Unlike other, more crowded arrondissements, there is a real community vibe here. Families walk or lounge around, smile at their neighbors, and enjoy some good Parisian living.

MONTMARTRE (18ÈME)

Montmartre might just be the most eccentric of Paris's neighborhoods. From the scenic vistas at the **Basilique de Sacre-Coeur,** to the historic **cabarets** and **Butte vineyard,** to the (ahem) colorful establishments on the **Red Light District** on bld. de Clichy, you'll see it all in the 18*ème*. Tourism in this part of town can be very difficult. While there aren't too many great options for staying in Montmartre, there are some fantastic sights, decent food, and fun local bars. Keep in mind that while wandering through this neighborhood, you might have to occasionally hike the 130m hill, or Butte, **Montmartre.**

BUTTES CHAUMONT (19ÈME)

In the mid-19th century, Baron Haussman's architectural reforms paved the way for a new working class neighborhood to be settled in the 19th arrondissement, on the northeastern outskirts of Paris. A quiet family neighborhood with a surprisingly lovely *Parc des Buttes Chaumont,* the 19*ème* is now making its best effort at a bohemian revival. The area is rapidly becoming the trendy new hotspot for young professionals and students, and now boasts a growing Asian and North African community. The modern macro-social engineering feat that is the *Parc de la Villette* is also well worth a visit.

BELLEVILLE AND PÈRE LACHAISE (20ÈME)

Belleville is one of Paris's most legendary working-class neighborhoods. Although far from the city center, it is home to one of Paris's most visited tourist sights, the Cimitière Père Lachaise (i.e. that cemetery where Jim Morrison's buried). During the late Second Republic, the 20*ème* became a "red" arrondissement, and was characterized as proletarian and ▓**radical.** The fighting that occurred during the Commune suppression caught the neighborhood reds between the Versaillais troops to the west and the Prussian lines outside the city walls. Forts at Parc des Buttes-Chaumont and the Cimitière du Père Lachaise expired, and on May 28, 1871, the Communards abandoned their last barricade and surrendered. Their legacy of class solidarity and progressivism still characterizes the "red" arrondissement today.

accommodations

ÎLE DE LA CITÉ AND ÎLE ST-LOUIS

One of the romantic centers of Paris, the isles attracts honeymooners, swooners, and the like; the hoteliers more than make good on it. Rooms are generally anything but budget and more in the "I need to seduce her" price range.

🏨 HÔTEL HENRI IV   ✦ HOTEL ❸
25 pl. Dauphine   ☎01 43 54 44 53 ▣www.henri4hotel.fr

It may not have modern-day "necessities" like TVs and hair dryers, but it does have some of the best, located and least expensive rooms in Paris. Henry IV's printing presses once occupied this 400-year-old and off-beat building; the hotel's porthole doors and a winding staircase make it looks like an ancient ship. Spacious rooms have large windows and charming views.

✣ ⓂPont Neuf. *i* Breakfast included. ⓢ Singles €42-59; doubles €49-78, twins €76-81.

CHÂTELET-LES HALLES

While affordable hotels in this trendy neighborhood tend to be pretty hard to come by, there are a few high-quality budget addresses that are worth checking out. Be sure to make your reservations far in advance—cheap spots in such a central location fill up rapidly at any time of year. Also, be sure to watch yourself around Châtelet. Other tourists will not stick up for you (or even tell you) when a pickpocket or mugger is about to pounce.

🏨 HOTEL DE ROUEN   ✦⑷⊛ HOTEL ❷
42 rue Croix des Petits Champs   ☎01 42 61 38 21 ▣www.hotelderouen.net

This cozy two star boasts the lowest prices you'll find in the 1st arrondissement for hotel accommodations. The friendly owner speaks English and is more than happy to tell you about the virtues of all the different rooms. Some of the rooms are decorated with liberated Metro signs and maps, so you won't even have to take advantage of the free Wi-Fi to plan your itinerary. While most rooms come equipped with showers, beware of getting the room without the shower on the first floor; you'll have to walk up five floors (the hotel doesn't have an elevator) to the hallway shower.

✣ ⓂPalais Royal Musée du Louvre, Les Halles. *i* Breakfast €6. Free Wi-Fi. ⓢ Singles €40-60; doubles €45-75. ⓩ Reception 24hr.

🏨 HOTEL TIQUETONNE   ✦⑆ HOTEL ❸
6 rue Tiquetonne   ☎01 42 36 94 58

Located a stone's throw from Marché Montorgueil and rue St-Denis's sex shops, Hotel Tiquetonne is surrounded by so many hip shopping spots it could send its hipster clientele into bankruptcy. Simple rooms are generously sized and boast unusually high ceilings (by Parisian standards). Amenities can be hit or miss; the hotel has an elevator, but some rooms don't have showers. Unbeatable prices for this location.

✣ ⓂÉtienne-Marcel. *i* Breakfast €6. Hall showers €6. ⓢ Singles €35, with shower €45; doubles with shower €55. ⓩ Reception 24hr.

🏨 CENTRE INTERNATIONALE DE PARIS (BVJ): PARIS LOUVRE   ⊛⑷ HOSTEL ❶
20 rue Jean-Jacques Rousseau   ☎01 53 00 90 90

In an unbeatable location right down the street from the Louvre, this massive hostel has taken over three buildings in total. All guests must be younger than

35, ensuring a young and international crowd. The decor in the lobby, dining hall, and rooms is utilitarian and vaguely influenced by the '60s. Spacious single-sex dorms are available with two to eight beds. A new location is coming to the Opéra district, so stay tuned.

 # [M]Louvre. i Breakfast included. Reservations can be made no more than 15 days in advance by phone or internet, except Jul-Aug, when they can be made 2 months in advance. Wi-Fi in dining hall €2 per hr., €3 per 2hr. $ Dorms €29. Extra bed €35. ⏰ Reception 24hr. 3-day max. stay; extensions can be arranged on arrival.

HOTEL MONTPENSIER 💳📶 HOTEL [3]

12 rue de Richelieu ☎01 42 96 28 50 💻www.montpensierparis.com

Hotel Montpensier is a swanky yet affordable option on a relatively quiet street, only a few blocks from the Louvre and other sights of the *2ème*. Tall ceilings and old-school decor grace the first two floors of the hotel. While the rooms upstairs aren't quite as gracefully decorated (and have spots on the walls), they offer much lovelier views of rue de Richelieu, if you can negotiate the doors' complex locks. The staff is warm and eager to help you get around the arrondissement, and Paris at large. Thirty-five of the hotel's forty-three rooms have ensuite bath.

 # [M]Palais Royal Musée du Louvre. i Free Wi-Fi. $ Singles €71; doubles €76-118; triples €139; quads €159. Petit Dej €9. ⏰ Reception 24hr.

THE MARAIS

As would be expected, the Marais and its surroundings provide budget accommodations with a bit of flare. Many basic rooms are wallet-friendly, done up in style, and situated in the center of Parisian action. The trendy yet down-to-earth *4ème* is also home to some of the best deals and worthwhile splurges in the city. There's a lot of good stuff to make (and take) home.

👍 **MAUBUISSON** 💳 HOSTEL [3]

12 rue des Barres ☎01 42 74 23 45 💻www.mije.com

Recognized as a 17th-century historical monument, Maubuisson is a former convent on a quiet street by the St. Gervais monastery. In keeping with the pious theme, the hostel only accommodates individual travelers, rather than groups. A member of the MIJE hostel group, Maubuisson can arrange airport transportation as well as reservations for area attractions; call for details. Breakfast, in-room shower, and sheets included (no towels).

 # [M]Hôtel de Ville or [M]Pont Marie. From Pont Marie, walk opposite traffic on rue de l'Hôtel-de-Ville and turn right on rue des Barres. i No smoking. English spoken. Public phones and free lockers (with a €1 deposit). Internet access €0.10 per min. with €0.50 initial connection fee. Individuals can reserve months ahead online and 2-3 weeks ahead by phone. $ MIJE membership required (€2.50). 4- to 9-bed dorms €30; singles €49; doubles €72; triples €96. ⏰ Reception 7am-1am. Lockout noon-3pm. Curfew 1am; notify in advance if coming back after this time. Quiet hours after 10pm. Arrive before noon the first day of reservation (call in advance if you'll be late).7-night max. stay.

👍 **LE FOURCY** 📶💳 HOSTEL [3]

6 rue de Fourcy ☎01 42 74 23 45 💻www.mjie.com

Le Fourcy surrounds a large, charming, mansion-worthy courtyard ideal for meeting travelers or for open-air picnicking. The adjoining restaurant is located in an authentic vaulted cellar, and offers a main course with drink (lunch only) and 3-course "hosteler special" *(€10.50)*. Breakfast, ensuite shower, and sheets are included (no towels).

 # [M]St-Paul or [M]Pont Marie. From St-Paul, walk opposite the traffic for a few meters down rue St-Antoine and turn left on rue de Fourcy. i No smoking. English spoken. Public phones and free lockers (with a €1 deposit). Internet access €0.10 per min. with €0.50 initial connection fee. Groups of 10 or more may reserve a year in advance. Individuals can reserve months ahead online and 2-3 weeks ahead by phone. $ MIJE membership required (€2.50). 4- to 9-bed dorms €30;

singles €49; doubles €72; triples €96. ⏰ *Reception 7am-1am. Lockout noon-3pm. Curfew 1am; notify in advance. Quiet hours after 10pm. Arrive before noon the first day of reservation (call in advance if you'll be late). 7-night max. stay.*

HOTEL PICARD
HOTEL [4]

26 rue de Picardie ☎01 48 87 53 82;hotel.picard@wanadoo.fr 🖥www.hotelpicardparis.com

A welcoming, family-owned hotel that's run more like a home with an open door policy. *Let's Go* readers will definitely feel like a member of the family; a 5% discount is given if you flash your copy. The bright and adorable rooms vary in size, but all of them are comfy. Many of them have private bathrooms, most of which have been recently renovated. All of the rooms come with TVs, safes, and showers.

 # [M]République. Follow bld. du Temple and turn right onto rue Charlot. Take the first right onto rue de Franche Comte, which becomes rue de Picardie. ℹ *Breakfast €5. Reserve 1 week ahead in summer and 2 weeks ahead the rest of the year.* $ *Singles with sink €53-68, with bath €74-93; doubles €59-74/89-112; triples €124-155. Shower €3.*

HÔTEL JEANNE D'ARC
HOTEL [4]

3 rue de Jarente ☎01 48 87 62 11 🖥www.hoteljeannedarc.com

Joan of Arc may have been one, but you certainly won't be a martyr for staying in this quaint hotel. Charming rooms decorated in mismatched patterns all come with bath or shower, toilet, cable TV, safe and hair dryer. Despite its modern amenities, the place feels more like a homestyle inn than a 2-star hotel; the dining area boasts an absurdly funky mosaic mirror, and serves a country-style breakfast.

 # [M]St.Paul. From St-Paul, walk against traffic on rue de Rivoli; turn left onto rue de Sévigné then right on rue de Jarente. ℹ *Breakfast €7. Free Wi-Fi. English spoken. Reserve 2-3 months in advance (longer for stays in Sept.-Oct.) by emailing or calling with credit card.* $ *Singles €62-90; doubles €90-116; triples €146; quads €160.*

LATIN QUARTER AND ST-GERMAIN

While hotels are generally a bit overpriced in these neighborhoods, it's to be expected given their central location in Paris. Nonetheless, the area boasts some truly luxurious accommodations at very reasonable prices. If you want to be well located while living the (somewhat) high life, *Let's Go* has a few good recommendations for you.

HÔTEL DE NESLE
HOTEL [3]

7 rue du Nesle ☎01 43 54 62 41 🖥www.hoteldenesleparis.com

An absolutely phenomenal place to stay. Every room is unique and represents a particular time period or locale. The Molière room is ideal for the comically minded, and an Oriental room is available for undying proponents of the colonial lifestyle (don't let that be you). The lobby's ceiling is adorned with bouquets of dried flowers, and the peaceful garden has terraced seating and a duck pond. Reserve a good deal in advance, because this unforgettable accommodation fills up quickly, especially during the summertime.

 # [M]Odéon. ℹ *Laundry facilities on-site.* $ *Singles €55-65; doubles €75-100. Extra bed €12.*

HOTEL DES ARGONAUTS
HOTEL [3]

12 rue de la Huchette ☎01 43 54 09 82 🖥www.hotel-les-argonautes.com

A hotel with extremely reasonable prices, especially considering its location on one of Paris's main thoroughfares. The intriguing decor includes leopard-print chairs perched under traditional rustic wood-beamed ceilings and insulates the guest from the hustle and bustle of rue de la Huchette. Keep in mind that rue de la Huchette is almost always buzzing with activity; if you need your peace and quiet, search elsewhere. All rooms have showers; more expensive options have toilets and bathtubs.

 # [M]St-Michel. ℹ *Breakfast €5.* $ *Singles €55-80; doubles €65-90; triples €90.*

YOUNG AND HAPPY HOSTEL

80 rue Mouffetard   ✆01 47 07 47 07 🖳www.youngandhappy.fr   ✈ HOSTEL ❶

A funky, lively hostel with 21 clean—if basic—rooms, some with showers and toilets in room. Friendly staff speaks English. A kitchen is available for guest use; the hostel is building a bar in the breakfast room which should be installed by late 2010. Breakfast included.

🚼 ⓂMonge. *i* Breakfast included. Sheets €2.50 with €5 deposit, towels €1. Internet €2 per 30min. ⑤ 2-, 3-, 4-, 5-, 6-, 8-, or 10-bed dorms in high season €28-84.90. ⌚ Strict lockout 11am-4pm.

INVALIDES

Budget travel isn't exactly synonymous with the elegant 7ème. Still, the centrally located arrondissement hosts a number of modern and decently affordable hotels with a friendly staff committed to good service. Many rooms also come with a view of the gilded dome of Invalides.

GRAND HÔTEL LÉVÊQUE

28 rue Cler   ✆01 47 05 49 15 🖳www.hotel-leveque.com   ✈ HOTEL ❹

Centrally located on the quaint and cobblestoned rue de Cler, this richly decorated hotel is just steps away from many of the arrondissement's main attractions. The hotel offers rooms with views of the street, courtyard, and some include full baths.

🚼 ⓂÉcole Militaire. *i* Breakfast €9. ⑤ Singles €62-74; doubles €95-130; twins €95-134; triples €132-55; quads €154-159.

HOTEL DE TURENNE

20 avenue de Tourville   ✈ HOTEL ❸
     ✆01 47 05 99 92

Somewhere between nice and nice enough, this hotel almost has a personality. It may have the squeaky floors and pin-striped wallpaper of forgettable hotels everwhere, but the bathrooms are huge and rooms are well-kept.

🚼 ⓂÉcole Militaire. ⑤ Singles €69; doubles €87; twins €100; triples €130.

HOTEL MONTEBELLO

18 rue Pierre Leroux   🅰🅚 HOTEL ❷
     ✆01 47 34 41 18 🖳hmontebello@aol.com

From the worn leather couch in the lobby to the faded old photographs lining the walls, Hotel Montebello feels more like a haven for long-lost French grand-children than an actual hotel. Provides clean and colorful rooms with purple curtains, at some of the best prices in the 7ème. It's a bit far from most of the neighborhood sights, but the elderly proprietor lends a genuine taste of old Paris. Be warned that credit cards are still considered a bit too new-fangled for this place; you will have to pay by check.

🚼 ⓂVaneau. *i* All rooms with bath. ⑤ Singles €49; doubles €59; triples €79.

CHAMPS-ÉLYSÉES

Catering to the Louis Vuitton clientele, accommodations in the posh 8ème come with a lot of stars and a hell of a nightly rate. Budget travelers might want to look elsewhere. For those absolutely set on location, there are a few quality options.

HÔTEL ALEXANDRINE OPÉRA

10 rue de Moscou   ✈ HOTEL ❷
     ✆01 43 87 62 21 🖳alexandrineopera@gmail.com

Nothing about this hotel could provoke anger (quite the contrary) but you'll still see red (decorators went a little crazy with the color scheme). Apart from that, rooms are well-sized, pleasant and come with a minibar (an unthinkable luxury at this price), hair dryer, TV, phone and shower.

🚼 ⓂLiège. *i* Breakfast €9. ⑤ Singles €65-80, doubles €75-100.

HÔTEL EUROPE-LIÈGE

8 rue de Moscou   ✈⬙ HOTEL ❸
     ✆01 42 94 01 51

Though you could certainly get more bang for your buck elsewhere, this borderline modern hotel is one of the only affordable options in the pricey *8ème*. Rooms are painted lilac, making guests feel slightly more cheerful despite the small size. Rooms come with TV, hair dryer, phone, and shower or bath.

✠ ⓂLiège. *i* Breakfast €7. Wi-Fi €4.50 per hr. Ⓢ Singles €81; doubles €94-120.

OPÉRA

🏠 PERFECT HOTEL
39 rue Rodier

✦⊗ HOTEL ❷
☎01 42 81 18 86

Possibly the best deal in Paris, the Perfect Hotel is, well, practically perfect. For super cheap, visitors have access to a kitchen available for their use whenever they need it. Some of the rooms have balconies, which may be available on request. The cordial owners owners are enthusiastic when it comes to new visitors; they're so concerned about their guests that they installed a surveillance system of the entire hotel to ensure privacy and safety. Or maybe just to watch you. No Wi-Fi, unfortunately, but it's coming soon with upcoming renovations (new painting, wallpaper, and showers).

✠ ⓂAnvers *i* Breakfast included. Reserve 2 months ahead; there are only 10 rooms, and given the cheap prices this hotel fills up weeks in advance during summer. Credit cards only for weeklong stays or longer. Ⓢ Doubles €50-70; triples €52-56. 🔑 No lockout.

HOTEL CHOPIN
10 bld. Montmartre, 46 passage Jouffroy

✦⊗ HOTEL ❸
☎47 70 58 10 🖳www.hotelchopin.fr

Appropriately titled given its location in Opéra (haha—get it?), Hotel Chopin is located at the end of a small and hyper-touristy indoor mall. The two-star hotel offers spacious, clean rooms with views of neighboring buildings' rooftops. The staff is fantastic, and goes out of its way to enhance your experience. The owner takes great pride in the hotel, and showcases his grandmother's paintings in the hallways. Phones, hair dryers, and TVs available in the rooms, but Wi-Fi is not, so geeks beware.

✠ ⓂGrands Boulevards *i* Breakfast €7. Reserve 2-3 months ahead.Ⓢ Singles €68 84; doubles €92-106; triples €125. 🕐 Reception 24hr. Check-out at noon.

CANAL ST-MARTIN AND SURROUNDS

Canal St-Martin boasts a wealth of dirt cheap options around **Gare du Nord.** The following accommodations are among the best that the arrondissement has to offer, but if they're full, ask the proprieters to recommend one of their many competing neighbors. People running hotels around here tend to be pretty no-nonsense, so they'll give you the inside skinny.

🏠 HOTEL PALACE
9 rue Bouchardon

✦ HOTEL ❶
☎01 40 40 09 45

Rock bottom prices and a safe (by 10*ème* standards), if not central, location are combined with a very warm and comfortable welcome. Prices are stupefyingly low, with singles going for €20; the greater tourist community is beginning to catch on to this bargain, so be sure to make reservations at least two weeks in advance.

✠ ⓂStrasbourg-St-Denis. *i* Breakfast €4. Ⓢ Singles €20-35; doubles €28-45; triples €60; quads €70.

HOTEL DE MILAN
17 rue de St-Quentin

✦⛄(ᵖ) HOTEL ❷

Offering a selection of rooms of varying sizes, Hotel de Milan is a good spot to stay if you feel safe making a short trek from Gare du Nord at night. Prices are potentially really cheap if you can go without a shower (*singles for €36*), and the hotel undoubtedly offers the best accommodations in Paris for any disabled patrons (the handicapped room is gi-normous). Friendly reception.

✠ ⓂGare du Nord. *i* Wheelchair-accessible rooms available. Breakfast €5. Wi-Fi €2 per hr.

Showers €4. $ Singles €36-60; doubles €52-71; triples €90. Extra bed €17. ⏰ Check-out 11am; check-in 2pm.

BASTILLE

The 11*ème* is littered with hotels (amongst other things), and offers a little bit of something for everybody. Accommodations range from the very cheap to the very not-cheap, but good quality budget hotels are in abundance. The neighboring 12*ème* offers relatively inexpensive and simple accommodations, which work hard to make up for being somewhat on the outskirts. The best options cluster around the **Gare de Lyon.**

AUBERGE DE JEUNESSE "JULES FERRY" (HI)

HOSTEL [2]

8 bld. Jules Ferry ☎01 43 57 55 60 🖳paris.julesferry@fuaj.org

A noble attempt to brighten up the hostel experience, and we mean that quite literally—the brown bunks have recently been painted neon green. A mural of sharks greets you on your walk up the stairs. Colorful rooms with sinks, mirrors, and tiled floors match the carefree atmosphere (though the sharks don't quite scream "Welcome Home!").

[M]République. i Kitchen available. Wi-Fi €5 per 2hr. $ Dorms €23 with breakfast. ⏰ Reception and dining room 24hr. Lockout 10:30am-2pm.

HOTEL BEAUMARCHAIS

HOTEL [5]

3 rue Oberkampf ☎01 53 36 86 86 🖳reservation@hotelbeaumarchais.com 🖳www.hotelbeaumarchais.com

The kind of place that would make hippies who traded their psychadelics for suits nostalgic for the old days. Funky, colorful decor. Spacious rooms come with hair dryers, cable TV, and a safe box.

[M]Oberkampf or Filles du Calvaire. i Breakfast €10. $ Singles €90; doubles €130; junior suite €170; triples €190.

HÔTEL RHETIA

HOTEL [3]

3 rue de Général Blaise ☎01 47 00 47 18 🖳hotel.rhetia@fere.fr

The communal bathroom may not have a toilet seat, but the owners tried damned hard to make all the colors match. Hotel Rhetia is saved from shoddiness by a feminine touch; rooms are surprisingly clean and pleasant, with decorative pillows and matching curtains.

[M]Voltaire or St-Ambroise. i Breakfast €3. $ Singles €30-48; doubles €53; twins €55. ⏰ Reception M-F 7:30am-9:30pm. Sa, Su 8am-9:30pm.

MODERN HÔTEL

HOTEL [4]

121 rue du Chemin Vert ☎01 47 00 54 05 🖳www.modern-hotel.fr

Contrary to its name, this hotel is all remnants of past grandeur—think worn marble and glass chandeliers. Rooms are clean, with plush carpets that visibly clash with the busy wallpaper and curtains. Avoid if high or suffering from OCD.

[M]Père-Lachaise. i Breakfast included. $ Singles €61-86; doubles €75-105; twins €78-109; triples €93-129; quads €154.

BUTTE-AUX-CAILLES AND CHINATOWN

Though perhaps not at the center of it all, the 13*ème* is home to several inexpensive accommodations in an ethnically-diverse and residential area, providing travelers with an opportunity to escape the steep prices and occasional phoniness of Parisian chic.

OOPS!

HOSTEL [1]

50 av. des Gobelins ☎01 47 07 47 00 🖳www.oops-paris.com

The first boutique hostel in Paris, Oops! has the fashion sense of a teen with an attitude problem. Animal print wallpaper, bold colors and a kaleidescope of patterns generate a fun, young feel. The rooms themselves are less remarkable than the decor, but are average in size and include a bathroom and shower, though no lockers are available. Guests are free to use the rainbow-colored lounge and its free Wi-Fi.

✦ ⓜLes Gobelins. *i Email to make a reservation. No deposit required if booking made through website. Cancel within 24hr. Breakfast included.* ⑤ *Dorms €23-30; private rooms €60-70.*

HOTEL MAGENDIE ✦ HOTEL ❸
2 rue Magendie, 6 rue Corvisart ☎01 43 36 13 61 ▣hotel-magendie@belambra.fr
A standard two-star hotel with the fake plants and whitewashed, concrete walls of a county hospital, Hotel Magendie offers clean and box-like rooms that are affordable if forgettable. The first floor atmosphere is a lot more welcoming, with warmer colors.

✦ ⓜLes Gobelins or ⓜCorvisart . *i Breakfast €8.* ⑤ *M-F singles €75; doubles €89; triples €110. Sa-Su singles €66; doubles €79; triples €98. Dec 27-Dec 31 singles €84; doubles €97; triples €119.*

MONTPARNASSE

HOTEL DE BLOIS ✦♿⑼ HOTEL ❷
5 rue des Plantes, 14ème. ☎01 45 40 99 48 ▣www.hoteldeblois.com
Conveniently located a 5min. walk from Denfert-Rochereau, and within walking distance of several tasty restaurants, Hotel de Blois is situated in a largely residential area of the 14ème on the popular rue des Plantes. Rooms are well-kept and relatively spacious, with full-sized bathrooms and showers. Amenities include hair dryer, phone, TV, and bathtubs. Don't fret about security—the exceptional hostess is extra vigilant about letting in strangers, given the hotel's central location. Her visitors show their gratitude in a proudly displayed collection of thank you notes. There are five floors and no elevator, so the hotel is far from wheelchair-accessible.

✦ ⓜMouton Duvernet or ⓜAlésia. *i Breakfast €12. Wi-Fi available. Reserve at least 1 month ahead* ⑤ *Singles €55-95; doubles €60-98; twin suite 65-80. Extra bed €3 5.* ⓚ *Reception 7am-10:30pm.*

HOTEL DU PARC ✦⑼❈ HOTEL ❸
6 rue Jolivet, 14ème ☎01 43 20 95 54 ▣www.hotelduparcparis.com
Located conveniently around the corner from Montparnasse, Hotel du Parc boasts bright red and somewhat small rooms with A/C, hair dryer, phone, and TV. Despite its central location, the setting is relatively tranquil; the sunny rooms overlook the small adjacent park, which doubles as a local pigeon's roost and outdoor bar. The staff is welcoming and eager to make your stay enjoyable.

✦ ⓜMontparnasse-Bienvenue. *i Breakfast €12. Wi-Fi included. Computers €2 per min., €5 per hr. Book at least a month ahead, especially in the summertime.* ⑤ *Singles €70-180; doubles €80-200; triples €90-200.*

PASSY AND AUTEUIL
Home to many the posh resident, things get expensive in the 16ème, amd accommodations are no exception. Budget hotels and hostels are hard to find and the few options available are a trek from the city's center. On the upside, the neighborhood's more reasonable hotels can offer a welcome respite from the sticky dorms of grungy hostels for those who can afford it.

▥ HOTELHOME PARIS 16 ✦ HOTEL ❹
36 rue George Sand ☎01 045 20 61 38 ▣www.hotelhome.fr
As its name would suggest, HotelHome offers a home away from home to the weary traveler. Each of the pre-outfitted apartments come with a kitchen, dishwasher, bathroom, living room, and delicious potpurri aroma. Thick plush carpets, rich colors, and dark wood make for the kind of luxurious atmostphere

one wouldn't dream of when traveling on a budget. Varying apartment styles can accommodate a range of people.

❖ Ⓜ*Jasmin.* *i Breakfast included.* Ⓢ *Junior suites (1-3 people) €123-260; twin suites €180-345; double suites (1-4 people) €207-385; family suites (1-6 people) €288-580. Discounts for early bookings.*

VILLA D'AUTEIL
28 rue Poussin

❖◦(•) HOTEL ❸

☎01 42 88 30 37 ✉VILLAAUT@aol.com

This two star hotel's uneven stairs will take you to homey, quaint rooms with patterned navy carpets and satellite TVs. All windows facing the street are double-paned for increased safety.

❖ Ⓜ*Michael-Ange Auteil.* *i Breakfast €6.* Ⓢ *Singles €70; doubles €74-80; triples €92.*

BATIGNOLLES

If you're going to stay this far out from the center of town, there better be something good to keeping you here. The 17*ème* hosts a number of more luxurious budget accommodations that will give you a soft bed to come home to after a long day of sightseeing, but it'll be a long Metro ride.

▨ HOTEL CHAMPERRET HELIOPOLIS
13 rue d'Héliopolis

❖♿(•) HOTEL ❹

☎01 47 64 92 56 ✉reservation@champerretheliopolis.fr
✉www.champerret-heliopolis-paris-hotel.com

Bright blue, white, and gold rooms with plush, comfy beds and flatscreen TVs. The hotel combines an intimate bed and breakfast vibe with the the amenities of a modern hotel. Book in advance.

❖ Ⓜ*Porte de Champarret..* Ⓢ *Singles €77; doubles €90, with bath €96; twins €96; triples with bath €120.*

HÔTEL PRINCE ALBERT WAGRAM
28, passage Cardinet

❖❄ HOTEL ❸

☎01 47 54 06 00 ✉hotelprincealbert.com

Located in a quiet alleyway, Hôtel Prince Albert Wagram offers reasonably sized, clean rooms in a quiet neighborhood. Rich dark colors and black leather couches in the lobby make for a more "manly" feel than in other small hotels. Guests are sometimes allowed to use the kitchen microwave. If you are American and of color, the proprietor might ask you if "Obama is your family" (he asked this Research Writer, anyway). Prices negotiable.

❖ Ⓜ*Malesherbes. Walk up bld. Malesherbes. Turn right onto rue Cardinet and then left onto passage Cardinet.* *i Breakfast €6. A/C €10.* Ⓢ *Singles €75-102; doubles €90-110. Check-in 2pm; check-out noon.*

MONTMARTRE

Montmartre's accommodations tend to be a bit pricier, given its position near the top of the list of Paris's most heavily touristed neighborhoods. That being said, we've picked out a few affordable options if you wish to be in the thick of things. Always remember to evaluate the noise level in the neighborhood of your accommodation; while none of these are located in noisy neighborhoods, most locations in the 18*ème* tend to be a bit rowdy at night.

▨ HOTEL CAULAINCOURT
2 sq. Caulaincourt

❖◦(•) HOTEL ❷

☎01 46 06 46 06 ✉www.caulaincourt.com

A friendly, cheap hotel that caters to a slightly younger crowd. Reception will do everything possible to make your stay enjoyable and happy. There's a TV in the lobby, and free internet access up to 30min. Rooms are generally clean, with the exception of a few grimy spots in the bathrooms. Keep in mind that there's a 2am curfew, and 11am-4pm is lockout time; this is not the place to be if you want to party really hard and then sleep in (*"faire la grasse matinée"* in French; doesn't that sound better?). The hotel is located at the top of a long staircase, so its rooms afford some fantastic views.

ⓂLamarck-Caulaincourt. $ Singles €50-60; doubles €63-76; triples €89. ⏰ Curfew 2am. Lockout 11am-4pm. Check-in 11am, check-out 4pm.

HOTEL ANDRÉ GILL — 📶 HOTEL ❷

4 rue André Gill — ☎01 42 62 48 48

A cozy family-run budget hotel, André Gill is located on a side street off rue des Martyrs, in the thick of the touristy section of Montmartre. The hotel's well-loved cat adds a homey touch, but if you're allergic you should think about heading somewhere else. The rooms here are clean and the reception is friendly. The location is a bit busy; if you're a city slicker, you should be able to sleep like a baby, but country bumpkins should search for something a bit farther out if you want to catch some z's.

 # ⓂPigalle, ⓂAbesses. i Breakfast €4. Computer use €1.50 per 30min. $ Doubles with sink €60, with bath €89. ⏰ Reception 24hr. Check-in 10am; check-out 2pm.

BUTTES CHAUMONT

Buttes Chaumont isn't known for its accommodations for a reason. Largely residential and far away from tourist destinations, hotels are generally a bit expensive, and impractical for a stay in Paris. La Perdrix Rouge is the great exception.

LA PERDRIX ROUGE — 📶 HOTEL ❷

5 rue Lassus — ☎01 42 06 09 53 🖥www.hotel-perdrixrouge-paris.com

Facing a gorgeous church and just steps from the Metro, La Perdrix Rouge offers a slightly pricey, peaceful home base away from the clamor of central Paris. Surrounded by a bank, grocery store, several bakeries, and restaurants, patrons will find the neighborhood tourist-free and generous in terms of the necessities (fresh bread, pharmacies, crêpes, etc.) Thirty clean, red-carpeted rooms come with bath or shower, hair dryer, toilet, telephone, and TV.

 # ⓂJourdain. i Breakfast €7.50. Minibar deposit €20. $ Singles €79; doubles €85-92; twins €98. Extra bed €12.

BELLEVILLE AND PÈRE LACHAISE

Belleville is pretty far out from most tourist destinations in Paris. Nonetheless, there are some pretty cheap accommodations here. The **Auberge de Jeunesse** has a fantastic sense of community; if you want to meet people at your hostel, but not be able to afford a taxi home after hitting the bars, the 20*ème* is the spot for you.

AUBERGE DE JEUNESSE "LE D'ARTAGNAN" — 📶 HOSTEL ❶

80 rue Vitruve — ☎01 40 32 34 56 🖥www.fuaj.org

A healthy walk from the Metro and a stone's throw from the Lachaise Cemetery, this Auberge boasts an unbecoming design, a friendly reception, and a huge community of transient students. Claiming to be France's largest Youth Hostel, this 440-bed backpacker's republic fosters a fun and irreverent atmosphere with flashing neon lights, a free in-house cinema, and a game room complete with those car-driving games you used to stuff with quarters as a kid. Rooms are clean and have all the basics down pat. The jovial elevator/social facilitator man will make otherwise ordinary elevator rides fun and social.

 # ⓂPorte de Bagnolet. $ Breakfast included. Internet and Wi-Fi €2 per hr. Sheets included, towel €2.50. Lockers €2-4 per day. Laundry €3 per wash, €1 per dry. Reserve online. Discounts for International Youth Hostels Association members. $ 9-bed dorms €21; 3- to 5-bed €23.50. Doubles €28. ⏰ Lockout noon-3pm. 4-night max. stay.

SUPER HOTEL — 📶 HOTEL ❷

208 rue des Pyrénées, place Gambetta — ☎01 46 36 97 48

🖥http://fr.federal-hotel.com/hotel_super-hotel-paris_2478.htm

Less than a block from several convenient pharmacies and stores, Super Hotel provides clean rooms with A/C, hairdryer, and TV vary greatly in size. The lobby boasts bright modern furniture, making it feel a little nicer than your average 2-star. Beware of steep Wi-Fi charges.

 # Ⓜ Gambetta. Hotel is right off the place Gambetta, off rue des Pyrénées. ℹ Wi-Fi €10 per stay, currently only reaches 3d floor. $ Breakfast €8. Singles €50.50-55, doubles €60, quad €79. ⏰ Check-in 2pm, check-out 11am.

sights

ÎLE DE LA CITÉ AND ÎLE ST-LOUIS

The ground zero of Paris, there are a lot of big hitters on the islands. If you're looking for grand architecture, hundreds of years of history, and mobs of tourists, Île de la Cité is a wonderful place to start. **Notre Dame Cathedral** is it the center of it all, rising above the lesser-known (i.e., not in a Disney movie) but equally impressive locations like **Ste-Chapelle**. Even without all the grandeur, the Île's sheer level of historical significance makes it worth a visit: the birthplace of Paris, the island's narrow streets offer a glimpse of the city's humble beginnings. Just across the way, the rue St-Louis-En-L'Île was historically home to some of the most famous Parisians in history. The main thoroughfare—the narrow, cobblestone **rue St-Louis-en-l'Île**—strings together a collection of clothing boutiques, gourmet food stores, galleries, and ice cream shops, including the famous **Berthillon glacerie.**

★ NOTRE DAME

◆ CATHEDRAL

Île de la Cité

☎01 53 10 07 00

Centuries before it witnessed Quasimodo's attempted rescue of Esmeralda, Notre Dame was the site of a Roman temple to Jupiter and three different churches. Parisian bishop **Maurice de Sully** initiated the construction of the cathedral in 1163. De Sully took care to avoid the poor interior design that characterized Notre Dame's dark and cramped predecessor, and worked to create a more airy structure that would fill with God's light; in the process, he helped engineer a new architectural style that would later be dubbed **Gothic.** De Sully died before his ambitious plan was completed, but the cathedral was reworked over several centuries into the composite masterpiece that stands today.

Like the Île de la Cite, Notre Dame has hosted a series of pivotal events in Western history. French royalty used the Cathedral for their marital unions, most notably the marriages of François II to **Mary Queen of Scots** in 1558, and of **Henri of Navarre** to Marguerite de Valois in 1572. The cathedral was also the setting for **Joan of Arc's** trial for heresy in 1455. In a fit of logic, secularists renamed the cathedral *The Temple of Reason* during the Revolution, and cleverly encased its Gothic arches in Neoclassical plaster moldings. The church was reconsecrated after the Revolution and was the site of **Napoleon's** famed coronation in 1804. However, the building soon fell into disrepair, and for two decades it was used to shelter livestock. Donkeys and pigs were cleared away when **Victor Hugo**, proving that books can change public opinion, wrote his famed novel *Notre-Dame de Paris* (*The Hunchback of Notre Dame*) in 1831, reviving the cathedral's popularity and inspiring **Napoleon III** and **Haussmann** to devote financial attention to its restoration. Modifications by **Eugène Viollet-le-Du** included a new spire, gargoyles, and a statue of himself admiring his own work, and rejuvenated the cathedral's image in the public consciousness, and Notre Dame once again became a valued symbol of civic unity. In 1870 and again in 1940, thousands of Parisians attended masses in the church to pray for deliverance from the invading Germans; God had a thing and couldn't make it, apparently. On August 26, 1944, **Charles de Gaulle** braved Nazi fire to visit Notre Dame and give thanks for the imminent liberation of Paris. His funeral mass was held there many years later, as was the mass of his successor, **Mitterand.**

Despite these centuries of upheaval—not to mention the herds of tourists who invade its portals every day—the Nortre Dame remains unscathed and as illustrious as ever. The Cathedral continues to keep up its political prominence, and its place in the public consciousness is demonstrated through its pop culture cameos in movies such as *Amélie*, *Before Sunset*, and *Charade*, as well as the animated films *The Hunchback of Notre Dame* and *Ratatouille*.

Exterior: Notre Dame has been undergoing a face-lift for a while now. Construction may have started in the 12th century to be exact, but detail work was continued all the way into the 17th, when artists were still adding Baroque statues to everything. The oldest part of the cathedral is above the **Porte de Ste-Anne** (on the right), and dates from 1165-1175. The **Porte de la Vierge** (on the left), which portrays the life of the Virgin Mary, dates from the 13th century. The central **Porte du Jugement** was almost entirely redone in the 19th century; the **figure of Christ** dates from 1885. Irreverant revolutionaries wreaked havoc on the facade during the frenzied rioting of the 1790s; not content with decapitating Louis XVI, Parisians attacked the stone statues of the **Kings of Judah** above the doors, under the mistaken impression that they represented the monarch's ancestors. The heads were found in the basement of the **Banque Française du Commerce** in 1977 and were installed in the **Musée de Cluny.**

Towers: Home to the cathedral's fictional resident, Quasimodo the Hunchback, the two towers are the cathedral's most prominent features. Streaked with black soot, they cast an imposing shadow on the Paris skyline for years, but after several years of sandblasting, the blackened exterior has been brightened, once again revealing rose windows and rows of holy saints and hideous gargoyles. It's a long way to heaven: there's always a considerable line to make the 422-step climb to the top of the towers, but the view of Paris is worth it. (20 visitors let in every 10min.). The narrow staircase leads to a spectacular perch crowded by rows of gargoyles that overlook the Left Bank's **Latin Quarter** and the Right Bank's **Marais**. In the **South Tower,** a tiny door opens onto the 13-ton bell that even Quasimodo couldn't ring: it requires eight people or one Sumo wrestler to move.

Interior: Notre Dame can seat over 10,000 churchgoers. The arched ceiling is achieved by the spidery **flying buttresses** that support the vaults of the ceiling from outside, allowing light to fill the cathedral through delicate stained-glass windows. Down the **nave** is the **transept** and a view of the **rose windows.** The 21m **north window** (to the left when your back is to the entrance) is still composed almost entirely of 13th-century glass. The Virgin is situated at its center, and depicted as the descendant of the Old Testament kings and judges who surround her. While the north window is spectacularly well preserved, the **south and west windows** have had to undergo modern renovations. The base of the south window shows Matthew, Mark, Luke, and John on the shoulders of Old Testament prophets, while the central window depicts Christ surrounded by his 12 apostles. The cathedral's **treasury,** south of the choir, contains an assortment of glittering robes, sacramental chalices, and other gilded artifacts from the cathedral's past. The **Crown of Thorns,** believed to have been worn by Christ himself is reverentially presented only on the first Friday of every month at 3pm.

⇞ Ⓜ Cité. $ €8, under 18 free. $ Cathedral €8, ages 18-25 €6, under 18 free. Treasury €3, ages 12-25 €2, ages 5-11 €1. Audio tours €5; includes visit to treasury. 🕐 Cathedral open daily 7:45am-7pm. Towers open Jan-Mar and Oct-Dec 10am-5:30pm, Apr-Sept 10am-6:30pm, June-Aug Sa-Su until 11pm. Last entry 45min. before close. Free tours begin at the booth to the right as you enter. In French M-F 2 and 3pm; call 01 44 54 19 30 for English-language tours. Treasury open M-F 9:30am-6pm, Sa 9:30am-5pm, and Su 1-1:30pm and 6-6:30pm. Last entry 15min. before close.

Mass Sept-June M-F 8, 9am, noon, 6:15pm; Sa 6:30pm; Su 8:30am, 10am Mass with Gregorian chant, 11:30am international mass with music, 12:45, and 6:30pm. Free recital by one of the cathedral organists at 4:30pm. Vespers Sa-Su 5:45pm.

🏛 SAINTE-CHAPELLE ❤♿ CHURCH

6 bld. du Palais; Île de la Cité ☎01 53 40 60 97 ▣www.monuments-nationaux.fr

Everybody needs the occasional diversion to get through a service. For French royalty in the 13th century, it was the color of the church's walls. When light pours through the floor-to-ceiling stained-glass windows in the **Upper Chapel** of Sainte-Chapelle, illuminating bright dreamscapes of biblical scenes, the church becomes one of the most stunning and mesmerizing sights in Paris. The 15 panes date from 1136, and depict 1113 religious scenes. They narrate the Bible from Genesis to the Apocalypse, and are designed to be read from bottom to top, left to right; the bottom-to-top organization of the stories is meant to represent and enable the elevation of the soul through knowledge. Sainte-Chapelle is the foremost example of flamboyant Gothic architecture, and a tribute to the craft of medieval stained-glass—at 618 square meters, there's more of it than stone. The chapel was constructed in 1241 to house King Louis IX's most precious possession: the Crown of Thorns from Christ's Passion. Bought along with a section of the Cross by the Emperor of Constantinople in 1239 for the ungodly sum of £135,000 (adjust that puppy for about 800 years of inflation), the crown required an equally grand home, though its cost far exceeded that of the chapel. Although the crown itself—minus a few thorns that St-Louis gave away in exchange for political favors—has been moved to Notre Dame, Sainte-Chapelle is still a sight to behold. Down on the bottom floor, the **Lower Chapel** has a blue vaulted ceiling dotted with golden *fleurs-de-lis*, and contains a few "treasures"—platter-sized portraits of saints. This was where mortals served God, while royalty got to get a little closer in the Upper Chapel upstairs.

✈ Ⓜ*Cité. Within Palais de la Cité. Ⓢ €8, ages 18-25 €5, travelers with disabilities and caretaker, EU citizens 25 and under free. Twin ticket with Conciergerie €11, ages 18-25 €7.50, under 18 and EU citizens 18-25 free. ⊙ Open daily Nov-Feb 9am-5pm, and Mar-Oct 9:30am-6pm. Last entry 30min. before close. Chapel closed M-F 1-2:15pm. Guided tours in French 11am, 3pm and 4:40pm; in English 3:30pm.*

🏛 MEMORIAL DE LA DÉPORTATION ♿ HOLOCAUST MEMORIAL

Paris's Holocaust memorial is a claustrophobic and deeply moving experience. Narrow staircases, spiked gates, and high concrete walls are meant to evoke the atmosphere of the concentration camps; only a few visitors are allowed to enter the exhibition at a time, and the solitude that the museum imposes upon its viewers only increases the pervasive sense of sadness. The focal point of the insitution is a tunnel lined with 200,000 lit quartz pebbles, one for each of the French citizens who were deported. The pebbles are an homage to the Jewish custom of placing stones on the graves of the deceased. Empty cells and walls bear the names of the most infamous camps, as well as a series of humanitarian statements by famous writers like Jean-Paul Sartre and Antoine de St-Exupéry. Near the exit is the simplest and most arresting of these quotes, "Pardonne. N'Oublie Pas." (Forgive. Do Not Forget.)

✈ Ⓜ*Cité. At the western tip of the island in square de l'Île de France, on quai de l'Archevêche. A 5min. walk from the back of Notre Dame cathedral, and down a narrow flight of steps. Ⓢ Free. ⊙ Open Tu-Su Oct-Mar 10am-noon and 2-5pm; Apr-Sept 10am-noon and 2-7pm. Last entry 11:45am and 30min. before close.*

CONCIERGERIE ❤ PALACE, PRISON

2 bld. du Palais ☎01 53 40 60 97 ▣www.monuments-nationaux.fr

Back in the day, the Conciergerie served as both palace and prison, where kings feasted and criminals rotted. Built by Philip the Fair in the 14th century, the

paris

building is a good example of secular medieval architecture—heavy, hard and, somber. The name "Conciergerie" refers to the administrative officer of the Crown who acted as the king's steward, the Concierge (Keeper). When Charles V moved the seat of royal power from Île de la Cité to the Louvre after the assasination of his father's advisors, he endowed the Concierge with the power to run the Parliament, Chancery, and Audit Office. Later, this edifice became a royal prison and was taken over by the Revolutionary Tribunal after 1793. Now blackened by auto exhaust, the northern facade casts an appropriate gloom over the building: 2780 people were sentenced to death here between 1792 and 1794. A full list of the bourgeosie who had their heads chopped up is hung inside. Among its most famous prisoners were Marie-Antoinette, who was kept for 5 weeks, Robespierre, and 21 Girondins.

At the farthest corner on the right, a stepped parapet marks the oldest tower, the **Tour Bonbec,** which once housed the in-house torture chambers. The modern entrance lies between the **Tour d'Argent**, the stronghold of the royal treasury, and the **Tour de César,** used by the Revolutionary Tribunal. Past the entrance hall, stairs lead to rows of cells complete with somewhat blank-faced replicas of prisoners and prison conditions. Plaques explain how, in a bit of opportunism on the part of the Revolutionary leaders, the rich and famous could buy themselves private cells with cots and tables for writing while the poor slept on straw and with each other in pestilential cells. A model of Marie-Antoinette's rather comfortable-looking room suggests the extent to which class distinction remained preserved during the Revolution. If you follow the corridor named for "Monsieur de Paris," the executioner during the Revolution, you'll be tracing the final footsteps of Marie-Antoinette as she awaited decapitation on October 16, 1793. In 1914, the Conciergerie ceased to be used as a prison. Occasional concerts and wine tastings in the **Salle des Gens d'Armes** have, happily, replaced torture and beheadings.
✠ ⓜ*Cité.* ⑤ *€7, students €4.50, travelers with disabilities and caretaker, EU citizens 18-25 and under 18 free. Includes tour in French.* ⌚ *Open daily Mar-Oct 9:30am-6pm; Nov-Feb 9am-5pm. Last entry 30min. before close. Tours in French daily 11am, 3pm.*

HOTEL DE DIEU
BUILDING, HOSPITAL
1 pl. du Paris ☎01 42 34 82 34
Upon realizing that it might be helpful to save actual people in addition to their Christian souls (this was the Dark Ages: the idea was new at the time), Bishop St. Landry built this hospital in 651 CE. Today, it is the oldest hospital in Paris. In the Middle Ages, Hôtel de Dieu confined the sick rather than cured them; guards were posted at the doors to keep the patients from escaping and infecting the rest of the city. Over a millenia later, world-renowned chemist and biologist Louis Pasteur utilized the hospital's resources to conduct much of his pioneering research. In 1871, the hospital's proximity to Notre Dame saved the Cathedral from the fires of hell, so to speak—Communards were dissuaded from burning the monument for fear that the flames would engulf their hospitalized comrades nearby. The hospital has seen quieter days for some time now. The serene and well-groomed gardens in the inner courtyard feature sculpture exhibits.
✠ ⓜ*Cité.* ⑤ *Free.* ⌚ *Open daily 7am-8pm.*

PALAIS DE JUSTICE
COURTHOUSE
4 bld. du Palais ☎01 44 32 51 51
This is *the* place to get a prison sentence. The Palais has borne witness to the German spy Mata Hari's death sentence; Sarah Bernhardt's divorce from the Comédie Française; Emile Zola's trial following the Dreyfus Affair; Dreyfus's declaration of his innocence; and the trial of Maréchal Pétain after WWII. The institution's architecture is organized around the theme of—unsurprisingly enough— "justice," and features symbolic representations of its basic concepts.

The portrayals of Zeus and Medusa symbolize royal justice and punishment; the swords and sunlight recall the general concepts of justice and the law. A wide set of stone steps at the main entrance of the Palais de Justice leads to three doorways, each marked with Liberté, Egalité, or Fraternité—words that once signified revolution and now serve as the bedrock of the French legal tradition, not to mention many a photo. All trials are open to the public, and even if your French is not up to legalese, the theatrical sobriety of the interior is worth a quick glance. Plus you don't have to pay to see justice (last time) served!

[M]Cité, within Palais de la Cité, use Ste-Chapelle entrance at 6 bld. du Palais. Enter through the Ste-Chapelle entrance, go down the hallway after the security check and turn right onto a double-level courtroom area. To go in the main entrance, turn right into the courtyard after the security check. $ Free. ⏰ Courtrooms open M-F 9am-noon and 1:30-end of last trial.

MUSÉE DU LOUVRE — ♿ MUSEUM

☎01 40 20 53 17 www.louvre.fr

The cultural importance of the Louvre cannot be overstated. The museum's miles (yes, miles) of galleries stretch seemingly without end, and the depth, breadth, and beauty of their collection spans thousands of years, six continents, countless artistic styles, and a vast range of media.

Successful trips to the Louvre require two things: a good sense of direction and a great plan of attack. *Let's Go* provides general information about the museum, followed by descriptions of its major collections. Those in search of a more detailed itinerary can choose from a selection of curator-designated "Thematic Trails," described on the Louvre's website. We wish you luck.

OVERVIEW

The Louvre is comprised of three connected wings: **Sully, Richelieu,** and **Denon.** These three buildings are centered on the **Cour Napoleon,** the museum's main entrance, which is accessible through I.M. Pei's large, glass **pyramid** (the Cour Napoleon is also accessible directly from the **Palais-Royal/Musée de Louvre Metro station,** by way of the **Carrousel du Louvre,** an underground gallery with high-end shops and a reasonably priced food court.) The Cour sports two ticket counters, a number of automated ticket machines, and a large information desk. Once you've secured your ticket, proceed up the escalators to Sully, Richelieu, or Denon to enter the museum itself on the basement level. Within the museum, each wing is divided into sections according to period, national origin, and medium. Each room within these thematic sections is assigned a number and color that correspond to the Louvre's free map.

[M]Palais-Royal-Musée du Louvre. i Audio tour €6, under 18 €2, disabled visitors and unemployed €4, ages 18-25 rent one audio tour get one free. Visitors with disabilities don't have to wait in line. All entrances except the Passage Richelieu have elevators. At the main desk, you can exchange a piece of identification for a temporary wheelchair. Concerts and films are held in the auditorium in the Cour Napoléon. Concerts €3-30; films, lectures, and colloquia €2-10. Check the website for scheduling and more information. There is a small theater in the hall with free 1hr. films in French relating to the museum (films every hr. 10am-6pm). 1½hr. tours in English, French, or Spanish daily 11am, 2pm, 3:45pm; sign up at the info desk $ €9, after 6pm on W and F €6, unemployed free after 6pm, under 26 free after 6pm. Free admission first Su of every month. Prices include both permanent and temporary collections, except for those in the Cour Napoléon. Tickets also allow same-day access to the Musée Delacroix. ⏰ Open M 9am-6pm, W 9am-10pm, Th 9am-6pm, F 9am-10pm, and Sa 9am-6pm. Last entry 45min. before close; closure of rooms begin to close 30min. before close.

NEAR EASTERN ANTIQUITIES

The cradle of civilization, the fertile crescent, and the land of epithets, Mesopotamia (also known as the Near East) was also the birthplace of Western Art. The Louvre's collection is one of the largest agglomerations of Egyptian and

Mesopotamian artifacts in the world, and includes works that are over ten thousand years old. This area of the museum is generally one of the calmer ones, so you can spend some time marveling at its ancient offerings without feeling overwhelmed by the frenetic crowds. The encyclopaedic exhibits include a few terrific *stelas* (no, not the beer you get ripped off for at the cafes around the Louvre; we're talking slabs of wood or stone inscribed with paintings, inscriptions, etc.) The *Victory Stela of Naram Sim (Room 2)* is a highlight of the collection, depicting the Akkadian King ascending to the heavens, trampling his enemies along the way and sporting the crown of a god. One of the Louvre's most historically significant pieces is the *Law Code of Hammurabi*, or the King of Babylon, currently holding things down in Room 3 of the museum's Near East section. The object itself is a modest *stela* inscribed with 282 laws for King Hammurabi's Babylonian civilization; unlike modern day LA, this code was deliberately written in simple language, so that the most people possible could understand it. The code's subjects ranged from family law to slavery to salary setting. The Babylonians didn't value criminals' civil liberties too highly—dismemberment was the sentence for minor crimes like petty theft.

⚔ *Richelieu. Ground fl.*

GREEK, ETRUSCAN, AND ROMAN ANTIQUITIES

The extensive collection boasts works dating from the Neolithic age, about fourth millennium BCE, up until the sixth century. Many of the works featured here can be traced back to the rich royal collections seized by the rebel government of the French Revolution—which is also, in large part, to thank for transforming the Louvre into a museum. Purchases of various other royal and private collections over the next century solidified the bulk of the modern-day exhibit. The armless *Venus de Milo* is, obviously, the main attraction. As you approach Room 74 on the first floor, you can hear the din of the crowd (not quite Mona Lisa level, but still a din), heartily oohing, ahhing, and snapping pictures of the lady. The *Winged Victory of Samothrace* proves that a head is not a prerequisite for Greek masterpieces; beware of large crowds.

⚔ *Denon and Sully. 1st fl., ground fl., and lower ground fl.*

THE ITALIANS

Da Vinci's *Mona Lisa*, purchased by Francois I in 1518 *(Room 6)* is the most famous painting in the world. While the lady's mysterious smile and plump figure are still charming, there is nothing charming about fighting for a good view of the painting; if you feel comfortable doing so, now's the time to throw some elbows. The crowds are fierce, the painting is hidden in a glass box that constantly reflects hundreds of camera flashes, and you won't be allowed within 15 ft of it. If you're pressed for time and/or physically unimposing, you might consider skipping the lady, or settling for a terrible view of her. In the adjacent hall, an astonishing group of Renaissance masterpieces awaits—everything from Da Vinci's *Virgin on the Rocks* to Raphael's *Grand Saint Michael* to Fra Angelico's *Cavalry*. The rest of the exhibit contains Renaissance masterpieces by Caravaggio, da Vinci, and more: an impressive bunch whose work documents the rise of Humanist art in the West. This wing is best visited as soon as the museum opens, as the entire thing turns into a zoo within 15-30min.; while crowds are smaller on Wednesday and Friday evening visit times, this part of the Museum is always pretty busy.

⚔ *Denon. 1st fl.*

FLANDERS, THE NETHERLANDS

A more relaxed Louvre experience awaits you on the second floor. Vermeer's majestic *Astronomer* and *Lacemaker* occupy Room 38. While Vermeer left behind no sketches or clues related to his preparatory methods, some scholars

sights · musée du louvre

believe that he used a camera obscura in composing his works; one can make out subtle effects of light that could not have appeared to Vermeer's naked eye without a little assistance, unless he was superhuman (granted, that's a distinct possibility). Also not to be missed is Rubens' *Galerie Médicis*; comprised of 24 huge canvases; the room's paintings are dedicated to episodes from the self-obsessed queen's life. The equally giant tableaux are worth a few minutes of your time. This section of the Museum is also filled with works by Rembrandt, Van Eyck, and Van der Weyden.

☏ *Richelieu. 2nd fl.*

AND NOW FOR THE FRENCH

French paintings? In the Louvre? You would never have guessed it. Extravagant works from the 17th, 18th, and 19th centuries dominate the second floor of the Sully wing. A room dedicated to La Tour, once one of the world's leading Caravaggesque painters, showcases his fascination with hidden sources of light, responsible for the haunting works that occupy Room 28. Once you've had your fill of modernity, peace, and quiet, head back to the first floor of Denon, where the French heavyweights neighbor the Mona Lisa. The second most famous painting in these galleries is Delacroix's chaotic *Liberty Leading the People*, in which Liberty is symbolized by a highly liberated (read: partially nude) woman. The rich use of color in the painting is considered seminal in its effect on the Impressionist school of art. Social science types should get a kick out of Ingres's body-twisting *Grande Odalisque* and Delacroix's *Death of Sardanapalus*. The combined chaos and richness of the tableaux are truly fascinating. Both paintings are good examples of Orientalism, a product of France's imperial adventures in North Africa. The latter painting depicts the suicide of Sardanapalus, an Oriental king of Antiquity, on a sacrificial pyre originally built to exterminate his slaves, women, and horses after military defeat. The legacy of French perception of the "Orient" as a paradise of indulgence, sexually generous women, and drugs, remains today.

☏ *Sully, 2nd fl. Denon, 1st fl.*

CHÂTELET-LES HALLES

Châtelet-Les Halles is perhaps Paris's most densely touristed area. And that's saying something. From the commercial indulgence of the Place Vendome, to the mind-numbing grandeur and beauty of the Louvre, to the bizarre trends on display at Les Arts Decoratifs, the 1st and 2nd arrondissements have it all.

🖼 JARDIN DES TUILERIES

⛦ GARDEN

pl. de la Concorde, rue de Rivoli   ☎01 40 20 90 43

Covering the distance from the Louvre to the place de la Concorde (and the Jeu de Paume and L'Orangerie), the Jardin des Tuileries are a favorite hangout for Parisians and tourists alike. The garden was originally built for Catherine de Medici in 1559, when she moved to the Louvre after the death of her husband, Henri II. The original designer was Italian Bernard de Carnesse, who modeled his masterpiece on the gardens of Catherine's native Florence, and the garden was used mostly for royal occasions. About a hundred years later, Louis XIV's superintendent, Jean-Baptiste Colbert, assigned the task of recreating the Tuileries garden to Le Notre (of Vaux-le-Vicomte and Versailles fame), the grandson of one Catherine's gardeners. Straight lines and sculpted trees became the decorative preference for this majestic plot of land, and several generations of kings employed the new and improved Tuileries for massive parties. You don't want to miss the beautiful views of Paris from the elevated terrace by the Seine. There are extremely expensive cafes scattered throughout the grounds. During the summer, confiserie stands, merry-go-rounds and a huge ferris wheel are installed near the rue de Rivoli entrance for the park's younger visitors.

⚐ Ⓜ*Tuileries.* $ *Free.* ⏲ *Open daily Apr-May 7am-9pm; June-Aug 7am-11pm; Sept 7am-9pm; Oct-Mar 7:30am-7:30pm. English tours from the Arc de Triomphe du Carrousel. Amusement park open July to mid-Aug.*

ÉGLISE ST.-EUSTACHE

CHURCH

2 rue du Jour ☎01 42 36 31 05 🖳www.saint-eustache.org

There's a reason why Richelieu, Molière, Louis XIV, and Mme. de Pompadour achieved greatness in their lives: they were all baptized and/or received communion in the truly awe-inspiring Église de St-Eustache. Construction of the Gothic structure began in 1532 and dragged on for over a century due to lack of funding. The situation was so dire that its head priest sent a letter to the Les Halles community (which was at that point almost entirely Catholic) soliciting money for the project. Construction was essentially completed in 1633, and the church opened in 1637. In 1754, the unfinished Gothic facade was demolished and replaced with the fantastic Romanesque one that stands here today; in this sense, the Church's dysfunctional building process ended up working in its favor. The chapels contain paintings by Rubens, as well as by the British artist Raymond Mason's seemingly misplaced relief, "Departure of the Fruits and Vegetables from the Heart of Paris," commemorating the closing of the market at Les Halles in February 1969. Today, St. Eustache stands up to almost any other church in terms of its physical beauty. Not to mention that it collects some serious points because it isn't as heavily touristed as the Basilique Sacre-Coeur, or, obviously, Notre Dame.

⚐ Ⓜ*Les Halles.* $ *Audio tours are available in English; the suggested donation is €3. A piece of identity is required to use one of the guides.* ⏲ *Open M-F 9:30am-7pm, Sa 10am-7pm, Su 9am-7pm. Mass Sa 6pm, Su 9:30, 11am, 6pm*

LES ARTS DECORATIFS

MUSEUM

107 rue de Rivoli ☎01 44 55 57 50 🖳www.lesartsdecoratifs.fr

The fashion-conscious among our *Let's Go* readers could easily spend a full day perusing the Musée des Arts Decoratifs. It itself houses four different museums, in addition to many smaller exhibits: **Arts Decoratifs** (Interior Design), **Mode et Textile** (Fashion and Fabric), **Publicite** (Advertisement), and the **Musée Nissim de Camondo.** The former three are dedicated to some funky, haute couture design that the average tourist has probably never experienced. In the Arts Decoratifs, you'll find sheep-shaped chairs, elephant-shaped fountains, and chairs whittled into the form of birds. The Mode and Textile Museum has exhibits on the evolution of fashion from the 1970s to the 1990s, featuring smaller exhibits on prominent fashion designers, including Yves St.-Laurent. The Advertisement Museum features, you guessed it, lots of ads. Fashion-conscious types balance their time in the museum between scrutinizing the exhibits and finding a mirror to make sure their hair is just so to impress their fellow fashionistas. The latter of the four museums is in the old home of the famous Camondo family; its three floors showcase wonderful artwork, furniture, and woodwork. Don't miss the Galerie des Bijoux; dark-room displays of some of modern mankind's finest jewels are breathtaking even for those helpless dudes who get their significant other a terribly homely piece of jewelry come Christmas and birthday times.

⚐ Ⓜ*Palais Royal-Musée du Louvre.* *i* *Audio tour included.* $ *Musées Rivoli (Arts Decoratifs, Mode et Textile, Publicite) €9, reduced €7.50. Musée Nissim Camondo €7, reduced €5.* ⏲ *Open Tu-W 11am-6pm, Th 11am-9pm, F-Su 11am-6pm. Last entry 30min. before close.*

COMÉDIE FRANÇAISE, SALLE RICHELIEU

THEATER

place Colette, southwest corner of Palais-Royal ☎08 25 10 16 80 🖳www.comedie-francaise.fr

In 1680 Louis XIV ordered that Paris's two most prominent acting troupes, that of the Hôtel Guénégaud and that of the Hôtel de Bourgogne, merge into the

Comédie Française. They were lodged originally at the former acting troupe's original location. After the Revolution, in 1799, the government provided for the troupe to move into its legendary location in Palais-Royal's Salle Richelieu. Molière, the company's founder, collapsed on stage here while performing in "Le Malade Imaginaire," and died several hours later. The chair onto which he collapsed is still on display, along with several busts of famous actors crafted by equally famous sculptors. Visconti's Fontaine de Molière is only a few steps from where Molière died at no. 40. Today, the Comédie Française also has locations at the Théâtre du Vieux-Colombier and the Studio-Théâtre.

✦ ⓜPalais Royal-Musée du Louvre. *i* Visits not available; you have to get tickets to one of the shows to see the Salle Richelieu. ⓢ Spectacles €6-47. Cheapest tickets are available minutes before the show, so try going on a weeknight. ⏲ Spectacle start times vary.

THE MARAIS

There's more to see in the Marais than strutting fashionistas and strolling rabbis. A unique mix of historic and new, the area boasts an impressive list of quirky and worthwhile sights. The eastern section of the arrondissement harbors a labyrinth of old, quaint streets, a smattering churches, and some of Paris's most beautiful *hôtels particuliers*, or mansions (particularly around the **pl. des Vosges**). The **Centre Pompidou**, the undisputed main attraction of the Marais, breaks up the beige monotony in the western part of the arrondissement. Though the Pompidou, quite like a spoiled child, tends to attract the most attention, there are a number of other museums that are less touristy and just as entertaining. The underrated **Musée Carnavalet** visually portrays the history of Paris, while the **Musée de la Chasse** tells the story of the animals that died here. Even if you aren't the museum-going type, **Vieille du Temple** and **rue des Rosiers** are great streets to explore.

▨ CENTRE POMPIDOU   ✐⁽ᵗ⁾ MUSEUM

pl. Georges-Pompidou, rue Beaubourg   ☎01 44 78 12 33 ▨www.centrepompidou.fr

Erected in Beaubourg, a former slum *quartier* whose high rate of tuberculosis earned it classification as an *îlot insalubre* (unhealthy block) in the 1930s, the Pompidou was and still is considered alternately an architectural breakthrough and a montrosity. Pioneered in the '70s by architects Richard Rogers, Gianfranco Franchini, and Renzo Piano at the commission of President Pompidou, the design features a network of yellow electrical tubes, green water pipes, and blue ventilation ducts along the exterior of the building. The range of functions that the Centre serves are as varied as its colors—a sort of cultural theme park of an ultra-modern exhibition, performance, and research space, it most famously hosts the **Musée National d'Art Moderne.** The **Salle Garance** houses an adventurous film series, and the **Bibliothèque Publique d'Information** (entrance on rue de Renard) is a free, non-circulating library with wireless, which is almost always packed with students. Located in a separate building is the **Institut de la Recherche et de la Coordination Acoustique/Musiqu**e (IRCAM), an institute and laboratory for the development of new technologies. The Pompidou was engineered to accommodate 5000 visitors a day, but the center now attracts over 20,000, making it more popular than the Louvre. The spectacular view from the top of the escalators, which can be reached only by purchasing a museum ticket or by dining at the rooftop restaurant, **Georges,** is well worth the lengthy ascent. From there, look out across at the Parisian skyline and observe the cobblestone square out front, filled with artists, musicians, punks, and passersby.

The **Musée National d'Art Moderne** is the Centre Pompidou's main attraction. While its collection spans the 20th century, the art from the last 50 years is particularly brilliant. It features everything from Philip Guston's uncomfortably adorable hooded figures to Eva Hesse's uncomfortably anthropomorphic sculptures. Those looking for a less provokative experience will want to see Cai

Guo-Qang's Bon Voyage, an airplane made of wicker and vine hanging from the ceiling and studded with objects confiscated from passengers' carry-on luggage at the Tokyo airport. A large part of its contemporary display is now devoted to work by women artists in a much-needed exhbition called elles@centrepompidou. On the museum's second level, early 20th-century heavyweights like Duchamp and Picasso hold court. Most of the works were contributed by the artists themselves or by their estates; Joan Miró and Wassily Kandinsky's wife are among the museum's founders.

⚓ ⓜRambuteau or Hôtel de Ville. RER Châtelet-Les Halles. ⓢ Library and Forum free. Permanent collection and exhibits €12, under 26 €9, under 18 and EU citizens under 25 free. First Su of month free for all visitors. Visitors' guides available in bookshop. ⚄ Centre open M 11am-9pm, W-Su 11am-10pm. Museum open M 11am-9pm, W 11am-9pm, Th 11am-11pm, F-Su 11am-9pm. Last tickets 1hr. before close. Library open M noon-10pm, W-F noon 10pm, Sa-Su 11am-10pm.

MAISON DE VICTOR HUGO
⚓🚻 HISTORIC HOME

6 pl. des Vosges ☎01 42 72 10 16 🌐www.musee-hugo.paris.fr

Dedicated to the father of the French Romantics and housed in the building where he lived from 1832 to 1848, the museum displays Hugo memorabilia, including little-known paintings by his family and the desk where he wrote standing up. On the first floor, one room is devoted to paintings of scenes from Les Misérables, another to Notre Dame de Paris, and a third to other featured plays and works. Upstairs are Hugo's apartments, a recreation of the bedroom where Hugo died, and the chambre chinoise, which reveals Hugo's flamboyant interior decorating skills and just how much of a romantic he was.

⚓ ⓜChemin Vert, St.Paul or Bastille. ⓘ Credit card min. €15. ⓢ Permanent collection free, special exhibits around €7-8, seniors €5, under 26 €3.50-4. Audio tour €5. ⚄ Open Tu-Su 10am-6pm, last entry 5:40pm.

IGOR STRAVINSKY FOUNTAIN
FOUNTAIN

pl. Igor Stravinsky

This novel installation features irreverent and multichromatic mobile sculptures by Niki de St. Phalle and Jean Tinguely. The whimsical elephants, lips, mermaids, and bowler hats are inspired by Stravinsky's works, and have been known to squirt water at unsuspecting bystanders. While the fountain's colorful quirkiness is in keeping with the Centre Pompidou, it stands in contrast to the nearby historic rue Brisemiche and Église de St-Merri.

⚓ ⓜHôtel de Ville. Adjacent to the Centre Pompidou on rue de Renard.

HÔTEL DE VILLE
🚻 GOVERNMENT BUILDING

Information office, 29 rue de Rivoli ☎01 42 76 43 43; 01 42 76 50 49

As the constant stream of tourists and their flashing cameras will attest, the Hôtel de Ville is the most extravagant and picture-worthy non-palace edifice in Paris. The present structure is the second incarnation of the original edifice, which was built in medieval times and, during the 14th-15th centuries, served as a meeting hall for merchants who controlled traffic on the Seine. In 1533, King François I appointed Domenica da Cortona, known as Boccador, to expand and renovate the structure into a city hall worthy of the metropolis; the result was an elaborate mansion built in the Renaissance style of the Loire Valley châteaux. On May 24, 1871, the Communards, per usual, doused the building with gasoline and set it on fire. The blaze lasted a full eight days, and spared nothing but the building's frame. Undaunted, the Third Republic built a virtually identical structure on the ruins, with a few significant changes. For one, the Republicans integrated statues of their own heroes into the facade: historian Jules Michelet graces the right side of the building, while author Eugène Sue surveys the rue de Rivoli. They also installed crystal chandeliers, gilded every interior surface, and created a Hall of Mirrors that rivals the original at Versailles. When Manet,

sights • the marais

Monet, Renoir, and Cézanne offered their services, they were all turned down in favor of the didactic artists whose work decorates the Salon des Lettres, the Salon des Arts, the Salon des Sciences, and the Salon Laurens. Originally called pl. de Grève, pl. Hôtel de Ville is additionally famous for its vital contribution to the French language. Poised on a marshy embankment (grève) of the Seine, the medieval square served as a meeting ground for angry workers, giving France the useful and ever necessary phrase *en grève* (on strike). In 1610, Henri IV's assassin was quartered alive here by four horses bolting in opposite directions. Today, place de Hôtel de Ville almost never sleeps: strikers continue to gather here, and the square occasionally hosts concerts, special TV broadcasts, and light shows. Every major French sporting event—Rolland Garros, the Tour de France, and any game the Bleus ever play—is projected onto a jumbo screen in the *place*. The information office holds exhibits on Paris in the lobby off the rue de Lobau.

[M]Hôtel de Ville. i Special exhibit entry on rue de Lobau. ⏰ Open M-Sa 9am-7pm when there is an exhibit; until 6pm otherwise. Group tours available with advance reservations, call for available dates.

LATIN QUARTER AND ST-GERMAIN

Sights, sights, sights, and more sights. There's more to see in the fifth and sixth than there is time to see it in. With that being said, there are a few things that you can't miss. The **Museums of the Middle Ages** (Musée de Cluny) and the **National Delacroix Museum** are two of the finest selections in Paris. The **Jardin de Luxembourg** is magnificent, and, alongside the Tuileries, one of the finest chill spots Paris has to offer. If you're the artsy type, you can't miss the slew of galleries in the **Odéon/Mabillon** area.

PANTHÉON — HISTORICAL MONUMENT, CRYPT

place du Panthéon ☎01 44 32 18 04 pantheon.monuments-nationaux.fr

Among Paris's most majestic and grandiose structures, the multi-faceted Panthéon is the former stomping ground and final resting place of many great Frenchmen and women of days past. In the 1760s, Louis XV recovered from a serious illness, and, having vowed to transform the basilica of Ste-Geneviève to something bigger if he survived, followed up on his promise. Though the building was originally designed to be an enlarged version of the Abbey of Ste-Geneviève, it was decided during the early stages of the French Revolution to use the massive structure as a secular mausoleum. Some of France's greatest citizens are buried in the Panthéon's crypt, including Marie and Pierre Curie, politician Jean Jaurès, Braille inventor Louis Braille, Voltaire, Jean-Jacques Rousseau, Émile Zola, and Victor Hugo. Now that's a list. There's something here for everybody; if you ever took a high school French class, you'll enjoy paying homage to Antoine de St-Exupéry, writer of "Le Petit Prince." Alexandre Dumas became the crypt's most recent addition, following his November 2002 interment. Compte de Mirabeau, a great Revolutionary orator, received the first nomination for a chunk of real estate at the Panthéon. Although interred there, the government expelled his ashes one year later when the public discovered his counter-revolutionary correspondence with Louis XVI. Beyondthe "ooh, look who's buried here," appeal of the crypt, the Panthéon's other main attraction is a famous science experiment any respectable nerd will have heard of: Foucault's Pendulum. The pendulum's plane of oscillation stays fixed as the Earth rotates around it, confirming the Earth's rotation. While you might be struck by the pendulum's oscillation, don't step in its path. The Earth's not gonna stop for ya.

[M]Cardinal Lemoine. i Dome visits Apr-Oct available in English. $ €7.50, ages 18-25 €4.80, under 18 free. Free 1st Su of the month Oct-Mar. ⏰ Open daily Apr-Sept 10am-6:30pm; Oct-Mar 10am-6pm. Last entry 45min. before close.

◾ LE JARDIN DU LUXEMBOURG   GARDEN
Main entrance on bld. St-Michel

"There is nothing more charming, which invites one more enticingly to idleness, reverie, and young love, than a soft spring morning or a beautiful summer dusk at the Jardin du Luxembourg," wrote Léon Daudet in a fit of sentimentality in 1928. The gardens were once a residential area in Roman Paris, the site of a medieval monastery, and later the home of 17th-century French royalty, when Marie de Medici hired architect Jean-François-Thérèse for the task of landscaping the garden's roughly 55 acres of prime Latin Quarter real estate in 1612. Revolutionaries liberated the gardens in the late 18th century and transformed them into a lush public park.

Today, Latin Quarter Parisians flock to Le Jardin de Luxembourg to sunbathe, stroll, flirt, drink, inhale cigarettes, and read by the rose gardens and central pool. The acres are patchworked by lawns of Wimbledon-esque precision, symmetrical pathways, and sculptures, taking in the garden can be a daunting task. Visitors saunter through the park's sandy paths, passing sculptures of France's queens, poets, and heroes. Nerds and chess phenoms challenge the local band of aged chessmasters to a game under shady chestnut trees. If you have kids, they can sail toy boats in the fountain, ride ponies, and see the *grand guignol*, or puppet show. Tennis courts in the garden generally fill up pretty quickly; you'll have a long wait to stretch out your muscles before showing off the skill set to passing French hotties. Undoubtedly the best, and most sought-after, spot in the garden is the **Fontaine des Médicis**, just east of the Palais, a vine-covered grotto complete with a murky fish pond and Baroque fountain sculptures. You might have to wait a few minutes, or hours, to get one of the coveted chairs bordering the Fontaine. Do not step on the portions of grass that bear a small divider from the walkways. There are tons of cops roaming the Garden at all times, so chances are you will get caught, *gueuled* (that's French for stank-faced), and, possibly, if you are so unlucky as to draw a supercop, fined. A more beautiful rest stop does not exist in Paris. The **Palais du Luxembourg,** located within the park and built in 1615 for Marie de Medicis, is now home to the **French Senate** and thus closed to the public. During WWII, the palace was used by the Nazis as headquarters for the Luftwaffe.

✦ ⓂOdéon or RER: Luxembourg. ✦ *Guided tours in French Apr-Oct 1st W of each month 9:30am. Tours start at pl. André Honorat behind the observatory.* ⚅ *Open daily.*

ÉGLISE ST-SULPICE   ♿ CHURCH
50 rue Vaugirard   ☎01 42 34 59 60 ▣www.paroisse-saint-sulpice-paris.org

The Neoclassical facade of Église St-Sulpice dominates the large square bearing its name, where children and street vendors gather around the meditative fountain. The church was designed by Servadoni in 1733, and, in classic French fashion, its Neoclassical facade was never finished. Today, it is in the middle of large-scale exterior renovations (or completions, maybe?). Despite its many practical complications, the church boasts a few unique attractions. A set of badly faded Delacroix frescoes, *Jacob Wrestling* with the *Angel and Heliodorus Driven from the Temple*, in the first chapel on the right are deeply moving. Jean-Baptiste Pigalle's similarly faded *Virgin and Child* is in a chapel in the rear of the building. A fantastically monumental organ (five keyboards!) is used in frequent concerts; check the bulletin at the front of the church for more information. Unfortunately, the poorly lit interior of the church provides an unbecoming setting for the church's artistic stronger points.

✦ ⓂSt-Sulpice or Mabillon. ⚅ *Open daily 7:30am-7:30pm*

INVALIDES

Visit this arrondissement more than once if you can. Unsurprisingly, the **Tour Eiffel** towers over all of the 7*ème* attractions, but the posh neighborhood also hosts the French national government, a number of embassies, and an astonishing concentration of famous museums. Be sure to stop by the **Musée de Rodin** and **Musée d'Orsay**.

EIFFEL TOWER
♥& TOWER

It doesn't need one. You can see it from everywhere   ☎01 44 11 23 23 🖳www.tour-eiffel.fr.

In 1937, Gustave Eiffel remarked on his construction, "I ought to be jealous of that tower; she is more famous than I am. "The city of Paris as a whole could share the same lament. A true French synecdoche, the Eiffel Tower has come to stand for Paris itself. Gustave Eiffel designed it to be the tallest structure in the world, intended to surpass the ancient Egyptian pyramids in size and notoriety. Parisians, per usual, were not impressed; the same city-dwellers who cringed at the thought of skyscrapers mumbled disapprovingly before construction had even begun. Critics called it, perhaps not unfairly, the "metal asparagus," and a Parisian Tower of Babel. Writer Guy de Maupassant thought it was so hideous that he ate lunch every day at its ground-floor restaurant—the only place in Paris where you can't actually see the Eiffel Tower.

When the tower was inaugurated in March 1889 as the centerpiece of the World's Fair, Parisians forgot their earlier displeasure. Nearly two million people ascended the engineering miracle during the event. Throughout its history, the tower has been more than an aesthetic controversy and photo backdrop. In WWI it functioned as a radio-telegraphic center that intercepted enemy messages, including the one that led to the arrest of Mata Hari, the Danish dancer accused of being a German spy. Since the expo, over 150 million Parisians and tourists have made it the most visited paid monument in the world. A Parisian icon represented on everything from postcards to underwear to umbrellas, Eiffel's wonder still comes under fire from some who see it as Maupassant did: a metal montrosity overrun with overly-tanned tourists, cheap trinkets, and false promises of cliché romance.

Still, at 324m—just a tad shorter than the Chrysler building—the tower is a tremendous feat of design and engineering, though wind does cause it to occasionally sway 6 to 7 cm. Though arguably ugly, it will still take your breath away with its sheer size, especially up close. The top floor and its unparalleled view especially deserve of a visit. And despite the 7,000 tons of metal and 2.5 million rivets that hold together its 12,000 parts, the tower appears light and airy. Its distinctive bronze color is repainted every seven years, and is graduated from a lighter tone at the summit to a darker one at the base to highlight the monument's elegant line of perspective.

The cheapest way to ascend the tower is by walking up the first two floors; the third floor is only accessible by elevator. Waiting until nightfall to make your ascent cuts down the line and ups the glamour. At the top, captioned aerial photographs help you locate other famous landmarks. On a clear day it is possible to see Chartres, 88km away. From dusk until 2am (1am Sept-May), the tower sparkles with light for 10min. on the hour.

✦ Ⓜ*Bir-Hakeim or Trocadéro.* Ⓢ *Elevator to 2nd fl. €8.10, ages 12-24 €6.40, 4-11 and handicapped €4, under 3 free; elevator to summit €13.10/11.50/9/free; stair entrance to second floor €4.50/3.50/3/free.* 🕓 *Open daily mid-June to Aug elevator 9am-12:45am (last entry 11pm), stairs 9am-12:45am (last entry midnight); Sept-mid-June elevator 9:30am-11:45pm (last entry 11pm), stairs 9:30am-6:30pm (last entry 6pm).*

CHAMPS DE MARS
& FIELD, WALK

Lined with more lovers than trees, the expansive lawn that stretches from the École Militaire to the Eiffel Tower is called Champs de Mars (Field of Mars).

Close to the neighborhood's military monuments and museums, it has historically lived up to the Roman god of war for whom it is named. In the days of Napoleon's empire, the field was used as a drill ground for the adjacent École Militiare, and in 1780 Charles Montgolfier launched the first hydrogen balloon from its grassy fields. During the Revolution, the park was the site of civilian massacres and political demonstrations. In 2000, a glass monument to international peace was erected at the end of the Champs in quiet defiance of the École Militiare across the way. Named the Mur pou la Paix (Wall for Peace), the structure consists of two large glass walls covered from top to bottom with the word "peace" written in 32 languages. Viewed through the monument's walls, École Militiare appears to have the word "peace" scrawled all over it.

✦ ⓜ*La Motte Picquet-Grenelle or École Militiare.*

▨ MUSÉE D'ORSAY

✦ ♿ MUSEUM

62 rue de Lille

☎01 40 49 48 14 🌐www.musée-orsay.com

Aesthetic taste is fickle. When a handful of artists were rejected from the Louvre salon in the 19th-century, they opened an exhibition across the way, prompting both the scorn of stick-up-their-arses Académiciens and the rise of Impressionism. Today, people line up at the Musée d'Orsay to see this collection of groundbreaking rejects, which were considered so scandalous at the time. Established in 1982 in a dramatically lit former railway station, the collection includes paintings, sculpture, decorative arts, and photography dating from 1848 to WWI.

The museum building is a story in itself. Built for the 1900 World's Fair, the Gare d'Orsay's industrial function was carefully masked by architect Victor Laloux behind glass, stucco, and a 370-room luxury hotel, so as not to offend the eye of the 7*ème*'s sophisticated residents. For several decades, it was the main departure point for southwest-bound trains, but newer trains were too long for its platforms, and it closed in 1939. After WWII, the station served as the main French repatriation center, receiving thousands of concentration camp survivors. Orson Welles filmed *The Trial* here in 1962. 24 years later, Musée d'Orsay opened in the station as one of Mitterrand's *Grands Projets*, gathering works from the **Louvre, Jeu de Paume, Palais de Tokyo, Musée de Luxembourg**, provincial museums, and private collections to add to the original collection the Louvre had refused.

The museum is organized chronologically from the ground floor up. The ground floor is dedicated to Pre-Impressionist paintings and sculpture, and contains the two scandalous works that started it all, both by Manet. Olympia, rumored to be a common whore whose confrontational gaze and nudity caused a stir, and Déjeuner sur l'Herbe, which shockingly portrayed a naked woman accompanied by fully clothed men. Back in the 19th century, scenes like that never happened. Or at least not publicly. The detailed section study of the Opéra Garnier is situated in the back of the room, and is definitely worth a visit as well. The top floor includes all the big names in Impressionist and Post-Impressionist art: Monet, Manet, Seurat, Van Gogh, and Degas. Degas' famed dancers and prostitutes are a particular highlight. In addition, the balconies offer supreme views of the Seine and the jungle of sculptures in the garden below. Beyond the permanent collection, seven temporary exhibition spaces, called *dossiers*, are scattered throughout the building. Call or pick up a free copy of *Nouvelles du Musée d'Orsay* for current installations. The museum also hosts conferences, special tours (including children's tours), and concerts. One of the most popular museums in Paris with the crowds to match, we recommend that you visit on Sunday mornings or Thursday evenings to avoid the masses.

✦ ⓜ*Solférino. Access to visitors at entrance A off the square at 1 rue de la Légion d'Honneur.*

ℹ Baby carriages not allowed. $ €8, ages 18-25 €5.50, under 18 and EU citizens 18-26 free (free tickets directly at museum entrance). Tickets available online. ⏰ Open T-W 9:30am-6pm, Th 9:30am-9:45pm, F-Su 9:30am-6pm. Visitors asked to leave starting 30min before close. Boutique open daily 9:30am-6:30pm. Restaurant on level 2 open M-W 11:45am-5:30pm, Th 11:45am-5:30pm and 7-9:30pm, F-Su 11:45am-5:30pm.

ÉCOLE MILITAIRE ♿ GOVERNMENT INSTITUTION

1 pl. Joffre

Demonstrating the link between sex, war, and power once again, Louis XV founded the École Militaire in 1751 at the urging of his mistress, Mme. de Pompadour, who hoped to make officers of "poor gentlemen." In 1784, 15-year-old Napoleon Bonaparte enrolled. A few weeks later, he presented administrators with a comprehensive plan for the school's reorganization, and by the time he graduated three years later, he was a lieutenant in the artillery. Teachers foretold he would "go far in favorable circumstances." Little did they know. Louis XVI turned the building into a barracks for the Swiss Guard, but it was converted back into a military school in 1848. Today, the extensive structure serves as the living quarters of the Chief of the National Army, and additionally houses the Ministry of Defense and a variety of schools for advanced military studies, such as the Institute for Higher Studies of National Defense, the Center for Higher Studies of the Military, the Inter-Army College of Defense, and the School of Reserve Specialist Officers of State.

➡ [M]École Militaire.

INVALIDES HISTORIC BUILDING

Situated at the center of the *7ème*, the gold-leaf dome of the Hôtel des Invalides glimmers conspicuously rain or shine, adding a touch of bling to the Parisian skyline. Most visitors assume that the building's history is just as scintillating, but Invalides has always led a life of seriousness and importance. Originally founded by Louis XVI in 1671 as a home for disabled soldiers, it is now the headquarters of the military governor of Paris and continues to serve, on a small scale, as a military hospital. Stretching from the building to the Pont Alexandre III is the tree-lined **Esplanade des Invalides** (not to be confused with the Champs de Mars, p. 42). The Musée de l'Armée, Musée des Plans-Reliefs, Musée des Deux Guerres Mondiales, and Musée de l'Ordre de la Libération are housed within the Invalides museum complex, as is **Napoleon's tomb,** which lies in the adjoining Église St-Louis. To the left of the Tourville entrance, the Jardin de l'Intendant is strewn with benches and impeccably groomed trees and bushes, a topiary testament to the army's detail-oriented (read: anal) mentality. A ditch lined with captured foreign cannons runs around the Invalides area where a moat used to be, making it impossible to leave by any means beyond the two official entrances. Be aware that certain areas are blocked to tourists, out of respect for the privacy of the war veterans who still live in the hospital.

➡ [M]Invalides. $ €9, under 18 and EU citizens 18-25 free. Free after 5pm.

CHAMPS-ÉLYSÉES

There's a reason that the *8ème* remains Paris's most touristed arrondissement, long after the Champs-Élysées ceased to be posh. The area harbors more architectural beauty, historical significance, and shopping opportunities than almost any other area in the city, and remains an exhilarating—if hectic—place to spend a day. Champs-Élysées also hosts a variety of art museums in its northern corners; they are often located in *hotels particuliers*, where they were once part of the private collections.

ARC DE TRIOMPHE ♿ HISTORIC MONUMENT

pl. de l'Etoile 💻arc-de-triomphe.monuments-nationaux.fr

The highest point between the **Louvre** and the **Grande Arche de la Defense,** the Arc de Triomphe offers a stunning view down the Champs-Élysées to the **Tuileries** and Louvre. Plans for the monument were first conceived by the architect Charles Francois Ribar in 1758, who envisioned an unparalleled tribute to France's military prowess—in the form of a giant, bejeweled elephant. Fortunately for France, the construction of the monument was not undertaken until 1806, when Napoleon conceived a less bizarre landmark modeled after the triumphal arches of victorious Roman emperors like Constantine and Titus. Napoleon was exiled before the arch was completed, and Louis XVIII took over its construction in 1823. He dedicated the arch to the French military's recent intervention in Spain and its commander, the Duc d'Angouleme, and placed its design in the hands of Jean-Francois-Therese Chalgrin. The Arc de Triomphe was consecrated in 1836; in honor of the emperor that conceived of its design, the names of Napoleon's generals and battles are engraved inside. The arch has been a magnet for various triumphant armies ever since. After the Prussians marched through the Arc in 1871, the mortified Parisians purified the ground beneath it with fire. On July 14, 1919, the Arc provided the backdrop for an Allied victory parade headed by Ferdinand Foch. After years under Germany's brutal occupation during WWII, a sympathetic Allied army ensured that a French general would be the first to drive under the Arc in the liberation of Paris.

Today, the arch is dedicated to all French army soldiers and veterans. The **Tomb of the Unknown Soldier**, illuminated by an eternal flame, is situated under the arch, and was added to the structure on November 11, 1920. The memorial honors the 1.5 million Frenchmen who died during WWI. Visitors can climb up to the terrace observation deck for a brilliant view of the **Historic Axis** from the Arc de Triomphe du Carrousel and the **Louvre Pyramid** at one end to the **Grande Arche de la Défense** at the other. There is also a permanent exhibit, "Between Wars and Peace," which reads like the Arc's autobiography.

✚ ⓜ*Charles de Gaulle-l'Etoile.* *i Expect daily, although you can escape the crowds if you go before noon. You will kill yourself (and face a hefty fine) trying to dodge the 10-lane merry-go-round of cars around the arch, so use the pedestrian underpass on the right side of the Champs-Élysées facing the arch. Tickets sold in the pedestrian underpass before going up to the ground level. ⓢ Admission €9, ages 18-25 €5.50, under 18 and EU citizens 18-25 free. ⓩ Open daily Apr-Sept 10am-11pm; Oct-Mar 10am-10:30pm. Last entry 30min. before close.*

AVENUE DES CHAMPS-ÉLYSÉES
� SHOPPING DISTRICT
from pl. Charles de Gaulle-Etoile southeast to pl. de la Concorde

Radiating from the huge rotary surrounding the Arc de Triomphe, the Champs-Élysées seems to be a magnificent celebration of pomp and the elite's fortuitous circumstance. As you ford through the swarms of tourists and walk slowly along the avenue, however, you'll quickly realize that its legendary elegance, for better or for worse, is fading away. Constructed in 1616 when Marie de Médicis ploughed the Cours-la-Reine through the fields and marshland west of the Louvre, the Avenue remained an unkempt thoroughfare until the early 19th century, when the city finally invested in sidewalks and installed gas lighting. It quickly became the center of Parisian opulence, and maintained a high density of flashy mansions and exclusive cafes well into the early 20th. More recently, the Champs has undergone a bizarre kind of democratization, as commercialization diluting its former glamor. Shops along the avenue now range from designer fashion boutiques to car dealerships to low-budget tchotchke shops: the colossal **Louis Vuitton** flagship emporium stands across from an even larger Monoprix, a low-budget all-purpose store. Overpriced cafes compete with fast-food outlets for the patronage of tourists, while glitzy nightclubs and multiplex cinemas draw large crowds well into the evening.

Despite its slip in sophistication, the Champs continues to be known as the most beautiful street in the world. In 1860, Louis Vuitton spearheaded a committee to maintain the avenue's luxury, and it still strives to do so today, installing wider sidewalks and trying to prevent certain shops from moving in—H&M was refused a bid in 2007, but eventually won out. With rents as high as €1.25 million a year for 1000 sq. m. of space, the Champs is the second-richest street in the world (New York's 5th Avenue is number one, if you really want to know). The Avenue also continues to play host to most major French events: on **Bastille Day,** the largest parade in Europe takes place on this street, as does the final stretch of the **Tour de France.** And while the Champs itself may be deteriorating into something increasingly (gasp!) bourgeois, many of its side streets, like **Avenue Montaigne,** have picked up the slack and ooze class in their own right.

⚑ Ⓜ*Charles de Gaulle.*

PLACE DE LA CONCORDE   HISTORIC MONUMENT
pl. de la Concorde

In the center of Paris's largest and most infamous public square, the 3300-year-old Obélisque de Luxor stands at a monumental 72 ft. The spot was originally occupied by a statue of Louis XV (whom the square was originally named after) that was destroyed in 1748 by an angry mob. King Louis-Philippe, anxious to avoid revolutionary rancor, opted for a less contentious symbol: the 220-ton red granite, hieroglyphic-covered obelisk presented to Charles X from the Viceroy of Egypt in 1829. The obelisk, which dates back to the 13th century BCE and recalls the royal accomplishments of Ramses II, wasn't erected until 1836. Gilded images on the sides of the obelisk recount its two-year trip to Paris in a custom-built boat. Today, it forms the axis of what many refer to as the "royal perspective"—a spectacular view of Paris from the **the Louvre** in which the Place de la Concorde, the **Arc de Triomphe,** and the **Grande Arche de la Défense** appear to form a straight line through the center of the city. The view serves as a physical timeline of the Paris's history, from the reign of Louis XIV to the Revolution to Napoleon's reign, and finally, all the way to the celebration of commerce.

Constructed by Louis XV in honor of, well, himself, the Place de la Concorde quickly became ground zero for all public grievances against the monarchy. During the Reign of Terror, the complex of buildings was renamed place de la Révolution, and 1343 aristocrats were guillotined there in less than a year. Louis XVI met his end near the statue that symbolizes the French town of Brest, and the obelisk marks the spot where Marie-Antoinette, Charlotte Corday (Marat's assassin), Lavoisier, Danton, and Robespierre lost their heads. Flanking either side of Concorde's intersection with the wide **Champs-Élysées** are reproductions of Guillaume Coustou's **Cheveaux de Marly,** also known as Africans Mastering the Numidian Horses, the original sculptures are now in the Louvre to protect them from pollution. The place is ringed by eight large **statues** representing France's major cities: Brest, Bordeaux Lille, Lyon, Marseille, Nantes, Rouen, and Strasbourg. At night, the Concorde's dynamic ambience begins to soften, and the obelisk, fountains, and lamps are dramatically illuminated. On **Bastille Day,** a military parade led by the President of the Republic marches through Concorde (usually around 10am) and down the Champs-Élysées to the Arc de Triomphe, and an impressive fireworks display lights up the sky over the place at night. At the end of July, the **Tour de France** finalists pull through Concorde and into the home stretch on the Champs-Élysées. Tourists be warned: between the Concorde's monumental scale, lack of crosswalks and heavy traffic, crossing the street here is impossible at best, fatal at worst.

⚑ Ⓜ*Concorde.*

OPÉRA

OPÉRA NATIONAL DE PARIS/OPÉRA GARNIER ☞⊗ THEATER
pl. de l'Opéra ☎08 92 89 90 90 ▨www.operadeparis.fr

Formerly known as the Opéra National de Paris before the creation of the Opéra Bastille in 1989, this splendid historic structure is now better known as Opéra Garnier. Architect Garnier was extensively inspired by his studies in Greece, Turkey, and Rome, and it definitely shows; the Opéra's wondrous frescoes and dazzling stone and marble designs regularly leave visitors speechless. That being said, visiting the Opéra is a roll of the dice. The building is periodically closed due to performances or set construction, and these interruptions are rarely listed on the website. We also advise that you take one of the guided tours, as the guides are all extremely knowledgeable. You might get a tour guide with a nearly incomprehensible French accent, so try to schedule this visit later in your stay when you're well accustomed to English a la frog.

✦ Ⓜ*Opéra.* ⑤ €9, under 25 €5. Guided visit €12, students €9, ages under 13 €8, over 60 €10, big families €30. ⓒ Open daily 10am-4:30pm; may be closed on performance days.

NOTRE DAME DE LORETTE CHURCH
18bis rue de Châteaudun ☎01 48 78 92 72 ▨www.notredamedelorette.org

Constructed between 1823 and 1836 by architect Hippolyte Le Bas, Notre Dame de Lorette is a remarkably ornate neoclassical church in an otherwise average residential neighborhood. At the time of its construction, it pushed the limits of socially acceptable extravagance, and even compelled a cadre of church officials, journalists, and other *Parisiens* to disapprove of its bordline-vulgar extravagance. The four massive and intricately carved pillars that support the church's blackening entrance will remind you of the Parthenon; splendid frescoes adorn the ceilings of each of the four chapels, and portray the Virgin Mary and the four principal sacraments (baptism, eucharist, wedding, and ailing, for those not in the know) in detail. Though a must-see for lovers of art and architecture, Notre Dame de Lorette remains an active neighborhood church, so try to avoid Mass times unless, of course, you want to go for Mass. Given some serious disrepair, the future of the church's renovation/closing is perpetually up in the air. Catch it while it's still here.

✦ Ⓜ*Notre-Dame-de-Lorette.* ⓒ Reception M-F 2:30-6:30pm, Sa 5-6:30pm. Open for visitors 9am-6pm daily.

PIGALLE ⊛ NEIGHBORHOOD

Like seedy strip clubs, sex shops, fake Gucci, and pigeon shit? Then the Quartier Pigalle is for you. Named after French sculptor Jean-Baptiste Pigalle (who perpetually rolls in his grave), this neighborhood is so nasty it's internationally famous. Sketchy old guys with stained shirts and way-too-small pants stumble after tired and scantily clad women, and an overwhelming colony of pigeons all vie for a hostile takeover of the area. If you aren't accustomed to the grimier things in life, you might get sick to your stomach even before you exit the Pigalle Metro stop. It is absolutely in no way a good idea to come here at night, whether you're a man or a woman, or together. Women beware of sexual deviants, and guys beware of getting roped into one of the cabarets or strip clubs. Stories of being forced—like, physically, by burly bouncers—into coughing up €100 for a drink are commonplace. The area does boast a few cool spots: famous cabarets like **Folies Bergère**, **Moulin Rouge**, and **Folies Pigalle** are all stationed here, as well as Elysee Montmartre, a rock/hip-hop/soul/alternative concert venue that always has something cool happening. Music gear is sold at several outlets a minute or so south of Pigalle place.

✦ Ⓜ*Pigalle.*

CANAL ST-MARTIN AND SURROUNDS

It seems that the number of sketchballs and number of cool sights in a given neighborhood are inversely related. While the 10*ème* doesn't offer much in the way of landmarks or museums, there are a few quick sights that you might want to check out; **Le Marché Saint-Quentin** could take a bit longer.

LE MARCHÉ SAINT-QUENTIN ♿ HISTORIC SIGHT, MONUMENT

Corner rue de Chabrol and bld. Magenta

The largest covered market in Paris, Le Marché Saint-Quentin was constructed in 1865 and renovated in 1982. A series of huge windows allow the sun to pour in, and keep the complex warm even in winter. Come here for the finest cheeses, fish, and meats, or just experience the delicious mix of aromas and mingle with veteran foodies who spend their days browsing for the finest permutation of camembert. There's a bistro in the middle of the market for those who can't wait until they get home to chow down on their produce.

 # [M]Gard de l'Est. ⏰ Open M-Sa 8:30am-1pm and 4-7:30pm, Su 8:30am-1pm.

BASTILLE

In the 11*ème*, the term "Sights" is a bit of a misnomer—there are few monumental ones that still exist in this neighborhood, aside from the **place de la Bastille.** Still, the symbolic historical value of the arrondissement remains, and the lively neighborhood provides many of its own contemporary diversions. The 12*ème* boasts giant monoliths of modern architecture, like the **Opéra Bastille** and the **Palais Omnisports.** Most of the construction is commercial, fitting the working-class background of the area, but a bit of old-fashioned charm can be seen in the funky **Viaduc des Arts** near the Bastille. There are generally more hospitals than museums in the neighborhood, but in October 2007 the arrondissement welcomed a new museum, the **Cité Nationale de l'Histoire de l'Immigration,** which is a must-see if only for its present relevance. It is housed in the **Palais de la Porte Dorée** along with the aquarium; if you make it there, hop on over to the nearby **Bois de Vincennes** for the impressive château and grounds.

paris

MALHIA KENT WORKSHOP

19 av. Daumesnil ☎01 53 44 76 76 💻www.malhia.com

Fulfilling every Project Runway fantasy, this workshop gives an up-close, behind-the-scenes look at fashion. Artisans weave gorgeously intricate fabrics that become *haute couture* for houses like Dior and Chanel. Also gives you a chance to buy clothing—mostly jackets and blazers—before a label is attached and the price skyrockets.

 # [M]Gare de Lyon. $ Usually €75-300. ⏰ Open M-F 9am-7pm.

BASTILLE PRISON HISTORIC LANDMARK

Visitors to the prison subsist on symbolic value alone–it's one of the most popular sights in Paris that doesn't actually exist. On July 14, 1789, an angry Parisian mob stormed this bastion of royal tyranny, sparking the French Revolution. They only liberated a dozen or so prisoners, but who's counting. Two days later, the Assemblée Nationale ordered the prison demolished. Today, all that remains is the ground plan of the fortress, still visible as a line of paving-stones in the *place de la Bastille.*

The proletariat masses couldn't have chosen a better symbol to destroy. The prison was originally commissioned by Charles V to safeguard the eastern entrance to Paris; strapped for cash, Charles "recruited" a press-gang of passing civilians to lay the stones for the fortress. Construction was completed by the end of the 14th century, and the Bastille's formidable towers rose 100 ft above the city. After serving as the royal treasury under Henri IV, the building was turned into a state prison by Louis XIII. Internment there, generally reserved for heretics and political dissidents, was the king's business, and as a result it was often arbitrary. But it was hardly the hell-hole that the Revolutionaries who tore it down imagined it to be. Bastille's titled inmates were allowed to furnish their suites, use fresh linens, bring their own servants, and receive guests; the Cardinal de Rohan famously held a dinner party for 20 in his cell. Notable prisoners included the ☙**mysterious Man in the Iron Mask** (made famous by writer Alexandre Dumas), the Comte de Mirabeau, Voltaire (twice), and the Marquis de Sade, who wrote his notorious novel *Justine* here.

On the day of the "storm," the Revolutionary militants, having ransacked the Invalides for weapons, turned to the Bastille for munitions. Surrounded by an armed rabble, too short on food to entertain the luxury of a siege, and unsure of the loyalty of the Swiss mercenaries who defended the prison, the Bastille's governor surrendered. His head was severed with a pocket knife and paraded through the streets on a pike. Despite the gruesome details, the storming of the Bastille has come to symbolize the triumph of liberty over tyranny. Its first anniversary was cause for great celebration in revolutionary Paris. Since the late 19th century, July 14 has been the official state holiday of the French Republic. It is a time of glorious firework displays and copious amounts of alcohol, with festivities concentrated in the pl. de la Bastille.

⚹ ⓜBastille

JULY COLUMN TOWER

Towering above the the always busy *place de la Bastille*, this light-catching column commemorates a group of French freedom fighters—though, somewhat illogically, not those who stormed the Bastille. Topped by the conspicuous gold cupid with the shiny bum, the pillar was erected by King Louis-Philippe in 1831 to pay homage to Republicans who had died in the *Trois Glorieuses*, three days of street fighting that engulfed Paris in July of 1830. Victims of the Revolution of 1848 were subsequently buried here, along with two mummified Egyptian pharaohs (we're not sure what their involvement was). The column is closed the public.

⚹ ⓜBastille. In the center of pl. de la Bastille.

BUTTE-AUX-CAILLES AND CHINATOWN

There are no monuments in the 13ème to speak of, and that's to its credit. Diverse, residential, and pleasantly odd, the neighborhoods here retain the daily rhythm of Parisian life, and remain uninterrupted by the troops of pear-shaped tourists in matching fanny packs that plague the more pristine arrondissements. Though short on medieval cathedrals, hidden gems from Paris's more recent legacy of perturbed Bo(hemian)-Bo(urgeoisie)s and globalization are scattered throughout the area. Adventurous wanderers will enjoy getting lost in the quirky and sprawling Chinatown, the and working class Butte-aux-Cailles harbors a thriving street-art culture.

▩ QUARTIER DE LA BUTTE-AUX-CAILLES   NEIGHBORHOOD

Intersection of rue de la Butte-aux-Cailles and rue 5 diamants

Once a working class neighborhood, the Quartier de la Butte-aux-Cailles was home to the *soixantes-huitards*, the activists who nearly paralyzed the city during the 1968 riots. Permutations of the district's original counter-culture remain alive and well: dreadlocks are the hairstyle of choice, and the fashionably disaffected tag walls with subversive graffiti and are armed with guitars at all times. Funky restaurants like **Chez Gladines** and **Le Temps des Cerises** line the cobbled streets, and attract a boisterous, artsy crowd. **L'Église de St. Anne**, which stands on the corner of rue Bobillot and rue de Tolbiac, boasts a gorgeous stained-glass collection that refracts the afternoon sun into red, blue, and purple light.

⚹ ⓜCorvisart. Exit onto bld. Blanqui and then turn onto rue 5 diamants, which will intersect with rue de la Butte-aux-Cailles.

QUARTIER CHINOIS

NEIGHBORHOOD

Just south of rue de Tolbiac

Spread out over four Metro stops just south of rue de Tolbiac, Paris's Chinatown is home to a significant population of Cambodian, Chinese, Thai, and Vietnamese immigrants. Signs change from French to Asian languages, and restaurants advertise steamed dumplings in lieu of *magret de canard.* Non-residents roam the streets looking for the best Asian cuisine Paris has to offer.

✣ ⓂPorte d'Ivry, Porte de Choisy, Tolbiac and Maison Blanche are near Chinatown.

BIBLIOTHEQUE NATIONALE DE FRANCE: SITE FRANCOIS MITTERRAND ✦ LIBRARY

11 quai Francois Mauriac   ☎01 53 79 59 59 ▣www.bnf.fr

With its wide windows and and towering steel frame, the library is an imposing piece of architecture worthy of the 13 million volumes it houses. Highlights of the collection include **Gutenberg Bibles** and first editions from the Middle Ages, and are displayed in rotation in the Galerie des Donateurs. The exhibit can be accessed for free. Scholars hunker down beneath the vaulted ceiling of the library's imposing reading room, or lounge on the extensive deck, surveying the Seine with cigarettes in hand.

✣ ⓂQuai de la Gare. Ⓢ Day pass to reading rooms €3.30, 15-day pass €20. Annual membership €35, students €18. Tours €3. ◫ Open M 2-7pm, Tu-Sa 10am-7pm, Su 1pm-7pm. Tours Tu-F 2pm, Sa-Su 3pm.

ÉGLISE DE ST. ANNE DE LA BUTTE-AUX-CAILLES   ♿ CHURCH

189 rue de Tolbiac   ☎01 45 89 34 73 ▣www.paroissesainteanne-paris.fr

Though this church is neither as grand nor as famous as the Notre Dame, its exceptionally gorgeous stained-glass windows make it worth a visit. Instead of depicting religious figures, the windows refract light through a series of intricate patterns, sending a shock of kaleidescoped light into the white marble interior of the church. Visitors are welcome to sit in the quiet pews.

✣ ⓂTolbiac. ⓘ Wheelchair-accessible entrance 11 rue Martin Bernard. ◫ Open M-F 10am-noon and 4-6:45pm, Sa 10am-noon and 4-6pm. Mass M 7 pm, Tu 9am and 7pm, W 9am and noon, Th 9am and 7pm, F 9am and noon, Sa 9am.

MONTPARNASSE

CIMITIÈRE MONTPARNASSE   CEMETERY

3 bld. Edgar Quinet   ☎01 44 10 86 50

Opened in 1824, Cimitière Montparnasse is the prestigious final resting place of countless famed Frenchman, and an escape from the touristy hustle and bustle of Montparnasse. Be sure to stop at the security station at the **Bld. Quinet** entrance for a map marking the resting places of the cemetery's celebrities. The map reads like a *Who's Who?* of French greatness; Charles Baudelaire, Alfred Dreyfuss, Guy de Maupassant, Samuel Beckett, Jean-Paul Sartre and Simone de Beauvoir (the two are buried together), among many others, hold real estate here. The presence of these great minds is surely enough to make humanities buffs shed a tear, and the graves continue to be lovingly adorned with cigarette butts, beer bottles, Metro tickets, and personal statements of gratitude in several languages. The rest of the cemetery, however, leaves a bit to be desired. The broken windows, bright green trash receptacles, and candy-cane-striped "Do Not Enter" signs detract from the solemn beauty of the cemetery. Local residents have co-opted the grounds for their own purposes; kids play tag, older kids from the "banlieues" bum cigarettes off tourists, and locals drink excessively. Nonetheless, the cemetery showcases some delightful architecture, an impressive list of tenants, and relatively few tourists.

✣ ⓂEdgar Quinet, opposite the Square Delambre. Ⓢ Free. ◫ Open 24hr.

paris

CATACOMBS
HISTORIC LANDMARK

1 av. du Colonel Henri Roi-Tanguy ☎01 43 22 47 63 ◻www.catacombes-de-paris.fr
The Catacombs were originally the sight of some of Paris's stone mines, but was converted into an ossuary (i.e. place to keep bones) in 1785 due to the stench arising from overcrowded cemeteries in Paris. A journey into these tunnels is not for the handicapped or the light of heart—it's a 45min. excursion, and there are no bathrooms, so we recommend that all middle-aged men double down on their Maxiflow the night before, and handle business before you descend into the abyss. The visitor enters down a winding spiral staircase, and soon thereafter, is greeted by a welcoming sign: "Stop, here is the Empire of Death." The visuals are quite unlike anything you've ever seen before. Morbid-themed graffiti lines the walls, and the view of hundreds of thousands of bones makes you feel, well, quite insignificant in the grander scheme of things. Try to arrive before the opening at 10am; nestled twice as deep below ground as the metro, the Catacombs offer a refreshing respite from the midday heat in the summer, and hordes of tourists form extremely long lines to try and get out of the beating sun. The visitor's passage is well-signed, so don't worry about getting lost. Try trailing behind the group a little for the ultimate creepy experience; you won't be disappointed.
✦ ⓜDenfert Rochereau. Cross av. Roi-Tanguy with lion on your left. ⑤ €7, over 60 €5.50, ages 14-26 €3.50, under 14 free. ⓩ Open Tu-Su 10am-4pm.

TOUR MONTPARNASSE
&. TOWER

33 av. du Maine ☎45 38 52 56
Built in 1969, this modern tower stands 59 stories tall and makes Paris look uncommonly small. The elevator is allegedly the fastest one in Europe, and spits you out to a mandatory photo line on the 56th floor. After being shoved in front of a fake city skyline an forced to smile for a picture that you probably don't want and will be pressured to pay for, you're finally allowed up to the 59th floor to take in the real, slightly more breathtaking view. From this obnoxiously lofty modern skyscraper, you can properly take in the beauty, uniformity, and meticulous planning behind Paris's historic streets. Thankfully, the city ruled that similar eyesores could not be constructed in Paris's downtown shortly after this one was built; the city's distinctive style are definitely here to stay. The Tour has a cafe, which provides a wildly overpriced selection of prepackaged food. The view can be a little much on hot summer days, but is nonetheless cool for those who aren't afraid of outdoor, non-enclosed heights.
✦ ⓜMontparnasse-Bienvenue. Entrance on rue de l'Arrivée. ⓩ Open M-Th 9:30am-10:30pm, F-Sa 9:30am-11pm, Su 9:30am-10:30pm. Last entry 30min. before close.

PASSY AND AUTEUIL
With streets named after Theopold Gautier, Benjamin Franklin, George Sand, and other illustrious figues, the 16ème echoes with previous eras of high culture. Remnants of these periods are now housed in the Quarter's many museums. Fans of *Last Tango in Paris* can wander onto the Bir-Hakeim bridge where scenes were shot, and Honoré de Balzac's devotees can lovingly touch the desk where he wrote. Though packed with tourists, Trocadero and its surroundings feature wonderful views of the Eiffel Tower, and boast a bustling center of street art, not to mention the graves of some of Paris's most notable residents.

▨ CIMITIÈRE DE PASSY
CEMETERY

2 rue du Commandant-Schloesing ☎01 53 70 40 80
Opened in 1820, this cemetery is home to some of Paris's most notable deceased, including the Givenchy family, Claude Debussy, Berthe Morisot, and Edouard Manet. The idiosyncrasies and enduring rivalries of these figures continue even

sights . passy and auteuil

in death; the graves here look more like little mansions than tombstones. The tomb of Russian artist Marie Bashkirtseff is a recreation of her studio, and stands at an impressive 40 ft. Morisot and Manet are buried in a more modest tomb together. We suspect that Morisot's husband would not have approved. Well-groomed and quiet, the graveyard is more of a shadowy garden, with a wonderful view of the Eiffel Tower.

⇄ [M]Trocadero. Veer right on Avenue Paul Doumer. $Free. 🕐 Open Mar 16-Nov 5 M-F 8am-6pm, Sa 8:30am-6pm, Su and public holidays 9am-6pm; Nov 6-Mar 15 M-F 8am-5:30pm, Sa 8:30am-5:30pm, Su and public holidays 9am-5:30pm. Last entry 30min. before close. Conservation office open M-F 8:30am-12:30pm and 2-5pm.

MAISON DE BALZAC MUSEUM

47 rue Raynouard ☎01 55 74 41 80 💻www.balzac.paris.fr

When he wasn't sleeping his way through Paris, Honoré de Balzac hid from the world in this three-story house, where he wrote most of *La Comédie Humaine*. Today, the house features drafts of his most famous work and various paintings, sculptures, and books related to his life. Visitors can also see the heavy-set desk where he worked. If you've never read Balzac, check out the select quotes lining the walls for a quick introduction to his style. If you have no interest at all in this literary figure, benches scattered amongst bushy trees and wireless access make the accompanying garden a beautiful and practical place to sit.

⇄ [M]Passy, La Muette. i Call ahead for guided tours. $ Permanent collection free. Temporary exhibits €4. 🕐 Open Tu-Sun 10am-6pm. Last entry 5:30pm. Library open M-F 12:30-5:30pm, Sa 10:30am-5:30pm.

STATUE OF LIBERTY STATUE

Île des Cygnes

One of the many replicas of the Statue of Liberty worldwide, this Parisian version faces toward the original in New York Harbor. Standing tall on the man-made Ile de Cygnes, the statue can be seen from the Pont Bir-Hakeim where *Last Tango in Paris* was shot. A peaceful walk down the Allee de Cygnes past runners and lovers will yield a close-up view.

⇄ [M]Passy. Walk down rue d'Albioni toward the Seine, cross av. du President Kennedy to the Pont Bir-Hakeim. Turn right onto Allee de Cygnes if you want a closer look.

PLACE DU TROCADERO SQUARE

One of the most bustling hubs in the 16th, Place du Trocadero offers one of the best views of the Eiffel Tower. Street artists dance to a melange of hip-hop and pop, vendors push their wares on foot, and angsty youth mill about with skateboards. The nearby cafe **Carette** has some of the best hot chocolate in Paris *(€7)*.

⇄ [M]Trocadero.

BATIGNOLLES

There's a reason the 17*ème* isn't a go-to tourist destination. Sights in the traditional sense are few and far between here, but the mostly residential neighborhood and its juxaposition of bourgeois and working class Paris is still worth exploring. The lively **Village Batignolles** is a highlight; stretching from **bld. de Batignolles** to **place du Dr. Félix Lobligeois,** the area is lined with hip cafes and populated by locals who believe in afternoon drinking. During warmer months, **rue de Levis** turns into an open-air market, and the local groceries and boutiques park their carts of bananas and hang their canopies of frilly skirts outside to tempt passerby.

SQUARE DES BATIGNOLLES SQUARE

Formerly a hamlet for workers, and then a storage sight for illicit ammunition, Square des Batignolles is now an English-style park where the trees grow wild, unfettered by neutoric French trimmings and metal bars. Monet once sat here to paint the Gare St-Lazare train tracks, before heading over to a favorite cafe at 11 rue de Batignolles. Today, less illustrious but just as ambitious artists line its winding paths, watching the local joggers go by. The gently flowing river and pooling lake make the park an idyllic respite from the bustle of the city.

➡ Ⓜ Brochant. Walk down rue Brochant. Cross place du Charles Fillion $ Free. ⏰ Open M-F 8am-9:30pm, Sa-Su and holidays 9am-9:30pm.

CIMITIÈRE DE BATIGNOLLES — CEMETERY

8 rue St-Just ☎01 53 06 38 68

Cemeteries are known for being creepy; this one does nothing to reverse that reputation. Mossy tombstones, unkempt streets, and a lingering smell of pee make for an unsettling cemetery-going experience; we'd bring Buffy along if we were you, just in case. If you can stand the heebie jeebies, verse poet Paul Verlaine and, fittingly, surrealist authors André Breton and Benjamin Peret are among its notable interred.

➡ Ⓜ Port de Clichy. Walk north along av. Port de Clichy and turn right onto av. du Cimitière des Batignolles. ℹ Request free map inside. ⏰ Open Mar 16-Nov 5 M-F 8am-6pm, Sa 8:30am-6pm, Su and holidays 9am-6pm. Nov 6-Mar 15 M-F 8am-5:30pm, Sa 8:30am-5:30pm, Su and holidays 9am-5:30pm. Conservation Bureau open M-F 8am-noon and 2-5:30pm. Last entry 15min. before close.

MONTMARTRE

One of Paris's most storied neighborhoods, Montmartre was once home to lots of famous artists. Today, the **Place du Tertre**, a former artist hangout, is dominated by drunk portraitists instead. From the hills of Montmartre to the seedy underworld of Pigalle, there's plenty to see here, and plenty of English spoken.

👍 HALLE ST. PIERRE — MUSEUM

2 rue Ronsard ☎01 42 51 10 49 🖥www.hallesaintpierre.org

Halle St. Pierre is a one-of-a-kind, abstract art museum located right down the street from the Basilica. Exhibits are constantly rotating, so the museum is naturally hard to pin down. The art on display tends to be a bit far out. One of Halle St. Pierre's more recent exhibits was on "Art Brut Japonais," or Japanese Outsider Art; during out visit, a stand out among the many mind-bending works there was a series of dirty pairs of underwear, or as the French call them, slips. Luckily they didn't smell. Halle St. Pierre also houses rentable workshops, a top-notch bookstore, and a constantly crowded cafe. The museum section is not closed off, so the soft din of cafe chatter accompanies any museum visit.

➡ Ⓜ Anvers, Ⓜ Abesses. $ €7.50, students €6. ⏰ Open Sept-July daily 10am-6pm; Aug M-F noon-6pm and closed on weekends. Annual closings on December 25, January 1, May 1, July 14, and August 15.

👍 CIMITIÈRE MONTMARTRE — CEMETERY

20 av. Rachel ☎01 53 42 36 30

A particularly vast cemetery, Montmartre was built below ground on the site of a former quarry, and stretches across a significant portion of the 18th arrondissement. It is now the resting place of multiple famous people: painter Edgar Degas, artist Gustave Moreau, writer Emile Zola, saxophone inventor Adolphe Sax, and ballet dancer Marie Taglioni are among the long term residents. Fans leave ballet shoes on Taglioni's grave, and coins, notes, etc. at some of the other famous gravestones. The Cemetery itself is in disrepair; several graves have broken windows, and could use some maintenance and cleaning. The mischievous crowd of the Red Light District is surely to thank for this.

➡ Ⓜ Place de Clichy. $ Free. ⏰ Open Nov 6-May 15 M-F 8am-5:30pm, Sa 8:30am-5:30pm, Su 9am-5:30pm; March 16-Nov 5 M-F 8am-6pm, Sa 8:30am-6pm, Su 9am-6pm.

BASILIQUE DU SACRÉ-COEUR — ♿ CHURCH

35 rue du Chevalier-de-la-Barre ☎01 53 41 89 00 🖥www.sacre-coeur-montmartre.fr

Situated 129m above sea-level, the steps of the Basilique offer what is possibly the best view in the whole city. This splendid basilica first underwent construction in 1870. Its purpose? To serve as a spiritual bulwark for France and the Catholic religion, under the weight of a pending military loss and German occupation. The basilica was initially meant to be an assertion of conservative, Catholic power, commissioned by the National Assembly. Today, the Basilica sees over 10 million visitors per year, and is accompanied by an attendant list of tourist traps; outside the Basilica, beware of men trying to "give you" a bracelet or other tourist trinkets, because they'll start to yell emphatically that you have to pay them once you don't. The Cathedral itself is home to two souvenir shops. The Museum has some interesting artistic and architectural features: its slightly muted Roman-Byzantine architecture was a reaction against the perceived excess at the recently constructed Opéra Garnier.

✦ ⓜLamarck-Caulaincourt. ⑤ Free. ⚂ Basilica open daily 6am-11pm. Mass M-Sa 11:15am, 6:30pm, 10pm; Su 11am, 6pm, 10pm.

BUTTES CHAUMONT

Sights in Buttes are pretty much limited to the **Parc des Buttes,** and the unique **Parc de la Villette,** a former meat-packing district that provided Paris with much of its beef before the advent of the refridgerated truck. In 1979, the slaughterhouses were replaced with an artistic park, and voilà. Architect Bernard Tschumi's three-part vision took 461 teams from 41 different countries to complete.

▨ PARC DES BUTTES-CHAUMONT ♿ PARK

This awe-inspiring neighborhood park shrewdly uses impressive, man-made topography to make visitors feel like they're in Atlantis, or some kind of movie. Napoleon III commissioned the park in 1862 to quell his homesickness for London's Hyde Park, where he spent a good deal of time in exile. Construction of the park was directed by designer Adolphe Alphand, whose main triumph was the park's central hill, with its breathtaking exposed crags. The park's area has been a well-trafficked part of Paris since the 13th century, but before Napoleon III it was famous for very different reasons. Once the site of a gibbet (an iron cage filled with the rotting corpses of criminals), a dumping ground for dead horses, a haven for worms, and a gypsum quarry (the source of "plaster of Paris"), the modern-day Parc des Buttes-Chaumont has come a long way. Today's visitors walk the winding paths surrounded by lush greenery and hills, and enjoy a great view of the 19ème, 20ème, and the rest of Paris from the Roman temple at the top of the cliffs. The lower rungs of the Parc provide a lovely and shaded respite on a warm summer's afternoon. Families, rebellious teens, and runners constitute the park's main demographics.

✦ ⓜButtes-Chaumont. ⑤ Free. ⚂ Open daily May-Sept 7am-10:15pm; Oct-Apr 7am-8:15pm.

▨ CITÉ DES SCIENCES ET DE L'INDUSTRIE ♥♿ MUSEUM

30 av. Corentin Cariou ☎01 40 05 12 12 ▧www.cite-sciences.fr

If any structure in Paris has ADHD, it's the Cité des Sciences et de l'Industrie; to call it a multi-purpose complex would be an understatement. The Cité houses the fabulous **Explora Science Museum,** one of the top destinations for the children of Paris. Highlights include a magnificent planetarium, a movie theater, a library, a massive cyber cafe, and an aquarium. The whole structure is an architectural tour de force. Outside of the Cité is the enormous **Géode,** a mirrored sphere that essentially looks like a gigantic disco ball, but somehow doubles as the Cité complex's second movie theater; the 1000 sq. m surface provides ample screen space. To the right of the Géode, the **Argonaute** details the history of (you guessed it) submarines, from the days of Jules Verne to present-day nuclear-powered subs. If the Argonaute looks like a real naval submarine, that's because it is. The exhibit is fantastic, but will cost you a little extra. At Level 1 in the Cité, you'll

paris

find consultation areas for jobs and health; while not exactly a fun outing with the kids, this stuff can be useful if you're looking for a job or wondering how to stay healthy during your time in Paris.

⚑ ⓂPorte de la Villette. i Admission includes English or French audio tours. Ⓢ Formule summer (access to all aspects of the Cite) €21, €19 reduced. Explora+Planetarium admission €11, under 25 €8. Argonaute admission €3. Cinaxe admission €4.80. Explora+Geode: €17.50, reduced €14, under 7 €9. ⏲ Open M-Sa 9:30am-6pm, Su 9:30am-7pm. Argonaute open Tu-Sa 10am-5:30pm, Su 10am-6:30pm. Cinaxe open Tu-Su 11am-1pm and 2-5pm, showings every 15min.

CITÉ DE LA MUSIQUE
⚑ MUSEUM

221 av. Jean Jaurès   ☎01 44 84 44 84 🖳www.citedelamusique.fr

Constructed by architect Christian de Portzamparc and opened in 1995, the Cité de la Musique's stunning glass ceilings and loops of curved steel house an impressive complex of musical venues and materials. Though nominally a music museum, the insitute also includes two concert halls, conference rooms, practice rooms and over 70,000 books, documents, music journals, and photographs. The museum is mostly geared towards classical music lovers; visitors don headphones that tune in to musical excerpts and describe the pieces comprising the museum's vast collection of over 900 antique instruments, sculptures, and paintings. The Cité de la Musique's two performance spaces—the 900-seat Salle des Concerts and the 230-seat Amphithéâtre—host an eclectic range of concerts, ranging from rock to jazz to classical. Check the website for details.

⚑ ⓂPorte de Pantin. i Extra charges may apply for temporary exhibits. Ⓢ Museum €8, under 18 €4. 1hr. French-language tour €10, under 18 €8. ⏲ Info center open Tu-Sa noon-6pm, Su 10-6pm. Musée de la Musique open Tu-Sa noon-6pm, Su 10am-6pm; last entry 5:15pm. Médiathèque open Tu-Sa noon-6pm, Su 1-6pm.

BELLEVILLE AND PÈRE LACHAISE

🏛 CIMITIÈRE DU PÈRE LACHAISE
CEMETERY

16 rue du Repos   ☎01 55 25 82 10

One of the most prestigious cemeteries in Paris, the Cimitière du Père Lachaise is the biproduct of innovative public health codes and 19th-century publicity stunts. Cemeteries were banned inside of Paris in 1786 after the closure of the Saints Innocents Cemetery (Cimitière des Innocents); the cemetery was located on the fringe of Les Halles food market, and local officials came to realize that this (shockingly) presented a health hazard. Père Lachaise, in the east of the city, was the biggest of the new cemeteries outside of the city's center, the others being Montmartre and Montparnasse. As any tourist who has visited the 20th arrondissement knows all too well, the 20ème is far removed from the heart of Paris, and the cemetery didn't attract many burials immediately after its creation. In a savvy marketing move, administrators made a grand spectacle of moving the remains of two renowned Frenchmen, Molière and La Fontaine, to Père Lachaise. The strategy worked. Thousands of burials occurred at Lachaise over the next few years, and the cemetery now holds over 300,000 bodies, and many more cremated remains. Today the well-manicured lawns and winding paths of the Cimitière du Père Lachaise have become the final resting place for many French and foreign legends. The cemetery's over-occupied graves house the likes of Balzac, Delacroix, La Fontaine, Haussmann, Molière, and Proust. Expat honorees include Modigliani, Stein, Wilde, and, most visited of all the graves at Lachaise, Jim Morrison.

You'll notice that many of the tombs in this landscaped grove strive to remind visitors of the dead's worldly accomplishments. The tomb of French Romantic painter **Théodore Géricault** bears a reproduction of his Raft of the Medusa, with the original painting now housed in the Louvre. On **Frédéric Chopin's** tomb sits his muse Calliope, sculpted beautifully in white marble. Although **Oscar Wilde** died destitute and unable to afford such an extravagant design, an American admirer added bejewelled Egyptian figurines to his grave in 1912. The sculpture was defaced in 1961, prompting false rumors that the cemetery director, finding a part of the sculpture's anatomy to be out of proportion, removed the offending jewels of the Nile and kept them as a paperweight. Despite an interdiction to kiss the tomb, dozens of lipstick marks from adoring fans cover Wilde's grave today. **Baron Haussmann,** responsible for Paris's large boulevards, originally wanted to destroy Père Lachaise as part of his urban renewal project; having relented, he now occupies one of the cemetery's mausoleums.

Upon entering the cemetery, you might feel a distinctly bohemian "vibe." Well, that's because The Doors's former lead singer, **Jim Morrison,** holds permanent real estate here at Lachaise. Apparently the crooner remains popular even in death. Honored with the most visited, though rather modest, grave in the cemetery, Morrison's final resting place is annually mobbed by hundreds of thousands of visitors. Admirers bearing beer, flowers, joints, poetry, Doors' T-shirts, bandanas, jackets and more surround the resting place of their idol daily.

While over a million people are buried at Père Lachaise, only 100,000 tombs exist. This discrepancy arises from the old practice of burying the poor in mass graves. To make room for new generations of the dead, corpses are removed from these unmarked plots at regular intervals. Even with such purges, however, Père Lachaise's 44 hectares are filled to bursting; hence, the government digs up any grave unvisited in ten years and transports the remains to a different cemetery. To avoid being disenterred, those who die alone hire professional "mourners" before their death to ensure against getting moved somewhere else.

The monuments marking collective deaths remain the most emotionally moving sites in Père Lachaise. The **Mur des Fédérés** (Wall of the Federals) has become a pilgrimage site for left-wingers. In May 1871, a group of Communards, sensing their reign's imminent end, murdered the Archbishop of Paris, who had been their hostage since the beginning of the Commune. They dragged his corpse to their stronghold in Père Lachaise and tossed it in a ditch. Four days later, the victorious Versaillais found the body. In retaliation, they lined up 147 Fédérés against the cemetery's eastern wall before shooting and burying them on the spot. Since 1871, the Mur des Fédérés has been a rallying point for the French Left, which recalls the massacre's anniversary every Pentecost. Near the wall, other monuments remember **WWII Resistance fighters** and **Nazi concentration camp victims.** The cemetery's northeast corner provokes greater solemnity than the well-manicured central plots' grand sarcophogi, so take playful activities elsewhere.

⇞ [M]Père Lachaise, [M]Gambetta. ℹ Free maps available at the Bureau de Conservation near Porte du Repos; ask for directions at the guard booths near the main entrances. Apr. to mid-Nov. free 2½hr. guided tour Sa 2:30pm. For more info on "themed" tours, call ☎01 49 57 94 37. $ Open mid-Mar to early Nov M-F 8am-6pm, Sa 8:30am-6pm, Su and holidays 9am-6pm; Nov to mid-Mar M-F 8am-5:30pm, Sa 8:30am-5:30pm, Su and holidays 9am-5:30pm. Last entry 15min. before close.

PARC DE BELLEVILLE ♿ PARK

27 rue Piat

A park on a hill with an urban twist, Parc de Belleville is in fact a series of terraces connected by stairs and footpaths. In between the paths, the abundant stretches of greenery beckon sunbathers, PDAs, and nature types. From its high vantage point, the park offers spectacular views of Parisian landmarks, including the Eiffel Tower and the Panthéon. The park features ping-pong tables, an open-air theatre, and a playground for kids. Shrieking children clamor around the park's playground near the entrance, while parents rest their weary legs on nearby benches. Dotted by flowers, napping couples, and gangs of youths (non-violent if a bit too energetic) in the summer, the serene oasis seems curiously far-removed from the city at night. The park's low fences make it easy to hop into, so it becomes a center for adolescent deviance at night.

⚑ Ⓜ*Pyrénées.* Ⓢ *Free.* 🕙 *Open dawn to dusk, roughly.*

food

ÎLE DE LA CITÉ AND ÎLE ST-LOUIS

The islands are dotted with traditional dimly lit French restaurants, ideal for the couples who walk hand in hand down the quais. But the old heart of Paris is now the tourist center of Paris, and a romantic meal here comes at a price. Expect to pay more than you would for an equivalent meal on the mainland—or just settle for some ice cream. Île St-Louis is perhaps the best place in Paris to stop for a crêpe or a cool treat while strolling along the Seine. And until you're rolling in dough, or dating someone who is, a snack will have to do.

▨ BERTHILLON
ICE CREAM ❶

31 rue St-Louis-en-l'Île
☎01 43 54 31 61

You just can't leave Paris without having a bit of this ice cream. The family-run institution has been doing brilliant marketing work since 1954, but it's not all false advertising; Berthillon delivers with dozens of flavors that cater to your every craving. If you can't stand the epic lines, you can get pints of the same stuff at nearby stores.

⚑ Ⓜ*Pont Neuf.* Ⓢ *Single scoop €2.20, 2 scoops €3.40, 3 scoops €4.80.* 🕙 *Open Sept-mid-July W-Su 10am-8pm. Closed 2 weeks in Feb and Apr.*

▨ CAFE MED
♥ 🍴 RESTAURANT, CRÊPERIE ❷

77 rue St-Louis-en-l'Île
☎01 43 29 73 17

There may not be doctors in attendance, but they'll fill that hole in your stomach and won't charge you an arm and a leg for your visit. One of the cheapest and most charming options on the isle. The 3-course menu at €9.90 is an astonishing deal.

⚑ Ⓜ*Pont Marie.* Ⓢ *3-course menus at €10, €10.50, €14, €20. Weekend special tea €6.* 🕙 *Open M-F 11am-3:30pm and 7-10:30pm, Sa-Su 11am-10:30pm.*

BRASSERIE DE L'ISLE ST-LOUIS
🍴🍷🍰 BRASSERIE ❷

55 quai de Bourbon
☎01 43 54 02 59

An old-fashioned brasserie that manages to feel just a tad bit inauthentic, with red checkered napkins and closely packed wooden tables. This island institution is known for regional specialties like southern *cassoulet* (*a casserole dish of meat and beans; €18*), which keep the Frenchmen coming. Outdoor quai seating with a view of the Panthéon makes up for the number of tourists dining here.

⚑ Ⓜ*Pont Marie.* Ⓢ *Appetizers €6-10; plats €17-45. Desserts €7-11.* 🕙 *Open M-Tu noon-11pm, Th-Su noon-11pm.*

AUBERGE DE LA REINE BLANCHE
🍴 TRADITIONAL ❸

30 rue St.Louis-en-l'Île
☎01 46 33 07 87

Miniature wooden chairs, bronze pans, and peasant dolls decorate the shelves, walls, and corners as subdued customers enjoy two to three course meals. Standard French dishes and simple salads featured on the menu.

⚑ Ⓜ*Pont Marie.* ℹ *Menu available in English.* Ⓢ *2-course lunch €15.50, dinner €19.50; 3 courses €19.50/25. Plat €12/15.* 🕙 *Open daily noon-2:30pm and 6-10:30pm.*

CHÂTELET-LES HALLES

Food in the Châtelet area is unabashedly overpriced and often touristy. Nonetheless, there are a few classics that you simply have to visit—Angelina comes to mind—and a couple neighborhood options with unique dining experiences that are not to be missed.

✎ LE PÈRE FOUETTARD ⬧♥⛄ TRADITIONAL ❸

9 rue Pierre Lescot ☎01 42 33 74 17

Boasting a cozy interior dining room and a heated terrace that stays open year-round, Fouettard serves tasty traditional French cuisine at slightly elevated prices. If you can bear to pass up the ambience of a cafe meal, it's better to sit inside; you'll be closer to the bar. Rich wood walls, ceilings and floors are decorated with wine bottles basically wherever they fit. Meals on the terrace are by candlelight at night; how romantic! The location is fantastic, in the midst of the Châtelet-Les Halles neighborhood.

✦ Ⓜ*Etienne Marcel.* Ⓢ *Formules Dej €15-20. Salads €14-14.50. Plats €12.50-23.50.* ☒ *Open daily 7:30pm-2am.*

ANGELINA ⬧ TEA HOUSE ❸

226 rue de Rivoli ☎01 42 60 82 00

A hot chocolate at Angelina will make you feel like Eloise at the Plaza. Located right across from the Jardin des Tuileries, this salon de the has been around since 1903; bright frescoes, mirrored walls, and white tablecloths have immortalized Angelina as a Paris classic. There's always a long line outside of Angelina; expect to wait 20-30min. to get a table. The wait can obviously get out of hand at peak times (weekends during the summer). The hot chocolate *(€7.50)* is to die for, even in the heat of the summer. In order to cut down on the line, all food items are available for take-out, but there's often a line for that as well.

✦ Ⓜ*Tuileries.* Ⓢ *Salads €17-19. Patisseries €5.90-8.90. Tea and coffee €4-7.50.* ☒ *Open daily 9am-7pm.*

ASSIETTE AVEYRONNAISE ⬧⛄ TRADITIONAL ❷

14 rue Coquillière ☎01 42 36 51 60

A neighborhood favorite; Parisians come from all corners of the city for the delicious traditional saucisse aligot (a sausage engulfed by a mix of mashed potatoes and cheeses), and they won't hesitate to initiate newcomers to the house's best dishes. A half-plate of the house specialty will leave most guests incapable of continuing onto the Millefeuille, the house's dessert specialty. The restaurant's dining room is no-frills and brightly lit, while the terrace (heated when necessary) unspectacularly looks out on the entrance to a parking garage. The service is extremely friendly despite being insanely busy with the droves of regulars.

✦ Ⓜ*Les Halles.* Ⓢ *Appetizers €7.20; plats €13.80. Formules €18.50, €23.80, €28.30.* ☒ *Open Tu-Su noon-2:30pm and 7:30-midnight.*

LE COUP D'ETAT ⬧⛄ CAFE, BRASSERIE ❷

164 rue Saint-Honoré ☎01 42 60 27 66

Perfectly located for a coffee or meal before or after your Louvre visit, Le Coup d'Etat looks out on the famous museum, if you're well placed on the terrace. Food is tasty and not ridiculously expensive, but nothing special: just traditional French cuisine. Le Coup d'Etat hopes there would never be a coup d'etat, because it would instantly lose all of its tourist customers.

✦ Ⓜ*Louvre-Rivoli.* Ⓢ *Appetizers €7-13; plats €13-18. Desserts €6.* ☒ *Open daily 7am-2am*

AU CHIEN QUI FUME ⬧ SEAFOOD, TRADITIONAL ❹

33 rue du Pont Neuf ☎01 42 92 00 24 ▣www.auchienquifume.com

Au Chien Qui Fume has been a staple of the Parisian dining scene since 1740. Chefs arrange mouth-watering seafood platters at the oyster bar (tantalizingly

paris

visible from the street). The seafood is fresh from the market the same day. A traditionally decorated dining room and terrace portray the unmistakable class of this establishment, which is arguably Paris's number one for oysters and seafood. The crowd here tends to be pretty old or touristy; the former just trying to revisit the "good old days" and escape the dreadfully multicultural modern Paris, the latter falling into a particularly delicious tourist trap.

➡ [M]Les Halles. $ Menus €25, 33, 38. Plats €17.50-29.60. ⏰ Open daily noon-2am.

THE MARAIS

Though at times it can feel like eating in the *4ème* is less about food and more about how you look eating it, there are a number of quality restaurants here, specializing in everything from regional French cuisine to new-age fusion. This is not the cheapest place to lunch, but if you're ready for a bit of a splurge your appetite will be more than sated here, even if your bank account is not. Satisfy them both with the unbeatable lunchtime menus, or by grabbing a sandwich from **Le Gay Choc** or a falafel on rue des Rosiers for €5. If you decide on dinner, make sure you make a reservation at the hotter venues. Dozens of charming bistros line rue St.-Martin, and kosher food stands and restaurants are located around rue du Vertbois and rue Volta.

CHEZ JANOU — 🍴🍸 BISTRO ❷

2 rue Roger Verlomme ☎01 42 72 28 41 www.chezjanou.com

The food is so good here it inspires desert-island hypotheticals: if you were stranded on a desert island, would you bring an endless supply of Chez Janou's *magret de canard* or the best lover you've ever had? It's a tough one. Tucked into a quiet corner of the *3ème*, this Provençale bistro serves affordable ambrosia to a mixed crowd of enthusiasts. The chocolate mousse *(€6.60)* is brought in an enormous self-serve bowl, though Parisians count on self-control. Over 80 kinds of pastis.

➡ [M]Chemin-Vert. ℹ Reservations always recommended, as this local favorite is packed every night of the week. $ Appetizers from €8.50; plats from €14. ⏰ Open daily noon-midnight. Kitchen open M-F noon-3pm and 7:45pm-midnight, Sa-Su noon-4pm and 7:45pm-midnight.

ROBERT AND LOUISE — 🍴 TRADITIONAL ❷

64 rue Vieille du Temple ☎01 42 78 55 89 www.robertetlouise.com

Defined by a firm belief that chicken is for pansies (let's not even talk about vegetarians), Robert and Louise offers a menu that's wholeheartedly carnivorous—we're talking veal kidneys, steak, prime rib, lamb chops. The only concession to white meat is their *confit de canard*. Juicy slabs are grilled in the open wood-fire oven and then served up on cutting boards. There's a definite homey vibe here; you'll feel like you've been given shelter by a generous French family who found you abandoned and shivering when they were coming back from a hunt.

➡ [M]St-Paul or Files du Calvaire. ℹ Reservations recommended. $ Appetizers €5-16; plats €8-18. Desserts €5-6. ⏰ Open Tu-Su noon-2:30pm and 7-11pm.

MARCHÉ DES ENFANTS ROUGES — 🍴 MARKET ❷

39 rue de Bretagne

The oldest covered market in Paris, The Marché des Enfants Rouges originally earned its seemingly politically incorrect name ("market of the red children"?) by providing shelter for orphans. The market is now a famous foodie paradise of hidden restaurants and chaotic stands. Comb through an eclectic selection of produce, cheese, bread, and wine, not to mention Japanese, Middle Eastern, Afro-Caribbean, and every other variety of ethnic cuisine. Parisians often duck in for lunch at one of the wooden tables, which are heated in the winter. The wine bar in the upper right-hand corner, *L'Estaminet*, is airy, relaxed, and offers some cheap glasses *(€3-3.50)* and bottles *(€5-25)*.

➡ [M]Filles du Calvaire or Arts et Métiers. $ Wine by the glass €3-3.50. ⏰ Open Tu-Th 9am-2pm and 4-8pm, F-Sa 9am-8pm, Su 9am-2pm.

EQUINOX 🍴 TRADITIONAL ❷

rue des Rosiers ☎01 40 41 95 03

After the falafel storm on rue des Rosiers, Equinox comes as a welcome respite. Traditional French fare and a few crowd-pleasers (ahem, pasta and salads) are served in a warmly lit, charming stone dining room. For the price of three falafel specials, the 3-course lunch or dinner meal comes at an unbeatable €15.

⇆ Ⓜ St-Paul or Hôtel de Ville. $ Appetizers €7-14.50; plats €12-17. ⏰ Lunch M-Sa noon-3pm. Su brunch noon-3pm.

LATIN QUARTER AND ST-GERMAIN

The rule with food in these neighborhoods is not to eat on **rue de la Huchette** or at a cafe with English menus on one of the main boulevards. You'll leave with higher cholesterol and a lighter wallet. Venture inland a bit to find a host of terrific selections. The Comptoir Méditerranée is a great cheap lunch option, Cosi is a great and convenient cheap eat at any time of day, and Le Foyer Vietnam provides a nice switch from heavy traditional French cuisine.

LE FOYER DE VIETNAM 🍴 VIETNAMESE ❶

80 rue Monge ☎01 45 35 32 54

It's easy to miss this restaurant, whose meager decor foreshadows this local favorite's meager prices. We suggest that you look for the crowds—Le Foyer de Vietnam is always packed, though it manages to keep hungry patrons waiting for only a few minutes tops. Portions are large but not unmanageable; try one of this hole in the wall's delicious meat- and spice-laced soups, followed by the duck with bananas *(€8.50)*. Wash it all down with the delicious and ambiguously titled Saigon Beer *(€2.60)*. Unconventional desserts prevail; ever heard of lychees in syrup *(€2.50)*...for dessert? The restaurant appeals to everybody except tourists, offering student discounts on certain menu choices.

⇆ Ⓜ Monge. $ Menus €9.20, students €7.50. Entrees €3.80-7.50. Plats €6.50-9.20 ⏰ Open M-Sa noon-2pm and 7-10pm.

CAFE DELMAS 🍴 CRÊPERIE, CAFE ❸

2-4 pl. de la Contre Escarpe ☎01 43 26 51 26

Two venues in one, Delmas is the place to while away the hours (stylishly) in a happening part of town. A modern crêperie and cafe on the stylish Pl. Contre Escarpe, Delmas's menu boasts a wide variety of choices, from stylish cocktails to traditional cuisines to crêpes. Don't sit inside; the painted library in the back corner is a rather tragic decorative decision.

⇆ Ⓜ Cardinal Lemoine. $ Sweet crêpes €3.50-8.50. Salads €13.50-18. Plats €16-24.50. ⏰ Open M-Th 7:30am-2am, F-Sa 7:30am-5am, Su 7:30am-2am. Happy hour 7-9pm.

CASA PEPE 🍴🍸 TAPAS, SPANISH ❸

5 rue Mouffetard ☎01 44 27 01 85 💻www.lacasapepa.com

The exterior of this charming Spanish restaurant on the tourist-frequented rue Mouffetard is decorated with pictures of past soirees and pictures of Pepe himself with various Spanish athletes and celebrities. Every night, there's a guitar serenade that generally persuades the clientele to get down on the floor. Food is pricey, flavorful, and copious.

⇆ Ⓜ Cardinal Lemoine. $ Menus €20-22. Paellas €14-29. Tapas €15-17. ⏰ Open daily noon-midnight.

JARDIN DES PATES 🍴🍸 ITALIAN ❷

4 rue Lacépède ☎01 43 31 50 71

Ideally located around the corner from the Jardin des Plantes, the Jardin des Pates combines a relaxed atmosphere and a lovely terrace with tasty, inventive, and fruity pasta dishes. Bright white plant-decorated walls and tiled floors evoke a yogi kitchen vibe. Selections are unconventional to say the least, like the entree, avocado in melon sorbet *(€6)*. Sweet tooths, be warned that ther is a somewhat paltry selection of desserts; for those with normal appetites, a meal here should do the trick.

⚡ Ⓜ️*Jussieu.* Ⓢ *Entrees €4.50-10. Pasta €9.50-14. Desserts €5.50-6.50. Wines €17-77.* 🕑 *Open daily noon-2:30pm and 7-11pm.*

GUEN-MAÏ
6 rue Cardinale

🖤 VEGAN, ÉPICERIE ❶

☎01 43 26 03 24

This healthy-living oasis might have more appeal for vegetarians and vegans than for carnivores (though they do have fish); anyone who craves seitan and soy will find a little slice of macrobiotic heaven here. Also a lunch restaurant, this is a great alternative to yet another heavy traditional French meal; flush out the butter, oil, and richness with one of Guen's homemade vegetarian options. The all-natural food products are made completely in-house. The lunch counter quadruples as a *salon de thé*, food market, bookstore, and vitamin boutique.

⚡ Ⓜ️*Mabillon.* Ⓢ *Lunch menu entrees €3-5. Plats €7-12.50. Desserts €5.* 🕑 *Open M-Sa 9:30am-8:30pm.*

INVALIDES
The chic *7ème* is low on budget options, but there are a number of quality restaurants that are worth shelling out the extra euros. **Rue St-Dominique, rue Cler,** and **rue de Grenelle** feature some of the best gourmet bakeries in Paris, and the steaming baguettes and pastries make for an ideal picnic by the nearby Eiffel Tower.

📷 LE SAC À DOS
4/ rue de Bourgogne

🖤🍴 TRADITIONAL ❸

☎01 45 55 15 35 🖥www.le-sac-a-dos.fr

A neighborhood favorite, this intimate restaurant does French dining right—excellent food, good wine and fresh bread cut to order. The standing red lamps and old books on mahogany shelves make Le Sac à Dos feel more like a living room than a restaurant, and the chummy proprieter's hearty jokes and attentive service really makes the experience; don't be surprised if he (jokingly) asks for some of your wine. The *midi* and *soir formule* (€16) will give you most bang for your buck.

⚡ Ⓜ️*Varenne.* Ⓢ *Gamas grille €25. Burger and frites €14. Desserts €5.* 🕑 *Open M-Sa noon-2:30pm and 7-10:30pm.*

📷 LES COCOTTES
135 rue St.-Dominique

🖤 TRADITIONAL ❷

☎01 45 50 10 31

Christian Constant, a famed Parisian chef, realized that not everyone wants to pay their left arm and right leg for a good meal. Then he opened Les Cocottes. The fourth of his restaurants on the street, the food is just as delicious and half the price. Unsurprisingly, the house speciality is the *cocottes* (€12-17), cast-iron skillets filled with pig's feet and pigeon or fresh vegetables. The decor is a sophisticated take on an American diner, with high upholstered stools at the tall tables, where you can get in and out pretty fast. The best quickie you'll ever have.

⚡ Ⓜ️ *Ecole Militaire or La Tour-Maubourg.* Ⓢ *Mousseline d'artichaut €16. Salads €10-12.Cocottes €12-17. Mousse au choclate €7.* 🕑 *Open M-Sa noon-4pm and 7-11pm. Closed on Sundays without reservation.*

📷 LA GRANDE ÉPICERIE DE PARIS
38 rue de Sèvres

🖤 SUPERMARKET, SPECIALITY SHOP ❹

If a skinny, chic, Chanel-toting Frenchwoman took on supermarket form, she would become La Grande Épicerie. In addition to its near obscene bottled water and wine display (*€30 for water? seriously?*), this celebrated gourmet food store features all things dried, canned, smoked, and freshly baked in itsy-bitsy packets. The butcher actually has a thin twirled mustache. We thought only cartoon French people looked like that. Most items here are overpriced, so it's better to treat La Grande Épicerie de Paris as a fascinating anthropological sample than a supermarket. You might want to avoid the American food section, which showcases such treasured "traditional" cuisine as marshmallows, brownie mix, and Hershey's syrup. The market's refined local patrons cluck their tongues disapprovingly as they walk down the aisle; it's kind of embarrassing.

[M]Vaneau. i No pets allowed. $ Water €30; this place is way too expensive for you. ⏰ Open M-Sa 8:30am-9pm.

CHAMPS-ÉLYSÉES

Once the center of Paris's most glamorous dining and world-class cuisine, the *8ème's* culinary importance is on the decline, but its prices are not. The best affordable restaurants are on side streets around **rue la Boétie, rue des Colisées,** and **place de Dublin.**

TY YANN — CRÊPERIE ❶

10 rue de Constantinople ☎01 40 08 00 17

The ever-smiling Breton chef and owner, M. Yann, cheerfully prepares outstanding and relatively inexpensive *galettes (€7.50-10.50)* and crêpes in a tiny, unassuming restaurant; the walls are decorated with his mother's pastoral paintings. Creative concoctions include La Vannetaise *(sausage sauteed in cognac, Emmental cheese, and onions; €10).* Create your own **crêpe** *(€6.40-7.20)* for lunch.

[M]Europe. i Credit card min. €12. $ Crêpes €7.50-10.50. ⏰ Open M-F noon-2:30pm and 7:30-10:30pm, Sa 7:30-10:30pm.

LADURÉE — TEA HOUSE ❷

16 rue Royale ☎01 42 60 21 79 💻www.laduree.com

Opened in 1862, Ladurée started off as a modest bakery; it has since become so famous that a Gossip Girl employee was flown over to buy macaroons here, so that Chuck could offer his heart to Blair properly. On a more typical day though, the Rococo decor of this tea salon attracts a jarring mix of well-groomed shoppers and tourists in sneakers. One of the first Parisian *salons de thé*, Ladurée shows its age but remains a must-see (and taste). Along with the infamous mini macaroons arranged in high pyramids in the window *(16 different varieties; €1.50)*, this spot offers little that hasn't been soaked in vanilla or caramel. Dine in the salon or queue up an orgasm to go.

[M]Concorde. $ Macaroons €1.50 each. ⏰ Open M-Th 8:30am-7:30pm, F-Sa 8:30am-8pm, Su 10am-7pm. Also at 75 av. des Champs-Elysées ☎01 40 75 08 75.

FAFOUQUET'S — CAFE ❺

99 av. des Champs-Élysées ☎01 47 23 50 00

Restaurants can only dream of this kind of fame. The sumptous, red velvet-covered cafe once welcomed the likes of Chaplin, Churchill, Roosevelt and Jackie Onassis. But as its gilded interior suggests, all that glitters is not gold. Today, Fouquet's owned by a hotel and dining conglomerate, and the only celebrity spottings you'll see are the framed pictures on the wall. Still, it's an experience of quintessential old-time Parisian glamour, easy on the eyes and devastating for the bank account *(starters run upwards of €30)*. Best to buy a coffee *(€8)* and see and be seen.

[M]George V. $ Plates €20-55. ⏰ Open daily 8-2am. Restaurant open daily 7:30-10am, noon-3pm, and 7pm-midnight.

OPÉRA

The Opéra district has a few classic food spots—**Chartrier** and **Saveurs et Coincidences** are particular favorites—but the area definitely suffered from the loss of one-of-a-kind restaurant Chez Haynes in 2009. Most of the high-quality, affordable options in the district are located in the St. Georges area.

SAVEURS ET COINCIDENCES

6 rue de Trévise ☎01 42 46 62 23 🖳www.saveursetcoincidences.com

Saveurs et Coincidences maintains a small, charming dining room; in the summertime, a few tables are set up outdoors and the front windows are flung open, letting the air waft in. Recently purchased by expert chef Jean-Pierre Coroyer—a former semi-finalist in a national gastronomical competition—the new Saveurs et Coincidences combines traditional French cuisine with Japanese, Italian, and other global favors for a succulent and entirely unique collection of entrees. Ingredients are ridiculously fresh. According to the chef, the restaurant doesn't even have a fridge; ingredients are ordered and received from suppliers in the mornings, then sliced, diced and stewed the same day. This process costs Coroyer a good deal of returns, but he proudly declares that he isn't interested in ripping off his customers. It certainly shows in his prices which are incredibly lower than those at most cafes. The lunch formules are such a deal, it should be illegal; an entree, plat, dessert and cafe combo is only €17.

✦ ⓜGrands Boulevards. ⓟ Appetizers €0.60; plats €14.20. Desserts €7.50. Formules midi €17, €12.50, €10.40.

CHARTRIER

7 rue du Faubourg Montmartre ☎47 70 86 29 🖳www.restaurant-chartrier.com

Chartrier has served French traditional cuisine, en masse, since 1896, and remains a unique experience that is not to be missed. Think Cheesecake Factory meets Friendly's family vibe, without the plethoric portions (portions are a good size here, just not disgustingly huge). We recommend the *tete de veau* (that's *sheep's head; €11.80*), and then some classic *profiteroles au chocolat chaud* for dessert (€4). If you go alone, you'll be seated with somebody you don't know, which can either be a fantastic experience or a boring, very awkward one. Waiters provide rapid service and are patient with Americans, but only to a point; know what you want to order, because they've got their hands full. If you want to be guaranteed a table, we recommend getting here early—the line stretches about 200m around the block by 7:30pm.

✦ ⓜGrands Boulevards. ⓢ Appetizers €2-10.30; plats €8.50-12.20. Desserts €2.20-4.50. Wine €6.50-34. ⓩ Open daily 11:30am-10pm.

KASTOORI

4 pl. Gustave Toudouze ☎47 70 86 29

Kastoori offers tasty, hearty Indian fare at a collection of tables on the lovely Place Toudouze; the indoor seating area is cozier, with plush chairs and couches in a small dining room that doubles as the kitchen. Pricewise, the place is a steal during the lunch hour, with a *thali du jour* tasting plate for just €10. There are alo plenty of veggie plates for the granola types among you. Waiters are quick to put their cigarettes down to replenish your carafe. Unfortunately, no alcohol is served here; we consider this to be a human right's violation.

✦ ⓜSaint-Georges. ⓢ At lunch (entrée, plat, naan) €10. Menu (entrée, plat, naan, cafe) €17. Desserts €5. Plats €7-13. ⓩ Open Tu-Sa 11am-2:30pm and 7-11pm.

CANAL ST-MARTIN AND SURROUNDS

The 10ème has a few all-star food spots, and both just happen to be located on the Canal St-Martin. Stay away from the brasseries on the main boulevards, and make the trip down to the Canal (specifically its side streets); great deals on great grub.

LE CAMBODGE

10 av. Richerand ☎01 44 84 37 70 🖳www.lecambodge.fr

Le Cambodge doesn't take reservations, and Parisians of all shapes and sizes regularly wait up to two hours for a table. You'd think Lady Gaga was in town; by the time the restaurant opens, the line at the door is already 20 ft. long. We

food · canal st-martin and surrounds

recommend that you arrive 30min. or so before opening, so as to secure a table on the terrace or in the more secluded dining room—and avoid wandering around the 10ème at night. Incredibly, Le Cambodge is not overrated. This is some of the best Asian food in Paris, and the plentiful main courses will only run you €9.50-13.

✢ ⓜRépublique. Ⓢ Appetizers €3-10.50; entrees €9.50-13. Vegetarian plates €8.50-11.50. Desserts €4.50-5.50. ⓠ Hours can vary day to day, giving locals a leg-up on early opening notices. Generally, however, M-Sa noon-2pm and 8-11:30pm.

LE FLASH
10 rue Lucien Sampaix

➥ MOROCCAN ❸
☎01 42 45 03 30

Within walking distance of République, Le Flash chefs up Tunisian and Moroccan specialties, Kosher-style. Seriously. This eccentric fusion of traditions comes with slightly elevated prices, but the dinners here are reliably tasty, and always blessed by the Beth-Din of Paris. Observant Jews understand that this is quite the rarity in Paris.

✢ ⓜRépublique, ⓜJacques Bonsergent. Ⓢ Plats €16-35. Sandwiches €8 (lunch only). ⓠ Open M-F 11:30am-3:30pm

BASTILLE

With as many kebab stands as people, Bastille swells with fast-food joints. But the diverse neighborhood also boasts a number of classy restaurants with an ethnic touch, many of which are cheaper than those in the more central arrondissements. The most popular haunts line the bustling **rues de Charonne, Keller, de Lappe,** and **Oberkampf.** In terms of food, the 12ème is a generally affordable arrondissement, where casual establishments serve a variety of cuisines, from North African to Middle Eastern to traditional French. Most of the better places are on side streets, scattered throughout the neighborhood. On **rue du Faubourg St-Antoine** there's a slew of nice but overpriced restaurants competing with cheap fast-food spots; the **Viaduc des Arts** hosts a couple of classy terrace cafes where designers take up residence.

▨ CAFE DE L'INDUSTRIE
15-17 rue St-Sabin

➥❦ CAFE ❷
☎01 47 00 13 53

There's a reason that podunk cafes specialize in coffee, but the menu at this one will make you forget it. Funky 20-somethings retreat in this always bustling, kind of dark spot, enjoying the extensive, fairly priced menu. The 3-course formule is a steal (€10.50); the chocolate cake is nothing short of divine (€3).

✢ ⓜBreguet-Sabin. Ⓢ Plats €8-14. Desserts €2.50-6. ⓠ Open daily 10am-2am.

▨ LE BAR À SOUPES
33 rue de Charonne

➥❦ SOUP BAR ❶
☎01 43 57 53 79 ▧www.lebarasoupes.com

It may not have the most personality in the world, but it does have some of the best soups in Paris. Making them fresh daily, the chef commits to creatively combining flavors like leeks and curry or zucchini and ginger. The salad and dessert selection is less spectacular.

✢ ⓜLedru-Rollin or Bastille. Ⓢ Soups €5-6. Formule midi includes soup, bread roll, salad, dessert or cheese plate, wine, iced tea or coffee. Take away available. ⓠ Open M-Sa noon-3pm and 6:30-11pm.

L'EMPREINTE
54 av. Daumensil

❦☿➥ TRADITIONAL ❸
☎01 43 47 25 59 ▧www.lempreinte.fr

A domesticated jungle theme extends from the food to decor; traditional French dishes are given an exotic twist, and potted plants grow freely inside.

✢ ⓜGare de Lyon. 𝒊 Credit card min. €15. ⓈSalads €11-12. Plats €13.50-15.50. Formules €12.80-13.80 ⓠ Open M-Sa 7am-11pm. Food served noon-2:30pm and 7-10:30pm.

MORRY'S BAGELS AND TOASTS

✿☪ BAGELS ❶

1 rue de Charonne

☎01 48 07 03 03

Trust the French to make bagels fancy; bold statements like the Magret de Canard, bagel with guacamole, cream cheese and sundried tomatoes (€5.80) and the *foie gras* (*self-explanatory; €6*) are daring but delicious.

⚡ Ⓜ*Bastille.* Ⓢ *Bagels with coleslaw or toppings €3-6. Dessert €1.50-3.35* 🕐 *Open M-Sa 8:30am-7:30pm.*

BABYLONE

✿ FALAFEL, SHAWARMA ❷

21 rue Daval

☎01 47 00 55 02

Distracted by the neon lights, snazzy music and trendy atmosphere, you might forget that you're overpaying for Middle Eastern fast food. Still, if you're tired of the semi-sketchy and hole-in-the-wall places that usually sell falafel here, this upscale joint might be a welcome upgrade.

⚡ Ⓜ*Bastille.* Ⓢ *Entrees €4.60. Shawarma plates €8.60-10. Falafel plates €8.60-9.50.* 🕐 *Open M 11am-3pm, Tu-F 11am-3pm and 6:30pm-midnight, Sa 11am midnight.*

BUTTE-AUX-CAILLES AND CHINATOWN

Unbeknownst to many a tourist, the 13ème is a haven for funky, fun and affordable restaurants. Bump elbows with locals over papier-maché tables in the crowded Butte-Aux-Cailles, or enjoy the unfathomable delights of Chinatown's many Asian restaurants. Eating on a budget never tasted better, especially in Paris.

📷 MUSSUWAM

✿ AFRICAN ❷

33 bld. Arago

☎01 45 35 93 67 🖥mussuwam.fr

The new kid on the block, Mussuwam offers Senegalese cuisine in an area dominated by Southern French restaurants. Creole music, chocolate brown walls, and a colorful decor creates an ethnic feel. Fresh juices (€5) are a highlight of the tropical menu.

⚡ Ⓜ*Les Gobelins.* Ⓢ *Plat du jour €15.* 🕐 *Open M-Sa noon-3pm and 7-11:30pm, Su 11am-3pm.*

LE SAMSON

✿ TRADITIONAL, MEDITERRANEAN ❷

9 rue Jean-Marie Jego

☎01 45 89 09 23

Run by a Franco-Greek owner, the restaurant offers reasonably priced options and generous portions. It attracts a slightly older, but local crowd.

⚡ Ⓜ*Place d'Italie, follow rue Samson off of rue de la Butte-aux-Cailles.* 𝒊 *Kids menu €11. Menu Complet €18.50.* 🕐 *Open daily noon-2:30pm and 7-11:30pm.*

MONTPARNASSE

📷 LE TROQUET

✿♀ SPANISH, FUSION ❸

21 rue François Bonvin

☎01 45 66 89 00

This place is worth budgeting for; if you have to eat at sweaty kebab take-out spots for a week, or even two weeks, to afford this, just do it. The food is simply sublime, and the prices are extremely reasonable given the quality. Original recipes developed under the supervision of master chef Christian Ethebest have their origins in traditional Basque cuisine, specifically from the Béarn region. Unlike some other super-gourmet restaurants you may have indulged in, the portions here are hearty. We recommend the caviar *d'aubergine* or the Basque *charcuterie* platter, which are both to die for. For main courses, go with the *joue de cochon* in red-wine sauce. The desserts are beyond tasty too. Menus change every three weeks, but the aforementioned items tend to make frequent comebacks. The service here is super professional and friendly. Could be tough for handicapped, since the dining room is very small and tightly packed. Expect long waits.

⚡ Ⓜ*Sevres Lecourbe, off of Boulevard Garibaldi.* Ⓢ *Dinner formule €32. Tasting plate €40.50. Wine €23-77.50 per bottle. Midi entrée, plat or plat-dessert combo €26.* 🕐 *Open Tu-Sa 12:30-2pm and 7:30-11pm.*

LE DIX VINS
57 rue Falguiere
♦♿❦ TRADITIONAL
☎01 43 20 91 77

Located on a side street uphill on Bld. Pasteur from the Metro stop, Le Dix Vins serves terrific traditional French cuisine at a reasonable price. This is undoubtedly a fine dining experience. In 2010, the restaurant won a prize from the prestigious *Confrerie Gastronomique de la Marmite d'Or* for its cuisine. Located on a quiet street, the restaurant's front windows open up on warm days, and air wafts through the two tightly packed dining rooms. The food is divine, but when we visited the chef told us to write down a few recommendations. For starters, try the artichoke hearts with *foie de veau*, then order the *filets de rougets à la Normande* for your first course. For dessert, the chef proposes the tartin de poires with a scoop of vanilla ice cream. The menu switches up periodically, but don't hesitate to ask the gregarious waiter for more suggestions. Technically wheelchair accessible, but it could be a bit tricky space-wise.

✿ Ⓜ*Pasteur.*

TANDOORI
10 rue de l'Arrivée
♦❦ INDIAN ❸
☎45 48 46 72

A trip to Tandoori will leave you incredibly full and mildly amused. The tablecloths and carafes are curry-stained, and the dining room has a funky, musky smell to it, which, unfortunately, smells nothing like curry. We advise sitting outside if the weather permits. The beer selections are quite limited to the comically generically-titled *bierre indienne* (€6). The food, however, is pretty good. Despite some grossly over-buttered (and nearly inedible) *naan*, the meat and vegetables were tasty and rich. The lunch formule of entrée-plat or plat-dessert is priced very reasonably (*€10 M-F, €12 Sa*). There's a nice selection of vegetarian options.

✿ Ⓜ*Montparnasse Bienvenue.* Ⓢ*Entrees €6-20, Plats €10-20, Desserts €6-8. Drinks €6-8.* ⏰*M-Sa noon-2:30pm and 7-11pm.*

PASSY AND AUTEUIL

Like everything in the 16*ème*, most dining options are on the pricier side, but the food is of the highest quality. If you're willing to spend a little more, the splurge is definitely worth it. Budget-friendly ethnic restaurants are clustered on **rue Lauriston**.

LES FILAOS
5 rue Guy de Maupassant
AFRICAN ❸
☎01 45 04 94 53 🖳www.lesfilaos.com

The first joint in Paris to specialize in Mauritian cuisine, Les Filaos provides an ethnic touch to the 16th restaurant scene. Delicious punches (*€5*) are made fresh behind the straw hut bar. Curries (*€15-16*) can be made as spicy as you like and are topped off with fresh fruit for dessert. Octopus is an island specialty. Saturday night features live Mauritian dancers.

✿ Ⓜ*rue de la Pompe.* 𝒊 *Prixe-fixe lunch €19.50; dinner €30.* ⏰ *Open Tu-Su noon-2:30pm and 7-10:30pm.*

LE SCHEFFER
22 rue Scheffer
BISTRO ❷
☎01 47 27 81 11

With red-checkered tablecloths, walls papered with posters, and an almost entirely local clientele, Le Scheffer is as authentic as French bistros get. Slightly tipsy diners chat loudly over the din of clattering plates and shouting waiters. Plats include fois de veau with honey vinegar (*€15*) and beef haddock (*€15*).

✿ Ⓜ*Trocadero.* Ⓢ *Entrees €15-20.* ⏰ *Open M-Sa noon-2:30pm and 7:30-10:30pm.*

BATIGNOLLES

If residents had to make a pilgrimage into central Paris every time they wanted a good meal, no one would live in the 17*ème*. Thankfully, good restaurants are a dime a dozen here, and the diverse population that lives here make for a wide array of choices, from ethnic to French to vegetarian.

▨ LE MANOIR   CAFE ❷
7 rue des Moines   ☎01 46 27 54 51

A true neighborhood favorite, Le Manoir is popular with the kind of cool, fun Parisians you'd want to hang out with. Local parents meet their children in front of the cafe's red awning to pick them up after school. The waiters here are so friendly you'd think there was a catch. When a certain intrepid Let's Go Researcher left her computer in her nearby apartment, the young waitress offered to watch her drink for her while she ran home to get it—even though the Researcher hadn't paid yet. The menu is comprized of local standards, and is particularly well-known for its salads (€11).

✚ ⓂBrochant. *i* Free Wi-Fi. ⓢ Plats €13, two-course menu midi €12, salmon tartare €13.20. 🕐 Open daily 7:30am-2am.

LA FOURNÉE D'AUGUSTINE   TRADITIONAL ❶
31 rue des Batignolles   ☎01 43 87 88 41

It's no mystery why La Fournée d'Augustine won Paris's medaille d'or in 2004. Luring in customers with the delicious aroma of freshly baked pastries, this boulangerie is everything you thought Paris would smell like: butter, chocolate, and heaven in general. The wide selection of desserts is reasonably priced (cakes €4; pain au chocolat €0.80). Fresh sandwiches (€3-4) and other lunch options are also available. The storefront can be hard to spot, so look for the boulangerie white, wooden tiles painted with lilacs, and follow the smell.

✚ ⓂRome. ⓢ Donuts €0.60. Loaf of brioche €4.60. 🕐 Open M-Sa 7:30am-8pm.

AU VIEUX LOGIS   BISTRO ❷
68 rue des Dames   ☎01 43 87 72 27

This standard French bistro serves standard French fare on standard red checkered tablecoths in a pleasant atmosphere. Would be utterly forgettable if not for its absolutely delicious food and generous portions. No wonder there are so many regulars.

✚ ⓂRome. ⓢ Plat du jour €10, plats €12-16, 2-course lunch menu €12. 🕐 Open M-Sa noon-3pm and 7-11pm.

BUTTES CHAUMONT

▨ L'ATLANTIDE   ❤🍴 NORTH AFRICAN ❷
7 av. Laumière   ☎01 42 45 09 81 🖥www.latlantide.fr

A relatively hard-to-find type of restaurant in Paris, L'Atlantide practices true North African gastronomie, using meats and spices coming directly from the mountains of North Africa. If you can stand a lot of Oriental-rug patterning (rugs, tablecloths, and waiters' aprons are all coordinated), you'll get a nice hearty plate of couscous you won't forget.

✚ Ⓜ Laumière. ⓢ Entrees €5.50-10. Couscous €11-19.50. Plats €13-19.50. Vins €12.50-22.50. 🕐 Open M-F 7-10:30pm, Sa-Su 12-2:30pm and 7-10:30pm.

LA KASKAD' CAFE   ❤ CAFE ❹
2 pl. Armand-Carrel   ☎01 40 40 08 10

Just outside the Parc des Buttes-Chaumont, La Kaskad' nets its fair share of unsuspecting—and suspecting—visitors. Their spacious, wrap-around terrace is a perfect place to relax after a stroll in the Parc des Buttes-Chaumont. Varied, American-friendly cuisine includes palatial sundaes (€7.50-9). You know what you're getting into, but you'll be properly fed and ready to get into the Buttes.

✚ ⓂLaumière. Ⓢ *Appetizers €5-13; plats €13-19. Lunch formule €15.* 🕐 *Open daily 7:30am-2am.*

BELLEVILLE AND PÈRE LACHAISE

Belleville doesn't compare to the 19*ème* in terms of food quality. It would behoove you to to hop on the Metro for lunch after your Cemetery visit.

LA BOLÉE BELGRAND
●⚐❄ CRÊPERIE, CAFE ❶

19 rue Belgrand ☎01 43 64 04 03

Across the street from the Gambetta metro exit, La Bolée Belgrand is a modest crêperie boasting American portions. A local crowd people watch through lace curtains and from outdoor tables while enjoying heaping crêpes and *galettes*. The La Totale, with cheese, eggs, tomatoes, onions, mushrooms, ham, bacon and salad, is a particular favorite.

✚ Ⓜ *Gambetta.* **i** *10% off takeout.* Ⓢ *Galettes €7.50-9.50. Crêpes €5-7. Glaces €5.50-7.50.* 🕐 *Open Tu-Sa noon-2:30pm and 7-10:30pm.*

LA MER À BOIRE
●⚐Ⴅ CAFE ❶

1-3 rue des Envierges ☎01 43 58 29 43 ▣la.meraboire.com

A three-, or, if you like a good view, four-in-one. This multi-purpose cafe/bar across from Parc de Belleville offers a spectacular view of Paris. Soak up the teenage revelry (accompanied by its unmistakeable scent) across the street. Or check out the venue's occasional contemporary art exhibits and live music concerts. Simple tasty food is perfect for those "petits faims," or small hungers, but won't suffice for a full meal. Hosts art exhibits and occasional concerts.

✚ Ⓜ *Pyrénées.* Ⓢ *Snacks €5-10. Wine glasses €2.50-7.50.* 🕐 *Open M-Sa noon-1am. Kitchen open noon-2pm and 7:30-9pm.*

nightlife

ÎLE DE LA CITÉ AND ÎLE ST-LOUIS

Far from a party spot, the islands are a bit of a nightlife wasteland. Still, there are a few overpriced brasseries that are worth a stop. The bars are a lot more fun and a lot less expensive on either side of the bank, in the neighboring 4*ème* and 5*ème* respectively.

▨ LE LOUIS IX
●⚐Ⴅ CAFE, BRASSERIE

25 rue des Deux-Ponts ☎01 43 54 23 89

The place where the isle's men go to drink, probably because it has the cheapest beer around. As unpretentious as it gets in this neck of the woods.

✚ Ⓜ *Pont Marie.* Ⓢ *Wine €3.50-4.60. Beer €3.80-5. Aperatif €3.80-4.50.* 🕐 *Open daily 7:30am-8:30pm.*

LE SOLEIL D'OR
●⚐Ⴅ❄ BRASSERIE

15 bld. du Palais ☎01 43 54 22 22

Its name doesn't quite make sense, but and after paying this much for a beer on terrace, you'll certainly wish the sun weren't so damned golden come morning. The view of the sparkling Seine on a quiet evening makes it a nice place for a drink.

✚ Ⓜ*Cité.* Ⓢ *Aperatifs €2.20. Beer €2.20/€4.50.* 🕐 *Open daily 7am-midnight. Happy hour 5-9pm.*

L'ANNEXE
●⚐Ⴅ❄ BRASSERIE

5 bld. du Palais ☎09 61 27 53 02

A neighborhood watering hole that remains as sequestered as possible from the dense troops of tourists in the areas. The €2 take-away beeris the only deal of note, otherwise you might consider drinking elsewhere.

➜ Ⓜ Cité. Ⓢ Wine €3.80-4.20. Beer €4.20-5. Aperatifs €4-8. ⏰ Open daily 7am-8pm.

SARL SAINT-REGIS 🎫🍸☀ BRASSERIE

6 rue Jean de Bellay ☎01 43 54 59 41

Less flashy than the nearby brasseries and about two inches further from the Seine, the Sarl Saint-Regis attracts Parisians willing to go the extra step and pay exorbitant prices for a cocktail, just to avoid the twittering tourist mob.

➜ Ⓜ Pont Marie. Ⓢ Wine €4.30-5.60. Beer €5-6.50. Cocktails €9.50. ⏰ Open M-Th 7am-midnight, F-Sa 7-1am.

CHÂTELET-LES HALLES

👍 BANANA CAFE 🎫🍸▼ BAR, GLBT

13 rue de la Ferronerie ☎01 42 33 35 31 💻www.bananacafeparis.com

Situated in the heart of one of Paris's liveliest areas for nightlife, Banana Cafe is the self-declared most popular GLBT bar in the *1er*—and rightly so. The club suits a wide range of clientele, ranging from the somewhat reticent and straight patrons who occupy the outdoors terrace, to the pole/striptease dancers stationed outside on nice days. During the summertime, there's always some kind of hot deal on beer or drinks, and the party regularly spills out onto the rue de la Ferronerie. Head downstairs for a piano bar and more dancing space. There are weekly theme nights, "Go-Go Boys" takes place every Th-Sa midnight-dawn.

➜ Ⓜ Châtelet. ℹ Happy hour pints €3, mixed drinks €4. Ⓢ Cover F-Sa €10; includes 1 drink. Beer €5.50. Mixed drinks €8. ⏰ Open daily 5:30pm-6am. Happy hour 6-11pm.

FROG AND ROSBIF 🎫🍸📶☀ BAR, BRASSERIE

116 rue St Denis ☎01 42 36 34 73 💻www.frogpubs.com

One of several Anglo-French "Frog and..." pubs in Paris. The Frog and Rosbif shows live rugby and soccer broadcasts; the floor gets sticky and loud. What makes this pub stand out in a neighborhood full of otherwise generic bars? Frog pubs brew their own beer: try the ginger twist and parislytic flavors. They're...interesting.

➜ Ⓜ Étienne-Marcel. ℹ Quiz nights Su 8pm. Free Wi-Fi. Ⓢ Happy hour pints €5; mixed drinks €5. Thirsty Th students €4.50 beer and mixed drinks, €2 shots. Beer €6. Mixed drinks €7. ⏰ Open daily noon-2am. Happy hour 5:30-8pm.

LA CHAMPMESLÉ 🎫📶🍸▼ CLUB, GLBT

4 rue Chabanais ☎01 42 96 85 20 💻www.lachampmesle.com

This welcoming lesbian bar is Paris's oldest and most famous; the owner still works the bar and enthusiastically promotes the bar's late-night spectacles (they don't always happen, but when they do it's at 2am). The crowd is friendly; straight folks are warmly welcomed. The club hosts weekly cabaret shows (Sa 10pm) and monthly art exhibits.

➜ Ⓜ Pyramides. ℹ Wi-Fi, but don't bring your computer at night, you nerd. Ⓢ Beer €5 before 10pm, €7 after. Cocktails €8-10. ⏰ Open M-Sa 4pm-dawn.

LE REX CLUB 🎫🍸 CLUB

5 bld. Poissonnière ☎01 42 36 10 96 💻www.rexclub.com

Definitely the place to be if you're looking to get down on the floor or rock out to a phenomenal DJ set. The club hosts top-notch DJs spanning pretty much any type of music that young people would have the slightest desire to dance to. The crowd is full of students, but due to the high quality of the DJs, there aren't too many Euro-trashy teenagers here. The large sweaty dance floor is surrounded by colorful booths.

➜ Ⓜ Bonne Nouvelle. Ⓢ Cover €10-15. Mixed drinks €9-11. ⏰ Open W-Th 11:30pm-6am, F-Sa midnight-6am.

a drunkard's guide to france

- **WINE:** Surprise! There's wine in France. There is also cheese and French people. Sarcasm aside, you can find it anywhere, but to go to the source, venture to **Bordeaux,** where Merlot grapes alone cover 50% of the region. Make sure to pick a wine that says *Mis en Bouteille au Château* on the label, which indicates that a wine was bottled at the château where the grapes were grown. If you go for Champagne, French law garentees that your bubbly white wine will have come from the area of the same name 100 miles east of **Paris**. André was barely champagne before, but it's definitely sparkling wine now.

- **PASTIS:** It's way too hot to eat much in **Côte d'Azur**, so sit back in your beach chair and sip Pastis. It's a yellow, licorice flavored alcoholic beverage similar to absinthe, and the French drink 130 million liters of the stuff a year. In Marseille be sure to call it *Pastaga*, and don't use the water served on the side as a chaser, it's supposed to be mixed in with the liquor (like ouzo). Hemingway coined the combo of champagne and Pastis as "Death in the Afternoon," warning us of the misery of a 5pm hangover.

- **KRONENBOURG BEER:** Not one to be outdone by beer chugging Germans, this beer brewed in **Alsace** hasn't changed much since the first pint was fermented in 1664. Its hopsy flavor and alcohol content will make the Alps, and your date, much prettier.

- **LIQUORS:** You can be sure that all those sweet fruits in the **Loire Valley**, in some form or another, have been fermented. If you like oranges, you should be familiar with Anger's Cointreau, but you might not know the cherry version Guignolet, which is also popular. There isn't a restaurant that doesn't have at least one of these liquors mentioned in their dessert menus. Soufflé AU COINTREAU, anyone?

- **ABSINTHE:** The poison of choice of **Parisian** artists of the 19th century, the newly legal spirit was central to Bohemian culture. Known in French as "The Green Fairy" for its, ahem, inspiring effects, absinthe was originally given to French troops as an anti-malarial. Whether you're feeling a bout a malaria coming on or if you're simply seeking hedonistic fun, the Green Fairy surely will not disappoint (unless you're expecting a hallucination).

THE MARAIS

There are as many bars and clubs in the Marais as people. It's indisputably the center of Paris's GLBT nightlife scene, and fun and fashionable men's and women's bars and clubs crowd **rue Ste Croix de la Bretonnerie**. Hotspots with outdoor seating are piled on top of one another on **rue Vieille du Temple**, from **rue des Francs-Bourgeois** to **rue de Rivoli**. The places on **rue des Lombards** have a rougher and more convivial—though often touristy—atmosphere. The scene in the 3*ème* is a little more laid-back—for the most part, women (and men, too) can leave their stiletto heels at home. There are a number of GLBT bars in the area on and around **rue aux Ours, rue St-Martin,** and **rue Michel Le Comte** but mostly casual bars do live music, especially around the Pompidou.

ANDY WAHLOO   ♥☺ BAR ❸
69 rue des Gravilliers   ☎01 42 74 57 81 ▦www.andywahloo-bar.com
Everything here is a twist on something else. Andy Wahloo, which means, "I have

nothing" in a certain Moroccan dialect, serves delicious and ambitious cocktails *(€10-14)* to a fashionable Parisian clientele in an open courtyard and dark bar. The stop sign tables and paint-can chairs are pushed aside for dancing later in the night. The incredibly attractive clientele will probably catch you staring.

✢ [M]Arts et Métiers. i A good place to wait for a table at 404. $ Cocktails €10-14. ⏰ Open Tu-Sa 5pm-2am.

👍 RAIDD BAR — 🍸▼ GAY BAR, CLUB [2]

23 rue du Temple — ☎01 42 77 04 88

If you want a penis or just want to see one, come here. Sparkling disco globes light up the intimate space, as do the muscular, topless torsos of the sexy bartenders. After 11pm, performers strip down in glass shower cubicles built into the wall (yes, they take it all off every hour on the hour starting at 11:30pm). Notoriously strict door policy—women are not allowed unless they are outnumbered by a greater ratio of (gorgeous) men.

✢ [M]Hôtel de Ville. $ Beer €4. Mixed drinks €10. ⏰ Open M-Th 5pm-4am, F-Sa 5pm-5am, Su 5pm-4am. Happy hour 5-9pm for all drinks, 5-11pm for beer.

STOLLY'S — 💰🍸☕ BAR [2]

16 rue Cloche-Perce — ☎01 42 76 06 76 💻www.cheapblonde.com

This small Anglophone hangout takes the sketchy out of the dive-bar and leaves behind the cool. The €13.50 pitchers of cheap blonde beer ensure that the bar lives up to its motto: "hangovers installed and serviced here." Come inside, have a pint, and shout at the TV with the decidedly non-trendy, tattoo-covered crowd. Occasional live music.

✢ [M]St.Paul. On a dead-end street off rue du Roi de Sicile. $ Cocktails €6.50-8. ⏰ Open M-F 4:30pm-2am, Sa-Su 3pm-2am. Terrace closes at midnight. Happy hour 5-8pm; mixed drinks and pints €5, pitchers €12.

LATIN QUARTER AND ST-GERMAIN

Nightlife is a bit stronger in the fifth arrondissement; plenty of pricey bars and jazz clubs line the main streets and boulevards around St-Michel. What better way to walk off a few beers than a stroll down the promenade along the Seine? The *6ème* is more of a bar and student-centered nightlife scene.

👍 LE CAVEAU DE LA HUCHETTE — 💰🍸 JAZZ BAR

5 rue de la Huchette — ☎01 43 26 65 05 💻www.caveaudelahuchette.fr

In the past, the Caveau was a meeting place for secret societies and directors of the Revolution; downstairs, you can still see the prison cells and execution chambers occupied by the victims of Danton and Robespierre. WWII brought American soldiers, bebop, and New Orleans jazz to the establishment. Now an eclectic crowd of students, tourists, and locals comes prepared to listen, watch, and participate in an old-school jazz show in this affordable, popular club.

✢ [M]St-Michel. i Live music nightly 10pm-2am. $ Cover M-Th €12, F-Sa €14, Su €12, students €10. Beer €6. Cocktails €8. ⏰ Open M-W 9:30pm-2:30am, Th-Sa 9:30pm-dawn, Su 9pm-2:30am.

LE WHO'S BAR — 💰🍸 BAR

13 rue Petit Pont — ☎01 43 54 80 71

This bar stays open super late right in the swing of things—a stone's throw from the Seine and in the heart of the Latin Quarter's bar scene. Live pop and rock music every night at 10:30pm is not exactly original, but it certainly gets the job done. Old and young alike get down on the often sweaty dance floor; the old folks take the cake in terms of funkiness (smell and dancing abilities included).

✢ [M]St-Michel. i Disco in the basement W-Su 10:30pm-midnight. $ Beer €5.50-12. Cocktails €10-12. Aperos €6-10. ⏰ Open M-Th 5pm-5am, F-Sa 6pm-6am, Su 5pm-5am.

FINNEGAN'S WAKE
@ IRISH PUB

9 rue des Boulangers   ☎01 46 34 23 65 ⬛www.finneganswakeparis.com

Claiming to be Paris's first, and best Irish pub Finnegan's has been around since 1989. The bar is a dark, renovated wine cellar with low ceilings and successfully combines a bougie French vibe with the unmistakeable feel of a gritty South Boston bar. Have a pint *(€6)* with the boisterous (i.e., as Irish as Paris can get) crowd of students and (drinking) professionals.

✦ Ⓜ*Jussieu.* *i Occasional live concerts of traditional Irish music in the downstairs cave from 5pm.* Ⓢ *Pints €5. Cocktails €6-7.* Ⓧ *Open M-Th 6am-2am, F-Sa 6pm-4am. Happy hour daily 5-9pm*

LE 10 BAR
@⚥ BAR

10 rue de l'Odéon   ☎01 43 26 66 83 ⬛www.le10bar.com

A classic student hangout; the "facade" of the bar makes it look more like a flop-house than a pub. Precocious Parisian youths indulge in philosophical discussions while getting drunk. After several glasses of their famous spiced sangria *(€3-3.50)*, anything can happen. Jukebox plays everything from Édith Piaf to Aretha Franklin.

✦ Ⓜ*Odéon.* Ⓢ *Beer €3.50-5.50. Sangria €3-3.50.* Ⓧ *Open daily 6pm-2am. Happy hour 4-8pm.*

INVALIDES

If you want to party into the wee hours of the morn, stumble home to your affordable hotel room, and pass out after consuming another €1 bottle of wine, then you probably shouldn't stay in the 7ème. Filled with sights but devoid of personality, the neighborhood gets quiet early. The corner-cafe bars at **École Militaire** are packed almost exclusively with tourists, and the **rue-St-Dominique** has some brassieres frequented by locals. The following venues are a solid bet.

▨ CHAMPS DE MARS
ROMANTIC

Droves of French youngsters march over to the Champs de Mars with the setting sun, schlepping bottles of wine, cases of beer, and packs of cigarettes with them. You'll be thankful it's legal to drink outside in Paris as you approach this grassy stretch in front of the the Eiffel Tower. Why? Because you'll find it overflowing with revellers playing guitar and Bocce, exploring the subtleties of each other's faces (read: PDA) and generally being merry. The Eiffel Tower lights up on the hour, and makes for a spectacular backdrop to the start of a good night.

✦ Ⓜ*École Militaire or La Motte Picquet-Grenelle.*

CLUB DES POÈTES
♠♿⚥ CLUB, POETRY

30 rue de Bourgogne   ☎01 47 05 06 03 ⬛www.poesie.net

If you want to drink and feel cultured, this restaurant by day and poetry club by night brings together an intimate community of literati for supper and sonnets. The hip patrons all seem to know each other and may seem intimidating at first, but you'll soon become fast friends as you cram in next to each other the L-shaped long table.

✦ Ⓜ*Varenne.* *i Poetry readings Tu, F, Sa at 10pm. Come a little before then, or wait for applause to enter.* Ⓢ *Prix-fixe appetizer-plat or plat-dessert €16. Lunch menu €16. Wine €4-8.* Ⓧ *Open M-F noon-2:30pm and 8pm-1am. Kitchen closes at 10pm.*

CHAMPS-ÉLYSÉES

Glam is the name of the game at the trendy, expensive bars and clubs of the 8ème. Whether you're going for a mystical evening at **buddha-bar** or a surprisingly accessible evening at **Le Queen,** make sure to bring your wallet, dashing good looks, and if possible, a super-important and/or famous friend.

▨ LE QUEEN
♠⚥▼ CLUB

102 av. des Champs-Élysées   ☎01 53 89 08 90 ⬛www.queen.fr

A renowned Parisian institution where drag queens, superstars, tourists, and go-go boys get down and dirty to the mainstream rhythms of a 10,000-gigawatt sound system. Her Majesty is one of the most accessible GLBT clubs in town, and has kept its spot on the Champs for a reason. Women have better luck with the bouncer if accompanied by at least one good-looking male.

 # [M]Georges V. i Disco M, Ladies Night W, '80s Su. $ Cover €20; includes 1 drink. All drinks €10 after that. ⏰ Open daily midnight-6am.

BUDDHA-BAR 🍸 BAR, RESTAURANT

8 rue Boissy d'Anglas ☎01 53 05 90 00 💻www.buddha-bar.com

Apparently too cool for overdone trends like capital letters, buddha-bar is billed as the most glamorous drinking hole in the city—Madonna tends to drop by when she's in town. If you're sufficiently attractive, wealthy, or well-connected, you'll quickly be led to one of the two floors of candlelit rooms, where your internal organs will gently vibrate to hypnotic "global" rhythms. A two-story Buddha watches over the chic ground-floor restaurant, while the luxurious upstairs lounge caters to those looking to unwind in style with one of the creative mixed drinks *(€16-21)*. A solid contingent of "atheist drinkers" think buddha is over-rated.

 # [M]Madeleine or Concorde. $ Mixed drinks €16-21. ⏰ Open daily noon-2am.

OPÉRA

CAFE LE BARON 🍸 BAR, RESTAURANT

11 rue de Châteaudun ☎01 48 78 13 68

A quintessential Parisian cafe—come here if you're really in the mood to receive some disdainful stares from behind sunglasses (if you're obviously American, that is), and cough up the fog of someone else's cigarette smoke. In a good way. Cafe Le Baron's sunny outdoors terrace is right in the thick of things near the Opera district; the scene here is simply classic and beautiful. Each cocktail looks like a work of art (*€2.20-7*), and drinks are accompanied by a complimentary tasting plate of olives, veggies, and cheese. Tasteful modern decor graces the interior, with whitewashed walls lined with red wine bottles and an assortment of maroon sofas. The food here is also quite delectable, but expensive; just about everything on the menu is delicious, so you probably won't regret it.

 # [M]Notre Dame de Lorette, Cadette. i Happy hour cocktails and pints €5. $ Beer €2.60-7. Wine (by glass) €2.60-5.50. Shots €5-18. Appetizers €14-19; plats €17-26. Desserts €9-10. ⏰ Open daily 11am-1am. Happy hour 5:30-8pm.

CORCORAN'S 🍸 CLUB, PUB

23 bld. Poissonnière ☎40 39 00 16 💻www.corcorans.fr

Corcoran's is located smack dab in the center of all things touristy, and offers American drinks and bar food for reasonable prices (by Opéra standards, that is). A cavernous room boasts a pool table and several TVs, while the outdoors terrace generally fills up with eager people watchers on balmy summer evenings. Any Irish pub should have decent Guinness, and that Corcoran's does, but your waitress might take 10min. to get it to you, and then take another 5min to add up your bill (at the table). The party gets jumpin' on Th-Sa nights, when Corcoran's hires house, rock, and R and B DJs. On the whole a great destination for young people on weekend nights.

 # [M]Grands Boulevards. i Other locations at Bastille, St. Michel, and Clichy areas. Happy hour cocktails and pints €5. $ Shots €4. Beer €4-6.50. Whiskey €6.50-8.50. Cocktails €8.50-9.50. ⏰ Open daily 11am-2am. Happy hour M-F 5-8pm.

CANAL ST-MARTIN AND SURROUNDS

Try to stay on big streets and avoid heading to the Metro on back streets in the 10*ème* late at night. Pickpockets, muggers, and scumbags abound.

[thumbs-up] CHEZ JEANETTE — 🍸🎟 BAR

47 rue du Faubourg Saint-Denis ☎01 47 70 30 89 💻www.chezjeanette.com

An old school brasserie à la 19th century, Chez Jeanette drips with authentic Parisian flavor, complete with candlelit tables and small red lamp chandeliers that hang from the cavernous white ceilings. Grab a seat at the marble counter or large windows of the spacious bar, though it tends to become standing room only at night. Given the old-school vibe here, the crowd is surprisingly down to earth, and generally a pleasant mix of twenty and thirty-somethings.

⇄ [M]Strasbourg Saint-Denis. $ Aperos €2.50-7.60. Beer €2.50-6.40. Cocktails €6.50-8. ⏰ Open daily 8am-11:30pm.

DELAVILLE CAFE — 🎟☀🍸 BAR, RESTAURANT

34 bld. Bonne Nouvelle ☎01 48 24 48 09 💻www.delavillecafe.com

Situated in a historic building, Delaville successfully mixes cutting edge design with classic Parisian architecture. If you start to feeling cobwebby or old at the old school, high-ceilinged bar, just slip into the ultra-modern lounge room, with its bright red cyclinder stools and couches. The crowd's a bit touristy, but not sickeningly so. DJs take the reins Th-Sa, causing the building's old proprietors to roll over in their graves.

⇄ [M]Bonne Nouvelle. $ Cocktails €8. Brunch €20. ⏰ Open M-Sa 11am-2am, Su noon-2am.

BASTILLE

Nightlife in the 11*ème* has long consisted of Anglophones who drink too much and the Frenchies who hide from them. With a few exceptions, **rue de Lappe** and its neighbors offer a big, raucous night on the town dominated by expats and tourist-types, while **rue Oberkampf, rue Amelot,** and **rue Thaillandiers** are more eclectic, low-key, and local. Both streets are definitely worth your time, even if you have only one night in the area. **rue Faubourg St-Antoine** is a world of its own, dominated by enormous nightclubs who only let in the well-dressed. **Rue du Faubourg St-Antoine** is the dividing line between the lively 11*ème* and tamer 12th. The hotspots overflow into the streets, and you can hop from one club-lounge to another all night—but it won't be cheap.

[thumbs-up] FAVELA CHIC — 🎟🍸 BAR, CLUB

18 rue du Faubourg du Temple ☎01 40 21 38 14 💻www.favelachic.com

A self-proclaimed Franco-Brazilian joint, this place is light on the Franco and heavy on the brassy Brazilian. Wildly popular with the locals, this restaurant-bar-club has an eclectic decor and equally colorful clients. Dinner in the restaurant segues into unbridled and energetic table-dancing to Latin beats. Exceedingly crowded with sweaty (in a hot way) gyrating bodies during the weekend and a long line snaking out the door. Regulars report that groups high on estrogen and ethnic diversity will get you in more easily.

⇄ [M]République. Walk down rue du Faubourg du Temple, turn right into the arch at no. 18; the club is to your left. $ F-Sa cover €10; includes 1 drink. Mixed drinks €9. ⏰ Open Tu-Th 8pm-2am, F-Sa 8pm-4am.

[thumbs-up] ZERO ZERO — 🎟 BAR

89 rue Amelot ☎06 68 84 28 57

A tiny, tiny bar covered from head to toe in stickers and graffiti, jammed with the artistic and the unpretentious. DJs spin hip-hop in the lowly-lit corner. The signature drink "Zero Zero," whose size you should not let deceive you, is a dangerously potent mix of dark rum, ginger, and lime *(€3).*

⇄ [M]Saint Sebastien Froissart. $ Beer €2.80-4. Cocktails €6.50-8.50. ⏰ Open daily 6pm-2am. Happy hour 6:30-8:30pm.

LE POP-IN
BAR, ROCK CLUB

105 rue Amelot ☎01 48 05 56 11 www.popin.fr

Leaning more towards "popping" than "pop-in," this two-level bar/rock club/90s time warp boasts a basement that's a favorite all-night hangout for Paris's hipster crowd. Pop, rock, folk, and indie fold concerts almost nightly.

[M]St-Sebastien Froissart. i Check website for concerts. $ Beer €2.80-5.50. Open daily 6:30pm-1:30am. Happy hour 6:30-9pm.

LA QUILLE
BAR, BILLIARDS, BOWLING

111 rue St-Maur ☎01 43 55 87 21 laquille.net

Knowing that Parisians were not going to bowl if they had to wear dumb shoes, this bar opted for a mini-version with no footwear specifications. Fashionable bowling and billiards complete with neon lights and a Top 40 playlist.

[M]Paramentier. $ Beer €2.20-3. Pint €4. Bowling €4 per person. Billards €13 per hr. Open daily 2pm-2am.

BUTTE-AUX-CAILLES AND CHINATOWN

Blessed with a young and unassuming crowd, the 13ème's local haunts are cluttered with vintage instruments, overflow onto maritime concert venues floating along the Seine, and maintain a chill atmosphere you never knew that a city as conscientiously chic as Paris could keep up. Walk down to the Porte de la Gare, grab a bottle of wine with some friends and watch the Seine go by.

LE MERLE MOQUER
BAR 1

11 rue de la Butte-aux-Cailles ☎01 45 65 12 43

Capturing the spirit of the neighborhood with its ecclectic mix of African art, uneven stools and spray-painted doors, this bar is a little funky, not at all fussy, and the best place on the street to dance. Homemade, flavored rum punches are well worth the €6. Ginger-apple-pear-cinammon is the bartender's choice.

[M]Place d'Italie. $ Drinks €4-€6. Open daily 5pm-2am.

LA DAME CANTON
BAR, CONCERT VENUE 2

Porte de la Gare ☎01 45 84 41 71 www.dame-decanton.com

A quirky alternative to all those passe land-locked watering holes, this floating bar is deliberately odd in the extreme, even by Butte-aux-Cailles standards. A seizure-inducing collection of fishing nets, musical instruments, books on Australia, postmodern takes on the Mona Lisa and small Chinese lamps decorate the walls and ceiling. The floor slopes, the patrons rock dreds, and the owner's been known to wear jean suits. The burly bartenders will serve you Pirate Punch *(€3)* and cocktails *(€7.50)* in plastic cups or out of cans. The lolling waters of the Seine make La Dame Canton a little less than stable, so we advise you avoid getting plastered on board. But the view of the Seine is spectacular, and the mix of soul funk, hip hop and reggae demonstrate excellent taste. Live concerts every night, starting at about 8:30pm.

[M]Quai de la Gare. i Cover T-Th €8, students €6; F-Sa €10. $ Cocktails €7.50. Open Tu-Th 7pm-2am, F-Sa 7pm-5am.

MONTPARNASSE

Montparnasse doesn't have much in terms of nightlife; at night, most of its younger residents are busy partying it up in other arrondissements. Older crowds frequent the bars along the main boulevards and avenues.

L'ENTREPÔT
BAR, RESTAURANT, CINEMA

7-9 rue de Francis Pressenc ☎01 45 40 07 50 lwww.lentrepot.fr

L'Entrepôt offers the potential for a quadruple-dip, boasting an art gallery, a three-screen cinema, a restaurant with garden seating, and a bar that hosts regular concerts. The young and nerdy clientele enjoys free lectures and discussions on topics ranging from modern literature to hip-hop. Until the end of 2010, the venue will host Ciné-Philo, a screening, lecture, and discussion cafe, held every other Sunday at 2:20pm *(€8)*; check the monthly schedule in the main foyer. Thursday jazz nights, and Friday and Saturday world music nights *(€7-10)*. Free improv theater with audience participation third Sunday of each month at 7:30pm. Check website for other special events, including jam sessions, scholarly debates, and slam poetry.

⚥ Ⓜ*Pernety.* Ⓢ *Lunch formule €15; brunch formule €25. Movie tickets €7, students €5.60, under 12 €4. Costs of other events vary.* ⚅ *Gallery open M-F 11am-7pm. Brunch Su 2:30-6:30pm. Bar open daily 9pm-midnight. Restaurant M-W noon-3pm and 7:30-10:30pm, Th-Sa noon-3pm and 7:30-11pm, Su noon-3pm and 7:30-10:30pm.*

LE REDLIGHT
⚥ ✦ ⚲ BAR, CLUB

34 rue du Départ ☎42 79 85 49 ▣www.leredlight.com

Formerly known as Enfer, Le Redlight is located at the foot of the Tour Montparnasse. Cozy red booths surround a disco-lit dance floor. DJs generally fall under the electro/dance/house genre, but they mix it up with R and B every once in a while. The party doesn't get jumping 'til late, and drinks are expensive, so start your night early and then head here; make-up you caked on will be quickly sweat off. Fauxhawks and fitted hats alike nod to the music. Crowd straddles the tween divide. Come for a great house DJ set or, just to get down.

⚥ Ⓜ*Montparnasse-Bienvenue.* Ⓢ *Admission €20; includes 1 drink.* ⚅ *Open only on weekends, opening time varies with DJ set, generally until 2am.*

PASSY AND AUTEUIL

The 16*ème* isn't the hottest spot in town, but it does feature a few stylish bars with reasonably priced drinks. You'll be hanging out with the chic and the too-cool-for-school, so leave those frayed sneakers at home.

SIR WINSTON
⚲ BAR, CLUB ❷

5 rue de Presbourg ☎01 40 67 17 37

This cafe/salon/bar/club is a sophisticated hotspot of the young Parisian Bobos (that's bohemian bourgeoisie, for those not in the know). Lean back into a leather chair and sip on a glass of wine (€5) or smoke attractively alongside a pensive Buddha. After all, Buddha would have totally done the same. There's a dance space downstairs, though the music is mainly jazz and lounge tunes.

⚥ Ⓜ*Kleber.* 𝒊 *French fries €5. Caesar salad €5.* ⚅ *Open daily 9am-4am.*

THE HONEST LAWYER
((ᵖ)) ⚲ BAR ❷

176 rue de la Pompe ☎01 45 05 14 23 ▣www.honest-lawyer.com

An unpretentious place to liquor up in the 16*ème* is about as hard to find as an honest lawyer, but The Honest Lawyer is definitely one of those things. The wood paneling, brass lamps, and free Wi-Fi are reminiscent of a law library; the blaring '80s pop, large-screen TVs, and the large painting of a judge nursing a tankard of beer, not so much. A regular and largely male crowd of dissheveled grad student types schlep their laptops and briefcases here for a relaxed and reasonably priced drink. Our intrepid researcher-writers report that the stella here is "bomb-ass" (€3.50).

⚥Ⓜ*Victor Hugo.* Ⓢ *Beer €3-5. Martini €4. Cocktails €8.*

BATIGNOLLES

If you're thinking of a wild night on the town in the 17*ème*, forget it. If the people who live here drink here, they do it by themselves; the craziest it'll get is a few drinks with old friends, and maybe a couple of new ones. Sometimes, though, that's all you need.

LE BLOC
CAFE, BAR ❷

21 rue Brochant ☎01 53 11 02 37

Like a good mistress, Le Bloc is always open, accommodating, and kind of cool. This former clinic turned industrial cafe/bar caters to the neighborhood's turtleneck-wearring types from morning till dawn, and will be whatever you want it to be. The food is decent enough *(penne au pisto €8.80)*, and drinks range from whatever to shocking. Look for the little nook under the stairs with the brown couch, pink walls, and fake skeleton.

♯ ⓂBrochant. *i* Free Wi-Fi. Ⓢ Salads €9-10.20. Most cocktails €6.50. Ⓩ Open daily 8:30am-2am.

SANS GÊNE BAR ❷

122 rue Oberkampf ☎01 46 27 67 82 🖥www.sansgene.fr

Like many of the hotspots in the 17*ème*, Sans Gêne is a good place for casual after-dinner drinks. Hot pink and black interior attracts a bigger crowd than neighboring bars, probably because it manages to be both punk and cutesy.

♯ ⓂBrochant. *i* Brunch Sa-Su noon-4pm. Ⓢ Cheese ravioli €14.50. Lamb with gratin dauphinoise €19. Wine €4. Cocktails €8.50. Ⓩ Open daily 9am-2am.

MONTMARTRE

Nightlife in Montmartre comes, of course, with the burden of not getting too drunk and staying away from the shady cabarets/strip clubs. The best way to stay safe is to keep your wits about you.

🖾 LE RENDEZ-VOUS DES AMIS 🍸Ⓨ BAR ❸

23 rue Gabrielle ☎01 46 06 01 60 🖥www.rdvdesamis.com

You know that you're in for a night of debauchery when the bar's owners and bartenders drink harder than their customers, pounding shots and beer at random. A true Montmartre institution, Le RVDA has been around for 17 years, and it's not hard to see why. Convivial and untouristed, this bar has a live free or die ethos. Patrons rock out to house music and experimental hip-hop, and occasionally live music. The mixed drinks are a rip-off, so stick to the beer. Welcome to Montmartre. Cigarettes are sold out front on an informal basis, but don't bring your drink outside—the burly but friendly bouncer will have words for you. Small appetizers are available to help you stomach the beer.

♯ ⓂAbbesses. Ⓢ Beer €2.30-7, pitchers €7. Ⓩ Open daily 8:30am-2am.

🖾 L'ESCALE Ⓨ🍸 BAR

32bis rue des Trois Freres ☎01 46 06 12 38

A very popular spot among the students of Montmartre, this restaurant serves famously strong cocktails for just €4.50. Young folks huddle around cozy, small tables, and the owner proudly proclaims on the website that L'Escale and its strong drinks are the #1 enemy of the police. There's generally a guest DJ playing house music, or whatever else is super hip at the moment, on Sunday nights.

♯ ⓂAbbesses. Ⓢ Beer €3.50-8. Cocktails €4.50. Ⓩ 2pm-2am. Happy hour 4pm-10pm.

CHEZ JULIEN 🍸Ⓨ BAR

2 rue Lepic ☎01 42 64 21 20

The vibe is, like, totally relaxed here dude. Old records and images of '60s celebrities decorate the walls. Locals flock here for the martinis served in beer glasses. While the attached restaurant is a bit pricey, the drinks are affordable by Red Light standards. A nice spot to start out the night, but it closes at midnight, so don't get too comfortable.

♯ ⓂBlanche. Ⓢ Aperos €2.60-6, wine €2.50-5, cocktails €7.50. Ⓩ Daily 7:30am-midnight.

THE HARP 🍸Ⓨ SPORTS BAR

118 bld. de Clichy ☎01 43 87 64 99

Feel like starting the day off wrong with a beer or two? The Harp's got your back. Open until 9am on weekends, this sports bar revolves around rugby, soccer, and booze, and hosts plenty of late-night partiers. Boasting a great selection of beer on tap, and pints that cost only €6, the Harp is a hell of a deal for the Red Light

District. If the Harp had an anthem, it'd be James Brown and Betty Newsome's "It's a Man's World"; expect lots of bros and the women who love them. Several big-screen TVs make this the ideal spot to watch the game.

➡ Ⓜ Blanche. $ Beer €4-6. ⏰ Open M-W 5pm-4am, Th-Sa 5pm-9am. Su 5pm-4am.

BUTTES CHAUMONT

Butte Chaumont doesn't have the most popping nightlife scene, and this is definitely not the safest neighborhood in Paris. That being said, drinks are generally cheap, and the company can get rowdy at the more student-ish bars. If you can only hit up one place, it has to be the Ourcq. The beer goes for only €2.50 and keeps the locals coming.

👍 OURCQ — 💲🍸 BAR, TEA HOUSE

68 quai de la Loire — ☎01 42 40 12 26

Where the students, hipsters, hippies, and other budget-conscious folks go to get down. There's always a party going on, whether it's a Tuesday or a Saturday night. During the day, this classic brasserie doubles as a tea salon, and provides its customers with a wide selection of board games and books to go along with their hot beverage of choice *(€2-3).*

➡ Ⓜ Laumière. $ Wine by the glass €2-3. Beer €2.50-4. Cocktails €5. ⏰ Open W-Th 3pm-midnight, F-Sa 3pm-2am, Su 3-10pm.

LE FAITOUT — 💲🍸 BAR

23 av. Simon Bolivar — ☎01 42 08 07 09 🖥www.lefaitout.fr

A cozy, relaxed bar located on the residential avenue Simon Bolivar. The decor is classic, the drinks are affordable, and the crowd is rowdy on weekends, a bit subdued on weeknights. The kitchen is open late, so you can grab a quick snack if you feel the need to wash something down besides your sorrows. Plenty of students, as is most often the case at bars in Buttes.

➡ Ⓜ Laumière. $ Shots €3. Wine by the glass €2.60-6.50. ⏰ Open daily 7am-2am.

BELLEVILLE AND PÈRE LACHAISE

Given that it's mostly a residential neighborhood, Belleville has very few nightlife options. Crowds tend to be exclusively local, so this is a great place to see how Parisians really get down.

👍 LOU PASCALOU — 💲🍸⛅ BAR

14 rue des Panoyaux — ☎01 46 36 78 10

The uncontestable #1 hotspot of the 20th arrondissement. On summer nights, a crowd floods out of the bar and vies for chairs on the terrace. The friendly staff handles drink orders en masse, and somehow keeps their wits about them.

➡ Ⓜ Ménilmontant. ℹ Sprawling terrace seating. $ Beer €2-6.50. Wine glasses €2-4.60. Cocktails €5-6.50. ⏰ Open daily 9am-2am.

LE MIROIR — 💲🍸 BAR

111 bld. du Ménilmontant

Cheap beer and strong cocktails attract a local crowd. There's no pretention here; the bar definitely worth checking out, but only come if you don't mind standing out among a crowd of regulars.

➡ Ⓜ Ménilmontant. $ Beer €2.70-3. Cocktails €5. ⏰ Open M-Sa 9am-1am.

arts and culture

THEATER

⬛ ODÉON THÉÂTRE DE L'EUROPE
🔷 LATIN QUARTER, ST-GERMAIN

2 rue Corneille
☎01 44 85 40 40 ▣www.theatre-Odéon.fr

The big fish in a theater-themed neighborhood, the streets leading towards the Odéon Theatre are named after some of France's most famous playwrights, including Corneille and Racine. The Odéon itself is a classically beautiful theater; gold lines the mezzanine, and muted red upholstery covers the chairs. Considering that this is the mecca of Parisian theater, the prices are stunningly reasonable. Works range from the classical to the avant-garde.

⚐ ⓂOdéon. ⑤ Shows €5-32. Limited number of extremely cheap rush tickets available right before the show. 🕐 Performances generally M-Sa 8pm, Su 3pm.

⬛ THÉÂTRE DE LA VILLE
🔷 CHÂTELET LES HALLES

2 pl. du Châtelet
☎01 42 74 22 77 ▣www.theatredelavilleparis.com

Built in 1862, the Théâtre de la Ville underwent a rapid number of name changes (and identity crises) in the 1870s. It has since come of age and is now one of the most renowned theaters in Paris—in the '80s it became a major outlet for avant-garde contemporary dance and, therefore, its attendant younger artists. A soiree here should fit into most travel budgets. Bravo!

⚐ ⓂChâtelet. ⑤ Tickets €17-23, students €15. 🕐 Box office open M 11am 7pm, Tu-Sa 11am-8pm.

CABARET

⬛ LE LAPIN AGILE
🔷 MONTMARTRE

22 rue des Saules
☎01 46 06 85 87 ▣www.au-lapin-agile.com

Halfway up a steep, cobblestoned hill that American tourists describe to be "just like San Francisco," Le Lapin Agile has been around since the late 19th century, providing savvy and physically fit (that hill was something!) Parisians and tourists with a venue for music, dance and theatre. The tiny pink, green-shuttered theater was a hotspot of the 20th-century bohemian art scene in Paris—Picasso and Max Jacob are on the list of people who cabareted (is that a word?) there.

⚐ ⓂLamarck-Coulaincourt. ⓘ Ticket price includes first drink. ⑤ €24, students under 26 €17. 🕐 Open Tu-Su 9pm-2am.

BAL DU MOULIN ROUGE
🔷 MONTMARTRE

82 bld. de Clichy
☎01 53 09 82 82 ▣www.moulin-rouge.com

Ever since Christina and Co's music video, the only thing people associate with "Moulin Rouge" is that universal question: *"Voulez-vous couchez avec moi?"* But the world-famous cabaret and setting for the song and film isn't just about sex; it's also about glam and glitz. Since its opening in 1889, the Moulin Rouge has hosted international superstars like Ella Fitzgerald and Johnny Rey, and now welcomes a fair crowd of tourists for an evening of sequins, tassels, and skin. The shows remain risqué, but the price of admission is prohibitively expensive. The late show is cheaper, but be prepared to stand if it's a busy night.

⚐ ⓂBlanche. ⓘ Elegant attire required; no shorts, sneakers, or sportswear permitted. ⑤ Ticket for 9pm €102, 11pm show €92; includes half-bottle of champagne. 7pm dinner and 9pm show €150-180. Occasional lunch shows €100-130; call for more info. 🕐 Dinner at 7pm. Shows nightly 9, 11pm.

CINEMA

👍 L'ARLEQUIN
LATIN QUARTER, ST-GERMAIN

76 rue de Rennes ☎01 45 44 28 80

A proud revival theater, L'Arlequin goes heavy on the Hitchcock, mixing in other classic European films and some more modern French selections. The same three films are featured each week, undoubtedly decreasing the prevalence of adolescent movie-hopping. Some films are in English, but beware of certain dubbed selections.

♯ [M]Saint-Sulpice. $ €9.50, students, ages 18 and under and over 60, and big families €6.50. No discount applies F night-Su night except to 18-under.

CINÉMATHÈQUE FRANÇAISE
BASTILLE

51 rue de Bercy ☎01 71 19 32 00 💻www.cinematheque.fr

Though it's had some problems settling down (it's moved over five times, most recently in 2005), the Cinémathèque Française is committed to sustaining film culture. A must for film buffs, the theater screens four-to-five classics, near-classics, or soon-to-be classics per day; foreign selections are usually Voice Over. The Française also features multiple movie-related exhibits, which include over 1000 costumes, objects, and apparatuses from the past and present world of film.

♯ [M]Bercy. ℹ Buy tickets 20min. early. $ €6.50, under 26 and seniors €5, under 18 €3. ⏰ Temporary and permanent collections open M and W-Sa noon-7pm, Su 10am-8pm. Ticket window open from noon-last showing M and W-Sa, from 10am-last showing on Su.

MUSIC

👍 ELYSÉE MONTMARTRE
MONTMARTRE

72 bld. Rochechouart ☎01 44 92 45 36 💻www.elyseemontmartre.com

Any hip-hop nerd will remember this historic music hall in the Roots' hit song, "You Got Me": "She said she loved my show in Paris at Elysée Montmartre/and that I stepped off the stage and took a piece of her heart." Catch various hip-hop, soul, reggae, rock, indie, and underground acts here.

♯ [M]Anvers. $ Prices vary, but generally €13.80-45. ⏰ Hall opens at 11:30pm for all shows.

POINT EPHÉMÈRE
CANAL ST-MARTIN

200 quai de Valmy ☎01 40 34 02 48 💻www.pointephemere.org

A continuously changing, grungy bar/restaurant/concert hall/dance studio/artist residence, where non-conformity and cigarettes reign supreme. Music acts are usually lesser known. On a concert night, the 300-seat space is packed with guys who collect tattoos and girls who tote helmets instead of purses.

♯ [M]Jaures. ℹ Don't walk back late alone. $ Tickets prices vary per show. ⏰ Open M-Sa noon-2am, Su 1-9pm.

OPERA

OPÉRA DE LA BASTILLE
♿ BASTILLE

pl. de la Bastille ☎08 92 89 90 90 💻www.operadeparis.fr

The Opéra Garnier's "ugly" other half, the Opéra de la Bastille tends to do pieces with a more modern spin. Though the building's decor is somewhat questionable, the operas and ballets tend to be breathtaking enough to compensate. There may not be gilded columns, but you'll still feel like you're at the opera.

♯ [M]Bastille. ℹ For wheelchair-access, call 2 weeks ahead 01 40 01 18 50. $ Tickets can be purchased by Internet, mail, phone, or in person. Rush tickets 15min. before show for students under 25 and seniors. Tickets €5-200. ⏰ Box office open M-Sa 10:30am-6:30pm.

OPÉRA GARNIER

♥☆ OPERA

pl. de l'Opéra ☎08 92 89 90 90 ▣www.operadeparis.fr

Imagine The Opéra (capital T, capital O) in Paris; now go to the Opéra Garnier. Hosts mostly ballet, chamber music, and symphonies.

✦ ⓜOpéra. *i Tickets usually available 2 weeks before the show. For wheelchair access call 2 weeks ahead.* ⓢ*Ticket prices vary; operas €7-160, ballets €6-80.* ⓩ *Box office open M-Sa 10:30am-6:30pm. Last-minute discount tickets go on sale 1hr. before show.*

GUIGNOL

MARIONNETTES DU LUXEMBOURG

In the Jardin du Luxembourg ☎01 43 26 46 47 ▣guignolduluxembourg.monsite-orange.fr

Dance, puppets, dance! In the fictional battle of the marionnettes, this one comes out on top. The best *guignol* in Paris has played the same classics since its opening in 1933, including *Le Petit Chaperon Rouge* (Little Red Riding Hood) and Pinocchio.

✦ ⓜ*Vavin.* ⓢ *€4.50.* ⓩ *Run time approx. 40min. Arrive 30min. early for good seats. Performances W 4pm, Sa-Su 11am and 4pm. Performances during the summer months daily at 4pm, matinée performance Sa-Su 11am.*

shopping

Depending on who you're talking to, Shopping and Paris are almost synonymous. It can be hard to keep yourself from going crazy, but you probably should (nobody likes credit card debt).

BOOKS

▦ SHAKESPEARE AND CO.

✦ LATIN QUARTER, ST-GERMAIN

37 rue de la Bûcherie ☎01 43 25 40 93 ▣www.shakespeareco.org

Shakespeare and Co. is an absolutely lovable English-language bookshop and miniature socialist utopia. Scenes from the film *Before Sunset* were shot here. Allegedly, the owners allow passing "tumbleweeds" to sleep for free, provided they volunteer in the shop and read a book a day. An adjacent storefront holds an impressive collection of first editions, with emphsis on the Beat Generation.

✦ ⓜ*St-Michel. i Bargain bins outside include French classics translated into English.* ⓩ *Open M-F 10am-11pm, Sa-Su 11am-11pm.*

▦ ABBEY BOOKSHOP

⊛ LATIN QUARTER, ST-GERMAIN

29 rue de la Parcheminerie ☎01 46 33 16 24 ▣www.abbeybookshop.net

Clear your afternoon; if you're going to to Abbey Bookshop, you'll need the time. Set in a back alley, you'll need a few minutes to get used to the sheer number of books surrounding you. With a collection that includes everything from *Why Sex is Fun*, to *Bin Laden: Behind the Mask of a Terrorist*, this Canadian-owned shop probably has what you're looking for, and if not they'll order it for you. Plus they carry *Let's Go*—they've obviously got the right idea.

✦ ⓜ*St-Michel or Cluny. i Books in English and other langauges available.* ⓩ *Open M-Sa 10am-7pm.*

LADY LONG SOLO

⊛ BASTILLE

38 rue Keller ☎09 52 73 81 53 ▣ladylongsolo.com

An odd assortment of counter-cultural books that includes communist pamphlets and guides to the wonders of medical marijuana. Basically, where the druggies who decide to write books sell them. Hours unreliable at best. Pamphlets advocating for the legalization of pota lying about.

✦ ⓜ*Bastille.* ⓢ *Books as low as €2.* ⓩ*Open M,Tu 11am-4pm, W 2-8pm, Th,F,Sa 11am-4pm. Sometimes Sunday.*

CLOTHES AND ACCESSORIES

⬛ LA SAMARITAINE

◆ CHÂTELET-LES HALLES

67 rue de Rivoli   ☎08 00 01 00 15 ▪www.lasamaritaine.com

Spanning three blocks of the city's prime real estate, La Samaritaine is one of the oldest and most obnoxiously large department stores in Paris, with 48,000 square meters of shopping space. The department store was founded in 1869 when Ernest Cognacq, a street salesman who had tired of selling his gentlemens' ties on the often rainy and windy Pont Neuf, decided to bring his operation indoors. La Samaritaine helped usher in the age of conspicuous consumption with an unforgettable slogan: "one finds everything at La Samaritaine." The roof cafe, accessible by a quick elevator ride, has a fantastic, free view of the city. Although the building was renovated in 1928, it closed indefinitely in 2006 for security renovations; murmurs of a reopening in late 2011 have been heard, but

look, but no touchy

Below you'll find a list of the big names that you automatically associate with the Paris shopping scene. Unless you found a Parisian ⬛**sugar daddy** (and props to you if you did) you probably won't be leaving with much, but who doesn't like looking at pretty things? Salespeople won't be jumping to help you, but they'll gladly answer your questions if you ask nicely.

- **CARTIER** (*23 pl. Vendôme* ☎*01 44 55 32 20* ▪*www.cartier.com* ⓂTuileries*).
- **CHANEL** (*42 av. Montaigne* ☎*01 47 23 74 12* ▪*www.chanel.com* ⓂFranklin D. Roosevelt*).
- **CHRISTIAN LOUBOUTIN** (*19 rue Jean-Jacques Rousseau* ☎*01 42 36 05 31* ▪*www.christianlouboutin.com* ⓂLes Halles or Louvre Rivoli*).
- **DIOR** (*8 pl. Vendôme* ☎*01 42 96 30 84* ▪*www.dior.com* ⓂTuileries*).
- **GIVENCHY** (*56 rue François 1er* ☎*01 43 59 71 25* ▪*www.givenchy.fr* ⓂGeorge V*).
- **GUCCI** (*60 av. Montaigne* ☎*01 56 69 80 80* ▪*www.gucci.com* ⓂFranklin D. Roosevelt*).
- **HERMÈS** (*24 rue du Faubourg Saint-Honoré* ☎*01 40 17 47 17* ▪*www. hermes.com* ⓂMadeleine*).
- **JEAN-PAUL GAULTIER** (*44 av. George V* ☎*01 44 43 00 44* ▪*www.jean-paulgaultier.com* ⓂCharles de Gaulle-Étoile*).
- **LOUIS-VUITTON** (*101 av. des Champs-Elysées* ☎*01 53 57 52 00* ▪*www. louisvuitton.com* ⓂCharles de Gaulle-Étoile*).
- **VALENTINO** (*27 rue Faubourg Saint-Honoré* ☎*01 42 66 95 94* ▪*www. valentino.com* ⓂMadeleine*).
- **VERSACE** (*45 av. Montaigne* ☎*01 47 42 88 02* ▪*www.versace.com* ⓂFranklin D. Roosevelt*).
- **YVES SAINT-LAURENT** (*32 rue du Faubourg Saint-Honoré* ☎*01 53 05 80 80* ▪*www.ysl.com* ⓂMadeleine*).

paris

those are about as reliable as any other construction timeline in France (read: very unreliable). Check online for progress.

✣ ⓂChâtelet/Pont Neuf. *i* Closed for renovation. ☑ Information available M-F 10am-6pm.

FORUM LES HALLES
Les Halles

☞ CHÂTELET-LES HALLES

☎08 25 02 00 20 █www.forumdeshalles.com

Like most of Paris's monuments, Les Halles history is closely tied to the whims of French royalty and, later on, its politicians. The mall began as a small food market in 1135; Philippe Auguste and, later, Louis-Philippe and François I all considered Les Halles a sort of pet project, and its expansion soon surpassed their expectations. The forum and gardens above ground attract a large crowd. Descend into the pits of one of Paris's storied historical sites to discover its bastard American child; a 200 boutique shopping mall (plus three move theaters), with selections ranging from the Gap, to H&M, to Franck Provost.

✣ ⓂLes Halles. ☑ Open M-Sa 10am-8pm.

ATELIER 33
33 rue du Faubourg St-Antoine

☞ BASTILLE

☎01 43 40 61 63

This boutique caters to the kind of people who wear studded jeans jackets (€34), or order custom-made dresses to be worn with diamonds (€300-€3000). Occasional sales.

✣ ⓂBastille. ⑤ T-Shirts from €9. ☑ Open M-Sa 10:30am-7:30pm.

LE GRAIN DE SABLE
79 rue St-Louis-en-l'Île

☞ MARAIS

☎01 46 33 67 27 █www.legraindesable.fr

Absolutely exquisite hats (€155) and head pieces (€45) that any 20-something-year-old probably can't pull off and certainly can't afford. The beautiful works are handmade, often at a wood table in the boutique. If you do spring for one, you'll attract admiring double-takes all day.

✣ ⓂPont Marie. ⑤ Hats €30-155. ☑ Open M 11am-7pm, Tu 3-7pm, W-Su 11am-7pm.

VINTAGE

▨ FREE 'P' STAR
8 rue Ste-Croix de la Bretonnerie

☞ MARAIS

☎01 42 76 03 72 █www.freepstar.com

Enter as Plain Jane and leave a star—from the '80s or '90s, that is. Wide selection of vintage dresses (€20), velvet blazers (€40), boots (€30), and military style jackets (€5) that all seem like a good idea when surrounded by other antiquated pieces, but require some balls to be worn out in the open. There's no way to go wrong with the €10 jean pile and €3 bin. Second location at 61 rue de la Verrerie (☎01 42 78 0 76).

✣ ⓂHôtel de Ville. *i* Credit card min. €20. ☑ Open M-Sa noon-11pm, Su 2-11pm.

COIFFEUR
32 rue de Rosiers

☞ MARAIS

Right next door to L'As du Falafel, Coiffeur brings in the type of people who are just as willing to battle a crowd in the name of a good bargain. High quality vintage clothing is sold at a such fair price that nothing stays in the store for very long. The sweater rack (€10-€15) is a local fave.

✣ Ⓜ Hotel de Ville. ⑤ Dresses €10-€22. Jackets from €25. ☑ Open daily 11am-9pm.

ADOM
35 and 56 rue de la Roquette

☞ BASTILLE

☎01 48 07 15 94 or 01 43 57 54 92

Think of every canonical high school film you've ever seen: *Fast Times at Ridgemont High, The Breakfast Club, Napoleon Dynamite*. The selection at Adom seems to be made up of the wardrobe department from all of them. Cowboy boots, acid wash jeans, and letterman jackets are in ample supply here. It's like totally awesome, duh.

shopping · vintage

⇞ [M]Bastille. $ Boots from €35. Cut-offs €15. ⏰ Open M-Sa 11am-8pm, Su 3-8pm.

MUSIC

CROCODISC
📍 LATIN QUARTER, ST-GERMAIN

40-42 rue des Ecoles ☎01 43 54 47 95; 01 43 54 33 22

It's the kind of shop that makes you feel like going out and buying cool sneakers to match your new record, if you don't already own a pair. Stretching across two storefronts, Crocodisc runs the genre gamut, carrying rock, reggae, Italian, sixties, North African, garage, psyche/acid, trip hop and soul. Listening stations are interspered between random objects.

⇞ [M]Maubert-Mutualité. $ Records €10-20. CDs €8-15. ⏰ Open Tu-Sa 11am-7pm.

BOULINIER
📍 LATIN QUARTER, ST-GERMAIN

20 bld. St-Michel

Are you old enough to miss cassette tapes? We're not, but lucky for you 40-somethings, Boulinier still carries them, old-school style. This multi-level music shop is your go to for records, CDs, DVDs, and yes, cassettte tapes. Unfortunately, they don't carry 8-tracks (sorry Disco Stu).

⇞ [M]Cluny or Odéon. $ Records €12-14. ⏰ Open M 10:30am-midnight, Tu-W 1:30-8:30pm, F-Sa 10:30am-midnight.

MONSTER MELODIES
📍 CHÂTELET-LES HALLES

9 rue des Décharges ☎01 40 28 09 39

From Jazz to Ska, from Bieber to Ziggy Marley, Monster Melodies probably carries what you're looking for. The lower level houses well over 10,000 used CDs, while the upstairs sells those vinyl things your parents are always talking about.

⇞ [M]Les Halles. ⏰ Open M-Sa noon-7pm.

SPECIALTY

👍 PYLÔNES
📍 MARAIS

57 rue St-Louis-en-l'Île ☎01 46 34 05 02 💻www.pylones.com

An adult version of a toy store with the kind of spunky things you'll impulsively buy, never need, but always marvel at. Like graters topped with doll heads (*€18*). More useful, but just as fun items include cigarette cases (€12) (you're in Paris now, tobacco's a part of growing up) and expresso cups (€6). The playful, artful objects are fun to look at even if you don't get any.

⇞ [M]Pont Marie. ℹ 5 other locations around the city. $ Cups €6. Wallets €24. ⏰ Open daily 10:30am-7:30pm.

👍 LA GRANDE ÉPICERIE DE PARIS
📍 INVALIDES

38 rue de Sèvres

The butcher actually has a thin twirled mustache. We thought only cartoon French people looked like that.

⇞ [M]Vaneau. ℹ No pets allowed. $ Water €30. this place is way too expensive for you. ⏰ Open M-Sa 8:30am-9pm.

essentials

PRACTICALITIES

- **TOURS: Bateaux-Mouches** *(Port de la Conférence, Pont de l'Alma, Rive droite ☎01 76 99 73 💻www.bateaux-mouches.fr ⇞ Pont de l'Alma. ℹ Free parking throughout the duration of the cruise. Tours in English. $ €10, children under 12 €5. ⏰ Apr-Sept 10:15am-7pm, every 20min. 7-11pm; Oct-Mar 11am-9pm, week-*

ends 10:15am-9pm.) **City Segway Tours.** *(24 rue Edgar Faure ☎01 56 58 10 54 💻www.citysegwaytours.com/paris. ℹ All tours leave from beneath the Eiffel Tower and last 4-5hr. $ €80. ⏰ Daily Jan-Apr 9:30am; Mar-Dec daily 9:30am and 2pm.)* **Canauxrama** *(13 quai de la Loire ☎01 42 39 15 00 💻www.canauxrama.com 🚏 ⓂBastille (Marina Arsenal) or Jaurés (Bassin de la Villette). ℹ Reservations recommended. Ticket desk open 40min. before departure or buy online. Departures either from Marina Arsenal or Bassin de la Villette. $ €16, students €11, children under 12 €8.50, under 4 free. ⏰ Both locations with tours between 9am and 11pm.)* **Fat Tire Bike Tours** *(24 rue Edgar Faure ☎01 56 58 10 54 💻www.fattirebiketours.com ℹ Tours last 4hr. $ €28, students €26. ⏰ Day tour daily 11am; Apr-Nov 11am, 3pm. Night tour Mar-Apr daily 6pm; Apr-Nov daily 7pm; Nov Tu, Th, Sa, Su 6pm.)*

- **DISABILITY RESOURCES: L'Association des Paralysées de France, Délégation de Paris.** In addition to promoting disabled individual's fundamental rights to state compensation, public transportation, and handicapped-conscious jobs, the association also organizes international and provencial vacations. *(17-19 bld. Auguste Blanqui ☎01 40 78 00 00)*
- **TICKET SERVICES: FNAC.** *(74 av. des Champs-Élysées ☎01 53 53 64 64 💻www.fnac.fr 🚏 Franklin D. Roosevelt. ℹ Also at 77-81 bld. St-Germain; 109 Porte Berger; 30 av. d'Italie, 13ème; 136 rue de Rennes, 6ème; 109 rue St-Lazare, 9ème; 26-30 av. de Ternes, 17ème. ⏰ Open M-Sa 10am-11:45pm, Su noon-11:45pm.)* **Virgin Megastore** *(52 av. des Champs-Élysées, 8ème ☎01 49 53 50 00 💻www.virginmegastore.fr 🚏 ⓂFranklin D. Roosevelt. ⏰ Open M-Sa 9am-6pm.)*
- **INTERNET: The American Library** provides free internet access for all members and those with Day and Week passes. Wireless internet available throughout library. Ask circulation desk for assistance. *(10 rue de Général Camou, 7ème ☎01 53 59 12 60 💻www.americanlibraryinparis.org 🚏 ⓂÉcole Militaire. ⏰ Open Tu-Sa 10am-7pm, Su 1-7pm. Reduced hours Jul-Aug. Reference desk closed Su.)*

EMERGENCY!

- **EMERGENCY NUMBERS: Police:** ☎17 (for emergencies only). **Ambulance (SAMU):** ☎15. **Fire:** ☎18. **Poison:** ☎01 40 05 48 48 (In French, but some English assistance available). **Rape:** ☎08 00 05 95 95. *(⏰ Open M-F 10am-7pm.)* **SOS Help!** *(☎17)* is an emergency hotline for english speakers in crisis.
- **CRISIS HOTLINES: AIDES** is the first French association against HIV/AIDs and viral hepatitis. *(☎0800 84 08 00 💻www.aides.org ⏰ Open 24hr.)* **Alcoholics Anonymous.** *(☎01 46 34 59 65 💻www.aaparis.org)* **Red Cross France** provides HIV testing. *(43 rue de Valois, 1er ☎01 42 61 30 04 💻www.croix-rouge.fr 🚏 Palais-Royal or Bourse.)* **International Counseling Service.** *(☎01 45 50 26 49 💻www.icsparis.com.)*
- **HOSPITAL/MEDICAL SERVICES: American Hospital of Paris.** *(63 bld. Hugo, Neuilly ☎01 46 41 25 25 wwww.american-hospital.org 🚏 ⓂPort Maillot, then bus #82.)* **Hôpital Bichat.** *(46 rue Henri Buchard, 18ème ☎01 40 25 80 80 🚏 ⓂPort St-Ouen.)*

GETTING THERE ✈

By Plane

Paris has three main airports: Roissy-Charles de Gaulle, Orly, and Beauvais.

Roissy-Charles de Gaulle (Roissy-CDG)

Most transatlantic flights land at Aéroport Roissy-CDG, 23km northeast of Paris (*💻www.adp.fr*). The two cheapest and fastest ways to get into the city from Roissy-CDG are by RER and by bus. The **RER train** from Roissy-CDG to Paris leaves from the Roissy train station, which is in Terminal 2. To get to the station from Terminal 1, take the Red Line of the Navette, a free shuttle bus that leaves every 6-10min. From there, the **RER B** (one of the Parisian commuter rail lines) will transport you to central Paris. To transfer to the metro, get off at **Gare du Nord, Châtelet-Les-Halles,** or **St-Michel,** all of which are RER and metro stops. The trip should take 35 minutes in either direction.

Taking a **shuttle bus** the whole distance from the airport to Paris is simple, and it takes about the same amount of time as taking the RER. The ▓**Roissybus** (☎*01 49 25 61 87)* leaves from rue Scribe at **place de l'Opéra** every 15min. during the day and every 20min. at night. You can catch the Roissybus from Terminals 1, 2, and 3 of the airport from 6am to 11pm. Roissybus is not wheelchair accessible.

Orly

Aéroport d'Orly (☎*01 49 75 15 15 for info in English)*, 18km south of the city, is used by char- ters and many continental flights. From Orly Sud gate G or gate I, platform 1, or Orly Ouest level G, gate F, take the **Orly-Rail** shuttle bus to the **Pont de Rungis/Aéroport d'Orly** train stop, where you can board the RER C2 for a number of destinations in Paris.

Another option is the RATP ▓**Orlybus** (☎*08 36 68 77 14)*, which runs between metro and RER stop **Denfert-Rochereau** (lines 4 and 6) in the 14*ème* and Orly's south terminal. You can also board the Orlybus at **Dareau-St-Jacques, Glacière-Tolbiac,** and **Porte de Gentilly.**

RATP also runs **Orlyval** (☎*01 69 93 53 00)*—a combination of metro, RER, and VAL rail shuttle—which is probably your fastest option. The VAL shuttle goes from **Antony** (RER line B) to Orly Ouest and Sud. You can either get a ticket just for the VAL, or combination VAL-RER tickets. Buy tickets at any RATP booth in the city, or from the Orlyval agencies at Orly Ouest, Orly Sud, and Antony. To Orly: Be careful; it splits into two lines right before the Antony stop. Get on the train that says **"St-Rémy-Les-Chevreuse"** or just look for the track that has a lit-up sign saying **"Antony-Orly."** From Orly: Trains arrive at Orly Ouest 2min. after reaching Orly Sud.

Beauvais

Ryanair, EasyJet, and other intercontinental airlines often fly into and depart from Aéroport de Paris Beauvais. Buses run between the airport and bld. Pershing in the 17*ème*, near the hotel Concorde Lafayette (Ⓜ**Porte Maillot)**. Tickets are €13 and can be purchased in the arrivals lounge of the airport, at the kiosk just oustide the bus stop, or online. Call ☎03 44 11 46 86 or consult ▓www.aeroportbeauvais.com for bus schedules.

By Train

- **GARE DU NORD:** Trains to northern France, Britain, Belgium, the Netherlands, Scandinavia, Eastern Europe, and northern Germany (Cologne, Hamburg) all depart from this station. To: **Amsterdam** *(4-5hr.);* **Brussels** *(1hr.);* **London** *(by the Eurostar Chunnel; 3hr.).*

- **GARE DE L'EST:** To eastern France (Champagne, Alsace, Lorraine, Strasbourg), Luxembourg, parts of Switzerland (Basel, Zürich, Lucerne), southern Germany (Frankfurt, Munich), Austria, Hungary, and Prague. To: **Luxembourg** *(4-5hr.);* **Munich** *(9hr.);* **Prague** *(15hr.);* **Strasbourg** *(1hr.);* **Vienna** *(15hr.);* **Zürich** *(7hr.).*

- **GARE DE LYON:** To southern and southeastern France (Lyon, Provence, Riviera), parts of Switzerland (Geneva, Lausanne, Berne), Italy, and Greece. To: **Florence** *(13hr.);* **Geneva** *(4hr.);* **Lyon** *(2hr.);* **Marseille** *(3-4hr.);* **Nice** *(6hr.);* **Rome** *(15hr.).*

- **GARE D'AUSTERLITZ:** To the Loire Valley, southwestern France (Bordeaux, Pyrénées), Spain, and Portugal. (TGV to southwestern France leaves from Gare Montparnasse.) To **Barcelona** *(12hr.)* and **Madrid** *(12-13hr.).*

- **GARE ST-LAZARE:** To Normandy. To **Caen** *(2hr.)* and **Rouen** *(1-2hr.).*

- **GARE MONTPARNASSE:** To Brittany and southwestern France on the TGV. To **Rennes** *(2hr.)* and **Nantes** *(2hr.).*

GETTING AROUND

By Metro

In general, the Metro system is easy to navigate (pick up a colorful map at any station), and trains run swiftly and frequently. Metro stations, in themselves a distinctive part of the Paris landscape, are marked with an "M" or with the *"Métropolitain"* lettering designed by Art Nouveau legend Hector Guimard. The earliest trains of the day start running around 5:30am, and the last ones leave the end-of-the-line stations (the *portes de Paris*) for the center of the city at about 12:15am during the week, and at 2:15am on Friday and Saturday. Connections to other lines are indicated by orange *correspondance* signs, exits indicated by blue *sortie* signs. Transfers are free if made within a station, but it is not always possible to reverse direction on the same line without exiting the station. **Hold onto your ticket until you exit the metro,** and pass the point marked *Limite de Validité des Billets;* a uniformed RATP *contrôleur* (inspector) may request to see it on any train. If caught without one, you must pay a hefty fine.

Don't count on buying a metro ticket late at night. Some ticket windows close as early as 10pm, and many close before the last train arrives. Also, not all stations have automatic booths. It's a good idea to carry one more ticket than you need, although large stations have ticket machines that accept coins. Avoid the most dangerous stations (**Barbès-Rochechouart, Pigalle, Anvers, Châtelet-Les-Halles, Gare du Nord, Gare de l'Est**) after dark. When in doubt, take a bus or taxi.

By RER

The RER *(Réseau Express Régional)* is the RATP's suburban train system, which passes through central Paris. The RER travels much faster than the metro. There are five RER lines, marked A-E, with different branches designated by a number: for example, the C5 line services Versailles-Rive Gauche. The newest line, the E, is called the Eole *(Est-Ouest Liaison Express)* and links Gare Magenta to Gare St-Lazare. Within Paris, the RER works exactly the same as the metro, requiring the same ticket. The principal stops within the city, which link the RER to the metro system, are Gare du Nord, Nation, Charles de Gaulle-Etoile, Gare de Lyon, and Châtelet-Les-Halles on the Right Bank and St-Michel and Denfert-Rochereau on the Left Bank. The electric signboards next to each track list all the possible stops for trains running on that track. Be sure that the little square next to your destination is lit up. Trips to the suburbs require special tickets. You'll need your ticket to exit RER stations. Insert your ticket just as you did to enter, and pass through. Like the metro, the RER runs 5:30am-12:30am and until 2:30am on weekends.

By Bus

Although slower and often costlier than the metro, a bus ride can be a cheap sightseeing tour and a helpful introductions to the city's layout. Bus tickets are the same as those used in the metro, and they can be purchased either in metro stations or from the bus driver. Enter the bus through the front door and punch your ticket by pushing it into the machine by the driver's seat. If you have a *Navigo* or other transport pass, flash it at the driver. Inspectors may ask to see your ticket, so hold onto it until you get off. Should you wish to leave the paradise that is the RATP autobus, just press the red button so the *arrêt demandé* (stop requested) sign lights up.

Most buses run daily 7am-8:30pm, although those marked **Autobus du nuit** continue until 1:30am. Still others, named **Noctilien**, run all night. Night buses run from Châtelet to the *portes* of the city every hour on the half hour from 12:30-5:30am (1-6am from the *portes* into the city). Look for bus stops marked with a bug-eyed moon sign. Check out **www.noctilien.fr** or ask a major metro station or at Gare de l'Est for more information on Noctilien buses.

excursions

VERSAILLES

If you descend the great steps of the Versailles garden slowly enough, you might just feel like royalty. A whopping 580m long, this crib won't fit in your camera frame. To be fair, the palace did house all 6000 members of the royal court and serve as the seat of goverment, after **Louis XIV** (1643-1715) decided in 1661 that his father's old brick and stone château needed an upgrade. No less than four men were needed to get it done. Louis XIV, or the Sun King, or the self-aggrandizing narcissist, commissioned two architects, Lous Le Vau and Jules Hardouin-Mansart, painter Charles Le Brun and landscape designer André Le Nôtre to create an unquestionable symbol of the awesome power of the French monarchy. Later, with the 1789 Revolution, Louis XVI and Marie-Antoinette would learn just how contestable that power was when set under a guillotine blade. In 1837, king Louis-Phillipe, initiated a clever piece of PR, opening up parts of the palace to the public and dedicating it to "all the glories of France," emphasis on all, emphasis on France. Since then, the château has remained largely unaltered, though a €370 million renovation and restoration campaign was launched in 2003, and visitors now are hardly ever of royal blood.

Orientation

As the Sun King demanded, a visit to the 800 hectares property must begin at the **terrace.** To its left, the **Parterre Sud** opens up to the **Orangery,** which onces boasted 2000 orange trees. The fresh-squeezed orange juice stands scattered throughout the sight today recall the orangery's historical production. The **Parterre d'Eau,** the first of many ponds and lakes on the premises, stands in the middle of the terrace. Past the **Bassin de Latone** and to the left is the **Jardin du Roi,** a fragant, flower-lined sanctuary only accessible from the easternmost side facing the **Bassin du Miroir.** Near the the grove's southern gate lies the **Bassin de Bacchus,** one of four seasonal fountains, which portrays the Roman god of wine, crowned in vine branches, reclining on a bunch of grapes. Some traveler's report having taken swigs of wine there in honor of the great god. Behind it, the **Bosquet de la Salle de Ball** is a semicircle of cascading waterfalls and torch holders, where royals once late-night bachanalias of their own.

Moving north to the center of the garden leads to the **Bosquet de la Colonnade,** an impressive arrangement of 32 violet and blue mable columns, sculptures, and white marble basins, created by Hardouin-Mansart in 1864. The northern gate to the Colonnade opens onto the 330m long **Tapis Vert,** the main walkway leading to the garden's most ostentatious fountain, the **Bassin d'Apollo,** in which the god himself charges out of the water on bronze horses. On the garden's northern side, you'll find the **Bosquet de l'Encelade.**When the fountain is on, a 25m high jet bursts from Titan's enormous mouth, which is plated, as all mouths should be, with shimmering gold and half buried under rocks.

The**Bassin de Flore** and the **Bassin de Cérès** show ladies, busts out, reclining in their natural habitats—a bed of flowers and wheat sheaves, respectively. The **Parterre Nord** overlooks some of the garden's most spectacular fountains. The **Allée d'Eau,** a fountain-lined walkway, provides the best view of the **Bassin des Nymphes de Diane.** The path slopes toward the sculpted **Bassin du Bragon,** where a beast slain by Apollo spurts water 27m into the air. Next to it, 99 jets of water issue from sea horns encircling Neptune in the **Bassin de Neptuune,** the gardens' largest fountain; make your way here at 5:20pm for a truly spectacular fountain finale.

If you get tired of the grandeur of the main gardens and groves, head up to Marie-Antoinette's Estate, where the quiet, flower-filled paths are much less of an ego display.

paris

CHÂTEAU

Though the Sun King's palace boasts a whopping 51,200 square meters of floor space, the public is granted access to only a small percentage of it. With over ten million visitors per year, the Versailles staff is practiced in the art of shuttling tourists through. After a walk through the **Musée de L'Histoire de France,** which briefly recounts French history in chronological order, visitors are shepherded down the halls in a single direction. The museum's 21 rooms feature stunning portraits of the royal family, including a smaller copy of Rigaud's famous **depiction of Louis XIV** with red-heeled shoes. Up the main staircase to the right is the two-level chapel where the King heard Mass, built in 1710. Here God competed with the Sun King for attention while the court gathered to watch him pray.

Through the hallway, where the ceiling is covered with marvelous frescoes (don't forget to look up!), are the luxurious **State Apartments,** which include both the king's bedroom, the **Room of Abundance**, the **Apollo Salon**, and the famed **Hall of Mirrors.** Note how tiny the bed is; like Napoleon, Sarkozy, and other French leaders that followed him, Louis XIV was a man of less than average height with an ensuing inferiority complex, and was known to wear shoes with 5" heels. The Apollo Salon houses the Sun King's throne; 3m tall, the throne enabled the King to tower over his subjects, and enjoy the view of the beautiful fresco of himself on the ceiling, which compares him to Apollo and portrays him as the bearer of Enlightenment. When they weren't trying to figure out how to kill him, French citizens showed great deference to the king and ritualistically bowed or curtsied when they passed the throne, even when great Louis wasn't there. As if the Apollo Salon wasn't elaborate (or pathological) enough, the sumptuous Hall of Mirrors exemplifies the King's opulent taste. Lined with the largest mirrors 17th century technology could produce, and windows that overlook to the grand gardens outside, the room served as a reception for great ambassadors. Today it can be rented out for a hefty sum.

The **Queen's Bedchamber,** where royal births were public events in order to prove the legitimacy of heirs, is much less ornate than the king's, but almost exactly as the queen last left it on October 6, 1789. A rendition of *Le Sacre de Napoleon* by French Neoclassicist David depicts Napoleon's self-coronation, and dominates the **Salle du Sacré,** also known as the **Coronation Room.** David painted Napoleon's mother, Letizia, into the scene even though she refused to be there. The more honest painting of **Battle of Aboukir** is positioned on the wall next to it, and portrays the gore of war— and perhaps the price of all the royal splendor that surrounds it.

GARDENS

Gardening *à la française* is nothing short of neurotic. The park of Versailles, with its parterres, groves, status, fountains, pools and trees boxed in metal frames, is no exception. Meticulously designed by André Le Nôtre in 1661 and completed by **Jules Hardouin-Mansart,** the château gardens are an impressive 800 hectares. During **Les Grand Eux Musicales,** almost all the fountains are turned on at the same time, and chamber music booms from among the groves. Wandering through the gardens many walks, you will find a number of marble statues and bursting fountains.

$ Free. Grandes Eaux Musicales Apr-Sept Sa-Su and holidays €8, students and under 18 €6, under 6 free. 🕒 Open daily Apr-Oct 8am-8:30pm; Nov-Mar 8am-6pm. Free.

TRIANONS AND MARIE ANTOINETTE'S HAMEAU

☎01 30 83 78 89 💻www.châteauversailles.fr.

Contrary to what officials will tell you, the walk up to **Trianons** and **Marie Antoinette's Hameau** does not take 25min. Less ambitious sightseers are overwhelmed by the prospect of leaving the main area, which makes for a quieter and infinitely more pleasant Versailles experience. The garden surrounding Petit Trianon and Marie Antoinette's hameau is one of the most beautiful and tranquil areas of the park. Inspired by Jean-Jacques Rousseau's theories on the goodness of nature, the Queen wanted a simple life, and so commissioned Richard Mique to construct a 12-building compound comprised of a dairy farm, gardener's house, and mill around a pristine and swan-filled lake. Complete with lilac beds, flower pots, and thatched roofs, Marie Antoinette played the peasant and held intimate parties in her **Temple of Love**. We doubt the irony of this idealized pastoralism escaped the Parisian masses of the time. **Petit Trianon** was built between 1762 and 1768 for Louix XV and his mistress Mme. de Pompadour. Some ways away from the palace, the more homey château was intended to serve as a love den. Unfortunately, Pompadour died before it was completed. The **Grand Trianon** was intended to be a château-away-from-château for Louix XIV, who reached the mini château by boat from the Grand Canal. Both the Petit and Grand Trianon provide a less ostentatious view of royal life and allow one to imagine the life of a man rather than the life of a king.

Ⓢ *Admission to palace and audio tour €15, reduced €13. The"passport" one-day pass allows entry to the palace, Trianon palace and Marie-Antoinette's estate €18. Day of Les Grands Eaux Musicales €25. Trianon palace and Marie Antionette's Estate €10, reduced €6. ⌂ Château open Tu-Su Apr-Oct 9am-6:30pm; Nov-Mar 9am-5:30pm. Last entry 30min. before close.*

Food

Eating in Versailles is less expensive than would be expected, considering the three million tourists that visit the town each year. Restaurants and vendors jack up the price about €1-2 for the privilege of eating where the kings once did, but prices outside of the gilded gates are more reasonable. The royal feasts rolled right out with Louis XVI's head; today, options are pretty much limited to sandwiches, crêpes and pizza. Wise visitors—that means you, fair Let's Go traveler—know that packing a long baguette, some fruit and a bottle of wine and spreading out on the grass is the best way to do it.

Essentials

Getting There

RER trains beginning with "V" run from Invaled or any stop on RER Line C5 to the **Versailles Rive Gauche station.** *(Ⓢ Round trip €5.80, advisable as ticket lines are long at Versailles station. ⌂ 30-40min., every 15min.)* Buy your RER ticket before going through the turnstile to the platform; when purchasing from a machine, look for the **Île-de-France ticket option.** While a Metro ticket will get you through these turnstiles, it won't get you through RER turnstiles at the other end and could ultimately result in a significant fine. From RER: Versailles, turn right down **av. du General de Gaulles,** walk 200m, and turn left at the big intersection onto av. de Paris. You'll know it when you see it.

Getting Around

The **tourist office** is on the left before the château courtyard. Info on accommodations, events, restaurants, and sightseeing buses. Not to be confused with office that sells guided tours of the château *(2bis av. de Paris ☎01 39 24 88 88 🖥www.versailles-tourisme. com ⌂ Open M 11am-5pm, Tu-Sa 9am-6pm, Su 11am-5pm.)*

LOIRE VALLEY

Named for the river running through it, the Loire Valley is home to some of the most beautiful renaissance castles and châteaux that France has to offer. Your childhood fairy-tale dreams come fully to life here as you take to the countryside to explore the homes of kings and queens.

Biking through the Loire is one of the more popular activities people undertake when visiting the region; the long river paths and hills provide a challenging but pleasant biking experience. Taking a bike provides freedom for the traveller who can bike between château and rest their behinds in exploring the grand gardens of Villandry or the fairytale setting of Chenonceau.

But there is more to do in the Loire Valley than just biking around green fields and gazing at châteaux. The cities themselves have fascinating histories and several brilliant and whacky museums to explore. Tours, one of the student capitals in France (after Paris), manages to combine a lively nightlife scene with an awful lot of historical buildings. Blois boasts an amazing château and a plethora of intricately designed churches, whilst Orléans prides itself in its Joan of Arc history. Whatever your pleasure, be it nightlife, museums, sights or food, The Loire Valley will suit even the most history-hating traveller with its stunning natural beauties and leisurely way of life.

greatest hits

- **SO MUCH BETTER IN DUMAS'S VERSION:** We're not sure if Catherine de Medici actually kept her poisons in that secret compartment in the Blois Chateau. We always liked Alexandre Dumas's versions of French history better anyway, though, so let's just play along (p. 104).

- **YOU THINK THEY LIKE JOAN OF ARC HERE?** She's our favorite saint too (at least until Mother Teresa makes the cut), but even by our standards Orléans venerates this woman to excess (p. 92).

- **BOW DOWN TO THE MASTER:** The *Mona Lisa* might be in Paris, but Leonardo Da Vinci himself is buried outside of Blois at the Chateau Amboise. Journey out to the elaborate gardens and pay your respects (p. 105).

Tired of living like a dirty, smelly, backpacker and ready to start living like a king? Well we can't promise that you'll be able to do that in the Loire Valley, but you can certainly see how kings lived. Known for the numerous châteaux peppered about the countryside, this is for the petit(e) prince(esse) in each and every one of us. **Orléans** and **Tours** are major cities of the region, but if you can only hit one make it **Tours.** You'll find other backpackers painting the town red in 🖼**Place Plumereau,** especially at Au Temps du Roi or La Guinguette.

orléans ☎02 38

The capital of the Loire Valley, Orléans (ohr-lay-ahn) compensates for its lack of lewd nightclubs and youth culture with its phenomenal amount of history. Joan of Arc, aptly known as the "Maid of Orléans," marched armies down these crooked cobbled streets when she liberated the city from a brutal seven-month English siege in 1429, a victory which rejuvenated French forces and contributed to their victory in the Hundred Years War. Medieval studies nerds eager to submerge themselves in all things pertaining to infected rats and feudal cat fights will find themselves completely at home here. The historic *petit vieille ville* and its tremendous Cathedral lie at the heart of Orléans, complete with the *patisseries* and *boulangeries* of any traditional French town. Though Orléans should definitely make an appearance on your Loire Valley itinerary, don't anticipate spending more than a few days (or even a day) here— unless, of course, you are a Joan of Arc fanatic and just can't get enough of her. The city devolves into a bustling but run-of-the-mill commercial area further out of the center, with shops and suburban streets which do not compare to the visual beauties on offer closer to the downtown.

ORIENTATION

The historic sights of Orléans are all within walking distance of the **train station,** and are so close to each other that you need not worry about taking public transport in between museums and buildings. The majority of interesting sights are located in the **vielle ville** and the surrounding streets, which makes access extremely quick and simple. Most streets are connected by small alleyways which should be avoided at night, but are safe to explore during the day. Almost all the streets in the area are historic, featuring Renaissance structures and intricate designs. Although it appears to be populated almost exclusively by geriatrics, Orléans does have a younger generation—they surface during the late afternoon, and head to the bars along **rue de Bourgogne** where a chilled and relaxed atmosphere dominates most of the establishments.

The train station is a 2min. walk north of the center on **bld. Alexandre Martin.** From this main road it is possible to reach the *vielle ville* by following the shopping street **rue de la République** (through the *centre commercial* and down the steps) which leads to **place du Matroi.** At pl. du Matroi, continue southwards where rue de la République becomes **rue Royale** and follow this directly southwards to reach the banks of the Loire. Rue Royale intersects with **rue Jean D'Arc,** which will take you to the Cathedral and Tourist Information Office at **pl. St Croix** ,and a little further down rue Royale connects with **rue de Bourgogne** where you will find the best of Orléans's bars and restaurants. A tram service runs between the Train Station and the river *(€1.40)* which makes transporting luggage nice and simple.

loire valley

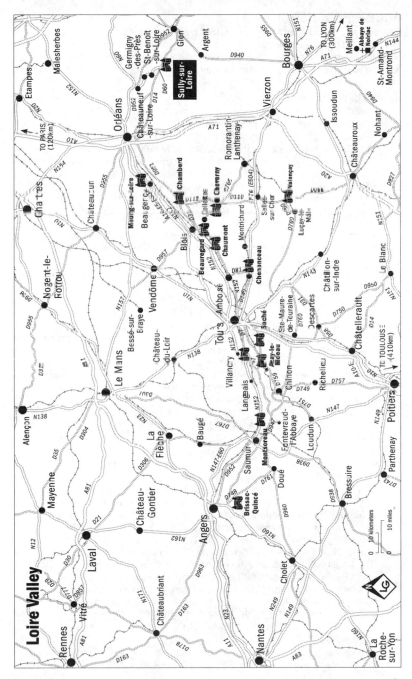

Loire Valley

ACCOMMODATIONS

Orléans isn't exactly thriving with budget hotels and funky hostels, but this does not mean that finding a bargain abode around town is impossible. Websites specializing in cheap hotel rooms often provide last-minute offers that are cheaper than advertised rates, so keep your chin up and keep Googling for that deal. Booking in advance for most places is advisable.

HOTEL ARCHANGE

💳🚭📶 HOTEL [4]

1 bld. de Verdun ☎02 32 54 42 42 💻www.hotelarchange.com

Owned by an outgoing and talkative local man and his son, Hotel Archange places you right near the train station and within walking distance of the major shopping district and historic sights. The hotel cultivates a bizarre yet comforting vibe that makes it an ideal place to set up shop for your stay in the town; murals of angels, rainbows and fairies are painted on the corridor walls, and an eccentric collection of hand-shaped chairs and Star Wars figurines clutter the reception area. The rooms are especially well suited for families or small groups, since pairs of rooms share a vestibule which is lockable from the outside. Free Wi-Fi and TV in all rooms.

➜ From the train station, walk through the commercial center, down the steps and the Hotel is on the other side of the street, next to the McDonalds. $ Singles with shower €43, with bath €47-57; double with bath €56-70; triples €70.

HOTEL DE L'ABEILLE

💳📶🚭 HOTEL [4]

64 rue Alsace Lorraine ☎ 02 38 56 54 87 💻www.hoteldelabeille.com

Boasting a range of rooms overlooking the main streets of Orléans that are scheduled to be fully renovated by 2011, The Hotel de L'Abeille takes pride in its heritage, and ensures that visitors don't forget the town's history by placing a statue of Joan of Arc in the reception area. This sense of history continues throughout the hotel, as each room is decorated with antique furniture and given its own unique character. Some rooms have bright blue bedding and beds covered in numerous throw pillows; others sport distinguished antique armchairs, positioned to look out over the street. The dining area where breakfast is served is reminiscent of an old French kitchen

➜Off of rue République, opposite the Train Station ℹ Breakfast €9. $ Singles with shower €47-76, with full bath €76-95; doubles €76-95; triples room available fo €99; family suite for up to 5 people €120.

HOTEL MARGUERITE

💳📶 HOTEL [4]

14 pl. du Vieux Marché ☎02 38 53 74 32 💻www.hotel-orleans.fr

Owned by a very welcoming gentleman who is keen to accommodate (unless you're traveling in a group, that is; Hotel Marguerite has refused to book group accommodations ever since items in the rooms were broken by a collection unruly school children), Hotel Marguerite boasts a range of lavish bedrooms and bathrooms with floors which you could eat the breakfast off of (for an additional €7, of course). The floral-patterned bedspreads will remind you of your grandmother's house, but so will the cleanliness and friendliness. The hotel's prime location, service, and cleanliness puts it in a higher price bracket than some of the other local digs more suited for the younger generation in the town. Perhaps this is a place to stay when your judgmental elderly relatives are following you around Europe.

➜ From the train station, take the tram in the direction of L'Hopital de la Source. Get off at De Gaulle Station and walk straight down rue des Minimes. The hotel will be on the far left of the street, tucked under another building. $ Singles €55-71; doubles €75.

L'HOTEL SAUVAGE

🍸🚭 HOTEL [3]

71 rue de Bourgogne ☎ 02 38 544848

Nestled amongst Orléans' most lively and busy bars, L'Hotel Sauvage may be savage by name, but it most certainly isn't savage by nature. Offering 30 cozy bedrooms complete with traditional low wooden beams (for those taller than 6ft., do watch your head!), the hotel feels almost as if it has been plucked from the 19th century. It may offer a piano in the corridor in lieu of Wi-Fi in the rooms, but The Hotel Sauvage will provide any tired and disoriented traveller with a home away from home.

Next to the barber shop near the rue de la Tour Neuve intersection on la Rue dee de Bourgogne. [$] Singles €35; doubles €45.

bridge over troubled waters

The Loire River was (and still is) a large, dangerous river to cross. Its tumultuous currents and breadth made sturdy bridges a necessity in France's early history. Being the most northern point on the Loire, Orléans became one of France's third richest cities, because of its monopoly on a river crossing.

Joan of Arc protected access to the bridge from the advancing English armies and, with the (alleged) help of God, defended the Châtlet des Tourelles ensuring her eternal favor with **Charles VII** and guaranteeing that she'd never get screwed over or burnt at the stake for heresy.

Louis XI used the bridge to extort merchants with high tolls to revitalize the saffron industry and tax rich castle owners to pass by the *val-de-Loire*, a sort of scenic toll road.

Duke of Orléans thought that the Mississippi looked so much like the Loire when the French settled America, that he named the settlement at its mouth Nouvelle Orléans, or New Orleans.

Jean Royer and Jean Kérisel rebuilt the bridges after WWII, making Orléans the first city to be rebuilt in France, even before Paris.

LE GRAND HOTEL

HOTEL [5]

1 rue de la Lionne, angle 21 rue Bannier ☎02 38 53 19 79 www.hotelorleans.com

Offers cheerful rooms that are not as cheap as you'd think they would be: expect average or above average rates for rooms which are by all means below average. Despite the price, the hotel is within walking distance of the three main squares in Orléans with shops lining the adjacent streets. Breakfast is available *(€10)*, and is free for guests under 16. Elevators make the rooms wheelchair-accesible.

From the train station, walk out through the Commerical Center, down the steps and turn right onto bld. Alexandre Martin. Follow the road until you reach place Gambetta, then take a left onto rue Bannier. Follow this road almost all the way to place du Martroi and rue de la Lionne will be on your right. [$] Singles €66; doubles or twins €73; triples €92.

LE BANNIER

HOTEL [2]

13 rue du Faubourg Bannier ☎02 38 53 25 86 www.lebannier.fr

If you roll into Orléans late at night and don't fancy straying too far from the train station, then the Bannier offers rock-bottom prices in a less affluent area of town. A single—which can be converted into a double in a pinch—will only set you back €33, and you can have a triple for just €48. But the prices seem to be the only thing going for this hotel, which is now dwarfed by a massive hotel complex on the corner of Place Gambetta. Expect to get what you pay for, and don't expect much in the way of space or comfort—the bathroom can only fit about one person in it!

Exit the train station and take a left onto av. de Paris. When you reach bld. Alexandre Martin head right until you reach rue du Faubourg Bannier on your right. The hotel is a few metres up the road. $ singles and doubles €33; triples €48.

ESCALE OCENIA HOTEL [4]

16 quai Saint-Laurent ☎02 38 54 47 65 www.oceaniahotels.com

If you enjoy pleasant walks along the river and want to avoid the hussle and bustle of the city center, then Escale Oceania can offer you such a leisurely stay. For a price, that is. Although the hotel claims to be 'steps' away from the center, it takes a good 10min. to get there. This is normally not a problem, but make sure you plan ahead—don't drink too much wine for dinner and get stuck on the way back to the hotel. A 24hr. reception and bar make the hotel feel very welcoming, but it is more often frequented by businessmen than the adventerous student traveler.

Take the tram in the direction of of L'Hopital de la Source from Orléans station. From the rue de Republiqe stop, head to le quai Châtelet (adjacent to river) and follow the road past the Pont George V and under the Pont Joffre. The hotel will shortly be on your right. i Breakfast €6.50. $ Rooms €57-90.

SIGHTS

The majority of the sights in Orléans are situated in and around **pl. St Croix** in the shadow its overbearring **Cathedral.** It is possible to walk between the major historical sights on your own, though the **Tourist Office** can provide you with some suggested routes and additional information. It was down the **rue de Bourgogne,** that Joan of Arc marched the triumphant French army in 1429. The street features multiple historic wooden houses, and is home to most of Orléans' nightlife. One wonders if the virginal saint would approve.

CATHÉDRALE SAINT CROIX CATHEDRAL

pl. St Croix

Towering over Orléans, the Cathedral is the biggest and most impressive sight to behold in the city. Its Gothic towers and 88m spires are visible throughout the city, and it is easy to imagine the young Joan of Arc marching past it centuries ago. The Cathedral was originally erected in the 13th century, and was built over the course of the next 200 years. When Joan liberated it from the English, it was still unfinished. The city's heroine is not forgotten inside the Cathedral— a statue of her stands in its north wing, flanked by two golden leopards that cower at her feet. Stand near the altar and gaze up to the stained-glass windows for a moment of breathtaking serenity.

From train station take Tram A in the direction of Hôpital and exit at pl. De Gaulle. Follow rue Jean d'Arc to pl. St Croix. i Tourist office provide tours. $ Free. Open daily 9:15am-6pm.

HÔTEL GROSLOT D'ORLÉANS MUSEUM

pl. de l'Etape ☎02 38 79 22 30 hotelgroslot@ville-orleans.fr

This grand and beautiful Renaissance mansion is situated just behind the cathedral in the *vielle ville*, and although it may not be as old as other historic homes in the area is most definitely rivals them in grandeur. The mansion was the local residence of the King for 200 years, and was later converted into the local City Hall; it remained a government building until the 1790s. Today, the areas of the house which is accessible to tourists spans 5 luxurious rooms, each of which focuses on a different element of local history. Explore the exhibit of Joan of Arc memorabilia (note the large painting of her on horseback above the fireplace in the first room), then pay your respects in the final resting place of 16-year-old François II. On the weekends, the regal rooms are often used for formal functions and weddings, which may mean the building is closed prematurely. Be sure to check ahead and see if the museum is open.

Left of the Musée des Beaux Arts. Walk through the gates and up the stairs to the entrance on

the left. ⑨ *Free. Brochure €1.* ② *Open Jul-Sept M-F 10am-6pm, Sa 5-8pm, Su 10am-6pm; Oct-June M-F 10am-1pm and 2-6pm, Sa 5-7pm, Su 10am-1pm and 2-6pm.*

MUSÉE DES BEAUX ARTS — MUSEUM
1 rue Fernand Rabier   ☎02 38 79 21 55 ▣www.musées.regioncentre.fr

A mural of Joan of Arc dominates the lobby of the Musée des Beaux Arts (we're sensing a pattern here), and her presence pervades this museum, which additionally showcases a collection of Italian, Flemish and French paintings and sculptures. Some intriguing modern art can be found here too, including a 3D representation of an evacuation of fruit and vegetables from Paris in the 19th century. The 19th-century painter Galle's "Nature Morte" conveys another interesting take on vegetarianism, and Reni's painting of David triumphantly holding the head of Goliath is a gory gem in the collection. In fact, gore and dead animals seem to be a lingering theme here—the second-floor lobby displays a large painting by Paul de Vos, depicting a horse being mauled and eaten by wolves. Less violent works in the collection include paintings by Van Dyck, Boucher, Delacroix, and Gaugin.

✦ *To the right of the tourist office, behind Cathedral.* ⑨ *€3, under 25 and over 65 €1.50, under 16 free.* ② *Free 1st Su of every month. Open Tu-Sa 9:30am-12:15pm and 1:30pm-6:30pm, Su 2-6:30pm.*

MUSÉES DES SCIENCES NATURELLES — ⊛ MUSEUM
6 rue Marcel Proust   ☎02 38 54 61 05 ▣www.ville-orleans.fr

For an excellent afternoon out, the Natural Science Museum near the train station fulfills the needs of both hyperactive children and adults. Ideal for families looking for an afternoon break, it can keep the children occupied with hands-on exhibits that explore light, sound, and sight. The first floor is home to an aquarium full of tropical fish and even a human-sized (fake) frog. A fun outing for all kids and big kids alike.

✦ *From the train station, exit to rue Albert 1er and follow it round until it bends into rue Proust. Next to bus station.* ⑨ *€3, students €1.50, under 16 free. Free every 3rd Sunday of the month.* ② *Open daily 2-6pm.*

PARC FLORAL DE LA SOURC — PARK
av. du Parc Floral   ☎02 38 49 30 00 ▣www.parcfloraldelasource.com

In 1967, a 12-hectare park was created here to host the International Flower Show. The Parc Floral may only host a few large geraniums these days, but it's still more than worth the trip. Spend the day entertaining the kids at the petting zoo, playing miniature golf, taking the petit train ride (*€2*) and visiting the butterfly reserve, which includes over 50 exotic species. The park also contains the mysterious source of the Loire River, hidden deep within the park's beautiful outdoor surroundings. A perfect family outing, especially if you choose to picnic.

✦ *By car, take RN-20 toward Vierzon-Bourges and exit at St-Cyr-en-Val. By tram take Tram A toward Hôpital and exit at Université/Parc Floral. Roughly a 30min. journey by tram.* ⑨ *€6, 6-16 yrs €4.50, under 6 free.* ② *Open daily mid-Mar-Sept 10am-7pm; Oct-mid Nov 10am-6pm! Nov-Mar 19 2-5pm. Open Tu-Su May-Oct 10am-2:30pm and 1:30-6:30pm; Nov-Apr 1:30-6:30pm.*

MAISON DE JEANNE D'ARC — ✦ MUSEUM
3 pl. de Gaulle   ☎02 38 52 99 98 ▣www.jeannedarc.com.fr

A tiny two-room museum based in one of Orléans's busy squares, the house was once the home of Joan of Arc herself during her brief time spent in the city. The house offers a unique and interactive learning experience, with models reconstructing the siege on the city in 1429. The third floor is dedicated to those who worked with or helped Joan in her quest. Ideal for history nerds interested in Medieval History or Joan of Arc.

✦*Opposite Post Office in sq. Charles de Gaulle* ℹ *Ring the doorbell outside* **many times** *if there is no response at first.* ⑨*€2, students €1, under 16s free, Free every second sunday of each month* ②*Tu-Su; May-Oct 10am-2:30pm and 1:30pm-6:30pm. Nov-Apr 1:30pm-6pm.*

CHÂTEAUX

Though plenty of tourists hire a car to reach the surrounding Châteaux from Orléans, taking the good old fashioned bus is both the cheaper and simpler option. Buses run from the **Gare Routière** (2 rue Marcel Proust). The **Gien Express** leaves M-F at 6am, 7am, noon and 12:30pm, and stops at **Germingy, Sully-Sur-Loire,** and finally Gien.

SULLY-SUR-LOIRE
✐ CHÂTEAU

Sully-Sur-Loire   ☎02 38 36 23 70 ▣www.sully-sur-loire.fr

Sully-Sur-Loire is one of the Loire's most striking castles, and has hosted a number of historically famous visitors, including Charles VII, Joan of Arc, and Louis XIV. Maintained by the Sully Family until the 1960s, the castle has since undergone renovations, and visitors are now able to climb up to the chamber of the guards, which yields a stunning view of the Loire and the surrounding valleys. One of the most interesting rooms in the house is dedicated to Psyche, the Greek goddess of the soul. The room, which dates back to the 17th century, contains tapestries bearring the Sully family's coat of arms. In mid-June, Sully-Sur-Loire is home to the world-famous **Festival de Sully et du Loiret,** which showcases worldwide classical music. **The Forest,** open daily 8am-sunset, provides a moment of peace away from the busy tourist attraction.

⚑ *Take the bus from Orléans to Gien, get off at Sully-Sur-Loire.* ⑤ *€7, groups €5.* ⚕ *Open Apr-Sept 10am-6pm; Oct-Dec M 10am-6pm, Tu-Su 10am-noon; Feb-Apr M 10am-6pm, Tu-Su 10am-noon.*

GERMINGY-DES-PRÉS (GERMINGY)
✐ CHÂTEAU

Germingy-des-Prés   ☎02 38 58 27 97 ▣www.tourisme-loire-foret.com

The Carolingian church of Germingy-des-Prés is about 30km southeast of Orléans, and dates back to 806 AD, making it one of the three oldest churches in France. The original pillar headings can still be observed in the re-plastered interior. One of the most fascinating displays in the church is a ninth-century "golden" mosaic. The mosaic was actually rediscovered by a group of schoolchildren in 1830 who happened to be playing underneath it. That was almost 200 years ago— see if you can discover anything new in the grand corridors and grounds of this medieval wonder.

⚑ *Take the bus from Orléans to Gien and get off at Germingy.* ⑤ *Free.* ⚕ *Open daily Apr-Oct 9am-7pm.; Nov-Mar 10am-5pm.*

FOOD

Restaurants in Orléans serve classic French cuisine and tastes from around the globe. If you're on a budget, check out the **Carrefour** supermarket, which can be found above of the train station at place D'Arc *(Open M-Sa 8:30am-9pm)*. A traditional French market can be found inside **Les Halles Châtelet,** where locals pick up essentials like bread, milk, fish and meats *(pl. du Châtelet.* ⚕*Open Tu-F 7:30am-7:30pm, Sa 7am-7:30pm, Su 8am-1pm.)* **La rue de Bourgogne** is the busiest street in Orléans, lined with Indian, Thai, British, Lebanese and traditional French cuisine. In the evening, most places don't open before 7pm, so an early dinner is rarely on the menu.

▧ LA MANGEOIRE
✐♈ RESTAURANT ❸

28 rue du Poirier   ☎02 38 68 15 38

This petit restaurant is an absolute must with filling French cuisine that won't empty the wallet. Specializing in *les tartines,* or bread topped with meats, cheeses, potatoes, and other ingredients, La Mangeoire provides some of the best portions and price-tags in town. Choose from numerous toppings, including vegetarian options, to create a gigantic rustic meal that could sustain a burly Gaul farmer for several days. For the truly hungry, try the Parisienne, which includes *bris,* beef, mushrooms, and potatoes. The manager, Florent, worked as a chef in NYC for five years and is fluent in English. He'll happily translate the menu for you or offer a few words of advice for making the most of the town. Families and big groups welcome. If you're coming in a big group, call in advance and special arrangements can be made, ranging from flexible opening hours to a set menu.

⌖ *Rue fu Poirier runs adjacent with rue de Bourgogne.* Ⓢ *Tartines €12, meat and fish €12-16.* Ⓓ *Open M-Sa noon-2pm and 7-10:30pm.*

AU BON MARCHÉ
♥ ♿ ✌ RESTAURANT ❸

12 place du Châtelet ☎02 38 53 04 35 ◾www.aubonmarche-orleans.com

Although not as "cheap" as the name suggests, this restaurant offers some high-class French dining for not-so-high-class prices. The restaurant bends around a bar and extends through to a seating area covered in red leather seats, with some high tables that create a modern vibe in an old building. The specialty beef dish (€15) comes served on a skewer which could be mistaken for a kebab, until you tuck into the tender meat. The plasma TV screen showing wildlife programmes adds a certain bizarre vibe to the whole setup.

⌖ *In the Châtelet Square which is a short walk from the Châtelet shopping complex.* Ⓢ *Lunch set menu €7, dinner set menu €18.* Ⓓ *Open M-F noon-2:30 and 7-10:30pm, Sa noon-2:30 and 7-11pm, Su noon-2:30 and 7-10:30pm.*

VOL TERRE
♥ ✌ RESTAURANT ❸

253 rue de Bourgogne ☎02 38 54 00 79

Dealing in organic and "experimental" ingredients (for the record, we're not sure what that means), Vol Terre will boost your eco-friendly street cred. This chill and funky restaurant features a rotating menu of culinary treats. The lunch menu (€12-16) allows you to taste the plate of the day, which varies from local, fresh meat to an experimental cold soup. In the evening, Vol Terre is ideal for the family or a group of people, with both indoor and outdoor seating that is more than able to accommodate large parties. Children are made extra welcome by the entertaining and energetic manager who is keen to promote the ideals of healthy eating and organic foods.

⌖ *Straight along rue de Bourgogne.* Ⓢ *Lunch set menu €12-16. 2- to 3-course menu €19.50 24.50.* Ⓓ *Open M-F noon-2pm, 7:30-11pm, Sa noon-2pm, 7:30-midnight.*

BAR DES TRIBUNAUX
♥ ✌ BAR ❸

29 rue de la Bretonnerie ☎02 38 62 71 86

Frequented by local businessmen and couples, Le Bar des Tribunaux epitomizes the French ideal of leisurely dining. Don't come here if you expect to be in and out quickly— the hostess will be too busy kissing the regulars. The restaurant's specialty fish and local sausage is worth the wait for service.

⌖ *Opposite the Palais de Justice.* Ⓢ *Appetizers €8-11; entrees €15-22, set menu €17.* Ⓓ *Open M-Sa 8am-6:30pm.*

AU DON CAMILLO
♥ ✌ RESTAURANT ❸

54 rue Ste Catherine ☎02 38 53 38 97

A taste of Italy with a French twist, the chaotic Au Don Camillo fills up as soon as the doors open for lunch, manages to serve a range of clientele until its doors close mid-afternoon, and repeating the bustling affair again that evening. The pizzas are large and include a generous number of toppings, and the *moules et frites* (mussels and fries) is a neighborhood favorite (€12.) Makes sure that you don't get in the way of the staff though; they seem so caught up in serving their customers that it's a wonder there aren't more head-on collisions in here.

Ⓢ *Lunch menu €10-13, evening set menus €17-24.* Ⓓ *Open M-Sa noon-2:30pm and 7:30pm-11pm.*

LES MUSARDISES
♥ ✌ PÂTISSERIE ❷

38 rue de République ☎02 38 53 30 98

Between faux-gingerbread walls and scrumptious cakes (€3), you would be forgiven for mistaking Les Musardises for Hansel and Gretel's gingerbread house.

Don't try to sample the walls; though we've only ever seen a sweet and attentive staff, there could be a little witch hidden under the counter. You never know.

Ⓢ *Most cakes €3, chocolates €6. 🕐 Tea shop open 8:30am-6:30pm. Pâtisserie open 8am-7:30pm.*

NIGHTLIFE

Orléans definitely isn't a discoteque and dance party kind of town, but this capital city still has some great spots for a few quiet (or during the summer, not-so-quiet) drinks as the evening draws to a close. Most bars are on **rue de Bourgogne,** which is populated by the students from the outskirts of Orléans during the weekends.

MCEWANS
⊛ PUB

250 rue de Bourgogne   ☎02 38 54 65 70

This very European pub is often the busiest on the street, as students and 20-somethings pour in to sample beer from around the world. The very small interior is perpetually inhabited by a few drinkers who never seem to leave; they appear to be afraid of sunlight. Try and name all of the European flags which appear on the bunting covering the walls and have a guess at the decade the current song is from (I wanna, I wanna, I really really wanna zigga zig ah!).

Ⓢ *Beer €3-8. 🕐 Open M-Sa 6pm-1am.*

L'ATELIER
⊛ BAR

203 rue de Bourgogne   ☎02 38 53 08 27

One of the cheapest bars on the strip, L'Atelier tries to keep its prices literally fixed by inscribing them on the wall behind the bar. This hasn't stopped prices from going *down* though, as indicated by a few choice red squiggles. Pieces of modern art lines the walls, and posters of satirical French political cartoons are peeling off the ceiling. The jazz music playing in the background creates a relaxed atmosphere, so kick back and sip your drink in one of the worn-out armchairs. If you ask with a smile, some of the regulars may even join you for a game of Monopoly.

Ⓢ *Beer €3, cocktails €6. 🕐 Open M-Sa 5:30pm-2am, Su 4-10:30pm.*

BAR D'HENDRIX
⊛✧ PUB

278 rue de Bourgogne   ☎02 38 54 64 47

A loud homage to Jimmy Hendrix painted on the ceiling here. Connect with your inner Woodstock and sip from one of the many rock-themed cocktails *(€8)* on offer; The Rolling Stones is popular, as is AC/DC. This pub overflows with students and rock music lovers alike, and the vast range of beer ensures something will take your fancy. Sing along with the manager as the night draws to a close or demonstrate your prowess on the dart board at the back of the pub. When you get a little hungry you can tuck into a plate of cheese or *charcuterie* for €8-13, which should give you enough stamina to down another Hendrix cocktail.

Ⓢ *Beer from €2.60. 🕐 Open M-Sa noon-2am.*

LA DATCHA
⊛ BAR

205 rue de Bourgogne   ☎02 38 81 00 11

Amongst the bars of Rue de Bourgogne lies a place which will take you back to the Cold War with a twist of funk. La Datcha boasts almost 30 different vodka drinks named after Soviet bloc cities, and is filled with the younger population of Orléans. The bar has its quirks, with dark wood pillars holding the building together and tables covered in graffiti.

Ⓢ *Vodka drinks €6. 🕐 Open M-Sa 5pm-2am.*

COCO AND CO
⊛ SHISHA BAR

260 rue de Bourgogne

Covered in purple drapes from wall to ceiling, this small nook of rue de Bougogne feels out of place in this Renaissance throwback of a town, but nevertheless provides a chill hangout for a young student population. Milkshakes and sheesha are a common combination during the early evening, as families gather in the front room and games of cards are played among friends. Fresh milkshakes can be made to your request and sheesha comes at an extra price, but as the sign on the wall reminds you, "Sheesha is not a product [in and of] itself, but merely an *accompaniment* to a drink".

Ⓢ *Milkshakes €5, sheesha €8.* ⌚*Open M-Sa 2pm-2am.*

ARTS AND CULTURE

Theaters

Both the **Cado** and **La Scene Nationale d'Orléans** are based at the **Théâtre d'Orléans,** but they offer different types of performances. The Théâtre d'Orléans is situated in the northeast part of Orléans, about a 10min. walk from the *vieille ville.*

CADO

Théâtre d'Orléans, bld. Pierre Ségelle   ☎02 38 54 29 29 📟www.cado-orleans.fr

Cado is the main arts company in Orléans providing theatrical entertainment, producing a combination of experimental theater, and traditional performances. Highlights include **Le Mec de la tombe d'à côté,** which is based on the novel by Katarina Mazetti and performances by the composer Roland Romanelli. Tickets are normally bought for more than one show, but can be bought separately if you contact the box office. Contact the box office for individual ticket prices.

Ⓢ *Combo tickets €25-98.*

LA SCÈNE NATIONALE D'ORLÉANS

Théâtre d'Orléans, bld. Pierre Ségelle   ☎02 38 62 75 30 📟www.scenenationaledorleans.fr

With a packed program throughout the year, La Scène Nationale provides music and dance lovers from across the Loire and even further afield with a plentiful mix of the expressive arts. Performances include modern dance, traditional dance, world music, and opera. Contact the box office for individual ticket prices.

Ⓢ *Tickets from €10.* ⌚ *Box office open Tu-Sa 1pm-7pm.*

ESSENTIALS

Practicalities

- **TOURIST OFFICE:** 2 pl. de l'Étape (☎02 38 24 05 05. 📟*www.tourisme-orleans. com.* ⌚*Open daily Apr-June 9:15am-6:15pm; July-Aug 9:15am-6:45pm; Sept. 9:15am-6:15pm; Oct 9:45am-5:30pm; Nov-Mar 9:45am-5pm.)*

- **BANKS:** ATMs along rue de la République.

- **LAUNDROMAT: Laverie Bourgogne.** 176 rue de Bourgogne. (Ⓢ*Wash €7 per 10kg, dry €1 per 10min.* ⌚*Open daily 7am-9pm.)*

- **HOSPITAL: Centre Hospatilier Régional.** 1 rue Porte Madeleine. (☎02 38 51 44 44).

- **POST OFFICE:** pl. du Général de Gaulle. (☎02 38 77 35 14. ⌚*Open M-F 8:30am-7pm, Sa 8:30am-12:15pm.)*

Emergency!

- **PHARMACY:** ☎15. (⌚*Line open daily 7am-9pm.)*

- **POLICE:** 63 rue du Faubourg St-Jean. (☎02 38 24 30 00).

Getting There

The main train station, **Gare d'Orléans** connects to the other train station **Gare Les Aubrais** by a shuttle which runs roughly every half hour (€1.20). You can reach Gare Les Aubrais from **Paris Charles de Gaulle** by a high-speed train (Ⓢ€30. ⌚1hr-1hr. 30min.) or take a train from **Paris Austerlitz** from the Gare d'Orléans (Ⓢ€20. ⌚1hr). There are frequent trains connecting Orléans with the rest of the Loire Valley, including **Blois** *($€10. ⏰40min.)* and **Tours** *($€18. ⏰1hr. 30min.)* The Info Desk at Gare d'Orléans is open M-Sa 6am-8pm, Su 8:30am-8pm.

Getting Around

The **tram** system runs in 2 directions: Jules Verne to the North and L'Hopital de la Source in the South. Tickets for one way on the tram costs €1.30 and must be bought at the stop before getting on. The tram stops at most main points of interest in Orléans, including **Rue de la République** and **De Gualle.**

Taxi Radio d'Orléans *(☎02 38 53 11 11).* Taxis run from underneath the train station and cost around €5 to reach the center of town *(€2.10-1.40 per km).*

Buses run around the Centre, but aren't really required for exploring the sights of Orléans, as they are all within walking distance from the vielle ville.

It is possible to hire a **bike** from newly installed Velo+ bike station outside the Tourist Information Office. The first half an hour is free, and it costs €1 for the next hour, and €2 for the hour after that. There are 33 stops in and around Orléans which are indicated on the map.

blois ☎02 54

The opposite of blah, Blois (blwah; pop. 51,000) is the hidden gem of the Loire Valley, and the perfect excuse for a few days of exploration and medieval meddling. Indulge your inner Disney princess with a waltz through the incredible Château that overlooks the Loire River, then hit the local bars for a night you'll never forget. The culinary offerings span a variety of palates, with an emphasis on traditional (and even medieval) French food. Though you shouldn't expect to find any banging clubs with massive crowds here, French 20-somethings kick back and bask in the sun outside the numerous bars and cafes in the town's main squares. So if you're looking for a knight in shining armor, rather than a night on the town, come use Blois also serves as your Camelot crash pad and château launch pad—it's close to Chambord and Cheverny.

ORIENTATION

Remember: what goes up must come down. In Blois, the **train station** rests at the top of a hill, and the main town (and the river) lies at its bottom. Luckily, this makes getting lost nearly impossible, since almost every path or road leading uphill heads towards the station, and every road heading down converges at the river. When in doubt, head down. It is also impossible to miss the **Château** and the **Cathedral**, the towering structures which dominate the town's skyline. There are relatively few museums and sights here, so head for a leisurely stroll along the river if you have extra time.

If you're still having trouble finding your way into the center, follow the **rue de Gambetta** down from the train station; when the street intersects **avenue Jean Laigret,** you will come across the **Château de Blois.** Keep walking round the road to reach the main shopping street on **rue de Commerce,** which connects to the commercial center of the town, **rue Denis Papin.** Continue down rue Denis Papin to reach the **place de la Résistance** and the **Loire River,** which is lined with a variety of restaurants and bars.

ACCOMMODATIONS

HOTEL DE FRANCE ET DE GUISE — HOTEL [4]

3 rue de Gallois — ☎02 54 78 00 53 www.franceetguise.com

You may feel as if you have just followed Alice down the rabbit hole as you find yourself winding through the twisting corridors of this hotel. We suppose that the creaking staircases and grand mirrors add to the charm of the place. Located a short walk away from all of Blois's attractions, the hotel is ideal for anyone wishing to explore to town.

➡ Just north of the rue de Commerce, the hotel is on a corner opposite the Jardins Augustin-Thierry. ℹ Breakfast €7. $ Singles €49-55; doubles €55-65; triples €70-85.

HOTEL DU BELLAY
💳 HOTEL [3]

12 rue des Minimes ☎02 54 78 23 62 🖥hoteldubellay.free.fr

Hidden away just at the top of porte Chartraine, this rustic old house has been converted into a small hotel, and it now offers a true home away from home. The location is ideal for getting away from the noisy streets and the center of town, but still provides easy access to all of Blois's sights. The hotel is also blessed with uncommonly accommodating owners.

➡ At the top of Porte Chartraine, take a right to the Old Quarter. ℹ Breakfast €6. $ Singles and doubles €35-50, triples and quads €65-75.

L'AUBERGE DE JEUNESSE
FARMHOUSE HOSTEL [1]

18 rue de l'Hôtel Pasquier ☎02 54 78 27 21 🖥www.fuaj.org.

This Youth Hostel is typical of where you would have stayed during sleep-away camp in high school. The boarders are sorted into single-sex dormitories, the setting is vaguely farm-like, and the owner is strict but maternal. The hostel's countryside surroundings are beautiful, but L'Auberge de Jeuness is a 10min. bus ride out of the city center, and is perhaps better suited to school groups than student travelers. Each dorm contains boxed-off areas for some kind of privacy, but that all falls apart when you nip outside for your morning wash.

➡ From the train station, take Bus #4 in the direction of Église les Grouts. ℹ Breakfast included. $ Single-sex dorms €11.50. ⏰ Lockout 10am 6pm.

SIGHTS

MAISON DE LA MAGIE
MUSEUM

1 pl. du Château ☎02 54 90 33 33 🖥www.maisondelamagie.fr

No hidden wires or trap doors here! "Enter a universe of illusion" at the Maison de la Magie, a museum opposite the Château that honours the life and works of Robert-Houdin, allegedly the most "famous magician of all time" (Houdini, who we think actually was the most famous magician of all time, stole his stage name from Robert-Houdin). The museum's biggest attraction is **The Hallucinoscope,** a large and vaguely sci-fi device that produces optical illusions, not to mention an interactive and spectacular show for kids and adults alike. A Magic Show is put on 3-4 times a day for children, though anyone who's attempted a card trick might enjoy it a little bit too.

➡ Directly opposite the Château. $ €8, students and seniors €6.50, and ages 6-17 €5. Combined tickets can be bought for the Château and the Maison de la Magie. ⏰ Open June daily 9:30am-1pm and 2-6pm; July-Aug daily 9am-7pm; Sept daily 9:30am-1pm and 2-6pm; Oct-Feb daily 10am-1pm and 2-5pm' Mar M-F 10am-1pm and 2-5:30pm, Sa 10am-1pm and 2-6pm, Su 10am-1pm and 2-5:30pm; Apr M 10am-1pm and 2-5:30pm, Tu-Su 10am-1pm and 2-6pm; May 9:30am-1pm and 2-6pm.

MUSÉE DE LA RÉSISTANCE, DE LA DÉPORTATION, ET DE LA LIBÉRATION
MUSEUM

1 pl. de la Gráve ☎02 54 56 07 02

A powerful memorial to the French victims and survivors of the Holocaust, the museum examines WWII-era Blois and features moving stories from survivors and veterans, including a hapless US pilot who almost hit the Château de Chambord during a flight over France.

➡ pl. de la Gráve. $ €3, students and under 18 €1. ⏰ Open M-F 9am-noon and 2-6pm, Sa 2-6pm.

CHÂTEAUX

From Blois as well as the renowned Château de Blois, the Tourist Office runs trips to two of the most magnificent Châteaux in the Loire: **Chambord** and **Cheverny**. A bus runs three times a day, departing from the train station at 9am, 11:10am, or 1:40pm, then stopping at Chambord and continuing on to Cheverny at three possible times. The last bus back leaves Cheverny at 6pm. The bus costs €6 for the whole day, and can be used for a reduced entrance into the three Châteaux *(€1.50 discount at Blois, €1.50 at Chambordm €1 at Cheverny).*

CHÂTEAU DE BLOIS — CHÂTEAU

pl. du Château ☎02 54 90 33 33 🖥www.châteaudeblois.fr

The highlight of a visit to Blois is by far a trip to its stunning Château. Renowned for its elaborate architectural design, which incorporates Gothic, Renaissance, late 16th-century, and Classical styles, the building will leave you in awe of the minds of those who conceived it. Seven kings and 10 queens of France once used Blois Château as their Royal Palace back in the day, and the rooms were recently renovated and restored to their former glory. Survey the royal study for the secret compartments hidden in the walls, where Alexandre Dumas made Catherine de Medici hide her poisons. Make sure you visit the **Musée des Beaux Arts** while you're here; it occupies what was formerly the Royal Apartments. The museum houses paintings from the 16th to 19th centuries, including portraits of the royal families and a very explicit painting of John the Baptist's head on a platter. **The Musée Lapidaire** provides insight into recovered rock pieces of other 16th- and 17th-century châteaux located nearby. For a particularly magical tour of Blois, a horse-drawn carriage ride departs from inside the Château every half hour in the afternoon. A light show is produced on the grounds every evening between Apr.-Sept.

*Follow the rue de Gambetta from the train station. The Château will be directly in front of you, with stairs leading to the courtyard on your right. **i** Guides available in English, but ring in advance to ensure someone will be there to provide it $ Tickets can be combined with the Light Show and the Maison de la Magie. All 3 together cost €18, students €13, ages 6-17 €10. The Château alone €8, students €6.50, ages 6-17 €4. ⏰ Open daily Apr- June 9am-6:30pm; July-Aug 9am-7pm; Sept 9am-6:30pm; Oct 9am-6pm; Nov-Dec 9am-12:30pm and 1:30-5:30pm; Jan-Mar 9am-12:30pm and 1:30-5:30pm. Last entry 30min. before close.*

CHAMBORD — CHÂTEAU

Chambord ☎02 54 50 40 00 🖥www.chambord.org

A truly royal experience awaits you as you grace the huge hallways and grand rooms of the former home of Louis XIV. The castle claims to be a "Place aux Rêves"; although Disney may soon want their slogan back, it's hard to deny that the Sun King's crib could take Cinderella's castle in the Magic Kingdom any day. The stunning Renaissance design includes a cool double-helix open staircase on which those who go up never actually cross paths with those going down. The stairs lead up to the chimney rooftops, which boast an exceptional view of the canal and the wildlife reserve below. To bring the château to life and keep the kids entertained, there is a 3D movie room which introduces the history and architecture of Chambord through computer animation. Summer activities on offer include a **Sound and Light show** and an **outdoor market** selling traditional products.

40min. from Blois by bus, departs from the Gare at 9am, 11:10am and 1:40pm. $ High-season €9.50, ages 18-25 €8; low-season €8.50/7. ⏰ Open daily Apr-mid-July 9am-5:15pm; mid-July-mid-Aug 9am-7:30pm; mid-Aug-Sept 9am-6:15pm; Oct-Mar 9am-5:15pm. Sound and light shows end of June-min-Sept.

CHEVERNY — CHÂTEAU

Cheverny ☎02 54 79 96 29 🖥www.château-cheverny.com

Cheverny was opened to the public in 1922, but those who are fans of TinTin may already know plenty about it— the Loire château heavily influenced Moulinsort's creation of the series. Since Cheverny has such a strong connection with the Belgian character, a life-size Tintin exhibition is open for you to enjoy, which includes models, life-sized drawings, and a retelling of the story set in this mysterious château. For those less interested in the activities of a cartoon explorer, the château has extensive grounds which can be explored by boat and electric car, both of which are ideal for experiencing the wildlife living in the flora. Inside the château, the furnished rooms make Cheverny look more like a homey castle than a museum of architecture.

55min. from Blois by bus; departs from the Gare at 9am, 11:10am and 1:40pm. $ €7.50. Open daily Apr-June 9:15am-6:15pm; July-Aug 9:15am-6:45pm; Sept 9:15am-6:15pm; Oct 9:45am-5:30pm; Nov-Mar 9:45-5pm.

AMBOISE — CHÂTEAU

Amboise ☎02 47 57 00 98 www.château-amboise.com

This late 15th-century building was once considered France's most beautiful châteaux, and it housed up to 4000 people during the 16th century. During the reign of Napoleon, most of the château was destroyed or sold off, and what you see now is the result of painstaking rebuilding renovations. Amboise château has a number of exhibits which change throughout the year; during the summer, it is also possible to embark on a guided tour of the underground tunnels, and enjoy the views of the castle by night on a guided "stroll under the stars." Unlike the royal history at most of the other Loire castles, the most interesting and historically fascinating past resident of Amboise was **Leonard da Vinci.** Da Vinci's grave is in the **Chapelle Saint-Hubert,** just next the the château; pay your respects to this genius, and reflect on all the salacious revisions Dan Brown has added to his legacy. The rooms are decorated with Gothic and Renaissance furniture that demonstrates the castle's royal history. A deserving resting place for one of the world's greatest artist and academics.

The small town of ***Amboise*** *is an hour's journey from Orléans by train (€14 every hr). The castle in Centre Ville between rue Victor Hugo and rue de la Concorde. For free parking follow signs for "parking du château." $ €9.70, students €8.30, ages 7-14 €6.30, under 7 free. Open daily Mar 9am-5:30pm; Apr-June 9am-6:30pm; July-Aug 9am-7pm; Sept-Oct 9am-6pm; early Nov 9am-5:30pm; late Nov-Jan 9am-12:30pm and 2-4:45pm; Feb 9am-12:30pm and 1:30-5pm.*

FOOD

Lots of little traditional restaurants can be found in and around the streets of **rue Saint-Lubin** and **place Poids de Rois.** Italian, Chinese, Indian and Greek cuisine can be found in the **place de la Resistance,** which faces the Loire river. You can pick up groceries from the **8 à Huit** at **11 rue de Commerce** *(Open M-Sa 8am-8pm, Su 8am-noon)* or the **Proxi Marché** at 6 Rue Henri Drussy. *(Open M 2:30-8pm, Tu-F 8:30am-1pm and 2:30-8am, Sa 9am-8pm, Su 9am-1pm).*

LE CASTELET — MEDIEVAL DISHES [3]

40 rue St-Lubin ☎02 54 74 66 09 castelet-restaurant@club-internet.fr

Set in a rustic old house, this restaurant offers medieval-themed dishes *(cider marinated chicken with seasonal vegetables; €13)* that will get you in the mood to see the local sights. The friendly owner will be happy to explain the origins and preparation of the dishes he serves. Vegetarian options available.

Situated on the corner of rue St-Lubin. From the bottom of the stairs to the Château, take a right. $ Set lunch menu €16, set dinner menu €21. Open M-Tu noon-2pm and 7-10pm, Th-Sa noon-2pm and 7-10pm.

LE CRÊPERIE DES ROIS — CRÊPERIE [2]

3 rue Denis Papin ☎02 54 90 01 90

Although finding a crêperie in Blois is about as difficult as finding a drunk at a college party, Le Crêperie des Rois is one place where you can eat like a king and pay like a peasant. In addition to classic tartines and crêpes, go for an interesting twist and try the "Sud-Oeust" *(€8.50);* if you're homesick, go for the the "Texas" *(steak, egg, tomatoes and potatoes; €9).* Vegetarian options also served.

➥ Right at the bottom of rue Denis Papin. $ Crêpes €6.50-9. ⏰ Open Tu-Su noon-2pm and 7-9:30pm.

NIGHTLIFE

The nightlife on offer in Blois is limited, and you shouldn't stop here if you are expecting a massive party. The following three hotspots are heavily trafficked and highly recommended by locals.

L'HENDRIX CAFÉ — ROCK BAR

1 rue du puits Châtel

A point of convergence for Blois's rock and roll lovers, L'Hendrix's late-night soirées regularly spill out onto its terrace during the summer. Hendrix himself is painted ad nauseum on the walls, and watches over partygoers like an approving patron saint as they binge, bump and grind. Provides coffee and drinks in the afternoon.

➥ Just off of place Avé Maria. $ Drinks €4-9. ⏰ Open M-Sa noon-2am.

LE SINGE VERT — COCKTAIL BAR

58 rue Foulerie ☎02 54 78 18 87

There isn't much time for monkeying around in Le Singe Vert, which holds salsa nights every Thursday and plays host to different DJs over the weekends. Jungle-themed with pint jugs of cocktails, the bar draws a diverse crowd in search of a good night. Make the most of half-price happy hour on F and Sa.

➥ Along rue Foulerie, just off rue Jeanne d'Arc. $ Drinks €5-9. ⏰ Open Th-Su 7pm-2am. Happy hour F-Sa 7-9pm.

LE VELVET JAZZ LOUNGE — JAZZ BAR

15 rue Haute ☎02 54 78 36 32 🖥 www.velvet-jazz-lounge.com

This cool and laid-back hangout puts on weekly jazz shows in what used to be a 13th-century abbey. An ideal place for the wannabe jazz musician, or someone in search of their muse, the lounge is one of the classier establishments in Blois's small nightlife.

➥ Just off of rue Denis Papin, by the bottom of the steps. $ Beer €5-7. Mixed Drinks €7-9. ⏰ Open Tu-Su 5pm-2am.

ESSENTIALS

Practicalities

- **TOURIST OFFICE:** 23 pl. du Château *(☎02 54 90 41 41. 🖥www.bloispaysde-chambord.com. ⏰Open daily June-Aug M-Sa 9am-7pm; Sept 9am-6pm; Oct-Mar 10am-5pm; Apr-May 9am-6pm.)*
- **BANKS:** ATMs available along rue du Commerce and along rue Denis Papin.
- **LAUNDROMAT:** 1 rue Jeanne d'Arc. *($Wash 8kg €4.90, dry €1 per 10min. ⏰Open daily 7am-9pm.)*
- **PHARMACY: Pharmacie des 3 Clefs.** 30 rue Denis Papin. *(☎02 54 74 01 35. ⏰Open Tu-F 9am-7pm, Sa 8:30am-7pm.)*

Emergency!

- **POLICE:** 42 quai St-Jean *(☎02 54 90 09 00.)*
- **HOSPITAL: Centre Hospitalier de Blois.** Maile Pierre Charlot *(☎02 54 55 66 33. 🖥www.ch-blois.fr.)*

Getting There

The train station is connected to the main Loire Valley stations as well as Paris. **Amboise** is a 20min train journey (€6) and **Tours** is a bit further along, taking about 40min. (€10). To reach Blois from **Angers**, which is further West, it takes around 1hr. 20min. (€23) and **Orléans** is a 30min. train journey east of Blois (€7.50). There are also connections to **Paris** which take under 2 hours (€26). The ticket office is open M-F 5:30am-8pm, Sa 8:30am-7pm, Su 7:30am-8pm.

Getting Around

Blois train station is within walking distance of the main city center and all the main sights can be reached on foot. Be prepared to walk up many sloping streets and sets of stairs to access different parts of Blois.

   Buses are run by TUB (☎02 54 78 15 66. 🖳www.tub-blois.fr) which depart from the station, going along the river in the direction of the Youth Hostel roughly every half an hour (Line 4, €1.10) and 24hr. **Taxis Radio** are stationed at the pl. de la Gare for longer journeys or for heading to the castles (☎02 54 78 07 65). **Bike rental** is provided by Bike in Blois (☎02 54 56 07 73) and is located at the pl. de la Gare (💲€9 per ½day, €14 per day, €30 per 3 days.) There are dropoff points all along the Loire, including Orléans, Amboise, Villandry, Saumur, Angers, and Nantes. A leaflet with all dropoff points and contact details are available from the Tourist Office or the Bike Shop.

tours ☎02 47

Tours (TOOR; pop. 142,000) is the liveliest of all the Loire cities; it may not have a grand château, but it can certainly be proud of its bustling nightlife. Historically, Tours lacks a local accent and is ultimately home to the "well spoken" of French society. Because of this, students from across the globe flock to Tours to polish their French speaking skills, and a follow student is never too far away. The grand Cathedral St-Gatien is one of the architectural highlights of the city, especially given that the Château de Tours has not withstood the test of time. Also home to some diverse museums and modern shopping complexes, Tours has a lot to offer in terms of history, sights, and entertainment for even the most jaded of travelers.

ORIENTATION

A lot of Tours was destroyed during WWII or has since been left to decay; only the *vielle-ville* really represents the true former glory of the town. Luckily, most of the activity in Tours centers on this area, which is very popular with students and younger crowds. **Place Jean Jaurès,** recognizable by its two grand fountains, marks the center of the city, with the Hotel de Ville positioned directly at its center; **bld. Heurteloup** runs east toward the train station, and **bld. Bérlanger** runs west away from the center. Running north toward the banks of the Loire is the main shopping street **rue Nationale,** which used to be part of the main road and trade route between Paris and Spain; **av. de Grammont** reaches south toward the Cher river. The majority of Tours's nightlife and restaurants are situated at **place Plumereau** in the northwest *vielle-ville*, which is a 10min. walk from pl. Jean Jaurès. Most of the sights and shopping complexes are closer to, or more east of, the center.

ACCOMMODATIONS

Tours is full of students, so finding a decently priced youth hostel is not difficult at all. For those looking for a bit more luxury, it is possible to bag some dirt-cheap hotel rooms (without actually getting the dirt). Booking in advance is a good idea, especially in the summer.

👍 AUBERGE DE JEUNESSE "VIEUX TOURS" (HI) 💳♿📶 YOUTH HOSTEL [1]

5 rue Bretonneau ☎02 47 37 81 58 💻www.ajtours.org

A hop, skip, and jump from Tours's best bars and nightlife (so perhaps more of a hop, a trip, and a drunken stumble), this former university housing block is the best deal in the city and is always full of students. Many long-term residents stay here to learn French at the renowned university, and as a result this HI feels more like you're back in the college dorms than your usual youth hostel. All rooms come with a sink and some with a balcony.

🧭 A 15min. walk from the train station. Head west along bld. Heurteluop, through pl. Jean Jaurès, and onto bld. Bérlanger. From there, turn right onto rue Chanoineau, which turns into rue Bretonneau. The hostel will be at the far end of the road, on your left. ***i*** *Breakfast included. Bedding provided, but bring your own towel. TV and common room/lounge area on 1st, 3rd, and 4th floors. All rooms with shared bath.* *$ Dorms €19. Required HI membership €7.* *⏰ Reception 8am-noon and 5-8pm.*

HÔTEL DES ARTS 💳📶 GUEST HOUSE [2]

40 rue de la Préfecture ☎02 43 05 05 00 💻www.hoteldesartstours.com

Tucked away right near Tours's Grand Théâtre, Hôtel Des Arts is a pleasant surprise as you climb the narrow winding staircase in what looks like a converted house. The real bargain is the one room on the top floor, which for €32 is a brilliant find; just look out for the low sloping roof. The rooms have a distinctly homey feel and come equipped with televisions and small but clean bathrooms. The owner herself serves breakfast in her rustic dining room *(€6.50)*; its slogan, "Calme et Charme," is a rather apt description for this cozy little guesthouse.

🧭 From the train station, cross the road and head straight down rue de Buffon. Keep heading down until you see rue de la Préfecture on the right. ***i*** *Breakfast €6.50.* *$ Loft room €32; singles €37-45; doubles €47-50.*

HÔTEL FOCH 💳🚭📶 HOTEL [2]

20 rue du Maréchal Foch ☎02 47 05 70 59 💻hotel-foch.tours@wanadoo.fr

If you want to explore the history of Tours, this is the place to stay. The very knowledgeable owner will spend hours discussing Tours's fascinating buildings, cathedral, and museums with you; make sure you ask him for the city walking guide. The decor is slightly out of date, but for the price and location (a 2min. walk from pl. Plumereau) you can't complain. The kindly owner and his wife serve their patrons breakfast in their living room.

🧭 From the train station, head west along bld. Heurteluop, through pl. Jean Jaurès, and onto bld. Bérlanger. Just after the post office on your right, turn right down rue de Marceau. Continue down this road until it intersects with rue du Maréchal Foch. Turn left, and the hotel is at the end of the road. ***i*** *Breakfast €6.* *$ Singles €32-40; doubles €33-€46; triples €37-58; quads €51-58.* *⏰ Reception 2-10pm.*

HÔTEL TERMINUS 💳📶🍸 HOTEL [3]

7 rue de Nantes ☎02 47 05 06 24 💻www.hotel-terminus-tours.com

This reasonable budget hotel is conveniently close to the train station. While it lacks the thrills of a more upscale hotel, Hôtel Terminus offers clean rooms and simple decorations. The cheapest single rooms are very small and offer nothing more than a bed and a bathroom, but for the price and the location they're unbeatable. As an added plus, the hotel has a bar area that's open late. Watch out for the elevator, which looks like it was built to withstand the weight of about one and a half people; it regularly withstands much more.

🧭 Right next to the train station. Exit through the main doors and turn right and right again. ***i*** *Free Wi-Fi.* *$ Singles and doubles €36-69.* *⏰ Reception 24hr.*

HÔTEL COLBERT 💳📶 HOTEL [3]

78 rue de Colbert ☎02 47 66 61 56 💻www.hotelcolbert.net

Hôtel Colbert is a prime example of not judging a book by its cover. The peeling wallpaper on the stairwell walls may be off-putting, but the luxurious rooms here are really something else. Each room is decorated to a different style and taste; highlights include a black-and-gold room complete with a golden mask hanging above the bed and a purple room with plush bed sheets fit for a French king. A fluffy white dog greats customers at the door.

➜ From the train station, head past the tourist office and down rue Bernard Palissy. Rue de Colbert is a 10min. walk on your left. ℹ Breakfast €7. $ Singles €37-52, doubles €43-59.

HÔTEL DES CHÂTEAUX DE LA LOIRE 💳♿📶🍸 HOTEL [4]

12 rue Gambetta ☎02 47 05 10 05 🖥www.hoteldeschâteaux.fr

Despite having an elevator that looks like it's been pulled from the Twilight Zone's Tower of Terror, this hotel offers a range of rooms at varying prices to accommodate different budgets. There's not much difference between the economy and standard rooms apart from size; both types of rooms are tastefully decorated and equipped with the basics required for comfortable living. If you want to go all out, however, the superior rooms come with a sofa, an armchair, and a much bigger space. But with a bigger space comes a bigger price tag.

➜ From the train station head west along bld. Heurteloup toward pl. Jean Jaurès. Take a right onto rue Nationale, past the Galleries Lafayette, and rue Gambetta is a bit further down on your left. ℹ Breakfast €7.50. $ Singles €47.50-54.50; doubles €47.50-68. 🕐 Reception 24hr.

HÔTEL MODERNE 💳♿📶 HOTEL [4]

1 and 3 rue Victor Laloux ☎02 47 05 32 81 🖥www.hotelmoderne37.com

Owned by a very excitable French woman who loves America (especially Boston), Hôtel Moderne is located in a rather grand building just off pl. Jean Jaurès and a few minutes walk from the train station. The lounge area looks more like a faux jungle with a very beautiful glass roof overhead, though it still feels like a relaxing hangout during the evening. The old-fashioned building lends itself to larger rooms with very clean bathrooms. There's one wheelchair-accessible room on the first floor—call in advance for more information.

➜ From the station, head west toward pl. Jean Jaurès, but take a right onto rue Victor Laloux. ℹ Breakfast €8. $ Singles with shower €43-53, with bath €62; doubles €52-54/70; triples €66/88; quads with bath €86. 🕐 Reception 24hr.

HÔTEL DU CYGNE 💳🚭📶 HOTEL [4]

6 rue du Cygne ☎02 47 66 66 41 🖥www.hotel-cygne-tours.com

One of the oldest hotels in the city of Tours, 18th-century Hôtel du Cygne has the appropriately elaborate architecture to prove its age, from massive doors leading to the grand hallway to the large, winding staircase. Each room is situated off a large corridor with very high ceilings, where the walls are covered with historic pictures of the city and the Loire Valley. If you are willing to pay the price, you can have a double room big enough to throw a massive party in *(€63)*, although the owners would probably not appreciate it. Other rooms are standard size and well-furnished, equipped with decor to match the history of the building.

➜ Just off rue Colbert. From the train station head down rue Bernard Palissy, just past the tourist info office. Rue de Colbert is a 10min. walk on your left. ℹ Breakfast €7. $ Singles €47; doubles €57.

ASSOCIATION JEUNESSE ET HABITAT LONG-TERM ACCOMMODATION [1]

16 rue Bernard Palissy ☎02 47 60 51 51 🖥www.asso-jeunesse-habitat.org

Accommodating the needs of the thousands of students who flock to Tours every summer, this association provides short- and long-term accommodations for 16 to 25-year-olds. The majority of rooms are singles with showers and toilets, though some double rooms are available upon request. The center also serves as a youth outreach program, answering questions on education, housing, and general rights for young people.

➜ From the train station, head past the tourist office and down rue Bernard Palissy. The center is

through an archway on your right, about halfway down 𝒊 *Breakfast €2. Lunch and dinner €5.55-7.80* Ⓢ *Singles €20; doubles €30.* ⏲ *Reception 9am-noon and 1:30-5pm.*

CAMPING LES RIVES DU CHER ✦ CAMPGROUND ❶
61 rue de Rochepinard ☎02 47 27 27 60 🖳www.camping-lesrivesducher.com

About 5km out of Tours lies this very modern-looking campground set in the town of St-Avertin. For those on a biking tour of the Loire and in need of a place to stop, or for those traveling in a caravan, this is the perfect campground along the Loire. With a swimming pool nearby and a village for daily amenities, you need not look any farther for a place to set up camp. Free hot showers.

✦ *From the train station, take bus 3B in direction of St-Avertin Center. Get off at termination, take a left out of the bus station and head toward a small bridge on your right. Cross the bridge and continue for 200m; the campsite is on your right.* 𝒊 *Internet €2 for 30min.* Ⓢ *€6.60 for tent and car. Electricity €3.30-5.30. 5% discount for second week.* ⏲ *Open Apr-Sept. Reception 8am-noon and 3-7pm.*

SIGHTS ◉

Museum-hungry tourists should pick up the 🖫**Carte Multi-Visite** at any museum for just €8. This little beauty gets you free entry into five of Tours's museums and a guided tour of the city. Just make sure to present the card to them at the museum.

🖫 MUSÉE DE COMPAGNONNAGE MUSEUM
8 rue Nationale ☎02 47 21 62 20 🖳www.ville-tours.fr

Imagine yourself as a child taking a few Lego bricks and building a small little house. Or building a gingerbread house with excessive amounts of frosting. Now, imagine if these designs you had in your head as a child were made in reality. And voila—welcome to the Musée de Compagnonnage, one of the most mind-blowing architectural wonders that you will ever experience. The building houses a semi-secret society of craftsmen from around the world who excel in all kinds of old-school artisanship; legend has it the society stems all the way back to King Solomon's construction of the Temple of Jerusalem. For any budding craftsman (and woman, of course), there is tough competition to ascend to the ranks of the Campagnons, as this museum demonstrates. Highlights include a medieval castle made entirely out of sugar cubes, a bird cage molded to look like a château, model versions of grand stairways, massive wooden clogs the size of a man, and a very impressive sculpture of the human hand. The museum is also connected to a **Museum of Wine,** which documents the history of wine-making in France.

✦ *From pl. Jean Jaurès, head straight down rue Nationale until you meet the Loire. The museum is on your right.* Ⓢ *€5, students and under 25 €3.30, under 12 free.* ⏲ *Open daily June4-Sept M 9am-12:30pm and 2-6pm, W-Su 9am-12:30pm and 2-6pm.*

🖫 CATHÉDRALE SAINT-GATIEN MUSEUM
pl. de la Cathédrale ☎02 47 70 21 00

After getting the French government on its side, this renovated 14th-century building once again rules the skyline of Tours. The highlight of this Gothic cathedral is undoubtedly its intricate stained-glass windows, which pattern the the floor of the cathedral with fragments of rainbow-colored light. Even more beautiful than the windows, however, is the choir which sings during Sunday morning mass *(11am)*. The cathedral is the final resting place for the children of Charles VII, and a very interesting 16th-century sculpture marks their tomb. A visit to the *Psalette* cloister is also a definite must for this sight; not only does it highlight the mix of styles present in the building, but there is also a Gothic library and early Renaissance records office.

✦ *From the train station, head east along bld. Heurteloup and take a left onto rue Jules Simon. The cathedral is just past the Musée des Beaux Arts on the right.* Ⓢ *Free.* ⏲ *Cathedral open daily June-Sept 9:30am-12:30pm and 2-6pm; Oct-Mar 9:30am-12:30pm and 2-5pm; Apr-May 10am-12:30pm and 2-5:30pm. Cloister open daily May-Aug 9:30am-12:30pm and 2-5:30pm; Sept-Mar M 2-5:30pm, T-Sa 9:30am-12:30pm and 2-5:30pm, Su 2-5:30pm; Apr daily 10am-12:30pm and 2-5:30pm.*

MUSÉE DES BEAUX-ARTS   MUSEUM

18 pl. François Sicard   ☎02 47 05 68 73 ▤musée-beauxarts@ville-tours.fr,
What was once home to the archbishop is now home to some of the world's most impressive pieces of fine art. The building, ranging from 17th- to 18th-century architecture, houses rotating collections as well as fixed works of art; featured artists include Rembrandt, Monet, and Rodin. At the top of the grand staircase in the entrance, take a moment to observe the very generous bust of the hero Hercules, then turn your head to the wall adjacent to the stairs. A towering, wall-size painting by Debré is easily missed due to its position; entitled *Royaye de Loire, Tourine*, this glowing painting sums up the beauty of the Loire with its mix of oranges and blues. But there are even more beauties outside the walls of the museum. Take time to wander round the gardens and gaze upon the ancient ▧Lebanon cedar tree which was planted in 1804 and the skeleton of the former circus elepant, "Fritz", now preserved in honor of the animal.

🕆 *From the train station, head east along blvd. Heurteloup and take a left onto rue Jules Simon. The museum will be on your right.* ⑤ *€4, students €2, under 13 free. Free 1st Su of every month.* ⌕ *Open M 9am 12:45pm and 2-6pm, W-Su 9am-12:45pm and 2-6pm.*

MUSÉE DU GEMMAIL   MUSEUM

7 rue du Mûrier   ☎02 47 61 01 19 ▤www.gemmail.com
Situated off a side street near pl. Plumereau, the Musée du Gemmail is a treat for the eye and a surprise for most visitors. The relatively unknown art form of gemmail uses stained glass to build pictures and designs with a backlight to emphasize them. These pieces differ from stained-glass windows in that no metal holds the pieces together, and the glass relies on layers for its design to look complete. The Musée du Gemmail houses a small collection of pieces in an ivy-strewn house that dates back to the 12th century. Be sure to visit the crypt, which is the oldest part of the building, and take care climbing up the extremely narrow, yet fascinating, winding marble staircase back into the gallery. The piece depicting the Mona Lisa is most certainly one of the highlights, as is *Les Aigles*. Some works are available to purchase.

🕆 *From pl. Plumereau, head along rue du Grande Marché and turn right onto rue Bretonneau. Follow the road until you reach the rue du Mûrier on your right.* ⑤ *€5.50, students and ages 12-18 €3, ages 6-12 €2.* ⌕ *Open Apr-Oct Tu-Su 2-6:30pm. Last entry 45min. before close.*

TOWERS OF BASILIQUE SAINT-MARTIN   CHURCH

Entrance to Basilique on rue Descartes   ☎02 47 05 63 87 ▤www.basiliquesaintmartin.com
The two ancient *tours*, or towers, mark out where the old Basilica used to be; the *tour de l'Horage* marked the western face of the former building, and the *tour Charlemagne* marks the end of what used to be the north transept. Both towers, although still standing, are not accessible to the public due to their fragility, caused by neglect after the French Revolution (in their defense, there was a lot going on). Although it's a shame that these are the only remains from the fifth-century building, the reconstruction of the Basilique St-Martin from the 19th century is nonetheless an impressive *fin-de-siècle* structure both inside and out. In fact, the architect who created the new designs, Victor Laloux, also drew the plans for the Hotel de Ville and railway station in Tours; he is best known for the famous Orsay railway station and museum in Paris. Inside the Basilica is the final resting place of St. Martin in a very peaceful and grand crypt; note the stones on the wall that have been inscribed with thanks and gratitude to the deceased saint.

🕆 *From pl. Plumereau head southward down rue du Change onto rue de Châteauneuf and head left to place de Châteauneuf. From here the tour de l'Horlage is to your right, the tour Charlemagne*

tours · sights

farther left, and the Basilique directly in front of you. $ *Free.* ⏰ *Open daily 8am-8pm.*

LE JARDIN DE BEAUNE SEMBLANÇAY GARDEN

Along rue Jules Favre

All that remains of Landlord Semblançay Jacques de Beaune's 16th-century mansion is the facade of the wall, a fountain, and a chapel which was built over semi-circular arches. The remainders show an early French Renaissance style of buildings, and the locals have a very charming tale about the fountain. According to legend, the fountain—nicknamed the "Lovers' Fountain"—was a present from a man to his wife. She had requested that he give her something that the whole town could share, since she already had everything she wanted. As the man and wife, deeply in love, walked hand in hand to the grand opening of the fountain, one of them spontaneously threw a golden coin into the fountain. The story says they both rose up on a brick which moved from the ground, so they could see into the fountain and their smiling faces were reflected for all to see. Nowadays, those madly in love should throw a coin in together and wish for everlasting love and happiness. Or a Ferrari. It's your call.

⇞ *From pl. Jean Jaurès, head down rue Nationale and take a right through one of the archways just after rue Berthelot.*

CHÂTEAU DE TOURS RUINS

rue Lavoisier ☎02 47 70 88 56

If you plan to take in the city on foot, make sure you head down rue Lavoisier to reach the remains of Château de Tours. Unlike the rest of the Loire Valley, this Renaissance building didn't withstand the test of time; only one tower is left over from the glory days. Henri III had his archrival's son, the second Duke of Guise, imprisoned here during the Wars of Religion, but the duke escaped by tricking his guards into hopping on one foot as he ran away. The tower now holds free temporary art exhibits throughout the year.

⇞ *Down rue Lavoisier from the tourist office.* $ *€3, students or under 18 €1.50.* ⏰ *Open Tu-Su 2-6pm.*

CHÂTEAUX

Getting to and from the châteaux of the Loire can prove difficult, as they are not well served by public transportation. For the eager châteaux explorer, there are a variety of options open to you at varying costs. The cheapest option, which offers some freedom, is to hire a bike and ride to the châteaux. **Détours de Loire** *(☎02 47 61 22 23 💻www.locationdevelos.com)* can provide you with a bike and a map, all for just €14 per day. But getting to and from more than two châteaux in a day by bike will prove difficult. The most freedom and ease is gained from hiring a car at a place like **Avis** *(in the train station ☎02 47 20 53 27),* but the prices are often prohibitive for the student traveler (upwards of €120 per day). Fortunately, many companies provide plush minibuses which offer half-day and whole-day trips to the châteaux, departing from the tourist office at 9am or 1pm. Some possible choices are **Touraine Evasion** *(☎06 07 39 13 31 💻www.tourevasion.com. $ ½ day €19-33, full day €44-51.),* **Quart de Tours** *(☎06 30 65 52 01 💻www. quartdetours.com $ ½ day €21-34, full day €45-50.),* **Alienor Excursion** *(☎06 10 85 35 39 💻www.alienor.com. $ ½ day €18-32, full day €43-49.),* **Acco-Dispo Excursions** *(☎06 82 00 64 51 💻www.accodispo-tours.com $ ½ day €20-33, full day €45-50.)*

CHENONCEAU 👍♿ CHÂTEAU

Château de Chenonceau ☎02 47 23 90 07 💻www.chenonceau.com

The best known of the Loire châteaux, Chenonceau is an incredibly beautiful sight, with Renaissance-era arches that stretch over the Cher River and gardens that expand around the moat. Chenonceau, more so than any of the other châteaux in the area, is a "lady's castle," due to the influence of women on its architectural innovations, restoration, and further development. The original owner, Thomas

Bohier, handed over the design of the château to his wife, Katherine, while he was away during the Italian Wars (1513-21). Due to official court rules, Henri II's mistress, Diane de Poitier, was given control of the building in 1547, to which she added luxurious gardens and a bridge that remain to this day. After the death of Henri II, his wife, Catherine de Medici, forced Diane out and designed her own gardens to assert her superiority above her dead husband's mistress.

For a more rural look at the château, follow the pedestrian route that takes you past a donkey field, a flower garden, and a 16th-century farm. The Master Gallery inside Chenonceau houses some stunning portraits, including works by Rubens and Tinoretto; the adjoining wax museum honors exceptional women throughout history. For a beautiful, and potentially wet, view of the river, you can hire a boat during the summer and make a splash on the current of the Cher. The truly magical ◼Night Walk in the summer, set to the music of Arcangelo Corelli, allows you to view the château in full illumination.

✛ *Trains run to Chenonceau from Tours every 1½hr.; the trip lasts 30min. The station is by the entrance to the château.* ✦ *Night Walks June F-Su 9:30-11pm; July-Aug nightly 9:30-11pm* ⑥ *€10.50, students and under 18 €8.* ◻ *Open daily Apr-May 9am-7pm; June 9am-7:30pm; July-Aug 9am-8pm; Sept 9am-7:30pm; Oct 9am-6:30pm; Nov-Jan 9:30am-5pm; Feb to mid-Mar 9:30am-6pm; late Mar 9:30am-7pm.*

VILLANDRY
🚲♿ CHÂTEAU

Château de Villandry ☎02 47 50 02 09 ◼www.châteauvillandry.com

Built in 1536, Villandry was the last Renaissance château to be built in the Loire but rests on the foundations of a former medieval castle. The only remains of the medieval influence nowadays are the moat that surrounds the château and the gardens. Although the château is an impressive Renaissance building, the real beauty of Villandry comes from its Italian gardens, which are composed of over 125,000 flowers and 85,000 vegetables. For those on a romantic tour of the Loire château, the Ornamental Garden is a must, with its floral representation of the four types of love: Tender Love, Passionate Love, Fickle Love, and Tragic Love. The maze in the Sun Garden is designed to offer a journey of self-discovery and spiritual fulfillment, although unlike the Greek labyrinths it was modeled after, this maze has no dead-ends.

Inside the château, the most impressive sight is the ceiling of the Oriental drawing room, which actually comes from the Maquedaducal Palace in Toledo, Spain. The room is surrounded by artwork and statues which the 20th-century owners of the château, the Carvallo family, built up over the century. Make sure you ascend to the ◼keep, which provides a phenomenal bird's-eye view of the gardens below you. The Cher and the Loire are visible through the valleys and forest that surround the château.

✛ *Follow the D7 west of Tours. Villandry is approx. 15km from Tours.* ⑥ *Château and gardens €9, students and under 18 €5, under 8 free. Gardens only €6, students and under 18 €3.50, under 8 free.* ◻ *Open Mar 9am-5:30pm; June 9am-6pm, July-Aug 9am-6:30pm; Sept-Oct 9am-6pm; first half of Nov 9am-5pm; mid-Dec to early Jan 9:30am-4:30pm.*

AZAY-LE-RIDEAU
🚲♿ CHÂTEAU

Château d'Azay-le-Rideau ☎02 47 45 42 04 ◼www.monuments-nationaux.fr

Unlike many of the Loire châteaux, Azay-le-Rideau was built not for defense purposes but rather to create a grand Italian-style residency for a noble in King François I's government. The noble, Gilles Berthelot, allowed his new wife Philippe Lesbahy to take over the restoration of the the 16th-century building, and it's said that Azay-le-Rideau has a feminine touch to it thanks to Lesbahy's influence. Passing hands many times due to corruption or revolution, Azay-le-Rideau finally became the property of the French state in 1905 and is now open to the public. The château and the English Gardens (the fields were drained to imitate the landscape of England) provide a peaceful and beautiful visit; the facades of the château are particularly impressive when viewed from the woodland pathways which lead away from the entrance and around the back. The Beauvais tapestries in the billiard room, complete with 18th-century decor, are a highlight of the interior.

🎏 *Follow the D7 west of Tours. Azay-le-Rideau is approx. 20km from Tours.* **i** *For wheelchair access call ☎02 47 45 42 04.* 💲 *€8, EU citizens under 26 free.* 🗓 *Open daily July-Aug 9:30am-7pm; Sept 9:30am-6pm; Oct-Mar 10am-12:30pm and 2-5:30pm; Apr-June 9:30am-6pm. Last entry 45min before close.*

---

all's fair in love and châteaux

If you thought that you had a complicated love life, check out the tale that accompanies the **Château Chenonceau** and **Diane de Poitiers,** the mistress of **Henry II**.

After her husband died, Diane became the most eligible bachelorette in Francis I's court, with her eyes set on the heir to the throne, Henry II. Despite his arranged marriage to **Catherine de Medici,** in 1533, Diane still pursued Henry and became his mistress shortly before the wedding. Rethink your normal ideas of gender roles and age differences in French affairs; Diane was 30, Henry was 14. Henry couldn't be bothered to sleep with his 18 year old wife, what with puberty and all, and ended up spending all of his time with Diane.

Diane was ever the pragmatist though, and was not keen on being the reason France was without an heir to the throne. She agreed to give Catherine some pointers in the sack in exchange for the freedom to continue to be with Henry. On any given night, Henry would lie with Diane, leave to be with his wife, and then return to Diane. Whatever the cool trick Diane taught Catherine, it worked. Henry fathered several other children, including the future Francis II, Henry III, and Charles IX.

Henry still very much loved Diane and, unbeknownst to Catherine, gave Diane the **Château Chenonceau** in the Loire Valley. Pedophilia clearly has perks, and Catherine resided at Chenonceau until Henry's death. After Henry died in a jousting tournament however, Diane found herself the enemy of the mother of the king. Suddenly without a bargaining chip, Diane was strong-armed into trading Châteaux and downgrading to the lesser Château Anet, where Diane died 7 years after Henry's death (still not a bad deal).

USSÉ 🚌♿ CHÂTEAU

37420 Rigny-Ussé ☎02 47 95 54 05 🖥www.chateaudusse.fr

Known as "Sleeping Beauty's Castle," Ussé truly is the home of fairy tales. The building was constructed in the 15th and 16th centuries, and it's a characteristically medieval cluster of cute white-brick turrets. The former garden designer of Versailles, Le Nôtre, was commissioned by the Marquis de Valentinay in 1664 to craft the ornate garden, which is complete with beautiful flowers and orange trees; some of the trees date back as far as 1789. Even by Loire Valley standards, the château has been meticulously maintained; the walls and seats of some of the royal chambers are still draped in their original cloths and sumptuous sheets, and the Ussé's furniture, bought from the country's best cabinet-makers, remains in the same locations that were described in an 1781 inventory of the palace's holdings.

🎏 *Follow the D7 west of Tours. Ussé is approx. 20km from Tours.* 💲 *€13, ages 8-16 €4.* 🗓 *Open* *daily Apr-Aug 10am-7pm; Sept to mid-Nov 10am-6pm; mid-Feb to Mar 10am-6pm.*

LANGEAIS 🎫♿ CHÂTEAU

Château de Langeais ☎02 47 96 72 60 💻www.chateau-de-langeais.com

King Louis XI built this grand château in 1465. Each room has different tiling, the chimney breasts have been finely sculpted, and the bedrooms and salons are covered in tapestries. Access the oldest fortress in France, **Foulques's Tower,** where Foulques Nerra (who seized Langeais in 994) resided during his invasion of Tours over a thousand years ago. There is a genuine reconstruction of the fortress that uses scaffolding to give you the feeling that you're the ferocious Comte d'Anjou directing the battle from your bed. The newest part of the château grounds can be found in the park where a recently installed viewing platform provides you with stunning views of the Loire Valley.

 # Follow the D7 west of Tours. Langeais is 5min. along the A85 which is exit number 7 from the D7. $ €8.50, ages 18-25 €7.20, ages 10-17 €5, under 10 free. ⏰ Open daily July-Aug 9am-7pm; Sept to mid-Nov 9:30am-6:30pm; second half of Nov-Jan 10am-5pm; Feb-Mar 9:30am-5:30pm; Apr-June 9:30am-6:30pm

FOOD

For students on a budget, Tours is a dream come true. Almost every restaurant in town will try to entice you with a decently priced set lunch menu *(usually €11-20)*. The restaurants along **rue Colbert** and **pl. Plumereau** are by far the least expensive and most popular, although it's possible to find some good bargains elsewhere. The indoor food market at **places des Halles** *(Open M-Sa 7am-7:30pm.)* can fix you up with fresh produce to make your own meals, and during the summer the market extends outside Wednesday and Saturday mornings *(7am-noon)*. The square in front of the tourist office has a weekly **marché traditionnel** *(Tu 8am-noon)*, where you can pick up typical traditional cheeses, meats, and vegetables. For daily groceries and everyday food, try the **ATAC** by the train station *(5 pl. du Maréchal Leclerc. ⏰ Open M-Sa 7:30am-8pm)* or the **Monoprix** supermarket. *(63 rue Nationale ⏰ Open M-Sa 9am-8:30pm.)*

MAMIE BIGOUDE 🎫♿🍸 CRÊPERIE 2

22 rue Châteauneuf ☎02 47 64 53 85

It looks like a house Grandma would build. But grandmas are always a little bit crazy, and Mamie Bigoude is no different; we're just grateful she left out the cats. Enter into her *maison*, which is complete with a kitchen, living room, lounge, garden, bedroom, and even a bathroom for you to eat in (don't worry, there are other bathrooms for when you need *pipi;* they are tastefully decorated with 1960s French advertisements). The restaurant serves crêpes, galletes, and salads named after famous figures. Fancy a bite of Harry Potter? Or a nibble on TinTin, perhaps? And let's not even get into the Chuck Berry salad. For the children, there is even a supervised play area, and for the adults there is enough humor hidden around the house to keep you entertained.

 # From pl. Plumereau, take rue de Change southward, which leads to rue Châteauneuf. $ Plates €5-15. ⏰ Open daily noon-2:30pm and 7-11pm.

LA SOURIS GOURMANDE 🎫🍸 FONDUE 2

100 rue Colbert ☎02 47 47 04 80

This place is cheap, cheerful, and very, very cheesy. Literally. Cow statues stand on the shelves, cow posters are plastered to the walls, and a cow clock tells the time. To top it all off, the toilet is complete with a cheese-shaped toilet seat and toilet-roll holder. This little restaurant naturally serves up cheese fondue *(€13-15, 2-person min.)* and an array of cheese dishes. The set lunch menu *(€10.75 for 2 courses, €12.50 for 3)* offers a brilliant bargain for anyone looking for some cheesy nosh to nibble on. Just watch out for the mouse traps.

 # Rue Colbert runs parallel with the bottom of rue de Buffon, which is directly opposite the train

station. $ *Plates €10-15. Fondue €13-15. Set menu €10.75-12.50* ⏰ *Open Tu-Sa noon-2pm and 7-10:30pm.*

LA DEUVALIÈRE
🍴🍸 TRADITIONAL ❸

18 rue de la Monnaie ☎02 47 64 01 57 🖥www.restaurant-ladeuvaliere.com

This award-winning restaurant proudly displays a newspaper clipping in a frame that declares, "the best restaurants don't have to be the most expensive." Hear, hear. Locals say that La Deuvalière serves the best food in Tours, and it will provide you with fine dining without that massive cost. The lunch menu is one of the most delectable things you will ever experience in Tours; the food is mouthwatering, and the prices will make your jaw drop *(€14 for 2 courses, €17 for 3).* Although prices become less reasonable in the evening *(€25-30 for set menus),* the restaurant's chic but simple setting is an ideal setting for an upscale night out in the center of Tours.

➜ *From pl. Plumereau, rue de la Monnaie is in the far southeast corner.* $ *Lunch €11-17. Dinner €15-30.* ⏰ *Open Tu-F noon-2pm and 7:30-10:30pm, Sa 7:30-10:30pm.*

LE LYS D'OR
🍴 ICE CREAM ❶

pl. Plum ☎02 47 20 88 88

Ice cream and sorbet are sold on every street corner in Tours, and it's hard to tell whether you're going to be eating the dairy of your dreams or sloppy milky mayhem. According to sweet-toothed local students, Le Lys d'Or serves the best ice cream in the square, and probably in all of Tours. It also features an ajoining crêperie and offers traditional treats. Ice cream flavors include Nutella and passion fruit.

➜ *In pl. Plumereau, southside.* $ *1 scoop €2, 2 scoops €3.30. Every 10th double scoop is free.* ⏰ *Open daily 10am-11pm.*

BISTROT BOCCACCIO
🍴🍸 ITALIAN ❸

9 rue Gambatta ☎02 47 05 45 22

Although you wouldn't expect to find the taste of Italy in the Loire Valley, Tours is swarming with Italian bistros that serve hungry businessmen. Finding Italian cuisine at a good value, however, is less than easy. Tucked away just off the main shopping street, Bistro Boccaccio is a favorite with local businessmen and women taking a speedy lunch break away from the daily grind. Although the lunch menu isn't revolutionary, it'll leave you satisfied, and the humorous decor will be worth the extra couple of euro. The walls are designed to appear as if they're falling down, and the missing bricks reveal large murals behind them. Be warned: when nature calls, you may feel like you've been called to Big Brother's crib to discuss your meal. The restrooms are entirely metal—the floors, the walls, and the ceilings.

➜ *From pl. Jules Jaurès, follow rue Nationale; rue Gambatta will be on your left.* $ *Set menu €12-16.* ⏰ *Open M-Tu noon-2:15pm, W-Th noon-2:15pm and 7:30-9:30pm, F-Sa noon-2:15pm and 7:30-10pm.*

LE GRILL DU ROY
🍴🍸 TRADITIONAL ❷

16 rue du Grand Marché ☎02 47 20 70 15

Although "Roy's Grill" sounds like somewhere you might end up looking for a burger after a night out on the town, Le Grill du Roy in Tours offers the cheapest three-course set menu in the square *(€11).* Choose from a small selection of local specialties, including pâtés, cheeses, and tartares to begin, and then indulge in the very generous entrees. For an extra €2, treat yourself to the leg of pork, which comes swimming in vegetables. For the more indulgent among you, a €17 "gourmet" menu is also available, which offers even bigger portions and slightly better cuisine. But why bother, when you can stuff yourself for €11?

➜ *Rue du Grand Marché is situated just off of pl. Plumereau, in the southwest corner.* $ *Set menus €11-17.* ⏰ *Open daily noon-12:30pm and 7-11pm.*

AU LAPIN QUI FUME

TRADITIONAL ❸

90 rue Colbert ☎02 47 66 95 49

Pictures of an Alice in Wonderland-esque white rabbit, complete with a smoking jacket and pipe, are painted on the walls of this small but pleasant restaurant along one of Tours's busiest streets. Well-known for the duck confit (€13.*50 with an appetizer or dessert)* and, of course, its rabbit dish (whether the rabbit had a pocket watch or a very important date is unclear), Au Lapin Qui Fume serves food suited for those in search of a more traditional taste of the Loire Valley. Those with eyes bigger than their stomach would do well to indulge in a *Plat Gourmet,* nicely translated as "the greedy plates." Piled high with meats of all kinds and surrounded by vegetables, these monster meals will fill you up and empty your wallet at €23.

✂ *Rue Colbert runs parallel with the bottom of rue de Buffon, which is directly opposite the train station.* ℹ *English menu translations available.* ⑤ *Set menus €13.50-30.* ☺ *Open Tu-Sa noon-2pm and 7-10.30pm.*

LA TAVERNE DE L'HOMME TRANQUILLE

TRADITIONAL ❹

22 rue du Grande Marché/17 rue de la Rotisserie ☎02 47 01 40 04

Tranquille by name and surprisingly tranquil by nature, this rustic restaurant offers a traditional Loire Valley menu. Make sure you look up as you enter to catch a glimpse of the rather large (and fake) swordfish hanging above the customers. The walls are adorned with grand murals of happy families, and given the prices of the set menus it's easy to see why. Three courses from the Traditional Menu will set you back €13.50, while the Gourmet Menu comes at the heftier price of €24.50. Of course, those travelers not eating out with the kids should sample some of local ▉wines. Booze aside, this place is still very good for families.

✂ *Rue du Grand Marché is situated just off of pl. Plumereau, in the southwest corner.* ⑤€13.50-€24.50. ☺ *Open M-Tu noon-2pm and 7-10pm, Th-Sa noon-2pm and 7-10pm.*

L'ATELIER GOURMAND

TRADITIONAL, FUSION ❸

37 rue Etienne Marcel ☎02 47 38 59 87 ▣www.lateliergourmand.fr

Owned by a very chatty couple who will happily discuss the menu options with you in English, this fine dining restaurant experiments with new and interesting dishes, while also providing some reliably high-quality favorites. Daily specials grace the board. The interior, if anything, tries to be too modern, with a somewhat nauseating jellyfish projection moving up and down the purple walls. The mellow background music and modern plastic chair/stools ensure that you will leave a lot more New Age Zen than you came in. You may also leave a little tipsy, given that alcohol can be added to many of their dishes. *Let's Go* recommends trying the sorbet with sparkling champagne for a real kick at the end of your meal.

✂ *Just off rue du Grande Marché, which runs off of pl. Plumereau.* ⑤ *Entrees €12-30.* ☺ *Open M 7:30-10:30pm, Tu-F noon-2pm and 7:30-10:30pm.*

RESTAURANT NOTABOU

NON-TRADITIONAL ❹

6 rue de la Rotisserie ☎02 47 64 95 34 ▣notabou37@gmail.com

Although Notabou's on the pricy side, the quote above the door should put your mind at ease: "It's forbidden to forbid anything." Perhaps that's just an attempt to convince you to indulge yourself and splurge on the menu at hand. The experience begins with the menu; Ronald McDonald, Alf the Alien and even a cow asking to be eaten all make an appearance encouraging you to indulge yourself. When your meal arrives, don't be surprised to find yourself eating out of fish bowls, small cooking pots, or other bizarre serving contraptions. Although the steak will set you back almost €30, the enormous serving looks like a small cow has been presented to you. The evening is likely to be rounded off with a humourous dessert—will you be lucky enough to have your ice cream served in the backpack of a maraca-wielding singing stuffed kangaroo? We certainly hope so.

⚜ *From pl. Plumereau head southward down rue du Change and rue de la Rotisserie will be on your right* ⑤ *Entrees €20-30.* 🕐 *Open Tu-Sa noon-2pm and 6-10:30, Su 6-10:30pm.*

NIGHTLIFE

The busiest and most popular location for students is around **pl. Plumereau,** where bars, restaurants, and a few clubs fill up with students both inside and outside during the summer months. The streets leading off the *place* are full of pubs and bars, especially the **rue du Commerce,** where finding an Irish pub is almost as easy as if you were in Dublin.

AU TEMPS DU ROIS   ⚲Ⓨ BAR

3 pl. de Plumereau   ☎02 47 05 04 51

Au Temps du Rois opens up before most people in Tours are awake and stays open long after most people have gone to bed. Owned by two best friends for over 20 years, the bar is decorated with fascinating tidbits, including a pair of golden boots, old theater posters, mosaic tables, and a collection of Petit Robert from across the years. With clocks telling you the time for Tours, Paris, London, New York City, and Japan, this bar manages to combine a traditional French feel with that of the modern world, making it a favorite with Tours's international and French student scene. They've had some very renowned customers in the past, including Mick Jagger, who signed the bar's guestbook. Perhaps second behind Mick was "Miss Mexico 2000," who before conquering the Mexican beauty world used to pull pints here on a Sunday evening when she lived in Tours.

⚜ *Northeast corner of pl. Plumereau.* ⑤ *All drinks €2.50-7.* 🕐 *Open daily 8:30am-2am.*

LA GUINGUETTE   ⚲Ⓨ BAR, RESTAURANT

This very bohemian hangout has neither a fixed address nor a telephone number, but that's because it's on the banks of the Loire river. Situated just by Pont Wilson, this outdoor bar and restaurant was founded around 5 years ago to combat the problem of the homeless not having anywhere to go. Now, the students of Tours populate the banks of the Loire in the summer and drink down beer, wines, and cocktails at La Guinguette while chillling to live music and sitting in chairs susupended from a tree or at the helm of a wooden boat. On summer weekends the riverside hangout is packed with an extremely diverse clientele, and everyone is made to feel welcome; just be careful when returning to the city at the end of the night. Walking home in groups is advisable.

⚜ *Down the steps by Pont Wilson, at the bottom of rue Nationale.* ⑤ *Drinks €3-8.* 🕐 *Open M-Th 11am-midnight, F-Sa 11am-2am, Su 11am-midnight.*

LES BERTHOMS   ⚲Ⓨ BAR

5 rue du Commerce   ☎02 47 20 01 66 🖳www.lesberthom.com

This rustic Belgian bar slightly resembles the inside of a treehouse, with its low wooden timbers and faux foliage on the walls. The oak tables and pillars provide a perfect setting in which to taste some of Belgian's finest beer; you'll soon forget that Belgium is a whole other country away. Packed in the early evenings of the week by students making the most of happy hour, this lively bar will keep a beer lover occupied for hours. Throughout the year, the bar plays host to a range of concerts and "slams," where the locals gather to chill out to some live music with their beer. Most busy on Thursday and Fridays, this is a mature student's haven, drawing punters from the thousands of graduate students studying and researching in Tours.

⚜ *Just past the intersection of rue Nationale and rue du Commerce.* ⑤ *Beer €3-5.* 🕐 *Open M-Tu 3pm-1am, W-Sa 3pm-3am, Su 3pm-1am. Happy hour M-F 7-9pm, Su 7-9pm.*

LE STRAPONTIN   ⚲Ⓨ BAR

23-25 rue Châteauneuf   ☎02 47 47 03 74

This bar in the shadows of the ancient Towers of the Basalique St-Martin could be mistaken for a modern art museum. Serving up some rather fruity beer (the peach and apricot varieties are highly recommended) to punters surrounded by statues emerging from the walls: a Mickey Mouse portrait and even TinTin's submarine hang overhead. Each table has an interesting and unique design to keep you amused; drink from Iggy Pop's chest or woo your date on the heart-shaped table.

From pl. Plumereau, head up rue du Change in the south corner which leads to Châteauneuf. Le Strapontin is on your right. $ Beer €5. ⏰ Open daily 7pm-2am.

BISTRO 64 — BAR, BISTRO

64 rue du Grand Marché — ☎02 47 38 47 40

Bistro 64 offers the casual drinker a little more culture than some of the other watering holes available. The ever-changing interior is offset by jazz music, which is often playing from the stereo, but if the jazz becomes old hat, the owner can make a selection from the hundreds of CDs behind the bar. The mosaic floor and grand doorway remind you that this bar is in one of Tours's medieval buildings, restored to its former glory. The first Thursday of every month, the bistro plays host to a DJ and a grand soiree that goes into the early hours.

From pl. Plumereau, head along rue du Grand Marché in the southwest corner. Walk past the intersection with rue Bretonneau and cross the road. Continue along and the bar will be on your left. $ Beer €3-5. Mojitos and other mixed drinks €6. ⏰ Open daily 3pm-2am.

THE OUTBACK — BAR

11 rue des Orfurus — ☎06 70 06 80 15

A piece of Australia dropped in the middle of Tours, The Outback is frequented by Australians, French, and the general international student crowd. The meter-high shots *(€18)* may have something to do with the crowds. Providing the cheapest and fiercest hangover you can afford on a budget, The Outback is a place to start and finish your night all in one round. For those wishing to take things a little more slowly, the bar also serves beer, wines, and cocktails, which will keep the traveling student happily watered.

Just off of pl. Plumereau. In the southeast corner, head to the far right intersection. $ Beer and mixed drinks €3-6. ⏰ Open Tu-Sa 6pm-2am.

ARTS AND CULTURE

LE GRAND THÉÂTRE — OPERA, SYMPHONY ORCHESTRA

34 rue de la Scellerie — ☎02 47 60 20 20 🖥www.operadetours.fr

This 19th-century theater was built over the remains of the Convent de Cordeliers; what's left of the church door is still visible on rue Voltaire. Steeped in history, Le Grand Théâtre provides Tours with its opera and orchestra and also plays host to the **Florilège Vocal de Tours,** where the best choirs from around the world compete in an annual competition at the end of May *(🖥www.florilegevocal.com).*

⏰ Box office open M-Sa 9:30am-12:30pm and 1:30-5:45pm.

NOUVEL OLYMPIA — THEATER

7 rue de Lucé — ☎02 47 20 17 26 🖥www.cdrtours.fr

The Nouvel Olympia offers up a wide variety of theatrical productions throughout the year and is Tours's regional dramatic base. Expect more experimental theater and local dramatic productions, including classic plays and original musicals. The artistic team, headed by Gilles Bouillon, offers around 15-20 productions per season; Gilles is often directly involved with three or five. The bar of Nouvel Olympia often holds events with artists and performers, or offers a place to grab coffee.

From pl. Jean Jaurès, follow rue Nationale halfway down and take a right onto rue de la Scellerie. Nouvel Olympia is just off rue de la Scellerie. $ €19, students and under 18 €11. Multi-show offers also available. ⏰ Box office open M-F noon-6pm.

VINCI 🎭 THEATER

67 rue Bernard Palissy ☎08 91 70 10 75 🖥www.vinci-conventions.com

Leonardo Da Vinci, the man of great ideas, is the inspiration behind this modern building which houses most of Tours's outside theater. Kitschy and family-friendly productions often travel through here—recent performances included *Scooby Doo* and *Dora the Explorer*—but performers such as Boyz II Men and Leonard Cohen have also graced the stage.

🚏 Just down the road from the tourist info. $ Prices depend on show. ⏰ Box office open Tu-F 1-7pm, Sa 2-7pm.

ESSENTIALS

Practicalities

- **TOURIST OFFICE:** 78-82 rue Bernard Palissy *(☎02 47 70 37 37 🖥www.ligeris.com ⏰ Open daily mid Apr-mid Oct M-Sa 8:30am-7pm, Su 10am-12:30pm and 2:30-5pm; mid Oct-mid Apr M-Sa 9am-12:30pm and 1:30-6pm, Su 10am-1pm.)* If you're looking for a comprehensive **tour** of Tours, the tourist office can suggest a route for you, and provides a **train** for guided tours of the city. *($ €6, under 18 €3.)*
- **BANKS:** ATM machines along rue Nationale. **BNP Paribas** *(86 rue Nationale ☎08 92 70 57 05 ⏰ Open M 2-6pm, Tu-F 9am-6pm, Sa 9am-12:30pm.)*
- **INTERNET ACCESS: Bureau d'Information Jeunesse (BIJ)** *(78-80 rue Michelet ☎02 47 64 69 13 $ 1hr. free internet access. ⏰ Open M-Tu 1-6pm, W 10am-noon, Th-F 1-6pm.)* **Tourist Office.** *($€0.50 per 15min.).* **Top Communications,** 68-70 rue du Grand Marché *(☎02 47 76 19 53 $ €0.50 per 15min., €2 per hr. ⏰ Open daily 10am-midnight.)*
- **POST OFFICE:** bld. Béranger *(☎02 47 60 34 05 ⏰ Open M-F 8:30am-6:30pm, Sa 9am-5pm.)* Branch office at 92 rue Colbert.

Emergency!

- **POLICE:** 70-72 rue de Marceau *(☎02 47 33 80 69).*
- **HOSPITAL: Centre Hospatilier Régional.** 2 bld. Tonnellé *(☎02 47 47 47 47).*

Getting There

The **train station** at Tours is one of the busiest in the Loire Valley. There are connections to most of the towns and cities of the Loire; you can reach Tours from **Orléans** in 1hr., and trains run frequently roughly every 30min. *(€17).* **Blois** can be reached on the same train in just over 30min. *(€10).* Tours is connected to **Paris Est** *($ €46. ⏰ 1½hr.)* by a high speed train. **Bordeaux** connects directly with Tours in under 3hrs *(€50).*

Getting Around

Tours can be easily traveled on foot. Be warned though: what you think is a pedestrian-only zone may very quickly become a road. To reach places farther south, east, or west of Tours, the bus company **Filbleau** *(9 rue Michelet. ☎02 47 66 70 70 ⏰ Open M-F 7:30am-7pm, Sa 10am-5pm.)* runs daily services. Bus tickets are bought on the bus, and cost €1.25 for a 1hr. ticket or €3.20 for a daypass. For those wishing to explore the Loire Valley by bike, the very helpful **Détours de Loire** can sort you out for €14 per day *(35 rue Charles Giles ☎02 47 61 22 23 🖥www.locationdevelos.com).*

Finally, for travel once public transportation stops running (around 11pm), **Taxis Radio** run 24hr. from outside the train station at €1.40 per km during the day and €2.30 at night *(☎02 47 20 30 40).*

BRITTANY AND NORMANDY

French culture is undeniably present in Brittany and Normandy's *centre-villes, crêperies,* and châteaux, but these two regions hold fast to their independent cultural identities, both of which are intimately tied to the ocean they border. In 911 CE, the Viking raider Rollo swung by Normandy unannounced and established himself as the region's first duke. His descendant William the Bastard confirmed Normandy's naval power when he conquered England in 1066 and earned himself a more flattering nickname: William the Conqueror. Eager to return the favor, England repeatedly invaded Normandy during the Hundred Years' War, and in 1431 they captured and burned Joan of Arc in Rouen. France's friendly neighbors didn't attempt another invasion until June 6, 1944 (better known as D-Day), when they returned—this time in the name of France—with North American allies to liberate Normandy from German control. Brittany and Normandy have both become considerably less tumultuous since then, and these days you're more likely to find sleepy towns with winding streets and steep, timbered houses than geopolitical conflicts. The dignified fortresses, haunting battlegrounds, and medieval tapestries make for an excellent daytrip on the train from Paris; while the beaches are more brooding than the perpetual sun of the Riviera, they're also less crowded and equally beautiful.

greatest hits

- **AMERICA WINS WAR FOR FRENCH:** Sign up for a tour and wander the haunting D-Day beaches (p. 146).
- **BASTARD'S CONQUEST...** Also known as the Battle of Hastings. Check out the jaw-dropping Tapisserie de Bayeux that documents William's historic victory (p. 145).
- **HUMAN HAMSTER WHEEL:** When the monks of the Mont St-Michel Abbey couldn't bear to sell off the stones of their monastery during the French Revolution, they sold their souls instead and allowed it to be converted into a prison. Wardens forced two to four prisoners to walk like hamsters on the giant wheel that is now on display to pull up supplies from the bottom of the mountain (p. 137).

student life

D-Day was over 60 years ago, but things haven't slowed down in Brittany and Normandy (though they're considerably less bloody). Caen and Bayeux are fine, but for the real student-travel experience you want to be in **Rennes.** With two universities, Rennes is Brittany's college town. During the summer months you'll be hard pressed to not find an outdoor bar full of young people ready to start the night off right. With student-budget friendly prices at places like **Ty Anna Taverne** and **Sunset Cafe** you'll get plenty of bang for your buck (if you're lucky that is).

rennes ☎0299

Quirky, colorful, and cool, Rennes (pop. 213,000) has the cosmopolitan attitude of Paris. but an independent Breton spirit. The result: a charming, unpretentious city where the culture is lively, the citizens are happy, and the booze is free flowing. Two hours from the French capital by train, the cityscape is a melange of medieval half-timbered houses, graffiti, ornate Neoclassical facades, and lively restaurants and bars that line winding cobblestone streets and hidden alleys. Unlike most of Brittany's coast, the town is at its best from September to June, when its 60,000 students are in town and the quintessentially French youth (counter) culture is throbbing.

ORIENTATION

The north exit of the **train station** will lead you to **av. Jean Janvier,** which runs over the **Vilaine River** that separates the train station from the **vieille ville.** Pleasant promenades line the canal that emerges briefly at **pl. de la République,** then resurfaces again at **pl. de Bretagne.** Turn left and walk along **Quai Châteaubriand** to reach **pl. de la République,** the city's cultural center. To the north on rue d'Orléans lies **pl. de la Mairie,** in the heart of the *vieille ville.* North of that, **pl. Ste-Anne** is always littered with idlers and bar-goers, booksellers, artists, and the occasional troublemaker. The most well-kept half-timbered houses can be seen on **pl. du Champ-Jacquet.**

ACCOMMODATIONS

👍 HOTEL VENEZIA 💳 HOTEL [2]

27 rue Dupont des Loges ☎30 36 56 💻hotel.venezia@wanadoo.fr

This absolutely lovable hotel is run by an endearring older couple, who carefully decorated the rooms themselves. It shows. Pattered wallpaper, elderly fireplaces, and 19th-century paintings give Hotel Venezia a taste of old France's intimacy and charm. Some rooms have views of the canal, from which ducks can be heard "singing" in the morning.

➡ [M]République. i Breakfast €5. ⓈSingles €30-42; doubles €40-48. Supplementary bed €10.

👍 HÔTEL DE NEMOURS 💳📶 HOTEL [4]

5 rue de Nemours ☎78 26 26 💻www.hotelnemours.com

Smelling like heaven, this beautiful hotel is way underpriced for the chic, modern rooms it provides. Mistakenly classed as a two-star hotel, it'll feel like a four to budget travelers, and to hostel virgins, a fair three. All rooms have satellite TV and hair dryers.

➡ [M]République. i Breakfast €8.50. Free Wi-Fi. Ⓢ Singles €64-74; doubles €74-87; triples €94; quads €97.

AUBERGE DE JEUNESSE(HI) 💳📶🍸 HOSTEL [1]

10-12 canal St-Martin ☎02 99 33 22 33 💻rennes@fuaj.org

Liberal on its interpretation of "jeunesse," this hotel shelters young travelers, the occasional weirdo, older couples, and students. Simple 2- to 4-bed rooms with lockers and showers that drain slowly. Some have canal views.

Ⓜ Ste-Anne. Walk to the right of the church on rue de St-Malo, which veers left into canal St-Martin. Cross the bridge; the hostel is on the right. i Kitchen, common room with TV, and cafeteria. $ Dorms €19.35. ⏰ Reception 7am-11pm. Lockout 10am-3:30pm. Night guard after 1am.

CAMPING DES GAYEULLES — CAMPGROUND ❶

rue Maurice Audin ☎36 91 22 www.camping-rennes.com

Far, far away from the town center, and deep, deep in the Parc des Gayeulles, you'll certainly be roughing it at Camping des Gayeulles (we suspect that's the point), but your wallet will certainly be happy.

In Parc des Gayeulles. Take bus #3 (dir.: St-Laurent) from pl. du Colombier or pl. de la République to Piscine Gayeulles. Go around the pool, turn left and follow the paved road through the park. i Laundry available, wash €3, dry €1.50.Internet €1 per 30min. $ €3.50; under 13 €1.50, €3-5.70 per tent; €1.50-€1.70 per car; €6.70-7.20 per caravan. Electricity €3.30 summer €3.50 winter. ⏰ Quiet hours 10pm-7am. Reception from mid-June-mid-Sept daily 7:30am-1pm and 2-8pm; from mid-Sept-Oct and from Apr-mid-June daily 9am-12:30pm and 4:30-8pm; Nov-Mar M-Sa 8-9am and 6-8pm. Gates closed from mid June mid Sept 11pm 7am; from mid Sept to mid June 10pm 7am.

HOTEL DE LA TOUR D'AUVERGNE — HOTEL ❷

20 bld. de la Tour d'Auvergne ☎02 99 30 84 16

Run out of a restaurant, the charming rooms in this makeshift hotel come as quite a surprise. Bathroom arrangements can be interesting (accordion doors), but the rooms are well decorated with multiple rugs. Rooms 10, 11, and 14 far outdo the rest.

Ⓜ République. i Free Wi-Fi. Reserve 15 days ahead. Check-in noon. Check-out 10:30am. Breakfast €6. $ Singles €32, with bath €42; doubles €37, with bath €47.

CITÉA RENNES — HOTEL ❸

35 rue d'Antrain ☎02 23 21 20 00 rennes@citea.com www.citea.com

Airy, spacious and affordable, the studios at Citéa Rennes fall somewhere between apartment and hotel room. Some bathrooms are large enough to accommodate orgies (if you're into that sort of thing). Rooms are furnished simply, but are cleaned daily with fresh linens provided.

Ⓜ Sainte Anne. i All rooms have kitchenettes. Wi-Fi available. $ Single studio €50-65 for stays of more than a week. Double studio €55-69. 4 person Studio €83-92. ⏰ Reception open M-F 1:30am-9pm, Sa-Su 8am-noon and 2pm-6pm.

HOTEL LANJUINAIS — HOTEL ❸

11 rue Lanjuinais ☎02 99 79 02 03 www.hotel-lanjuinais.com

This standard hotel located near Pl. de la République provides rooms that are clean, if not particularly homey. One of the few hotels in Rennes that is wheelchair accessible.

Ⓜ République. i Breakfast €7. Internet €5. $ Singles €47; doubles €60-69. Supplementary bed €7.

ANGELINA — HOTEL ❸

1 quai Lamennais ☎02 99 79 29 66 angelina-hotel@voila.fr

After trekking up to the third floor, coming back to this adhoc hotel may feel like coming home. Each room has its own personal touch: some pink curtains, others sun-printed comforters. Conveniently located close to Pl. de la République.

Ⓜ République. i Payment by credit card only. $ Singles and doubles €45-65. Breakfast €7.50. Supplementary bed €7.

HOTEL RICHEMONT — HOTEL ❸

8 rue Dupont des Loges ☎02 99 30 38 21

This small hotel on a quiet street is a little musty, but affordable and clean. Bathrooms resemble those on boats but are bit bigger.

Ⓜ République. i All rooms come with Wi-Fi and TV. Breakfast €6.50. $ Singles €46-52; doubles 56-64; triples €69. ⏰ Door code required at night.

SIGHTS

MUSÉE DES BEAUX ARTS   🕭 MUSEUM

20 quai Emile Zola   ☎02 23 62 17 45 🖳www.mbar.org

Like the city itself, the museum's collection is an odd assortment. Art objects range from an Egyptian mummy—the oldest piece on display—to contemporary exhbitions. Though there are no "must-see before I die" pieces here, there are a few works from Picasso's Surrealist period of the '20s, namely *The Bather*, and some paintings by Gauguin and Caillebotte. The Baroque collection is also impressive, especially Ruben's *The Tiger Hunt*. Many paintings offer less dramatic depictions of famous moments, which lend a fresh perspective to some of the grandiose paintings of Versailles and Paris.

Ⓢ €5-8, students, handicapped, unemployed €3, art history students free. Guided tours €10.30. ⚙ Open Tu 10am-6pm, W-Su 10am-noon and 2-6pm. Closed on holidays.

JARDIN DU THABOR   GARDEN

5 bld. de la Duchesse Anne   ☎02 99 28 56 62

A former orchard, these lush grounds are now some of the most beautiful in France. The Jardin du Thabor is rich with fountains, wild trees, neat flower beds dotted by marble statues, an aviary of chirping parakeets, and a former medieval jousting area where actors now fight for the spotlight on a stage lovingly referred to as "hell." The target-shaped rose garden boasts 980 varieties of the *fleur d'amour*; love abounds on the grassy flat of the central quad. A small gallery on the north side of the gardens exhibits local artwork. On Wednesday evenings in July, Les Mecredis du Thabor brings Breton song and dance to the gardens.

✝ Entrances at pl. St-Melanie, rue de la Palestine, rue de Paris, and bld. de la Duchesse Anne. Ⓢ Free. ⚙ Open 8am-sunset.

PARC DES GAYEULLES   PARK

av. des Gayeulles

As woodsy as it gets here, Parc des Gayeulles is the only place in Rennes where Frenchmen feel comfortable jogging. Every so often the imposing trees clear up and reveal an indoor pool, several lakes, sports fields, tennis courts, minigolf course, or a campground. Walking and bike paths also wind through the park. Maps are posted at regular intervals.

✝ #3 bus. *i* Paddle boats available in summer. Ⓢ Free. ⚙ Open July-Aug. 8am-8:30pm; Sept-June 8am-5:45pm.

CATHÉDRALE SAINT-PIERRE   CATHEDRAL

carrefour de la Cathédrale

Some people may say that God is unmoving, but His churches certainly move all the time. Cathédrale Saint-Pierre is the third cathedral to stand on this site; the plot was previously occupied by a pagan temple, a Roman church, and a Gothic cathedral. Subsequent reconstructions of the cathedral were prompted by the ravages of decay and the French Revolution. The church that stands here today is a 19th-century masterpiece, finished by a massive Neoclassical facade, with huge columns inside holding up the painted and gilded ceiling. The one noticeable 20th-century addition is the altar, a large block of green bronze. The fifth chapel on the right houses the cathedral's treasure: a delicately carved 16th-century wooden altarpiece that traces the life of the Virgin Mary. The great organ was built with funds granted by Napoleon III when he visited Rennes in 1858.

✝ Ⓜ Sainte-Anne. Ⓢ Free. ⚙ Open daily 9:30am-noon and 3-6 pm. Sunday mass -10:30am.

PORTES MORDELAISES   🕭 ARCH

rue des Portes Mordelaises

Dukes and earls once gathered before these gates, restored in 1440, to pledge their fidelity to the rights and freedom of Brittany. Today, the picturesque stone arch is overgrown with flowers and the hanging chains of a former drawbridge. Rennes no longer needs city walls and valient noblemen to protect itself; these days, France has a nuclear deterrent.

♯ Ⓜ*Sainte-Anne.* Ⓢ *Free.*

PLACE DES LICES
                                                        ♿ SQUARE

pl. des Lices

Before it turned into the place where the heavily caffeinated get their next hit, and the slighly tipsy fight the urge to go home with homely stranger, the Places des Lices was a medieval jousting ground used for festivals and tournaments. Built in the 17th century for parliamentarians, its northern side is lined with large timber-framed townhouses. France's second largest food market is held here every Saturday morning.

♯ Ⓜ*Sainte-Anne.*

SAINT MELAINE ABBEY
                                                                   ABBEY

pl. St. Melaine

Right next to Jardins du Thabor, this abbey is the only surviving example of Romanesque architecture in Rennes. The abbey was founded after the death and burial of Saint Melaine, a 6th century bishop of Rennes and trusted advisor to King Clovis I. An abbots' residence was added in the 17th century.

♯ *Entrance at Jardin du Thabor.*

TY-KOZ
                                                     HISTORIC BUILDING

3 rue Saint Guillaume

Built in 1505, this timber-framed house hides it age well with bright red paint but seems to have trouble standing upright, not unlike a dolled up grandma. Rennes' master carpenters and sculptors built Ty-Koz in the Gothic style, replete with psychedelic stone statues. The intricacy and color of the facade is striking. Alcohol is supposedly served inside, though bar hours are unreliable.

♯ Ⓜ*Saint-Anne.* ⏱ *Noon-1am; hours vary.*

FOOD

Rennes's culinary center northwest of the city boasts an astounding number of ethnic restaurants; **rue de Saint-Malo** alone has Haitian, Lebanese, Indian, and Chinese cuisine, with Greek and Italian restaurants nearby. There are plenty of kebab stands on and around **pl. Sainte-Anne,** and more traditional restaurants around **pl. Saint-Michel** and in the **centre-ville.** On the other side of the city, brasseries and creperies line **rue Saint-George.** Rennes also has several markets, that often provide affordable alternatives to eating out. The city's largest market is on **pl. des Lices** (open Sa 7am–1pm); others are held from Tuesday to Sunday throughout the city (ask at the tourist office for a list). Local supermarkets include a **Champion,** (20 rue d'Isly, in a mall near the train station ⏱ Open M-Sa 9:30am-8pm), a **Supermarché Hoche** (9 Pl. Hoche ⏱ Open M-Sa 8am-9pm, Su 9am-noon),and a **Marché Plus** (43 Pl. de la Rance, in an apartment complex off rue de St-Malo near the hostel; open M-Sa 7am-9pm, Su 9am-noon). There are several local grocery stores along **rue Jean Janvier** by the train station.

LA CASA PEPE
                                         ☕ PIZZERIA, ITALIAN ❷

29 rue St. Georges   ☎02 99 38 99 55

Among the countless pizzerias in Rennes, La Casa Pepe is considered one of the best. The huge, creative pizzas (€7-10) and pastas (€8-9) draws a steady crowd into the warm, red interior. You might forget you're in France for a little bit, unless you take advantage of the outdoor seating to take in the views of the city.

♯ Ⓜ*République. From station, head east on Quai Emile Zola. Left on rue Jean Janvier, continue on rue Gambetta Left on rue St. Georges.* Ⓢ *Salads €7-9. Gratins €8-9. Plat du jour €7.20. Formule midi €9.25.* ⏱ *Open M-W, Th noon-2pm and 7pm-11pm, F-Sa noon-2pm and 7pm-10:30pm.*

L'EPICERIE
                                                       ☕ BISTRO ❶

2 rue des Fossés   ☎02 99 38 76 70

This tartines-bistro fosters an authentic and homey vibe; as you take a seat at one of the long wood tables under the quirky assortment of hanging hammers, stacked teacups, and bronze candelabras, you'll mistakenly think a Frenchie took you home with him. You can easily order a delicious meal for less than €10 here.

✦ ⓂSainte-Anne. *From pl. Sainte-Anne, continue to rue de la Visitation, L'Epicerie is at intersection of rue des Fossés and rue de la Visitation.* ⓘ *Credit card min. €15.* Ⓢ *Tartines €3.80-6.20.* Ⓐ *Open daily noon-midnight.*

STAR KEBAB
●⚲ KEBABS ❶
3 pl. St-Anne
☎02 99 79 07 34

An innocuous storefront with pastel blue walls, Star is one the best *kebaberies* around, and one of the cheapest ways to eat in the bumping pl. St-Anne. Vegetarian options available. Take your food to the outdoor seating to people-watch in Pl. Sainte-Anne.

✦ ⓂSainte-Anne. Ⓢ *Sandwiches with fries €3.50-4.50.Plats €7-10.50* Ⓐ *Open daily 11am-1am.*

CRÊPERIE DES PORTES MORDELAISES
✦⚲ CRÊPERIE ❶
6 rue des Portes Mordelaises
☎02 99 30 57 40

This worn-in, family-run crêperie serves quality *galettes* (€2.50-12) right inside the historic Portes des la Mordelaises. The cluttered courtyard proves that most of the proprieter's attention goes to the food. Feel free to get creative, and make your crêpe your own way.

✦ ⓂRépublique. ⓘ *Menu also available in English.* Ⓢ *Most crêpes €6-7.* Ⓐ *Open M, Th-Su noon-2pm and 7pm-11pm.*

CAFÉ BRETON
⚲ CAFE ❸
14 rue Nantaise
☎02 99 30 74 95

Celebrating Rennes' culinary diversity, this high-quality restaurant presents diners with an ever-changing, fabulously creative menu in a stylish dining room. Sit down beneath portraits of soldiers and take in the smells of dishes like *tarte fine au guacamole, confites basilic,* or *capaccio de beouf.*

✦ ⓂRépublique. ⓘ *Reservations recommended on the weekend.* Ⓢ *Entrées €6-7. Plats €12-16.* Ⓐ *Open M, noon-2pm, Tu-Th noon-2pm and 7:30pm-10:30pm, F-Sa noon-2pm and 7:30-11pm.*

LE ST-GERMAIN DES CHAMPS
✦⚲ VEGETARIAN ❸
12 rue du Vau St-Germain
☎02 99 79 25 52

Granola meets homey in this popular organic and vegetarian restaurant. The walls are adorned with ethnic looking tapestries, and the outdoor terrace is set in a calm courtyard. The food is tasty and fresh, and you're guaranteed a healthy dose of feel-good.

✦ ⓂRépublique. ⓘ *Reserve ahead for evenings.* Ⓢ *Sandwiches €5-6. Plats €11-20.* Ⓐ *Open Tu-Sa noon-2:30pm.*

LE NABUCHODONOSOR
⚲✿ CAFE ❷
12 rue Hoche
☎02 99 27 07 58

A small, unpretentious cafe with character serving simple dishes at fair prices. Graphic-art paintings, varied tables and piles of books create artsy charm.

✦ ⓂSainte-Anne. Ⓢ *Tartines €5. Salads and Plats €8-10. Desserts €4.50.* Ⓐ *Open Tu-Sa noon-1am.*

LEON LE COCHON
✦ BISTRO ❸
1 rue Maréchal Joffre
☎02 99 79 37 54 ▣www.leonlecochon.com

Imagine a stylish, modern barn where the animals were dead and seasoned on your plate; that's Leon le Cochon. Conveniently located in the center of Rennes, this elegant, swine-themed restaurant is decorated with happy-looking, unaware pig statues. Vegetarians avoid.

Ⓢ *Entrées €9.50-13.50. Plats€9-28. Formule midi €11.* Ⓐ *Open M-Th noon-2pm and 8-10:30pm, F-Sa noon-2pm and 8-11pm, Su noon-2pm and 8-10:30pm.*

LE PHOENICIEN
✦⚲ LEBANESE, MEDITERRANEAN ❸
22 rue de Saint-Malo
☎02 99 79 27 78 ▣www.lephoenicien.com

Fierce competition between the city's many Lebanese restaurants makes sure those

brittany and normandy

that come out alive are top-notch; Le Phoenicien's tasty *mezzes*, grilled meats, and other Mediterranean specialties are excellent, thanks to natural selection.

✚ ⓜSainte-Anne. *i* Reservations reccommended in the evening. Ⓢ Mezzes €8.50-14.50. Grilled plates €8.50-15. ⓩ Open M-W 6:45pm-midnight, Th-Su noon-2pm and 6:45pm-1am.

NIGHTLIFE

At every turn of Rennes' cobblestoned streets, there seems to be another bar. People spend more time drinking in this college town than anything else. At night, the population seems to double as watering holes swell with students and retired hippies. **rue St.-Michel,** lovingly referred to as rue de la Soif, is the chosen haunt of the young and the restless; **Pl. St-Anne** and **Pl. des lices** are also hot spots for liquoring up. Nightclubs are spread throughout the city, often a little ways outside the city center where streets are a little less populated.

LA CITÉ D'YS
✦ ✹ ⑴ ♨ BAR
31 rue Vasselot ☎02 99 78 24 84

Named after a legendary Breton city, this slightly run-down bar is full of mythic charm. A spiral staircase leads to a sloping flat, lined with decaying couches and young things wearing decaying clothing to match. If you're not up for an alcoholic beverage, this bar also serves 11 different types of hot chocolate. Yum.

✚ ⓜRépublique. *i* Free Wi-Fi. Happy hour 7-8pm; pints €3.50. Ⓢ Teas €2.50. Coffee €1.30. Beer €2.50. ⓩ Open M-Sa noon-1am, Su 3pm-1am.

TY ANNA TAVERNE
✦ BAR, LIVE MUSIC
19 pl. Ste.-Anne ☎02 99 79 05 64

A hang-out for the area's budding musicians, the tavern overflows with guitar-toting types at all hours of the day. Homemade rum punches (€2.50) comes in a variety of flavors, including mint, mango, ginger, and banana.

✚ ⓜSainte-Anne. *i* Credit card min. €10. Live music at 9pm during the week Ⓢ Wine €2.50. Beer €2.50-3.50 ⓩ Open M-Sa 10-1am. Sunday 4pm-1am.

WEBB ELLIS
✦ ✹ ♨ SPORTS BAR
20 pl. des Lices ☎02 99 65 04 07 🖳www.lesitewebb.com

A hip spin on a sports bar, with rugby art and the occasional picture of a naked man (and one naked girl) spray-painted on deep red walls. Beer is available in pitchers (€9-11). Unofficially student night every day of the week, with special rugby nights for the bloodthirsty knee-sock lovers.

i Outdoor seating available. Ⓢ Wine €2.50-3. Beer €3-5. ⓩ Open M-F 10am-1pm, Sa 8am-1am, Su 3pm-1am.

SUNSET CAFE
✦ ✹ ⑴ ♨ BAR
22 rue St. Michel ☎02 99 79 09 63

Sunset Cafe's flashing neon lights and diamond-studded bottles of vodka are deceiving; the bar attracts a laid-back crowd sipping on some of the cheapest pints on rue St.-Michel. Try some of the specialty shots like a *cervelle de single* (Bailey's, vodka, grenadine; €3).

✚ ⓜSainte-Anne. *i* Free Wi-Fi. Ⓢ Wine €2-2.50. Cocktails €2.50 5. Beer €2 2.50; pitchers €12-15. Pints €3-4. Cafe €1 ⓩ Open M-Sa noon-1am, Su 3pm-1am.

L'DETERNAM
✦ ✹ ⑴ ♨ BAR
5,7 rue Saint-Michel ☎02 99 79 13 63

Slightly more expensive than other bars on the street, L'Deternam manages to attract a dreads-wearing, boisterously drunk crowd. It feels more like a place for men who fell off punk and into hippie; reggae plays in the background as you sip your drinks under the low red ceilings.

✚ ⓜSainte-Anne. *i* Free Wi-Fi. Credit card min. €10. Ⓢ Cocktails €6. Pint €4.30-5.70. Bottled beer €3-4. Wine and shots €2.50-3. ⓩ Open M-Sa 11am-1am, Su noon-1am.

BERNIQUE HURLANTE
✦ ✹ ♨ BAR
40 rue Saint-Malo ☎02 99 38 70 09

This quirky watering hole deserves its place on the rowdy rue St.-Malo. The foosball table, shattered glass walls and random objects hanging from the ceiling make the bar even more random, but lovable.

🚇 ⓂSainte-Anne. *i* Credit card min. €10. Ⓢ Cocktails €5-5.50. Beer €2.30-2.50. Wine €2.50. ⓉOpen Tu-Sa 4pm-1am. Su 6pm-1am.

LE CROIX DU SUD
❤ Ⓨ🪑 BAR
42 rue Vasselot
☎02 99 79 69 14
The kind of bar that you treat like your best friend's basement; almost home but not quite, and definitely a good place to get drunk. The well-worn couches downstairs and the slightly teenage crowd definitely contribute to that feeling. Shoot some pool on the billiards table upstairs, or try your hand at chess in the outdoor area.

🚇 ⓂRépublique. Ⓢ Cafe €1.20. Cocktails €4.50. Wine €2.20. Beer €2.30. Ⓣ Open M-Sa 10am-1am.

DÉLICATESSEN
Ⓨ🪑 CLUB
7 Allée Rallier du Baty
☎02 99 78 23 41
Formerly a jailhouse, this club now attracts prisoners of alcohol and electronica. What was once the prison courtyard has been turned into several bars; be sure to check out the neighboring La Tourelle.

🚇 ⓂSainte-Anne. *i* 18+. Ⓢ Cover Tu-Th €5 cover with drink, after 1:30am €10. F-Sa €10 with drink, after 1:30am €15 with drink. Mandatory coat check €2, bags €5. ID required. Ⓣ Open Tu-Sa midnight-5am.

L'ESPACE
Ⓨ▼ CLUB, GAY
45 bld. de la Tour d'Auvergne
☎02 99 30 21 95
Oh, L'Espace. Some things are better after 2am and a round or three of drinks—like grinding to thumping music under video screens, for instance, and the idea of strobe lights, disco balls, and cages. Townees report it's the gay hotspot.

🚇 Enter through the corridor. Ⓢ Th-F students free before 1am, after 1am €8 with drink. Heineken €3. Cocktails €6. Champagne €10. Mandatory coat check €2, bags €5. Prices go up after 2am and on Saturday. Ⓣ Open Th-Sa 11pm-5am.

ARTS AND CULTURE

With as many students as there are in Rennes, you can be sure there are plenty of festivals and concerts to keep them busy.

🎟 LES TOMBÉES DE LA NUIT
FESTIVAL
☎02 99 32 56 56 🖥www.tdn.rennes.fr
A riot of music, theater, mime, dance, interactive performances and general revelry overtakes the city.

Ⓢ Free. Ⓣ First week of July.

FESTIVAL LES MYTHOS
FESTIVAL
☎02 99 79 26 🖥www.festival-mythos.com
A celebration of fairy tales and other oral traditions.

Ⓣ In April.

MUSÉE DE LA DANSE
MUSEUM
38 rue St.-Melaine
☎02 99 63 88 22 🖥www.muséedeladanse.org
We would try to describe Musée de la Danse, but the museum staff has already done a pretty good job of it themselves with the motto painted in their window: "a room where you are free to think about what you are going to do." A self-proclaimed anti-national choreographic center, this challenge to the very idea of a museum functions as a space to think, encounter and do dance. Pretention occasionally abandoned; temporary exhibitions also shown.

🚇 ⓂSainte-Anne. *i* Part of National Choreographic Centers network.

LA CRIÉE
GALLERY
pl. Honoré Commeurec
☎02 23 62 25 10; la-criee@ville-rennes.fr 🖥www.criee.org
With only two galleries, this center for contemporary art can only put on five

brittany and normandy

exhibitions per season. But entrance is free, and if you get hungry Rennes's covered market is right next door.

[M]République. $ Free. ⏰ Open Tu-F noon-7pm and Sa-Su 2pm-7pm. Closed holidays.

SHOPPING

Clothes

CHIC AND TROC — VINTAGE

10 rue de la Psalette ☎02 99 65 48 78

This charming vintage and secondhand store is full of tempting things you may never quite find the right occasion to wear within the ecclectic assortment of brandname shoes, bags, jackets, dresses, and coats.

[M]République. $ €10-895. ⏰ Open M 3pm-7pm, Tu-Sa 10am-1pm and 2-7pm.

KAKI CRAZY — CLOTHES

27-29 rue du Champ Jacquet ☎02 99 79 33 95

A one stop shop for casual clothing, including every type of sweatshirt you could ever want, the sneakers all the French kids wear *(€20-25)*, and underwear if you're running low on clean ones. Have a look at the wide selection of brand name jeans at a slightly cheaper price than competitors *(€60-80)*

[M]Sainte-Anne. $ Shoes €20-€25. ⏰Open M-Sa 10am-7pm.

Jewelry

PALOMA — JEWELRY

9 rue de Nemours ☎02 99 79 08 63

Reminding girls that jewelry is an art form, this small boutique has individual pieces that are colorful, classy, and have character. Fairly priced for a droplet of beauty.

[M]République. $ Earrings €20-65. ⏰ Open M 2-7pm, Tu-Sa 10am-7pm.

LES FILLES — JEWELRY

2 rue Motte Fablet ☎02 99 27 28 55

The French equivalent of Claire's, with a bit more authenticity. Large selection of costume jewelry *(€6-10)*, hats, bags, headbands *(€2)*, and scarves. Piercings also done.

[M]Sainte-Anne. $ Jewelry €6-€10. ⏰ Open M 1pm-7pm, Tu-Sa 10am-7pm.

Books

COMÉDIE DES LANGUES — BOOKSTORE

25 rue de Saint-Malo ☎02 99 36 72 95

This independent bookstore has a rather random collection of English titles, from *Bob Marley: A Complete Guide to His Music* to *Lolita*. Russian, Spanish, Portuguese, Scandanavian and Asian literature also available in French translation.

$ Novels starting around €9. ⏰ Open Tu-Sa 10am-7pm. Closed M from June 6-Aug 31.

LIBRAIRE GREENWICH — BOOKSTORE

1 rue Jean-Jaurès ☎02 99 78 34 90 💻 librariegreenwich@free.fr

Playing on the crossroads between languages, this bookstore specializes in foreign literature in translation. Cultured and cool, the dark wood bookshelves, vines and clean white walls in the small store make for pleasant browsing.

⏰ Open Tu-F 10:30am-12:30pm and 2-7pm, Sa 10:30am-7pm.

ESSENTIALS

Practicalities

- **TOURIST OFFICE:** Free maps, directions, public toilets, and lists of hotels, restaurants, and shops. Info for disabled travelers.(*11 rue St-Yves. From pl. de la République, turn right onto rue George Dottin, then right on rue St-Yves. The office is on the right.* ☎*02 99 67 11 66* 💻www.tourisme-rennes.com *i Lockers €1.*

1-2hr. tours of centre-ville in French Jul-Aug. daily, Sept-June 1-3 per week. Tours in English or Spanish offered Aug, 2 per week. €6.80, students and handicapped €4, under 7 free. Ticket office for tours, festivals, and concerts. ☼Open July-Aug M-Sa 9am-7pm, Su 11am-1pm and 2-6pm; Sept-June M 1-6pm, Tu-Sa 10am-6pm, Su 11am-1pm and -2-6pm.) **France Randonnée,** *(9 rue Portes Mordelaises* ▆www. france-randonnee.fr ⓘ *Info on Grande Randonnée (GR) trails (several daylong to weeklong hikes), as well as shorter walks. ☼ Open from mid-Mar-mid-Oct M-T, W 9:30am-12:30pm, Th-F 10am-12:30pm and 2-6pm, Sa 10am-1pm; from mid-Oct-mid-Mar M-F 10am-12:30pm.)*

- **LAUNDRY: Café Laverie,** *(18 rue de robien* ☎ *02 99 38 86 62 ⓘ Cafe, bar, foosball, and free Wi-Fi. Open T, Th, F 2pm-1am, W 2pm-1am, Sa 3pm-1am.)* Laundromats for mortals at *(23 rue de Penhoët ☼ Open daily 7am-8pm)*, *(59 rue Duhamel ☼ Open daily 7am-10pm)*, and *(3 pl. de Bretagne ☼ Open daily 7am-10pm)*.

- **POST OFFICE:** *(pl. de la République ☎02 23 20 02 05 ☼ Open M 10am-6pm, Tu-F 8:45am-12:15pm and 1:45-6pm, Sa 8:45am-12:15pm.)*

- **POSTAL CODE:** 35000.

Emergency!

- **POLICE:** *(22 bld. de la Tour d'Auvergne* ☎02 99 65 00 22*).*

- **PHARMACY: Pharmacie de la Gare,** *(9 pl. de la Gare* ☎02 99 30 83 27 ☼ *Open M-F 8:30am-7:30pm, Sa 9am-12:30pm).*

- **HOSPITAL: Centre Hospitalier Régional Hôtel Dieu,** *(2 rue de l'Hôtel Dieu* ☎02 99 28 43 21).

Getting There

Trains leave from pl. de la Gare. Info and ticket office open M-Th 5:40am-9:05pm, F 5:40am-9:15pm, Sa 6:45am-8:05pm, Su 7:40am-10:05pm. To: **Caen** *(☼3hr., 4 per day.* Ⓢ€33.)*;* **Nantes** *(☼1-2hr., 6-11 per day.* Ⓢ€22.)*;* **Paris** *(☼2hr., every hr.* Ⓢ€53-65.)*;* **Tours** *(☼2-3hr., every hr.* Ⓢ€37.)*.*

Buses come from 16 pl. de la Gare *(*▆*www.cg49.fr)* right next to the train station serves **Dinan** *(☼1hr., M-Sa 5 per day, Su 4 per day.* Ⓢ *€3.90, reduced €3.10.),* **Angers** *(☼ 2hr., 2 per day.* Ⓢ *€14.60.),* **St-Malo** 2hr. Regional buses run to Mont St-Michel *(☼1hr.; 4 per day* Ⓢ€11.10, under 25 or over 60 €8.30 Open M-Thu 6am-8pm, F 6am-8:15pm, Sa 7am-7:45pm. Closed Sundays but buses still run.)

Getting Around

The easist way to get around Rennes is by foot. Buses are also a good option. **Star** *(12 rue du Pré Botté* ☎08 11 55 55 35 ▆www.star.fr ☼ *Office open M-F 7am-7:30pm, Sa 9am-6:30pm. Buses run M-Sa 5:15am-12:30am, Su 7:25am-midnight.)* To get to Parc des Guyelles, take the #3 bus *(☼ M-Sa every 10 min., Su every 40min., last bus midnight).* Buy tickets on board, at the bus office, or at tabacs. A **Metro** line runs through the heart of Rennes and accepts the same ticket. Taxis pick up at the train station and on pl. de la République. **Guedard** rents bikes. *(13 bld. Beaumont* ☎02 99 30 43 78 Ⓢ *€13 per day. ☼ Open M 2-7pm, Tu-W 9am-12:30pm and 2-7pm, F 10am-7pm, Sa 9am-6:30pm.)*

rouen ☎02

Rouen's spectacular medieval architecture has survived centuries of storms, cold winters, and even a tornado in 1999. These days, an influx of crass moderniza-tion encroaches on the city's historical wonders—try to overlook the excessive numbers of sunglasses boutiques, McDonald's, and Foot Locker outlets—but the town's beauty still persists. There are a few must-sees, including the absolute steal that is the Musée Beaux Arts, the Abbatiale St.-Ouen, the Cathedral, and the Gros Horloge.

ORIENTATION

To get to the *centre-ville* from the **train station,** exit the station onto **pl. Bernard Tissot** and turn onto **rue Jeanne d'Arc,** the city's main thoroughfare. After several blocks and an extraordinary number of (sigh) sunglasses boutiques, you'll arrive at the **rue du Gros Horloge** in the heart of town. Start your tour with a left, leading toward **place de la Cathédrale.** The city's **tourist office** is located on the *place.* After you've collected your free English map, backtrack to the intersection of rue Jeanne d'Arc, and keep walking straight across on rue du Gros Horloge to **place du Vieux Marché,** where Joan of Arc was burned at the stake, and where droves of natives drink beer and catcall tourists for a living. Joan would approve. If you continue down rue Jeanne d'Arc instead, you'll reach the **Seine** and (on the right) the **bus station.** Although there is public transportation, most sights are within easy walking distance—and given the richness of Rouennaise cuisine, walking to burn off the calories isn't necessarily a bad thing.

ACCOMMODATIONS

Accommodations here range from austere and antiseptic rooms in one-star hotels, to overpriced luxury digs, to cozy and well-run family hotels. The best deal in Rouen is without a doubt **Hotel Morand,** which falls into the third category. No matter what hotel you select, make sure to book well in advance. *Let's Go* only recommends the best, so you have to get in line early to guarantee yourself a suitable accommodation. If you plan to spend the weekend in Rouen, reserve ahead and ask about the **"Rouen, vos Week-ends"** deal, an initiative funded by the tourist office. Some hotels also offer seasonal deals on internet purchases or multi-night stays.

👍 HOTEL MORAND
HOTEL ❷

1 rue Morand ☎ 02 35 71 46 07 🖥 www.morandhotel.com

This is the place to be if you're on a budget and looking for a classy option. The hotel is conveniently located across from the Musée Beaux Arts, and is a breezy 5min. walk from downtown. The antique Norman decor gives Hotel Morand an uncommonly swanky and homey ski lodge vibe for a two-star hotel. Wooden beams span the walls of spacious rooms. The owner and his wife speak English, Spanish, and Japanese between them. Amenities include laundry services, a bar, free Wi-Fi, and a delightful living room with a fireplace where visitors can read.

ℹ Breakfast in the dining room €7.50, with room service €8. $ Singles €32.60-47.60; doubles €57.20; triples €70.80. ⏰ Check-out 11am, check-in noon.

HOTEL DES ARCADES
HOTEL ❷

52 rue des Carmes ☎ 02 35 70 10 30 🖥 www.hotel-des-arcades.fr

Conveniently located right near the Cathedral, this cozy one-star offers clean rooms that overlook the action in the heart of downtown Rouen. Rooms are all equipped with at least a *lavabo*, and, for a slightly steeper price, a shower, toilet, hairdryer, and TV.

ℹ Breakfast €6.50. Television €4.50. Phones in rooms €0.40 per min. Wi-Fi included. $ Singles €32-46; doubles €36-54; triples €57. ⏰ Reception 24hr.

HOTEL DE LA CATHÉDRALE
HOTEL ❸

12 rue Saint-Romain ☎ 02 35 71 57 95 🖥 www.hotel-de-la-cathedrale.fr

This lush hotel boasts a leafy garden, a cavernous rustic dining room, and spacious rooms equipped with the works. The hotel really fills up, so make sure to reserve well in advance of your arrival in Rouen, or as it's described on the hotel's site, "this little corner of Normandy." Rooms can accommodate up to five guests with the addition of an extra bed.

ℹ Breakfast €8.50. Free Wi-Fi. $ Singles €56-79; doubles €66-96; triples and quads €119. Extra bed €15. Parking €5 per day.

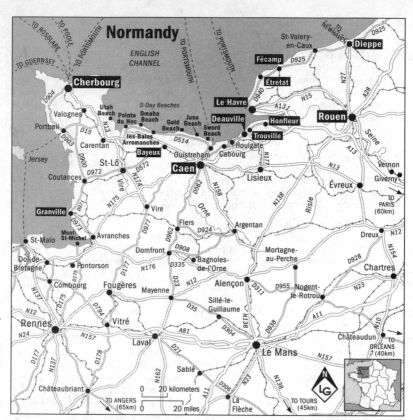

SIGHTS

🖼 MUSÉE BEAUX ARTS
MUSEUM

esplanade Marcel Duchamp, off sq. Verdrel   ☎02 35 71 28 40 💻www.rouen-musées.com

A fantastic, cheap, and almost perpetually uncrowded museum located off the main boulevard in Rouen, Musée Beaux Arts is sure to thrill several different types of art lovers. The museum's permanent collection spans from the 15th to the 21st centuries, so a walk through the exhibits reveals a greatest hits of Western artistic styles; there's a little bit of everything here, from idealized and austere religious paintings to Dutch still lifes to rich 18th-century Italian *tableaux*. More impressively, the Musée Beaux Arts boasts an Impressionist collection second in size only to that of the Musée d'Orsay. The museum attracts some of its visitors simply by virtue of having tableaux from Moreau, Caravaggio, and Delacroix, but the museum also has plenty of slightly quirkier offerings. Keep on the lookout for a comically misplaced 1970s photograph of a Joan of Arc impersonator in a room full of 19th-century paintings, a Jean Baptiste Deshays depiction of an older man indulging in a younger woman's luscious breasts (tween-aged readers, take note), a room dedicated solely to the depiction of hunting, and a chess board (nerd alert!) in the modern painter Marcel Duchamps's salle.

i *16th- and 17th-century collections closed -1-2pm. Special soirées 2nd Th of each month.* ⑤ €5, *ages 18-25 and groups €3, free under 18.* 🕐 *Open M 10am-6pm, W-Su 10am-6pm.*

GROS HORLOGE

rue du Gros Horloge   ☎02 32 08 01 90

You can't miss this gilded 16th-century "Big Clock," located on a bridge across the street that bears its name, rue du Gros Horloge. The spectacle of the tower is dazzling, and the clock continues to keep two types of time. A rotating disk denoted by Greco-Roman divinities marks the passing days, while an orb at the top of the clock marks the moon's phases. An audio tour of the clock and its tower is readily available; the tour culminates in a vista of the roofs of Rouen's medieval architecture.

✦ *Left onto rue du Gros Horloge walking away from the Gare Rouen.* ⓘ *Audio tour 40min.* Ⓢ *€6, ages 6-18 €3, under 7 free.* Ⓓ *Open Tu-Su Apr-Oct 10am-1pm and 2-7pm; Nov-Mar 10am-1pm and 2-6pm. Last entry 1hr. before close.*

CATHÉDRALE NOTRE DAME

CATHEDRAL

3 rue Saint-Romain   ☎02 35 71 85 65 ▣www.cathedrale-rouen.net

The closest thing to a skyscraper in Rouen, this Gothic masterpiece's Lantern Tower is the tallest cathedral spire in France at 495 ft., and it marks nearly unparalleled architectural extravagance. The Tour de Beurre (Tower of Butter) on the righthand side was funded by parishioners, who chose to pay for the extravagance rather than focus on the actual services and go butterless during Lent (sounds like something Americans would have done if we'd been around back in the 16th century). Somehow, the cathedral and its multitude of stained-glass survived the Wars of Religion, French Revolution, and WWII bomb raids. Given these many tests of durability, the cathedral today is in a state of constant renovation and repair; specialists are still cleaning and restoring the statues damaged by a tornado that hit Rouen in 1999. Parts of the church are periodically closed, so check the cathedral's website to see what is being worked on leading up to your visit. Bring your binoculars or bifocals; if you find the keystone that represents Mary and Jesus in the nave, you will allegedly have your craziest prayers answered. Don't miss the tombs of Richard the Lionheart and the first bishop of Rouen inside, and (if you visit in 2010) the oddly misplaced abstract portraits of Korean priest Kim En Joong.

Ⓢ *Free.* Ⓓ *Open Tu-Su 9am-6pm, but respectfully avoid visiting during Mass times, (Tu 10am, W 8am, 10am, Th 10am, F 8am, 10am, Sat 10am, and Su 8:30am, 10:30am, and noon) unless, of course, you plan to worship.*

ABBATIALE ST. OUEN

CHURCH

pl. du Générale de Gaulle

Often confused by lost tourists for the Notre Dame Cathedral because of its gargantuan dimensions, this abbey was founded in the year 750, when, as a French man told *Let's Go*, "America was but a whisper in the testicles of England." A fantastic example of Gothic architecture, the abbey took the better part of the 14th and 15th centuries to construct, and it didn't stop there; the current facade was reconstructed by Henry Gregoire in the middle of the 19th century. For music lovers, the church holds one of the largest organs in the world, a *Cavaillé-Coll* made by Crespin Cartier in 1830 that boasts four keyboards and 64 stops. Famed composer Charles-Marie Widor's *Symphonie Gothique no. 9, op. 70* is dedicated to the organ. A great view of the abbey is to be had from the gardens of the Hotel De Ville.

Ⓢ*Free.* Ⓓ *Open Apr-Oct Tu-Th 10am-noon and 2-5pm, Sa-Su 10am-noon and 2-5pm; Nov-Mar Tu-Th 10am-noon and 2-5:30pm, Sa-Su 10am-noon and 2-5:30pm.*

MUSÉE DE LA CÉRAMIQUE

MUSEUM

1 rue Fauçon   ☎02 35 07 31 74

Located right around the corner from the Musée Beaux Arts on the former site of Hotel d'Hocqueville, the Ceramics Museum is off the beaten path and can be difficult to find. Some travelers report that it's not uncommon to find students smoking things (hint: it's not cigarettes, but not crack) outside the museum. Fear not. It's all

rouen • sights

good. The museum itself has just undergone some serious renovations. Behind the enormous doors of this imposing building is an impressive collection showcasing the development of ceramic art from the 16th through 19th centuries.

Ⓢ €4, under 18 free. ⓩ Open M 10am-1pm and 2-6pm, W-Su 10am-1pm and 2-6pm.

FOOD

Rouen offers a wealth of overpriced brasseries around **pl. du Vieux Marché** and **place de la Cathédrale**; some are better than others, but all serve basic cafe fare at unreasonable prices. If you're in the mood for a kebab or sandwich (and want to save money), there are plenty of cheap and tasty options along **rue de la République** and **rue du Gros Horloge**. If you plan to enjoy a meal on the **pl. du Vieux Marché**, it's better to go to one of the recommended restaurants (you'll pay a bit more, but for a high quality gastronomical experience instead of generic brasserie fare).

🏷 LA COURONNE
FINE DINING ❹

31 pl. du Vieux Marché ☎02 35 71 40 90

Recommended by the tourist office as the place to go for traditional Rouennaise cuisine, La Couronne claims to have been in existence since 1345. The food and elegant atmosphere of this sophisticated restaurant make for quite the splurge, but it's definitely worth it. Housed in the oldest *auberge* in France, this restaurant drips in refinement, snubbing the general public with rich red and gold drapes at dinnertime. The menu offers a wide array of choices, but its specialty is *canard à la Rouennaise à la Presse* (serves 2; €42). Photos and autographs of famous patrons—including Salvador Dalí and Audrey Hepburn—proudly grace the walls. If a meal here isn't in your budget, come for dessert and coffee. Make a reservation for dinner; just about every local and travel guide in town recommends this place.

Ⓢ Lunch and dinner formules €25-48. Appetizers €13-26. Plats €28-67. Desserts €11.40-13. Wines €22-50. ⓩ Open daily noon-2pm and 7-10pm.

POMME D'ÉPICES
TRADITIONAL ❷

66 rue Bouvreuil ☎02 35 71 73 57 🖳www.pommesdepices.fr

Located right across from the Tour Jeanne d'Arc on a quiet side street, but still removed from the touristy bustle along Jeanne d'Arc and the Vieux Marche, this is a cozy family restaurant offering affordable and tasty lunch formules that go with its trademark dessert, *pomme d'epices à la mode*. Formerly just a lunch place, Pomme d'Épices has now expanded to serving dinner. Don't arrive too late for lunch, as it often fills up.

⚡ Across from the Tour de Jeanne d'Arc. ⓘ For dinner, menu is à la carte. Ⓢ 1 plat €10, 2 plats €12, 3 plats €16. Wine bottles €12.50-24.50. ⓩ Open M-W noon-1:45pm, Th-Sa noon-1:45pm and 7-10:30pm.

ROLAND CRÊPERIE
CRÊPERIE ❷

22 rue Saint Nicolas ☎02 32 10 19 76

Looking for a classic Norman *galette* for a hearty meal, or a sweet dessert crêpe to finish off your night just right? Roland Crêperie is located right across from the Cathedral, and offers an intimate two room set-up. Try some of the delicious house ice creams: the *Poire Belle-Helène* combines pear syrup, *chantilly*, and chocolate sauce over vanilla ice cream. Occasionally open on Mondays.

Ⓢ Galettes (salty) €2.30-11. Sweet crêpes €2.30-6.80. Drinks €5.50. ⓩ Open Tu-Sa noon-3pm and 8-11pm.

LE TERRE NEUVAS
SEAFOOD ❸

3 pl. du Vieux marché ☎ 02 35 71 58 21 🖳www.terre-neuvas.fr/

Boasting an outdoors on-ice display of its delicious fresh fruits of the sea, Le Terre Neuvas and its friendly waiters serve customers 365 days a year, either outside on its spacious terrace or in its well lit dining room. The food is delicious, even down to the selections on the cheaper menu (€16.50), but may dishes leave something to be desired in terms of quantity. If you're in the mood for seafood a la Rouennaise, this is the place to be, but you might want to catch a hearty butter-and-something crêpe afterwards.

$ Menus with differingly delicious options €16.50, €28, €38. Tasting plates €18-45. Entrees €12-20. Plats €16-35. Desserts €6.50 with menu. €11 a la carte. Kids' menu €8.50. Wine by the glass €16-19. ⏰ Open daily noon-2pm and 7-11pm.

NIGHTLIFE

PUB YESTERDAY

BAR

3 rue Moulinet ☎02 35 70 43 98

Want a taste of the real Rouen? Pub Yesterday's a beloved local spot, though the highly prized Guinness is hardly the traditional drink of the Rouennaise. Irish music drifts in the background as regulars stop in for a pint after work, or park a bar stool for most of the night. The regulars proudly claim that this is the best Guinness in all of France, since the owner tastes and approves it himself every day. The upstairs is a bit cramped and poorly decorated, but things can get excited and sloppy downstairs in the basement.

$Beer €4.10-6.30. Cocktails €2.30-7.60. ⏰ Open daily 5pm-2am.

L'EURO

CLUB, BAR

41 pl. du Vieux Marché ☎06 28 48 66 53

A chic spot preferred by locals for an after-work *coupe de champagne* (€9.50-10) or a beer. L'Euro has your best interests at heart, providing every cocktail lover with a complimentary carb boost of prosciutto and chips; they don't want customers drinking on an empty stomach. Later at night Thursday-Saturday, L'Euro draws a younger crowd, despite the outrageous price of its red bull supplement (€12). This club space upstairs is used for dancing, and hosts guest DJs regularly. If you get tired of boogying, the downstairs room is perfect for cozying up (hopefully with somebody) in the luscious magenta sofas lining the dimly lit main bar room.

$ Champagne by the glass €9.50-10. Wine by the glass €4-5.50. Cocktails €3.50-7.50. ⏰ Open daily -3pm--2am.

ESSENTIALS

Practicalities

- **TOURIST OFFICE:** *(25 pl. de la Cathédrale 🖥 www.rouentourisme.com).* In the oldest Renaissance building in Rouen. Free English map. Currency exchange available. *($ €2.50 commission ⏰ M-Sa 9am-noon and 1:30-6:30pm.)* The French-language guide *Le Viking*, published once a year in Sept, lists local hot spots.
- **TOURS:** Audio tours of the city available in English for €5 from the tourist office. *(⏰ Open May-Sept M-Sa 9am-7pm, Su 9:30am-12:30pm and 2-6pm; Oct-Apr M-Sa 9:30am-12:30pm and 1:30-6pm.)*
- **CURRENCY EXCHANGE AND ATMS:** Banks line rue Jeanne d'Arc, including **BNP Paribas.** *(40 rue Jeanne d'Arc ☎08 20 82 43 00 ⏰ Open Tu-F 8:45am-noon and 1:30-5:45pm, Sa 8:45am-1:30pm.)* There are **ATMs** across from the train station. **Société Genérale.** *(34 rue Jeanne d'Arc ☎02 35 70 03 97)*
- **YOUTH CENTER:** Centre Régional Information Jeunesse (CRIJ). Provides information for young people interested in working, volunteering, or living in the region for 1 month or more. *(84 and 94 rue Beauvoisine 🖥www.crij-haute-normandie.org ⏰ Open Tu-F 10am-6pm; closed for 3 weeks in July and Aug)*
- **LAUNDROMAT:** *(56 rue Cauchoise near pl. du Vieux Marché. $Wash €3.70-8,70, dry €1 per 11min. ⏰Open daily 7am-9pm. Other locations on av. Pasteur near pl. de la Madeleine or 55 rue d'Amiens. Same prices and hours.)*
- **PUBLIC TOILETS:** *(pl. du Vieux Marché $ Free. ⏰ Open Tu-Sa 8-11:45am and 1:30-6pm.)*

- **INTERNET ACCESS:** Cyber@Net (*47 pl. du Vieux Marché, near Église St-Maclou. ☎02 77 76 90 21 $€1 per 15min., €5 per 3hr. if you buy the "Gamer" package. ⏰ Open M 2:30pm-12:30am, Tu-Th 10:30am-12:30am, F-Sa 10:30am-3am, Su 2:30pm-12:30am.)* **E-mega.** (*50 rue de la République $ €1 per 15min., €3 per hr. ⏰Open M-F 1pm-12:30am, Sa 3pm-2am, Su 3pm-12:30am.)*
- **POST OFFICE:** (*45bis rue Jeanne d'Arc, to the left of the train station ☎02 32 10 55 60 ⏰Open M-W 8:45am-6pm, Th 9:15am-6pm, F 8:45am-6pm, Sa 9am-noon.)*
- **POSTAL CODE:** 76000

Emergency!

- **POLICE:** (*9 rue Brisout de Barneville, across Seine from centre-ville ☎02 32 81 25 00)*
- **PHARMACY:** Grande Pharmacie du Centre (*29 pl. de la Cathédrale ☎02 35 71 33 17 ⏰Open M 10am-7:30pm, Tu-F 9am-7:30pm, Sa 9am-7pm)*
- **HOSPITAL:** Hôpital Charles Nicolle (*1 rue de Germont ☎02 32 88 89 90)*

Getting There

By Train

The train station is on rue Jeanne d'Arc, at pl. Bernard Tissot. *(⏰ Main office open M-Sa 8am-6:30pm; smaller office open M-F 5:30am-10pm, Sa 6:30am-10pm, Su 6:45am-10:30pm; ticket office open M-F 5:10am-9pm, Sa 5:50am-9pm, Su 6:10am-10:30pm.)* Trains run to **Caen** *($ €22. ⏰ 1-2hr., 5-9 per day.)* and **Paris.** *($ €19.30. ⏰ 1hr., every hr.)*

By Bus

VTNI/TVS has a station at 11 rue des Charrettes. *(☎0800 25 07 60 27 ⏰ Ticket office open M-Sa 8am-6pm.)* Buses run to various towns in the area. All tickets cost €2.

Getting Around

TCAR operates the **public transportation** in Rouen, including a subway and municipal buses. *(9bis rue Jeanne d'Arc 💻www.tcar.fr $ 1hr. ticket €1.40; 1-day pass €4, carnet of 10 €11.* ⏰ Open M-Sa 7am-7pm. Most buses run 6am-10pm. Night bus runs Sept-June M-Th 11pm-1am, F-Sa 11pm-3:30am, Su 11pm-1am. Subway open 5am-11pm.) There are always plenty of **taxis,** including **Radio Taxis** *(8 av. Jean Rondeaux ☎02 35 88 50 50),* at the train and bus stations as well as on rue Jeanne d'Arc. **Cyclic,** offered by the city of Rouen, rents **bikes.** *(40 rue Orbe ☎02 35 07 94 80 💻www.cylclic.fr ℹ Credit card required. $ €1 per 30min. 1st hr. €2, €4 per hr. thereafter.)*

brittany and normandy

mont st-michel ☎02 33

Rising out of a vast expanse of sand at lowtide and water at hightide, the island of Mont St-Michel immediately elicits images of medieval grandeur and timeless majesty, replete with monks, knights and desperate damsels. It's really no wonder that pilgrims in the Middle Ages considered Mont St-Michel (mohn-sehn-mee-shell; pop. 50) to be an image of paradise on earth, and were willing to risk their lives against the treacherous tides to try to get to it. A trip inside the millennium-old abbey, with or without a tour, is an indispensable part of the experience; no less intoxicating are the panoramic views from its fortified walls. Expanses of sandy marshland seem to extend into the horizon, with the perfectly preserved Mont standing out in idyllic isolation.

ORIENTATION

Situated on the border between Brittany and Normandy, Mont St-Michel is a small island connected to the mainland by a sturdy causeway. **Grande rue** is its only major street, which leads up to the entrance to the **Abbey. Pontorson,** 9km due south down D976, has the closest **train station,** as well as several affordable hotels; there's also a **supermarket** (open daily 8am-8pm) and cheap cabins at the **campground** across the causeway, 1.8km from the Mont. There's no public transportation off the Mont after 8pm, and the last bus to Rennes leaves at 5:25pm. Biking to or from Pontorson takes about 1hr. on terrain that is relatively flat but not always bike-friendly; the path next to the **Coucsnon River** is the best route.

ACCOMMODATIONS

👍 CAMPING DU MONT ST-MICHEL

🎟 📶 CAMPGROUND [1]

☎02 33 60 22 10 🖥www.camping-montsaintmichel.com

Back in the days when people made pilgrimages, they would walk for miles to reach the Mont, surviving on the bare essentials. Camping here puts you far enough out of town to re-invoke that pilgrim spirit, but Camping du Mont St-Michel adds some 21st-century comforts. This is the closest affordable lodging to the Mont, with spotless dorms and great facilities. At night, you can see the dramatically illuminated Abbey. Only supermarket around is located next door.

🪧 1.8km from the Mont on route du Mont St-Michel. Get off at caserne, the stop before the Mont, on Manéo line 6 from Pontorson. ℹ Laundry wash €4.50, dry €1.90. Wi-Fi at adjoining Hôtel Motel Vert €3 per 30min., €5 per hr. [$] €3.60-4.30 per person, children €2-2.50; €5.30-6.50 per site. Electricity €2.10-2.80. Dorms €9. Bikes €5 per hr., €8.30 per ½ day, €16.40 per day. ⏰ Open Feb-mid Nov. Reception 24hr. Gates closed -11pm--6:30am.

CAMPING HALIOTIS

🎟 📶 CAMPGROUND [1]

chemin des Soupirs ☎02 33 68 11 59 🖥www.camping-haliotis-mont-saint-michel.com

Whoever said camping was hard was wrong—the three-star cabins and camp sites here might as well be part of a luxurious mini-resort. If you get tired of the abbey, Camping Haliotis boasts a heated pool, hot tub, sauna, tennis and volleyball courts, game room, bar, and a playground with a bouncy castle, badminton, and ping pong tables.

🪧 In Pontorson. ℹ Breakfast €5. Laundry €3, dry €2. Wi-Fi free. [$] €5-6 per person, children €2-3.50; €6-7 per tent and car or RV. Electricity €2.50-3. Cabins €18.50-26. Mobile homes also available. Bike rental €5 per 1/2-day, €9 per day. ⏰ Open Apr-Nov. Reception -7:30am--10pm.

SIGHTS

ABBEY

🎟 ABBEY

At the end of Grande rue ☎02 33 89 80 00

Named after the archangel Saint Michael, who in the Christian tradition is responsible for driving the devel out of heaven, Mont St-Michel's illustrious abbey dates back to 708. Well before the time of highways, Christians would make the treacherous 7km trip to the mount, walking fast to beat the tide. If they made it, they considered getting to heaven a done deal. If, however, the quicksand sucked them under, then it was thought that the Devil had pulled the wayward pilgrims down to hell. The tides continue to be a perilous force here; the biggest in Europe, they come in horizontally at a stunning 1m per second. Luckily, cars and roads have made life easier here. Travelers can now easily visit the village, which grew up around the abbey in the 14th century, and the impressive structure itself; the church is a product of ingenious planning, considering the incredible constraints of its hilltop location. The entire building rests on only 200 square meters of solid rock; the choir, both sides of the transept, and the entire nave are held up by pillared crypts below the church floor.

During the Revolution, when Frenchmen weren't too keen on God, the monks couldn't bear to sell the stones of the monastery as many others did. Instead, they sold their souls, allowing the abbey to be used as a prison in 1863. The **Chapelle Saint-Martin** under the Southern transept, became a cistern; next door, the abbey's **ossuary**—once filled with the bones of deceased monks—was converted into a supply depot. Wardens forced two to four incarcerated men to walk like hamsters on the **giant wheel** that is now on display; the conversion of their muscular energy then pulled supplies up the side of the walls on a sled. In 1874, the abbey was classified as a historic monument, and there was another selling out—this time to the tourist industry. Forgetting the ascetic life the monks once held here, chattering imbeciles rush through the **refrectory**, where the monks once took their meals in silence. Don't be surprised by the loud and color-coordinated school groups in the **Chapelle Saint-Étienne**, or the chapel of the dead, where deceased monks rotted down to bones before being moved to the ossuary. Still, the abbey is a magnificent structure, as are the gardens that cling to the side of the eigth-century rock on which it was built.

Ⓢ *Free for handicapped and companion. €8.50, ages 18-25 €5, 18-25 EU citizens and under 18 free. 1st Su of the month free. Tours free. Audio tour €4. ☼ Open daily May-Aug -9am--7pm; Sept-Apr -9:30am--6pm. Last entrance 1hr. before close. Tours of abbey daily; 2 in English (11 am and 3 pm), 8 in French; more in summer. Tours of crypts daily July-Aug; Sept-June Sa-Su 1hr. Mass daily 12:15pm, Su 11:30am; enter for service 15min. before.*

FOOD

LA SIRÈNE
Grande rue
🗣⊗♆(ᵗᵖ) CRÊPERIE ❷
☎02 33 60 08 60
After walking through the boutique entrance and sitting at one of the long bench-like tables, you may feel like a tourist, but at least you won't feel like the dumb, bank-breaking ones next door.
✦ *Entrance through the boutique.* 𝒊 *Wi-Fi available.* Ⓢ *Galettes €2.50-8.50. ☼ Open M-W 10am-6pm, Th-Sa 9:30am-9pm, Su 10am-6pm.*

LE GRILLON
37 rue Couesnon
🗣♆ BRASSERIE ❶
☎02 33 60 17 80
The place where all 10 residents of Pontorson gather. Just about the only place close to the Mont that's affordable.
✦ Ⓜ*Pontorson.* Ⓢ *Dinner and dessert crêpes €1.95-4.50. Galettes €6.25-8. Salads €2.50-7.20. ☼ Open M-W noon-2:30pm and 6:30-9:30pm, F-Su noon-2:30pm and 6:30-9:30pm.*

ESSENTIALS
Practicalities

- **TOURIST OFFICE:** Mont St-Michel's tourist office (*Located at the start of Grand rue* ☎*02 33 60 14 30* 🖥*www.ot-montsaintmichel.com*). The helpful multilingual staff provides info on sights and lodging. Currency exchange is also available. (☼ *Open July-Aug daily 9am-7pm; Sept M-Sa 9am-6pm, Su 9am-noon and 2-6pm; Oct-Mar M-Sa 9am-noon and 2-6pm, Su 10am-noon and 2-5pm; Apr-June M-Sa 9am-12:30pm and 2-6:30pm, Su 9am-noon and 2-6pm*). There's also an office in **Pontorson** (*pl. de l'Hôtel de Ville, off rue St-Michel* ☎*02 33 60 20 65* 🖥*www. mont-saint-michel-baie.com*). Offers free maps and info on walking tours, accommodations, and the Mont (𝒊 *Internet €4.50 per 30min., €8 per hr.* ☼ *Open M-Th 9:15-11:45am and 2:30-7pm, F-Sa 3:45-7:30pm, Su 1:30-7:30pm*)

- **LAUNDROMAT:** (*rue St-Michel* ☎*02 33 49 60 66*). Pontorson (*Next to the Carrefour* Ⓢ *Wash €4-10, dry €1 per 10min.* ☼*Open daily 7am-9pm*)

- **PUBLIC TOILETS:** By the Mont tourist office. (Ⓢ*€0.40*) Pontorson. (*In the train station* Ⓢ*Free.*)

- **POST OFFICE:** (*Grande rue about 100m inside the walls* ☎*02 33 89 65 00 Cur-*

rency exchange available ⏰ Open July-Aug M-Sa 9am-5:30pm, Su 9am-12:15pm and 1:15-5:30pm; from Sept-mid-Nov; June M-F 9am-5:30pm, Sa 9am-4pm; Mar-May M-F 9am-noon and 2-5pm.) Pontorson (*18 rue St-Michel across from the tourist office ☎02 33 89 17 76 ⏰ Open M-F 8:30am-noon and 2-5:30pm, Sa 8:30am-noon.)*

- **POSTAL CODE:** 50170

Emergency!

- **POLICE:** (*☎02 33 89 72 00 on duty in July-Aug to left of the Porte de l'Avancée before you enter the Mont*) Also in Pontorson (*2 chaussée de Ville Chérel*)
- **MEDICAL SERVICES:** (*7 chaussée de Ville Chérel in Pontorson ☎02 33 89 40 00*)

Getting There

The only way to get to Mont St-Michel by **train** is through **Pontorson**. Station is at Pl. de la Gare, Pontorson. (*⏰ Open M-Sa 9am-noon and 3-6:60pm, Su 1:20-7:35pm.)* To: **Caen** (*$ €24.50 ⏰ 2hr., 2 per day)*; **Paris** (*$ €47.70 ⏰ 4hr., 1-3 per day)* via **Caen**; Alternatively, buses from **Rennes** (*💻www.illenoo.fr) ($ €11.10⏰1 hr., 4 per day)* can be taken directly to the Mont.

Getting Around

Veolia Manéo (*💻www.cg50.fr*). **Buses** leave Mont St-Michel from the entrance at Porte de l'Avancée and leave Pontorson from pl. de la Gare. Shuttles between Pontorson and the Mont run 7 times per day; more July-Aug. The first bus from Pontorson is at 6:54am, and the last bus from the Mont is around 6:20pm. (*$ €2.20; tickets available on board.)* Its subsidiary Illenoo (www.illenoo.fr) runs to Rennes (*⏰ 1hr.; M-Sa 6 per day, Su 1 per day. $ €3.50*) and St-Malo (*⏰ 1hr., 2-3 per day. $ €2.50*).

caen ☎02 31

At the end of WWII, three-quarters of Caen (KAI-ehn; pop. 200,000) had been destroyed and two-thirds of its citizens were left homeless. The city of William the Conqueror has since been skillfully restored to its pre-war condition and is now part historical monument, part sizzling university city of busy bars and brasseries. It makes a good base from which to explore the D-Day beaches and has a decidedly younger feel and cheaper prices than its neighbors along the Côte Fleurie.

ORIENTATION

Caen's **train station** and **youth hostel** are relatively far from the ***centre-ville*** (1km and 3km, respectively). Ambitious travelers can walk from the station, but it's best to take the tram or bus to and from the hostel. Trams stop running just after midnight, so plan accordingly. The **two tram lines,** A and B, leave from the train station and cut through the centre-ville; take either line to St-Pierre (5min.). The St-Pierre stop is on bld. des Alliés, which intersects avenue du 6 Juin and rue Saint-Jean. These parallel streets run toward the *centre-ville* and border the lively districts between rue Saint-Pierre and rue de l'Oratoire.

ACCOMMODATIONS

HOTEL DE L'UNIVERS HOTEL [3]

12 quai Vendeuvre ☎02 31 85 46 14 💻www.hotelunivers-caen.com

Without a doubt, this is the best place to stay in Caen. The owner who recently bought the hotel used to work as a lights man for concerts and spectacles around Europe. His experience traveling in hotels inspired him to open this gem in the middle of downtown Caen, providing a friendly environment, cheap prices, a convenient location, and beautiful airy rooms. Americans take note: there's a room set aside for you if you reserve a few months in advance. A double on the top floor, the "New York room" boasts a beautiful view of the port, as well as paintings of New York on the walls and...the shower curtains. Great stay, friendly service.

 # Off the Bassin St-Pierre. i Reserve in advance. Only 21 rooms available. $ Doubles €48-57; quads €62. ⏰ Reception M-F 7:15am-10pm, Sa-Su 8:30am-10pm.

HOTEL IBIS ♿ HOTEL 3

33 rue de Bras ☎02 31 50 00 00 www.ibishotel.com

One of the benefits of staying in a chain is knowing exactly what you're going to get, and at Ibis it's friendly service, clean, decently spacious rooms, and quite a few older customers. The chain boasts three hotels in the D-Day beaches area; this one is the most central to Caen. The hotel has a cozy bar perfect for a nightcap after a long day on the beaches.

 # Facing the marina downtown. i Breakfast €8. Recommended to book at least two months in advance. $ Singles and doubles €64-85. ⏰ Reception and bar open 24hr.

HOTEL DE LA PAIX HOTEL 1

14 rue Neuve St-Jean ☎02 31 86 18 99

The prices are just right at this small, no frills accommodation near the château. A deliciously saggy black leather couch and a mirror grace the lobby, just in case you wanted to spend your time in beautiful Caen indoors admiring yourself.

 # Off avenue du 6 Juin, near the château. i Breakfast €5. Extra bed at €8. Reserve ahead in summertime. $ Singles €29-35; doubles €32-39; triples €40-41. ⏰ Reception 24hr.

AUBERGE DE JEUNESSE: RÉSIDENCE ROBERT RÈME HOSTEL 1

68 rue Eustache Restout ☎02 31 52 19 96 www.fuaj.org/Caen

Like most HI hostels, Résidence Robert Rème is about 3km from the center of town. Guests at this spot sacrifice convenience for quite possibly the lowest accommodation prices in all of France. This spot boasts spacious 4-person single-sex rooms with toilets, sinks, and showers. There is a communal kitchen and TV room.

 # Take tram B to Rostand-Fresnel, walk half a block to the roundabout, and turn right onto rue Armand Marie. Make another right on rue Restout. $ Dorms €11. Breakfast €2. Linen €2.50. Laundry €3. ⏰ Reception open 5-9pm.

SIGHTS

MEMORIAL DE CAEN MUSEUM, MEMORIAL

☎02 31 06 06 44 www.memorial-caen.fr

By far the best of any of the (too many) WWII Memorial Museums, the Memorial de Caen uses a striking set of visual exhibits to immerse visitors in the historical moment, allowing them to feel the war's significance, human impact, and legacy. After a few hours here, you should have all the WWII info you need to furnish the rest of your D-Day beach tours. The Memorial is unlike any other WWII museum you have ever visited; its portrayal of the lead-up to the war seriously questions the resolve of the French in the face of German occupation, examines the propaganda used to support Hitler's genocide, and pays homage to American and British involvement. The Museum does not end at WWII, however, and it contains a fantastic exhibition on the aftermath of WWII and the arrival at the Cold War. Finally, there is a silent film that plays every 40min. Plan to allot a few hours to this visit. It's worth it.

$ The memorial's price system operates on a high-season (May-September) and low-season (October-April) system. All prices listed below are €0.50 more expensive during high season. Adults €17, reduced tarif €14.50, visit and lunch in memorial's cafe €21.50, visit and lunch in memorial's restaurant €29.50, under 10 free. i Written guide €5. Audio tour €3. Available in 7 languages. ⏰ Open Jan Tu-Su 9:30am-6pm; Feb-Oct daily 9am-7pm; Nov-Dec Tu-Su 9:30am-6:30pm.

CHÂTEAU
Allée du Chat Qui Veille

            HISTORIC MONUMENT
☎02 31 30 47 70

Work on the Château began all the way back in the 11th century under the direction of William the Conqueror, the duke of Normandy. Throughout the hundreds of intervening years and proprietors, the Château was gradually improved and fortified. In 1182, a Grand Christmas Court was held here; Henry II and his sons, Richard the Lionheart and John Lackland, hosted over 1000 knights. In 1204, it was surrendered along with the rest of Normandy to King Phillip Augustus of France. Today, however, chivalry has departed from the Castle. You're now more likely to find local kids drinking beer and smoking joints on its premises; it might be difficult to imagine what the Kings would say about these uncouth activities, but then that's why they were ousted in the Revolution. Luckily, however, the Castle survived the Revolution and some bombing in WWII to provide beautiful views of Caen from its ramparts. And if you're lucky, the drunkard who stands in a back alley all day to wave at tourists might not be passed out, and you might even get to have a conversation with him (French required).

Today, the Château grounds are home to a few other sights: the **Musée des Beaux Arts de Caen**, the **Musée de Normandie**, the **Saint Georges Church**, the **Echiquier de Normandier** (Exchequer of Normandy), and the **Jardin des Simples**. The Church was built back in the 10th century, but only a few vestiges of its original architecture remain. Nonetheless, these small remnants are rather fantastic: the walls of the nave and some Roman windows remain from the 10th to 12th centuries. Important renovations in the 15th and 16th centuries left the church as it is today. It remains a rare example of medieval Church architecture. The Jardin des Simples showcases medicinal plants from the Middle Ages, but is wholly unremarkable, beyond being a shady retreat from the midday heat.

⑤ *Free.* ⌚ *Open M and W-Su 9:30am-6pm.*

MUSÉE DES BEAUX ARTS DE CAEN
Inside the Château

         ✦ **MUSEUM**
☎02 31 30 47 70 ▪www.mba.caen.fr

Located in a somewhat obnoxiously modern building inside the Château's grounds, the Museum of Fine Arts of Caen has a tremendous collection to offer to visitors. The repertoire of the free permanent collection encompasses 15th-20th century Western art. The early stuff is fantastic: you don't want to miss "La Vierge à L'Enfant," by Cosme Tura, and the "Marriage de la Vierge" by Pérugin. It houses works by some famous French painters, including Charles Le Brun, the man responsible for decoration at Château Vaux-le-Vicomte and Versailles. Household names from the 19th and 20th centuries—think Delacroix, Monet, and Boudin—all hold permanent real estate here. The museum boasts probably the most French painting ever created, even though the artist is Italian (Mimmo Paladino): the 1948 tableau entitled *A L'Huile et Pain Sur Étoile*, which actually has pieces of bread on it. Be careful, while in the permanent collection, not to accidentally wander into the temporary collection, which you have to pay to enter; given that borders between the two don't exist, it's easy to do so, and you'll get a huge stinkeye from the security staff.

⑤ *Permanent collection free. Temporary exhibit €5.20, students €3.20. under 18 free.* ⌚ *Open M and W-Su 9:30am-6pm.*

LE MUSÉE DE NORMANDIE
Inside the Château

         MUSEUM
☎02 31 30 47 60 ▪www.musée-de-normandie.eu

The Musée de Normandie is a hidden gem in the Castle. Curiously, despite the Museum's free entry, few visitors choose to venture inside. As the French would say, *tant pis* (too bad for them)! The Museum tells the story of Normandy starting from 1000 B.C.E. The Museum shows everything from ancient tools used in the neolithic ages, to diaramas of Norman villages, to warrior helmets from

caen • sights

the Bronze Age (1100-900 B.C.E.), to religious sculptures and art in the 4th-7th centuries. The Museum also contains old WWII memoribilia, and some splendid Norman ceramic pottery that will have artistically attuned housewives drooling on the floor. This is a great visit to make before you tour the D-Day beaches.
💲 Free. 🕘 Open M 9:30am-6pm, W-Su 9:30am-6pm.

FOOD 🍴

It's difficult to find quality cuisine in Caen, given the fact that almost the entire restaurant industry services tourists. There are plenty of fast food places throughout the city; sit-down restaurants are almost never cheap. However, there are a few prime spots worth checking out.

BOEUF ET COW — 💳🍸 TRADITIONAL [3]

6 bld. des Alliés — ☎02 31 86 37 75 💻www.boeufandcow.fr

Located right across from the château, Boeuf et Cow proposes hearty portions of tasty, fresh meat at decent prices during lunchtime. The staff is usually quick and capable. Situated conveniently on one of Caen's major thoroughfares, the terrace affords a fantastic opportunity for some rich people watching.
➔ From train station, take Avenue du 6 Juin until you reach Boulevard des Alliés, and turn left. ℹ Vegetarians might prefer dining elsewhere. 💲 Plat, dessert, cafe €14.50, plat and cafe €9.50, entree, plat, dessert €25. Wine bottles €18-49. Beer €3.50-4.50. Cocktails €6.50-7.50.

LA TRATTORIA — 💳🍸 ITALIAN [2]

13 rue du Vaugueux — ☎02 31 47 97 01

Situated in the heart of Caen's tourist district, La Trattoria serves tasty Italian food in a cozy, lush setting. The terrace provides a great place to watch the history nerds walk by. Nothing remarkable, but you'll leave full, with a little money in your pocket and some lasting characters in mind.
➔ From the train station, take rue de la Gare to Pont Winston Churchhill. Continue onto Avenue du 6 Juin, and turn right at Boulevard des Alliés. Continue onto Avenue de la Libération. Turn left on rue du Vaugueux. 💲 Lunch €14-19, menu a l'italienne (entree, plat, dessert) daily at any meal €26. Entrees €8-11. Pasta €11-15. Wines €17.50-27.50.

AU MAITRE CORBEAU — 💳🍸 TRADITIONAL, FROMAGERIE [3]

8 rue Buquet — ☎02 31 93 93 00 💻www.caen.maitre-corbeau.com

Cows are the name of the game at Au Maitre Corbeau; they grace photos and paintings on the wall, the napkins, and are even caricatured in a few sculptures. The restaurant boasts two floors of dining rooms; both are spacious and comfortable. Diners should not be cowed by all these cows, but rather by the *oeuf cocotte*, a delicious yet dangerously filling cheese appetizer, consisting of three eggs in a soup a melted cheese of your choice. If you plan to enjoy one of the Maitre Corbeau's delicious, artfully decorated main courses to the fullest extent, stay away from an appetizer; they're delicious but won't leave you with much maneuvering room. The cheese fondues *(€14.10-14.40)* are legendarily delicious, and despite the menu's advice, can be comfortably be shared by three or four participants.
➔ From the train station, take rue de la Gare to Pont Winston Churchhill. Continue onto Avenue du 6 Juin, and turn right at Boulevard des Alliés. Continue onto Avenue de la Libération. Turn right at rue Montoir Poissonnerie, and then right on rue Buquet. 💲 Menu midi entree, plat or plat, dessert €10. Dinner €21-25. Entrees €6-8.60. Salads €8-14. Plates €8.50-18.60. Desserts €5.80-7.40.

AU P'TIT GRUMEAU — 💳🍸⛅ CRÊPERIE [2]

3 rue du Vaugueux — ☎02 31 93 64 75 💻www.auptitgrumeau.e-monsite.com

Tucked cozily into the restaurant-laden rue du Vaugueux, Au P'tit Grumeau offers deliciously tasty and hearty crêpes. Nothing out-of-this-world, but the *galettes* are stuffed with meat, and sweet crêpes are doused in *chantilly* (whipped cream). Help is friendly and quick. Come with three friends and grab one of the coveted tables on the terrace bordering the rue du Vaugueux.

⇄ From the train station, take rue de la Gare to Pont Winston Churchhill. Continue onto Avenue du 6 Juin, and turn right at Boulevard des Alliés. Continue onto Avenue de la Libération. Turn left on rue du Vaugueux. $ Formule midi €11.50 for galette, crêpe or salad, crêpe. Galettes (salty crêpes) €8.40-12. Sweet crêpes €2.80-6.30. Salads €8.40-12. Beer €3.50-4. ⏰ Open Tu-Sa noon-3pm and 7pm-late.

NIGHTLIFE

DUBLIN — BAR

bld. des Alliés ☎02 31 85 79 87

Dublin has a prime real estate terrace on Quai Vendeuvre, a main thoroughfare in Caen, and a cozy, chic indoors barroom which just might turn into a dancefloor on Friday and Saturday nights. There is also an oddly separate windowed room in the back for...who knows?

$ Cocktails and beer €3-5.50. ⏰ Open 6pm-4am.

CAFE DES BRUMES — CAFE, BAR

21-23, bld. des Allies ☎02 31 95 20 83

Boasting a scenic terrace on one of Caen's main party thoroughfares, Cafe des Brumes offers a fun student vibe. Hip-hop and house music rattle the barroom as students' conversations progressively become slower-paced and more scandalous.

$ Happy hour pint €4. Coupe champagne €4.50. Verre de vin €2.50. ⏰ Open daily 9am-1am.

ESSENTIALS

Practicalities

- **TOURIST OFFICE:** Hotel booking, useful brochures, and free maps. Sortir à Caen, printed every 3 months, lists concerts and events. *(12 pl. St-Pierre ☎02 31 27 14 14 🖥www.tourisme.caen.fr)*
- **TOURS: Le Petit Train Touristique.** 45min. bus tour in French and English. *($€5, under 12 €4. ⏰ Runs June-September daily 10am-noon and 2-7pm; Apr-May Th-Su 10am-noon and 2-7pm.)*
- **INTERNET ACCESS: L'Espace.** *(1 rue Basse ☎02 31 93 37 14)*
- **POST OFFICE:** *(pl. Gambetta ☎02 31 85 11 95 ℹ Currency exchange available.)*
- **POSTAL CODE:** 14000.

Emergency!

- **POLICE:** *(10 rue Thiboud de la Fresnaye ☎02 31 29 22 22).*
- **PHARMACIES: Pharmacie Danjou-Rousselot.** *(5 pl. Malherbe ☎02 31 30 78 08 🖥www.danjourousselot.com)*
- **HOSPITAL: Centre Hospitalier Univsersitaire.** *(av. Côte de Nacre ☎02 31 06 31 06)*

Getting There

Caen's **train** station is located at pl. de la Gare *(⏰ Ticket office open 5am-8:30pm.)* Trains run to **Cherbourg** *($ €19.50. ⏰ 1hr., 7 per day)*; **Paris** *($ €31.20. ⏰ 2hr., 11 per day)*; **Rennes** *($ €32.50. ⏰ 3hr., 2 per day)*; **Rouen** *($ €23.10. ⏰ 1hr., 5-9 per day)*; and **Bayeux** *($€4.25, under 26 €3.60. ⏰ 1hr., M-F 3 per day).*

Buses run by Bus Verts *(☎08 10 21 42 14)* leave from the *gare routière*to the left of the train station *(⏰ Open July-Aug M-Sa 7:30am-7pm, Su 9am-3pm; Sept.-June M 6:30am-7pm, Tu-F 7:30am-7pm, Sa 8:30am-7pm)* and a kiosk at pl. Courtonne *(⏰ Open M 7:30am-7pm, Tu-F 7:45am-7pm, Sa 9am-7pm).* Bus destinations include **Bayeux** *($ €4.25, under 26 €3.60. ⏰ 1hr., M-F 3 per day).* The **Carte Liberté** gives unlimited rides in a set period. There is also a day pass *($ €13. ⏰ 3 days €25.16, 1 week €36.12.)*

Getting Around

Twisto, the local bus and tram system, supplies schedules and maps at its information office, across the street fron the château *(15 rue de Geôle ☎02 31 15 55 55 💻www.twisto.fr 💲 Tickets €1.20, pack of 10 €10.60, 1-day pass €3.55, 3-day pass €7. ⏰ Open July 15-Aug. 15 M-F 9am-5pm; Aug. 16-July 14 M-F 8am-6:30pm, Sa 10am-12:30pm and 1:30-5pm. Hours vary by season.)* The city's two **tram lines,** A and B, leave from the train station and cut through the *centre-ville (5min.)* Take either line to the St-Pierre stop on bld. des Alliés, which intersects avenue du 6 Juin and rue Saint-Jean. These parallel streets run toward the *centre-ville*, and border the lively districts between rue Saint-Pierre and rue de l'Oratoire. **Taxis** are also readily available; try **Abbeilles Taxis Caen,** which runs 24hr *(52 pl. de la Gare ☎02 31 52 17 89).* There's also a **late-night taxi stand** at bld. Maréchal Leclerc near rue St-Jean. *(⏰ Open daily -10pm--3am.)*

bayeux ☎02 31

Bayeux (bah-yuh; pop. 28,000) may be most famous for its 900-year-old tapestry narrating William the Conqueror's victory over England, but the lively city offers more than historical needlework. After narrowly escaping the devastation of WWII and surviving both Nazi occupation in 1940 and Allied liberation in 1944, Bayeux today retains its charming architecture and a resplendent cathedral. The city's Old World atmosphere, pleasant—if slightly touristy—pedestrian byways, and manifold D-Day tour operators cater to a map-toting middle-aged crowd, but Bayeux makes an equally appealing base for younger travelers looking to tour WWII sites.

ORIENTATION

To get to the *centre-ville* from the **train station,** bear right to reach **bld. Sadi Carnot,** then turn left and follow it to a roundabout. Go right at the roundabout up **rue Larcher** to reach the **cathedral.** Past the cathedral on rue de Nesmond, which becomes rue de la Maitrise, lies **place Charles de Gaulle.** Several *ponts* (bridges) traverse the **L'Aure River,** which runs through the city.

ACCOMMODATIONS

HOTEL REINE MATHILDE 💳♿📶 HOTEL [3]

23 rue Larcher ☎02 31 92 08 13 💻www.hotel-bayeux-reinemathilde.fr

A cozy, swank, yet reasonably priced hotel located in as central a location as Bayeux has to offer, within a stone's throw of the Cathedral and the Tapisserie. Reactionaries will feel at home here; the hotel has curiously chosen to name its rooms after various Anglo-Saxon kings and queens. The 22-room hotel also offers a cozy cafe, and a beautiful terrace overlooking the River Aure.

➡ About five blocks from the Cathedral down rue Larcher; before the rue Larcher roundabout, right before the Hospital. ℹ Hotel will have two handicapped rooms by early 2011. 💲 Prices vary by season. June 1-August 31 doubles €60-63; triples €73; quads €85. Sept 1-May 31 doubles €55-58; triples €68; quads €80. ⏰ Reception M 9:30am-6pm, W 9:30am-6pm.

HOTEL LE MAUPASSANT 💳📶 HOTEL [2]

19 rue Saint Martin ☎02 31 92 28 53 💻www.hotel-le-maupassant-bayeux.com

A 10-room, no-frills hotel located centrally to all that you may need in Bayeux: shopping, fast food, sight-seeing, and fine dining. Rooms are sufficiently spacious, and all boast private showers; the amenities are impressive for a 1-star hotel. Bathrooms are all ensuite except for the singles, where you have to make a short trip down the hall to take care of business. Le Maupassant also offers cheap eats at its cafe/brasserie, and a nice view of Bayeux thoroughfare rue Saint Martin.

ℹ Reception at bar. We approve. 💲 Singles €29; doubles €40; quads €85.

THE FAMILY HOME/AUBERGE DE JEUNESSE
HOTEL ❷

39 rue Général de Dais ☎02 31 92 15 22

A cozy hostel with clean rooms and some seriously cut rates. A stone courtyard and small dining room deftly mix a ski-lodge decor with classic Normandy styles. Keep in mind that there's no age limit here; there can be some older characters puttering around this Auberge. Shower and toilet are down the hall, but most rooms have a sink. The kitchen is also available for guest use.

i Breakfast included. Dinner €10, offered at 7:30pm. $ Dorms €22; singles €32.20. ⏰ Reception 8am-11am, 6pm-9pm.

CAMPING MUNICIPAL
HOTEL ❶

bld. Eindhoven ☎02 31 92 08 43

The campground offers volleyball, a playground, and swimming pool. Plenty of camper cars here, but also plenty of campers *sans voiture*. There are plenty of down-to-earth families here, as well as a few social renegades who just want to live the camper lifestyle, man.

i Electricity €3.50. $ 1 person €3.45, under 7 €1.80. €4.25 per tent/caravan/car. ⏰ Office open M-Sa 8-10am and 5-7pm, Su 8-10am and 6-8pm. Gates closed 10pm-7am.

SIGHTS

TAPISSERIE DE BAYEUX
MUSEUM

13 bis rue de Nesmond ☎02 31 51 25 50 🖥www.tapisserie-bayeux.fr

This jaw-dropper is the only thing that you really need to see in Bayeux. A whopping 68.3 sq. m, the tapestry tells one of the most important stories of Western history. In 1066, after a grueling 14hr. final battle, William triumphed in the invasion of England, switching his name to William the Conqueror from William the Bastard, in what most would call a rather flattering improvement. The tapestry tells the story in 58 fantastic frames; from the mind-blowing detail of the hundreds of characters, to the hidden symbolisms, to the inscriptions and contextual depictions at the bottom of the tapestry, watching it unfold is a roll-ercoaster ride through the the Middle Ages. The shock value is only enhanced by an understanding of the tribulations that the tapestry has been through. The Bayeux Cathedral it was housed in burned down twice, but the tapestry survived. It was even used as a tarp to cover a chariot loading with weapons during the Revolution. We highly recommend the complimentary audio tour, but be warned that it moves very fast. Use the pause button liberally, and take a go-around at your own pace after you've listened to it once. After you check out the tapestry, a fantastic exhibit and film (English and French) upstairs discusses the history behind its trials and tribulations.

$ €7.80, students €3.80, under 10 free. ⏰ Open Mar 15-Nov 15 daily 9am-6:30pm; May-Aug daily 9am-7pm; Nov 16-Mar 14 daily 9:30am-12:30pm and 2pm-6pm. Last entry 45min. before close.

LA CATHÉDRALE
CHURCH

rue du Bienvenue ☎02 31 92 01 85

The original resting place of the tapestry, this cathedral has burned down twice and undergone one too many stylistic redirections. It thus encompasses many different architectural traditions in one building. From its 11th-century origins under the direction of Bishop Odon, the Cathedral retains its towers, crypt and some of its nave. From the 13th century, the chancel remains, as well as several Gothic windows which shed a bit too much light on faded 15th century frescoes; some of these windows have been replaced with newer undecorated ones. The real jaw-dropper is the facade, which boasts amazingly detailed, yet tragically decaying, sculptures. Some visitors will be lucky enough to hear an organ performance by the church organist, and maybe even be solicited for coins (or bills, if the Spirit so move you) outside the church's entrance.

$ *Free.* ⏰ *Open daily July-Sept. 9am-7pm, Oct-Dec and Apr-June 9am-6pm, and Jan-Mar 9am-5pm.*

FOOD 🍴

Kebab and fast food joints line rues St-Martin and St-Jean. The best options are hidden here and there; Bayeux has some deliciously small restaurants to offer.

👍 ASSIETTE NORMANDE — 💳🍸 TRADITIONAL [2]

3 rue de Chanoines ☎02 31 22 04 61 💻www.lassiettenormande.com

Highly recommended by locals, L'Assiette Normande serves you up fine traditional regional cuisine at an incredibly low price, especially at lunch time. Ingredients are harvested locally, from the meat to the cheese (obviously) to the fish. You don't want to miss this cozy little restaurant; a glass of wine and a tasty, filling meal could not be better set than in L'Assiette's rustic Norman dining room. As the French would say, *"un petit resto sympa,"* or a nice little restaurant.

$ *Menus €12-33. Formule midi plat poisson, dessert, coffee, wine glass €11. Plat du jour €6.60.* ⏰ *Open Tu-Su noon-2pm and 7-9:30pm.*

LE P'TIT RESTO — 💳🍸 BISTRO [3]

6 bld. des Alliés ☎02 31 86 37 75 💻www.boeufandcow.fr

Self-dubbed "creative cuisine," this small little restaurant has mind-bending offerings, like zucchini cappucino, and a deliciously salty micuit chocolate. While the food is fantastic and original, the portions are quite small, so don't come here in the middle of a long day of exploring if you like to eat; you'll have to stop for a kebab or a crêpe later on. The restaurant only has a few tables, so reserve if you want a table at night.

$ *Formule midi €15.50, formules soir €20-30.* ⏰ *Open M-F lunch and dinner, Sa dinner only.*

CAFÉ INN — 💳 CAFE [3]

6 bld. des Alliés ☎02 31 86 37 75 💻www.boeufandcow.fr

From the outside, this hidden gem may look more like a tourist shop than an eatery; pottery and Normandy trinkets crowd the windows. Café Inn, however, offers a wide variety of delicious options for beakfast, lunch, and early evening snacks. Tea connoisseurs will be happy to select from over 80 choices, and vegetarians will be pleased with a wide collection of fresh, heaping, delicious salads.

$ *Breakfast formuls €6-9.25, teas €3.25-8, sandwiches €4-5.* ⏰ *Open M-Sa 9am-7pm.*

ESSENTIALS ℹ

Getting There ✈

Bus Verts *(☎08 10 21 42 14)* runs buses from **Caen** to Bayeux during the week (*$€4.25, under 26 €3.60. ⏰1hr., M-F 3 per day).*

d-day beaches ☎02 31

In 1943, German forces occupying France fortified their defenses with the "Atlantic Wall"—a series of bunkers, and batteries all along France's northern coasts. The Allies learned the difficulty of attacking a major port from the failed 1942 Dieppe raid, in which thousands of Canadians were either killed or taken prisoner. However, convinced that the only way to overthrow Hitler was to assault his "Fortress Europe" by sea, Allied commanders decided that Normandy would be their beachhead for the liberation of France. Allied forces set the stage for the invasion by flooding German intelligence services with false information and planting dummy tanks near Norway to confuse General Rommel and his troops. The action began in the pre-dawn hours of June 6, 1944, when 29,000 troops tumbled onto the coast between the Cotentin Peninsula and Orne. A few hours later, 130,000 more troops arrived by sea; by the end of June 850,000 had landed. The losses incurred on D-Day were devastating to both sides; the Allies alone lost 10,300 troops. The Allied victory was a key precursor to Paris's August 25 liberation.

ORIENTATION

The Americans who landed at the westernmost beaches—code-named **Utah** and **Omaha**—witnessed the bloodiest battles. **Voie de la Liberté** (Liberty Rd.) follows the US Army's advance to Bastogne, Belgium. British troops landed in the east at **Gold** and **Sword,** and Canadians landed at **Juno.** In the center, between Omaha and Gold, lies **Arromanches,** where the Allies hastily constructed one of two crucial offshore ports. Bayeux makes the best base for the western and central beaches (Utah, Omaha, and Gold) and is home to companies that offer great guided tours, but Caen has better access by bus to Juno and Sword.

The best way to see the sights is undoubtedly by car—not only can you get farther and go at your own pace, but you'll also have the opportunity to stop at any of the countless museums along the route. Even with a car, it is extremely difficult to get to all of the sights in a single day, as the beaches span over 50 mi. For a quick visit, it's best to focus on a single beach or a group of neighboring beaches; if you are careful with your bus connections, Juno and Sword Beaches can both be visited in one day, as can Utah and Omaha. **Bus Verts** is by far the cheapest way to get around and offers many interesting routes, especially from July through August, when service expands. Numerous companies offer guided minibus tours of the major sights. These tours, typically geared toward visitors from a particular country involved in the D-Day Invasion, are pricey but educational—quality ranges widely among different tour guides even within the same company, so it's a bit of a gamble. Call in advance to reserve. For the budget-conscious and physically fit, **biking** to the beaches is a viable option, though cyclists will only be able to visit a limited number of sites. Walking from beach to beach is practically impossible.

ACCOMMODATIONS

Accommodations in the areas surrounding the D-Day beaches tend to be extremely expensive, especially in high season. It's best to stay in one of the nearby "major cities," Caen or Bayeux, than to try to get a spot near one of the beaches. Both cities have a few interesting sights, and a wealth of restaurants and accommodations, to offer their visitors. Transportation to and from the beaches from these towns is easy; it's the getting between the beaches that can be a headache.

SIGHTS

POINTE DU HOC   BEACH
Cricqueville-en-Bessin

Located between Utah and Omaha beaches, the Pointe du Hoc is the most aesthetically stunning and possibly the most historically impressive of all the D-Day beach sights. the beach is located on top of 100 ft. of steep craggy cliffs, and marks an important point of attack by the U.S. Army Ranger Assault Group during Operation Overlord in WWII. The German coastal operation commanded, by Field Marshal Erwin Rommel, had used the point in the coastline to establish six casemates, fortified bunkers that were armed to to the teeth with 155mm guns. Pointe du Hoc represented a crucial strongpoint, since it provided the Germans with an opportunity to fire on both Omaha and Utah beaches. Led by Lieutenant Colonel James Rudder, 250 U.S. Army Ranger Assault Group troops scaled the crags, suffering about 25 casualties. They found, upon their ascent, that the guns had been removed to an alternative location; this forced them to simultaneously defend the bunkers, block off the adjacent road, and search for the guns. The stalemate lasted two days until the guns were found and destroyed with thermite grenades. Today, there are still several preserved bunkers at Pointe du Hoc, albeit filled with urine, soda cans, and other tourist debris. Deep bomb craters are frequently scattered across the Pointe—don't come here after a few drinks, because you'll fall in.

$ Free. ⏰ Information center open Apr-Sept daily 9:30am-1pm and 2-6pm; Oct-Mar F-Su 10am-1pm and 2-5pm.

AMERICAN CEMETERY CEMETERY

The American Cemetery is arguably the "must-see" of the D-Day Beach tour. The cemetery was designed to be perfectly symmetrical, on a cliff overlooking Omaha Beach and the English Channel. 9,387 American soldiers lay at rest here. The Walls of the Missing, located in a garden on the east side of the memorial, displays 1,557 names of those who went missing in action, never to be recovered. The Memorial at the top of the cemetery consists of a semicircular colonnade with a loggia at each end containing large maps and narratives of the military operations, and in between the lies a bronze statue, "Spirit of American Youth," crafted by sculptor Donald De Lue. An orientation table overlooking the beach depicts the landings in Normandy. In the middle of the burial area lies a circular chapel, the walls of which bear the prominent inscription: "Think not only upon their passing. Remember the glory of their spirit." The American Cemetery is a moving display; it puts your visit to the other D-Day Beaches in a palpable human context.

⏰ Open daily -9am--5pm.

OMAHA BEACH 👍 BEACH

Avenue de la Liberation, Normandie ☎02 31 21 97 44 💻www.musée-memorial-omaha.com

Spread across the beaches of three French villages, Vierville-sur-Mer, Colleville-sur-Mer, and Saint-Laurent-sur-Mer, Omaha Beach was the code name for the main point of American debarkment in Normandy. The initial assault waves, manned by U.S. Army Rangers, the 1st, and 29th Infantries, consisted of an amphibian attack, combining infantry and tank attacks on the German 352nd Infantry Division. The conditions for the attack were terrible, and many of the bombs that were supposed to hit the Germans missed, leaving the Americans with a larger contest than they had anticipated. It took three thousand casualties for the American attack waves to ultimately win out. The Beach now features a fantastic Visitor Center *(open 9am-5pm)*, featuring cool displays of German beach obstacles, clunky field radios, boots, helmets, knives, and ration boxes. Along the left side of the exhibit, there is a historical discussion of the Omaha Beach operation's larger context in the Allied Attack, and some striking statistics: we for one did not know that the Germans had installed 500,000+ obstacles on the beaches in anticipation of Allied attacks. Another feature of the Omaha Beach area is the souvenir-oriented Memorial Museum of Omaha Beach. Operated privately, the museum showcases military tanks, uniformed mannequins, rare documents, and rations, among other things.

$ €6, students €4.60. ⏰ Open July-Aug daily 9:30am-7:30pm; Sept 16-Nov 15 daily 9:30am-6:30pm; Feb 15-Mar 15 daily 10am-12:30pm and 2:30-6pm; Mar 16-May 15 daily 9:30am-6:30pm.

JUNO BEACH 👍 BEACH

Voie des Francais Libres ☎02 31 37 32 17 💻www.junobeach.org

Juno Beach is generally thought of as one of the more minor beaches, and therefore receives less of a tourist mob, even during D-Day tourist season. Its role in the Allied invasion, however, was critical. Situated between Sword and Gold Beaches and stretched between French towns Saint-Aubin-sur-Mer and Courseulles-sur-Mer, Juno Beach was one of the five primary disembarking beaches; 14,000 Canadian troops flooded into the beach, which was the second most heavily defended of all the D-Day Beaches by the Germans. While the attack was mostly amphibian, like the others, a remarkable feature of the Juno

Beach was that some soldiers traveled on land by bike, extending their reach of power 10km into the coastline. Ask for directions to the **Croix de Lorraine,** a special type of cross which bears two horizontal beams. A majestic symbol of the the Free French, it marks the spot where General de Gaulle, leader of the Free French movement, first disembarked onto French soil after the German occupation. The **Centre Juno Beach,** opened in 2003, commemorates Canadian military efforts in Juno Beach. The Centre offers seven permanent exhibits, featuring your standard fare of photos, documents, and even model amphibious vehicles. However, it also offers rotating temporary exhibits on historical and cultural features of the Allied efforts; admission to this part of the museum is a good deal cheaper. Groups should call in advance to reserve a tour in English.

$ €6.50, students €5. Temporary exhibition only €2.50. Park only €5, students €4. Center and park €10, students €8. ⏰ Open Apr-Sept daily 9:30am-7pm; Oct daily 10am-6pm; Nov-Dec and Feb daily 10am-5pm; Mar daily 10am-6pm.

ARROMANCHES

BEACH

chemin du Calvaire ☎02 31 22 30 30

Located in the tranquil French town Arromanches les-Bains, Arromanches is today remembered not as one of the primary debarkment beaches, but rather as the location which provided the entrance and survival of Allied troops in their sustained efforts to defeat the Germans after D-Day. After the failed Dieppe raids of 1942, the Allies realized that they'd need to have a port along the northern French coast other than Cherbourg to oust the Germans from the territory. In pursuit of a solution to this problem, the Brits towed 600,000 tons of concrete across the English Channel to build two artifical military ports, called Mulberries. Once in place, the Mulberries did the trick. The ports provided for the passage of 2.5 million men, half a million vehicles, and 4 million tons of raw materials. Today Arromanches is ironically home to one of the best, and most popular D-Day museums, **Le Musée du Débarquement.** Be sure to check out the **Arromanches 360°**, a cinema up the street from the beach which offers an historical account of the disebarkment in a circular 360° presentation made up of 9 screens, and even simulates ships landing on the beach. The only caveat is that you really can't sit down, unless you have a wheelchair. Don't stress; the film lasts only 20mins.

$ €4.20, students €3.70, 10 and under free. ⏰ Open daily Feb 10:10am-4:40pm; Mar 10:10am-5:10pm; Apr 10:10am-5:40pm; June 9:40am-6:40pm; Sept 10:10am-5:40pm; Nov 10:10am-5:10pm; Dec 10:10am-4:40pm.

GOLD BEACH

BEACH

2 pl. Amiral-Byrd ☎02 31 22 58 88 💻www.goldbeachmusée.org.uk.

Situated a little west of Sword Beach, Gold Beach was the primary sight of British disembarkation. The 50th Infantry Division invaded the beautiful beaches of Ver-Sur-Mer in an effort to establish power between Arromanches and Ver-sur-Mer, with the ultimate goal of cutting off German access to highway Route 13 and establishing Allied control over Caen and Bayeux. While Gold Beach boasts nothing extraordinary in terms of D-Day Beaches, it does offer one of the more offbeat D-Day museums, Le Musée America Gold Beach. The Museum boasts an emphasis on things aeronautical. Half of the museum is dedicated to the 42 hours of the first aeropostal flight from the U.S. to France, while the other half examines British preparations for landing on Gold Beach.

$ €4, children €2.40. ⏰ Open July-Aug daily 10:30am-5:30pm; Sept and Apr M and W-Su 10:30am-5:30pm.

FOOD

The best idea as far as food goes is to pack a sandwich. Restaurants around the beaches (Juno especially) are tourist exploitation joints. Besides, does it get any better than picnics on the beach? Pack a blanket and some sandwiches for the day, and forget about having to shell out euros for the best view you could have imagined. Near Omaha and Juno, there are a few good spots that are worth a college try.

LA SAPINIÈRE — TRADITIONAL [3]

100 rue de la 2ème infanterie US, St. Laurent-sur-Mer ☎02 31 92 71 72 www.la-sapiniere.fr

A sunny dining room graced with high ceilings and homey woodwork. The restaurant is part of an expensive hotel, and its lovely outdoors terrace reaches into a garden, creating an immeasurable and delectable distance from the tourist mayhem of the beaches. The cuisine is nothing extraordinary, but is as about as un-touristy as you're going to get a stone's throw from Omaha Beach.

$ Menus €14-35. Tasting plate €38. Kids menu €10, a la carte from €12. ⏰ Open March 10th-November 2nd.

D-DAY HOUSE — SEAFOOD [3]

1 rue Désiré Lemiere, Eleu-dit-Leauwette ☎02 31 92 66 49 www.d-dayhouse.com

It may be a tourist trap, but it's our tourist trap. Once again, it's tough to find good deals on dining out in the D-Day beaches area, and this spot is no exception. Good seafood and Norman dishes are served in a smartly decorated dining room, maybe after a drink at a run-of-the-mill bar. No complaints as far as convenience goes; a stone's throw from Omaha beach.

$ Menus €14-35, tasting menu €38. ⏰ Open daily 9am-10:30am, 11am-1pm, and 8-10pm.

ESSENTIALS

Getting There

Bus Verts *(☎08 10 21 42 14)* has offices at the Gare Bayeux and Gare Caen. Special D-Day lines run once a day July-Aug from Caen and Bayeux, and visit the 3 "major beaches" (Omaha, Gold, and Juno). Ask at office for complete listing of lines *(i Cash only. Depending on distance, can be purchased on board the bus. $ Tickets €1.60-10.60, under 26 €1.35-9.)* From **Bayeux,** Line #70 serves the area of Omaha Beach, with stops near Pointe du Hoc and the American Cemetery *(M-Sa 2 per day);* Line #74 serves Gold and Juno Beaches, with stops at Arromanches, Ver-sur-Mer, and Courselles-sur-Mer *(M-Sa 3 per day).* In July-Aug., line #75 runs from Bayeux to the sights on Gold, Juno, and Sword beaches. From **Caen,** Line #1 serves Sword Beach; a transfer to line #3 will take you to Juno; another transfer to line #74 can take you on to Gold, but you'll have trouble returning to Caen the same evening.

Getting Around

Getting to and from the beaches is virtually impossible on foot, and most easily accomplished by car. Chances are you probably don't have one, in which case you should try to take a **tour. Normandy Sightseeing Tours** *(www.normandywebguide.com),* is based in **Bayeux.** The tours stop at the most famous beaches, various museums, and lesser-known (or often completely unmarked) sights. Guides are enthusiastic, knowledgeable, and English-speaking; the tour picks up passengers at the Bayeux at the train station in pl. du Québec, or will stop at your hotel. Packages include the **morning tour** *($ €40, students €30, under 10 €20. ⏰ 3hr.),* **afternoon tour** *($ €55, students €45, under 10 €35. ⏰ 4hr.)* and **day tour** *($ €85, students €65, under 10 €45. ⏰ 9hr.)* **Overlordtour** *(www.overlordtour.com)* provides anecdotes and historical photos, which adds flair to 7 package tours in English and French. Tours depart from pl. du Québec in Bayeux. Personalized tours also available *(⏰ ½-day tour €50, full-day tour €85.)*

STRASBOURG

Strasbourg (strahss-boorg, pop. 270,000) suffers from a confusing history. Much like the beloved toy of a pair of siblings, Alsace went back and forth between France and Germany throughout history as the two countries squabbled over who should control it. After the Second World War, France reclaimed the region, but this couldn't eliminate its heavy Germanic influences. In Strasbourg, you're just as likely to hear German as you are French, and among the older generations you may even catch a few words of Alsatian, a mix of the two languages that is now dying out. As you wander through the streets of Strasbourg and explore the Alsace region, you will be blown away by the beautiful buildings, which have a certain Germanic appearance about them. Many streets and areas have German-sounding names, and this Germanic influence also extends into the city's meaty cuisine. The region prides itself on its food, and a trip to Strasbourg would not be complete without sampling these delights.

Although the long history of conflict hangs over the head of the region, the capital of Alsace is now the home of a beacon for European democracy. Several European Union institutions, including the Council of Europe (which includes the European Court of Human Rights), lie just outside of the city and Strasbourg is full of Eurocrats working for the good of Europe (or at least that's what they say) Visiting the European institutions is a highlight of a trip to Strasbourg.

greatest hits

- **THE WORLD'S GREATEST FAVORITE CUCKOO CLOCK:** Watch a procession of miniature apostles march out of the Strasbourg Cathedral's clock tower every day at 12:30pm (p. 154).
- **CARNIVORES OF THE WORLD, UNITE:** Eat your way through the traditional local *winstubs* (p. 154).
- **AT LAST, SOME CHEAP BEER:** Immerse yourself in the student crowds and hunker down with a pint (p. 158).

student life

You might have been a little tipsy when you got on that early morning train, but don't worry you didn't wake up in Germany. Strasbourg definitely has a distinctly German feel to it as you'll find as you explore. 50,000 students attend three universities in Strasbourg, and while you'll find a lot of student bars the club scene isn't what you'll find in some other cities. Don't fret though; head out to a *winstub* with the group you met at your hostel and sample some *Alsacien* cuisine and beer; you'll be glad you did.

orientation

Strasbourg has a good mix of sights to see, museums to visit, and bars to end the night with; you won't be sitting alone in your hostel room in this city. The main streets swarm with tourists, both foreign and French, during the summer. They flock like fireflies to a flame to visit the grand cathedral that dominates the city center. The city itself is very beautiful, and in summer the streets are worth exploring by foot—pedestrian zones and large parks make doing so very easy. The mass of green space on the outskirts of Strasbourg means you can escape the inner city noise for the peace of a calm park. With the Council of Europe situated northeast of the center of the city, Strasbourg is the core for a lot of European political debates and discussions.

The *vielle ville* is surrounded completely by the **River Ill,** making it a lemon-shaped island reachable by a series of bridges, which connect quais running on either side of the river. The **train station** is a short walk northwest of the city's **center;** to reach the center on foot, head down **rue du Mairie Kuss,** over pont Kuss, then make a sharp right onto **quai Desaux** and take the immediate left onto **Grande rue.** This continues to one of Strasbourg's busiest squares, **place Gutenberg.** Pl. Gutenberg reaches east to **place de la Cathedral;** head north up **rue des Grandes Arcades** to reach **place Kléber,** and to the southwest of the square is **Petite France.**

accommodations

Accommodations in Strasbourg can vary greatly in prices, and the farther out of the center you go, the less you'll have to pay. Cheaper chain hotels can be found around the train station and the surrounding streets. Hotels in the center and near the cathedral will cost upward of €100 a night. Check whether you will be visiting during a Parliamentary sitting; this will affect both price and availability. It's cheaper and easier to find a hotel when the Parliament isn't sitting in Strasbourg.

CENTRE INTERNATIONAL D'ACCUEIL DE STRASBOURG ♿ HOSTEL [2]

7 rue Finkmatt ☎03 88 23 89 21 www.ciarus.com

The bright and colorful CIARUS hostel is fantastic for families, groups, or even the lone traveler looking for a few days' stay. With competive rates and a location that puts you a short walk from Strasbourg's main squares and the cathedral, CIARUS will not disappoint. The simply furnished hostel also has a game room and bar to keep you occupied. For those who don't wish to venture far for their meals (and want to save a bit of cash), the restaurant serves up cheap daily menus for guests. Rooms are spacious, with bunk beds, shelving, and ensuite bathrooms.

A short walk from the train station. Take rue du Maire-Kuss to the canal, turn left, and walk along quai St-Jean. Turn left onto rue Finkmatt; the hostel will be on your left. ℹ *Sheets and blankets provided. Wi-Fi €1 per day. Disco night on M and W, crêpe party night on Tu and Th.* $ *Dorms €19.50-26.50; singles €45-50; doubles €58. Rooms €3 more during Parliamentary sessions.* ⏰ *Reception 24hr.*

AUBERGE DE JEUNESSE RENÉ CASSIN (HI) HOSTEL [1]

9 rue de l'Auberge de Jeunesse ☎03 88 30 26 46 🖥www.fuaj.org

This countryside hostel allows you to avoid the hustle and bustle of central Strasbourg while staying within walking distance of the main sights and city center. With a beautiful canal setting, you can easily forget the Eurocrats and the political nature of Strasbourg and relax by the calm flowing waters before heading out into the city. The hostel is well served by public transport into the evening, and is open 24hr. *(swipe access after 1am).* For entertainment, there's a bar and a game room with an arcade and table tennis. Rooms are large and clean with a sink and communal bathrooms. The English-speaking staff will happily help you out with restaurant recommendations and transportation queries.

 # From the train station, take bus #2 in direction Campus d'Illkirch. Get off at Auberge de Jeunesse and take a left under the bridge. The hostel is on your left after the bridge. ℹ Breakfast included. Internet €3 per hr.; Wi-Fi €5 per day. $ Dorms €20.50; singles €40.50; doubles €20.50. ⏰ Reception 7am-noon, 1-7:30pm, and 8:30-11pm.

CAMPING DE LA MONTAGNE VERTE CAMPING [1]

2 rue de la Montagne Verte ☎03 88 30 25 46 🖥www.aquadis loisirs.com

This campground provides minimal privacy at each site, as it is basically an open field situated next to a picturesque river and canal. The camp compensates with a fantastic location close to Strasbourg, easily reached by public transportation. The tranquil setting also suits travelers or families who want to escape the center of a busy city. Bar serves up drinks and snacks throughout the day.

 # From the train station take bus #2 in direction Campus d'Illkirch. Get off at Nid de Cigognes. Turn right onto rue du Schokeloch and right again onto rue Robert Forrer. ℹ Free showers. $ €9.60 per person; €14.20 per 2 people; with electricity €18.40. ⏰ Reception 8:30am-9:30pm. Closed to cars after 10pm.

HOTEL WEBER HOTEL [3]

22 bld. de Nancy ☎03 88 32 36 47 🖥hotel.weber@free.fr

This cheap and cheerful hotel doesn't suffer from the price inflation that many others in Strasbourg experience during the Parliamentary season, and for that reason you can find a basic room for a smaller price. Located a short walk from the train station, the hotel is set in a large house and offers both "modest" rooms for budget travelers and rooms with a few more comforts (at a higher price). While the faded outside may be off-putting, and the disorganized owner a concern, the modern and clean bedrooms will be worth it.

 # From the train station, head along bld. de Metz, which turns into bld. de Nancy. Hotel Weber is just past the bus stop on your left. ℹ Breakfast €4.50. Bookings in advance recommended. Ring bell to enter. $ Singles €28-38; doubles and triples €44. ⏰ Reception 2:30-7pm.

HOTEL LE GRILLON HOTEL [3]

2 rue Thiergarten ☎03 88 32 71 88 🖥www.grillon.com

A short walk from the train station, this hotel boasts a lively bar and a modern interior. Although the outside facade is fading, the hotel's interior is plush and modern. The plainly decorated rooms will keep you comfy, but more importantly, the bar downstairs and the fast-food restaurants surrounding the hotel will keep you well fed and watered. For those wishing to spend a little more on their accommodations, "superior rooms" are available for a higher cost.

 # From the train station, head down rue Kuhn. The hotel is on the corner on the left. ℹ Breakfast €8. $ Singles €36, with shower €46-61; doubles €43-51/53-76. ⏰ Reception 24hr.

LE 21ÈME HOTEL [3]

21-23 rue du Fossé des Tanneurs ☎03 88 23 89 21 🖥www.hotel-cyber-21.com

Although this hotel has expensive week rates, its prices plummet on the weekends—making it ideal for a weekend break in Strasbourg. Prices are slashed by almost half from F-Su. Rooms are plainly furnished and are equipped with clean bathrooms.

 # Just off pl. Kléber. $ Singles and doubles M-Th €40-48, Sa-Su €80-95. ⏰ Reception 24hr.

sights

CATHEDRAL — CHURCH

pl. de la Cathedral

Towering above the Strasbourg skyline and visible from almost every part of the city, this stunning cathedral draws people from across the world to Strasbourg's city center. There are continually crowds moseying around the adjacent square, posing for pictures outside the grand towers of the building. Step inside and you'll see some of the oldest stained-glass windows in Christian history as well as an organ that dates back to 1385 (it was most recently renovated in 1981). One of the cathedral's most beautiful sights is the statue depicting Jesus's moment of doubt on the Mount of Olives. Round to the southern trancept is the **Pillier des Anges,** which portrays humanity rising for judgment as Jesus sits on his throne. Next to the Pillier is the famous **Horlage Astronomique,** which was built by 16th-century watchmakers. At 12:30pm, tiny apostles march out of the face of the clock and a rooster greets St.-Pierre. Ascend the 33m tower *(€3)* for a beautiful panoramic view of the city.

$ €3, students €2.30. ⏰ Open daily 9am-6pm. Su Mass 10am. Tower open daily July-Aug 8:30am-7pm; Sept-Oct 9am-6:30pm; Nov-Feb 9am-4:30pm; Mar-June 9am-6:30pm.

LA PETITE FRANCE AND PONTS COUVERTES — NEIGHBORHOOD

Formerly part of an old tanners' district, La Petite France's steep-roofed houses and old colored facades are southwest of the grand cathedral. The picturesque little neighborhood can easily be explored on foot. Walking along the cobbled streets by the canal, you will find numerous cafes and plenty of Alsatian restaurants to keep you fed and watered. The canals can be crossed by a system of bridges connecting the two sides of the river. For a real tour of the canal area, take the Batorama Tour (booked through the tourist office), which will take you along the canals of Strasbourg and through La Petite France. The Ponts Couvertes, or the covered bridges, aren't actually covered, since the roofs were removed in the 18th century, but the name stuck. These bridges border the towers, which are the remains of the 14th-century city walls.

✈ Southwest of pl. de la Cathedral.

L'ÉGLISE ST PETERS — CHURCH

3 rue de la Nuée Bleue ☎03 88 32 41 61

Strasbourg has many churches and a grand cathedral for you to ogle at, but perhaps one of the more interesting and lesser-known churches in the city will also impress you with its grand history and intricate murals. The current building rests on the remains of a seventh-century church, and what you see here today was built between 1250 and 1320, resulting in a beautiful Gothic building that has a Romanesque cloister and some very grand interior furnishings. On the West Wall is the church's crowning glory, the Navicella, which is supposed to represent God's word being brought to the people (make sure you ask for it to be illuminated). Turn your gaze to the now-faded, but still visible, mural of the European nations marching by horseback towards the cross. Each country (or empire) is depicted to represent its strength and power from the time. The grand organ above the altar is also a brilliant sight in this church, which looks as if it's crumbling down with every step you take through it.

✈ Just off of Pl. Kléber $ Free. ⏰ Open daily 10am-6pm.

food

Traditional Alsatian dishes are the order of the day in Strasbourg; with a strong emphasis on classics like *choucroute garnie* (sauerkraut with meats), Strasbourg's foods outlets are a carnivore's dream. Vegetarians can still find some options, though it will be more difficult than usual. **La Petite France** is populated with traditional *winstubs*, which serve platefuls of Alsatian dishes. For the end of a night, head to the roads surrounding the train station (especially **rue Kuhn**) for cheap takeout and kebab shops. Supermarkets are easy to find in the center of Strasbourg. A **Monoprix** is located at 5 rue des Grandes Arcades. *(☎03 88 52 25 00 ⏰ Open M-F 8:30am-8:30pm.)*

AU PONT SAINT-MARTIN
🍴🍸 WINSTUB ❸

15 rue des Moulins ☎03 88 32 45 13 💻www.pont-saint-martin.com

Although you have to pay a bit extra for this *winstub*, the extra dent in your wallet will definitely be worth the beautiful view of the river and Strasbourg's more traditional Alsatian streets. This four-story, Germanic house is always busy with tourists and locals alike. Make sure you request a window table to make the most of the meal, or for a large party you may be lucky enough to request the outdoor platform situated on the river itself. A rotating set lunch menu serves up Alsatian classics, including hefty amounts of meat and cheese, while a more expensive three-course menu is offered all day long *(€18.50)*. Vegetarian options are available.

⇟ Situated over the bridge in Petite France. Follow rue du Boucher, which is off of Grand Rue. $ Entrees €7-25. Set menu €18.50. ⏰ Open daily 11:30am-10:30pm.

JEANETTE ET LES CYCLEUX
🍴🍸📶 CAFE ❷

30 rue des Tonneliers ☎03 88 23 02 71

Jeanette et les Cycleux serves up dishes of meat and cheese in a do-it-yourself picnic style. Choose three *(€4.70)*, four *(€5.70)*, or even six *(€12)* items off of the chalkboard menu, which features sausage, ham, salad, and a variety of local cheeses. Salads from Jeanette's adventures are also available; why not sample something from her time in Italy or even a farm-influenced salad *(€9.50)?* Ideal for a small lunch at a very good price.

⇟ Rue des Tonneliers is just south of pl. Guttenberg. $ Plates €4.70-10. ⏰ Open daily for picnic 11:30am-2pm. Open for drinks daily 5-8:30pm.

L'ÉPICERIE
🍴🍸 TARTINES ❶

6 rue du Vieux-Seigle ☎03 88 32 52 41 💻www.lepicerie-strasbourg.com

This dirt-cheap restaurant specializes in tartines, or bread covered in meats, cheeses, and a paste base of your choice. They are reasonably priced and a popular lunchtime snack or evening boost. Choose from a wide selection of toppings, including goat cheese and sausage. The interior is defined by a series of Van Gogh portraits and resembles a rustic kitchen more anything else. As you visit the bar watch out for the fresh bags of bread that surround the counter.

⇟ Rue du Viexu-Seigle is just off rue des Francs Bourgeois or rue Grands Arcades. $ Tartines around €5. ⏰ Open daily 11:30am-1am. Kitchen open noon-midnight.

EL PIMIENTO
🍴♿🍸 TAPAS ❸

52 rue du Jeu des Enfants ☎03 88 21 94 52

A surprising find in the center of Strasbourg, this Spanish tapas bar makes its love for chilis well known by covering the walls with them, having large faux-chilis as light fixtures and even propping up tables with massive plastic red chilis. The only thing lacking is the Red Hot Chili Peppers in the background, but a buzzing Spanish soundtrack adds a bit of spice to your night out instead. The waitstaff will help out with some English translations for these traditional tapas dishes. For a true Spanish experience, be sure to order a pitcher of sangria to accompany your meal.

⇟ Just off of pl. de l'Homme de Fer. $ Tapas bowls €3-5. ⏰ Open M-Sa 11:45am-2pm and 6pm-1am, Su 6-11pm.

LA CORDE À LINGE
🍴🍸 WINSTUB ❸

2 pl. Benjamin Zix ☎03 88 22 15 17 💻www.lacordealigne.com

If you're looking for a *winstub* with a bit of pizazz, this German-style restaurant has a menu that will at least make you smile (but the excessive carbs might just make you fat). The staff has named their salads after certain articles of clothing; Le Corset will certainly keep you tight and skinny, and the Mini Jupe is available for the more fashionable among you *(€9)*. The restaurant also offers hefty portions of more traditional Alsatian dishes, such as flannelle, ketsch, and taffetas.

⇟ Pl. Benjamin Zix can be reached from the Grand Rue by heading down petite rue Des dentelles. $ Plates €7-20. ⏰ Open daily 10:30am-midnight or 1am. Kitchen open 11:45am-11pm.

FLAM'S 🍴🍸 TRADITIONAL [2]

29 rue des Frères ☎03 88 36 36 90 💻www.flams.fr

On the weekends, locals and tourists alike line up out the door for this popular restaurant, which serves a wide selection of *Flammekueche* (Similar to a *tarte flambée).* Toppings include special mushroom mixes, sausage, meats, and vegetarian options. The quirky restaurant will serve larger portions for you to share. To start your night out right, attempt to conquer the 2.5L of beer, which is served in a large tube to your table *(€17.50).*

➡ Just off of pl. du Château, behind the cathedral. i Reservations recommended on weekends. $ Plates €4-11. Set menus €10-18. ⏰ Open daily 11:30am-midnight.

AUX ARMES DE STRASBOURG 🍴🍸 WINSTUB, BAR [3]

9 pl. Guttenberg ☎03 88 32 85 62 💻www.auxarmesdestrasbourg.com

Those who really want to taste the Alsatian diet ought to head over to pl. Guttenberg, where, in the shadow of Guttenberg himself, you can devour some of the most interesting (and meaty) Alsatian dishes around. The sausages and the blood sausage are a must for anyone looking to taste Alsace, and the sauerkraut too is a plentiful dish. But for the truly adventurous, why not try a veal's head? Vegetarian options are more difficult to find on this menu.

➡ Pl. Guttenberg is south of pl. Kébas via rue Grands Arcades. i Small plates available. $ Plates €10-23. ⏰ Open daily 11:30am-midnight.

LA STUB 🍴🍸 WINSTUB [3]

4 rue du Saumon ☎03 88 21 05 00

The restaurant tries to mix tradition with modernity and winds up looking like something out of a sci-fi film. But La Stub, despite dropping the "win" from its name, still can't shake the *winstub* image—the checkered tablecloths outside are a massive give away. Specializing in *tartes flambées*, as well as other Alsatian dishes, the restaurant is tucked inbetween two of Strasbourg's busiest shopping streets. For those looking for something more filling than set menus, a mixture of Alsatian dishes is available *(€12-17.)*

➡ Rue du Saumon is between rue des Francs Bourgeois and rue des Grands Arcades. $ Tartes flambées €5-7. Set menus and other dishes €12-20. ⏰ Open M-Sa 11am-12:30am. Kitchen open noon-midnight.

LE GLACIER FRANCHI 🍴 ICE CREAM [1]

5 rue des Francs Bourgeois ☎03 88 23 16 15

On a hot summer's day, Strasbourg is full of places to grab a *glace* (ice cream to you) and cool off in the sun. But Le Glacier Franchi offers up some exciting flavors, including a bizarre tasting *Schtroumpf* (The Smurfs!), which come served in zany colored glass dishes. Also ideal for an ice cream sundae date.

➡ Rue des Francs Bourgeois runs southwards from Place de l'Homme Fer. $ €1.50 for 1 scoop. €3 for 2. Sundaes €3-€7 ⏰ Open M 1-7pm, Tu-Sa 8am-11pm, Su 1-6pm.

LE TROC'AFÉ 🍴🍸 BAR, CAFE [2]

8 rue du Faubourg de Saverne ☎03 88 23 23 29

Describing itself as *bistrot d'objets*, Le Troc'afé certainly has a brilliant collection of tidbits to admire. The cafe is decorated with classic French horror movie posters, an old wireless radio, and a gnome that guards the door. Anyone thrown overboard can try grab onto the lifeguard ring hanging from the ceiling, though there is unfortunately no David Hasselhoff in sight. The cafe plays host to a variety of small concerts and other events throughout the year, some of which will have a small *(€4-5)* entry fee.

➡ Rue du Faubourg de Saverne can be reached from the train station. Rue Kuhn connects pl. de la Gare and rue du Fauburg de Saverne. $ Drinks €3-5. Food €4-10. ⏰ Open M-F 7:30am-10pm, Sa 11am-8pm.

GOTHAM 🍴🍸 BAR [4]

21 rue du Fossé des Tanneurs ☎03 88 16 07 39 💻www.gotham-strasbourg.fr

Although there is no Dark Knight to be found in this restaurant and bar, Gotham fills its tables with those looking for a fine dining experience. The lamb is a delectable dish that will leave you smiling and asking yourself, "why so serious?" ⚐ *Just off pl. Kléber.* Ⓢ *Plates €8-25.* 🕐 *Open Tu-Sa 10am-1:30am, Su 10am-2pm.*

AU POITRON   ⚲🍴 VEGETARIAN ❷
24 rue St Madeline   ☎03 88 35 49 86

This very orange-looking restaurant specializes in vegetarian dishes, which is a welcome break from the meat-heavy *winstubs* that crowd Strasbourg. Out of the way from the busy streets, just off the south banks of the Ill, Au Poitron offers up a varied mix of the classic *tarte flambée*, Italian-style pizzas, and a variety of *gratins* (an Alsatian style of baking various foods topped with cheese and breadcrumbs). During the summer, take the opportunity to sit outside on the cobbled streets, watch the world drift by, and be pleased you're doing your cholesterol level an awful lot of good.
⚐ *From pl. du Château (behind cathedral), head south down rue du Bain aux Roses over the bridge, which then leads into rue St-Madeline.* Ⓢ *Lunch menu €10.50; set menu €20.* 🕐 *Open M-Sa noon-2pm and 7-10:30pm.*

L'ANCIENNE CHAPELLE   🍴⚲ TRADITIONAL ❸
2 pl. des Orphelins   ☎03 88 35 35 37

This small little restaurant is a hub of high-quality Alsatian dishes as well as some traditional southwestern French cuisine. During the summer, customers spread out into the square and enjoy their food in the beauty of the old surroundings. The owner will discuss the dishes with you and help you to decide whether to pig out or rein it in. A large goose-shaped chalkboard marks the specials of the day outside.
⚐ *p. des Orphelins is just off rue St Madeline. From pl. du Château (behind cathedral), head south down rue du Bain aux Roses, over the bridge, which then leads into rue St-Madeline.* Ⓢ *Plates €9-24.* 🕐 *Open M 7-10:30pm, Tu-Sa noon-2pm and 7-10:30pm.*

LE GRUBER   🍴⚲ TRADITIONAL, ITALIAN ❸
11 rue du Maroquin   ☎03 88 32 23 11 🖳www.legruber.com

Although claiming to be a traditional Alsatian restaurant, Le Gruber also serves up some mean pizzas that might make you wonder if you're in Italy rather than France. Their expansive indoor and outdoor seating area means that although it will get busy, you will be able to find a seat. Pizzas are large and have plentiful toppings, ideal for a family meal.
⚐ *Just off of pl. de la Cathedral.* 🛈 *Kids' menu available (under 10).* Ⓢ *Pizzas €7-12. Kids menu €7.* 🕐 *Open M-Th 11:30am-10:30pm, F-Sa 11:30am-11pm, Su 11:30am-10:30pm.*

LE HANNETON (CHEZ DENIS)   ⚲🍴 WINSTUB ❸
5 rue Ste-Madeleine   ☎03 88 36 93 76

This traditional *winstub* provides some very tasty classics on a *petit* street with views of the Ill River. Plates come with hefty servings and make finishing your meal near impossible. Don't annoy the host; the *sorcières* (witch dolls) that hang overhead might just put a spell on you.
⚐ *From pl. du Château (behind cathedral), head south down rue du Bain aux Roses, over the bridge, which then leads into rue Ste-Madeline.* Ⓢ *Plates €12-20.* 🕐 *Open Tu 7-11pm, W-Su noon-2pm and 7-11pm.*

AU VIEUX STRASBOURG   🍴⚲ WINSTUB ❸
5 rue du Maroquin   ☎03 88 32 41 89

This traditional *winstub* is one of the few places in town that provides English translations of their dishes. For those wishing to try the variety of pork options Alsatians eat, try the Choucroute Alsacienne au Rieslingene *(€15.50)*, which comes with six different types of pork chops and sausages covering a bed of cabbage (not for the faint-hearted). Both the inside and outside seating areas are perfect for a leisurely lunch in the shadow of the cathedral behind.
⚐ *Just off pl. de la Cathedral.* Ⓢ *Entrees €8-22.* 🕐 *Open daily noon-2:30pm and 7-10:30pm.*

food

nightlife

Strasbourg's many squares are home to the majority of the city's nightlife, but you may want to approach them in groups, as the city can become a little bit dodgy in the wee hours. **pl. Klébar** and the surrounding streets have many bars and lounges to relax, while some older crowds gather at **place Gayot.** A student crowd heads to the bars in and around **rue des Frères,** while some traditional Irish pubs can be found in **pl. Austerliz.**

■ BAR EXILS
♦ ❖ (ᵗᵖ)) BAR

28 rue de l'Ail   ☎03 88 32 52 70 ▣www.barexils.com

This extremely popular student hangout may not be the classiest of establishments, even if the bouncer at the door in his best suit will at least give the image that Bar Exils is an upscale venue. Once you get your wallet out to pay, you'll realize this will be the cheapest round of drinks you will buy in Strasbourg. Bar Exils is the watering hole of choice for a lot of Strasbourg's students who are looking for a cheap beer or a fine (yet inexpensive) cocktail. On those warm summer nights, you can gather round a table on the small but cozy terrace and enjoy a beer for just €2 (*€2.50 after 10pm*).

⚑ *Just off pl. Gutenberg.* ⓢ *Beer €2-3. Mixed drinks €3-7.* ⌚ *Open M-F noon-4am, Sa-Su 2-4am.*

■ LES BRASSEURS
♦ ❖ PUB, PIANO BAR

22 rue des Veaux   ☎03 88 36 12 13 ▣www.au-brasseur-strasbourg.com

This busy Belgian-style pub and bar serves food during the day, but as the evening approaches it transforms into a haven for local music lovers and those in search of a cheap drink. The generous happy hours mean you can get two pints for the price of one. The weekend brings free concerts of varying variety, so stop off here to see the talent that Strasbourg has to offer (and by talent we don't just mean the good musicians).

⚑ *From pl. du Château (behind the cathedral), head east along rue de la Rape, turn right onto rue des Ecrivans, and turn left onto rue des Veaux. Les Brasseurs is at the end of the street* ⓘ *Free live music on weekends.* ⓢ *Beer €2-5. Cocktails €3-8.* ⌚ *Open daily 11am-1am. Happy hour daily 5-7pm and 10:30-11:30pm. Last call 12:30am.*

LA PASSELLE
♦ ❖ BAR

38 quai des Bateliers   ☎06 79 42 89 45

La Passelle's unassuming facade doesn't do it justice. As you walk inside, you come one step closer to a night full of techno, salsa, or "Celine Diop" (for those not in the know, this is a West Coast-influenced avant-garde dance music), depending on which night of the week you decide to visit this busy bar. The chic and modern red design, along with the very inviting, comfy sofas, will make La Passelle either a great place to start the evening or (especially after 11pm) a fantastic one to end the night. Wednesday night is Celene Diop, and Thursday is salsa night. The weekend is dominated by techno and popular music.

⚑ *From pl. du Château, head south down rue du Bain aux Roses, over pont Ste-Madeleine, and left onto quai des Bateliers.* ⓢ *Drinks €3-9.* ⌚ *Open W-Sa 8pm-4am.*

JAVA BAR
♦ ❖ BAR

6 rue du Faisan   ☎03 88 36 34 88 ▣www.lajava.net

Java promotes itself as a student bar and makes the most of Strasbourg's thriving student population; Wednesday and Thursday nights are student soirées. Locals say that these events can be hit and miss—it's best to go in a group of friends to make sure that the night doesn't fall too flat. The upstairs bar, dimly lit to add some sort of atmosphere, is a small space filled with one long table through the middle and smaller tables around the edge of the room. The real action happens in the dungeon-like rooms downstairs, where the DJ works his magic, with two more bars and a dance floor to aid you in busting out your moves.

⚑ *From pl. de la Cathedral, head round the east side of the cathedral onto rue des Frères. Rue du Faison is the final left, just before pl St-Etienne.* ⓘ *Student nights on W-Th.* ⓢ *Drinks €3-5.* ⌚ *Open M-Sa 8pm-4am.*

strasbourg

L'ALCHEMISTE
🍺🍸 BAR

3 rue des Soeurs ☎03 88 37 02 83

L'Alchemiste really has cast a few magic spells over this place, with witches and wizards hanging from the ceiling and mystical objects sitting in the windowsill. The bar of this quirky place has a large (most likely fake) tree sprouting out from behind it. Don't let this put you off, though, as this bar is staffed by some extremely welcoming staff who will help you navigate your way through the beer and wines on offer. Head downstairs to the small seating area, which is decorated black and red in keeping with the theme from upstairs.

 # From pl. de la Cathedral, head round the east side of the cathedral onto rue des Frères. Rue de Soeurs is the final right just before pl. St-Etienne. $ Beer €3-6. Other drinks €6-12. ⏰ Open Tu-Sa 9pm-4am.

RETRO CLUB
🍺🍸 CLUB

pl. des Halles ☎03 88 22 32 22 💻www.leretro.com

The draw of this club, one of the few in the city, is its special ladies' nights; every Friday is "Lovely Girls" night, where only women are allowed entrance. After 11:30pm everyone is allowed in. The club provides entertainment (mostly in the male form) for women's bachelorette parties, birthday parties, or just a girls' outing.

 # Underground, just in front of the shopping center Halles. $ Cover €15. Drinks €5-12. ⏰ Open W-Sa 10pm-4am.

GOTHAM
🍺🍸 BAR

21 rue du Fossé ☎03 88 16 07 39 💻www.gotham-strasbourg.fr

If the price of the menu at Gotham is a bit off-putting, make sure you return for the more affordable drinks that the lounge bar serves after dining has ended. That way, you can enjoy the classy atmosphere without having to pay for the upscale food. The candlelit tables and modern seating areas will give you the feel of having eaten in Gotham, even if you are just sampling their cheapest bottle of champagne.

 # Just off pl. Klébar. $ Drinks €4-12. ⏰ Open Tu-Sa 10am-1:30am. Food stops being served at midnight.

ZANZIBAR
🍺🍸 BAR

1 pl. St Etienne ☎03 88 36 66 18 💻www.zanzibar-strasbourg.com

Zanzibar has a good selection of over 60 beer and 50 whiskeys for you to sample. The dartboard inside provides a break from all the air-guitaring the locals like to perform when the rock music gets playing. AC/DC and other bands can often be heard shaking the wooden doors as the music gets cranked up high. Both old and young gather to rock out in the center of Strasbourg all night long.

 # From the Cathedral, head along rue des Frères. $ Beer €3-5. Other drinks €4-8. ⏰ Open M-Sa noon-4am, Su 2pm-4am.

MOLLY MALONE'S
🍺🍸 IRISH PUB

1 pl. Austerlitz ☎03 88 52 94 26 💻www.pubmollystrasbourg.fr

The grand terrace outside Molly's is always buzzing on weekends, but with an older crowd that wants to watch the world go by with a pint of Guinness in one hand and a cigarette in the other. For a more quiet evening head to the bar and pick up one of the special brews the pub prides itself on, and make sure you get there for the happy hour, which halves the prices of beer and brews.

 # From the Cathedral, follow rue d'Austerlitz. $ Drinks €4-9. ⏰ Open M-Sa 11am-1:30am. Happy hour 6:30-8:30pm.

LE GAYOT
🍺🍸 BAR, RESTAURANT

18 rue des Frères ☎03 88 36 31 88

Place Gayot starts filling up by mid-afternoon, and by 10pm it is overflowing with people, so get there early if you want to grab a table. That said, the crowd is generally in their 30s (and upward) and the prices may explain why. Le Gayot isn't out of everyone's price range, but don't expect to come here for some cheap cheers and laughs—Le Gayot means business. The area is very family-friendly, with smaller children exploring the concrete artwork in the middle of the square.

 # Just off pl de la Cathedral. $ Drinks €4-10. ⏰ Open M-F noon-12:30am, Sa-Su noon-1am.

L'AUBETTER BAR

BAR, LOUNGE

31 pl. Kléber ☎03 88 13 71 30

L'Aubette, a busy shopping center in the middle of Strasbourg, has its very own bar, which stays open long after the shoppers have headed home. Inside is a plush sofa lounge with a very modern design, providing the perfect setting for a few glasses of Alsatian wine. During the summer, families and locals head outdoors onto the seating area that spans across the square to enjoy their drinks al fresco.

Just north of the cathedral, along rue des Grandes Arcades. $ Drinks €3-7. ⏰ Open daily noon-1:30am

TAPAS CAFÉ

BAR, TAPAS

16 rue du Bain Finkwiller ☎03 88 24 57 30

Although in Petite France you don't expect to find lively nighttime spots, this tapas bar stops serving food at midnight and continues the party for another hour and a half (at least). Very different from the bars on offer in the city center, this Tapas Café will make you wonder if you're dancing in Petite France or Madrid.

From Grand Rue, head down rue de Martin Luther. $ Drinks €3-8. ⏰ Open M-F 11am-1:30am, Sa 5pm-1:30am. Kitchen open until midnight.

arts and culture

FESTIVALS

FESTIVAL DE MUSIQUE DE STRASBOURG

MUSIC FESTIVAL, CLASSICAL

Wolf Musique, 24 rue de la Ménsage ☎03 88 32 43 10 www.festival-strasbourg.com

This annual event has been running for years and attracts some of Europe's best classical musicians. The concert takes place in and around Strasbourg, and is organized by Wolf Music, who can be contacted for tickets and program of events.

⏰ 2 weeks in June.

CONTRE TEMPS

MUSIC FESTIVAL, ELECTRONIC

☎06 49 41 67 04 www.contre-temps.net

The Electro Groove Festival is a brilliant 10-day event that attracts up-and-coming artists who specialize in urban culture music and electro groove. Although seemingly a very niche festival, Contre Temps will open up your horizons to the music of some of Europe's biggest future stars. You can choose to buy individual day/event tickets or a full-access pass. Check the brochure or online for more specific details for each performance. Tickets are sold by third party groups (Fnac, Ticketnet.fr, and digitix), and at La Culture Boutique by the Cathedral *(☎03 88 23 84 65 ⏰ Open Tu-Sa noon-7pm).*

Various locations across Strasbourg. i Some venues will sell out faster than others, depending on size. $ Full-access pass €35. ⏰ 2nd week of June.

THEATERS

THÉÂTRE NATIONALE STRASBOURG

1 av. de la Marseillaise ☎03 88 24 88 24 www.tns.fr

Strasbourg's main theater will entertain you with an array of performing arts, ranging from professional productions all the way to a young European directors' festival in the summer.

Tram B, C or E to [M]République. $ €16-25, students €13.50-16. ⏰ Box office open M 2-6pm, Tu-Sa 10am-6pm.

PALAIS DE LA MUSIQUE ET DES CONGRÈS

pl. de Bordeaux ☎03 69 06 37 00 www.philarmonique-strasbourg.com

The 2011 season of Strasbourg's outstanding Philarmonic Orchestra includes Beethoven's *Symphony No. 9* (April), Stravinsky's *Pulcinella* (May), and Schönberg's *Gurrelieder* (June). Housed in the beautiful building of the Palace of Music and of Congress, the philarmonic is a must for any classical music lover.

🚊 *Tram Line B direction Hoenheim (get off either Kléber or Wacken).* ℹ *Student rates available.* Ⓢ *Gala tickets €5-57.* 🕐 *Box office open M-F 10am-6pm.*

OPERA

OPERA NATIONAL DU RHIN
19 pl. Broglie   ☎03 88 75 48 00💻www.operanationaldurhin.eu

Strasbourg's beautiful Opera House has a fantastic 2011 season waiting to entertain you with some rather big classics in ballet and opera as well as some lesser-known performances. The big name for 2011 is *Hamlet*, which will be shown from June 9 until June 28. Other highlights of the program include *Triologie Russe* and *Le Lac des Cygnes (Swan Lake)*.

🚊 *Tram to Broglie.* ℹ *Student rates available.* Ⓢ *Tickets €15-90.* 🕐 *Box office open M-F 11am-6pm, Sa 11am-4pm. Also open 1hr. before curtain.*

shopping

FNAC
22 pl. Kléber   ✒♿ DEPARTMENT STORE
☎08 25 02 02 02 💻www.fnac.com

Fnac is one of France's best-known-department stores, and provides customers with electronics, books, CDs, DVDs, games, and other miscellaneous items. For long term students in need of some electronic essentials such as a kettle or microwave, Fnac will also be able to set you up.

🚊 *Pl. Kléber is just south of the tram stop l'Homme de Fer.* ℹ *Tickets to concerts and other events often available here.* Ⓢ *DVDs €10-20. Books €10-20.* 🕐 *Open M-F 10am-7pm, Sa 9am-7pm.*

LA CURE GOURMANDE
5 rue Mercière   ✒♿ CANDY STORE
☎03 88 32 97 49

This brightly colored sweet shop specializes in classic Alsatian biscuits and sugary treats. Pick a box (€4) and cram it full of delicious, handmade goodies, or try the "olives," the hard-boiled sweets colored green and black to resemble olives. Selection boxes also available if you'd rather not make the choice yourself. Also sells candy canes and lollipops.

🚊 *Rue Mercière runs to the cathedral.* Ⓢ *Fill a box for €4.* 🕐 *Open daily 10am-9pm.*

BOOKWORM
3 rue de Pâques   ✒ BOOKSTORE
☎03 88 32 26 99 💻www.bookworm.fr

Hidden away down a small street between two Alsatian *winstubs*, this little shop will provide you with a little piece of home if you are truly missing it. The friendly staff all speak English and will happily guide you through a wide selection of fiction, nonfiction, and language-resource books.

🚊 *Take rue du Faubourg de Saverne off quai St-Jean, northwest of the center. Rue de Pâques will be on your right.* ℹ *No longer sells secondhand books.* Ⓢ *Also sells calendars.* 🕐 *Open Tu-F 9:30am-6:30pm, Sa 10am-6pm.*

essentials

PRACTICALITIES

- **TOURIST OFFICE:** 17 pl. de la Cathédrale near the Cathedral. English-speaking staff. Free map available, or a more in depth map for €1.(☎03 88 52 28 28 💻www. otstrasbourg.fr 🕐 *Open daily 9am-7pm.*) Offers the **Strasbourg Pass** (€12.40, children €6.20), which covers free entrance into one of Strasbourg's 12 main museums,

essentials · practicalities

the cost of ascent to the cathedral platform, a boat tour of the city, half a day's bicycle hire and a view of the astronomical clock. The **Pass** (valid for 3 days) can also be used for half entry into another museum, half price on the audio tour tour of the city and half price on the minitram tour.

- **CONSULATES: USA.** *(15 av. d'Alsace ☎03 88 35 31 04 ✈ Next to Pont John F. Kennedy. ⏰ Open M-F 9:30am-noon and 2-5pm.)*
- **YOUTH CENTER: CROUS** offers info on housing, employment and student opportunities. *(1 quai du Maire-Dietrich ☎03 88 21 28 00 💻www.crous-strasbourg.fr ⏰ Open M-F 9am-noon and 1:30-4pm.)*
- **INTERNET ACCESS: TaxiPhone.** *(24 rue du Faubourg de Pierre ☎03 88 23 91 70 $ €0.50 per 15min. ⏰ Open daily 9am-9pm.)* Second location. *(3 quai Saint-Jean ☎03 90 93 53 70 $ €0.50 per 15min. ⏰ Open daily 9am-9pm.)*
- **POST OFFICE:** *(5 av. de la Marseillaise ☎03 88 52 35 50 ⏰ Open M-F 8:30am-6:30pm, Sa 8:30am-1pm.)* Branch at pl. de la Cathedral. *(⏰ Open M-F 8:30am-6pm, Sa 8:30am-5pm.)*
- **POSTAL CODE:** 67000.

EMERGENCY!

- **POLICE: Local police.** *(11 rue de la Nuée Bleue ☎03 88 15 37 17).* **Police Nationale.** *(34 route de l'Hôpital ☎03 90 23 17 17).*
- **PHARMACY: Association SOS Pharmacie.** *(☎03 88 61 03 83)*
- **HOSPITAL: Hôpital Civil de Strasbourg,** 1 pl. de l'Hôpital, south of the vielle ville across the canal *(☎03 88 11 67 68).*

GETTING THERE

Strasbourg can be reached by land or by sea, depending on where you're coming from. If you're in France already, then taking the **train** is likely the cheapest and most efficient means of travel. Strasbourg now has a high-speed connection to **Paris Est** *($ €60. ⏰ 2hr.),* which runs every hour. Trains to **Nancy** run every hour *($ €22. ⏰ 1½hr.)* and it's possible to reach **LUX** *($ €34. ⏰ 2-3hr.)* and **Zurich** *($ €43. ⏰ 2½hr.)* Train tickets can be bought from the train station. *(⏰ Open M-F 5:45am-8pm, Sa 5:45am-8:50pm, and Su 7am-9:10pm.)*

To get to Strasbourg by **plane,** the airport has connections with **London, Lyon,** and **Paris,** as well as other countries. An **Air France** travel agent can be found on 7 rue du Marché *(☎08 20 82 08 20).* The airport is about 15km from the center of Strasbourg and is served by **Tram Line A** and a **shuttle bus,** which runs there roughly every 20mins. Tram tickets can be bought on the tram. The tram for the airport stops at the terminus, Baggarsee, where you must then take the shuttle bus. Three trams run every hour until 10:30pm.

GETTING AROUND

Traveling around Strasbourg is best done on foot; all the museums, sights, bars, and restaurants are very close to each other, and the paths and parks in Strasbourg make walking a convenient option. For making longer journeys, five **tram** lines run through the city, stopping at most major squares and locations in Strasbourg. Tickets can be bought on board *(€1.70, roundtrip €2.60),* or head to the Compagnie des Transports Strasbourgeois. *(14 rue de la Gare aux Marchandises ☎03 88 77 70 11, 03 88 77 70 70 💻www.cts-strasbourg.fr).* CTS also runs **buses** that travel between the train station and most major points in the city. Tickets for the tram are also valid on the bus.

LYON AND RHÔNE-ALPES

As the Alps-bound train leaves the rolling countryside and begins its long climb into the mountains, riders abandon their newspapers to watch a stunning transition: hills give way to craggy peaks, calm rivers to rushing torrents, and lazy cows to dashing mountain goats. High in the Alps, vast snowfields and glaciers look down on mountainsides blanketed with wildflowers. The region's stunning beauty draws not only those who want to admire it but also those who want to experience it up close: world-class athletes descend on the area each year to hike, bike, ski, and climb its majestic peaks. A trip to the region isn't complete without a glimpse of Mont Blanc—Western Europe's highest peak—but the gentler hikes and hidden trails throughout the area are dotted with tiny glacial lakes, and provide an equally rewarding visit.

Of course, you could hide yourself away in the solitude of the mountains, but why? Students dominate the cities of Grenoble and Lyon, which creates an international scene that makes drinking cheap and partying easy. Never fear if you don't know the French for "two pints of your finest beer, please"—the barman will probably serve you in English. The nightlife in the area is generally fast-paced, and you will move from grungy bars to dark nightclubs. You'll eventually end up back at your hostel. Just don't count on remembering how you got there. Beyond mountains and booze, Lyon hosts what are indisputably the best kitchens in the country (and possibly the world), and the smattering of historical sights are more than enough to keep you busy. The historic is juxtaposed with the modern in this region, and you can easily spend a morning in the middle of an ampitheater and be looking at a Picasso by the afternoon.

greatest hits

- **BEST CALORIE INTAKE EVER:** Splurge on Lyon's world-famous cuisine (p. 172).
- **BEST CALORIE BURN EVER:** Make the treacherous hike up to Grenoble's Bastille (p. 184).
- **SHOOTERS IN BULK:** A happening college town, Grenoble has one of cheapest and most happening drinking scenes we've seen in the country. Prepare to be up all night (p. 187).

Lyon and Rhône-Alpes don't make it to the top of most student tourists' lists, but they should. Tucked away in the French Alps, Grenoble is a total student town. In case you were worried that they didn't have college bars in France, head to ⊠**Les Berthom** for a cheap Belgian beer. When you don't want to remember what you've done the next morning, head to **Bukana** (just be sure to count your shots).

lyon 04

Ultramodern, ultra-friendly, and undeniably gourmet, Lyon (lee-ohn; pop. 453,000) is more relaxed than Paris and claims a few more centuries of history. Its location at the confluence of the Rhône and Saône Rivers and along the Roman road between Italy and the Atlantic made Lyon an easy choice for the capital of Roman Gaul. Today, Lyon has shed its long-standing reputation as a gritty industrial city, emphasizing its beautiful parks, a modern financial sector, and a well-preserved Renaissance quarter. The city is best known as the stomping ground of world-renowned chefs Paul Bocuse and Georges Blanc and as an incubator of contemporary culinary genius.

ORIENTATION

Like Paris, Lyon is split into neighborhoods that have then been numbered, and are often referred to by their number (1èr, 2ème, etc.) For the purposes of this guide, we've split Lyon into four main areas: Presqu'ile, Vieux Lyon, Croix-Rousse and Terreaux. All these areas are west of the Rhône river. To the east of the Rhône, the only landmark of note is the main train station, **Gare Part-Dieu**. The Rhône and the Saône split Lyon into three sections, with the Vieux Lyon on the far west, Croix Rousse to the far north of the center section, Terreaux to the center, and Presqu'ile to the South of the center.

Vieux Lyon

Vieux Lyon is the most beautiful and oldest part of city, with its cobbled streets, religious buildings, and large parks. The Metro stop Ⓜ️Vieux Lyon is in the center of the old town, near the Cathedral Saint Jean. The River Saône is to the east; the busy pedestrian streets of **rue du Boeuf, rue Saint Jean,** and **pl. du Change** run north to south, and are lined with traditional restaurants. The Funicular at the Metro stop takes you to the top of the Fourvière, where the **Basilica Nôtre Dame de Fourvière** is located with the HI hostel at Saint-Jean.

Croix-Rousse

Croix-Rousse is at the north of the city and perched on top of a very large hill. Head here for some wonderful views of Lyon, and to explore the older buildings of the city, the **Traboules** and the **La Maison des Canuts.** From the Metro Stop (Ⓜ️Croix-Rousse), **Grand Rue de la Croix Rousse** runs northwards, passing many small shops, boutiques, and La Maison des Canuts. Head eastwards to **rue d'Austerlitz** for some amazing views of the river below and the expansive parks to the northeast; this area is also a hotbed of some brasseries and cafes, so stop and grab a drink before climbing down the hundreds of stairs.

Terreaux

Place des Terreaux (Ⓜ️Hôtel de Ville) is to the north of the city center, and mainly in the 1èr. The area is one of the most diverse in Lyon, and hosts the breathtaking buildings of the Hôtel de Ville and the Musée Beaux Arts. From Place Terreaux three

lyon and rhône-alpes

streets run southwards; **rue Chenavard** and **rue Herriot** which both lead to **Place des Jacobins,** while **rue de la République** runs to **Place de la République.** North of the square, up the hilly roads, is the Croix Rousse area.

Presqu'île

The center of Lyon is focussed around **pl. Bellecour,** where you will find the tourist office and lots of restaurants around the square. **Rue Herriot** and **rue de la République** both run from the northeast corner of Place Bellecour, which has a lot of shops and cafes along them. **Rue Victor Hugo** runs southwards from the square towards **pl. Ampère,** around which you will find a lot of budget hotels close to train station Gare de Perrache. **pl. de la République** and **pl. des Jacobins,** both north of Place Bellecour, have fountains, restaurants, and shops around them and are useful for orientating yourself.

ACCOMMODATIONS

Most student travelers heading to Lyon check into the only hostel available in Vieux Lyon, consequentially, it can book up pretty fast. If you can't get into the hostel, or if you're in search of more comfortable accommodations, you can find some very quaint and charming places in the city's center, where a single room averages at €40-60.

Vieux Lyon and Presqu'île

AJ DU VIEUX LYON
⚡(ŋ) HOSTEL ❶

41-45, montée du Chemin Neuf ☎04 78 15 05 50 🖥www.fuaj.org

After conquering the massive hill in Vieux Lyon you may be ready to collapse (remember, there *is* a cable car), but the views you get from the HI Hostel in Vieux Lyon are worth the massive climb any day. Sitting on the terrace of the hostel you see the whole city expanding below you, cut by the two rivers, and during the summer you can lounge out and top up your tan. As this is the only hostel in the area, it's full of fellow students. If you can, try and request a room with a view of the city.

🚶 Ⓜ*Vieux Lyon. Walk up the hill or, take the Funicular to Pl. Saint-Jean.* 🛈 *Breakfast and sheets included. Bring your own towel.* 💲 *6-bed dorms €18.* 🕐 *Reception 7am-1pm, 2-8pm, and 9pm-1am.*

HÔTEL DE THÉÂTRE
⚡ 🍴(ŋ) HOTEL ❸

10 rue de Savoie ☎04 78 42 33 32 🖥www.hotel-du-theatre.fr

The owners of this very homey hotel open up their radiant rooms for rent. The reception area has a petite dining area, complete with wooden floors and a very authentic-looking leather sofa, while the standard rooms are a good size and feel very homey. For those with a few extra euro, the superior rooms are bigger, more spacious, and very plush, promising a peaceful night's sleep in the center of Lyon.

🚶 Ⓜ*Bellecour* 🛈 *Breakfast €6.* 💲 *Singles €59-64; doubles €64-70.* 🕐 *Reception open 7am-11pm.*

HOTEL DE LA MARNE
⚡(ŋ) HOTEL ❹

78 rue de la Charité ☎04 78 37 07 46 🖥www.hoteldelamarne.fr

The exterior connecting the reception area to the rooms is slightly odd in Hotel de la Marne; passing along the mosaic floor from the modern reception, you're led to what feels like a small backyard. The plush and well-decorated rooms make it worth it.

🚶 Ⓜ*Perrache* 🛈 *Breakfast €6.* 💲 *Singles €57-63; doubles €63-73; triples €79-85; quads €87.* 🕐 *Reception 24hr.*

HOTEL ALEXANDRA
⚡(ŋ) HOTEL ❸

49 rue Victor Hugo ☎04 78 37 75 79 🖥www.hotel-alexandra-lyon.fr

Conveniently close to the Perrache train station, the Hotel Alexandra is more

lyon and rhône-alpes

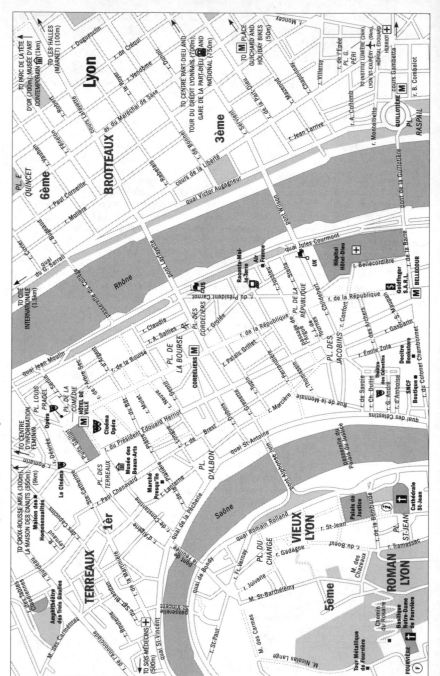

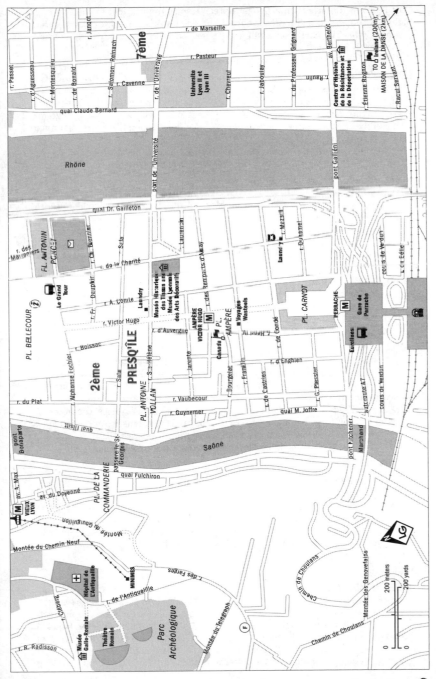

lyon • accommodations

of a terraced house than a budget hotel. Despite the old feel to the building, the bedrooms and bathrooms are modern and simple with a distinctly Mediterranean vibe. The chatty staff will make sure your stay in the city is as pleasant as possible.

🐸 ⓜ*Ampère.* 𝒊 *Breakfast €7.* ⓢ *Singles and doubles €45-60.* ⓩ *Reception 24hr.*

HOTEL D'AINAY
⟋⟍⁽ᵗᵖ⁾ HOTEL ❸

14 rue des Remparts d'Ainay   ☎04 78 42 43 42 🖳www.hotelainaylyon.com

Right next to the Place Ampère, this old-feeling hotel has faded rooms and a grand staircase. The location makes the cheap price well worth it. If you go for one of the cheaper rooms you will have to sacrifice a toilet; there are communal bathrooms down the hall.

🐸 ⓜ*Ampère.* 𝒊 *Breakfast €5.* ⓢ *Singles with shower €41, with shower and toilet €46; doubles with shower €45, with shower and toilet €50.* ⓩ *Reception 6am-10:30pm.*

HOTEL D'AZUR
⟋⟍⁽ᵗᵖ⁾ HOTEL ❸

64 rue Victor Hugo   ☎04 78 37 10 44 🖳www.hotelazurlyon.fr

Once you've gotten over the intense colors on the walls of the corridors (each floor has its own bright color, including a bright lime green and almost glowing yellow), you can enjoy these large and plainly furnished rooms with a good view of the old-looking street below.

🐸 ⓜ*Ambrère.* 𝒊 *Breakfast €6.* ⓢ *Singles €43-57; doubles €48-53; triples €73; quads €78.* ⓩ *Reception 24hr.*

HOTEL LE LYS BLEU
⟋⟍⁽ᵗᵖ⁾ HOTEL ❸

60 rue de Charité   ☎04 78 37 42 58 🖳www.lelysbleuhotel.com

Small and simple rooms in what feels like a former manor house, with high ceilings, sky blue walls, and a tremendous winding staircase to reception.

🐸 ⓜ*Ampère.* 𝒊 *Breakfast €6.* ⓢ *Singles €32-37; doubles €43.* ⓩ *Reception 24hr.*

HOTEL D'ENGHIEN
⟋⟍ᵞ HOTEL ❸

22 rue d'Enghein   ☎04 78 37 42 63 🖳www.enghien-lyon.fr

Situated above a local restaurant, this cozy budget hotel has an old stone staircase leading to some interesting rooms. They have a bit of an odd layout; the shower and the toilet are located at opposite corners of the room, and each room has a rather bright green door. Despite these idiosyncrasies, the hotel offers cheap comforts near the center of the city, and the rooms are quite spacious. Most rooms have fireplaces, and several were renovated in 2010.

🐸 ⓜ*Perrache.* ⓢ *Singles €38-42; doubles €43-47; triples €63-69.* ⓩ *Reception 9am-10pm.*

Croix-Rousse

HOTEL DE LA POSTE
⟋ HOTEL ❸

1 rue Victor Fort   ☎04 78 28 62 67

A small hotel with modest rooms on top of the steep hill in Croix Rousse. If you want a hotel that's slightly out of the center, and you don't mind either taking the Metro to reach your home or climbing the massive stairs, this will suit you fine.

🐸 ⓜ*Croix-Rousse.* 𝒊 *Breakfast €6.* ⓢ *Singles €37-45; doubles €42-53; triples €65-75.* ⓩ *Reception 7am-1pm and 5-9:15pm.*

Terreaux

▨ HOTEL LE BOULEVARDIER
⟋⟍ᵞ⁽ᵗᵖ⁾ HOTEL ❸

5 rue Fromagerie   ☎04 78 28 48 72 🖳www.leboulevardier.fr

This quirky hotel is definitely worth checking out if you want a more interesting stay in Lyon. Compared to the standard offerings in the city center, Hotel le Boulevardier is one of the more eclectic (and good value) places to stay, from the colorful clocks covering the bar wall downstairs, to the old tennis rackets and golf clubs lining the hallways, to the modern art guiding you up the steep staircase to the rooms. The beds themselves are even covered with zany but tasteful covers like pink and green stripes or green polka dots.

✴ ⓂCordeliers. *i* Breakfast €6. Ⓢ Singles €41-51; doubles €47-53; triples €62; quads €74. Ⓩ Reception open from 7am.

HÔTEL IRIS
✦ HOTEL ❸

36 rue d l'Arbre Sec ☎04 78 39 93 80 ▧www.hoteliris.fr

The owner of this hotel personally ensures that the rooms are cleaned to the utmost in this hotel, which used to be a convent. The history of the building shines through, as the high vaulted ceilings make rooms feel much larger than they actually are. Potted plants contribute to an earthy and rather Mediterranean atmosphere for the place.

✴ ⓂHôtel de Ville *i* Breakfast €6. Ⓢ Singles €55; doubles €60. Ⓩ Reception 7am-8pm.

HÔTEL DE PARIS
✦⊶ HOTEL ❹

16 rue de la Platière ☎04 78 28 00 95 ▧www.hoteldeparis-lyon.com

Despite the misleading exterior, this hotel is a haven of plush and modern amenities; the lounge area comes complete with what looks like a cow-skin rug. Although the standard rooms smell a bit stale, you may want to stretch out on the plush comfort rooms, which match up with the modern design downstairs. Don't get confused by the metal walls in the hallways—the hotel's just trying to be ultra-modern.

✴ ⓂHôtel de Ville. *i* Breakfast €7. Ⓢ Singles €49-69; doubles €65-100. Ⓩ Reception 24hr.

HOTEL DE BRETAGNE
✦⊶ HOTEL ❸

10 rue Dubois ☎04 78 37 79 33

This small hotel has plainly furnished rooms whose only quirk is the cowprint toilet seat and toilet roll holders installed in all the bathrooms. The brown and white rooms won't revolutionize interior design, but they'll keep you comfortable and warm for a night in the city.

✴ ⓂCordeliers. *i* Breakfast €6. Ⓢ Singles €47.50-55; doubles €55-65; triples €63-75 Ⓩ Reception 7am-11pm.

HOTEL SAINT VINCENT
✦⊶ HOTEL ❸

9 rue Pareille ☎04 78 27 22 56 ▧www.hotel-saintvincent.com

It's a shame this traditional hotel closes in August; their large rooms are a great place to stay if you are looking for somewhere with a bit more character. The large staircase leads up to long rooms with fireplaces, large wooden doors, closets behind more wooden doors and...wooden floors.

✴ ⓂHôtel de Ville. Head along rue d'Algérie until you hit the river. Follow quai de la Pêcherie until you see pl. St Vincet on your right. The hotel is on your right. *i* Breakfast €6. ⓈSingles €55; doubles €70; triples €80-90. Ⓩ Reception 24hr. Closed in August.

SIGHTS
🔾

Vieux Lyon

Vieux Lyon is by far the most beautiful part of the city, with its cobbled streets, the Fourvière Hill, and mazes of streets and spiral staircases. For a more structured tour the Tourist Office provides a guide upon request.

▩ BASILIQUE NOTRE DAME DE FOURVIÈRE
✦ BASILICA

8 pl. Fourvière ☎04 78 25 86 19 ▧www.lyon-fourviere.com

Despite being built just over 100 years ago and gaining its status as a Basilica in 1897, the Basilica (known in English as *Our Lady of Forvière*) is the crown of the skyline of Lyon. Locals call it *un éléphant renversé*, because the white marble facade makes it look like Dumbo has fallen over at the top of the hill. The beauty of the building is clear as you approach from below, but the closer you get, the more the real spectacles begin to emerge. Inside, there is a fantastic painting dedicated to the Virgin Mary, for whom the Basilica was named as thanks for her protection during the Franco-Prussian Wars. The **Tour de l'Observatoire** is open from July-Sept and offers a fantastic panaromic view of the city below. For a free view, head to the back of the basilica and gaze at Lyons sprawling below. Make sure you descend via the Chemin du Rosaire for a peaceful walk through a sloping park.

✠ ⓂVieux Lyon. *Climb the hill until you reach the top, or take the Funicular from Vieux Lyon to Fourvière.* 𝒊 *Two tours of Tour de l'Observatoire are offered. The 45min. short tour takes you up 188 steps of the tower. The 1½hr. long tour takes you up the full 466 steps of the tower.* Ⓢ *Basilica free. Short tour €3, under 12 €1.50. Long tour €5, under 12 €3.* ☾ *Chapel open daily 7am-7pm. Basilica open daily 8am-7pm. Tours July-Sept daily 2:30pm, 4pm.*

lyon: 2000 years and counting

Over the course of two millennia, Lyon has managed to preserve sites from Roman times all the way through the Renaissance. It's your one-stop history tour of Europe in France:

43 BCE to 395 CE: Get a taste of Europe under the iron fist of the Romans by visiting the **Fourvière District**. The original site of the first Roman settlement Lugdunum, you can still visit the amphitheater and basillica, which has been converted to a Catholic Church now featuring a giant golden statue of the Virgin Mary.

12th-16th Centuries: The Middle Ages still very much exist in this district, with narrow streets and open market squares that offered a haven for painters and booksellers on the **rue Mercière** in the 15th and 16th centuries. Visit the Museum of Printing, and you'll find that no one could read back then.

Renaissance: In **Vieux-Lyon**, the 5th arrondissement is separated into three sections, all bearring the name of a Saint. St. Paul section is home to expensive hotels, given the original inhabitants were bankers; St. George has corridors and secret passageways that confound unsuspecting tourists and St. Jean is, appropriately the focus of political power in Lyon.

Late Renaissance 17th-18th Centuries: The "Slopes of **Croix Rousse**" are home to the original European artisan: the silk spinner. In the **place Tolozan**, you can find the still standing silk industry building, built in the 17th century, and old silk storage buildings that are connected by a series of passageways built by secretive silk workers.

MUSÉE GALLO-ROMAINS AND ARCHEOLOGICAL SITE　　　　RUINS

17 rue Cléberg　　　　　☎04 72 38 49 30 ▣www.musées-gallo-romains.com

Lyon, or "Lugunum," as it was known to the Romans 2000 years ago, was one of the most important cities in the Empire back in the day. The top of this hill was the cultural hub for the city, with amphitheaters and other meeting points for the locals. These beautifully preserved ruins can now be explored and exploited for the great view of the city below. Even more exciting is the fact that the Théatre Romain is used for concerts; Vampire Weekend, Iggy Pop, and REM have all performed here. To learn more about the history of the archaeological site and discover more remains from Lugunum, head to the museum at the top of the site.

✠ ⓂVieux Lyon. *Climb the hill and take a right at the Archéologique.* Ⓢ *Archaeological site free. Museum €4, students €2.50, under 18 free.* ☾ *Ruins open daily Apr 15th-Sept 15th 7am-9pm;*

Sept 16th-April 14th 7am-7pm. Museum open Tu-Su 10am-6pm.

CATHÉDRALE SAINT-JEAN CATHEDRAL

pl. Saint Jean

Lyon's Cathedral isn't as stunning as the other religious buildings that dominate French cities, but the interesting quirks of this place are worth checking out. The stained-glass window at the east side of the building depicts Lucifer's rejection from Heaven, with Lucifer displayed as a ★**dragon.** Not all the windows in the cathedral are religious. During the Nazi's retreat in 1944 some of the windows were destroyed, and have since been replaced with non-religious abstract designs. The 14th-century ★**Astrological Clock** chimes several times a day, and features popping automatons that reenact the Annunciation.

➔ Ⓜ Vieux Lyon $ Free. ⏰ Open daily M-F 8am-noon and 2-7:30pm, Sa-Su 2-5pm.

Croix-Rousse

LA MAISON DES CANUTS 👍 MUSEUM

10-12 rue d'Ivry 💻www.maisondescanuts.com

At the top of the Croix Rousse area (up a very steep set of stairs; you may want to take the Metro) is the location of Lyon's silk haydays. Lyon dominated silk production in Europe for centuries, and in La Maison des Canuts you can have a guided look at how to make silk the old-fashioned way. There's also a free exhibit with information on the history of the city's silk industry; the adjoining shop sells handmade silk scarves, ties, and handkerchiefs, which are expensive but impressive *(handkerchiefs €8.50).*

➔ Ⓜ Croix Rousse. Take the Metro from pl. Terreaux. $ Shop and exhibition free. Tours €6, students and under 25€3, under 12 free. ⏰ Guided tours daily 11am and 1:30pm; groups can call to arrange a tour.

Terreaux

MUSEÉ DES BEAUX ARTS 👍 MUSEUM

20 pl. des Terreaux ☎04 72 10 17 40 💻www.mba-lyon.fr

Located in the ornate Palais St Pierre, the museum's exhibits range from Egyptian mummies and hieroglyphics to the Ancient Roman bronze models of deities to 14th- and 15th-century Italian artwork. The first floor features an Islamic art collection with some beautiful pieces. Ascend the grand marble staircase to explore artwork from the 20th century, including some zany Picasso pieces. Classical pieces by Monet and Boucher are in the 15th- to 19th-century section, with a big collection of religious artwork further along the floor. Make sure you check out the gardens of Palais St Pierre, which have sculptures by Rodin and Bourdelle.

➔ Ⓜ Hôtel de Ville. $ €7, students and under 26 free. Audio tour €3, under 26 and students free. ⏰ Open M 10am-6pm, W-Th 10am-6pm, F 10:30am-6pm, Sa-Su 10am-6pm.

PARC DE LA TÊTE D'OR PARK, ZOO

quai Charles de Gaulle/bld. des Belges ☎04 72 69 47 60 💻www.lyon.fr

This 16-hectare park across the river and slightly north of the Terreaux area is a beauty that you have to visit if you're craving a green park. The zoo is fully equipped with lions, elephants, giraffes, and other typical exotic animals. The botanical gardens to the west of the park are extremely pretty, and the large open fields provide plentiful opportunities to kick back on a blanket and catch some rays. You can even get a boat out across the lake in the middle of the park.

➔ Buses #41 and #58 stop near the park at Parc Tête d'Or–Churchill. $ Park and zoo free. ⏰ Open daily Apr-Oct 6:30am-10:30pm; Nov-Mar, 6:30am-8:30pm.

PLACE DES TERREAUX

                                                 ♿ SQUARE

Heads might roll when you see this square; it was used as a place of guillotine beheadings during the French Revolution. Of course, with the Musée des Beaux Arts on one side and the Hôtel de Ville on the other, no one would suspect that morbid history today. On the far north side is a grand fountain built by Frédéric-Auguste Bartholdi; it used to belong in Bordeaux, but the mayor was unable to afford its upkeep, so in 1890 the mayor of Lyon bought it and transported it to his own city center. The four horses bursting out of the water represent the four tributaries of the Saône river that runs through Lyon.

✠ ⓂHôtel de Ville.

Presqu'ile

MUSÉE DES TISSUS
                                            ⚑ MUSEUM

34 rue de la Charité   ☎04 78 38 42 00 🖳www.musée-des-tissus.com

This museum is more for those who like their fashion, but it's not all Gaga and Chanel here. From 4000 year old Egyptian Tunics and fashions from the Ottoman Empire to French fashion from a few years ago, this museum provides a long history of what we wear and why we wear it. At the entrance, check out the family tree that maps a fierce history of fashion. Who knew that your jeggings have ancient Chinese and Italian roots.

✠ ⓂAmpère Victor Hugo. ⑤ €5.50, students and under 26 €3. ⌚ Open Tu-Su 10am-5:30pm.

FOOD
                                                             🔃

Lyon is the home of high quality and top notch French cuisine and many will say that this is the city where you will find traditional food alongside modern fusions. Walking through the cobbled streets, you will see areas lined with traditional *bouchons*—little restaurants that serve dishes such as *andouillette* (sausage in a variety of sauces), duck, snails, and frog legs. Most restaurants are accessible on a budget, and every restaurant offers daily set menus; you can expect to pay anything from €12 for set menus, and the more expensive (but oh-so-worth-it) set menus are often worth the splurge. Fast-food options can be found around many squares in the center and just off of Pl. des Terreaux, along with many kebab joints along **rue d'Algérie**. Daily food markets appear along the banks of the Saône from 8am-1pm hawking wares from fruits and vegetables to cheeses and other locally sourced produce.

Vieux Lyon

Vieux Lyon's cobbled streets are lined with *bouchons* and little alcoves housing all types of restaurants. Strolling along **rue Saint Jean** and the little streets off here will throw up many delightful places to sample the local cuisine.

LE PETIT GLOUTON
                                  🍴☕ CRÊPERIE, LYONNAIS ❷

56 rue Saint Jean   ☎04 78 37 30 10

This cheery little restaurant feels very homey, with its checkered tableclothes and attentive waiters. If you're in a hurry and don't want to sit down, don't fret—you can grab a cheap crêpe to go (€2.90-€5.55), and watch as the man makes it in front of you. For a more indulgent meal, we recommend the salmon (€12), or a special pork cooked in a mustrad sauce (€14.20). Their three-course set menu is cheaper than those at other restaurants in the area, but may be slightly less plentiful than other offerings (€14.25).

✠ ⓂVieux Lyon. rue St Jean runs north from the Metro station ⑤ Meals €10-15. Crêpes €2.90-5.55. ⌚ Open daily 11:30am-11:30pm.

LES PAVES DE SAINT JEAN
                                     ☕⚑ BOUCHON ❸

23 rue Saint Jean   ☎04 78 42 25 13

This traditional *bouchon* offers cheaper set menus than the other restaurants in

lyon and rhône-alpes

the area but without sacrificing the standard of the food. The restaurant boasts dishes such as cold pork meats, *andouillette*, and duck in pepper sauce. The high-ceilinged dining area makes it feel like the family are serving you dinner in their own kitchen, and the food is served quickly but still feels as if it's been freshly prepared.

✈ Ⓜ*Vieux Lyon.* Ⓢ *Set menus €12.50-21. Meats €9.90-15. Fish €9.90-16.* 🕙 *Open daily noon-2pm and 6:30-10:30pm.*

LIBRAIRIE CULTURE CAFÉ
16 quai de Bondy

Ⓦ✈ CAFE ❶
☎04 78 25 56 19 ▣www.book-livre.com

The old owner of this little bookshop has doubled it up as a "culture café," providing a great place to grab a drink, read a book, and watch the locals go by. With a view of the river, this cafe is a great little place to rest your feet, but make sure you explore the crypt of books under the first floor. The menu boasts a great range of 25 teas *(€3 each).*

✈ Ⓜ *Vieux Lyon.* Ⓢ *Drinks €1.60 3.* 🕙 *Open daily 10:30am 7:30pm.*

LE VIEUX LYON
44 rue Saint Jean

✈✈⌣ BRASSERIE ❸
☎04 78 42 48 89

Since 1947, Le Vieux has catered to locals and tourists alike; they've been there long enough to claim the name of the actual neighborhood. For the hungry among you, dive into their four-course gourmet menu *(€23),* where you have a wide range of dishes including local sausages, tripe and vegetarian options. For a cheaper option, the restaurant has a house speciality of steak and frites *(€13).*

✈ Ⓜ*Vieux Lyon. Rue St Jean runs north from the Metro station.* Ⓢ *Set menus €13-23. Entrees €12-18.* 🕙 *Open daily noon-2:30pm and 6-11pm.*

LE LAURENCIN
24 rue Saint Jean

✈✈ LYONNAIS ❸
☎04 78 47 97 37

The fake meats hanging from the ceiling and crates dangling above your heads in Le Laurencin makes you feel like you're in the kitchen where this traditional Lyonnais food is being prepared. With a range of set menus to choose from, you can sample some of Lyon's fine cuisine with a cheap "St Jean" menu *(three courses; €12).* For a larger range of plates on the set menu you can have the three-course gourmet menu *(€15),* or you can pick fish and meat dishes straight off the menu.

✈ Ⓜ*Vieux Lyon.* Ⓢ *Set menus €12-15. Meat entrees €9-12. Fish €11-15.50.* 🕙 *Open M-F noon-2:30pm and 6:30-11pm, Sa-Su noon-11pm.*

MAÎTRE BOEUF
6 pl. de la Baleine

✈✈ STEAK HOUSE ❹
☎04 78 37 37 90 ▣www.maitre-boeuf.fr

This modern-looking, bright red steak house offers a break from the Lyonnaise gastronomy. Although the menu is a bit pricier than at some of the cheaper options in the area, the portions and the meat make the spending worth it. For a cheaper option go for their three-course Lyonnais menu *(€21)* which has a choice of three different appetizers, entrees, and desserts.

✈ Ⓜ*Vieux Lyon. Place de la Baleibe is just off of rue du Boeuf.* Ⓢ *Beef dishes €16-28. Lyonnais menu €21; Maître Boeuf menu €26.* 🕙 *Open daily noon-2pm and 7-10pm.*

TERRE ADÉLICE
1 pl. de la Baleine

Ⓦ ICE CREAM ❶
☎04 78 03 51 84 ▣www.terre-adelice.fr

Terre Adélice is a glacier with a difference—they specialize in bio-ice cream and sorbets. This ice cream is locally made in the Lyon area, and comes in 200 different flavors (though not all of them are served at the same time), including pear sorbet, clementine sorbet, and caramel ice cream.

✈ Ⓜ*Vieux Lyon. On the corner along rue Saint Jean.* Ⓢ *1 scoop €2.30.* 🕙 *Open daily noon-midnight.*

lyon · food

LE PIQUE ASSIETTE

♥♥♨ TRADITIONAL ❸

4 rue de la Baleine

☎04 78 37 38 78

This cute little venue is a little removed from the busy square, but still packs a punch like the other Lyonnaise restaurants in the area. With a grand statue of armor standing in the doorway, le Pique keeps the theme of Vieux Lyon alive. The menu features traditional fare like *Plats Conailles* (a traditional pork dish from Lyon) and a three-course set menu *(€16.50)*.

❧ Ⓜ*Vieux Lyon. Rue de la Baleine is just off of place de la Bateine, which is along rue du Boeuf.* Ⓢ *Meat €16-18. 3-course menu €16.50.* ☒ *Open daily noon-2pm and 7-10:30pm.*

Croix-Rousse and Terreaux

Rue Austerlitz is lined with brasseries, which are usually open from 10am until late; entrees generally start at €10. **Place Croix Rousse** features lots of boulangeries and supermarkets for the real cheapskates among you. Head down the hill into the Terreaux area for a great selection of traditional and modern cuisine.

L'ESPRESS'O'

♥♥(ᵗᵖ) PIZZA, PASTA ❷

39 rue Paul Chenavard

☎04 78 91 86 64

Despite a plethora of expensive set menus that rarely dip below €15, L'Espress'o' offers slightly cheaper options in heaping portions. During the week, you can get a steak and chips *(€8)*, and for an extra €2 you can add a drink and a coffee. The traditional pizza and pasta offerings will fill you up nicely if you'd rather not eat steak, and the outside terrace opposite the restaurant is perfect for getting some sun.

❧ Ⓜ*Cordeliers* Ⓢ *Pizza and pasta €9-12. Set menu €13.50.* ☒ *Open daily 8am-10pm.*

LE NORD

♥♥ LYONNAIS ❸

18 rue Neuve

☎04 72 10 69 69

Although the food is slightly more expensive, heading north will give you some of the best Lyonnais cuisine available, from snails to *quenelle*. Although splurging on a meal here may break your budget, the three-course set menu *(€23)* gives you a rather lavish selection of Lyonnais cuisine. Grab a seat on their covered terrace, complete with faux stained-glass windows.

❧ Ⓜ*Hôtel de Ville.* Ⓢ *Meat entrees €15-26, 2-course set menu €20, 3-course set menu €23.* ☒ *Open daily noon-2:30pm and 7:30-11pm.*

LÉON DE LYON

♥♥ LYONNAIS ❸

1 rue Pleney

☎04 72 10 11 12

The man in a suit at the door says it all; Léon de Lyon is all about fine cuisine and high class dining, and the higher prices that come along with it. The menu rotates every two months, so the food offerings reflect the season, but you can expect pork and beef dishes, grand sausages, veal, and snails. The set menus are slightly more affordable but will still break some budgets.

❧ Ⓜ*Hôtel de Ville.* Ⓢ *Meat €14-26. Set menus €19.60-22.60.* ☒ *Open daily noon-2:30pm and 7-10:30pm.*

CHOCOLATIER BOUILLET

♥ CHOCOLATIER ❶

15 pl. de la Croix-Rousse

☎04 78 28 90 89 ▣www.chocolatier-bouillet.com

This chic little chocolate shop is high on the hill of Croix-Rousse, and sells delectable *petit gateaux* and a variety of macaroons. Though things here are a little more expensive than at your average candy shop, the attention to detail and the artistic nature of the chocolates and cakes make the price worth it.

❧ Ⓜ*Croix-Rousse.* Ⓢ *Most chocolates €3-6.* ☒ *Open Tu-F 8:30am-7:30pm, Sa 8am-7:30pm, Su 8am-1pm.*

lyon and rhône-alpes

Presqu'ile

The center of Lyon is great for cheap eats and traditional Lyonnais cuisine. Restaurants line **rue Mercière** and **rue des Marronniers** all boast set menus *(€14-25)*, where you will find typical dishes from the south of France. Splurging is not necessarily a bad thing here, as you get what you pay for—spending a few extra euro on dinner will give you a very tasty dining experience.

LA CLÉANOA 🍴 TRADITIONAL [3]
33 rue Mercière ☎04 78 37 78 37
Although their set menus are slightly more expensive than some of the others in the area, this ultra modern restaurant serves some mouthwatering dishes. This is one of those places where dishing out a little extra pays off. The duck dressed in lavender sauce and pork with peppercorn sauce may cost you a bit more, but you won't care about the damage to your wallet when the immaculate dishes are sizzling in front of you.
➔ [M]Cordeliers. ℹ English menu translations. $ Set menus €20-26. Lunch menu €12. Meats €14-20. ⏰Open daily noon-2pm and 7-11pm.

LA MARONNIER 🍴 LYONNAIS [3]
5 rue des Marronniers ☎04 78 37 30 09
This homey *bouchon* serves Lyonnais cuisine of all varieties. The helpful staff makes you feel like you're eating in someone's house rather than a restaurant. A brilliant three-course menu *(€14)* allows you to choose from several pork dishes, including a sausage in a red wine that which comes complete with potatoes. If you're after a more indulgent cuisine, there is a more expensive set menu giving you a choice of snails, mullet, and duck liver *foie fras*.
➔ [M]Bellecour. $ Set menus €14-23. Meat €8.50-18. ⏰ Open M 6-11pm, W-Su 6-11pm.

CHEZ MARIE-DANIELLE 🍴 BOUCHON [3]
29 rue des Remparts d'Ainay ☎04 78 37 65 60
Pictures of the Queen of England and Prince Charles indicate which toilet is for the *femmes* and which is for the *hommes* in the quirky Chez Marie. The small restaurant gives off a relaxed vibe, and you don't need to own your own island to pay for your meal. Everyone is made welcome by the staff, even the traveler in shorts and flip-flops. A lot of the dishes are served the "Marie-Danielle way," with a traditional flare to the cooking. Their beef steaks, covered in creamy and sauces, are popular and tasty *(€15-18)*.
➔ [M]Amère Victor Hugo. $ Lunch menu €16. Meat entrees €14-22. ⏰ Open M-F noon-2pm and 7:30-10pm.

LE CYRANO 🍴 BOUCHON, TRADITIONAL [3]
49 rue Mercière ☎04 78 38 13 44
The owner of this traditional *bouchon* may decide to join your table for a quick drink as you choose from his steaks, sausages, and more expensive (but equally as delightful) duck or salmon dishes. You can also choose from a set menu of the day, which includes a fish dish and a couple of meat dishes, as well as an entree and a dessert *(€17)*. The more lavish set menus allow you to sample some more gourmet offerings of the Lyonnais cuisine world.
➔ [M]Cordeliers. $ Set menus €17-26. ⏰ Open daily noon-2pm and 7-11pm

CHEZ MOUNIER 🍴 LYONNAIS [2]
3 rue des Marronniers ☎04 78 37 79 26
The marionettes in the window of this small restaurant add a quirky—albeit creepy—edge to traditional Lyonais fare. Punch and Judy guard the door with their guant wooden faces, and other puppets watch over you as you eat. Expect traditional dishes like *tripe* or *quenelle* on these simple but plentiful menus.
➔[M] Bellecour. ℹ Reservations recommended. $ Set menus €12.50-17.50. ⏰ Open Tu-Sa

noon-3pm and 7-11pm, Su noon-3pm.

CHABERT ET FILS ♥ ♈ 🍴 BOUCHON ❸

11 rue des Marronniers ☎04 78 37 01 94 🖵www.chabertrestaurant.fr

The family who owns this restaurant, *la famille* Chabert, owns three other restaurants on this street, though this one is the biggest, and offers the widest menu options. Their indulgent set menu *(€36)* may break budgets, but you'll leave with a belly full of Lyonnais goodness.

♯ ⓂBellecour. Ⓢ *Set menus €18-36.* 🕐 *Open M-Th noon-2pm and 7-11pm, F-Sa noon-2pm and 7-11:30pm, Su noon-2pm and 7-11pm.*

LE SUD ♥ ♈ MEDITERRANEAN ❷

11 pl. Antonin Poncet ☎04 72 77 80 00 🖵www.brasserie-bocuse.com

The *Bocuse* brasseries have four different locations in the city, but the one in the south is their nicest establishment. Serves pizza, pasta, and Mediterranean cuisine. The metallic golden sun hanging on the wall represents the *cuisine du soleil*, and the well-dressed waiters serve up plentiful southern dishes. The three-course menu includes a mix of Lyonnais and Mediterranean classics *(€23).*

♯ ⓂBellecour. Ⓢ *Pizza and pasta €12-14. Set menus €20-23.* 🕐 *Open M-Th noon-2:30pm and 7-11pm, F-Sa noon-2:30pm and 7-midnight.*

NIGHTLIFE 🏩

With Irish, English and Scottish pubs in the Vieux Lyon area, busy and noisy boat bars and clubs along the river, cocktail bars and classy establishments near the center, and rum bars specializing in rum cocktails, Lyon's nightlife scene has something for everyone and a bit of everything. A more relaxed scene can be found by sipping wine after your dinner, outside on one of the brasseries' terraces until the early hours.

🏩 LE PERROQUET BOURRÉ ❀ ♈ RUM BAR

18 rue Ste Catherine ☎06 68 68 03 12 🖵www.perroquetbourre.com

After having a few of the bar's famous cocktails ("Sex'n'Fresh," anyone?), you'll be stumbling on to the next bar like a *perroquet bourré* (drunken parrot). The dancing barmen chuck, throw, toss, and mix the cocktails in time with the music; if they like the looks of you you might even get in on their special handshake. If you're lucky, you might get a glowstick and some candy sweets in your cocktail.

♯ ⓂHôtel de Ville. Ⓢ *Rum shots €2-5, cocktails €5-7.* 🕐 *Open daily 6pm-1am.*

🏩 THE SHAMROCK ❀ ♈ IRISH PUB

15 rue Ste Catherine

Although this is an Irish pub, complete with the Guiness signs outside, a step inside the 🏩Shamrock will quickly remind you that you're in Lyon. Inside the small room with skateboards and buckets hanging from the ceiling, locals show off their musical talents in jam sessions on Wednesdays and jazz nights on Mondays. The back room offers a more chill atmosphere, with old leather sofas where students gather to drink a large bowl of cocktails *(€20),* or work through a meter of shots *(€16).* The place can get pretty crowded, though, so be prepared to tussle to get to the bar.

♯ ⓂHôtel de Ville. Ⓢ *Beer €2-6. Cocktails €6.50.* 🕐 *Open daily 7:50pm-late.*

SIRIUS ❀ ♈ BAR

4 Quai Augagneur

With treasure chests hanging from the top of the boat, a quirky collection of nets and diving suits, and even barrels for bar tables, this boat bar really gets in touch with its pirate side. Order a mojito complete with a glowstick *(€8),* or try the special "secret" punch that comes in bottles *(€10).* As the boat gets busier, the heat turns up, so expect to get sweaty on the dance floor in the early hours on the boat.

⇄ Ⓜ Cordeliers. Over pont Lafayette and along the waterfront. $ Drinks €3-10. ⏰ Open daily 9pm-3am.

AYERS ROCK CAFÉ
🍸 ROCK BAR

2 rue Désirée ☎08 20 32 02 03 💻www.ayersrockcafe.com

No, not *that* Ayers. With music so loud that the bartenders can only just hear your order, Ayers really isn't the place to come for a chat, but it's definitely the place if you're in the mood for a busy and wicked night of loud music, excited barmen, and Australian fun. Bouncers (and a fake kangaroo) guard the door on weekends when it gets busy, so you may have to dress to impress if you want to get in. Watch in awe as the barmen juggle bottles, balance glasses on their arms, and serve you a cocktail or beer with a few other party tricks they've learned along the way. They occasionally bang on the lights that hang above them, so mind your head!

⇄ Ⓜ Hôtel de Ville. $ Beer €3-6. Cocktails €6.50. ⏰ Open daily 8pm-3am.

THE SMOKING DOG
🍸 PUB

16 rue Lainerie ☎04 78 28 38 27

With pictures of dogs in smoking jackets and English music playing over the system, The Smoking Dog is a wonderful, if slightly out-of-place, watering hole. There is an old bookshelf full of French and English books in the back seating area, as well as empty boxes of whiskey. For a test of your brain power, visit on Tu night at 9pm for the weekly quiz, including the "Hamster Question" round and the "Yank or Manc" section. Even though the bar is English, the locals lap up the atmosphere, and you will find French people amongst the Anglophones.

⇄ Ⓜ Vieux Lyon. $ Beer €2-6. ⏰ Open daily 5pm-1am.

WALLACE
🍸 BAR

2 rue Octavio ☎04 72 00 23 91 💻www.wallacebarlyon.com

This pub is a self-confessed Anglophone bar, where you'll be served by an English-speaking (and most likely Scottish) barman, who'll help you through the menu of over 200 whiskies. The wall of whiskey dominates the back of the bar, and requires a library-style ladder to reach the top. It offers an endless list of delights; bottles are worth up to €60 a glass. English football and the Premiership play on the TV, and classic tunes beat out over the sound system. You might just forget France and begin to think you're in the Highlands.

⇄ Ⓜ Vieux Lyon. $ Beer €2.50-6. Tasting plate of 3 different whiskies €11. ⏰ Open M-Sa 11am-2am, Su 11am-midnight.

EDEN ROCK CAFÉ
🍸 BAR

68 rue Mercière ☎04 78 38 28 18 💻www.edenrockcafe.com

With a slogan like "Rock'n'Roll is not dead," you know that you're in for a treat at Eden. The classy cocktail bar isn't pumping with rock tunes, but rather chilled American 'rock', so expect some Elvis and other classics from the 1960s. The bar is American-themed, with a car hanging over the door, guitars on the wall, and even a statue of a woman in a very revealing dress. Although a little more expensive, the cocktails are delicious and provide you with a classy end to your night.

⇄ Ⓜ Bellecour $ Cocktails €8.50-14. ⏰ Open Tu-Sa 4:30pm-2am.

ON THE DECK
🍸 BAR

4 Quai Augagneur

Although there's a restaurant inside the boat, the big draw here is their "On the Deck" bar. Waitresses dart through the crowds, serving cocktails and wine into the early hours. If you're lucky, you might catch live music on the boat; otherwise, kick back and relax in the deck chairs.

⇄ Ⓜ Cordeliers. Over pont Lafayette and along the waterfront. $ Beer €4-5. Cocktails €8. ⏰ Open daily 6pm-late.

COSMOPOLITAN
BAR

4 rue Desirée

Next door to the Ozzy bar is a very American bar, where the Top 40 is all that you will hear. The music and style is completely American, with pictures, posters, and murals of all things USA. All the cocktails are American-themed, so you can grab a Bikini (not literally) or head down to 5th Avenue through the bottom of a glass. The happy hour "Downtown Cocktails" are just €4 (regularly €6).

✿ ⓜHôtel de Ville. *i* Owned by same people who own Ayers Rock Cafe. Student Night on Tu. Ⓢ Beer €2-6. Cocktails €6-8. Ⓧ Open daily 8pm-3am. Happy hour Th-Sa 8-10pm.

Q BOAT
CLUB, BOAT

17 Quai Augagneur ☎04 72 84 98 98

This is one of the more exclusive liners docked on the river Rhône. On the weekends, don't expect to get in unless you've made a reservation beforehand (or, if you're *known* to the bouncers)—the 3-strong bouncer team will make sure of that. Nights here come with good music and lots of drinks. During the week the entrance is less strict, and you can grab a cocktail on the deck of the boat with ease.

✿ ⓜCordeliers. Over pont Lafayette and along the waterfront. *i* Strict door policy. Ⓢ Drinks €3-8. Ⓧ Open daily 10am-late.

ST JAMES PUB
IRISH PUB

19 rue Saint Jean ☎04 78 37 36 70

This pub is definitely traditional. Just not traditionally French. Everything in the small pub reminds you of Ireland and the UK; a red phone box sits in the corner of the bar, while imported beer and ciders from across the ocean line the chalkboard. There's even a massive wooden leprechaun that points out where the bar is, and reminds you the place is "bar service only." Install yourself into one of the wooden booths to sip your pint.

✿ ⓜVieux Lyon Ⓢ Beer €3.70-5.70. Ⓧ Open daily noon-2am. Happy hour noon-9pm.

ROCK'N EAT
ROCK BAR

4 rue Octavio May ☎04 78 28 22 66 🖳www.myspace.com/rockneat

If you're into your Metallica and other heavy metal groups, then you'll find like-minded people at this classic rock bar in Vieux Lyon. The crowd is often dressed in black, and the music inside is loud and banging. Skulls adorn the walls, and posters of some rock classics look down on you from the second floor balconies.

✿ ⓜVieux Lyon Ⓢ €2-7. ⓧOpen daily 10am-1am.

ARTS AND CULTURE

Festivals

LES NUITS DE FOURVIÈRE
MUSIC, DANCE, THEATER

1 rue Cléberg ☎04 72 57 15 40 🖳www.nuitsdesfourviere.fr

Every summer, this massive arts festival takes place in Lyon with everything from public showings of black and white horror classics such as *Dracula* to another kind of vampire, Vampire Weekend. In 2010 Iggy and the Stooges even graced the Théâtre Romain as well as performances of The Tempest, "Let it Be," opera, and classical music performances. Every year Lyon trumps with its selection of arts and performances. Tickets can be bought by calling or visiting the Théâtre Romain or the FNAC store on rue de la République.

Ⓢ Tickets from €10. Some performances are free. Ⓧ June-July.

TOUT L'MONDE DEHORS
ARTS

🖳www.tlmd.lyon.fr

Tout L'Monde Dehors is an annual festival of free arts performances and classes in Lyon with all kinds of theater, dance, performances and music at your fingertips. Each year from June to September, there are hundreds of spectacles, most of which you can get involved in and all for free. The website has detailed information of all the performances for 2011 and about how to get involved.

i 2011 program to be announced. $ Free. ⏰ June 21-Sept 5.

LE FESTIVAL DE CINÉMA LUMIÈRE — FILM FESTIVAL

☎04 78 76 77 78 🖥www.lumiere2011.org

The annual film festival in Lyon lasts over a week in October with independent filmmakers from all over Europe showcasing their work. Film buffs flock to the city to see what the local filmmaking talent has to offer.

i Program announced in early July. $ Film tickets €5. ⏰ First week in October.

FÊES DES LUMIÈRES — LIGHT FESTIVAL

🖥www.lumieres.lyon.fr

In honor of the Virgin Mary, locals put candles in their window every Dec 8th and ascend to the Basilica to honor the Virgin Mary. In the city center there are impressive light displays and events all across Lyon.

⏰ Dec 8th.

ESSENTIALS

Practicalities

- **TOURIST OFFICE:** In the Tourist Office Pavillion at place Bellecour, 2ème. *(☎04 72 77 69 69 🖥www.lyon-france.com. ⏰Open daily 9am-6pm.)* Offers free accommodation bookings, a free public transport map and the 👍**Lyon City Card** *($1 day €20. 2 days €30. 3 days €40.).* It gets you free entry into Lyon's 21 museums, free public transport for the period, a city tour, a boat tour *(Apr-Oct)* and reductions at certain places, including the National Opera and bicycle rentals. Student reductions on the price of the card are available upon request.
- **TOURS:** Audio tours are offered in English and organized by the Tourist Office. To book one, either call or go into their office *($ €9, students €5).* **Le Grand Tour** is also offered. English guides are available *($ €17, students €15, ages 4-11 €8 ⏰ 1hr. 15mins.)*
- **CONSULATES: USA** *(1 quai Jules Courmant, 2ème ☎04 78 38 36 88).* **Canada** *(17 rue Bourgelat, 2ème ☎04 72 77 64 07).* **UK** *(24 rue Childebert, 2ème ☎04 72 77 81 70).*
- **CURRENCY EXCHANGE: Goldfinger SARL.** No commission *(81 rue de la République ☎04 26 68 00 12 ⏰ Open M-Sa 9:30am-6pm).*
- **ATMS:** 24hr. ATMs line the Bellecour Square in the Hôtel de Ville area. An **HSBC** Bank is located at 18 Pl. Bellecour *(☎04 78 92 31 00 ⏰Open M-F 8:45am-12:15pm and 2-5pm).*
- **LAUNDROMAT:** 19 rue St-Hélène, 2ème. *($ €4 per 7kg ⏰Open daily 7:30am-8:30pm).* Another branch at 51 rue de la Charité, 2ème *(⏰ Open daily 6am-9pm).*
- **INTERNET ACCESS:** Free Wi-Fi at the **Bellecour McDonald's. Raconte Moi la Terre** has Wi-Fi and internet access *(14 rue du Plat ☎04 78 92 60 22 $€3 per hr. ⏰Open M noon-7:30pm and Tu-Sa 10am-7:30pm.)*
- **POST OFFICE:** Pl. Antoine Poncert, 2ème, next to pl. Bellecour. *(☎72 40 65 22 ⏰Open M-W 9am-7pm, Th 9am-8pm, F 9am-7pm, Sa 9am-noon).*
- **POSTAL CODES:** 69001-69009; last digit corresponds to arrondissement.

Emergency!

- **POLICE:** 47 rue de la Charité (☎04 78 42 26 56).
- **HOSPITAL: Hôpital Hôtel-Dieu** (1 pl. de l'Hôpital, 2ème☎08 20 08 20 69; central city hospital line).
- **EMERGENCY SERVICES:** ☎17.

Getting There

By Plane

Lyon's main airport is **Aéroport Lyon-Saint-Exupéry.** You can reach the city proper from the airport by train run by **Rhônexpress** (🖳www.rhonexpress.fr ⑤€13, roundtrip €23; ages 11-25 €11, roundtrip €19. ⏱30min., daily 5am-midnight). You can pick the train up at **Lyon Part-Dieu** station or **Vaulx-en-Velin La Soie** station. Tickets can be bought online in advance to save time. For information on flights, **Air France** has an office on 10 quai Jules Courmont, 2ème (☎08 20 32 08 20) and runs 10 daily flights to Paris's Orly and Charles de Gaulle aiports (⑤from €125. ⏱Open M-Sa 9am-6pm.)

By Train

Lyon is served by two main train stations. The main station is **Gare de la Part-Dieu,** where all national and international trains depart from (5 pl. Béraudier ✠ ⓂPart-Dieu. ⏱ Info desk open daily 5am-12:45am. Ticket window open M-Th 8am-8pm, F 7am-10pm, Sa 8am-8pm, Su 7am-10pm.) **Gare de Perrache** is where most trains that end their route in Lyon finish. (Pl. Carnot ✠ Ⓜ Perrache ⏱ Ticket office open M 5am-9:45pm, Tu-Sa 5:30am-9:45pm, Su 7am-9:45pm.) Trains leave both stations to **Dijon** (⑤€27. ⏱ 2hr, every hr.), **Grenoble** (⑤ €20. ⏱ 1½hr, every hr.), **Marseille** (⑤ €44. ⏱ 2hr., every hr.), **Nice** (⑤ €70. ⏱ 6hr., 3 per day.), **Paris** (⑤ €80. ⏱ 2hr., 17 per day.), **Strasbourg** (⑤ €53. ⏱ 5hr, 6 per day.), and **Geneva, CHE** (⑤ €28. ⏱ 2-4hr., 6 per day.). The trains are run by **SNCF.** Their office is located at 2 pl. Bellecour, near the tourist office (⏱ Open M-F 9am-6:45pm and Sa 10am-6:30pm).

Getting Around

Bordeaux can easily be tackled by foot. For longer journeys, the following options are available:

By Bus, Tram, and Metro

All public transport in Lyon is run by **TCL** (☎08 20 42 70 00 🖳www.tcl.fr). There are TCL information offices at the bus and train stations **Part-Dieu** and **Perrache,** and also at major metro stations. A very useful plan of the bus routes and map of the city is available from the Tourist Office or the info centers. All **tickets** are valid for the metro, bus, and tram, and last either one hour (€1.60), or are valid for 10 separate journeys (€13.70; connections and changes included). Public transport runs daily from 5am-12:20am. Th-Sa there is an additional night bus service that runs from Pl. Terreaux to the University areas (every hr., Th-Sa, 1am-4am). The **T1 Metro** line connects the two **train stations,** Part-Dieu and Perrache directly. For reaching the top of **Fourvière** in Vieux Lyon, there are **funiculars** (cable cars) which run between ⓂVieux Lyon, Pl. St-Jean hostle, and St-Just/Fourvière Basilica, until midnight (€2.20).

By Bike

Vélo'v (🖳www.velov.grandlyon.com) has bike rental spots all around the city center, which makes grabbing a bike cheap, simple and easy. A day card costs €1, which allows you to take a bike from the docking station and use it at your leisure. The first half an hour of travel is free, and the second half hour is €1. Every half hour after that costs €2. You can pick up a map with the points from the internet, the bike points, or the tourist office.

grenoble ☎04 76

A popular safe haven for hard-drinking students and grungy granola freaks, this college town hosts a crushing amount of diversity. Grenoble's suburbs are home to the city's immigrants; the old city houses an eclectic mix of Indian and North African cultures, not to mention an extensive international student population. Ringed by the pristine French Alps, the city is a cheap and relaxing option for eco-conscious types who aren't as into nature as they'd like to be, but still love the odd hour-long hike or afternoon ski; regular buses to various trailheads transport diehards to the beginning of their seven hour treks through the mountians and snow. Refreshingly, Grenoble's bars cater almost exclusively to local students as opposed to tourists, and as a result are some of the cheapest in France.

ORIENTATION

The heart of Grenoble is the *Vieux Ville*, which is bounded by the River l'Isère to the north, Cours de Jean Juarès (the longest straight road in France) to the west, and the **Museum of Grenoble** to the east. One of Grenoble's largest suburbs, Échirolles, is about 4 km to the south, and is connected to the *centre ville* by the #1 bus and the A Tram. The other side of the River l'Isère is mostly residential, though there is a thin avenue of shops and cafés that runs along its bank. Towering over the city is the **Bastille**, a mountain fortress with stunning views of the new and old city, as well as the mountain ranges surrounding Grenoble.

ACCOMMODATIONS

Crashing in Grenoble proper can get pricey. To stay in the center of town cost-efficiently, *Let's Go* advises that you stay for longer than a week, and/or travel with someone to split the cost of a double room in the vieux ville. If you're budget travelling for a short period, you're going to have to sacrifice location and stay in the 'burbs.

LE FOYER DE L'ÉTUDIANTE — FOYER [1]

4 rue Ste Ursule ☎04 76 42 00 84; fax 42 96 67 www.foyer-etudiant.org

Located close to the vieux ville, Le Foyer de l'Étudiante is by far the cheapest and most convenient option for anyone planning on spend at least a week in Grenoble. The large kitchen offers multiple stoves and four refrigerators, while the main hall and courtyard provide eating and mingling space. The simple, clean rooms are furnished with a bed and desk, with double rooms lofted for studying (or other kinds of) privacy.

From the train station, take Tram B in the direction of Plaine de Sports to Notre Dame-Musée. Facing the direction you came, turn left on to rue Très Cloîtres, make your thrid left at rue Commandant l'Herminier, and rue Ste. Ursule is the first on the left. ℹ *Kitchen, laundry €2, and Wi-Fi included.* $ *Weekly singles €110, doubles €80. Monthy for €350/250.* ⏰ *Check in after 2pm, check-out before 10am. Non-EU citizens staying longer than 90 days must provide a visa upon check in.*

HÔTEL DE LA POSTE — HOTEL [3]

25 rue de la Poste ☎04 76 46 67 25

A small but pricey home away from home. The quilts on the European sized beds and couches will remind you of your grandma's house, and the wooden cabinets in the kitchen would make *grande-mère* herself weep for her pre-war home. We're sure if you ask, the hotelesse will tuck you into bed.

Located in the heart of the vieux ville on the block bonded by the A and B Trams, and Bld. Agutte-Sembat. ℹ *Located on the first floor of an apartment building. Kitchen. Wi-Fi included. Kitchen use and cable TV.* $ *Singles €39; doubles €41.* ⏰ *Reception 24hr.*

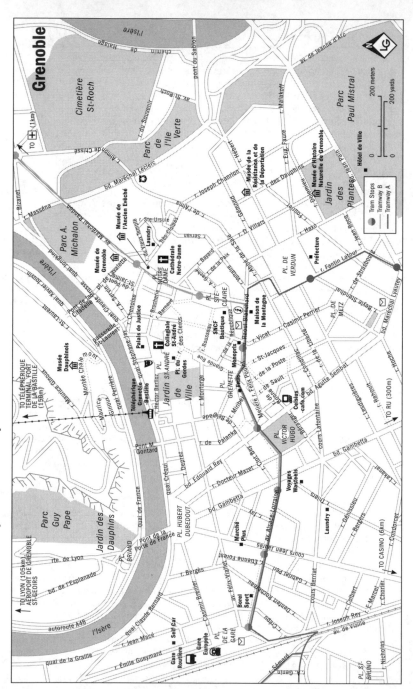

lyon and rhône-alpes

Grenoble

AUBERGE DE JEUNESSE (HI)

HOSTEL [2]

10 ave. de Grésivaudan ☎04 76 09 33 52; fax 38 99 🖳www.fuaj.org

The rooms are clean and spacious, and the incessant eco-friendly reminders won't let you forget to turn off the light or flush less. HI is completely and totally out of the way of Grenoble (it's in Échirolles, a local suburb) but there is a bus that runs often right by the hostel. Though the majority of boarders are French, the staff speaks very good English, and is willing to futher perfect their language skills by giving prospective patrons guided tours of the hostel. If you are a solo traveller staying less than a week, this is your affordable option.

#Take bus 1 (dir. Pont Rouge) from the corner of rue Alsace-Lorraine and cours Jean Juares to Quinzaine, in front of the Casino Supermarché. Facing the direction from which the bus came, turn left onto Grésivaudan; the auberge is three blocks on the right. Or take Tram A (dir. Echirolles-Denis Papin) to La Rampe-Centre Ville. Walk in the direction from which the tram came, turn left at the first intersection at the McDonalds. Trust the signs that point towards the Auberge: the street snakes for a good 15 20 minutes through multiple, dimly lit intersections that make you think you're lost. You'll come to the the Casino Supermarché. The Auberge is three blocks up on the left. Look for the orange triangle symbol. ℹ *Wi Fi, breakfast and linens included.English speaking staff.* $ *€19/person/night in rooms between 2 and 6 beds shared bath ensuite.*

HÔTEL VICTORIA

HOTEL [3]

17 rue Thiers ☎04 76 46 06 36 🖳www.hotelvictoria.com

Hôtel Victoria's fancy china and old world glam-tastic dining room make up for its simple rooms, which come with either ensuite or shared bathrooms. Located in a calm enclave of the vieux ville, this hotel is on the pricey side for the average backpacker, but remains a pretty good deal when you factor in the ridiculously cheap covered parking (*€3 a day*). It's best to bring a buddy and a car to make this place worth it.

 # From Place Victor Hugo with the Bastille fort on your right, walk along Alsace-Lorraine two blocks. Turn left on rue Thiers. ℹ *Wi-Fi included. Covered parking. Breakfast for €7.50* $ *Singles without bath €42, with bath €51; doubles without bath €50, with bath €58.* ⏰ *Closed from 20 July to 20 August, because absolutely NO ONE goes on vacation in August.*

3 LE 3 PUCELLES

HOTEL [1]

58 rue des Allobroges ☎04 76 96 45 73 🖳www.camping-trois-pucelles.com

Located in Seyssins, a suburb 4km from the old city of Grenoble, 3 Le 3 Pucelles is more of an assortment of campers than a hostel, with a decent-sized campground behind the suspiciously green pool. The location of this affordable option can get inconvenient; service at the nearby bus stop is limited at night, and the local route does not run to the *centre ville*. Clean and pleasantly rustic, once you get past the tents and trucks.

 # From the Gare, take Tram A (dir. Seyssins Le Prisme) to Mas des Îles. Turn left, and walk down rue de Dauphin. towards the river. ℹ *Parking and electricity available.* $ *1 person, tent and car €10, two persons €14.50. Electricity €2.50.* ⏰ *Office open 8am 1pm, 3 9pm.*

SIGHTS

TÉLÉPHÉRIQUE GRENOBLE-BASTILLE

PANORAMIC VIEW

Quai Stéphanie Jay ☎04 76 44 33 65 🖳www.bastille-grenoble.com

Brave the gondola (read: small plastic ball about 5 feet in diameter) and crawl 262 meters up to this venerable 16th century fortress, which held a key defensive position for the Alps division of the French Army. If you know French, visit the free military museum with the free audio tour. If you don't know French, visit the free military museum and snicker at the plastic life-sized replicas. No angry peasants made it up this hill, so this Bastille fared better than its cousin in Paris and remains well preserved. It additionally houses a **Museum of Contemporary Art** (☎*04 76 54 40 67;* 🖳*www.cab-grenoble.com*) and restaurant. The Bastille is also the starting point of multiple breathtaking trails of varying difficulty, ranging from leisurely walks to vertical rock climbs.

i Right alongside the river. Look for the cable cars. $ One way/Round trip: €4.40/6.50; Students €5/3.45 ⏰ Jan-Feb and Nov-Dec: M-Tu 11am- 6:30pm, W,Th,Su 10:45am-6:30pm, F-Sa: 10:45am-12:05 am; Mar: Same except Su 10:45am-7:25pm; Apr/May/Oct: M 11am-7:25pm, Tu 11am-11:45pm, W-Sa 9:30am-11:45pm, Su 9:30am-7:25pm; Jun: M 11am-11:45, T-Sa 9:15am-11:45pm, Su 9:15am-7:25pm; Jul/Aug: M 11am-12:05am, T-Su 9:15am-12:05am; Sept: M 11am-11:45pm, T-Sa 9:15am-11:45pm, Su 9:30am-7:25pm.

MUSÉE DE GRENOBLE — MUSEUM

5 pl. de Lavalette ☎04 76 63 44 44 🖳www.muséedegrenoble.fr

The pride of the museum is its 20th century French art collection, which features works by Matisse and Chagall, as well as a whimsical sculpture garden that Tim Burton would be fond of.

i Guided 1.5hr. tour in French or English audio tour for €4. $ €5 entrance, students €2. Under 18 free, first Su of every month is free. ⏰ Open M, W-Su 10am-6:30pm. Closed Jan 1, May 1, and Dec 25.

THE GREAT OUTDOORS

Skiing and Snowboarding

Oisans

Grenoble's biggest ski areas are to the east of Oisans. **Alpe d'Huez** is where Lance Armstrong kicked ass in the mountain portion of the Tour de France, and where you can ski 250km of trails, ranging from bunny slopes for beginners to balls-to-the-wall vertical drops (*Tourist office: ☎04 76 11 44 44 🖳www.alpedhuez.com Ski area ☎04 76 80 30 30.$ Lift tickets €40.50, students €36 in late Dec-early May, €25/€22.50 Mar-Dec*). For those who left the bunny slopes long ago, head for **Les Deux Alpes**, the largest skiing glacier in Europe (*Tourist office:☎ 04 76 79 22 00; 🖳www.les2alpes.com. Ski area: ☎04 76 79 75 01.$Lift tickets per day in winter: €38.90, summer €33.50*).

Belledonne

Devoid of the towering heights and pristine conditions of Oisans but boasting lower prices, **Chamrousse** offers 90km of downhill trails and 40km of alpine skiing. With a **FUAJ youth hostel**nearby (*☎04 76 89 91 3*), the atmosphere is more lively for those interested in a less intense introduction to skiing or snowboarding on easier trails. (*Tourist office: ☎04 76 79 22 80; 🖳www.chamrousse.com $Lift tickets €17/€14 for students/€5 seniors over 70*).

Vercors

South of Grenoble, and more popular with the locals, the resort **Grass-en-Vercors** boasts a 1000m vertical drop. The dirt cheap prices here are difficult for students to take advantage of, since the lodge can only be reached by car (*⏰ 40min from Grenoble. Tourist office: ☎04 76 34 33 40 🖳www.gresse-en-vercors.com $Lift tickets: €17, under 18 €14*).

Hiking

The Bastille

The hikes that depart from the Bastille range from romantic strolls to adrenaline fixes. **Mont Jalla** (*⏰ 30min, 1.5km*) is among the less strenuous. The trail is about as wide as a car, and is all switchbacks. A memorial to the fallen of WWII is situated at the top of the trail, where hikers are treated to panoramic views of the local city and the rivers. On a clear day you can see **Mont Blanc**, France's highest mountain. Only .4km from the Bastille, the **Grotte de Mandaran** features a long and exciting (read: dimly lit and slippery) series of tunnels carved out of the mountain, which loop back around to the Bastille after reminding you why you were so afraid of the dark as a kid (*lit until 9pm Apr-Sept, 7pm Oct-Mar*). If that's not enough of to curb your death wish, **Via Ferrata** is an Alpine climbing wall an hour up from the Bastille *(Porte closes at 6pm Sept*

16-Mar, 8pm Apr-Sept 15). Let's Go advises that you rent your equipment at **Barel Sport** *(42 rue Alcase-Lorraine ☎04 76 46 47 46 $ Also offers ski and snowboard packages for €13/17, weekly €67/90 ⏰ Open year round M-Sa 9am-noon, 2-7pm. Nov-Mar open Su 8-11am)*

The Parc Guy Pape is a relaxing cool down after a day of bandeliering, and the easiest way to walk down from the Bastille for free. Be careful on this trail when it's raining— the trail is mostly dirt and slippery concrete steps. To keep from getting lost, walk towards the signs to Porte de France or Jardin de Dauhpin, then follow the signs to Grenoble once about 20 minutes down the hill *(closes at 5:30pm Sept 16-Mar, 7:30pm Apr-Sept 15)*. For more information on your Bastille hiking pleasures, hit the **Maison de la Montagne** and pick up a copy of the free and useful Carte des Sentiers des Franges Vertes, which will direct you to the most scenic trails at the top of the Bastille.

Other Hikes

Though the Bastille trails are among the most easily accessible, Grenoble is surrounded by mountains, which provide both the casual hiker and the granola munching BAMF with a diverse range of hikes to choose from. **Chamechaude** is among the most strenuous. The first section of the hike follows GR9 "Tour de Chartreause," marked with red and white lines on trees and rocks. At Habert Chamechaude, take trail B on the climb up a near vertical rock face using a wire cable for assistence; it can be dangerous, especially when wet. Descend along same route. *(14.2 km, 6-7 hr. roudtrip, 1068m elevation change. Take VFD bus #7140 to Le Sappey-en-Chartreuse (30 min, 2-3 per day, €1.40). The bus stops after the church; follow the street to the right downhill. The trailhead is marked with yellow signs on the left.)* We recommend that the less hard core try **Le Moucherotte**. Follow the road to the left of the church and cemetery to the trailhead of the GR9, across the street from the panoramic viewpoint. This leads to the summit marked by red and white lines. A red and white "X" indicates you're leaving the route. Descend by the same route. *(8.4 km, 4 hr. round trip; 731m elevation change. Take Transière bus #5110 (dir. Lans en Vercors) to St-Nizier du Moucherotte (40 min, 1-3 per day, €3.20) and turn right toward the church)*.

Almost all of Grenoble's hiking trails can be reached by public transport, and are free. The #31 bus takes you out to the the trailhead of an Alpine pass. More isolated hikes are accessed by car or infrequent buses. While the trails are well marked, we suggest splurging on a IGN hiking map at any bookstore or newstand in France for around €8. All bus schedules are available at the TAG info desk at the **Maison du Tourisme.**

Biking

Chamrousse offers trails 40min. from Grenoble during the summer. The buses *(6 per day, €4.30)* take you to the four bike paths the mountain has to offer.

FOOD

Grenoble's *vieux ville* plays host to almost any kind of food you can think of, from the Asian and North African restaurants sandwiched between **Place Notre Dame** and the river, to the cafes lining the **Place Saint André** and the river on **Rue Saint Laurent.** Traditional French restaurants are scattered along the opposite side of Place Notre Dame. The best bets for cheap food are fast food shawarma joints throughout the city, or the **U Express** *(17 rue Alsace-Lorraine; ⏰Open M-Sa 8am-9pm, Su 8am-12:30pm, and on 2 rue President Carnot; ⏰Open M-Sa 8am-8pm, Sun 8:30am-1:30pm)* where you can find groceries and toiletries. The one on **Rue President Carnot** sells hard liquor. There is also a **Casino Marché** next to the HI Auberge at 46 rue Jean Jaurès *(⏰Open M-Sa 8:30am-8pm)*.

LA CRÊPERIE CADET ROUSELLE — CRÊPERIE [1]

3 rue Millet — ☎04 76 46 02 24

This new Bretton Crêperie is packed with mini wooden tables and chairs that make you feel Hobbit-sized. The incredibly well priced menu ranges from cheap cheese crêpes (€1.60) to croque monsieurs and club sandwiches, which give you a little more bang for your buck (€4.60). The Spéciale is the by far the best deal (*cheese, egg and ham; €4.60*) and ideal for a late brunch—which is just as well, since the place opens at noon.

🕐 *M-Sa 12-2pm and 7-11pm. Oct 30-Apr open non-stop on Saturdays from 12-11p. Closed on M and Su.*

▨ LE PETIT TABLE

🍴🍷 BISTRO ❸

16 rue Barnarve ☎04 76 54 19 64

Wine bottles and emptied glasses hang from the ceiling and the walls at this funky Parisien bistro. Tucked away in a small corner between the Place Notre Dame and Place aux Herbes, this Parisien bistro is the ideal place to impress a significant other without making an impression on your wallet. The decadant 3 or 4 course *prix-fixe* here features rack of lamb, rouget a la Nisoise, or Saint Jaques des gambes (€22/33). Dessert of the chef's choice included.

Ⓢ *Three course prix-fixe €22, four course €33.* 🕐 *Open daily 7-9:30pm.*

LA TABLE RONDE

🍴♿ 🍷⦙ TRADITIONAL ❸

7 pl. Saint Ándre ☎04 76 44 51 41 ▨www.restaurant-tableronde-grenoble.com

Centrally located both physically and in French history books, this restaurant/café has been serving patrons since well before the Revolution. Decorated in turn of the century *belle-epoche* style, the place is covered in old alcohol advertisements and mirrors decorated with scantily-clad women (by 19th century standards, that is).

Ⓢ *Espresso €1. Cappucino €2. Fixed menu for €22 featuring French Alpine cuisine.* 🕐 *Open daily 9am-1am.*

LA FERME A DEDE

🍴♿ 🍷⦙ TRADITIONAL ❶

1 pl. aux Herbes ☎04 76 54 00 33 ▨www.restaurantlafermeadede.com

A throwback to old-fashioned French dining, this *au naturale* restaurant is complete with a radio playing old French music and flickering candles in pickle jars on each of the wooden tables. Try either the steak tartare (€10.90) or the Dauphinois salad with egg, potato and mushroom (€8.70). Sustainability nuts of the world rejoice: all the ingredients are fresh from the farm (*la ferme* en français).

Ⓢ *Lunch Plat du Jour for €7.90, €10.90 with dessert. Changes weekly.* 🕐 *Open M-Sa 7pm-midnight.*

LE COUP DE TORCHON

🍴♿🍷 TRADITIONAL ❷

8 rue Dominique Villars ☎04 76 63 20 58

A 10-table jewel on the outskirts of the old city with a domineering grandfather clock, Le Coup de Torchon features basic, traditonal food and a fully stocked bar. This is a slightly cheaper option for those who want to delve into authentic French cuisine; the *prix-fixe* menu includes lamb, a simple salad, and fromage blanc for dessert.

Ⓢ *Afternoon menu: €12.50 for a plat du jour and dessert or entre and plat du jour. Night menu: €16 for 3 course prix-fixe menu.* 🕐 *Open Tu noon-1:15pm and 7:30-8:45pm, W noon-1:15pm, Th noon-1:15pm and 7:30-8:45pm, F-Sa noon-1:15pm and 7:30-9pm.*

AU CLAIRE DE LA LUNE

🍷♿ EPICERIE, VEGETARIAN ❶

54 rue Thiers ☎04 76 51 17 61 ▨www.atelier-culinariemanou.com

Environmentalism has never been so exclusive (wait, yes it has). This restaurant biologique in the old city offers a reasonably cheap lunch featuring organic, mostly vegetarian options, though tht *epicerie* also serves up fish and a vegetable salad (€12). Dinner is reserved for groups of 12+ with a reservation in advance. Gather some hippie friends and also sign up for the cooking classes

(€49) offered during the day.
Ⓢ *Vegetarian dish €9. Fish plus vegetable salad €12.* ⌚ *Open at noon Tu-Sa, open for dinner Th-Sa by reservation after 7pm.*

LE COUSCOUS
Ⓐ♿☺ CAFE ❷

19 rue de la Poste
☎04 76 47 92 93

Small, simple, and cheap. Offers outside seating when it's packed (a frequent occurence). If you're not sure what to order, maybe its namesake might give you a clue.
✴*Right next to the Hôtel de la Poste.* Ⓢ*€7.90 plat du jour. Couscous from €4.20 to €14 for the Royale.* ⌚*M 7-11pm, Tu-Su 12-2pm, 7-11pm.*

NIGHTLIFE

🏛 LES BERTHOM
♥♿🍸 BAR

1 rue Saint Hugues
☎04 76 01 81 17 🖥www.lesberthom.com

For those who are tired of cheap urine-flavored beer, but don't want to give up on the college scene just yet, this Belgian bar is calling your name. While not the cheapest joint around (1 pint; €6), you for sure get what you pay for and then some with a Meredsous Blonde or Westmalle Triple (a whopping 9.5% alcohol by volume). The cobblestone floor and fake tree in the middle of the bar will make you think you're in a Belgian beer garden.
✴ *An offshoot of the Place Notre Dame.* ⌚ *daily 3pm-2am.*

🏛 SUBWAY
♥♿🍸☺ BAR

22 rue Gambetta
☎04 76 87 31 67

No, not the sandwich chain. Far away from the old city, but close enough to keep the students coming, this young hipster hangout will leave you in awe of their complex and cheap drink specials. Thursdays are the night to go, with €1 flavored shots of rum lasting until 1am. Tuesdays host themed nights and a choice of 19 flavors of vodka (€3).
i Happy hour 5-9pm, Th 5pm-1am. Ⓢ *Cocktail of the week for €2. Half pint €1.60 euro. Pastis €1 euro.* ⌚ *Open M-W 10am-1am, Th-F 10am-2am, Sa 2pm-2am, Su 2pm-1am.*

🏛 BUKANA
♥((•))🍸 BAR, INTENSE

1 Quai Créqui

There's no listed phone number. No website. Bukana is like the '60s: if you can remember anything about it, you weren't really there. Indulge in a fun and sweaty night you'll most likely forget, and gain automatic free entrance to Le Vertigo or Vieux Manoir. The happy hour here is a misnomer—it's 4hrs. long—and the infinitely affordable tequila and vodka shots (€1) and pints (€3) will provide an excuse for your dance floor makeover.
✴ *Along the river, past the téléphérique towards i Credit card min. €10. Pool table, fooseball table. Wi-Fi avaiable. Group drinking encouraged: €20 giraffes and 10 shots for €18. Happy hour 6-10pm.* ⌚ *Open daily 6pm-2am.*

BARBEREUSSE
♥🍸 BAR

8 rue Jean-François Hache
☎04 76 51 14 53 🖥www.grenoble-barberousse.com

This packed and pirate-themed shooters bar is where the party really gets started. If the crowd isn't hot enough for you, it will be when the bartender sets the bar on fire. No really. He lights the bar on fire. Shooters and mixed drinks (€3.50) and a rum-and-orange-juice concoction called Sous Marin (€5) will have you singing "A Pirate's Life For Me" in French in no time, though you may have trouble recalling it again in the morning.
✴ *Behind Place Notre Dame, around the corner from le 365. i Happy hour 6-8:30pm.* ⌚ *Open M-Sa 6pm-1am .*

LONDON PUB
🍺🍸 PUB

11 rue Brocherie ☎04 76 44 41 90

Let's Go does not necessarily advise that you join Lucy in the sky with diamonds, but if you ever did pull a Tim Leary it would probably look something like the London Pub. The black lights are groovy, the walls are lined with English football jerseys and John Lennon posters, and the shots (€2) keep the party going. Free club entrance with patronage.

ℹ Happy hour from 6:30 to 9, all beer €4. Credit card min. €10. $ Mon-Wed Stella nights €3.50 and Ladies Nights (€1 off selected mixed drinks). Come 2011, W nights will offer joint deals with London Pub and Spanish pub next door. ⏰ Open Mon-Sat 6:30-2am.

COUCHE TARD PUB
🍺🍸 PUB

1 rue de Palais ☎04 76 44 41 90

This dark, cramped bar is covered with the scribblings of drunken patrons. This bar is designed for the young 20-somethings, but catches more of a just-out-of-school crowd eager to take advantage of the very generous Happy Hour. The cheap full pints (€3) are a draw, as well as the friendly staff, who are eager to practice their English.

✢ Stone's throw from Place Notre Dame. ℹ Happy hour 6pm-midnight. Credit card min. €10. $€1.80 shooters and €3 Stella and mixed drinks. ⏰ Open M-Sa 6pm-2am.

AU VIEUX MANOIR
🍺🍸 CLUB, BAR

50 rue Saint Laurent ☎04 76 42 00 68

It may not be the cheapest, but you won't find another club or bar that stays open until 7am. The three-room club features a wide variety of music from the previous three decades or so. Shooters seem to be the best deal here (€30), since the beer is definitely not (€7.50). Odds are you're well on your way to hangover-ville if you end up here. An assortment of dancing cages and a giant airplane hanging from the ceiling generate some considerable thematic confusion.

✢ Across the river from the Vieux Ville. ℹ Free entrance if coming from Bukana Pub. $ €5 cover to the discotheque, free entrance to bar. ⏰ Open daily 10:30pm-7am. Closed in August.

LE 365
🍺🍸 BAR, CLASSY

3 rue Bayard ☎04 76 51 73 18

If you've outgrown the heavy college drinking scene (we haven't), this classy bar will suit your more mature needs, or at least serve as a good launch point for your night out before Grenoble's cheap shooters force you to lose your composure. The glass tables and modern funky lighting add to the chic, artsy vibe.

✢ Near the place Notre Dame. ℹ Happy hour 6-8:30pm. $ €2 wine glasses during happy hour. Mixed drinks €6-16. ⏰ Open Tu-Sa 3pm-1am. Closed August.

ARTS AND CULTURE 🎵

The main **theater** in Grenoble features frequent plays and musical preformances. Info and tickets are available at the *billererie* across from the Place Saint André (*☎04 76 44 03 44. ⏰ Open Tu-F 10am-noon, 1-6pm, Sa 1-6pm*). **Theatre St. Marie-en-Bas** is another, lesser known theatre on the outskirt of the *vieux ville*; built in the neo-classical style of Louis XVI, the building used to be a convent. It is located on Rue Très Cloîtres, and is recognizable by its all white marble collonade facade (*☎04 76 42 01 50 ⏰ Ticket office open M-F 4-7pm*). **Grenoble's Maison de la Culture** (*4 rue Paul Claudel, [M]MC2, Tram A, dir. Grand Place from le centre-ville ☎04 76 00 79 00 🖥www.mc2grenoble.fr ⏰ Open Sept-Jun Tu-F 12:30-7pm, Sa 2-7pm*) organizes cultural events throughout the year.

Practicalities

- **TOURIST OFFICE:** Offers a Grenoble City Pass, which features a *petit train* ride, entry to the Grenoble Museum, a gondola lift to the Bastille, and an audio tourd walking tour. Ask for the Guide de l'Étudiant if you are interested in long term student housing. (*14 rue de la République From the train station, turn right onto pl. de la Gare and take the third left onto av. Alsace-Lorraine. Follow the tram tracks through rue Félix Poulat and rue Blanchard. The concrete modern art-esque tourist office is on the left, before the tracks split. Also, Trams A and B (dir. Échirolles and Gières) stops right in front of the office at Hubert Dobedout-Maison du Tourisme.* ☎ *04 76 42 41 41* ▣*www.grenoble-isere.info* ⌚ *Open May-Sept Mon-Sat 9-6:30pm, Sun 10-1pm and 2-5pm; Oct-Apr Mon-Sat 9-6:30pm, Sun 10-1pm*)

- **TOURS:** Available from the Tourist office. Tours of the *vieux ville* are audio tourd in French or English and last 4hrs. Set rental is avaiable during tourism office hours and costs €5 for everyone. Must leave ID with set rental.

- **GLBT RESOURCES:** (▣*www.grenoble-glbth.com*)

- **LAUDROMAT:** Laverie (*14 rue Thiers* ☎*04 76 96 28 03* ⌚ *Open daily 7a-10p.* ⑨*5kg for €2.30, 7kg for €2.90, and 18kg for €6.40*)

- **HIKING INFO:** Maison de Montagne (*3 Raoul Blanchard, one street over from the tourist office* ☎*04 76 44 67 03* ▣*www.grenoble-montagne.com* ⌚ *Open M-F 9:30am-12:30pm and 1-6pm, Sa 10am-1pm and 2-5pm*) Get the free trail map, *La Carte de Sentiers des Franges Verts.* Weather Info: ☎*08 92 68 02 38* Snow Info: ☎*08 92 68 10 20*

- **INTERNET ACCESS:** Celcius Cafe (*11 rue Gutéal* ☎*04 76 46 43 36 Although there are many around the outskirts of the city, this one is centrally located in the middle of the vieux ville. English speaking.* ⑨ *15 min €1, 1 hour €3.30. Printing available. B/W €10/page. Color €20* ⌚ *Open from 9am-11pm*)

- **POST OFFICE:** (*12 rue de la République, right next to the Tourism Center* ☎*04 76 63 32 70* ⌚ *Open M 8am-noon and 1:15-6pm Tu-F 8am-6pm, Sa 8:30am 12:30pm and 1:30-5pm. Currency exchange available as well as ATM. Postal Code: 38000*)

Emergency!

- **POLICE STATION:** (*36 bld. du Maréchal Lyautey* ☎*04 76 60 40 40*).

- **PHARMACIE:** Ask for the **pharmacie de garde** (*Take bus #31 (dir. Malpertuis) to Hôtel de Police*)

- **HOSPITAL:** Northern Hospital: bld. de la Chantourne; Southern Hospital: av. de Grésivaudan. (☎*04 76 76 75 75 same number for both depending on where you call from*).

Getting There

Flights: Aéroport de Grenoble Saint-Geoirs. (☎*04 76 65 48 48*). International flights only. Ryan Air flies to **Stockholm, Sweden**, British Airways and easyJet fly to **London GAT, UK**. Buses and trams run between the airport and stations (€1.40).

Trains: Gare Europole (*pl. de la Gare* ⌚ *Ticket office open M-F 5:45am-8:45pm. Sa 5am-7:45pm, Su 6am-8:45pm*) SNCF (*Office across from the Maison du Tourisme at 14 rue de la République* ⌚ *Open M-F 9am-6:30, Sa 10am-6pm*) To **Annecy** (⌚ *1.5 hr. 18 per day* ⑨ *€18.60*); **Lyon** (⌚ *1.5hr 30 per day* ⑨ *€19.10*); **Marseille** (⌚*15 per day, 2.5 hr.* ⑨ *TGV €51* ⌚*4.5hr.* ⑨ *TER €35*); **Nice** (⌚ *6-7 hr. 15 per day* ⑨ *€69*); **Paris** (⌚ *3hr 9 per day* ⑨ *€75*).

Buses: Next to the Gare (⌚ *Open M-Sa 6:15am-7pm, Su 7:15am-7pm*) VFD (☎ *08 20 83 38 33*

🖳 *www.vfd.fr*) goes to **Geneva** (⏰ *3 hr. 1 per day* $ *€43 adult, €32 25 and under*). Frequent services to ski areas.

Getting Around

The *viex ville* is very pedestrian friendly. Above-ground **Trams** (*4 lines* $ *€1.40 per trip*) are clearly marked, and car access is limited. **Buses** (*€1.4 per trip*) also run frequently (daily 6am-9pm. Night buses run Th-Sa until midnight). Best way to see the city is to rent a bike at **Metro Velo** (*3 rue Malakoff* ☎*04 76 59 59 59*) where you can rent bikes by the day (*€5, students €3.50*) by the weekend (*€9, students €6*) or by the week (*€15, students €10*). Every bus and tram stop also includes a *"vous êtes ici"* sticker on the maps.

BORDEAUX AND WINE COUNTRY

Bordeaux's world-famous wines have been in high demand since the Romans first conquered the area. However, the marriage of Eleanor of Aquitaine and King Henry II of England in 1152 altered the region's fate considerably. The Plantagenet King refused to be deprived of his *claret* (or as the rest of the world calls it, red Bordeaux wine) and bestowed speical shipping rights on Bordeaux, opening it up to the unquenchable British market. At first, the *Bordelais* simply shipped wines produced farther up the Garonne River, but the money flowing in sparked a local planting mania. Soon Bordeaux gained a monopoly over the market by refusing to ship wines to its clients that had been produced elsewhere. Today, the region produces some 800 million bottles of wine every year. In fact, wine is so integral to the economy that 4 in every 10 adults in Bordeaux and the surrounding region are somehow connected to the wine industry.

greatest hits

- **STAIRWAYS TO HEAVEN.** Your Stairmaster never had views this nice. Climb 230+ steps in either the Pey-Berland bell tower (p. 194) in Bordeaux or the Le Phare lighthouse in Biarritz to see absolutely postcard-perfect panoramas.

- **IN VINO VERITAS.** Learn what words like "vanillin," "maderized," and "herbaceous" mean at a château *dégustation* (p. 203).

- **COASTING ALONG.** The Dune du Pyla (p. 211), Europe's highest sand dune, is so buffeted by sea winds that it actually moves a few centimeters every year. Go see it before it hops the border into Spain.

Time to embrace your inner wino (he's probably not hiding too far under the surface away). The viticultural center of the world, a trip to **St-Émilion** is a great way to learn to wine taste. It may also be the place that you learn what kind of wine will leave you with a bitching hangover. Either way, memories to last a lifetime will be made there. When you're tired of drinking (wine) head over to **Biarritz** and lounge with a cocktail on the beach.

bordeaux ☎05

In addition to its well-deserved reputation as the wine capital of the world, Bordeaux's grand 18th-century architecture makes this city by the river a photographic marvel. In some of France's most elegant streets, hipsters hang out at Pl. de la Victoire in the student quarter, children splash in the waters of the *miroir d'eau*, and tourists with purple-stained mouths taste the best wines on the planet from the legendary vineyards of St-Émilion, Médoc, Sauternes and Graves. Come to Bordeaux first and foremost for the viticulture, but stay for the panoramic views, the sophisticated culture, and the vibrant nightlife.

ORIENTATION

For a mental map of the city of Bordeaux, picture the Garonne River flowing north to south, then add Bordeaux on its west bank. Now let's fill in the details. At the southern end of the city is the **Gare St-Jean** train station, which is a hike from *centre-ville*. To get to town, walk past the sex shops on **cours de la Marne** until you reach **pl. de la Victoire,** the student nightlife quarter. From here, turn right under the arch onto the pedestrian street **rue Ste-Catherine.** *Centre-ville* in a straight shot ahead. You can also take tram C or bus #16 from the train station and get off at Pl. de la Bourse or the Esplanade de Quinconces, but that's jumping the gun.

At the heart of *centre-ville* is **pl. de la Comédie.** If you're walking along Rue Ste-Catharine from the train station, this is where you'll end up. The square is immediately recognizable by its opulent Grand Théâtre. Ahead on **cours 30 Juillet** (the continuation of rue Ste-Catherine) you'll find the **Tourist Office,** right before the **esplanade des Quinconces,** a large plaza and an important public transportation hub. Back at Pl. de la Comédie, you can get to **pl. Gambetta,** another one of Bordeaux's centers of activity, by walking west for a short distance along **cours de l'Inentendance.** Most budget hotels are located north of Pl. Gambetta, while the best cheap eateries are south of the Grand Théâtre in the streets coming off rue Ste-Catherine. Head west one one of them, **rue St-Rémi,** to hit the **pl. de la Bourse.** This square by the Garonne River is across the street from Bordeaux's iconic public art installation, the ▨**miroir d'eau.**

ACCOMMODATIONS

Although Bordeaux's youth hostel is conveniently situated near the train station, the area is home to many a sex shop, and the 5-10min. walk from the nearest tram stop can be freaky at night. Great deals, especially for groups of travelers, can be found farther from the station in the *centre-ville*, on the streets around **Pl. Gambetta.** Reserve one to two weeks ahead in the summertime.

▨ **HOTEL STUDIO**   ✦(ᵗ) BUDGET BOUTIQUE ❷
    26 rue Huguerie   ☎05 56 48 00 14 ▨www.hotel-studio-bordeaux.fr
    A long-time Let's Go favorite, Hotel Studio's got a mixture of old and newly reno-

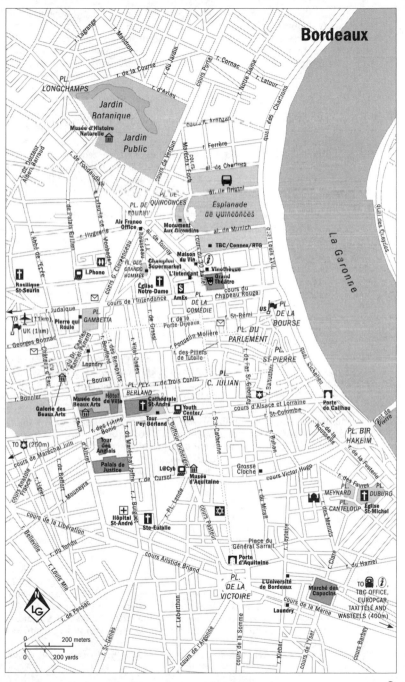

Bordeaux

PL. LONGCHAMPS

Jardin Botanique

Jardin Public

Musée d'Histoire Naturelle

PL. DE QUINCONCES

Esplanade de Quinconces

Air France Office

Monument Aux Girondins

TBC/Cennex/RTG

La Garonne

Maison du Vin

Champion Supermarket

L'Intendant

Vinothèque

Grand Théâtre

I.Phone

PL. DES GRANDS HOMMES

Basilique St-Seurin

Église Notre-Dame

AmEx

cours du Chapeau Rouge

Pierre qui Roule

UK (1km)

PL. GAMBETTA

PL. DE LA COMÉDIE

US

PL. DE LA BOURSE

Laundry

PL. DU PARLEMENT

PL. ST-PIERRE

Galerie des Beaux Arts

Musée des Beaux Arts

Hôtel de Ville

PL. C. JULIAN

Cathédrale St-André

Tour Pey Berland

Youth Center/ CIJA

Porte de Cailhau

PL. BIR HAKEIM

Tour des Anglais

Palais de Justice

L@Cyb

Musée d'Aquitaine

Grosse Cloche

cours Victor Hugo

PL. MEYNARD

PL. DUBURG

Église St-Michel

PL. CANTELOUP

Hôpital St-André

Ste-Eulalie

Place du Général Sarrail

Porte d'Aquitaine

PL. DE LA VICTOIRE

L'Université de Bordeaux

Marché des Capucins

Laundry

TO TBC OFFICE, EUROPCAR, TAXI TÉLÉ AND WASTEELS (400m)

TO (260m)

N

0 200 meters

0 200 yards

bordeaux · accommodations

vated rooms that might not be spacious, but have everything you need. From extra-comfy double beds, to cable TV, to futuristic tin showers in the full baths, you'll be hard pressed to find better value in Bordeaux's *centre ville*, especially given the caring staff who makes this hotel feel like home. Ask for a spiffier renovated room and reserve ahead of time in July and August.

From Pl. Gambetta, walk along Rue Georges Clémenceau until a left turn onto Rue Huguerie just before the statue and traffic circle of Pl. de Tourny. $ Singles €28, renovated €33; doubles €30/38; triples €49; quads €65; quints €70. ⏰ Reception daily 7:30am-8:30pm.

HOTEL CHIC DE LYON

BUDGET HOTEL 2

31 rue des Remparts ☎05 56 81 34 38

It seems like everything in this lovely hotel sparkles, from the crisp sheets to the white walls. Combined with the fresh smell, the high windows that let in ample air and light, and the occasional garden of potted plants, you're in for a refreshing treat in a superb location. Every room has a full bath, and the staff is warm and welcoming.

Rue des Remparts is the street running past the Hôtel de Ville from Pl. Pey-Berland (where the St-André cathedral is) to Pl. Gambetta. $ Singles €35-37; doubles €49-53; triples €69. ⏰ Reception 24hr., although there is an access code for guests to enter late at night.

HOTEL BALZAC

HOTEL 3

14 rue Lafaurie de Monbadon ☎05 56 81 85 12

Full of character, Hotel Balzac's creaky staircase climbs to irregularly shaped and spacious rooms with rather sensual art on the walls. Between the dim reception, the hotel's namesake, and its *passé* feel, you might just write the next great novel here. If you're not a tortured artist with a rolled cigarette in hand, then at least you have a cheap place to stay and shower in central Bordeaux.

From Pl. Gambetta walk 1 block up Rue Georges Clémenceau and turn left at a 70 degree angle onto Rue Lafaurie de Monbadon. $ Singles €33; doubles €46.

AUBERGE DE JEUNESSE

HOSTEL 2

22 cours Barbey ☎05 56 33 00 70 www.auberge-jeunesse-bordeaux.eu

Shiny metal, bright colors, and lots of glass characterize the impressive modern architecture of Bordeaux's municipally owned Auberge de Jeunesse. Nevertheless, given the water damage in need of repair and the location near Bordeaux's red-light district, travelers will find better value in *centre-ville*. Dorms for 2, 4, or 6 sleep a total of 108 people in 30 rooms with bunk beds; most rooms come with interior showers, and some with toilets, in addition to cabinets for personal affairs. Relax in the lounge with a flatscreen and a foosball table.

3 large blocks along Cours de la Marne from Gare St. Jean. Follow well-marked signs. i Breakfast, sheets, and internet included. $ Dorms €22. ⏰ Breakfast 7:30-9:30am. Lockout 10am-2pm. Check-out by 10am. Doors close at 2am.

SIGHTS

Bordeaux isn't short of fun, educational, or quirky ways to pass the time between glasses of wine. Admission to all of Bordeaux's museums is free the first Sunday of every month.

TOUR PEY-BERLAND

TOWER

pl. Pey-Berland ☎05 56 81 26 25

For the best views of Bordeaux, climb 231 steps through an ever-narrowing spiral staircase to the top of the 50m-high Pey-Berland bell tower, named after one of the great archbishops of Bordeaux. Built in 1440 at a distance from the *Cathédrale St-André* in order to protect it from the bell's vibrations, the tower ironically had no bells until 1853.

$ €5. ⏰ Open daily June-Sept daily 10am-1:15pm and 2-6pm; Oct-May daily 10am-12:30pm and 2-5:30pm.

⬛ MIROIR D'EAU — PUBLIC ART

Accessible from the grand buildings of Pl. de la Bourse and beside the banks of the Garonne River, Miroir d'Eau is a spectacular public art installment, and an icon of modern Bordeaux: a mirror made of water. Designed by the architect Michel Corajoud and installed in October of 2006, 2cm of water transform 130m by 42m of black granite into a reflective surface that captures a stunning panoramic view of the city. In additon to releasing billows of fog in computer-controlled cycles, the *miroir d'eau* is a particular favorite of little and not-so-little kids, who love to splash and play in its waters. Bring your camera, sketchpad, and people-watching glasses, especially at sunset.

Ⓢ *Free.* Ⓕ *Open 24hr.*

CATHÉDRALE ST-ANDRÉ — CATHEDRAL

pl. Pey-Berland — ☎05 56 52 68 10

Sculpted angels and apostles adorn the cathedral's facade, while Gothic windows allow natural light to illuminate an interior that has been home to many important royal weddings (a.k.a. alliances)—Eleanor of Aquitaine and Louis VII got hitched here in 1137. Louis XIII and Princess Anne of Austria also tied the knot here in 1615, whereupon Louis walked through the "royal portal" on the north side of the church, an entrance that has allegedly not been used since. Today, the cathedral is a UNESCO World Heritage Site, and one of the stops for pilgrims walking the Camino of Santiago de Compostella.

Ⓕ *Open daily 10am-12:30pm and 2:30-7:30pm. Guided visits June-Sept Tu-Su 3-5pm.*

MAISON DU VIN — 🍷 WINERY

3 cours du 30 Juillet — ☎05 56 00 43 47

If you're desperate to become a sophisticated oenophile (wine-lover) and you don't have time to venture into the nearby wine country, then head to the *Maison du Vin*, an immense building directly across from the Tourist Office. The *Maison* houses industry offices, an extensive *Bar à Vin* (wine bar) staffed by professionals who guide tastings and an *École du Vin* (wine school) that offers a 2hr. "Introduction to Bordeaux Wines" in English and French with a comparative tasting of two reds and two whites. Those appropriately impressed can purchase the goods at two nearby wine shops. **L'Intendant,** a more intimate wine shop across the street, has an impressive selection of regional wines and a knowledgeable staff. (*2 Allée de Tourny* ☎*05 56 48 01 29* Ⓕ *Open daily 10am-7:30pm).* Conoisseurs can then venture across the square to buy high-end bottles, crystal pitchers, and obscure gadgets at the classy **Vinothèque,** a store specializing in all things *vin.* (*8 Cours du 30 Juillet* ☎*05 56 52 32 05* 🖥*www.la-vinotheque.com* Ⓕ *Open M-Sa 10am-7:30pm).*

🚶 *Directly across from the tourist office.* ℹ *Tickets for the course can be purchased at the Maison du Vin or at the tourist office.* Ⓢ *Wine-tasting course €25. Bar à Vin €2-8 per glass of wine.* Ⓕ *Courses offered M-Sa 10am in English and 3pm in French. Bar à Vin open M-Sa 11am-10pm.*

CENTRE JEAN MOULIN — MUSEUM

48 rue Vital — ☎05 56 10 19 90

A fascinating museum that chronicles France's WWII history with one of its three floors, dedicated entirely to the remarkable life story of Jean Moulin, a politican, high-profile member of the Resistance against the Nazis, and French national hero. Exhibits include documentary films, photographs, newspaper clippings, letters, old uniforms, weapons, and all kinds of artifacts of war. Unfortunately, this history buff's delight is entirely in French, although temporary exhibits housed on the second floor often have English brochures accompanying them.

🚶 *Across from the Cathédrale St-Andé.* Ⓢ *Free.* Ⓕ *Open Tu-Su 2-6pm.*

bordeaux · sights

FOOD

Bordeaux boasts a range of local specialties, including oysters straight from the Atlantic, *foie gras* from Les Landes, and beef braised in St-Émilion wine. Restaurants cluster around **rue St-Rémi** and **pl. St-Pierre,** while small and budget-friendly options line the narrow streets between **pl. du Parlement** to the east of **rue Ste-Catherine.** *Bordelais* don't usually eat before 9pm in the summer and restaurants typically serve meals until 11pm or midnight. Sample local fish and produce at the **Marché des Capucins** *(Tu-Su 6am-1pm)* off **cours de la Marne,** or head to the conveniently located **Centre Commerical des Grands Hommes** for all your grocery needs. The *Centre*is in the middle of the triangle made by **pl. Gambetta, pl. de la Comédie,** and **pl. de Tourny.** Inside there's a huge **Carréfour** grocery store with super-cheap prepared roasted chicken meals for €3.50. *(Open M-Sa 9am-9pm.)*

👍 LA PAPAYA ⊛ AFRICAN [2]

14 rue Ferdinant Philippart ☎05 56 44 76 88 💻www.lapapaya.populus.org

A wonderful Malagasy and Réunionese restaurant (that's the cuisine of Madagascar and the subtropical French island of Réunion due east) that serves up spicy, fruity, and all-round tasty stews on beds of white rice. Try the mutton cooked in *massalé*, a traditional Réunionese composite of cardamum, black pepper, coriander, cumin, and five other spices. Turns out that island food still goes down beautifully with a Bordeaux.

⇄ From Pl. de la Bourse, with your back to the 3 Graces Fountain and the Garonne River, take the left fork ahead of you. The restaurant is on your left. [$] Appetizers €4.10-8. Plates €9.50-11.80. ⏰ Open M-Sa 7:30-10:30pm.

O'MIRROIR D'O CAFE 💳⛅ TRADITIONAL, SEAFRONT [2]

2 quai Louis XVIII ☎05 56 44 59 59

As close to the banks of the Garonne as you can eat, this friendly cafe serves French dishes like *steak frites* and *confit de canard* that are simply delicious, especially when accompannied by Bordeaux's world-famous wines. Skip dessert—it pales in comparison to the main courses. Afterwards, stroll down the river to the café's namesake, the 👍**miroir d'eau,** which looks best at sunset on a full stomach.

⇄ Quai Lousi XVIII is the avenue that follows the Garonne River. The restaurant is in between Pl. de la Bourse and Esplanade des Quinconces. [$] Menu (appetizer + plate or plate + dessert) €14. Appetizers €5-7. Plates €9.50-13. Salads €9-11. Pizzas €9-11. Desserts €4-6. ⏰ Open daily 8am-midnight.

TWIN TEA WINE 💳🍸 SMALL PLATES [1]

16 rue des Argentiers ☎05 56 44 63 71 💻www.twinteawine.com

Looking for a truly gourmet experience? Come to this trendy small plates restaurant that doubles as a tea house and wine bar. Using seasonal and fresh produce, the owners have never cooked the same dish twice, but you can expect the likes of lamb and eggplant tajine or organic zucchini sautéed in fennel. If you're not famished, one small plate (€4) and a basket of bread is enough, although 2 plates and a glass of sangria (€10) will ensure your satisfaction. Multi-talented, the owners also prepare homemade cakes and pastries, in addition to entertaining every evening during "happy time" with discounts on wine-tastings.

⇄ From Pl. de la Comédie and the Grande Théâtre, walk down rue Ste-Catherine until a left turn onto rue de la Devise. When the street opens into a small square, rue des Argentiers is at the far end beside the church. [$] Small plates €4. 2 plates and a drink €10. 4 plates a drink for brunch €12. Desserts €3,50. Dégustation of 2 wines with a plate €7. Glasses of wine €3. Sangria €2. ⏰ Open Tu-W 11am-11pm, Th-Su 11am-2am. "Happy time" 7:30-9:30pm.

L'OMBRIÈRE 💳🍸 TRADITIONAL [3]

14 pl. du Parliament ☎05 56 48 58 83 💻www.restaurantlombriere.com

Perfectly prepared French cuisine tastes better when it's enjoyed beside a bubbling fountain amidst this chic restaurant's ever-present crowds. Fixed menus include fusion choices like Yakitori-style Scallop and King Prawn Skewers *(€15-25)*, but there are plenty of French staples available, including a meal-size salad with baked goat cheese and *foie gras*.

➡ From Pl. de la Comédie and the Grande Théâtre walk down Rue Sainte Catherine until a left turn onto rue St-Rémi. Your next left will be on rue des Lauriers which leads to the open square of Pl. du Parliament. $ Menus €15-25. Appetizers €5.50. Plates €12-16. Desserts €4.50. Wines €3-5.50. ⏰ Open daily July-Aug 10am-2am; Sept-June 10am-3pm and 6pm-midnight.

CASOLETTE CAFÉ — 🍸 TRADITIONAL, CAFE ❷

20 pl. de la Victoire — ☎05 56 92 94 96 🖥www.cassolettecafe.com

This immense, bright-orange cafe seems to have enough space to entertain all of Bordeaux's university students, especially with its foosball table. The kitchen loves cheese and *cassolettes*, red clay dishes that go straight in the oven with your soon-to-be dinner. You'll find the occasional tandoori among mostly French classics, like the hearty *bardado du morue* (cod with potatoes, garlic, and salt). Check out the awesome five-course tasting menu.

➡ Straight down Rue Ste Catherine to the student hub of Pl de la Victoire. $ Menu du jour €11. Salads €9-11.10. Fresh pastas €8.50-11.20. Plates €9-12.00. 5-course tasting menu €14. ⏰ Open daily noon-midnight.

PIZZERIA LA SQUADRA — ITALIAN ❷

50 rue du Palais Gallien — ☎ 05 56 44 00 55

A pizzeria that is forever full of local families and young people. La Squadra's excellent pizzas and pastas will fuel you up for more life on the road. Besides two flat-screens and flags of the world to enterain you, there's also the gregarious owner, who is guaranteed to chat you up with a smile. The *pasta formule* comes with three kinds of home-cooked pasta and a chocolatey dessert, which gets you more than you pay for.

➡ Off Pl. Gambetta. $ Menu (appetizer + plate or plate + dessert/coffee) €11 or €14. Appetizers €3.50-7. Salads €6.50-9.20. Calzones €9-9.50. Pizzas €7.70-11. Meals €9.50-15. ⏰ Open M-F 11am-11pm year-round except for July-Aug M-F 11am-11pm and Sa-Su 7-11pm.

NIGHTLIFE

Given its student population of 70,000, Bordeaux is full of bars. **pl. de la Victoire** is *the* student party quarter, and the streets around **pl. de la Comédie**—especially those south of the Place off of **rue Ste-Catherine**—are well-stocked with nightlife opportunities. For Bordeaux's large nightclubs, clustered south of the city by mayoral decree, head to **quai du Paludate** behind the **Gare St-Jean** train station. Travelers should exercise caution when walking in this area at night.

LA CALLE OCHO — 🍸 CLUB

24 rue des Piliers de Tutelle — ☎05 56 48 08 68

This never-ending bar is covered floor-to-ceiling with a love for all things Cuban, not to mention filled wall-to-wall with insane crowds of the young, beautiful, and partying from around the world. Move your hips to rockin' Latin music until you can't resist the allure of a *mojito* any longer.

➡ From Pl. de la Comédie walk along Cours de l'Intendance with the Grand Théâtre to your left. Rue des Piliers de Tutelle is the second right turn. $ Beer €4. Mixed drinks €6. ⏰ Open daily 5pm-2am.

EL BODEGON — 🍸 BAR

14 pl. de la Victoire — ☎ 05 56 96 74 02

This place dominates nightlife in la Victoire, the most popular student party quarter. DJ plays the latest club hits, and bartenders light booze on fire, while the exuberant crowd dances and drinks the night away. Come for karaoke on Wednesdays or weekly theme nights—"Foam Night" and "Vodka Redbull Night" are particularly popular. In addition to the huge drink menu, the bar also serves food daily *(11am-3pm)*.

⚡ *A straight shot down rue Ste-Catharine to Pl. de la Victoire.* ℹ *W karaoke or theme nights.* Ⓢ *Beer on tap €2.80-4.50.* 🕐 *Open daily 6am-2am. Kitchen open 11am-3pm. Happy hour 6-8pm.*

LE TROU DUCK
♥℃▼ BAR
33 rue des Piliers-de-Tutelle ☎05 56 52 36 87
An intimate gay bar that's really more of an excuse to gyrate to '90s music, modern French hits and everyone's favorite: Rihanna. When you're not ordering a drink at the zebra-striped bar or watching wall-size music videos on the projector, take your pick from the young and cute guys.

⚡ *From Pl. de la Comédie walk along Cours de l'Intendance with the Grand Théâtre to your left. Rue des Piliers de Tutelle is the second right turn. The bar is at the very end of the street.* Ⓢ *Beer €3.50. Mixed drinks €6.* 🕐 *Open daily 10am-2am.*

LE NAMASTHÉ
♥℃ TEA HOUSE
16 rue de la Devise ☎06 67 52 69 68
You and the multiple Buddha statues can mellow out together on the leafy brews all night long on the satiny red cushions. This awesome alternative to any ordinary bar has dozens of teas from the Far East in addition to alcoholic beverages, so long as they're not from France. Who knew tea could be so sexy?

⚡ *From Pl. de la Comédie walk town Rue Ste-Catharine until a left turn on Rue de la Devise.* ℹ *Credit card min. €10.* Ⓢ *Tea pot €3.80-6. Beer €5. Foreign wine €5.* 🕐 *Open M-Sa 7pm-1:30am.*

ARTS AND CULTURE
To indulge in other kinds of *Bordelais* culture besides wine, pick up **Clubs and Concerts** at the Tourist Office, which lists every musical happening of all genres in the city. This town is a treasure trove for the indie music scene. Also inquire about a list of weekly free concerts on some of Bordeaux's 40 organs; you're guaranteed a visit to a beautiful church and a dose of good ol' Baroque fun. Of course, for the big daddy of them all, visit the Grand Théâtre, whose ballets, operas, plays, and concerts run from Sept-Jun. When the theater isn't in season, you can still take a guided tour of its magnificent interior.

▨ GRAND THÉÂTRE
 OPERA HOUSE
pl. de la Comédie ☎05 56 00 85 95 🖳www.opera-bordeaux.com.
The austere facade of this 18th-century opera house conceals a breathtakingly intricate Neoclassical interior, with a blue dome you will never foget. To see it, attend an opera, concert, ballet, or play—or give your wallet a bit of a break by taking a daytime tour in English or French.

Ⓢ *Tickets €8-80. Special student discount offers 3 shows for €24. Tours €3.* 🕐 *The Opera House is closed for performances July-Aug, but open for tours. Ticket office open Sept-Jun Tu-Sa 1-6:30pm.*

ESSENTIALS
Practicalities

- **TOURIST OFFICES:** The main tourist office distributes an 80-page *Welcome to Bordeaux* guide and provides maps, brochures, and help with same-day hotel reservations. There's an entire desk dedicated to arranging visits to the *vignobles* (wineries). *(12 cours du 30 Juillet.* ☎05 56 00 66 00 🖳www.bordeaux-tourisme.com ⚡ *Tram line B or C, pl. de Quinconces.* 🕐 *Open July-Aug M-Sa 9:30am-1pm and 2-7pm, Su 10am-1pm and 2-6pm; Sept-Oct M-Sa 9:30am-1pm and 2-6pm, Su 10am-1pm and 2-6pm; Nov-Apr M-Sa 10am-1pm and 2-6pm, Su 2-6pm; May-June M-Sa 9:30am-1pm and 2-6pm.)* **Tourist Office Gare St-Jean** helps with transportation and hotel reservations. *(*☎05 56 91 64 70 🕐 *Open May-Oct M-Sa 9am-noon and 1-6pm, Su 10am-12pm and 1-3pm; Nov-Apr M-F 9:30am-noon and 2-5:30pm.)*

bordeaux and wine country

- **TOURS:** The tourist office offers organized tours in English and French. **Walking tours** take place July 15-Sept 15 daily at 10am and 3pm; Sept 16-July 14 daily at 10am. (☎*05 56 00 66 24* Ⓢ *€8, students €7.* Ⓩ *2hr.*) There are also tours with the same duration and price on roller skates, bikes, boat, taxi and *cabriolet*. Woah. More importantly, there are affordable *(€27)* and excellent bus tours to the wine regions of **St-Émilion, Graves,** and **Médoc.** Of course, there are also fancier day-excursions for €90.

- **CURRENCY EXCHANGE:** You have to ring multiple doorbells and climb one flight of stairs to reach the security-heavy **Bureau de Change Kanoo.** *(11 cours de l'Intendance* ☎*05 56 00 63 33* Ⓢ *€8 fixed commission on all cash exchanges. 2.5% commission on traveler's checks.* Ⓩ *Open M-F 9:30am-5:30pm.)*

- **YOUTH CENTER: CIJA** helps with employment and long-term accommodations. Free internet access and SNCF train ticket purchase inside. Also distributes *LINDIC*, a student guide to Bordeaux. *(125 cours d'Alsace Lorraine.* ☎*05 56 56 00 56* Ⓩ *Open July-Aug M 1-6pm, Tu-F 9am-6pm; Sept-June M 1-5pm, Tu-F 9am-5pm. Closed for 1 week in Aug, usually around the 2nd week.)* A branch office is around the corner on 5 rue Duffour Dubergier. (Ⓩ *Open M-Th 9:30am-6pm, F 9:30am-5pm.)*

- **INTERNET ACCESS: I.Phone.** *(24 rue Duplais Gallien* ☎*05 57 85 82 62* Ⓢ *€0.50 per 15min.* Ⓩ *Open M-Sa 10am-10pm, Su noon-10pm.)* **L@ Cyb.** *(23 cours Pasteur* ☎*05 56 01 15 15* Ⓢ *€0.75 per 15min.* Ⓩ *Open M-Sa 10am-2am, Su 2pm-midnight.)*

- **POST OFFICE:** The post office has Western Union and **Poste Restante** with Postal Code 33065. *(32 pl. Gambetta* ☎ *05 57 14 24 60* Ⓢ *€0.58 per letter received.* Ⓩ *Open M-F 9am-6pm, Sa 9am 4pm.)*

Emergency!

- **EMERGENCY NUMBERS: Police** ☎17. **Ambulance** ☎15.

- **POLICE: L'Hôtel de Police.** *(23 rue Francois Sourdis* ☎*05 57 85 77* Ⓩ *Open 24hr.)*

- **HOSPITAL:** Hôpital St-André. *(1 rue Jean Burguet* ☎*05 56 79 56 79)*

Getting There

By Plane

There's an airport in **Mérignac** 11 km. west of Bordeaux. (☎*05 56 34 50 50* ▣*www. bordeaux.aeroport.fr)* A *navette* run by **Jet'bus** goes from *centre ville* to the airport. (Ⓢ *€7, under 26 €6; round-trip €12/10.* Ⓩ *45min., every 45min. 7:45am-10:45pm.)* There are stops at **Gare St-Jean,** the **Tourist Office,** and **pl. Gambetta.** Air France has an office at 37 Allée de Tourny. (☎*36 54* Ⓩ *Open M-F 9:30am-6:30pm, Sa 9:30am-1:15pm.)*

By Train

Gare St-Jean *(rue Charles Domercq* ☎*36 35* Ⓩ *Ticket office open M-Th 5am-9:40pm, F 5am-10:35pm, Sa 5:40am-9:40pm, Su 6am-10:30pm.)* sends trains to **Lyon** (Ⓢ *€67.40.* Ⓩ *8-10hr., 1 per day.);* **Marseille** (Ⓢ *€75.40.* Ⓩ *6-7hr., 5 per day.);* **Nantes** (Ⓢ *€45.70.* Ⓩ *4hr., 3 per day.);* **Nice** (Ⓢ *€93.40.* Ⓩ *9-12hr., 2 per day.);* **Paris** (Ⓢ *€69.80.* Ⓩ *3hr., 20 per day.);* **Poitiers** (Ⓢ *€36.70.* Ⓩ *2-3hr., 16 per day.)* **Rennes** (Ⓢ*€58.50.* Ⓩ *6hr., 3 per day either through Nantes or Paris.);* **Toulouse** (Ⓢ *€36.30.* Ⓩ *2-3hr., 17 per day.)*

By Bus

Réseau TransGironde (☎*05 56 43 68 43* ▣*www.citram.com)* buses travel to many small towns surroudning Bordeaux including **St-Émilion** (301 and 302) and **Pauillac** (705), both important viticulture destinations. Ask at the tourist office for schedules and prices. Be aware that buses are decentralized and leave from Esplanade de Quinconces, Gare St-Jean, and several other centers throughout the city.

Getting Around

By Public Transportation

Tbc runs a bus and tram system. *(☎05 57 57 88 88 💻www.infotbc.com, www.reseautbc.com $ 1 ticket €1.40; carnet of 10 or a 7-day-pass €10.60, under 28 €8; 1-day pass €4.10; night pass valid from 7pm-5am €2.30. ⏰ Trams A, B, and C run daily 5am-1am.)* Ticket and information offices at 9 pl. Gambetta *(⏰ Open M-F 8am-7:30pm, Sa 9:45am-12:25pm and 2-6pm.)*, esplanade des Quinconces *(⏰ Open M-F 7am-7:30pm, Sa 9:45am-12:25pm and 2-6pm.)* and at the Gare St-Jean train station *(⏰ Open M-F 7am-7:30pm, Sa 8:30am-3pm.)*

By Bike

Pierre Qui Roule. *(32 pl. Gambetta ☎05 57 85 80 82💻www.pierrequiroule.fr $ €10 per day, €20 per weekend, €45 per week. In-line skates and pads €6 per half-day, €9 per day. ⏰ Open M 2-7pm, Tu-Sa 10am-7pm.)*

By Taxi

Taxi Télé. *(☎05 56 96 00 34 $ €1.46 per km during the day, €2.19 per km after 7pm. €30-45 to the airport.)*

saint-émilion ☎05

Located 35km northeast of Bordeaux, the famed viticulturists of St-Émilion have been refining their technique since Roman times—and it shows. Local winemakers nourish over 5400 acres, gently crushing the grapes to produce two and a half million liters of wine each year. The medieval village's antiquated stone buildings, twisting narrow streets, and religious monuments ensure a charming visit.

ORIENTATION

St-Émilion is a tiny village, surrounded by miles of vineyards. Indeed, it's small enough that you can walk from one end of town to the other in less than ten minutes. If you arrive at the **train station,** turn right onto the main road and walk 2km north into town on **rue Porte Bouqueyre** (or take a cab). Once you arrive, there are well-marked signs for the **tourist office,** which is located on **rue du Clocher,** just opposite the belltower of the *Église Monolithe* church, the tallest structure in the village and your principal landmark. South of the Tourist Office is **rue Guadet,** where you'll find several wineries and **Montagne D122,** a highway that leaves town. The highway leaves town at the traffic circle, **pl. Bourgoise,** where **bus #302** from Bordeaux drops you off. Less than one block north on highway D122, where you'll find St-Émilion's grocery store. Continue straight for another 3km to reach the campsites.

ACCOMMODATIONS

It's difficult to plan more than a daytrip to the lovely village of St-Émilion, since you'll be hard pressed to find budget accommodations. St-Émilion's least expensive bed and breakfasts are many miles outside of town, and hotels in the village proper start at €70 per room. Your best option is the campsite, which is 3km north of town on highway D122.

DOMAINE DE LA BARBANNE CAMPSITE ❷

route de Montagne D122 ☎05 57 24 75 80 💻www.camping-saint-emilion.com

St-Émilion's closest campsite and most affordable accommodation is 3km outside in the heart of the wine country. With leafy tent sites, an emerald lake for paddleboating, a sparkling pool, and amenities like on-site kitchens, a grocery store, and a restaurant *(plates €9-13)*, the campground is better value than any budget hotel. And, since you won't find budget hotels in St-Émilion, it's your only choice. The downside is the distance from town, so it's best to rent a bike, although take extreme care on the highway.

 # From Pl. Bourgeoise, walk north on Route Montagne or highway D122 through 3km of vineyards. You'll be turning right at the sign for "Camping." The walk takes 30-45min. but BE CAREFUL since you are walking on a highway. i Reserve in advance. Bike rental available. $ Apr-June and Sept-Oct tent sites €18, with electricity €22; €6.50 per additional camper. July 2-8 tent sites €26.50/30.50; €8 per additional camper; July 9-Aug tent sites €30/35; €9 per additional camper. ⏰ Reception M-Th 8:30am-9pm, F-Su 8:30am-10pm.

FOOD

St-Émilion's only grocery store is perfect for a picnic among the vines. If you plan to sit down at one of the town's restaurants, expect to pay €10-20 for a plate and search **pl. du Marché** for typically French fare.

L'ÉPICERIE — GROCERY ①

pl. Bourgeoise ☎05 57 24 70 08

This cute grocery store is the optimal way to eat for budget travelers. There is an impressive cheese counter, four kinds of fresh bread, fruits, vegetables, all kinds of packaged goods and of course, jars of Nutella.

 # 20m on highway D122 past Pl. Bourgeoise, the northern border of town where bus #302 from Bordeaux drops you off. A 2min. walk from the tourist office. ⏰ Open M-Sa 8am-7:15pm, Su 8am-6:15pm.

BAR DE LA POSTE — CONTINENTAL ②

6 pl. du Marché ☎05 57 24 70 76

A casual, reasonably priced restaurant that serves a little of everything beneath the belltower of St-Émilion's *Église Monolithe*. In warm weather, you'll join the crowds outside for healthy portions of salad, pizza, pasta, fish, or meat—accompanied, of course, by the *pièce de la resistance*, St-Émilion red wine.

 # In the square beneath the belltower of Église Monolithe. It's easiest to follow the signs for the church from the Tourist Office. $ Salads €8.50-12. Sandwiches €4.80-6. Galettes €6.50-13.50. Pastas €9.50-16.30. Pizzas €9-13. Plates of meat and fish €12-18. Menu du jour €14.50. ⏰ Open daily 9am midnight.

RECETTE DES VÉRITABLES MACARONS — BAKERY ②

9 rue Guadet ☎05 57 24 72 33 www.macarons-saint-emilion.com

Not only are the macaroons in this shop made with a 400-year-old recipe, the little almond cookies also took part in the 1867 World Fair in Paris. As the story goes, the secret recipe was concocted in a convent in 1620 under Mother Superior Sister Lacroix, and was subsequently passed down to the widow, Mrs. Goudichaud, to whom the recipe is attributed today. After all the hype, an actual bite reveals the macaroons to be delicate and flavorful. Sadly, they are none too cheap. Ask for a taste before you purchase a box of 36.

$ €10 for a box of 36 macaroons. ⏰ Open M-Sa 8am-7pm, Su 9am-7pm.

SIGHTS

ÉGLISE MONOLITHE — CHURCH

Carved by Benedictine monks out of solid rock over the course of three centuries, the *Église Monolithe* is the largest and best preserved subterranean church in all of Europe. Giant iron clamps keep the columns from collapsing under the combined stress of the heavy bell tower, which was added in the 17th century. The damp underground catacombs, a burial place for infants and wealthy monks, and the adjacent cave of the hermit Émilion, represent only a small portion of the 70 acres of underground galleries that have yet to be excavated. To visit, you must take one of the 45min. guided tours, which depart from the tourist office.

$ €6.70, students €4.20. ⏰ Tours in French at 10:30am, 11:30am, and 2pm-6pm every hr. Tours in English at 2:30pm and 4:30pm.

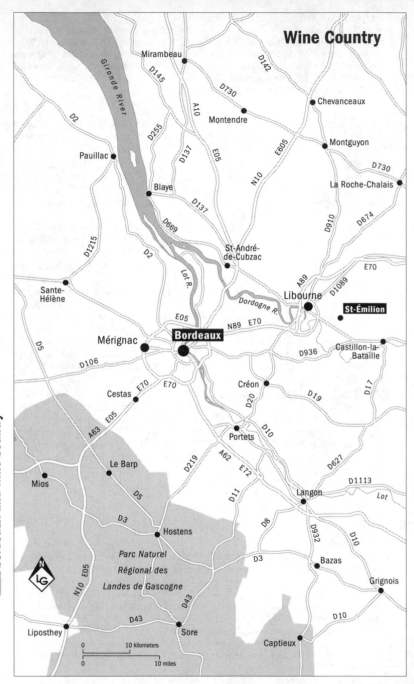

Wine Country

Gironde River

Mirambeau

D145

D142

D730

Chevanceaux

Montendre

A10

E05

D255

D137

E605

N10

Montguyon

D730

Pauillac

Blaye

D137

La Roche-Chalais

D910

D674

D669

D1215

D2

Lot R.

St-André-de-Cubzac

Dordogne R.

A89

D1089

E70

Libourne

St-Émilion

Sante-Hélène

E05

N89

E70

Bordeaux

Mérignac

D5

D106

E70

E70

D936

Castillon-la-Bataille

Cestas

E05

Créon

D20

D19

D17

A63

Portets

D10

Le Barp

D219

A62

E72

D627

Mios

D5

D11

Langon

D1113

Lot

D3

D8

D932

D10

Hostens

Parc Naturel Régional des Landes de Gascogne

D3

Bazas

Grignois

D43

D43

D10

Liposthey

D43

Sore

Captieux

0 10 kilometers

0 10 miles

bordeaux and wine country

VINEYARDS

The easiest way to experience the vineyards is to register at the tourist office for guided visits (starting at €18 for a 3hr. tour). Free spirits can pick up a map from the tourist office, rent a bike, and travel to the collection of châteaux several miles outside of town. Plan ahead, since many of them require reservations several days in advance. Luckily, it's not hard to experience St-Émilion wine in the village itself, with a handful of châteaux, associations, and shops offering tours, *dégustation* or wine-tastings and a generally thorough education in some of the world's most renowned red wine.

CHÂTEAU VILLEMAURINE CARDINAL

🍷 WINERY
☎05 57 24 64 40

The only château within 2min. of the village promises to teach you all the basics in under an hour. A tour in English or French of this family-run winery comes with a fabulous explanation of the production process, from its hand-picked beginnings to the final corking. Thousands of bottles and barrels in the dark and clammy caves are a sight to behold, and the *dégustation* at the tour's end covers all five steps of wine-tasting. Pay €5 to become an oenophiliac. It sounds dirty, but it means you're beginning a lifelong love affair with wine.

From Pl. Bourgeoise, walk briefly on Saint-Cristophe des Bardes which is highway D243 East and at the fork, veer right. Continue 10m straight ahead, passing the similarly named Château Villemaurine and Château Villemaurine Cardinal will be on your left across from the field of grape vines. $ Visit and dégustation €5. Bottles from €15 and up. ⏰ Open M-F 9:30am-12:30pm and 1:30-5:30pm. Open by appointment on the weekends.

CLOTS DES MENUTS

🍷 CAVES, WINERY

pl. du Chaptire ☎ 05 57 74 45 77

Explore the cool and creepy caves with thousands of bottles from eight regional *châteaux*, just waiting for you to tase their contents at the *dégustation* table upstairs. Although the wine-tasting is free, it's polite to pay a token amount if you don't plan on purchasing a bottle.

On rue Guadet 2min. from the tourist office $ Bottles from €6. ⏰ Open daily in summer 10am-7pm; in winter 10am-6pm.

MAISON DU VIN

🍷 GALLERY, WINE SHOP

pl. Pierre Meyrat ☎ 05 57 55 50 55 💻www.vins-saint-emilion.com

Over 400 wines at wholesale prices, wine-tasting classes run by oenologists, daily visits from St-Émilion châteaux offering free *dégustation* and best of all, an *oflactif* (nasal) guessing game with aromas from raspberry to thyme.

Around the corner from the tourist office next to the church. $ 1½hr. wine-tasting class €21. ⏰ Open daily Aug 9:30am-7pm; Sept-Oct 9:30am-12:30pm and 2-6:30pm; Nov-Mar 10am-12:30pm and 2-6pm; Apr-July 9:30am 12:30pm and 2-6:30pm. Wine-tasting classes July-Sept daily 11am.

ESSENTIALS

Practicalities

- **TOURIST OFFICE:** To get to the office from the train station, take a right on the main road and walk 20min. up rue de la Porte Bouqueyre toward the clock tower. From the bus stop, just follow the signs. The office distributes *Le Guide St-Émilion,* which details the town's history, provides maps and itineraries, and lists vineyards, accommodations, and restaurants. Note that many of the *châteaux* require reservations to visit. The office organizes daily tours in English and French to the surrounding vineyards: €18 for a 3hr. bus tour of the wine-country with *dégustation* included. *(pl. des Créneaux ☎05 57 55 28 28 💻www.saint-emilion-tourisme.com $ Bike rental €12 per half-day, €15 per full day. ⏰ Open daily June-Sept 9:30am-8pm; Sept-Oct 9:30am-12:30pm and 1:30-6:30pm; Nov-Mar open 10am-12:30pm and 2-5pm;*

Apr-June 9:30am-12:30pm and 1:30-6:30pm. Tours M-Sa 2:30pm.)

Getting There

Trains go from **Bordeaux** to the **St-Émilion** train station, 2km outside of town, several times a day; it's a 40min. trip. *($ €7.70. ⏰ M-F 5:56, 7:06am, 1:33, 4:03, 4:51, 7:19pm; Sa 7:06, 10:42, 10:51am, 1:04, 2:28, 4:03, 7:19pm; Su and holidays 8:33, 10:42, 10:51am, 4:03, 7:19pm.)* **Bus** #32 leaves from the tourist office and takes 1hr. to get to St-Émilion. The benefit is that it drops you off right in the village, whereas the train station is 2km away. Buses leave at 9:20am and 12:25pm.

graves and médoc ☎05

Though St-Émilion vineyards are easiest to visit, they're certainly not the only worthwhile stop in the area. South of Bordeaux, the **Graves** region, named for its gravel topsoil, is said to be the birthplace of Bordeaux viticulture. Graves's dry and semi-sweet wines were the drink of choice in Eleanor of Aquitaine's time and though the reds of the **Médoc,** north of Bordeaux, overtook their popularity in the 18th century, it was not due to a change in quality. At the southeastern end of Graves is the **Sauternes** region, celebrated for its sweet dessert wines. Médoc, situated between the Gironde Estuary and the ocean, gets its name from the Latin *in medio aquae* (in the middle of the water). Within the region is the town of **Pauillac**, home to 3000 acres of vineyards including some of the world's most famous premier *Cru* reds: Lafite-Rothschild, Latour, and Mouton-Rothschild.

Given that Graves and Médoc comprise miles of vineyards with fewer or no centralized towns like St-Émilion, the easiest way to visit is through the Bordeaux tourist office's guided tours that include two châteaux, a *dégustation*, and transportation by bus. *($ Students €27. ⏰ Tours Apr-Nov 1:30-6pm. Médoc on Th and Sa; Graves on F; St-Émilion on W and Su.)*

biarritz ☎05

The resort town of Biarritz is synonymous with glitz—and not just because they sort of rhyme. Once a minor whaling village, Biarritz became an aristocratic playground in the mid-19th century. Its natural beauty has drawn the likes of Napoleon III, Alphonse XIII of Spain, Nicholas II of Russia, and the Shah of Persia. While today Biarritz remains an opulent getaway for jet setters from around the world, its crowded beaches and vibrant clubs are still within the reach of both blonde-haired surfer dudes and budget travelers.

ORIENTATION

The train station, **Biarritz-la-Négresse,** is 3km. outside of town along **av. du Président John Fitzgerald Kennedy.** Av. du JFK turns into **av. du Maréchal Foch** once it enters town. It's a 40min.-1hr. walk, or a 10min. bus ride on **#2.** On Sundays, **bus B** travels the same route. To walk, turn left outside of the train station. If you're staying at the **Auberge de Jeunessse.** it's an easy 10min. walk from the train station. Follow the signs and expect to quickly turn left off av. du JFK onto **rue Phillipe Veyrin.**

Once you've made it to town, you can orient yourself using the central square **pl. Georges Clémenceau.** From this square, **av. Édouard VII** passes the **Casino** and heads north, following Biarritz's main beach, the **Grande Plage,** to one side. At the far northern tip is Biarritz's lighthouse. **rue Gambetta** leaves the square to the west and curves south following the beach in the other direction. Taking **rue Mazagran,** the right fork where rue Gambetta leaves pl. Clémenceau leads to **pl. Sainte Eugénie,** another square with a church, gazebo and beautiful view of the waves. Continue along Rue Mazagran to find hotels, restaurants and bars and eventually **rue du Port Vieux** will take you to the water's edge.

ACCOMMODATIONS

Bargains are hard to find in this upscale vacation town. To get the best deals, it's important to plan at least a month ahead for stays in July and August or enlist the help of the tourist office.

HOTEL LA MARINE — HOTEL ❸

1 rue des Goélands ☎05 59 24 34 09

The best deal in central Biarritz. Run by an attentive family for some 30 years, the 9 blue-and-white rooms with double beds, wicker furniture, full baths, and mini-TVs put you in a superb location just 5min. from the beach, and right next to Biarritz's best food and nightlife. Reserve weeks in advance for July and August, or you'll be out of luck.

From pl. Clémenceau, take the right-forking rue Mazagran and walk downhill. After the open square at pl. Saint Eugénie with an ocean view to your right, climb uphill and take your first right onto rue des Goélands. The front door to the hotel is immediately on your left. ℹ *Cable internet provided.* $ *July-Aug singles €40-45; doubles €50-55; triples €82. Sept-Nov singles €40; doubles €45; triples €68. Apr-June singles €35; doubles €40; triples €68.* ⏰ *Reception 8am-8pm. Access code for entry after 8pm.*

AUBERGE DE JEUNESSE — HOSTEL ❶

8 rue chiquito de Cambo ☎05 59 41 76 00 💻biarritz@fuaj.org

One of the best hostels around, with a laid-back surfer crowd and a well-stocked bar. Dorms for 2-4 with bunk beds, personal cabinets, and full baths inside. When it comes to eating, the hostel provides both free kitchen access and a glassy cafeteria for complimentary breakfast *(lunch and dinner €9-10.50)*. When you're not at the beach, make friends with super-cool Halim at reception. This place is popular, so make your reservations weeks in advance, or just show up and pray. Management offers to drive guests to the Auberge de Jeunesse in Anglet if there's space.

Exit the train station and turn left at the sign for the Auberge. Walk on a steep downhill past a park and continue straight down, for 5min. until the Auberge on your right. Near a beautiful lake. ℹ *Breakfast included. Lunch and dinner €9-10.50. Wi-Fi €1 per 45min.* $ *Dorms May-Sept €19.50; Oct-Apr €18.50.* ⏰ *Reception 8:30am-12:30pm and 6-10pm. Check-out 8:30am-11am.*

HOTEL BARNETCHE — HOTEL ❷

5 av. Charles Floquet ☎05 59 24 22 25 💻www.hotel-barnetche.fr

A two-star, family-run hotel with rooms beyond your budget, but a secret and affordable dormitory in back designed for young travelers like you. There are 12-14 small bunk beds, a basic communal shower, and a tight-squeeze toilet; the dorm's large windows open onto the hotel's garden. Although pricier than the Auberge de Jeunesse and lacking comparable services (no cafeteria, we're afraid), the huge benefit of Barnetche is that you're 5min. from the beach. The owners will store your surfboard in the garage.

From pl. Clémenceau walk away from the water on av. de Verdun. Turn right up rue P. Moussempés. At the small square pl. de la Libération, take av. Charles Floquet. ℹ *No food, drink, or alcohol; no guests from the outside. Keep passport at reception.* $ *12- to 14-bed dorms €25.* ⏰ *Open May-Sept. Reception 7:30am-10:30pm. Pay daily at 10am.*

SIGHTS

When you're not sunbathing or surfing, Biarritz has some nifty sights, including some very cute baby seals at the Musée de la Mer. Unfortunately, nothing's free except for Le Rocher de la Vierge, but it's worth paying to catch the view from the lighthouse.

☆ LE PHARE — LIGHTHOUSE

av. de l'Impératrice ☎05 59 22 37 10

Why would you ever pay money to climb 248 stairs? The only reasonable answer: to gaze dreamily at the Basque coast and the Pyrenees Mountains beyond from 73m above sea-level. Built in 1834, Biarritz's lighthouse offers a breath-taking visit, if the climb up hasn't already winded you.

Follow av. Edouard VII with the beach to your left. Keep going uphill as it becomes Av. de l'Impératrice and the lighthouse is at the far tip of the beach on your left. $ €2.50. ⏰ Open July-Aug daily 10am-1:30pm and 2-7pm; Sept daily 2-7pm; Oct-June 2-6pm.

LE ROCHER DE LA VIERGE — ♿ HISTORIC SITE

Legend has it that whalers caught in a tempest were guided to shore by a light from this rocky outcropping. The grateful men erected a statue of the Virgin Mary on the miraculous spot. Linked to the beach by a metal bridge built in the Eiffel workshops, the rocks were also chosen by Napoleon III as the anchor point for the sea wall of Port du Refuge. Napoleon's gone, but Mother Mary's still there.

At the very end of esplanade du Rocher de la Vierge, around the corner from Musée de la Mer.

MUSÉE DE LA MER — AQUARIUM

esplanade du Rocher de la Vierge ☎05 59 22 75 40 💻www.museedelamer.com

Crowds stare at the seal tank on the second floor for hours, especially the uber-cute baby *phoques* inside. Yes, the French word for seal is *phoque*. Get over it. There's also a small shark tank in a nearby fake cave; their proximity to the baby *phoques* is a little ominous. The aquarium also has manta rays, eels, and over 150 species of fish from the Bay of Biscay, as well as exhibits on the history of fishing in Biarritz. Displays are only in French, but the fish don't know the difference.

Take rue Mazagran straight until it connects with rue du Port-Vieux. Walk towards the water then curve right on esplanade du Rocher de la Vierge until the museum on your right. $ €8, students €5.50. ⏰ Open daily July-Aug 9:30am-midnight; Sept and June 9:30am-7pm; Oct-May 9:30am-12:30pm and 2-6pm. Seal feeding daily 1:30, 5pm.

PLANETE MUSÉE DU CHOCOLAT — MUSEUM, CHOCOLATE

14-16 av. Beaurivage ☎ 05 59 23 27 72 💻www.planetemuseeduchocolat.com

A small and private museum dedicated to the art of chocolate-making on the Basque Coast. Thanks to Sephardic Jews who fled to the area from the Spanish Inquisition in 1609, the secret of South American chocolate production came to nearby Bayonne early on, where it has been safeguarded and developed for 400 years. Museum exhibits chronicle this history through displays of cocoa sculptures, machines, old posters, ads, knick-knacks, and a chocolate shop. There's also a 14min. film in French. Best of all, your somewhat pricey ticket includes chocolate coins and thick hot cocoa. It might be worth skipping right to the chocolate shop.

Take rue Gambetta to the traffic circle Rond-point d'Héllanthe. Continue straight along av. Beaurivage with the sea to your right. Pass a garden and the museum is ahead on your right. A 10min. walk from the center of town. i Explanations and film offered in English upon request. Explanations and film offered in English upon request. $ Entry €6, students €5. Chocolate coins €3.50. Chocolate bars €4. ⏰ Open July-Aug daily 10am-6:30pm; Sept-June M-Sa 10am-12:30pm and 2-6:30pm.

FOOD

In dining, as with everything in Biarritz, style trumps substance. Restaurants can get away with charging gourmet prices for gruel if they provide the right view. Accordingly, the restaurants around the **Grande Plage** and **pl. Sainte Eugénie** tend to be expensive. Go to **rue Mazagran** and at **pl. Clémeanceau** for cheap *crêperies* and sandwich joints instead. In addition to nightly live music, ☆**New Quay** has ridiculously awesome tapas, which are actually large plates of wings, fries or calamari (€4-6). There are some good finds on **rue du Port Vieux** and on **rue du Centre** near Biarritz's **Halles,** fantastic covered markets with fresh fruits, veggies, cheese, breads, meat and fish (🕐 *Open daily 7am-1:30pm.)* Just next to the Halles is a **Carrefour** grocery store. *(2 rue du Centre* ☎*05 59 24 18 01* 🕐 *Open M-Sa 7am-9pm, Su 9am-1pm.)*

🏅 CASA JUAN PEDRO
Port des Pêcheurs

♥✓❄ SEAFOOD ❷
☎05 59 24 00 86

Nestled in a rocky cove at the fishermen's port, this outdoors-only seafood restaurant boasts a sensational ocean view, not to mention a muscular and tattooed cartoon fish as their badass logo. Owned by identical twins, the patio is always packed with locals enjoying fish fresh off the grill. You can only order right here; choosing anything from the large selection of tasty seafood dishes including mussels, tuna, sardines, hake, and sea bream.

⚒ *From pl. des Clémenceau, take rue Mazagran to pl. Sainte Eugénie. Walk towards the water and turn left onto bld. du Maréchal Leclerc. Take the path on your right leading down toward the Port des Pêcheurs. The restaurant is right on the water.* ⑨ *Plates €6-13.50. Sangria €3.* 🕐 *Open daily July-Aug noon-3pm and 7:30-11:30pm; Sept-June noon-2pm and 7.30-10.30pm. Closed in bad weather.*

LE PALMARIUM
7 rue du Port Vieux

♥❄ SPANISH ❷
☎05 59 24 25 83

You'll recognize this family-run place by their specialty: a mammoth pot of paella being dished out for dinner in and to-go. Since it's an all-you-can-eat plate of rice, mussels, shrimp, fish, and the occasional piece of chicken, the homey paella is one of the best ways to fuel up after a long day of traveling. When you're not chowing down on seafood, you can also enjoy excellent salads, pizzas, or various meat dishes among the palm trees in this outdoor restaurant. It's not called the Palmarium for nothing.

⚒ *Facing the water on rue Mazagran at the open square of pl. Sainte Eugénie head left and walk slightly uphill. You're now on rue du Port Vieux so walk straight. Easy, right? You're welcome.* ⓞ *Menu €12.50. House paella €15 for all-you-can-eat. Pizzas €7.50-13. Meats €13-18. Fish €10-11.50. Cocktails €6.* 🕐 *Open daily July-Aug noon-11:30pm; Sept-June noon-3pm and 7-10pm.*

LA TIREUSE
29 rue Mazagrin

♥✓❄ WAFFLES, BEER ❷
☎05 59 24 26 18

Waffles hot off the griddle topped with sugar, whipped cream, chocolate, Nutella, and other decadent things. Easily the best euro you'll spend today.

⚒ *At the end of rue Mazagran where it opens into pl. Ste-Eugénie, a square with a church, gazebo, and view of the sea.* ⑤ *Waffles €2.50-5. Beers €3-5.* 🕐 *Open July-Aug daily 11am-2am; Sept-June Tu-Sa 5pm-2am.*

NIGHTLIFE

🏴

In this town, every summer's night is a weekend. Start your night off with groups of young people drinking on the **Grande Plage,** then move around 11pm to the bars on **rue Mazagran** and **pl. Clémenceau.** At 2am, as bars close, long lines form outside Biarritz's fancy *boîtes* (clubs.)

🏅 NEW QUAY
20 pl. Clémenceau

♥((ꞁ)) BAR, LIVE MUSIC

A laid-back bar during the day with 🏅**terrific tapas** like fries, chicken wings, and calamari (€4-6). "Tapas" are so large that just one makes a meal. Once the live music starts at 11pm, there's barely an inch to move. Just wait for the student crowd to spill out onto lively pl. Clémenceau around 2am.

i *Free Wi-Fi.* ⑤ *Big fries €4. Nachos €6. Heaps of chicken wings €6. Calamari €4. Fish and chips, burgers, salads €4-10. Beer €5.40 for a pint.* 🕐 *Open daily 9am-2am. Nightly concerts at 11pm.*

IBIZA 🍸 MEDITERRANEAN

Grande Plage ☎05 59 24 38 34 🖳www.ibiza-biarritz.fr

Two-in-one: the bar takes a page from Coyote Ugly with uber-attractive bartenders serving drinks amid the grunge. DJ mixes Spanish music that's a party for your hips. The adjacent and swanky *boîte* (club) opens at 2am for a young crowd. A mosaiced bar, mirrors, and a smoky purple-lit dance floor that's occasionally frequented by male and female go-go dancers mean that your party keeps on going on.

⇅ From pl. Clémenceau walk along av. Edouard VII. Turn left onto bld. Général de Gaulle with the fancy Hôtel du Palais on your right and the Grande Plage ahead of you. The club is to the left around the corner. $ Cover €10. Beers on tap €3. Mixed drinks €6-8. ⏰ Open July-Aug daily 10pm-6am; Sept-June Tu-Sa 10pm-6am. Club doors open at 2am.

CASINO BARRIÈRE DE BIARRITZ 🍸 CASINO

1 av. Edouard VII ☎05 59 22 77 77

Biarritz's Casino stands over the Grande Plage in all its Art Deco glory. A red-carpeted ocean of slot machines welcomes gamblers on the first floor, and card tables are shuffling and dealing on the second floor starting at 8:30pm. If you're not an EU citizen, remember to bring a passport. Remember us at Let's Go if you win the multi-million-euro jackpot.

*⇅ Where pl. Clémenceau meets av. Edouard VII, climb down the stairs towards the Grande Plage. The Casino is on your right before the beach. **i** 18+. ⏰ Open daily July-Aug 10am-4am; Sept-June 10am-3am.*

LE CAVEAU 🍸▼ BAR

4 rue Gambetta ☎05 59 24 16 17 🖳www.lecaveau-biarritz.com

A fun-loving bar that keeps the champagne flowing and the dance music playing in the pink upstairs, while the DJ turns heavier beats in the red-lit basement *boîte*. Biarritz's first gay club is true to its roots, but you're also sure to find a mix of men and women, mostly 30-somethings. Check yourself or someone else out in the shards of mirror arranged in a mosaic by the bar, and full walls of the stuff in the basement.

⇅ Follow the left-forking rue Gambetta as it leaves pl. Clémenceau. $ Cover €10. Beer €7. Mixed drinks €8. Champagne €10. ⏰ Open daily 11pm-5am.

ESSENTIALS

Practicalities

- **TOURIST OFFICES:** A super-friendly English-, French-, and Spanish-speaking staff track down same-day hotel reservations or campsites for free. Very useful in the overbooked summer months. Pick up the free *Guide Loisirs* to find out about Biarritz's sights and leisure activities, *Biarritzscope* for monthly event listings, or the *Hebergement* guide to the resort town's expensive accommodations. *(sq. d'Ixelles. ☎05 59 22 37 10 🖳www.biarritz.fr $Internet €2 per 15min.)* Finally, there's a tourist office outpost at the **Biarritz-La-Négresse** train station. *(⏰ Open July-Aug daily 9am-7pm; Sept M-F 9am-6pm, Sa-Su 10am-6pm; Oct-Mar M-F 9am-6pm, Sa noon-5pm, Su 10am-1pm; Apr-June M-F 9am-6pm, Sa-Su 10am-5pm.)*
- **TOURS:** The **Petit Train** departs every 30min. from the Grande Plage (Casino) or the Rocher de la Vierge and gives multilingual 30min. guided bus-disguised-as-train rides of the Port des Pêcheurs, the Port Vieux, and the Perspective Côte des Basques. The Grande Plage booth is located at 39 av. de la Marne. *(☎06 07 97 16 35 🖳www.petit-train-biarritz.com $ €5.20. ⏰ Open daily July-Aug 10am-10pm; Sept and May-June 10am-5pm; Oct and Apr 10:30am-1pm and 2-5pm.)*
- **CURRENCY EXCHANGE: Change-Plus.** *(9 rue Mazagran ☎05 59 24 82 47 **i** No extra commission on traveler's checks. ⏰ Open July-Aug M-Sa 9am-6pm;*

Sept-Jun M-F 9am-6pm, Sa 9am-noon.) Currency exchange also available a the post office.

- **BEACH INFORMATION AND EMERGENCIES:** Info on Biarritz's beaches. *(☎08 05 20 00 64)* **Grande Plage.** *(☎05 59 22 22 22 ⏰ Lifeguards on duty July-Aug 10am-8pm; Sept 11am-7pm.)* **Miramar.** *(☎05 59 24 34 98 ⏰ Lifeguards on duty July-Aug 10am-7pm; Sept occasionally 11am-7pm.)* **Le Port Vieux.** *(☎05 59 24 05 84 ⏰ Lifeguards on duty July-Aug 10am-8pm; Sept 11am-7pm.)* **Marbella.** *(☎05 59 23 01 20 ⏰ Lifeguards on duty July-Aug 10am-8pm; Sept 11am-7pm.)* **La Milady.** *(☎05 59 23 63 93 ⏰ Lifeguards on duty July-Aug 10am-7pm; Sept occasionally 11am-7pm.)* **La Côte des Basques.** *(☎05 09 24 39 72 ⏰ Lifeguards on duty July-Aug 10am-8pm; Sept 11am-7pm.)*
- **INTERNET ACCESS: Formatic.** *(15 av. de la Marne ☎05 59 22 12 79 $ €5 per hr. ⏰ Open July-Aug M-F 9am-10pm, Sa-Su 10am-7pm; Sept-June M-F 9am-noon and 2-8pm, Sa-Su 10am-noon and 2-6pm.)*
- **POST OFFICE: Biarritz Principal.** *(17 rue de la Poste ☎05 59 22 41 12 ℹ Western Union and currency exchange inside. ⏰ Open M-F 8:30am-12:30pm and 2-6pm.)*
- **POSTAL CODE:** 64200.

Emergency!

- **EMERGENCY NUMBERS: Police** ☎17. **Ambulance** ☎15. **Aquatic emergencies** ☎18.
- **POLICE: Commissariat.** *(rue Louis Barthou. ☎05 59 01 22 22 ✈ 1 block from the tourist office. ⏰ Open 24hr.)*
- **HOSPITAL: Centre Hospitalier Côte Basque.** *(13 av. Interne Jacques Loeb. Bayonne ☎05 59 44 35 35)* **Médecin en Garde.** *(☎05 59 24 01 01 ⏰ Doctor on duty 24hr.)*
- **PHARMACIES:** For a pharmacie de nuit after 8pm on weekdays, call the Commissariat, under **Police,** above. A list of rotating *pharmacies de garde* that remain open on Sundays is posted outside the door of all pharmacies in Biarritz.

Getting There

By Plane

To get to **Aéroport de Parme** *(7 esplanade de l'Europe ☎05 59 43 83 83)* on Monday-Saturday, take bus #6 (dir: Bayonne Gare) from the Hôtel de Ville *(every 30min. 7:02am-7:33pm)*; on Su take bus C (dir: Aéroport). Flights head to local destinations in France as well as **Dublin, London, Bimringham, Amsterdam,** and **Helsinki.**

By Train

Biarritz-la-Négresse *(☎36 35 ✈ 3km from town or 15min. on bus #2. ⏰ Ticket office open M-Sa 9am-7pm, Su 10am-7pm.)* has trains to: **Bayonne** *($ €2.50-3.20. ⏰ 10min., 23 per day.)*; **Bordeaux** *($ €29.40-32.90. ⏰ 2hr., 12 per day.)*; **Paris** *($ €74.40-98.20. ⏰ 5hr., 6 per day.)*; **Pau** *($ €18.30. ⏰ 2hr., 3 per day.)*; **Toulouse** *($ €42.70-54.90. ⏰ 4hr., 4 per day.)*. There is an SNCF agency in town at 13 av. Maréchal du Foch, three blocks from the intersection with av. de Verdun. *(☎05 59 50 83 34 ⏰ Open M-F 9am-12pm and 2-6pm.)*

By Bus

ATCRB *(☎05 59 26 06 99)* runs buses form the sq. d'Ixelles in front of the tourist office. Schedules are subject to change in the near future, so consult the tourist office. Purchase tickets from the driver. Buses go to: **St-Jean de-Luz** *(ℹ Line 26. $ €4. ⏰30min., 22 per day.)*; **Hendaye** *(ℹ Line 25 from St-Jean de-Luz. $ €4. ⏰20min., 7 per day.)*. **PESA** *(🖥www.pesa.es)* services buses to **San Sebastian,** Spain. *(⏰ M-Sa at 12:15pm and 4:45pm.)*

Getting Around

By Public Transportation

A **VTAB** ticket and information office is on rue Louis Barthou next to the tourist office. Purchase tickets at the office or on the bus. *(☎05 59 52 59 52 💻www.bustab.com $ 1 ticket €1.20; 5 trips €4.75; carnet of 10 €9.50, students €8. ⏰ Open M-Sa 8:15am-noon and 1:30-6pm. Buses #1, 2, and 6 run M-Sa 6am-8:30pm; buses A, B, and C run Su 7:30am-8:30pm. Bus de la nuit runs daily in summer 9pm-5am.)* The Passeo bus leaves every 30min. from the Hôtel de Ville and passes the train station near the **Auberge de Jeunesse,** perfect for party-oriented hostel-dwellers. The Chronobus leaves every hour from Sq. d'Ixelles and heads to Bayonne. In January 2011, Biarritz's public transportation system will be revamped so that schedules, routes and prices are likely to change. Consult the tourist office for up-to-date information.

By Bike And Scooter

CYCLE OCÉAN

24 rue Peyroloubilh ☎05 59 24 94 47 💻www.cycle-ocean.com

This bike-rental shop also rents scooters; an ID is required, so take a big gulp and show 'em your passport photo.

$ €5 per hr., €8 per 4hr., €12 per 8hr., €15 per 24hr. €153 credit card deposit. ⏰ Open daily June-Sept 9am-8pm; Oct-Mar 10am-6pm.

By Taxi

Taxi de Biarritz *(☎05 59 03 18 18 💻www.taxisi-biarritz.fr $ €13-15 to the airport. ⏰ Open 24hr.)* has a taxi stop at the corner of av. de Verdun and av. Edouard VII.

arcachon ☎05

One of the most relaxed and beautiful beach towns on the Côte d'Argent (Silver Coast), the thin strip of sand that runs along 200km of France's southern Atlantic seaboard, Arcachon was created a mere 160 years ago by French aristocrats suffering from bad lungs and boredom. It remains a posh resort town, and a hotspot for vacationing families and content retirees. But more than its dozens of beaches, what makes Arcachon worth a daytrip from Bordeaux is the **Dune du Pyla,** Europe's highest sand dune and a slice of the Sahara in France. It's an absolute must-see. The **Bassin d'Arcachon** (bay of Arcachon) is also known for the **Banc d'Arguin**, a 1000-acre sand bar in the form of a crescent across the waters from the Dune. Pack a picnic lunch, hop the train and prepare to play in white sand and swim in the azure water.

ORIENTATION

By happy coincidence or clever urban planning, Arcachon's **train station** and **tourist office** are on the same block, both on **bld. du Général Leclerc.** The bus to the **Dune du Pyla**, which is 5km south of town, stops right at the train station. To reach Arcachon's beaches from the tourist office, take **av. Gambetta.** It's only three blocks until the beach. You can bike or walk along the **bld. de la Plage** which follows the town's many beaches as they curve around the bay. Travelers who opt to bike to the Dune should expect a 45min.-1hr. ride, half of which is on specified bike paths, while the other half is on highways. Except for the intense hill right before the Dune, it's a great bike ride.

ACCOMMODATIONS

The siren song of Arcachon might leave you wanting more than a daytrip from Bordeaux. Unfortunately, if you're planning on staying the night, it's tough to find student-friendly prices in the heart of town. The cheapest rooms start at €50, and only go up. You'll have slightly more luck with the bed and breakfasts 1-2km from town. Ask at the tourist office for a list. You can also consider the very basic **Auberge de Jeunesse** located in **Cap Ferret**, a 30min. ferry across the bay from Arcachon. *(87 av. Bordeaux ☎05 56 60 64 62 ⑨Dorms €11.70.☒Open daily July-Aug 8am-1pm and 6-9pm.)* To get to the Auberge, take the **Line 1** ferry operated by **Union Bateliers Arcachonnais.** Finally, there's also the **Camping Club d'Arcachon**, 1.5km from the town center. *(5 allée de la Galaxies les Abatilles ☎05 56 83 24 15 ◼www.camping-arcachon.com)* The campsite is open year-round and has tent sites for €13 in July and August.

SIGHTS

▩ DUNE DU PYLA   BEACH

Rising from the edge of a pine forest 5km south of town, the extraordinary Dune du Pyla seems more like a section of the Sahara than a French beach. The 104m mountain of white sand stretches for 2.7km along the coast, and has a total volume of 60,000L. Every year without fail, the west winds that created the dune move it a few centimeters east; as a result, the army barracks constructed at the summit in 1942 now hug the water's edge. Where sand meets the azure ocean, there is a small lifeguarded beach for swimming and sunbathing. Take care, though: a strong undertow makes deep swims unwise. Expect to spend a few hours, at least, on this geographic marvel. Afterwards, if you have wheels— either a bike or car—the campsites 3-5km south of the Dune offer hang-gliding lessons. Try **Waggas School** at Pyla Camping from April to October. *(☎06 32 04 32 07 ◼www.waggaschool.com ⑨ €120-140 for 2hr., including instruction.)*

✦ *City bus #1 runs from the train station to "Dune de Pyla" within 5min. of the sand. From the bus stop "Dune de Pyla" walk straight into the park. Follow the signs to the tourist office. Continue 500m past shops and restaurants to reach the staircase leading up the dune. The adventurous can climb direclty on the sand slope. ⊕ Free. ☒ Dune open 24hr. Parking lot open 7am-2am.*

FOOD   ◖

There's a daily market *(☒ Open 7am 1pm.)* in the parking lot on bld. du Général Leclerc next to the train station. Here, you can stock up on fresh fruits, vegetables, cheeses, deli meats and mouth-watering *rôtisserie* chicken after disembarking from the train. For an even greater selection, visit the enormous **Casino** supermarket directly behind the train station. *(☒ Open M-Sa 8:30am-8pm.)* For a sit-down meal, hold off until the **Dune de Pyla,** where there are a series of touristy but reasonably priced restaurants with lots of seafood like *moules et frites (€8-10).* In Arcachon proper, there are restaurants all along the beachfront with beautiful views and higher prices.

ESSENTIALS   �

Practicalities

- **TOURIST OFFICE:** The tourist office distributes an excellent tourist guide to the Bassin d'Arcachon in English and French. It also has information about accommodations, restaurants, and things to do like water-sports centers, surf spots, beaches and hikes. *(1 esplanade George Pompidou ☎05 57 52 97 97 ◼www.archachon.com ✦ After exiting the train station, turn left. The tourist office is 1 block ahead on your left. ☒ Open July-Aug daily 9am-7pm; Sept M-Sa 9am-6pm, Su 10am-1pm and 2-5pm; Oct-Mar M-F 9am-6pm, Sa 9am-5pm; May-June M-Sa 9am-6pm, Su 10am-1pm and 2-5pm.)* **Dune du Pyla Tourist Office.** *(☒ Open Apr-Sept M-Sa 10am-1pm and 2-6pm, Su 10am-2pm.)*

Getting There   ✕

Trains (bld. du Général Leclerc ☒ Ticket office open M-F 6am-8:25pm, Sa 7:10am-8:25pm, Su 8:50am-9:25pm.) chug off to **Bordeaux** *(⑨ €10.10. ☒ 1hr., 23 per day.)* and **Paris** *(⑨ €73.60. ☒ 4-4½hr.; in summer 2-3 per day, in winter 1 per day.)*

Getting Around

By Public Transportation

Baia *(3 rue du Général Castelnau ☎08 10 20 17 14)* runs bus #1 to the **Dune du Pyla.** *($ €1. ⏰ 20-30 min., every hr. 6:45am-7:45pm.)* In addition, **ého!** runs free electric *navettes* around the center of town.

By Ferry

Union Bateliers Arcachonnais *(☎05 57 72 28 28 🖥www.bateleirs-arcachon.com)* is the ferry company of choice to **Cap Ferret.** *($ €7, after 7pm €8; round-trip €11.50/13.50. ⏰ 30min.; July-Aug every hr. 9am-midnight, Sept-Dec 5 per day 9am-5:30pm, Jan-Mar 4 per day 9am-5:30pm, Apr-June 6 per day 9am-5:30pm.)* Ferries leave from **Jetée Thiers,** a dock on the main beach. To get there from the tourist office, walk until av. Gambetta hits the sand.

By Bike

Exiting the train station, turn left onto bld. Général Leclerc. At the following traffic circle, turn right onto av. Gambetta. When you get to the promenade by the beach, turn right again. **Dungovelos** is down the next side street to the right. *(1 rue Grenier ☎05 56 83 44 09 🖥www.dingo-velo.com $ Bike rental €13 per day. 10% discount for students. Multi-person bikes, for 3 or 6 adults, €11 or €16 per 30min. ⏰ Open daily July-Aug 9:30am-11pm; Sept-June 9:30am-7pm.)*

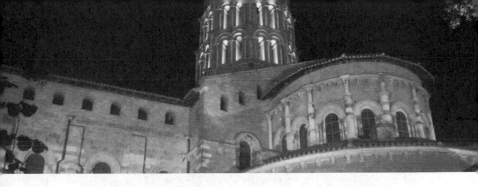

TOULOUSE AND MONTPELLIER

Located in Languedoc-Roussillon, Toulouse and Montpellier might not be as chic as Paris or wealthy as Nice. But these are two of the most free-thinking cities in France—and given the sheer number of naked people we've seen here, that's saying something. A stronghold of iconoclastic behavior for at least a millennium, Toulouse is the hometown of Thomas Aquinas; historically, the city objected to the excesses of the French monarchy so strongly that an eight-man council defiantly governed the city themselves until the Revolution. Today, the city is crowded with alternative students during the school year, who browse through mom-and-pop bookstores and galleries by day and go to poetry slams in local caves by night. Also a university town, Montpellier has achieved its rebellious rep a little more recently. The city hosts some of the best gay nightlife in the entire country, as well as some of France's oldest gay bars.

greatest hits

- **CAVEMAN'S THEATER:** Be sure to attend a poetry jam or dramatic performance in Toulouse's La Cave Poésie, a local cave that has been renovated into an intimate theatrical space (p. 220).
- **CHURCH GETS KINKY:** In addition to its glorious architecture, the Basilique St-Sernin is known for its collection of holy relics, some of which date back to Charlemagne's reign (p. 217).
- **EVERYONE ELSE GETS KINKY:** Montpellier is famed for its colorful gay nightlife. Put on some chaps and get to it (p. 229).

You've got nothing Toulouse by letting loose in Languedoc-Roussillon. If you happen to be in the region during the schooll year, head on over to **La Cave Poésie** in Toulouse to get in touch with your Beat side. You don't have to be in Paris to wear a beret.

toulouse ☎05 61

Known as *La Ville en Rose* ("the pink city"), zany Toulouse is the place to go when all French cities begin to look alike. During the school year, 110,000 scholars fill the cafés and brasseries in the narrow streets where Thomas Aquinas once discussed Aristotle with fellow theologians. At the heart of *centre ville* sits the massive Capitole building, whose eight grand columns symbolize the eight headstrong *capitouls* (councilors) who defied counts and kings to govern the city until the Revolution. An abundance of museums and concert halls makes France's fourth-largest city the region's cultural capital, with family-owned art galleries, indepenent theaters, and a diverse music scene to support the city's free-thinking tradition. Whether it's the Garrone River or the flourishing arts scene that makes your heart pound, it's hard not to fall in love with Toulouse.

ORIENTATION

While residential Toulouse sprawls along both sides of the Garonne River, the thriving *centre ville* occupies a manageable area east of the river bounded by **rue de Metz** to the south, **bld. de Strasbourg** to the north and **bld. Carnot** to the east. At the heart of things is the grand *Capitole* building, which is no more than a 20min. walk downhill on **allées Jean Jaurès** from the **Gare St. Jean** train station. The hub for Toulouse's efficient metro system is located at the intersection of allées Jean Jaurès and bld. de Strasbourg, only blocks away from the *Capitole* building.

ACCOMMODATIONS

On the whole, accommodations in Toulouse tend to be somewhat pricey. Thankfully, there are a handful of excellent options close that are only a 10-20min. walk from the action in the *centre ville*. Your best bet for budget hotels is to search the side streets off **allées Jean Jaurès,** in between the **Gare St. Jean** train station and **pl. Wilson.**

HOTEL BEAUSÉJOUR ●((•)) HOTEL ❷

4 rue Caffarelli ☎05 61 62 77 59 ▦www.hotelbeausejourtoulouse.com

An immaculate and newly renovated family-run hotel, perfectly situated a 5min. walk from the train station in one direction and the Capitole building in the other. Bright and airy rooms with double beds, most of which come with interior baths and the option of a flatscreen TV, ensure a beautiful stay in *La Ville en Rose*. The good-natured owner, *Gerome*, just loves Let's Go travelers. Introduce yourself with a smile and he'll take care of you.

⚑ *From the train station, walk downhill for 5 min. on allées Jean Jaurès until a right turn onto rue Caffarelli.* **i** *Reserve in advance.* ⑤ *Singles €25-46; doubles €38-48; triples €45-55. €0.50 daily tax per person. Reception open daily -7am--11pm. Hotel closed July 14 - Aug 1.*

RÉSIDENCE JOLIMONT ●((•)) HOSTEL ❶

2 av. Yves Brunaud ☎05 34 30 42 80

A member of the French youth hostel league that doubles as a *résidence sociale*, helping 18-25 year olds get on their feet. Luxury by hostel standards, the relatively private two- or three-person rooms come with full baths, convenient lockable cabinets, and sizeable windows. A vibrant social scene is accentuated

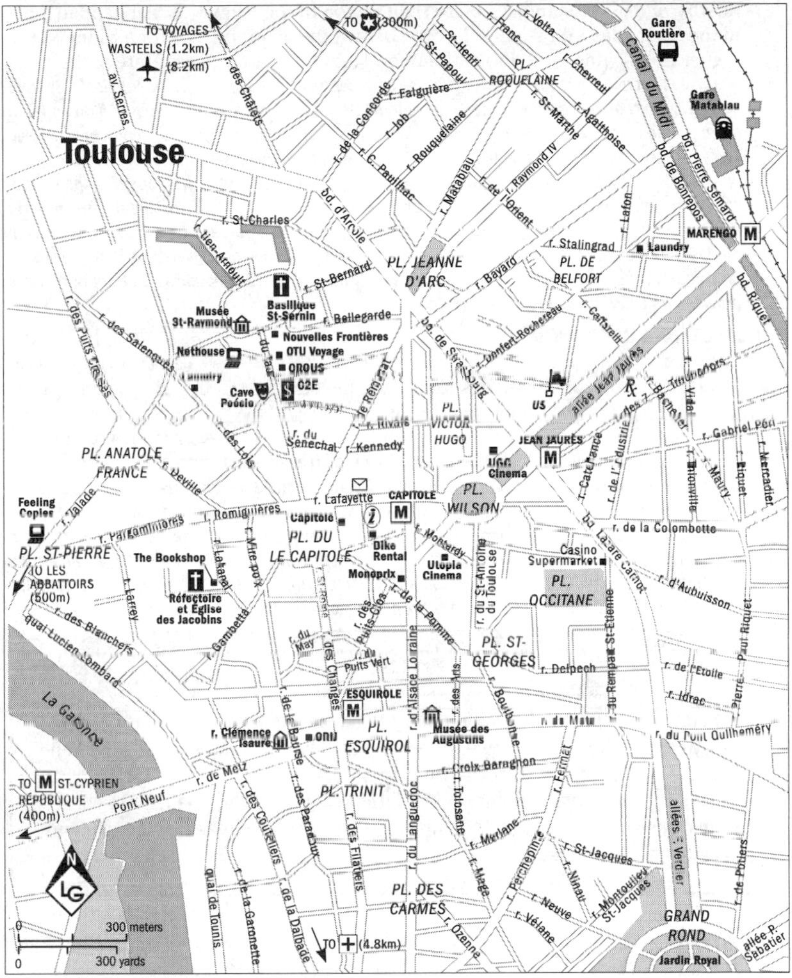

by a basketball court, lounge, pool, ping-pong tables, kitchen, weight room, and organized outings. The staff is kind, but they're sticklers for the rules.

Exit the train station and turn left onto bld. Pierre Sémard (road with train station that parallels the Canal du Midi river). Take your next left and walk straight on av. G. Pompidou. It passes underneath the Mediathèque (big building in front of you), then continues uphill for 10min. The residence is at the top of the hill as the road curves. Alternatively, take the metro one stop to Jolimont. The residence is beside the metro stop. ℹ *Breakfast €3.50.* $ *Dorms €16.50.* ⏰ *Breakfast -6:30--8:30am, lunch -12-1:30pm, and dinner -7-8pm. Rooms must be vacated by -10am.*

HOTEL DES JARDINS HOTEL ❷

9 rue Laganne ☎05 61 42 09 04 🖳www.hoteldesjardins.com

With only nine cozy and fragrant rooms, you're bound to feel at home in this family-run inn just off the banks of the Garonne River. Although it's a 30min. walk through Toulouse's old city to the Capitole, there's a free shuttle with pick-up nearby, and in the summer you're right on top of the festivities that happen daily in the Praire des Filtres park. For the best of the beautiful, ask for a room on the higher floors which overlooks the river. Mix of ensuite and separate baths.

➜ *The easiest route is to take the free navette from centre ville which runs every 7-8min. M-Sa from 9am-7pm and can be hailed where rue du Taur meets the Capitole. Get off at cours Dillon and turn left onto the first street at the traffic light. Alternatively, from centre ville walk along rue d'Alsace Lorraine away from the Capitole building until you reach pl. Esquirol with the Musée des Augustins on your right. Turn left and follow rue de Metz until the Pont Neuf bridge. After crossing the bridge, veer down your second left immediately after the bus depot/park (precisely where the free navette drops you off). This is rue Laganne. Follow the walls next to the gardens for 5min. The hotel is in the last block on rue Laganne before it hits the traffic circle. Look carefully for the tiny green sign on your right.* $ *Singles or doubles €26; €33-40 with bath.* ⏰ *Reception M-Sa 8am-8pm. Keys provided for entry when reception is closed.*

HOTEL CROIX-BARAGNON 📶 HOTEL ❸

17 rue Crois-Baragnon ☎05 61 52 60 10 💻www.hotelcroixbaragnon.com

Distinctively bright blue doors just down the street from the St. Etienne Cathedral welcome you into a boutique hotel that puts you in walking distance of all the hotspots in *centre ville*. Fifteen tastefully decorated rooms are arranged along blue and white hallways with an open interior for an astro-turf garden that caters to loungers and smokers alike. Tastefully decorated rooms have double beds, TVs, telephones, and Wi-Fi. Ask for the newly renovated ones at the same price.

➜ *From the Capitole, take rue d'Alsace Lorainne one block past the Musée des Augustins. Turn right onto rue Croix-Baragnon and look for the blue doors on your right. If you hit the Cathédrale St.-Etienne, you've gone too far.* ℹ *Breakfast €5. Reserve in advance.* $ *Singles €45; doubles €55; triples €70; quads €80. €0.50 daily tax per person.* ⏰ *Reception 8am-8pm.*

rogue graffiti and naked ladies

If pictures of plump, scantily clad women painted on the walls, buses, and subways make you uncomfortable, you aren't alone. Painting under the alias of Miss Van, this rogue graffiti artist got her start in 1993 painting the "pink city," as Toulouse is called, with what are now considered **"Hanky Panky Girls."** The defiant curves and declensions of colors of Fafi, Kat and Plum are silhouettes of the city and source of citizenry pride.

CAMPING LE RUPÉ 📶 CAMPSITE ❶

21 chemin du Pont de la Rupé ☎05 61 70 07 35 💻www.camping-toulouse.com

One of Toulouse's most affordable accommodations, Camping Le Rupé is near the gorgeous Lac de Sesquières, but otherwise surrounded by little greenery and lots of suburban industrial parks, highway, and fast food. Tent sites could use more grass, but there are excellent campground facilities, including a solar-heated kitchen and shower facility, and a convenient mini-grocery store at the reception. Be prepared for an hour or more commute to *centre ville* due to the infrequent bus schedule, particularly on weekends.

➜ *Be prepared for a long trip: From pl. Jean Jaurès, take metro B towards Borderouge. Get off at La Vache and take bus #59 until Le Rupé. The campsite is across the road (be careful crossing!) and 200m straight (don't turn left toward the lake!) on chemin du Pont de la Rupé.* ℹ *Wi-Fi €5 per hr.* $ *June 15-Sept 15 €5 per tent; €2.80 per additional person. Sept 15-June 15 €13 per tent; €2.50 per additional person. €0.20 daily tax per person.* ⏰ *Reception M-F 9am-12:30pm and 3-8pm, Sa-Su 9am-12:30pm and 5-8pm.*

SIGHTS

Walking or biking in Toulouse's vibrant *centre ville* is the best way to get around, and exploration never goes unrewarded, since *La Ville en Rose* has stunning cathedral architecture and fine arts museums. Multi-sight passes are sold at all museums: visit three museums for €6, or six museums for €9. In July and August, travelers should make their way down to the **Praire des Filtres** park on the banks of the Garonne River, across the **Pont Neuf.** There's a beach party all day, every day, with activities like volleyball and water-skiing on the river.

BASILIQUE SAINT SERNIN — BASILICA

pl. Saint-Sernin ☎05 61 21 80 45

The Basilica of Saint Sernin is the longest Romanesque structure in the world, with an enormous brick steeple that rises in five double-arched terraces like a massive wedding cake. St. Dominic, head of the Dominican order of friars, made this ornate church his base of operations in the early 13th century, and in so doing departed from the monastic tradition of ascetic architecture. Be sure to walk all the way to the end of the elegant Romanesque nave, where you'll find vivid frescoes above the altar. Behind the altar and to the left is a crypt that keeps holy relics, ranging in type from engraved silver chests to golden goblets—some from Charlemagne's time.

 # At the end of rue du Taur off of pl. du Capitole. $ Crypt €2. ⏰ Open daily July-Sept 8:30am-6:30pm; Oct-June 8:30am-noon and 2-6pm. Crypt open July-Sept M-Sa 10am-5pm, Su 11:30am-5pm; Oct-June M-Sa 10am-11:30am and 2:30-5pm, Su 2:30-5pm. Free guided tours in English July-Aug daily 4-6:30pm.

FONDATION BEMBERG — MUSEUM

pl. d'Assézat ☎05 61 12 06 89

A lovely fine arts museum, organized according to popular themes and movements, like 18th-century Venetian Art or the Fauves and Pointillists. Works are housed in the beautiful Hotel D'Assézat, a rose-brick building that makes the visit especially worthwhile. Among the collection are 35 Bonnard paintings in Room 7, as well as a modest number of works by Gaugin, Pisarro, and Toulouse-Lautre,c and the occasional Matisse, Picasso, Braque, and Renoir. Learn about these big names and more on daily guided tours with museum staff.

 # From pl. du Capitole, walk down rue d'Alsace Lorraine and turn right onto rue de Metz. Continue straight until pl. Assézat. The museum is to the right. $ Students €3, students of fine arts free. ⏰ Open Tu-W 10am-6pm, Th -10am-9pm, F-Su 10am-6pm. Guided visit Tu-F 3:30pm, Sa-Su 2:30 and 4pm.

MUSÉE DES AUGUSTINS — MUSEUM

21 rue de Metz ☎05 61 22 21 82 💻www.augustins.org

This 14th- to 15th-century Augustinian monastery now serves as a museum, with over 4000 paintings and sculptures in Romanesque and Gothic styles; the fifteen howling gargoyles are particularly entertaining. Look for the harrowing Rubens painting *Christ Entre les Deux Larrons* inside the church, in one of the insets to the left of the rose window. Come back for a second visit on Wednesday evenings, when there are free organ concerts.

 # At the corner of rue d'Alsace Lorraine and rue de Metz. $ Free entry for students. Permanent exhibit €3. Temporary exhibits of sacred art €3, students €1.50. ⏰ Open M-Tu 10am-6pm, W 10am-9pm, Th-Sa 10am-6pm. Free organ concerts W 8-8:30pm.

ENSEMBLE CONVENTUAL DES JACOBINS — MONASTERY

rue Lakanal ☎05 61 22 23 81 💻www.jacobins.mairie-toulouse.fr

A 14th-century Romanesque church so beautiful that in 1368 Pope Urban V decided it was worthy of St. Thomas Aquinas' remains. His ashes take center stage in a dramatically backlit golden tomb. Be sure to gaze into the mirror installed at the apse to reflect the vaulted roof above, which is said to resemble palm trees. Beyond the church, the peaceful cloister has occassional piano concerts, and the réfectoire houses temporary exhibits of world art.

From pl. du Capitole, walk down rue Gambetta and turn right onto rue Lakanal. $ Entry free. Cloister €3, students free. Art exhibit and cloister €5, students €2.50. For piano concerts, inquire at the Tourist Office. ⏰ Open daily 9am-7pm. Guided visits daily at -4:30pm.

CAPITOLE — GOVERNMENT BUILDING

This grandiose brick building in the heart of Toulouse's old city looks out onto a plaza of restaurants, occasional political protests, and hundreds of students taking a break from their books on the stone benches. In short, it's an ideal spot for people-watching. The palace was once home to the bourgeois *capitouls* who unofficially ruled the city—which technically controlled by counts—for many years. Inside, there are two gorgeous rooms. **La Salle Henri Martin** has 10 Post-Impressionist tableaux by Martin that represent Toulouse in all four seasons. Next door, the **Salle des Illustres** paintings from wall-to-wall and frescoes on the ceiling, all of which were created by Toulousain artists. In a lovely tradition of the city, all couples who marry must pass through the *salle*'s ornate walls.

i Building often closed Sa for marriages. ⏰ Salle des Illustres and Salle d'Henri Martin open daily 10am-7pm.

FOOD

For food that pleases your stomach and your budget, head directly to **rue du Taur,** where cheap eateries serve *plats* at €5-10. On Tuesdays and Saturdays, **pl. du Capitole** becomes an open-air market, selling organic food and consumer goods *(8am-3pm);*the city's daily *halles*, or covered farmer's markets, can be found at **pl. Victor Hugo, pl. des Carmes,** and **pl. Saint-Cyprien.** *(⏰ Open Tu-Su 6am-1pm.)* There's a **Monoprix** supermarket at 43 rue d'Alsace Lorraine *(⏰ Open M-Sa 9am-10pm.)* with cheap lunches on the third floor *(€5),* and another, smaller branch inside the Jean Jaurès metro stop. *(⏰Open M-Sa 8am-10pm.)* Students who want a good hot meal also have the option of trying the *restaurants universitaires* scattered throughout the city.

LA FAIM DES HARICOTS — VEGETARIAN [2]

3 rue du Puits Vert — ☎05 61 22 49 25

The scenario: A giant and menacing lima bean ran you through with a sword and you've gone to vegetarian heaven, stocked with five buffets of pastas, salads, *tartes*, creative veggie dishes of the world like couscous and curry, and, *bien sûr*, dessert. You can't eat the cartoon vegetables on the sign above the door, but you can certainly try.

From the Capitole, walk down rue St. Rome and run right onto rue du Puits Verts. $ Buffet €10 lets you pick 1 of 4 options for all-you-can-eat; €1 extra for each additional all-you-can-eat option; €15.50 for an apéritif, café, and buffet. ⏰ Open M-Sa noon-2:30pm and 7-10:30pm.

LE SHERPA — CRÊPERIE [1]

46 rue du Taur — ☎05 61 23 89 29

If you're wondering why a French crêperie is called Le Sherpa, just peruse the mountainous selection of Eastern teas listed on the menu, including dried leaves flown direct by air-sherpa from Nepal. Like the eclectic menu, the restaurant's decor is a mix of the French, the poetic, and the absurd, with wooden tables, dark red booths, painted murals with philosophical musings and jester's hats on dangling lightbulbs. The tasty crêpes go surprisingly well with black and green teas.

Rue du Taur is one of the main streets radiating off pl. du Capitole. $ Salads €5.50-7.20. Crêpes €3-6.50; sweet crêpes €1.70-5. Ice cream €1.40-3.50. Tea €2.50. ⏰ Open daily noon-midnight.

LE BARBU — TRADITIONAL, LARGE PORTIONS [2]

9 rue Clémence Isaure — ☎05 61 21 96 62

A restaurant that prides itself on winter portions, even in the summer. Heaping *plats* of Southwestern French cuisine (read: meat) are accompanied by delicious soups and enjoyed beneath red brick arches. Funky artifacts like an old bicycle, boots, and a music stand serve as decor. Adventurer can inquire about the downstairs cave, or satisfy their craving for hte unknown by trying the *boudin* (*blood sausage; €12.50*). Meanwhile, those with the appropriate credit card limit should splurge on a three-course menu of duck, duck, and dessert (*€30*). Now you know what became of Donald and Daisy after they retired from Paris Disney.

🍴 *From pl. du Capitole, walk along rue Gambetta. When you eventually arrive at a fork, go left and follow the road as it continues to curve to the left. Make the third possible left onto rue Clémence Isaure.* Ⓢ *Plat du jour €12. Plates €12-16. Desserts €1.50.* 🕐 *Open daily 7:30pm-midnight.*

REGALS
☙ VIOLETS ❷
25 rue du Taur ☎05 61 21 64 86 🖥www.regals.fr

Both Toulouse's official flower and the candied treat for sale in Madame Charron's renowned shop, violets are pricey, but that's because you're eating candied beauty. You really can't go wrong here. Don't get turned off by the 🔷**Lonely Planet** sticker on the door—we promise this is still a good place.

Ⓔ *70g package of candied violets €8.* 🕐 *Open daily 9am-7pm.*

MAISON DE THÉ SLONGQUAN
❂ CHINESE ❶
2 rue Lakanal ☎06 65 76 96 24

Tranquil music, shelves laden with teas, traditional clay teapots, and a cute older couple preparing homey noodle and rice dishes in the miniature kitchen—this is just what you'd expect in a mom-and-pop Chinese restaurant. Lakanal's menu features the usual suspects at great prices, especially the beef, shrimp, or vegetable dishes. You might not expect a psychedelic red and yellow yin-yang on the lime green walls, but that's what you'll get anyway.

🍴 *From pl. du Capitole, take rue Gambetta until a left turn onto rue Lakanal. The joint is almost on the corner.* Ⓢ *Menu including tea, dinner, and desssert €8. Salads €5. Plate of fried rice or noodles €3.50.* 🕐 *Open M-Sa 11:30am-9:30pm.*

LE POTTOK
☙ SOUTHWESTERN CUISINE, SEAFOOD ❷
8 rue Arnaud Bernard ☎05 61 23 64 54

With a huge menu with huge value, Le Pottok offers delicious meals from the southwest of France. Although the kitchen favors meats like *steak frites* and roasted chicken, there are also vegetarian options, from pizza to the *cassolette fromage*, a 3-cheese pie, baked to melted perfection. We don't think the locals here believe in vegans, unfortunately. The used books hanging from the ceiling make the decor intellectual and hip, as do the piano and bass waiting in the corner for the frequent live music conerts.

🍴 *From pl. du Capitole, follow rue du Taur until it meets the Basilique St. Sernin. Curve left around the cathedral and take your first right onto rue d la Chaine. Walk one block on this residential street to pl. des Tiercerettes and the restaurant is on your right.* Ⓢ *Plat du jour €9. Fish of the day €9. Lunch menu with an appetizer, plate, dessert and wine or coffee €11.60. Dinner menu €13.40. Plates €10-15. Pizzas €10.20-13.20. Desserts €3.70-4.20.* 🕐 *Open daily noon-2:30pm and 7:30-11:30pm.*

NIGHTLIFE

Toulouse always has something going on, though things are calmer in the summer months when the university isn't in session. Thankfully, you can always make a bee-line for **pl. St. Pierre** for a raucous party no matter what time of year. Not only is the student crowd lively, but the Garonne river is beautiful at night.

🏠 CHEZ TONTON—PÂSTIS Ô MAITRE
☙🍸 BAR, CLUB
pl. St. Pierre ☎05 61 21 89 54

The only thing wilder than the cartoon graffiti plastered on the bumblebee yellow walls here is the horde of plastered students having a blast. Inside, it's chaos under bright lights as groups dance to pop and servers careen around tables, precariously balancing trays of "Le Maitre" *(€27-38)*. If you're sober enough, try to tease out the multiple puns in the name *Pâstis Ô Maitre*.

From pl. du Capitole, follow rue Romiguières to pl. St. Pierre. Note that along the way, it changes names to rue Pargaminières. i Happy hour special: buy 10 bottles of beer or pastis and get 20. $ Beer €2.40-3.50. Le maitre of 17 beer €27-38. Bottle of namesake pastis €43. ⏰ Open M-F 7am-2am and Sa 9am-4am. Happy hour 7-8pm.

CAFÉ POPULAIRE — BAR

9 rue de la Colombette ☎05 61 63 07 00

Another hot destination for a motley crowd of fun-loving students with beer flowing more freely than the Garonne River after a thunderstorm. The menu is scrawled on the walls, so look around while you're sitting at the wooden tables to people watch and pick what you want, if you can see the walls through the crowds.

Walking towards pl. Wilson on allées Jean Jaurès, turn left onto bld. Lazare Carnot and turn left again onto rue de la Colombette. i Pints on the 13th of the month €1. $ Pint €4. 13 glasses of beer €21, or of pastis €20. ⏰ Open M-F 11am-2am, Sa 2pm-4am. Happy hour 7:30-9:30pm.

PURE PURPLE — CLUB

2 rue Castellane ☎05 62 73 04 67 www.purepurple.fr

Well-dressed and beautiful, just like the clientele, Pure Purple manages to combine an upscale vibe with reasonable prices and a friendly ambience. Lounge in white booths or on purple antique furniture when you're not moving to R and B, house, or electro on the spacious wooden dance floor.

Walking towards pl. Wilson on allées Jean Jaurès, turn left onto bld. Lazare Carnot and turn left again onto rue Castellane. $ Cover €10. Drinks €8-13.50. Bottles €100. ⏰ Open M-Sa midnight-6am.

LE SHANGHAI — BAR, LGBT FRIENDLY

12 rue de la Pomme ☎05 61 23 27 80

It doesn't matter if you're gay or straight at Le Shanghai, so long as you love to dance. Except for the occassional drag queen at the bar, the small upstairs is tame compared to the downstairs club, which first opens its doors at -2am and is aptly equipped with lighting for every color of the rainbow. The "Men Only" bar and backroom is best avoided by modest travelers. Dress to impress the bouncers (that goes for men and women).

From pl. du Capitole, walk down rue d'Alsace Lorraine until a left turn on rue de la Pomme. $ Cover €8. Drinks €8. Bottles €77. ⏰ Open daily midnight-6am.

BREUGHEL L'ANCIEN — BEER HALL

30 rue de la Chaîne ☎05 61 21 66 54

A dark tavern for Belgian beer and live music during the school year, this is a neighborhood favorite among Toulouse's university crowd. Calmer in the summer, the crowd takes over pl. des Tiercerettes, turning the square into one big outdoor chill-sesh. For a delicious French beer, try the Desperados.

From pl. du Capitole, follow rue du Taur until it meets the Basilique St. Sernin. Curve left around the cathedral and take your first right on rue de la Chaine. Walk one block on this residential street to pl. des Tiercerettes. i Concerts every Sa and every third Th of the month. $ Beer €2.30-6.50. Cocktails €3-6. ⏰ Open M-Sa 5pm-2am.

ARTS AND CULTURE

Theater

LA CAVE POÉSIE

71 rue du Taur ☎05 61 23 62 00 www.cave-poesie.com

La Cave Poésie is located in one of the old city's hundreds of **caves,** which was excavated and transformed into an extraordinary theater for creative expression in all its forms. The intimate space privileges drama with an ever-changing program of plays and performances, but the rock walls also frequently resound with the music of renowned and undiscovered artists alike, in addition to poetry readings every Monday during the school year and open-mike nights with the full moon. It doesn't get cooler, and that's not just because you're in a cav.

⚔ *On rue du Taur off pl. du Capitole.* ℹ *Free poetry readings on Mondays when the university is in session.* Ⓢ *Seats €12, students €8; public readings €5; open-mike nights €2.* ⌖ *Ticket office open 10am-7pm. Theatrical, musical and literary performances Tu-Sa 7:30 and 9:30pm.*

Cinema

UGC (*9 allée Roosevelt in pl. Jean Jaurès*, ☎08 92 70 00 00) is your centrally located cinema of choice for Hollywood hits. Open daily 10:30am-midnight with the last screenings starting at 10:30pm. Students pay €4.20, whereas regular fare is €5.70 before noon and €8.70 for all other screenings. If it's independent cinema you want, head to **Cinema Utopia** (*24 rue Montardy*, ☎05 61 21 22 11), where you'll find *art et essai* films in their original languages with French subtitles. Open daily 11am-midnight and customers pay €4 at noon or €6 for all other screenings.

---

summer lovin'

For 20 days straight during the summer, starting on July 15 and ending on August 7, the festival **Toulouse d'Été** hosts a range of French music from classical to reggae, with free entrance half of the days, and charging €8 the other days. The 7 concert venues ensure that wherever you go in the city, you'll be sure to have a sound track to your visit. Visit www.toulousedate.org/?page=festival or call ☎ 05 62 27 60 71 for more info.

SHOPPING

The following listings are intended for those travelers wishing to backpack through France on talent and tomfoolery alone. If tomfoolery isn't your thing, you can always shop for brand name clothing on the streets off **rue d'Alsace Lorraine** south of **pl. du Capitole**. But let's face it, you'll look better in a clown nose.

Circus Supplies

PSYCHOJONGLEUR

2 rue de Metz   ☎05 61 32 74 47 📧www.psychojongleur.com

Your local go-to for juggling and circus supplies. Clown noses are about the same price as a *baguette* at the nearby *boulangerie*, but are more worthwhile. Pick up a unicycle, juggling pins, or old-fashioned balls in every color. There's also rope for acrobatics or for lashing that new unicycle to your backpack.

⚔ *From pl. du Capitole, walk down rue d'Alsace Lorraine and turn right onto rue de Metz. The shop is on your left before the bridge.* Ⓢ *Clown nose €1. Circus supplies from €18.50.* ⌖ *Open Tu-Sa 10am-12:30pm and 2-7pm.*

Music Supplies

LE CROQUENOTES

19 rue Sainte Ursule   ☎05 61 23 17 82 📧www.croquenotes.com

Walls of sheet music for all instruments but percussion. Whether you're desperate to learn the traveling accordion, can't live without Beethoven's Sonata No. 8, or just want to jam on a stylish white upright piano, Le Croquenotes can make it happen.

⚔ *From pl. du Capitole, take rue Gambetta until your first turn onto rue Sainte Ursule. The shop is on your right.* ⌖ *Open M 10am-noon and 2-7pm, Tu-Sa 10am-1pm and 2-7pm.*

Those visiting Toulouse for more than a day or two should pick up a **Toulouse en Liberté** city card at the Tourist Office. For a mere €10, the card provides you with up to 30% discounts at participating museums, hotels, restaurants, theaters and shops. Notably, cardholders receive free *apéritifs* at many of Toulouse's restaurants. The Tourist Office has a list of over 300 participating establishments.

ESSENTIALS

Practicalities

- **TOURIST OFFICE: Donjon du Capitole** gives out a free and extensive guide to the city that lists hotels, restaurants, museums, transportation information, and cultural events. It also distributes *LINDIC*, a student guide to the city published every September. (*sq. Charles de Gaulle* ☎08 92 18 01 80 ▪www.toulouse-tourisme.com ⌚ *Open M-Sa 9am-7pm, Su 10am-5:15pm.*)

- **YOUTH CENTER:** The **Centre Régional Information Jeunesse** has friendly faces and helpful information regarding work, study, and travel. You can beat lines and avoid hastle by buying **SNCF** train tickets here. (*17 rue de Metz* ☎05 61 21 20 20 ▪www.crij.org ⌚ *Open M-F July-Aug 10am-1pm and 2-6pm; Sept-June 10am-6pm.*)

- **CURRENCY EXCHANGE: C2E.** (*30 rue du Taur* ☎05 61 13 64 25 ▪contact@C2Echange.fr ⑤ *€1.50 commission on all exchanges.* ⌚ *Open June-Aug M 9am-12:30pm and 2-6pm, Tu-F 9am-7pm, Sa 10am-noon and 2-6pm; Sept-May M 9am-12:30pm and 2-5:30pm, Tu-F 9am-6:30pm, Sa 10am-noon and 2-5:30pm.*)

- **INTERNET ACCESS: Nethouse** is a very luxurious internet cafe with coffee and chocolate bars for sale. (*1 rue des 3 Renards* ☎05 61 21 98 42 ⑤ *€3 per hr.* ⌚ *Open M-Sa 9am-11pm, Su noon-8pm.*) The area around rue du Taur has other establishments with similar value.

- **POST OFFICE:** (*9 rue Lafayette* ☎36 31 *i* *Western Union inside.* ⌚ *Open M 8am-7pm, Tu 8am-9pm, W-F 8am-7pm, Sa 8am-5pm.*)

- **POSTAL CODE:** 31049.

Emergency!

- **POLICE:** (☎17) **Commissariat centre-ville.** (*17 rue du Rempart St-Etienne* ☎05 61 12 81 97 ⚓ *On allée Jean Jaurès facing pl. Wilson, turn left onto bld. Lazare Carnot. Continue straight until rue du Rempart St-Etienne branches off to the right.*) **Commissariat Central** is the main police station outside of *centre ville.* (*23 bld. de l'Embouchure* ☎05 61 12 77 77 ⚓ *At the Canal du Midi metro stop on the B line.*)

- **HOSPITALS: Hospital CHR Rangueil.** (*av. Jean Poulhès* ☎05 61 32 25 33 ⚓ *Take the B line until Ramonville, then bus #88 to the hospital.*) **S.O.S. Medecins** has doctors on call 24hr. (☎05 61 33 00 00)

- **PHARMACY:** If you need a pharmacy at night M-Sa, head to the **Pharmacie du nuit.** (*76 allée Jean Jaurès* ☎05 61 62 38 05 ⌚ *Open M-Sa 8pm-8am.*) For Sunday service, use the *pharmacie de garde* system by calling ☎32 37 to identify the *pharmacie de garde* nearest you.

Getting There

By Plane

Aéroport Toulouse-Blagnac is outside of the city. *(☎08 25 38 00 00)* **Flybus** runs a **navette,** or airport shuttle, directly from the **Gare Routière.** There are shuttle stops at **pl. Jean Jaurès** and **pl. Jeanne d'Arc.** *(☎05 61 41 70 70 $ €5. ⏰ Every 20min. 5am-12:15am.)* **Air France.** *(2 bld. de Strasbourg ☎36 35 ⏰ Open M-F 10am-6:30pm, Sa 10am-5:30pm.)*

By Train

Gare SNCF Matabiau *(64 bld. Pierre-Sémard ☎36 35 ⏰ Ticket office open daily -7am--9:10pm.)* sends trains to: **Bordeaux** *($ €35.40. ⏰2hr., 15 per day.);* **Carcassonne** *($ €14.40, TGV €16.50. ⏰ 1¼hr., 21 per day.);* **Lyon** *($ €66. ⏰ 4½hr., 5 per day.);* **Marseille** *($ €53.50. ⏰ 3½hr., 8 per day.);* **Paris Montparnasse** *($ €85.60. ⏰ 5½ hrs., 5 per day.);* **Paris Austerlitz.** *($ €74.70. ⏰ 6½-7½hr., 4 per day.)* Reserve as far as possible in advance (three months!) to benefit from mega-discounts of up to 50% on all destinations.

By Bus

From the **Gare Routière** *(68 bld. Pierre-Sémard ☎05 61 61 67 67 ⏰ Open M-F 8am-7pm, Sa 9am-1pm and 2-6pm, Su 9:30am-1pm and 2-4:30pm.).* Buy tickets from the driver. **Eurolines** runs buses to all major European countries and Morocco in North Africa. *(☎08 92 89 90 91 🖥www.eurolines.fr ⏰ Ticket office open M-F 9am-12:30pm and 1:30-6pm, Sa 9am-12:30pm and 2-5pm.)*

Getting Around

Toulouse has an extensive and awesome **Metro** system *(☎05 61 41 70 70 🖥www.tisseo.fr)* that runs M-Th 5:15am-midnight, F-Sa 5:15am-1am, Su 5:15am-midnight. The A line crosses the city from northeast to southwest, while the B line runs north to south. The two intersect at pl. Jean Jaurès in the city center. Buses leave from major Metro stops. Purchase passes at Metro stops or from bus drivers. *($ €1.50; round trip €2.70 as long as you go and come back within 1hr. Day pass €5, ages 4-25 €4. 10 trips €12.50/9. Unlimited evening service 7pm-close €2.50. 12 trips for 2-6 people €4.20.)*

Capitole **Taxi** is a good bet in case public transportation has stopped running. *(☎05 34 25 02 50 $ €1.80 per km during the day, €2 per km at night. €25-30 from the train station to the airport. ⏰ Open 24hr.)*

There are 253 automated Vélô Toulouse stations throughout the city for renting **bikes** between 5:30am and 2am. A station is located in pl. Wilson near the tourist office. Machines accept MasterCard and Visa but can be finnicky. *(☎08 00 11 22 05 🖥www.velo.toulouse.fr $ €200 deposit on credit card. €1 base fee for 24hr. €2 for the first 2hr., €2 per hr. thereafter.)*

montpellier ☎04 67

It's hard to find locals who were born in Montpellier. A college town and cultural center, Languedoc-Rousillon's capital seduces visitors and then compels them to stay. Reputed to be the most light-hearted place in the south, Montpellier prides itself on a diverse population of partygoers and some of the best gay nightlife in France. Amateur theatrical and musical performances take place in pl. de la Comédie, academics browse trendy bookstores, and tourists shop for funky flair in hip boutiques.

ORIENTATION

The right fork in front of the train station, **rue Mageulone,** leads to **place de la Comédie,** Montpellier's spectacular central square, with the three Graces fountain, a carousel, the tram station, and cafes everywhere. The tourist office is at the far right end of the square, just before the entrance to the tree-lined **esplanade Charles de Gaulle**. The *vieille ville* is an oval bounded by main arteries on all sides: **bld. de Pasteur/bld. Louis**

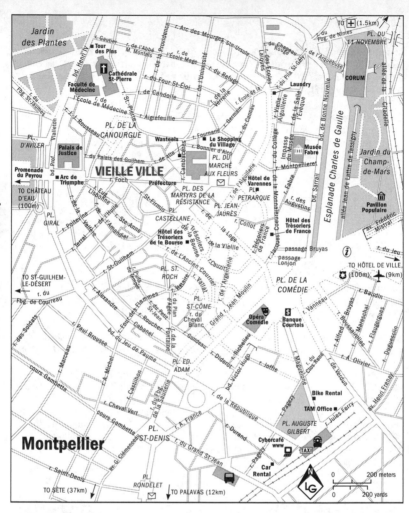

Blanc (the slash signifies that the road changes names) to the north, **esplanade Charles de Gaulle** and **bld. Victor Hugo** to the east, and **bld. Henri VI/bld. du Jeu de Paume** to the west and south. From pl. de la Comédie **rue de la Loge** is what you'll walk daily to reach **pl. Jean Jaurès**, the heart of the *vieille ville*.

ACCOMMODATIONS

Montpellier offers many excellent budget options in *centre ville*. For other reasonably priced hotels not listed below, search the peripheries of the *vieille ville*, especially in the sidestreets coming off of **cours Gambetta** or along **rue Auguste Brousonnet**.

HÔTEL NOVA
HOTEL ❷

8 rue Richelieu ☎04 67 60 79 85 www.hotelnova.fr

Stone walls and a pleasant musk throughout the building make you feel like you're retiring to your chambers in an old castle, and even the least expensive "student" rooms have baby-blue walls and cushy double beds that are supremely grand by budget standards. The incredibly priced options fill up quickly, so be smart, reserve in advance, and make sure to bring your *Let's Go* guide, since the family that runs Hotel Nova generously offers users a 5% discount. Other bonuses include an electronic pass system that gives guests 24hr. access and an automatic espresso machine in the lobby at €1 a shot.

Walk around to the back of Opéra de la Comédie. Look downhill along rue Richelieu, and you'll see the hotel sign. Go! i Breakfast €5. $ Singles €21, with bath €27, with bath and TV €43; doubles without bath €24/€34-€36/€48; triples with bath €45, with bath and TV €57; quads with bath and TV €64. Daily tax €0.85. 5% Let's Go discount. ⏰ Reception M-Sa 7:30am-11pm.

AUBERGE DE JEUNESSE HOSTEL [1]

rue des Écoles Laiques ☎04 67 60 32 22 www.fuaj.org

You too can experience what it would be like to don your habit and live as a nun in the old convent that now houses Montpellier's friendly youth hostel. The beer-stocked vending machines and foosball table must have arrived after the ecclesiastical stained glass, but it all makes a nice combo. (Do nuns pay foosball?) Spacious dorms sleep three to six people, although private doubles are available for couples upon request. There are some quirks to the building, like circular toilets without traditional seats and an elementary school on the first floor, but the vibe is all warmth and fun.

Coming off of bld. Louis Blanc, turn into the archway of rue des Écoles Laiques. Walk 10m or less and make your 1st left. There are no signs, but the hostel is the 1st open doorway you find. i Breakfast Included. $ €16.70 with an HI card (€15). ⏰ Reception 8am-noon and 3pm-midnight. Hostel doors are open until 3am. Breakfast 7:30-9am. Lockout 10am-3pm.

HÔTEL LITTORAL HOTEL [3]

rue Anatole France ☎04 67 92 28 10

Like a painfully awkward first date, you'd better not write off Hôtel Littoral too quickly—what doesn't look like much from the front turns out to be just what you're looking for inside. Long blue and yellow hallways, airy rooms, and comfortable double beds offer all the space you need to breathe a sigh of relief at the great price tag, so long as you don't mind opting for communal showers.

hôtels particuliers

The secret courtyards and intricate staircases of Montpellier's nearly 80 **hôtels particuliers** (mansions), built from between the 17th- and 19th-centuries, hide behind grand oak doors. **Hôtel de Varennes,** once Montpellier's treasury, has two small, free museums inside. The **Musée du Vieux Montpellier,** on the first floor, traces Montpellier's history through furniture, maps, ceramics, and other artifacts *(2 pl. Petrarque. ⏰Open Tu-Su 10:30am-12:30pm and 1:30-6pm. $€3, students free.)* Upstairs, the adorable second-floor **Musée Fougau** reconstructs 19th-century lifestyles in Montpellier *(⏰Normally open W-Th -3-6pm but closed 14 July-Aug 17. ☎04 67 84 31 58).* Next, the **Hôtel des Trésoriers de France** houses the **Musée Languedocien,** an archaeological museum that contains medieval artwork, 18th-century perfume bottles and tons of artefacts in between *(7 rue Jacques Coeur. ☎04 67 52 93 03. www.musée-languedocien.com. $€6. ⏰Open 15 Jun-15 Sept M-Sa 3-6pm and 15 Sept-15 Jun M-Sa 2:30-5:30pm.)* For the intent and interested, continue your visit with **Hôtel des Trésoriers de la Bourse,** which has unique 16th-century architecture *(4 rue des Trésoriers de la Bourse)* and **Hôtel Sabatier d'Espeyran,** the new location of Musée Fabre's decorative arts collection.

You'll have to wait for the Musée Fabre to see any artistry, but you're paying for a good bed—not Van Gogh—and that's exactly what you'll get.

⚑ *From the train station, take the left fork and walk along bld. de la République until the traffic circle. Turn left onto rue Anatole France and look for a right turn down an alley with a large blue sign.* ⓘ *Breakfast €5.* Ⓢ *Singles without shower €28, with shower €35-€38, with bath €44-€46; doubles without shower €30-€35/€38-€41/€47-€50; triples with bath €52-54; quads with bath €56-58.* ⓩ *Reception open M-Sa 7am-11pm, Su 7am-11am and 11am-7pm.*

HÔTEL DES ÉTUVES

24 rue des Étuves ☎04 67 60 78 19 ▪www.hoteldesetuves.fr HOTEL ❸

This family-run hotel nestled in a row of former medieval bathhouses (an *étuve* is, in fact, the steamroom of a bathhouse) is an intimate experience from top to bottom, with narrow staircases and hallways that lead to 12 simple rooms on three floors. Defying constraints, the warm couple who own the place have managed to fit in all the amenities, such as mini-TVs and fans for the summer heat. Pay a little extra and you can live the building's legacy by floating in one of the hotel's bathtubs. You'll have to bring your own rubber duckie.

⚑ *Facing the opera house at pl. de la Comédie, walk the road direclty ahead to the right of the building. The hotel is just downhill on rue des Étuves.* ⓘ *Reserve ahead of time.* Ⓢ *Singles €37-42; doubles €39-49.* ⓩ *Reception M-Sa 7am-11pm, Su 7am-1pm and 6:30-11pm.*

HÔTEL ACAPULCO

445 rue Auguste Broussonnet ☎04 67 54 12 21 ▪www.acapulcohotel.fr HOTEL ❸

The bamboo garden may be exotic, and the name certainly implies a sombrero or two, but this family-run hotel couldn't be truer to its French heritage given the Gaugin and Van Gogh prints on the walls and the pastel colors in lovely rooms. The prices are great for the comfort but beg a trade-off with location, since the old home is a full 30min. walk from pl. de la Comédie. Luckily, it's only 5min. from the nearest tram stop. And if it's the university you're looking for, then there's no better, especially for the air-conditioning.

⚑ *From Le Corum, walk left on bld. Louis Blanc, which becomes bld. Pasteur, then intersects with the main artery, bld. Henry IV. Continue straight and the bld. turns into rue Auguste Broussonnet. The hotel is on your left, 2 long blocks after the intersection with bld. Henry IV.* ⓘ *Breakfast €6.* Ⓢ *Singles €41-52; doubles €46-66; triples €69-75; quads €78. Daily tax €0.85.* ⓩ *Reception in summer 7am-11pm; in winter 7am-10:30pm.*

HÔTEL DU PALAIS

3 rue du Palais ☎04 67 60 47 38 ▪www.hoteldupalais-montpellier.fr HOTEL❺

A charming old mansion in a tranquil square, minutes from the heart of Montpellier's *vieille ville*. The tall windows let ample natural light into rooms that are each unique but all decorated with elegance and care. You pay for the ambience, air-conditioning, and the occasional luxurious bathtub, but it's a lovely splurge if you can afford it.

⚑ *Follow the signs at the end of rue Foch just before the Arc de Triomphe.* ⓘ *Breakfast €7-16.* Ⓢ *Singles €68; doubles €75-90; triples €110. Daily tax €0.85.*

SIGHTS

For sightseeing, nothing beats **place de la Comédie,** which is spectacularly illuminated every evening and hosts open-air performances that range from traditional French accordion to hot Spanish fire dancing. For more established sights, there are ample museums in the ornate *hôtels* (mansions) of the *vielle ville* (old city), as well as the big-ticket ▪**Musée Fabre**, which contains one of France's major fine arts collections. The ▪**Jardin des Plantes** is France's oldest botanical garden and for the intrepid, Montpellier even has an aquarium just a tram ride away. (⚑ *Tramway line 1: Station Place de France and Odysseum* ☎04 67 13 50 50 Ⓢ *Students €10.50.* ⓩ *Open Sept-June M-Th 10am-7pm, Fri-Sa 10am-8pm, Su 10am-7pm; July-Aug daily 10am-10pm.*)

👍 MUSÉE FABRE ➤ FINE ARTS MUSEUM

39 bld. des Bonnes Nouvelles ☎04 67 14 83 00 💻www.muséefabre.fr

Built on a site where Molière performed from 1654 to 1655, this beautifully renovated museum holds one of the largest collections of (very) fine art outside of Paris. It will take you hours to wander through the 59 rooms on three floors—and that's just the permanent collection. Focusing on 17th- to 19th-century painting, the museum features works by bigwigs like Courbet, Ingres, Poussin, and Delacroix. If you don't know those names, it's even more reason to visit. The permanent collection is complemented by temporary collections on exhibit for several months at a time.

➡ From pl. de la Comédie walk on the left side of esplanade Charles de Gaulle until you hit the opulent facade. $ Permanent collection €6, students €4; entire museum €8. ⏰ Open Tu 10am-6pm, W 1-9pm, Th-F 10am-6pm, Sa 11am-6pm, Su 10am-6pm.

👍 JARDIN DES PLANTES ♿ BOTANICAL GARDENS

163 rue Auguste Broussonnet ☎04 67 63 43 22

Montpellier's lush botanical gardens were initially created to grow medicinal herbs for the Faculty of Medicine. Today they are France's oldest and make for hours of relaxed wandering, romantic canoodling, or artistic inspiration. Everywhere you look there are scented herb gardens and thick forests. There are also several historical greenhouses, one of which has a ginkgo tree that dates back to 1795. After the botanical gardens, you can check out the green **promenade du Peyrou** a few blocks away on Bld. Henri IV. This walk links the **Arc de Triomphe**—erected in 1691 to honor Louis XIV—to the **Château d'Eau,** the arched terminal of an aqueduct. Though locals claim it dates back to antiquity, it just turned 500. Climb to the top for a view of the surburbs that surround Montpellier.

➡ These incredible gardens take up several blocks on bld. Henri IV near it's intersection with bld. Pasteur. From pl. de la Comédie, walk up rue de la Loge until pl. des Martyrs de la Résistance, then turn left onto rue Foch. Turn right when you exit through the Arc de Triomphe and walk straight until the gardens. i Guided tours of gardens are offered with a reservation. $ Free. ⏰ June-Sept Tu-Su noon-8pm; Open Oct-May Tu-Su noon-6pm.

JARDIN DU CHAMPS DE MARS ♿ GARDEN

esplanade Charles de Gaulle ☎04 67 66 13 46

These lovely public gardens centered on a large pond are just above pl. de la Comédie to one side of esplanade Charles de Gaulle. They are a great spot to picnic on fruit from the nearby farmer's market and crepes from the concession stands. The **Pavillon Populaire** is a small building in the gardens that holds free photography exhibits.

➡ Pavillon Populaire. ⏰ Pavillon Populaire open Tu-Su 10am-6pm.

FOOD

In Montpellier's *vieille ville*, it is no exaggeration to say that you can't walk two steps without bumping into another cafe or restaurant. All of the squares, notably **pl. de la Comédie** and **pl. Jean Jaurès,** are packed with people in the evenings. For the most budget meals, hit up the North African snack and sandwich places on **rue de l'Aiguillerie** and **rue des Écoles Laiques.** If it's a sit-down meal you want, search the streets around **Église Saint-Roch,** where the young crowds flock around dinnertime. There's an awesome market with local produce, meat, dairy, and other goods sets up in **Les Halles Castellane** at the top of pl. Jean Jaurès (*⏰Open M-Sa 7am-8pm),* and there's a smaller farmer's market at pl. de la Comédie beside the tourist office. *(⏰Open M-Sa 7am-1pm.)* Finally, there is a large **INNO** supermarket in the basement of the Polygone commercial center. *(⏰Open M-Sa 8:30am-8:30pm.)*

👍 CRÊPERIE LE KREISKER ➤ CRÊPERIE ❶

3 passage Bruyas ☎04 67 60 82 50

Since they are so awesomely priced, it's highly recommended that you treat yourself to at least two of Le Kreisker's superb crêpes. The first is a savory buckwheat crêpe filled with anything from your standard cheese and sausage and the homemade *ratatouille*, and the second is a dessert crêpe with Nutella, *crème au maron* (chestnut cream), raspberries, and whipped cream. If you are not salivating at this point, you've either just eaten, or you're illiterate. Better yet, find friends and order half the menu.

🧭 A left turn off of pl. de la Comédie just before the esplanade starts. $ Meal crêpes €2-6.80; desert crêpes €2-5.40. Salads €2.50-7.10. ⏰ Open M-Sa 11am-3pm and 6:30-11pm.

👍 LA CASE DU SALOUM
🍴 SENEGALESE [1]

18 rue Diderot ☎04 67 02 88 94

An unassumingly hip Senegalese restaurant that is simply too good for the price tag. Selections like jumbo shrimp in creamy coconut milk, steak in a savory peanut sauce, and the especially succulent grilled lamb all come with sides of crispy vegetable fritters and sticky white rice. There are equally delicious fish and vegetable options. Warning: eating here may cause you to (a) want to steal the cool Senegalese wooden chairs for your room or (b) impulsively board the next flight to Dakar.

🧭 From pl. de la Comédie, walk downhill for 2 quick blocks on bld. Victor Hugo until a right turn onto rue Diderot. $ Appetizers €5. Salads €9. Appetizer and plate €12.80. ⏰ Open Tu-Su noon-3pm and 8-11pm.

👍 TRIPTI KULAI
🍴 VEGETARIAN [2]

20 rue Jacques Coeur ☎04 6 66 30 51

A peaceful restaurant, where the waitresses wear bright saris and even brighter smiles while serving cleansing plates of vegetarian and vegan food. Enjoy avocados in raspberry dressing to start, followed by plates of tofu, broccoli, or mushroom *tartes*, polenta in a tahini sauce, and just about every other scrumptious species of veggie under the sun. While you're crunching on your radish like a rabbit or chewing your seitan like a regular yogi, you can browse the library of books on meditation and aromatherapy or commune with the photo of Sri Chinmoy, an Indian swami whose sayings adorn the walls. Go for the food, stay for ever-lasting enlightenment.

🧭 From pl. de la Comédie, walk up rue de la Loge and make your 1st right turn onto rue Jacques Coeur. ℹ Credit card min. €10. $ Appetizers €4-5.80. Plates €9.50. Plat du jour €9. ⏰ Open M-Sa noon-9:30pm.

CHEZ DOUMÉ
🍴 LYONAIS [2]

5 rue des Tessiers ☎04 67 60 48 76

For authentic Lyonais in Montpellier, dine *chez* Doumé. What more can we say? Frog's legs, lamb's brain, and calf's head are dished out here daily. A huge menu provides options that are less cray-cray as well, and the student crowds plus hearty food are damn good reasons to pay.

🧭 From pl. de la Comédie, walk uphill on rue de la Loge and turn left onto rue de l'Argenterie just before you get to the open plaza of pl. Jean Jaurès. March downhill until pl. St-Côme (there'll be a fountain!) and turn right onto rue St-Côme. You'll hit the crowds of pl. St-Roch, as well as the Church. Rue Tessiers is straight past both. $ Lunch €9.50. Lunch plates €12. Dinner plates €15-20. Dinner menu €16 or €22. ⏰ Open M-F noon-2pm and 8-10:30pm, Sa-Su 8-11pm.

PASTA CAMPA
🍴 PASTA [1]

66 rue de l'Aiguillerie ☎04 67 56 38 78 💻www.pasta-campa.fr

Point to a pasta, gesture at a sauce, and the folks at Pasta Campa will do everything else for you. There's spicy arrabiatta, meaty bolognese, nutty pesto, 5 cheeses, and a few more sauces to choose from in a tiny joint with unbeatable prices and containers of noodles that induce satisfied tummy-rubbing for backpacking heroes.

🧭 From pl. de la Comédie walk uphill on rue de la Loge and turn right onto rue de l'Aiguillerie. Walk

for 5-7min. and look to your right. $ *Classic €5.50. Farcies €6.50. Salads €3.50-5.50.* ⏰ *Open M-F 11am-3:30pm and 5-10pm, Sa 11am-10pm.*

YÖMI
🏷 FROZEN YOGURT [1]

16 rue Sain Guilhem ☎04 99 61 86 74 🖥www.yomi-glaces.fr

First it was the wheel. Then it was Facebook. Now, it's frozen yogurt—the newest phenomenon to successfully take over the world. Don't be fooled by the angelic deliciousness of Yömi's froyo with fruit, candy, and chocolate toppings. This refreshing mid-afternoon snack is a highly addictive substance produced by dairy farmers intent on world domination. New York's Pinkberry was only the first. Be especially wary of the cheescake flavor, which has double the mind-numbing power.

From pl. de la Comédie, walk up to pl. Halles Castellane on rue Loge. Turn left past the market onto rue Saint Guilhem. *i* *Credit card min. €10.* $ *Small €2.80-3.50, medium €3.50-5, large €4.50-7. Cheesecake €3. Salads from €4. Smoothies €3.50-5.50.* ⏰ *Open M 2-7pm, and Tu-Sa 11:30am-7pm.*

SUCRE-SALE
🏷 FAST FOOD [1]

20 rue de la Loge ☎04 67 66 04 17

If you've been indulging for hours at one of the popular *café*-brasseries on pl. Jean Jaurès, and you're craving a fix of fast food, make a bee-line (or a zig-zag, depending on your mental impairment), for this one-stop shop. Salads, burgers, fries, doughnuts, pizza, ice cream, and fresh orange juice are all available until 2am. The prepared food sometimes waits a while for customers, so your tastiest and freshest option is to order off the menu for hot and crispy fries.

One of the 1st joints you'll see on your left as you walk uphill on rue de la Loge to the hoppin' pl. Jean Jaurés. $ *Plates €7-7.50.* ⏰ *Open daily 8pm-2am.*

NIGHTLIFE

Although Montpellier is particularly famous for its gay nightlife, there is something for everyone in this student capital. Without a doubt, start your night off at one of the vibrant *café* brasseries in **pl. Jean Jaurès.** Once you're ready to go, hit up the popular bars, concert venues, and clubs listed below, or take L'Amigo buses from the train station on the weekend to the 13 major discos on the outskirts of town.

✓ LE REBUFFY PUB
🏷🍸☀ PUB

2 rue Rebuffy ☎04 67 66 32 76

Packed with local and international students, this pub is plastered to the ceiling with old posters and has more than just beer on tap, with events like annual film festivals, rotating art exhibits for local talent, and chess tournaments. The main activity for the night still involves one or more of the 14 Dutch and Belgian beer on the menu. Say hello to the two pink elephants on the storefront, Le Rebuffy's mascots and your drinking buddies for the night.

From pl. des Martyrs de la Résistance, head 1 block along rue Foch. The pub is in a nook-type squarish opening on the left. $ *Beer €2.50-4.50. Cocktails €2.50-7.* ⏰ *Open daily in summer 9pm-2am; in winter 9pm-1am.*

✓ CAFE DE LA MER
🏷🍸☀▼ BAR, GLBT FRIENDLY

5 pl. du Marché aux Fleurs ☎04 67 60 79 65

The rainbow flag at Montpellier's first openly gay cafe and bar is still waving proudly after 21 years. Sip a coffee in the afternoon while browsing gay-themed magazines, appreciate the funky portraits on the walls, and make new friends over a beer once the crowds of cute boys flock to La Mer at night.

Facing the Préfecture at pl. des Martyrs de la Résistance, turn right into pl. du Marché aux Fleurs and look for the cafe in the far corners. *i* *Credit card min. €10.* $ *Coffee €1.50. Beer on tap €2-€6.40; bottles €3.20-4.50. Alcohol €3.20-8. Cocktails €6-10.* ⏰ *Open M-Sa 8am-2am, Su 3pm-2am; in winter M-Sa 8am-1am, Su 4pm-1am.*

LE ROCKSTORE ✎ CONCERT VENUE

20 rue de Verdun ☎04 67 06 80 06 🖥www.rockstore.fr

The 1950s Cadillac that's sticking out of Le Rockstore's facade is impressive, but so is the fact that Radiohead and Lenny Kravitz performed in this concert space, which accommodates up to 900 people. Black walls, graffiti, and not too much light are the key to good old grunge in the front bar and the electro disco upstairs, which are both waiting for the party to start once the live music stops.

⇄ Rue de Verdun comes off pl. de la Comédie on the opposite side of rue de la Loge. $ Concerts €15-25. Beer €3.80. Cocktails €7. Bottles of liquor €70. ⏰ Open in summer Tu-Sa 11:30am-5am; in winter Tu-Sa 11am-5am. Open Su and M when there are special concerts. Concerts start 7-8pm.

LE HEAVEN ✎🍸▼ GAY BAR

1 rue Delpech ☎04 67 60 44 18

You're guaranteed to meet lots of intense gazes in this narrow bar and club, which plays lounge and house every night of the week. In addition to the mirrors, glitz, and plastic blow-up whale above the dance floor, there are theme nights like Wednesday's "drink the thing"—a Montpellier version of a stoplight party. For men looking to meet men, this is heaven. Women are welcome, but there aren't many.

⇄ 5m from Café de la Mer. $ Beer €3. Mixed drinks €7. Bottles €60. ⏰ Open daily in summer 8pm-2am; daily in winter 8pm-1am.

ARTS AND CULTURE

Montpellier is a musical mecca throughout the year, but the scene amps up the volume every July for the **Festival Radio France et Montpellier Languedoc-Roussillon.** Musicians of all genres come from around the world come to perform. *(☎04 67 02 02 01 🖥www.festivalradiofrancemontpellier.com.)*

LE CORUM ✎ OPERA, SYMPHONY

esplanade Charles de Gaulle ☎04 67 79 39 40 🖥www.opera-montpellier.com

Montpellier has two concert halls at either end of the open plaza made by pl. de la Comédie and the tree-lined Esplanade Charles de Gaulle. Although **Opéra de la Comédie** at pl. de la Comédie is closed for restoration until 2012, its modern sister **Opéra Berlioz** in the massive performing center, **Le Corum,** continues to host operas, symphonies, and chamber music year-round. Attention students (which includes all young men and women less than 26 years old): take advantage of the sweet discount package of four concerts for only €15.

⇄ From pl. de la Comédie, walk straight to the end of esplanade Charles de Gaulle. The ticket office is down the stairs. $ Ticket prices for the opera €14-45; the symphony €14-24; and chamber music €16. Students can purchase a package with 4 concerts for €15. ⏰ Open M-Sa noon-6pm.

SHOPPING

For boutique clothing shops, search **Grand Rue Jean Moulin** and **rue Saint Guilhem,** which both come off **rue de la Loge. Rue de l'Aiguillerie** has the funkiest collection of consumer goods along the lines of comic books and old records.

POLYGONE ✎ MALL

rue Michelet ☎04 67 99 41 60 🖥www.polygone.com

Zara, Gap, Dolce and Gabbana, United Colors of Benetton, and dozens of European brand names you may not know (yet) can be found in Polygone, Montpellier's *centre ville* mall. So close that you can see it beckoning from the middle of pl. de la Comédie, you might want to leave your credit card at the hostel. Go straight to the basement to shop for groceries at the **INNO** supermarket.

⇄ Turn right past the tourist office and walk straight to the mall that looms before you. ⏰ Open M-F 10am-8pm, Sa 9am-8pm.

LE COMPTOIR DU DISQUE MUSIC

12 rue de la Petite Loge ☎04 67 60 91 71

The record industry is still alive and kicking in this shop for aficionados. Their full stock consists of 170,000 records and 25,000 CDs, although not all of it is displayed on the jam-packed walls. The selection ranges from Black Sabbath to Beethoven, with the greatest emphasis on rock and pop.

Walk up rue de la Loge until pl. Halles et Castllane. Turn left onto rue de l'Aiguillerie, and the shop is your 1st right into the mini-square. $ Records €5-35. ⏰ Open M-Sa 11am-1pm and 2-7pm.

IMAGES DE DEMAIN STATIONERY, POSTCARDS

20 rue de la Vieille ☎06 67 66 23 45

Attention travelers looking for that oh-so-elusive postcard to send home or study-abroad students in eager search of dorm decor: Images de Demain stocks 5000 postcards, supposedly the largest stock in France. The inside of the store is practically an Andy Warhol and Gustav Klimt exhibit inside. You're pretty much guaranteed to find the print that's right for you.

Walk uphill on rue de la Loge until the farmer's market at pl. Halles Castellane. Turn left before the market and turn left again. The shop is in the narrow street straight ahead. $ Posters from €16. ⏰ Open M-Sa 9:30am-7:30pm.

ESSENTIALS

Practicalities

- **TOURIST OFFICE:** A godsend of free maps, guides to lodging, eating, sightseeing, friendly faces, and help with just about anything, including same-night hotel reservation. Student guide *L'INDIC* is published annually in September. Various **city passes** on offer for discounted rates on public transport, guided tours, museum visits and other sights. *(30 allée Jean de Lattre de Tassigny.☎04 67 60 60 60. 💻www.ot-montpellier.fr $€12-18 per 24hrs., €19-25 per 48hrs., and €25-31 per 72hrs. ⏰Open Oct-June M-F 9am-6:30pm, Sa 10am-6pm, Su 10am-5pm; July-Sept M-F 9am-7:30pm, Sa-Su 9:30am-6pm.)*
- **TOURS:** Eight different guided tours of the city run July-Sept such as "Montpellier at night" visits to the Faculty of Medicine, the *hôtel particuliers,* and the medieval city, among other options *(guided visits €6-14).* Audio tours available in English, Spanish, Italian, and German. The **petit train** offers a 40min. tour of the old city, starting from pl. de la Comédie. *(☎04 67 66 24 38 💻www.petit-train-demontpellier.com. $ Regular fare €6, but 33% discount with a valid student card. ⏰Every 30min., runs daily July-Aug 10:30am-7pm; Sept-Nov 5-6 per tours per day 11am-6pm; Dec-Feb 5-6 tours per day 11am-4pm; March-June 5-6 tours per day 11am-5pm.)*
- **CURRENCY EXCHANGE: Banque Courtois.** Traveler's checks accepted. *(Pl de la Comédie. ☎04 67 06 26 16 $ 1.20% commission if more than €700, €8 if less ⏰Open M-F 9:45am-12:15pm and 1:45-4:45pm.)*
- **GLBT RESOURCES: Le Shopping du Village.** In addition to fashionable shopping, the store has current copies of *Nous*, a national gay magainze with info on restaurants, shops and clubs *(3 Rue Fournarié.☎09 54 34 91 70 ⏰Open M-Sa noon-7pm.)*
- **LAUNDROMAT: Matik Lavarie.** Free wi-fi *(35 rue de Verdun. ☎06 63 43 25 99. $Wash €3-4, dry €1 per 10min. Detergent €0.50. ⏰Open M-Sa 7am-7pm.)*
- **INTERNET ACCESS: Cyber Stadium.** *(6 rue Jules Ferry.☎04 99 63 87 78. 💻www. cyberstadium.fr. $€2 per hr. ⏰ Open daily 9-1am.)* There are other cybercafés on rue de Verdun and off of rue de la République.
- **POST OFFICE: Post Restante.** Western Union inside. *(15 rue Rondelet. ☎04 67 34 50 00. ⏰Open M-F 8:30am-6:30pm, Sa 9am-12:30pm.)*

- **POSTAL CODE:** 34035. There is another large post office in *centre ville* at pl. des Martyrs de la Résistance.

Emergency!

- **POLICE:** ☎17. **Bureau Centre Ville.** *(pl. de la Comédie next to the Tourist Office. ☎04 99 74 26 74. ⏰ Open M-Sa 10am-6pm.)* **Commissariat Central.** *(206 av. Comté de Melgueil. ☎04 99 13 50 00.)*
- **PHARMACY:** Call ☎32 37 to find the *pharmacie de garde* for evening and weekend service. Otherwise, there are ample pharamcies in and around pl. de la Comédie.
- **MEDICAL EMERGENCY: Ambulance** ☎15. **Centre Hospitalier Universitaire** *(37 av. du Doyen Gaston Giraud.☎04 67 33 67 33.)* **Anti-Poison** *(☎04 91 75 25 25.)*

Getting There

By Plane

The closest airport to Montpellier is the **Aéroport International Monteplier Mediterranée** in Mauguio *(☎04 67 20 85 00.)* There is a 15min. **navette** from pl. de l'Europe to the airport *($ €5. ⏰ 12 shuttles daily -5:45am--7:50pm.)* **Air France** is located 1min. from the Tourist Office, just outside the Polygone Shopping Center *(⏰ Open M-F 9am-6:30pm, Sa 10am-1pm and 2-6pm.)*

By Train

Gare Saint Roch. *(pl. Auguste Gibert.☎36 35. ⏰ Ticket office open M 5am-9pm, Tu-Sa 6:30am-9pm and Su 6:30am-9:45pm., station open 4:45-12:30am daily.)* Trains run to: **Paris** *($ €99.70. ⏰ 3hr., 10 per day)*; **Marseille** *($ €27.50. ⏰ 2-3½hr., 10 per day)*; **Nice** *($ €51.30. ⏰ 4hr., 2 direct per day)*; **Toulouse** *($ €35.90. ⏰ 2½hr., 11 direct per day)*. For reduced fares, buy your ticket more than 10 days in advance.

By Bus

Buses run from the **Gare Routière,** a parking lot at 20 Rue Grand Saint Jean. To get there, exit the train station and turn left along the tram tracks. Continue until you see the depot on your right. Buses to surrounding towns, the beach and the airport are run by **Hérault Transport** *(☎04 34 88 89 99 🖥www.herault-transport.fr.)* Purchase tickets directly from bus drivers, but go the **Tourist Office** to pick up bus schedules. To: **Millau** *(⏰ 2hr.; M-Sa 13 per day, Su 2 per day)*; and **St. Guilhelm le Désert,** reputed to be France's prettiest town *(⏰ 1hr.; M-Sa 6 per day, Su 2 per day.)*

Getting Around

By Bus and Tram

Local buses and trams are run by **TAM** *(6 rue Jules Ferry. ☎04 67 22 87 87. 🖥www.tam-way.com. $ €1.40, 10 trips €11.50, day pass €3.40, week pass €10 for students. ⏰ Office open M-Sa 7am-7pm.)* Runs local **buses** and **trams** connecting the *centre ville* to the outskirts *(⏰ 5am-1:30am. Every 7min. 7am-8pm.)* Buy bus tickets from the driver and tram tickets from automated dispensers at the tram stops. **L'Amigo** line connects the **Gare Saint Roch** to the 13 major clubs and discotheques on the outskirts of the city *(⏰Runs Th-Sa, departures at midnight and 1am, return trips 2:30, 3:30 and 5am.)*

By Taxi

There is a small dispatch office next to the train station. Exit the station and turn left. *(☎04 67 58 10 10. $ Base €1.80. €1.56 per km. 7am-7pm, €2.34 per km. 7pm-7am. €6.10 minimum fare. €20-25 to the airport.)*

By Bike

Tam Vélo. *(27 rue Mageulone. ☎04 67 22 87 82. $ €1 per 4hr., €2 per day. ⏰ Open daily in summer 8am-8pm; in winter 9am-7pm.)*

PROVENCE

Paris might have the world-class paintings, but Provence is the region that inspired them. One of France's most diverse regions, Provence boasts ancient Roman ruins, luxurious hilltop castles, and endless fields of lavender. Fierce mistral winds cut through olive groves in the north, while pink flamingoes, black bulls, and white horses gallop freely in the marshy Camargue to the south. With 2600 years of tumultuous history, Marseille is France's second largest city, and a chaotic melting pot of French, African, and Middle Eastern cultures. The former stomping ground of medieval popes, Avignon combines a fun student vibe with a lively arts scene and world-renowned theater festival. Come summertime, Parisians head to Provence to "escape" the city, while foreigners come to see if there's any truth behind all the hype. What they find keeps visitors coming back year after year—a dip in the jewel-green sea, a stroll through earthy vineyards, and a taste of *la vie en rose.*

greatest hits

- **LIFE'S A BEACH.** At least it is in Cassis, where you can work on your tan without working your way around massive tourist crowds (p. 253).
- **SURF 'N' TURF.** Hike your way through the rocks of the calenques and cap off the adventure with a dive into the lagoon (p. 241).

You want to experience *provençal* life and you'll definitely go to **Marseille**. You should, but if you limit your time in Provence to what is arguably the Jersey Shore of France (sorry Snooki), you'd be doing yourself a disservice. Cities like **Avignon** are definitely nicer with lots of great bars like ☒**Wall Street**. Get your tan on in Cassis - you'll be glad you got out of the touristy area when you lay out at **La Plage de l'Arène**.

marseille ☎04 91

We could call Marseille a "true immigrant city" with a "vibrant local culture," but we prefer to think of it as the Tijuana of France. A Tower of Babel, produced by the train-with-cut-brakes that is globalization, this (in)famous port town is the stomping ground of sailors, backpackers, mobs of immigrants, and (we suspect) unsavory characters involved in the import-export business. Expect color, chaos, and a lingering smell of trash. The city is most famous for its dense North African population, and parts of the city are more akin to Algiers or Fez than southern France. People from throughout the Mediterranean converge here to barter and argue loudly with each other in the downtown. Tourists generally observe them from behind the plastic windows of the dinky tour buses. Located in the center of Provence, Marseille is an ideal home base for visits to the *calanques* along the coasts, or to the Provencal cities of Avignon, Arles, or Cassis. This is not the prettiest town on the French Riviera, but it hosts the closest train station to the prettiest towns on the Riviera. Avoid certain neighborhoods, and schlep it to the sweet smell of lavender only an hour away.

ORIENTATION

Marseille is organized into three main districts. The area bounded by **rue Canebière** and the **calanques** to the East is **Vieux Port; Notre Dame de la Garde** is situated on its central hilltop. Up a few blocks and to the west is **Belsunce,** Marseille's immigrant quarter. Explore "Little" Algeria, Morocco, or Tunisia and people-watch from carpet shops and tea lounges. Just don't walk around there at night. The old quarter to the furthest West is **Le Panier,** where you'll find Marseille's oldest buildings and cramped 6ft.-wide alleys. The **quai du Port** is lined with expensive hotels, boutiques, and upscale seaside cafes.

Vieux Port

Bordered by cours Julien to the east and the tourism office to the west, Vieux Port is where the bars, restaurants, shopping, and other vibrant parts of the city contain themselves. Crowned by **Notre Dame de la Garde** which overlooks its center, the neighborhood boasts the oldest *boulangerie* in Marseille, not to mention its most happening nightclubs. The port is hemmed by bars and cafes that turn into hotspots at night; upscale restaurants are situated further inland around **place aux Huiles.** Frustrated single men beware: at night in the Vieux Port, it can be particularly difficult to differentiate between clubs, bars, and strip clubs. The entrepreneurial young women beckoning you to come in at the door are a pretty good hint.

Le Panier

When the Greeks landed in Marseille 2,600 years ago, this is where they landed. Today, le Panier is the oldest and most cramped part of the city, though the area around La Vieille Charité might give it a run for its money. Mostly devoid of bars and clubs at night, this area is best to visit during the day, where the stores and the kooky cafes add charm to the winding narrow streets. At night, the same alleyways are shadowy and somewhat intimidating, since you might be the only one on them.

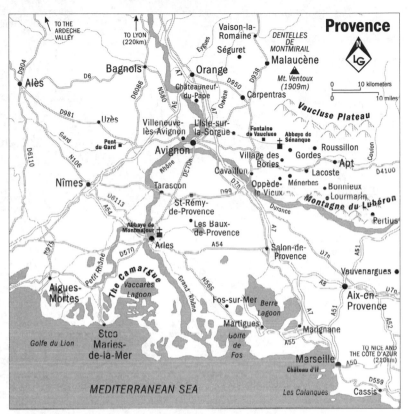

Belsunce

Little North Africa is bounded by **av. Belsunce** and the **Canebière**, and teems with little kebab stands and carpet stores; this is an ideal place to shop cheap, and perhaps stop in and enjoy a pastis with a group of old Algerian men. Once dark, the stores close, and the few bars in the area become packed with the city's local flair. Unless you're large, male, and handy in a knife fight, however, take the long way to the port and skip Belsunce at night.

ACCOMMODATIONS

Accommodations in Marseille range from the affordable to the absurd. Stick to Belsunce or on the city's outskirts for the cheapest hotels and hostels, or spend a little more at Vieux Port's quiet B and Bs and nicer, centrally located hotels. If you have money to burn, stroll over to Le Panier and quai du Port for some hotels that are as close to the marina as they are expensive. Unless you're splitting the cost of a terrace room, avoid the area if you're on a budget.

Vieux Port

BALAENA   (ᵞ)占   HOTEL ❷

83 av. de la Pointe Rouge   ☎06 68 42 21 22 ▣www.hebergement-marseille.fr

Conveniently located next to the beach and attached to a wetsuit/dive shop, this spotless hostel remains happily unlisted on English sites because Celine, the

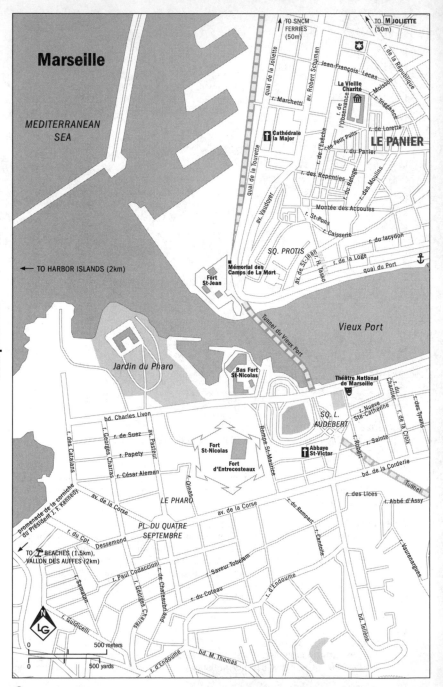

Marseille

MEDITERRANEAN
SEA

← TO HARBOR ISLANDS (2km)

TO SNCM
FERRIES
(50m)

TO ⓜ JOLIETTE
(50m)

LE PANIER

quai de la Joliette

av. Robert Schuman

r. de la République

Jean-François Lecas

r. Moisson

r. de l'Observance

La Vieille
Charité

r. Tisserand

r. Marchetti

Cathédrale
la Major

r. de l'Evêché

r. du Petit Puits

r. de Lorette

r. du Panier

r. des Repenties

r. du Refuge

r. des Moulins

quai de la Tourette

Montée des Accoules

r. St-Pons

r. Caissene

av. Vaudoyer

r. du lacydon

SQ. PROTIS

r. de la Loge

quai du Port

Mémorial des
Camps de La Mort

av. de St-Jean

r. H. Tasso

Fort
St-Jean

Vieux Port

Tunnel du Vieux Port

Jardin du Pharo

Bas Fort
St-Nicolas

Théâtre National
de Marseille

SQ. L.
AUDEBERT

r. du Chantier

r. Nueve Ste-Catherine

r. de la Croix

r. des Trrats

bd. Charles Livon

r. des Catalans

r. Georges Charas

r. de Suez

av. Pasteur

r. Papety

Fort
St-Nicolas

Rampe St-Maurice

Abbaye
St-Victor

r. Robert

r. Sainte

r. César Aleman

Fort
d'Entrecosteaux

bd. de la Corderie

Promenade de la corniche
du Président J. F. Kennedy

r. Quitasol

LE PHARO

av. de la Corse

r. des Lices

Tunnel

r. Abbé d'Assy

av. de la Corse

r. du Cpt. Dessemond

PL. DU QUATRE
SEPTEMBRE

r. du Rempart

r. Candolle

r. Vaurenargues

TO ⚓ BEACHES (1.5km),
VALLON DES AUFFES (2km)

r. Samatan

r. Paul Codaccioni

de Chateaubriand

r. Georges Chyas

Saveur Tobelem

r. du Coteau

r. d'Endoume

bd. Tellène

N

LG

r. Guidicelli

0 ——— 500 meters

0 ——— 500 yards

r. d'Endoume

bd. M. Thomas

provence

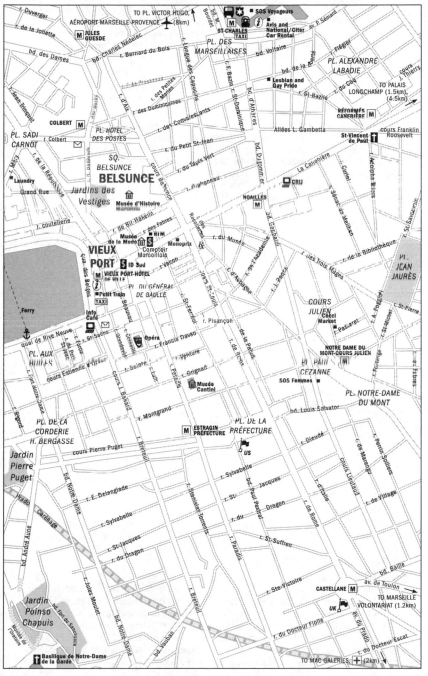

owner, speaks no English. A must for those focused on outdoor activites such hiking the calanques or diving/windsurfing/kiteboarding.

✈ Ⓜ*Metro line #2 to Castellene then take Bus #19 (dir. Madrogue de Montredon) to Tibulon. At the end of the alleyway.* ℹ *Wi-Fi, breakfast, and linens included.* ⑤ *Shared rooms €22.50 per person; triples €81.*

🏠 AUBERGE DE JEUNESSE   ♿(ᵗᵖ)♈☂ HOSTEL ❶
impasse du Docteur Bonfils   ☎04 91 17 63 30 💻www.fuaj.com

Far away from the city, but close to the beach. All the way out in the 8th arrondissment (something most FUAJ hostels have in common) the brightly colored, spacious reception welcomes you with a pool table and bar right as you walk in. Clean, but bare rooms. Organizes wind surfing (*€14 per person for a half day*) and kayaking half days on Saturday (*€25*) and full days on Su (*€44*).

✈ Ⓜ*Castellene. From there, take bus #44 to Clot Bey Leau. Walk in direction of bus to traffic circle and take a right onto av. Joseph Vidal. Pass the bike rental store and turn left onto Impsse du Docteur Bonfils. Its at the end of the street. Look for Orange circle around blue triangle.* ℹ *FUAJ Card required. Bar, restaurant, Wi-Fi, kitchen, breakfast included.* ⑤ *€19/night. Three nights maximum in summer.*

🏠 MONTGRAND   ♒♿(ᵗᵖ)♈ HOTEL ❺
50 rue Montgrand   ☎04 91 00 35 20 💻www.hotel-montgrand-marseille.com

Clean and well-lit rooms with wide windows that let in lots of sunshine. Tripples and quads avaiilable.

✈ Ⓜ*Estrangin, walk along rue Montgrand.*⑤ *Singles €59-65; doubles €75; triples €85; quads €95.*

HOTEL RELAX   ♒⊗❄ HOTEL ❹
4 rue Corneille   ☎04 91 33 15 87 💻www.hotelrelax.fr

Boutique hotel that screams Belle Époque, but without the bankroll. Pink, upholstered, and slightly mismatched furniture is scattered throughout the reception. All rooms are doubles, so not the most affordable for the single traveller. Awesome location next to the Opera and many cafes. Book in advance in the summer.

✈ Ⓜ*Vieux Port. To the right of the Opera if facing colonnade.* ℹ *Parking available. Breakfast €7. Mini fridge and TV in each room.* ⑤ *Rooms €60-65; triples €75.*

ST LOUIS   ♒♿(ᵗᵖ)♈ HOTEL ❺
2 rue des recolettes   ☎04 91 54 02 74 💻www.hotel-st-louis.com

Quiet, easily accessible hotel near the Vieux Port. Tiled bathroom floor and comfy bed are welcomed amenities. Patio rooms overlook main Place as well as bright white dining room. Ask for student rate upon reservation.

✈ Ⓜ*Vieux Port* ℹ *Renovated in 2007. Breakfast €8.* ⑤ *Singles €67; doubles €72; triples €90. Reduced prices in winter.*

Le Panier

The hotels in this area are freakishly expensive. A few of the better finds on the water sport exceptional views and will only cost you your right arm (unless you're left handed, in which case they will ask for that). For any of the other ones, come back when you've made it in life.

HOTEL HERMES   ♒♿(ᵗᵖ)❄ HOTEL ❹
2 rue Bonneterie   ☎04 96 11 63 63 💻www.hotelmarseille.com/hermes

Location, location, location. Hotel Hermes is right on the quai du Port, and next to an innocuous hotel that charges €180 per night. In light of these factors, the prices aren't that bad at this Greek-themed hotel with terrace rooms. While the rooms are reminiscent of a porno shot in a Motel 6 back in 1970's Miami (think pink sheets, loudly patterned carpets, and lingering smell of smoke in the halls), the proximity to cafes and the port more than make up for it.

➡ Ⓜ Vieux Port. ℹ TV, A/C, newly renovated. Breakfast €8. $ Singles €50; triples with terrace €90. We reccommend springing for the terrace.

Belsunce

LE VERTIGO
💳♿📶🍸☀ HOSTEL [2]

42 rue des Petites Maries ☎04 91 91 07 11 💻www.hotelvertigo.com

Right next to the train station. Funky flea market finds decorate the walls and comprise the furniture at this dedicated, youthful hostel. The outside patio explodes with reds and blues and yellows, mimicking the festive streets of Marseille. Clean, cozy shared kitchen is a welcoming haven in this English speaking, laid-back establishment.

➡ From the train station, walk down the Grand Staircase onto bld. d'Athèns. Take the first right. rue des Petites Maries will be on the left, hostel is 20 yards down on the left. ℹ Wi-Fi, shared kitchen, 24hr reception, bar open til midnight. $ 2-6 person dorms €23.90; doubles €55-65.

HOTEL DU PETIT PARIS
💳📶🚭 HOTEL [2]

33 rue Tapis Vert ☎04 91 90 89 94 💻www.hotelpetitparismarseille.com

Stay here when you want to stay someplace quality and close to the train station and Le Vertigo is fully booked, as Petit doesn't fill up as quickly. Not to be confused with the luxury Parisan hotel. Good for splitting a double or triple.

➡ Ⓜ St-Charles Gare. Walk down stairs onto rue d'Athens for 5-6 blocks (depending on your defnition of a block) Make a right on rue Tapis Vert. $ Singles €40; doubles €50.

SIGHTS

Most of the must-see sights here are located in the Vieux Port of the city, which hosts **Notre Dame de la Garde** and the **Abbaye St.-Victor**. The museums are decent, and will hypnotize afficionados of 20th-century Cubism, Fauvism or any of those other "-isms" you studied in art school. If you are less than intellectually inclined (you are on vacation, after all), we recommend that you spend most of your time getting out of the city to see **Ile d'If** or the **callanques**. **Le Panier** has the one of the oldest orphanages in France, which also served as a baroque church and now is a museum for Marseille's ancient history. To experience 1,000 years of North African culture in the Med, explore **Belsunce,** which is a sight and smell of its own.

Vieux Port

NOTRE DAME DE LA GARDE

Top of the hill ☎04 91 13 40 80

You simply won't get a better view of the city than this. As awesome as it is windy, this is where shipwreck survivors went to thank God, and it's where you will too, provided you survive the walk up (take the #60 bus instead). Towering over the Basilica is an 11.2m-tall golden Madonna and Child, which weighs just shy of 10,000 kilos. Services are still held in the crypt of the church, a tradition that's probably a holdover from the days when the Nazis were shooting at the basilica; you can still see the bullet holes in the east wall.

➡ Take bus #60 from Vieux Port all the way to the end. $ Free. ⏰ Open daily 7am-7:30pm.

MUSÉE CANTINI

19 rue Grignan ☎04 91 54 77 75 💻www.marseille.fr

Housed in a chic warehouse, this museum hosts a permanent collection of Picasso, Cezanne, and Dubuffet paintings. Focuses on Surrealist, Fauvist, and Cubist movements of the last century. The museum is currently undergoing renovations and is expected to be completed in 2013. The new and improved museum is expected to house French artists from all over the country as well as Europe (France is scheduled to be the EU's culture capital in that year).

➡ Ⓜ Prefecture. $ €2.50 entrance fee. Under 10 free. ⏰ Open daily 10am-5pm. Jul-Oct open til 7pm.

⬛ CHÂTEAU D'IF

quai des Belges   ☎04 91 59 02 30

The legendary home to the 🍴**Man in the Iron Mask** and **Count of Monte Cristo**, this island fortress turned prison is less exciting than Alcatraz, but more exciting than just any rock in the middle of the harbor. Forget about the cool, fictitious noble prisoners, though since you were more likely to find Huguenot leaders jailed here during the religious purges of the 1600s. While it's an equally horrific story, somehow it just doesn't have the same ring to it.

🍴 Ⓜ*Vieux Port. Quai des Belges.* Ⓢ *Boat tickets €15, students €10. Château entrance €5. Studnets free.* 🕐 *Open 9:30am-6:15pm, as a function of the last operating boats to the island.*

---

hollywood

They may look peaceful to you, but these oceanside promenades and narrow streets are the stomping grounds of spies, pirates, drug lords, international intrigue, and plain old-fashioned revenge (well, at least on the silver screen.)

- **THE COUNT OF MONTE CRISTO.** Edmond Dantès escaped Château d'If, the island prison off the coast of Marseilles, by dressing himself in his dead friend's burial shroud. (Ew.) Over 3500 Huguenots and scores of real-life political detainees found this feared fort-turned-prison escape-proof, but not so with our friend the Count. The prison is open today and frequented by tourists.

- **THE FRENCH CONNECTION.** Sit in a seaside cafe and await your shipment of smuggled heroin from Turkey. (*Let's Go* does not recommend smuggling drugs, because Doyle *will* find you. And he will shoot.) What most people don't know is that the ring leader, Paul Corbone, also smuggled Parmigiano-Reggiano cheese between Italy and France. But whether you're carrying illegal drugs or just illegal dairy products, you'll need to take a break and take in the harbor.

- **THE BOURNE IDENTITY.** If you manage not to fall off the ferry to Corsica, you will officially be more coordinated than Jason Bourne. No, seriously. He takes a spill off the ferry in the opening scene of the movie (two gunshot wounds may have had something to do with the fall, but *Let's Go* doesn't believe in excuses).

ABBAYE ST-VICTOR

3 rue de l'Abbaye   ☎04 96 11 22 60

An early Christian burial site for saints, the history of the Abbaye St-Victor is (naturally) characterized by power struggles, mob violence, and other things Jesus would totally do. The abbey was originally fortified against pagan invaders, and successfully repelled the barbarian hordes until part of it was destroyed and looted by ⬛**disgruntled** plebeians during the French Revolution. Though Napoleon attempted to restore the Abbey upon taking leadership, many of its treasures had been mysteriously misplaced. In their infinite respect for the dead that are buried here, the Christian faithful have more recently dug up the deceased saints and put their bones on display for tourists in the museum. Hallelujah. The Church also hosts a crypt that is way cooler than **Notre Dame de la Garde,** though you do have to pay for added awesomeness.

🍴 *At the end of rue Sainte.* 𝒊 *Serves F-Su.* Ⓢ *Free. Crypt entrance is €2.* 🕐 *Open daily fro 7am-7pm. Will be closed until February 2011.*

provence

Le Panier

👍 VIEILLE CHARITÉ ♿

2 rue de la Charité ☎04 91 14 58 80 💻www.vieille-charite-marseille.org

The Vieille Charité was originally intended to be a tolerant place of worship for the homeless, but they tended to crowd the entrances and make church awkward for the other parishioners. The men and women of the cloth delicately transformed the church into an orphanage, perhaps in an effort to service more lovable charity cases. A wooden plank was strategically placed in front of certain windows so that the nuns couldn't see the local Mother or Father of The Year dropping their kid off in front of the Church. Today, the building hosts the **Baroque Chapel** and the **Musée des Arts Africains, Océaniens, et Amérindiens,** as well as the **Musée d'Archéologie Méditerranée,** where you can peruse local ancient history from before and after Roman times.

[$] Permanent exhibits €3, students €1.50. French university students (even exchange students) and children under 12 free. Temporary exhibits €4, students €2.50 for students. 🕐 Tu-Sa noon-7pm.

Belsunce

👍 MUSEE DE LA MODE — MUSEUM

11 La Canebière ☎04 96 17 06 00 💻www.espacemodemediterranee.com

The ultimate window shopper's dream, this museum houses a history of clothing from the 1940s to the present, and boasts 6000 garments. Lady Gaga's Kermit the Frog dress is sadly omitted. Closed until further notice in preparation for 2013.

➜ [M]Vieux Port, walk up three block, on your left. [$] €2 entrance, students free. 🕐 Oct-May 10am-5pm, Jun-Sep 11am-6pm.

LA CANEBIÈRE — MARKET

La Canebière

If you were expecting an open market with the local medicinal hash, we hate to disappoint: "la canabière" is a false cognate. Deriving its name from the Provençal for "hemp," this bustling shopping street is named after Marseille's historic ropemakers and sailors. Look for the really long street that separates Vieux Port from Belsunce.

➜ [M]Vieux Port. Turn around and walk up.

THE GREAT OUTDOORS

Beaches

LA PLAGE POINTE ROUGE

Popular with local windsurfers and kite-boarders, and an oasis for SCUBA divers. Small but awesome windbreak, protected by a jetti.

➜ #19 bus to Toulon.

PRADO PARC

When residents complained about not having easy access to local beaches, this park was created to provide both a community hangout and a buffer between more relaxed tanning beaches and the main road. Packed with both tourists and locals in summer, the park is pretty big, and is conveniently broken up into 4 smaller beaches: Benneveine, Borely, Roucas Blanc, and Vieille Chapele.

➜ Either the #19 bus of #83 to La Plage bus stop.

Hiking

👍 SORMIOU CALANQUE

One of the easiest and most breathtaking of the calanques, this trail leads down to a small cove where it's just too pretty to not swim, even if it means donning your underwater or birthday suit to enjoy it.

➜ *Take the #23 bus to the end of the line, and follow the signs for Sormiou down a hike that is all downhill, and takes 25 min.*

LUMINY CALANQUE

The calanque to the East of Sormiou, and equally pretty. Windy trail for 30min downhill to the water's edge where cliff jumpers are seen jumping from the high ledges into the lagoon.

➜ *End of bus #23, follow signs for Luminy.*

CALLELONGE

☎08 11 20 13 13

Why go around the mountain when you can go over it? Hike across the peninsula from the end of the #19 bus (dir. Madrague de Montredon) up 432m to the port city of Callelongue (*1 ½hr. hike*).The path is paved with limestone, yields glorious views, and can be dangerous when windy; stick to the trail and follow the yellow brick road (read: stick to the yellow and black markers which mark the local trails, as opposed to bivouacking through any roads less traveled by). Be sure to pay attention to the trails' color-coding, since this trailhead is also the begining of the 28km trail to Cassis. Optional detour to the summit of Marseilleveyre (*1½hr.*).

➜ *Take #19 bus (dir. Madrogue de Montredon) all the way to the end from the Castellene metro stop.* **i** *Be sure to calle about wind safety and closures regarding all of the calanques automated, multi-lingual. Black means closed, red means open 6-11am and green means open all day.*

MARSEILLE TO CASSIS

The adrenaline junkie's dream starts at the end of the #19 bus (dir. Madrague de Montredon). Follow the road up 100 ft. to the trailhead on the left. This "hike" is actually a 28km trek to the nearby town Cassis. Not recommended for beginners or whiners, the rocky trail winds up and over Marseilleveyre and into the small port town. Bring proper supplies and gear (read: water)—it's a long hike through dry areas.

➜ *Take #19 bus (dir. Madrogue de Montredon) all the way to the end from the Castellene metro stop.*

FOOD

Vieux Port

LE SUD DE HAUT — AFRICAN, HAITIAN ❸

80 cours Julien ☎04 91 33 75 33

This hippie African/Haitian restaurant specializes in French attitude and American cinema, and is more than willing to provide a little kitsch whenever needed. Few other places offer sit down service with dessert for €10. The walls are painted in bright African colors and papered with American movie and music posters. Oddly enough, the Declaration of Independence too; we've just become more of a fan. The dessert is especially awesome—check out the chocolate covered fried banana.

➜ *[M]Notre Dame-Cour Julien.* $ *€10.50 lunch menu with plat du jour and dessert du jour. Make it a three course for €16. Plats €11-16. Cocktails €7.* ⏰ *Open T-Sa noon-2:30pm, 7-10:30pm.*

AU FALAFEL — FALAFEL, SHAWARMA ❶

5 rue Lulli ☎04 91 54 08 55

Kickass Israeli falafel and shawarma joint. The hummus is homemade, and the falafels are assembled in-house and served hot. The framed pictures of local graffiti art that line the walls are a particular treat, but we nonetheless recommend that you sit outside; the fryer is situated right by the entrance, and the place can get pretty hot. Take-out availible.

➜ *[M]Vieux Port.* $ *€4.50 Falafel, Chicken curry and dishes €6.* ⏰ *Open M-Th noon-midnight, F noon-4pm, Su noon-midnight.*

FOUR DES NAVETTES   ♿ BOULANGERIE ❶

136 rue Sainte   ☎04 91 33 65 69 ◼www.fourdesnavettes.com

Founded in 1781, the oldest *boulangerie* in Marseille is famous for its secret recipe of a lemony, hard biscuit that every February 2, the abbey of St-Victor blesses as they first come out of the oven at 6am. Almond cakes and other biscuits fill the air with aromas of marzipan and glazed sugar.

☞ *Down the street from the Abbaye St-Victor.* ⑤ *1 Navette €0.75, for a dozen €8.* ☒ *Open M-Sa 7am-8pm, Su 9am-1pm and 3-7:30pm. Aug daily 9am-1pm and 3-7:30pm.*

CAFE LULLI   ◕♿♻ CAFE ❷

26 rue Lulli   ☎04 91 54 11 17 ◼http://lecafelulli.over-blog.com

The tea jars stacked high behind the register demonstrate the number of available options at this tea cafe. As far as food goes, try the quiche and salade lunch combo (€7.50) or splurge on the dessert maison (€2-6).

☞ ⓜ*Vieux Port, near the Opera.* ⑤ *Open Lunch menu from €7.50-11.*

EATING   ◕♻ TRADITIONAL ❷

40 rue Montgrand   ☎04 91 33 76 88 ◼www.ilove-eating.fr

Eating gets straight to the point. The ideal place to pick up a hefty picnic lunch before hitting the beach, the menu changes with the seasons, and the prices remain remarkably reasonable (*salad, cheese dish and wine; €7.80*). A large framed picture from Paris in the '20s takes you back to when people actually went on picnics.

☞ ⓜ*Vieux Port.* ⑤ *Seasonal lunch menu €7.80. Bakery items €.50-3.* ☒ *Open M-F 8am-4pm.*

LA KAHENA   ◕♿♈♻ NORTH AFRICAN ❸

2 rue de la République   ☎04 91 90 61 93

Tunisian restuarant which serves heaping bowls of couscous in handpainted blue plates. Map of Tunisia and mosaics of camels kick the kitsch up a notch to an almost annoying level.

☞ ⓜ*Vieux Port.* ⑤ *Entres €5-6 while couscous plates will set you back €10-16.* ☒ *Open daily noon-2:30pm and 7:30-10:30pm.*

Le Panier

▨ CHEZ MANON   ◕♻ TRADITIONAL ❷

2 rue Rodillat   ☎06 21 42 30 91

This small cafe may only have 3 tables, but the light blue walls with yellow stripes are oddly soothing, and the proprietess Nacira is a sweetheart who goes out of her way to take care of you. Whether looking for a sandwich (€3.50-4.50) or a more substantial penne dish with salmon, or a combo of three French cheeses (€9-12), this is the perfect escape from the busy *quai du port*.

⑤ *Tucked away in plain sight 100m from the Vieille Charité.* ☒ *Open daily 10:30am-6pm.*

LE SOUK   ◕♿♈♻ NORTH AFRICAN ❸

100 quai du Port   ☎04 91 91 29 29 ◼www.restaurantlesouk.com

Tall people watch out in this low-ceilinged (we're talking 6' here) restaurant, which serves Maghreb style tea, tahini, and couscous. Tables are accompanied by small cushions in lieu of seats, and dishes served in traditional pottery from across the Med. Choose from wines from Morocco, Algeria, or France to acompany your menu du jour (€13.50).

⑤ *Plates from €8-25. Menu du jour offers plat du jour and dessert du jour or entree du jour and plat du jour.* ☒ *Open Tu-Su noon-2:30 and 7:30-10:30pm.*

CHEZ MADIE LES GALENETTES   ◕♿♈♻ PROVENÇAL ❸

138 quai du Port   ☎04 91 90 40 87

A provençal cafe specializing in traditional Marseillaise cuisine, located in Marseille? Blasphemy! Not only that, but the beach theme trend applies here as well. Located right on the harbor, the fish tastes fresher and the tourists are louder.

marseille • food

Splurge here for dinner when it's not as crowded on the boardwalk.
Ⓢ *Three course menu featuring local fish and lamb chops €25. Desserts €6.* Ⓩ *Open M-Sa noon-2pm, 8-11pm.*

LE WICH

◉⎔ PANINI, CRÊPERIE ❶

Passage Pentécontore, in between quai du Port and rue de la Loge.

A one window panini and crêpes shop identifiable by the light pink and green storefront and the long line that winds to the other end of the alley. The fare here is sweet and wicked cheap, and features sweet paninis that are rare in a world of grilled ham and cheese (*nutella and banana panini; €4*).
Ⓢ *Paninis and sandwiches from €3-5.* Ⓩ *Open daily 10am-5:30pm.*

MIRAMAR

◆⎔♈♨ PROVENÇAL ❺

12 quai du Port   ☎04 91 91 10 40 🖳www.bouillabaisse.com

If food is more important to you than housing, splurge here for over-the-top fish and lobster dishes and more over-the-top service. Named one of France's gourmet restaurants of the year in 2009, Miramar has sure taken pains to keep up its reputation; the outside seating is covered and enclosed, to keep out noise and riff-raff like yourself. Right on the water, reserve a table well in advance, preferably with someone else paying for you. This may well be the best meal you'll have in Southern France.
Ⓢ *Dishes between €25-44. Daily fish specials.* Ⓩ *Open T-Sa noon-2pm, 7-10pm.*

Belsunce

▩ MARCHÉ PROVENÇAL

◉⎔ MARKET ❶

7 rue Vacon   ☎04 91 54 44 87

Belsunce may well host a largely North African population, but we've noticed that there's plenty of cross-over between French and North African culture—and that most of these commonalities have to do with food. This open air fruit and vegetable market is the heart of Belsunce, and specializes in seasonal fruits from both sides of the Med. Incredibly, given the its size, the market is run by a single local Algerian family.
Ⓢ *Market prices.* Ⓩ *Open daily 8am-8pm.*

▩ ARABESQUE

⎔ NORTH AFRICAN ❶

20A rue d'Aix   ☎04 91 91 96 75

Algerian bakery and tea salon on a main, well-populated street in Belsunce. The neighborhood favorite boasts an array of finely decorated sweets covered in various amounts of carmelized sugar (*€1-3*). A lunch menu comprised of your standard couscous and kebabs is also available (*€7*). Try it with the mint tea, which is brewed with real mint leaves.
Ⓢ *Bakery items €1-3. Lunch kebab or couscous €6.70.* Ⓩ *Open daily 6am-8pm, lunch from 12-3pm. Tea salon open after 3pm.*

NIGHTLIFE

Most of the bars and clubs here are located in Vieux Port. The more artsy (read: kooky) watering holes are in the area around cours Julien, while the more hopping, and more expensive hotspots can be easily spotted along the port. Le Panier is devoid of bars, since it's devoid of people at night anyway. Belsunce is where you go when you want to get lost at night and quickly regret doing so.

Vieux Port

PETIT NICE

◆♈♨ BAR

28 pl. Jean Jaurès

The giant covered patio seating dominates this local fixture of the Cours Julian neighborhood, and is almost three times the size of the bar itself. The inside is decorated with a seemingly random assortment of ropes, hats, Nice posters, and

life rings that adhere to the restaurant's general Nice theme (we guess).
⚑ Ⓜ*Cours Julien.* Ⓢ *Half pints €2. Pints €4. Rum and mixed drinks €3.50.* Ⓩ *Open Tu-Th 11am-2am, F-Sa 8am-2am.*

SHAMROCK
⬤♿🍸♨ IRISH PUB

17 quai de Rive Neuve

A tried and true Irish bar where the city's students and youth hostel workers can always depend on to be open. In true ☘shamrock fashion, the Shamrock encourages patrons to drink above and beyond the legal limit—on Mondays, all pints are half-off all night. Soccer and rugby scarves cover the walls.
i *Happy hour Tu-Su 6-8pm.* Ⓢ *Pints €5.50-6.* Ⓩ *Open daily 4pm-2am.*

DAN RACING
🍸♿ BAR

17 rue Andre Poggioli ☎06 09 17 04 07 ▨www.dan-racing.tk

This Harley-themed bar is about as loose and fast as its owner, who never listens to a band before letting them play on stage. More often than not, this tolerant system of letting anyone play only adds to Dan Racing's fly-by-the-seat-of-your-pants vibe, but it occasionally results in the hiring of slasher head-banging groups who sound like some cross between Jacques Cousteau and Iron Maiden.
⚑ Ⓜ*Cours Julien.* Ⓢ *Free entry. Beer €2.50.* Ⓩ *Open F-Sa 6:30pm-2am.*

EXIT CAFE
⬤♿🍸 BAR

12 quai de Rive Nueve ☎04 91 54 29 43

The Euro-trashy Exit Cafe mixes loud electronic music with bright neon lights for a local clientele. Patrons are generally slicked-back-hair types who unbutton their shirts to their mid chest, so the inside is a bit to much to handle. The outside seating area is the perfect place to enjoy their 2 for 1 drinks deal at their generous happy hour.
Ⓢ *Beer €5-6. Cocktails €8. 2 for 1 happy hours (5pm-10pm)* Ⓩ *Open Tu-Sa noon-2am.*

TROLLEYBUS
⬤🍸♿▼ CLUB

24 quai de Rive-Neuve ☎06 72 36 91 10 ▨www.letrolley.com

One of the few clubs in Vieux Port that's not a strip club, this Trolleybus features different kinds of rock, electonica, and world beat in each of their three rooms. Whoever's in charge of the lights here should definitely get a pay raise: when this research-writer visited, a rock concert was projected onto the wall in the first room, fast-paced strobelight pulsed in another, and some moodier, groovier lighting was dappling the third.
Ⓢ *€10, free drink with entry.* Ⓩ *Open Jul-Aug W-Sa 11pm-6am, Sep-Jun Th-Sa 11pm-6am.*

BARBAROUSSE
⬤🍸⊗ CLUB

7 rue Glandèves ☎04 91 33 78 13 ▨marseille.barberousse.com

The Marseille branch of this three-club chain is the original, and the pirate theme makes much more sense at this port city. A shooters bar of flavored rum and vodka, Barbarousse usually has a line out the door to get in, so arrive early, and preferably with a group of attractive females to get past the bouncers.
i *No cover, just one mean line. Happy hour 7-10pm.* Ⓢ *Shooters €2, bottles for €23.* Ⓩ *Open Tu-Sa 6pm-2am.*

LA POSTE A LA GALENE
⊗🍸 CLUB, CONCERT VENU

103 rue Ferrari ☎04 91 42 16 33 ▨www.lapostealagalene.com

This club/concert venue is a little out of the way and can charge steep covers, so check their website to see who's playing before heading out. Big open area on two floors and beer bar with large stage. Hosts local bands, DJs, and international groups. Themed nights vary from mask to '80s Nights.
⚑ *Off of pl. Juan Juares.* Ⓢ *€1 membership required. Cover €5-18. Beer half-pint €3 full-pint €5.* Ⓩ *Open Tu-Sa 8pm-1am (concert nights start at 9, club nights start at 10:30pm). Closed from Jul-20-Sept 2.*

Le Panier

👍 BAR 13 COINS 🍸 BAR

pl. 13 Coins

Identifiable by its dark red exterior and the loud portraits of people painted in bright African yellows, greens, and reds along the walls, this chill bar is ideal for an early start in the afternoon or the first drink of the night. Posters advertising African and Maghreb music concerts paper the doors and windows. While the beer here is not the cheapest, the groovy vibe makes the place more than worth it.

$ Beer €3-4.50. Mixed drinks €5. ⏰ Open daily 8am-midnight (or later depending on the scene).

ARTS AND CULTURE

Festivals

FESTIVAL DE MARSEILLE

Going strong since 1996, this ginormous music, dance, and movie festival features everything from ballet performances to special screenings to rock concerts. The festival is technically a celebration of Marseille's illustrious history, but appears to be more of an excuse for a two-month party. The festivities start in Le Panier and gradually move east across the city.

$ Prices vary accoring to event. ⏰ June and July. Check out 6 place Sadi Carnot, or www.festival-demarseille.com for specific information on times.

FÊTE DE LA MÉDITERRANEÉ

pl. Bargemon (Hôtel de Ville) 🖥www.lafetedelamediterranee

Features music from France, le Maghreb and throughout the Mediterranean.

$ Free. ⏰ Early May.

provence

SHOPPING

👍 PLACE AUX HUILES 🛍🍸 SPECIALTY

2 pl. Daviel ☎04 91 90 05 55 🖥www.placeauxhuiles.com

You can get your standard pastis, dish soap, and other amenities at place aux Huile too, but people come here for the olive oil. The store sells over 16 different kinds, and a series of bottles line the back walls. Samples availible.

$ Half liter €11.50. Full liter €22. Bring your own bottle to fill for €10. ⏰ Open daily 10am-1pm, 2-7pm.

MAISON DU PASTIS 🛍🍸 SPECIALTY

108 quai du Port ☎04 91 90 86 77 🖥www.lamaisondupastis.com

For those of you who've been living in a very small hole during your time in Marseille, pastis is that yellow drink all the cool people drink here. As its names suggests, Maison du Pastis sells it in spades, and for good measure provides more than enough absinthe too—the store stocks over 95 varieties of each. The bottles are ideal for gifts or a discreet personal party on the beach.

$ Half liter €12. Full liter €20. ⏰ Open daily 9am-5:30pm.

BOUTIQUE D'OLYMPIQUE DE MARSEILLE 🛍 SPORTS

44 Canebière ☎04 91 33 20 01 🖥http://boutique.om.net

Get your Olympique Marseille gear here so you don't look like you're a Grenoble fan. While the scarfs (€7) aren't much of a deal, you'll find discounted jerseys from last year upstairs that will make you look like you've always been a fan.

⏰ Open M-Sa 10am to 7pm.

LE SOMMELIER 🛍♿🍸 LIQUOR

42 rue de Rome ☎04 91 33 53 53 🖥www.lesommelier-marseille.com

Organic is only the tip of the iceberg when its come to bio awareness at this wine store. Wines marked with "Lutte Raisonee" stickers were farmed with the least amount of ecological harm possible, and the grapes used in wines marked with "Bio Dynamic" stickers were planted during the full moon. We're not sure what the moon has to do with it. Were these vineyards blessed by baked Wiccans or farmed by the Wolfman or something?

Ⓢ *Wines from €4.50 to €200+.* Ⓓ *Open M-Sa 9am-6:30pm.*

H&M
☛ APPAREL

16 rue de la République   ☎04 96 17 57 10 ▦www.hm.com/fr.

Yeah, yeah, we know. But it's really cheap and their selection is tailored to whatever country they're in.

i *Foreign credit cards require ID verification.* Ⓢ*Slightly higher than home, because of the exchange rate.* Ⓓ *Open M-Sa 10am-7pm.*

LAFAYETTE
APPAREL

Centre Bourse   ☎04 91 56 82 12 ▦www.centre-bourse.com

Upscale gallery of men's and women's clothing features everything from T-shirts to suits. When you want something more exclusively French than H&M.

Ⓢ *From €10 sundresses to €2000 suits.* Ⓓ *Open M-Sa 9:30am-7:30pm.*

FNAC
☛ ELECTRONICS, CDS, DVDS

Centre Bourse   ☎08 25 02 00 20 ▦www.fnac.com

Sure. Its an electronics store. But for you, it's oh so much more. Around the corner from the entrance is a booth that sells tickets to practically every possible museum, concert, and art show in the South of France. This researcher would have killed to see Elton John in Nice. Oh well.

Ⓓ *Open M-Sa 9:30am-7:30pm.*

COUNTRY LIFE
☛ ✢ SPECIALTY

14 rue Venture   ☎04 96 11 28 00 ▦www.countrylife.fr

If the organic wine store wasn't enough for you, try this restaurant/cafe/soap-and-bath products store for all your vegan needs. Sells popular Provençal items without the guilt of having it ever come close to an animal. All ingredients locally grown in France.

Ⓢ *€6.70 buffet lunch.* Ⓓ *Open M-Th 10am-7pm. Open Friday for tea salon and restaurant only 11am-2:30pm.*

LE KELLY
☛ ACCESSORIES

53 rue Francis Davso   ☎04 91 33 22 99

Discount handbag store features brands like Lupo, Frederic, and Lancaster Paris. Up to 30% off retail prices on luggage, purses, and handbags.

Ⓢ *€100-280.* Ⓓ *Open daily 10am-7pm*

DURANCE
PERFUMERIE

40 rue Francis Davso   ☎04 91 33 52 47 ▦www.durance.fr

If you can't make it to Grasse to get your personalized perfume, come here instead, since this is one of their cheaper outlets. Also sells Provençal cosmetics, candles, and fragrances.

Ⓢ *Anywhere from €4 handsoaps to full blown packages.* Ⓓ *Open daily 10am-7pm*

L'OCCITANE
SPECIALTY, PERFUMERIE, SOAP

20/22 rue Hexo   ☎04 91 55 06 82 ▦www.loccitane.com

We would be lying to you if we didn't put this in here for Provence. This popular French soaps/lotions/good-smelling-stuff producer is world famous for a reason, and it's slightly cheaper here than the rest of the world. Defy mortality for only €72 with their Divine Cream, although we're betting you'll die just like everyone else. At least you'll look fabulous.

Ⓢ *€3 soaps to more money than you want to spend on fancier soaps.* Ⓓ *Open M-Sa 10am-7pm.*

L'ESCALE MARINE

22 quai du Port ☎04 91 91 67 42

It may not have the ring of "La Maison du Pastis," but it is slightly cheaper. Liquor, soaps, and everything else that you need is sold here, right on the harbor.

[$] Pastis for €21 per liter. ⏰ Open daily 10am-8pm.

ESSENTIALS

Marseille is essentially an immigrant town, so if the local resources seem to be overwhelmingly intended for a North African/Arab population, thats because they are. Never fear! There is help for tourists here!

Practicalities

- **TOURIST OFFICE:** Free maps and accommodations bookings. Marseille City Pass includes RTM day pass, access to 14 museums, a walking tour, ferry to Île d'If and varying discounts for city music festivals and events *(4 La Canebière ☎04 91 13 89 00 💻www.marseille-tourisme.com [M]Vieux Port [$] City Pass 1 day, €22; 2 day €29 ⏰ Open M-Sa 9am-7pm, Su 10am-5pm.)* Annex (*At train station ☎04 91 50 59 18 ⏰ Open M-F 10am-12:30pm, 1-5pm)*
- **TOURS:** Tourist office offers walking tours of the city in French daily (*One tour in English per week; ask for schedule*). **Petit Train:** Almost always full of families and tourist groups, this Disneyland-esque trolley takes tourists around the the major sites of the city (*☎04 91 25 24 69* *i* Departs on 3 different tracks: Notre-Dame de la Garde basilica, Old Marseille, and Frioul archipelago. ⏰ *From quai Belges every 30min.; from Port Frioul to the Saint Estève for the archipelago. The first two routes run Apr-Nov 10am-12:20pm and 2-6pm; the one to the archipelago runs Jul-Aug 10am-12:20pm and 2-6pm. $€7/4 for children, €6/3 for children and the one to the archipelago runs Jul-Aug $€3.5/2.5 for children.)*
- **CONSULATES:** UK *(24 av. du Prado ☎04 93 15 72 10 ⏰ Open M-F 9:30am-noon and 2-4:30pm by appointment only).* US (12 pl. Varian Fry *☎04 91 54 92 00 ⏰ Open M-F 9:30am-noon and 2-4:30pm by appointment only).*
- **LOST PROPERTY:** Although it's probably already been resold or put on a ship to Algeria. Good luck. *(41 bld. de Briançon ☎ 04 91 14 68 97.)*
- **YOUTH CENTER:** Centre Régional Information Jeunesse (CRIJ) Information on long term housing, short term employment, vacation planning (once you get that job) and services for the disabled. *(96 Canebière ☎04 91 24 33 50 💻www.crij.com [M]Noailles ⏰Open M 10am-5pm, Tu 1-5pm, W-F 10am-5pm. Limited hours July and Aug.)*
- **GLBT RESOURCES:** *(💻www.gay-sejour.com)*
- **LAUNDROMATS:** Most hostels have laundry services, even if it's not listed; just ask. (*8 rue Rudolf Pollack. ⏰Open daily 9am-7pm.*)
- **INTERNET ACCESS:** Free internet at the CRIJ. There are also many internet cafes scattered around Belsunce and the Vieux Port. Look for the North African flags in the windows– they advertise that international calls can be made from that cafe.
- **POST OFFICE:** *(1 pl. Hôtel des Postes. Take La Canebière toward the sea and turn right on rue Reine Elisabeth as it becomes Hôtel des Postes. ☎ 04 91 15 47 00 i Currency exchange availible. ⏰ Open M-W 8am-6:45pm, Th 9am-6:45pm, F 8am-6:45pm, Sa 8am-12:15pm. Branch at St-Charles as well scattered libeally around the city. Postal Code 13001.)*

Emergency!

- **SOS VOYAGEURS:** *(Gare St. Charles ☎04 91 62 12 80.)*

- **POLICE:** *(2 rue du Antoine Becker Branch at train station next to Platform A.* ☎*04 91 39 80 00).*
- **PHARMACY:** *(7 rue de la République* ☎*04 91 90 32 27* *i* *English and French spoken.* ☒ *Open daily 8:30am-7pm.)*
- **HOSPITAL: Hôpital Timone.** (264 rue St-Pierre Ⓜ️Timone. ☎*04 91 38 00 00).*

Getting There

By Plane

Aéroport Marseille-Provence (☎04 42 14 14 14 ▣*www.mrsairport.com).* It's a popular destination, so many carriers offer service to Marseille (*airport code MRS).* Air France offers flights from Paris. Ryan Air also has service to London Airports and to various offshoots of main airports throughout Europe. Shuttles (☎ *08 91 02 40 25* Ⓢ *€.30 per min)* run every 20 minutes between the airport and Gare St-Charles (Ⓢ *€8* ☒ *25min.).*

By Train

Gare St-Charles is the hub of the city, with frequent trains within France. International trains go through Paris (stations differing by ultimate destination). Trains to **Lyon** (Ⓢ *€58.* ☒ *1hr., 20 per day*), **Nice** (Ⓢ *€32.* ☒ *2hr., 20 per day*) and **Paris** (Ⓢ *€105.* ☒ *3hr., 15 per day)* For up-to-date, accurate fare information go to www.sncf.com. For those of you under 25, you can get a TER pass for €15, valid one year, and get a 50% discount on regional travel in Provence Alps Côte d'Azur (PACA), or anywhere else for that matter. Trust us, you don't want the TER from Marseille to Paris—its a long haul.

By Bus

Depot at pl. Victor Hugo, behind train station (☎*08 91 02 40 25* ☒ *Gare St-Charles. Ticket counters open M-F 6:15am-7:30pm, Sa 6:30am-6:30pm, Su 7:45am-noon, 12:45-6pm.)* Depending on location, you can buy tickets on board the bus (i.e. the closer the destination, the more likely) but we reccomend buying tickets at the window and follow ticket-window-guy's advice. To **Aix-en-Provence** (Ⓢ *€5.50.* ☒ *every 10-15min. 6:30am-8:30pm, 2 per hr. 9-11:30pm.),* **Nice** (Ⓢ *€28, students €19.* ☒ *2hr., 1 per day.),* and **Cannes.** (Ⓢ *€25, students €19.* ☒ *2-3hr., 4 per day.)*

By Ferry

SNCM (*61 bld. des Dames* ☎*08 25 88 80 88* ☒ *Open M-Sa 8:30am-8pm. Office open M-F 8am-6pm, Sa 8:30am-noon and 2-5:30pm)* **Corsica Ferries** (*7 rue Beauvau* ☎ *08 25 09 50 95* ▣*www.corsicaferries.com* ☒ *Open daily 8am-8pm.* To Corsica: *€32-65; Algeria €105-315; Sardinia €60-85)*

By Taxi

Expensive, but if you must... **Marseille Taxi** (☎*04 91 02 20 20).* **Taxi Blanc Bleu** (☎*04 94 51 50 00).* 24 hr stands surroung the Gare St-Charles and Vieux Port. To Vieux Port from Gare St-Charles €20-30. To airport €40-55.

Getting Around

Public transport is easily navigable here, with only two metro lines, and two trams covering Belsunce and Vieux Port. Le Panier is only accessible by foot (which adds to the charm, we guess) but buses run along its perimeter. Bus passes can be bought for one journey (*€1.50),* three days (*€10.50)* or 7 days (*€16).* Solo passes can be bought on the buses, and are good for MetroTram or the bus for one hour after they are first validated. All public transport runs frequently Su-W 6am-11:30, Th-Sa 6am-1am. There are Le Vélo bike stands, but they only work with European bank cards, and require a €150 deposit on your credit card. If you do have a European bank card, though it's a screaming deal at €1 an hour (under 30min free, like in Paris). Buses that you'll care about leave from Gare St-Charles and from Castellene, as well as from Vieux Port. Around the Marina though, walking is your fastest and easiest option.

Avignon is most famous (and rightfully so) as the historical home base for seven rebellious Popes who left Rome during the Babylonian Captivity. Those 39 years made Avignon a center for religion and politics in France, and its famous bridge provided one of the few passes of the river Rhone. A popular camping destination for French campers and historical buffs alike, the medieval alleys and architecture have still held up, making Avignon a city trapped in the 13th century. Its a totally doable daytrip to see everything and not leave feeling disappointed that you didn't see more, while still wondering what was over that little bridge or around that stone turret. Come here and you'll expect to hear tamborines and pipes in the background while you walk around, but it will actually just be the city's vibant bars and cafes with the occasional annoyance of a tourist tram or school group.

ORIENTATION

The town of Avignon is surrounded by a giant wall, so there are only so many ways you can get lost in it. **Rue de la République,** the main road from the train station, leads straight to the **Palais des Papes,** and divides the town into halves. Most of the cafes and restaurants are on the west side of the street, while the east side is generally comprised of hotels and private housing. Most of the shopping areas are clustered further down the main drag, or at **Halles,** the large shopping center in the middle of town. The **Rhône river** runs right by the city, and sports a very large island, the **Île de la Barthelasse.** There is camping here for those on a budget, as well as a hostel. The entire town is very walkable, and it would almost be more of a hassle to figure out the public transport; Avignon is comprised of a tangle of one-way streets and alleyways that date back to the 1200s. While you may get lost easily, it's always easy to look up and see the Palais des Papes and re-orient yourself.

ACCOMMODATIONS

HOTEL MIGNON
⬥♿(ᵗⁱ)✣ HOTEL ❸

12 rue Joseph Vernet ☎ 04 90 82 17 30 🖵www.hotel-mignon.com

Small and neat, Hotel Mignon lives up to its name. The centrally-located hotel's wood floors and pristine carpeting make it look like a model home in a Home Depot advertisement. The closet-sized bathrooms appear to be barely able to fit a person, but amazingly pack in a personal sink, toilet and shower. Book well ahead of time in July.

✤ *From the main square, go down rue St. Agricole towards the pharmacy. Make your second right onto Joseph Vernet. Hotel on the left.* **i** *Breakfast included.* ⑤ *Singles €45-55; doubles €64-80; triples and quads €81-110.*

CAMPING AUBERGE BAGATELLE
⬥♿(ᵗⁱ)✣⌂ CAMPGROUND, HOSTEL ❶

25 all Antoine Pinay- Île de la Barthelasse ☎04 90 27 16 23 🖵www.campingbagatelle.com

Over the river and through the woods, you can find cheap camping and hostelling less than 5min. from the town center. Auberge features an attached convenience store, as well as a free breakfast for basic double, quad or sextuple rooms. Both camping or hostel options have access to the establishment's facilities, which include a soccer field, basketball court, and pool.

✤ *From the Pont d'Avignon, cross the Daladier bridge, and go down staircase on the right on other side. Turn left towards signs and walk into the campground. Reception is hidden kind of next to the convenience store.* **i** *Camping and Auberge. Wi-Fi, breakfast, and linens included (unless camping).* ⑤ *Camping €6 per night; 2 people, car, camp is €10 per night in winter, €15 per night in summer; €16 for a bed in a dorm.*

provence

SIGHTS

PALAIS DES PAPES
PALACE

☎04 90 27 50 00 🖥www.avignon-tourisme.com

This giant Gothic palace was built at the height of the Catholic Church's power, when Pope Clement V decided the Vatican was too cramped. The next 6 popes that followed him remained in Avignon during a period known as the Babylonian Captivity (for the record, it wasn't in Babylon, and the popes weren't held captive). Their Palais des Papes is a maze of small passageways that lead abruptly into huge painted chambers. Painted tiles and giant murals ornately decorate select areas, most notably the papal throne room.

[i] Free audio tour with entrance. $ Nov-Feb €8.50; Mar-Sep €10.50. Includes entrance to Bridge. ⏰ Open Nov-Feb 9:30am-5:45, Mar 1-14 9am-7pm, Mar 15-Jun 9am-7pm, Jul 9am-8pm, Aug 9am-9pm, Sep 1-15 9am-8pm, Sep 16- Nov 1 9am-7pm.

PONT D'AVIGNON
BRIDGE, HISTORIC SIGHT

Port du Rhône ☎04 00 27 51 16

Step aside Palin; the Pont d'Avignon is literally a bridge to nowhere. Stopping half-way across the river Rhône, this bridge is the brainchild of St. Benezet, a shephard who one day heard angels tell him to build a bridge to Avignon. When the townspeople laughed at him, he miraculously threw a large stone into the river, laying foundation for the first arch. No one laughed at him ever again. The bridge eventually collapsed due to flooding and poor construction, and was closed until the 20th century, when they decided to open it again as a museum.

[i] Free audio tour with entrance. $ Open Nov-Feb €4, Mar-Sep €4.50. Palais and Pont ticket, €11 Nov-Feb, €13 Mar-Sep. ⏰Nov-Feb 9:30am-5:45, Mar 1-14 9am-7pm, Mar 15-Jun 9am-7pm, Jul 9am-8pm, Aug 9am-9pm, Sep 1-15 9am-8pm, Sep 16- Nov 1 9am-7pm.

MUSÉE DU PETIT PALAIS
MUSEUM

pl. du Palais des Papes ☎04 90 86 44 58 🖥www.petitpalais.com

The Musée du Petit Palais starts out slow, with your run of the mill exhibits of 19th-century paintings of saints on wooden boards. We recommend spending more time in the exhibits toward the back, which feature the works of Giotto and other quattrocento Italian artists, 14th century attempts at perspective, and the trials and tribulations of a burgeoning Renaissance. Also of note is the gory 14th century equivalent of the Passion of the Christ, "The Calvary," depicting a gold, sad, and bleeding Jesus that would make even Mel Gibson cringe.

 # Behind Palais des Papes at then end of the square. [i] Info brochures on what you're looking at scattered around the museum. $ €6, students €3. ⏰ Open M 10am-1pm and 2-6pm, W-Su 10am-1pm and 2-6pm.

FOOD

RESTAURANT NANI
ITALIAN [1]

rue de la République ☎04 90 82 60 90

Two story Avignonais restaurant specializes in *assiettes*, a pseudo calzone stuffed with meat, olives and tomatoes. Designed to resemble a small farmhouse, you'll definitely rub elbows with the locals in this popular (read: packed like sardines) restaurant.

 # Corner of rue Théodore Aubanel and rue du Provôt. $ Express lunch with salade, coffee and grande assiette €9.60. Lunch menu for €14 gets you a choice of assiette, chocolate fondue and coffee. Dinner plates €7-15. ⏰ Lunch M-Sa 11:30am-2:30pm, Dinner F-Sa 7-11pm.

FRANÇOISE
TRADITIONAL [1]

6 rue du Général Léclerc ☎04 32 76 24 77

A weird but trendy combo of cafeteria seating, baked goods and to-go sandwiches. Jams and jellies lure students and *gouteurs* (that's snackers to you) in to chill out for an hour or more over a hot cup of coffee.

i Free Wi-Fi. Credit card min. €10. $ Baked goods and sandwiches €1-5. Salads €4-9. Cafe €1.50 ⏰ Open M-Sa 8:30am-7pm.

NIGHTLIFE 🍸

WALL STREET — 💳🍸♿⛅ BAR

32 rue du Chapeau Rouge — ☎06 61 07 11 62

Unlike Wall St., this youthful bar is justly popular with just about everyone. Students and *jouers* alike come on Friday for the stockmarket theme night, where the prices at the bar increase or decrease as randomly as the market itself every 100 seconds. Twice a night the market will "crash" and all prices are slashed by 50%. Prices are posted on their projector screen. Thursday is student night and Saturday is theme night, which changes weekly. Don't let the threat of an economic bubble scare you away—the prices never rise more than €4.50 for pints and shots, and can drop as low as €2. And you thought i-banking was boring.

$ Shooters €2.50. Half-pints €2.50; pints €4.50. Does not include market night. ⏰ Open M-Sa 6pm-1:30am.

LEVEL ONE — 🍸♿ BAR

pl. Pie

For the dyed hair and grunge types, this dive bar is both the cheapest and most rough around the edges. Enjoy the 1970s American soundtrack featuring the likes of Janis Joplin and Hendrix while you shoot pool or play fooseball. The orange pleather booths are pretty groovy, unless someone more peirced than you are is sitting in it already.

i Happy hour half-priced pints. $ Shooters €2. Pints €4. Group drinking with €18 giraffes and 10 vodka shooters for €18. ⏰ Open daily 10am-1:30am. Happy hour 5-8pm.

LE CAGE — 🍸♿▼ BAR, GLBT FRIENDLY

1 av. des Sources — ☎04 90 27 00 84 💻www.thecage.fr

Avignon's hottest gay bar. Contact the bar for themed nights and special soirees.

$ Cover €10; includes 1 drink. ⏰ Open F-Su 11pm-5am.

ESSENTIALS [i]

Practicalities

- **TOURIST OFFICE:** Offers maps, guidance, and a free pass that discounts Avignon sights by 20-50%. *(41 cours Jean Juarès. Walk straight down the main drag from the train station. Its on your right after 200 m ☎04 32 74 32 74 💻www.avignon-tourisme.com ⏰ Open Apr-Oct M-Sa 9am-6pm, Su 9am-5pm. Nov-Mar M-F 9am-5pm, Sa 9am-5pm, Su 10am-noon. Closed Dec 12-Jan 1)*
- **PETIT TRAIN:** Lets be real, Avignon is a small city that's easily walkable in a day, so the Petit Trains are mostly packed with, um, let's just say those who are most susceptible to the annual flu. Takes you to all the major sights in Avignon. (*Leaves from Palais des Papes every 20min ⏰ Open daily 10am-8pm. $ €7, children €4*)
- **GLBT RESOURCES:** Le CIDcafe. Loud and proud cafe with brochures to the popular GLBT clubs and bars, such as Le Cage and L'esclave, and a schedule of GLBT theme nights in Avignon *(pl. St Pierre ☎04 90 82 30 38 💻www.lecidcafe.com).*
- **LAUNDROMAT:** La Blanchisseuse (*24 rue Lanterne ⏰ Open daily 7am-9pm.)*
- **INTERNET:** You can find free internet almost anywhere in Avignon; look out for the green sticker on the entrance to cafes, laundry mats, and stores. Both Françoise or the Laundry mat occasionally have free (but patchy) internet.
- **POST OFFICE:** *(Cours President Kennedy ☎04 90 27 54 10 ⏰ Open M-F 8:30am-6pm, Sa 9am-4pm.)*

Emergency!

- **POLICE:** Caserne de Salle. (*Bld. St. Roch* ☎*04 90 16 81 00*).
- **PHARMACY:** *(11 rue St. Agricole* ☎*04 90 82 14 20 Open daily 9am-7:15pm.)*
- **HOSPITAL: Hôpital Timone.** (264 rue St-Pierre Ⓜ️Timone. ☎*04 91 38 00 00*).

cassis   ☎04 42

This small fishing village is one of Provence's best kept secrets, at least from Americans. European tourists swarm the petit train, the quais, and the beaches to the West. However packed the port area is, you can always escape up the hill and into the *centre-ville* to the shade of the church and the peace of the central fountain, which retain the sleepy vibe of a pre-tourism era. Walk along the shore in any direction and you are guaranteed to spot pristine coves and the occasional nude sunbather (vive le France).Show off your own kibbles and bits if you must, so long as you can withstand the gawkers nearby.

ORIENTATION

Cassis is extremely walkable. Before you know it, you will have walked its circumference about 200 times. The main port is bounded by the **marina** (quai des Baux, St. Pierre, and JJ Barthelemy). **Av. Victor Hugo** is the main drag here, and leads to the *centre-ville,* as well as an array of cheaper bars and restaurants. **Rue de l'Arene** takes you East towards the **secluded beaches;** residents appear to preserve those to themselves, because a series of signs point all the tourists West instead, towards the **calanques** and more popular beaches. There is one bus from the gare to the main stop in front of the Casino on **rue de l'Arene,** putting you right in the middle of the calmer side of town. The closer you get to the port and to the beaches, the higer the prices will be.

ACCOMMODATIONS

LE COMMERCE
    🛏️🍴📶♿ HOTEL ❸

12 rue St. Clair   ☎04 42 01 09 10

Tucked away from the crazy quai des Baux, but so far as to diminish the rooms' ocean views, this hotel/restaurant offers a cheaper option for those who don't want to shell out their college fund, but still want to be close to the *centre-ville.* Way more relaxed and youthful than anywhere else in town.

☀ *One block up from quai JJ Barthelemy, on the "left" side of the marina if facing the sea.* ⓘ *Bar and restaurant. Wi-Fi available. Breakfast €7.* Ⓢ *Singles €45-50; doubles €55-75, €70-75 for ocean facing rooms.*

LE CLOS DES ARÔMES
    🛏️♿📶🍴 HOTEL ❸

10 rue Abbé Paul Mouton   ☎04 42 01 71 84 ▣www.le-clos-des-aromes.com

Adorable Riviera villa that's shockingly affordable. Definitely where your parents would stay on a budget—it's tucked away from the noise but nice enough. The shady terrace restaurant features quaint tiled roofing and wrought iron furniture that takes you back a century.

☀ *From the pl. de la République, walk up rue Adolphe Thiers until it becomes rue Abbe Paul Mouton. Hotel on your right.* ⓘ *Bar and restaurant attached. Terrace in the back. Wi-Fi as well as guides available to help with excursions and car rental.* Ⓢ *Singles €49-79; doubles €69-89; quad for €89.*

CAMPING LES CIGALES
    🛏️♿🍴 CAMPGROUND ❶

av. de la Marne   ☎04 42 01 07 34 ▣www.campingcassis.com

This shady campsite comes complete with a bar, snack shack, and electricity. It's far from the beach (1.5km), but the bus stops at the corner and will take you directly to the *centre-ville*. 205 plots for tents, cars, or campers.

From the train station, take the bus to av. de la Marne. You will have to ask bus driver to stop for you. If walking, its 2.5 km from the train station down av. Marechal. Turn left at route de Marseille, site on your left. i Bar, general store and electricity. $ €6.25 per person. €2.25 for electricity. ⏰ Open Mar 15-Nov 15.

AUBERGE DE JEUNESSE — HOSTEL [1]

La Fontasse ☎04 42 01 02 72 www.fuaj.org

Without fail, FUAJ hostels guarantee the cheapest stay that's the farthest away from anything, and this Auberge de Jeunesse is no exception. Clean rooms, a bar and youthful atmosphere don't quite make up for the 12km hike from town, although you'll be sure to encounter the most dedicated of hostel-goers way out here.

No bus. Walk 12 km on D559 towards Marseille. $ €19/night/person.

BEACHES

PRESQU'IL — BEACH

The Presqu'il features stunning views of the other calanques along the coast. A small hike will take you to its edge, where you can survey the a long strip of the coast, and where the rich Cassis population keeps their yachts.

Located on the very edge of the calanque.

LA PLAGE DE L'ARÈNE — BEACH

A farther walk, but in the opposite of all the tourists, this rocky beach is both the most secluded and the most stunning in the area.

From the bus stop, walk uphill on av. du Revestel past the fancy Châteaux and the vineyard. There will be a sign pointing you to the right. Follow it to the stairs, which lead you to the beach. The bay is called Anse de l'Arène.

LA PLAGE BESTOUAN — BEACH

Learn the extent to which old people have no shame at this packed and very French beach. You will see exposed body parts well past their prime here; maybe the Dove campaign was too successful.

Walk to the side of the harbor opposite the lighthouse. Continue uphill on av. de l'Admiral Ganteaume and follow the signs. To avoid excess nudity, keep to the left and follow the stairs around the corner. Flat white rocks to lay on as well as a view of the boats going in and out of the harbor.

LA PLAGE BLEUE — BEACH

La Plage Bleue is less of a beach and more like a series of sharp ledges of rock that jut out over the water. The water is shallow, so don't go **jumping**. Less crowded, but beware of gawkers above you.

On the way to the calanque and presqu'il. Follow directions to La Plage Bestouan, and continue av. des Calanques, and follow signs to Presqu'il. You will walk past residential areas and eventually to the end of the road. Go through the parkinglot and arrive at the beach on the other side.

FOOD

LE GRANDE MARNIER — CRÊPERIE [1]

12 quai des Baux ☎04 42 01 81 19

A crêperie that specializes in Grand Marnier specialties for cheap. They'll serve up any crêpe you can think of, and then add in some orange liqueur. If the alcohol content isn't high enough, there's a 2l bottle that's self-serve right on the walk up bar.

i Bottles of specialty Grand Marnier for sale. $ €3-5. ⏰ Open M-Sa 3-8pm.

LA VIEILLE AUBERGE — PROVENÇAL [4]

14 quai Barthelemy ☎04 42 01 73 54

Hands down, the nicest restaurant in town. Splurge here for the white tablecloths and sommelier, not to mention the traditional Provençal food. The *prix fixe* menu makes this place an affordable option, while the wood beams and Picasso-esque paintings will try to convince you otherwise.

i *Reservations accepted.* Ⓢ *Plates €15-35. Prix-fixe €24 and €33 for three course menu.* ⏰ *Open daily noon-2pm and 7-10:30pm.*

CROQUE SOLEIL
⊛⛅ DELI ❶

34 av. Victor Hugo ☎06 61 71 29 85

A one-window cafe that sells basic sandwiches, salads, and crêpes. Serves sandwiches named after various world locations, although the Californian deceivingly named *(€4.50)* is more like a Philly cheese steak. Two mini tables out front provide seating.

Ⓢ *Paninis and Sandwiches €2.50-5. Salades €5.* ⏰ *Open daily 10am-5pm.*

SAVEURS LATINES
💳♿🍸⛅ SEAFOOD ❸

3 rue S. Icard ☎04 42 72 21 24 🖥http://saveurslatines.com

Corsican restaurant hidden down a small alley in the heart of the *centre-ville*. The seating is entirely outdoors, and lures in passerby to enjoy their fixed 3 course menu of seafood and crème brulee *(€16)*.

Ⓢ *€16 lunch menu, €19 dinner menu.* ⏰ *Open M noon-1:30pm and 7-11:45pm, and W-Su noon-1:30pm and 7-11:45pm.*

NIGHTLIFE

Far from friends of the backpacker budget, the bars are expensive, don't offer happy hours, and close relatively early. The closer you are to the port, the more expensive they are.

👍 BAR DE LA FONTAINE
♿🍸⛅ BAR

31 av. Victor Hugo ☎04 42 01 72 28

A local favorite with lower prices. La Fontaine caters to a slightly older crowd who are already over the excessively hormonal scene at the port. The walls covered in Pastis posters will convince you to finally try some, if you haven't blacked out on it already.

Ⓢ *Pastis €2.50. Half pints €2.90. Mixed drinks €5.* ⏰ *Open daily 6am-midnight.*

XX SIECLE
💳♿🍸⛅ BAR

17 av. Victor Hugo ☎04 42 01 70 76

Trendy bar with New York-themed decor that's a ways from the port, but not the port's prices. The large mirror along the back wall makes the bar look bigger and more packed than really is, so don't be intimidated.

Ⓢ *Half pint €2.50. Pints €4. Mixed drinks €5.* ⏰ *Open daily 2pm-1:30am.*

BAR LE FRANCE
💳♿🍸⛅ BAR

4 quai de Baux ☎04 42 01 79 02

Bar le France is right on the water, and boasts beautiful views of the boats going in and out of the harbor. You pay for it though; the place is expensive and, like the other bars along the port doesn't host happy hours.

Ⓢ *Pints €7. Bottles €3-4. Espresso €1.80.* ⏰ *Open daily 10am-1:30am.*

ESSENTIALS

Practicalities

- **TOURIST OFFICE:** Offers brochures, maps, and advice on housing (*quai des Moulins* ☎*08 92 25 98 92* 🖥*www.ot-cassis.com* ⏰ *Open Nov-Feb M-F 9:30am-12:30pm, 2-5:30pm. Sa 10am-12:30pm, 2-5pm. Su 10am-12:30pm; Mar-Jun M-F 9am-12:30pm, Sa 9:30am-12:30pm, 2-5:30pm, Su 10am-12:30pm; Jul-Aug M-F 9am-7pm, Sa-Su 9:30am-12:30pm, 3-6pm; Sept-Oct M-F 9am-12:30pm, Sa 9:30am-12:30pm , 2-5:30pm, Su 10am-12:30pm.)*
- **TOURISM TRAIN:** This is a hilly palce and walking to the calanque could take up to

an hour from the *centre-ville*. (☎*04 42 01 09 98* 🖳*www.cassis.fr* Ⓢ *€7*. Ⓓ *daily every hour from 11:15am-6:15pm)*

- **BUS:** Bus stops at train station and takes you to La Poste. (*rue l'Arène, near the centre-ville.* Ⓓ *Runs every 20-40 min from 7am-7pm.* Ⓢ *€0.80.*)
- **POST OFFICE:** Western Union and ATM available. (*15 rue l'Arène* ☎*04 42 01 98 38* Ⓓ *Open M 8:30am-noon and 2:30-5pm, Tu 9am-noon, 2:30-5pm, W 8:30am-noon and 2:30-5pm, Th 8:30am-noon and 2:30-5:30pm, F 8:30am-noon, Sa 8:30am-noon and 2:30-5:30pm.*)
- **CALANQUE BOAT TRIP:** Stand at the port (☎*06 86 55 86 70* 🖳*www.cassis-calanques.com* Ⓓ *Boat trips from 45min-1h30.* Ⓢ*€13-19, children €7-13.*)

Emergency!

- **PHARMACY:** (*34 rue l'Arène* ☎*04 42 01 71 71* Ⓓ *Open daily 10am-6pm.*)

la ciotat ☎04 42

One stop away from Cassis, La Ciotat manages to escape the excess tourists during the low season, and even the beginning of the summer. However, once summer comes along, this sleepy fishing village explodes with parties and clubs. The town's overnight transformation from an innocuous port where middle-class Frenchmen dock their boats to party central is like Extreme Makeover Port Edition. La Ciotat's old town seems to be very confined to the port, but expanded development along the beaches has made the technical city limits somewhat undefinable. The expansion has shifted the focal point of tourism to the beaches, leaving the old port uniquely untouched by the pasty masses searching for sun in the summer. A good place for low key sailing or SCUBA diving, not to mention a calanque hike and beach time, Ciotat is sure to remain a budget traveler's paradise, so long as the rest of the world doesn't find out there is a low priced seatown in Southern France.

ORIENTATION

The town is divided into two main areas: the **Vieux Port,** and the **Beaches.** the Vieux Port is cluttered with restaurants, cafes, and bars as well as an expensive hotel or two; bring your parents or their credit cards. Getting to the **main bus stop** from the **SNCF trains station** requires a bus (#10 or 40, €1), which runs frequently from 6am-8pm. It will take you past the beaches on **av. President Wilson** and **av. Roosevelt** (Party in the USA) until the **tourist office,** which is at the dividing line between the two areas. North of the beaches is the **av. Guillaume Dulac,** which has some bars and mostly bakeries and markets; the #20 bus runs by this neighborhood, as well as the campgrounds on the city's outskirts. On the other side of the Vieux Port are the **calanques** and **Parc du Mugel,** and access to **Île Verte.**

ACCOMMODATIONS

🖾 **HOTEL AFY** 🏨 HOTEL ❹

39 quai François Mitterand ☎04 42 08 42 98

Located above a restaurant and next to the port, Hotel Afy gets a little noisy, but it's ridiculously central location makes up for it, so long as you're a heavy sleeper. Clean, simple rooms with sparse decor, but chances are you won't care what they look like; if you're staying in this neighborhood in summer, you probably don't plan on sleeping much anyway. ⚐ *From the Train station, take #10 or #40 bus to Vieux Port. Continue in direction of large warehouse (Yacht Club) until you get to Restuarant l'Louverteau. Hotel is inside restaurant. ⓘ Wi-Fi.* Ⓢ *Singles and doubles €50 winter, €60 in summer.*

HOTEL KEROR

⊛☺⊛ HOTEL ❷

12 av. Frédéric Mistral ☎04 42 83 49 49

Small family-run inn that is within spitting distance from the beach. Seven small, simple rooms are all Mme. Valentin has to offer in her home, but her homey bed and breakfast is quiet, not to mention the exact opposite of touristy. Breakfast included for additional charge.

🍴 *From the Gare Routiere, walk back from where the bus came until where av. President Wilson and rue Frédéric Mistral connect via a sharp left. Walk up the way, and the hotel is on your right; with a bike store at the corner opposite to it.* **i** *Breakfast €5.20.* Ⓢ *Low season singles €22; doubles €25-31. High season singles €23; doubles €28-33.*

CAMPING PLEIN AIR

⒲ CAMPGROUND ❶

av. Eugène Julien ☎04 42 83 07 68 🖳www.campingceyreste.com

Not totally out of the way, and accessible by bus, this campgound is clean, with a helpful reception area and space for both cars and campers. If you really don't like camping, you can rent a mobile home to stay in for the night. Plenty of shade. Shockingly, though, this is not the area's cheapest option.

🍴 *Washing machine available. Wi-Fi available. Electricity €6.26.* Ⓢ *Low season €14-24. High season €24-30.* 🕐 *Reception open til 8pm.*

HOTEL LA CROIX DE MALTE

🍸☺⒲♿🍸 HOTEL ❸

4 bld. Jean Juarès ☎04 42 08 63 38 🖳www.croix-de-malte.com

Small hotel close to the beach and away from the touristy areas, with ocean views from terraced rooms. The light blue walls have a calming effect we can't explain. Whatever it is, it makes Hotel la Croix de Malte quiet and relaxing.While more expensive than other options, it is more established than some lady's home.

🍴*From the Gare Routiere, walk back from where you can until you pass the port of Plaissance. Jean Juarès is on your left. Hotel is 30m up.* **i** *Wi-Fi, parking, breakfast, and restaurant on premises.* Ⓢ *Singles €43-50; doubles €54-71; triples €65-73; families €76-84.*

SIGHTS

◉

GRANDE PLAGE

BEACH

bl. Beaurivage.

One of the busiest 🔖**beaches** in Ciotat, Grande Plage is mostly visited by families and children. Though generally as pebbly as the rest of the coastline in the South of France, there are some sandy areas that are easier on the feet.

🍴 *Easily accessable from the #10, 40, and 20 bus, which run right along the coast.*

PARC DU MUGEL AND ROUTE DES CRÊTES

PARK

☎06 23 79 55 92

Situated right in the middle of the Bec l'Aigle massif, this lush garden of rare plants is a jarring contrast to the bustling streets that surround it. Go in the morning when it's not too hot, since the walk uphill can be a little daunting. There's a built-in shaded picnic area here as well, so bring some food in case you want to hike the route des Crêtes. The path around the massif is well laid out and has some awesome viewpoints of Marseille islands and the Bay of Ciotat.

🕐 *Open Apr-Sep 8am-8pm, Nov-Mar 9am-6pm.*

MASSIF DES CALANQUES

TRAIL, BEACH

At the end of av. des Figuerolles is the trailhead that leads down to the Calanques Figuerolles (go figure). At the end, there is a small beach. Keep in mind that the term "beach" is used very loosly here; the Massif des Calanques is more similar to a rocky cove on the waters edge. On the other side of the the peninsula, towards La Chapelle Notre Dame de la Garde (of Ciotat).

la ciotat . sights

FOOD ◨

☺⊻♿ LOULOU LA MALICE   ☺⊻♿ CAFE, TAKEOUT ❷

4 bld. Anatole France   ☎04 42 71 83 47

Unusual combination of sitdown cafe and sandwich/crêpes takeaway. Situated on the raised street above the main road, Loulou la Malice has turned the nearby parking lot into a mini garden with shaded seating, providing diners with a view of the beach and bay. Takeout available for hot/cold sandwiches and crêpes.

Ⓢ *Formule du Jour €14 for entree, plat, and dessert. Sandwiches €3.80-4. Hot panini and omelets €3-3.50.* ☼ *Open daily 10:30am-12am*

LE DÉTOUR   ☺♿ VEGETARIAN ❷

5 rue Canolle   ☎04 42 08 00 15

Bohemian and deliberately unconventional, this hole-in-the-wall establishment serves Caribbean and Mediterranean vegetarian fare. Look out for the grafitti tags and the bright red window panes. Take out available.

Ⓢ *Plates from €5-10. Take out usually €2-3 cheaper.* ☼ *Open Tu-Su 12-5:30pm.*

LES FLOTS   ☛♿⊛⊻ SEAFOOD ❶

3 rue Gueymard   ☎04 42 08 24 61 ▣www.restaurant-les-flots.com

Small seafood restaurant tucked away in an alley on the edge of the Vieux Port. Specializes in shellfish and grilled fish plates. At night, the rstaurant turns into a bar with live music until 11pm.

i *Wine cellar. Wi-Fi available.* Ⓢ *Three course special €12.* ☼ *Open daily 12-3pm, 7-11pm.*

SOUS LAS LAMPIONS   ☛♿⊻☺ CRÊPERIE ❷

quai François Mitterand   ☎04 42 71 55 06

Cute little crêperie situated right in the center the Vieux Port, but sequestered from the city's midday rush. Outdoor seating is covered and shaded by the tree growing right out of the center of the street, which makes the area feel more like an enchanted forest than a busy avenue. A bit expensive for crêpes, but a worthwhile place to relax and get out of the sun.

Ⓢ *Plates €11-16, Midi Formule €11 for plat and dessert.* ☼ *Open M-F 9am-6pm, Sa 9am-midnight.*

NIGHTLIFE ◧

☒ BAR L'ABRI CÔTIER   ☛♿⊻☺ BAR

1 rue Jean Jaures   ☎04 42 08 64 23 www.restaurant-abricotier.com

Popular with local youth, sailors, and girls who love sailors, this marina bar is not as rough around the edges as you'd expect, but still provides some salty air ambience and attitude. Come around sunset when the boats return to harbor after a long day at sea.

Ⓢ *Beer €2.80. Rum and vodka €5.* ☼ *Restaurant open noon-4pm. Bar from 6pm-midnight.*

☒ L'ASPHALTE   ☛♿⊛⊻☺ JAZZ BAR

1160 av. Guillaume Dulac   ☎04 42 70 65 46 ▣www.lasphalte.com

Brand new rock/jazz bar in the new part of town. Though it's name suggests otherwise, l'Asphalte is actually meticulously clean; the bar makes up for its straight edge by cranking up American rock music to enhance their grunge factor.

♯ *#20 bus to pl. Guillaume Dulac.* *i* *8 beer on tap, live music on Tu and Sat.* Ⓢ *Shooters €2.50. Pints €3-4. Wi-Fi €3 per hour.* ☼ *Open M-Sa 8am-midnight.*

BAR CRISTAL AND LOUNGE   ♿⊻☺ BAR

quai François Mitterand   ☎04 42 08 41 33

Bar on the port at the corner of the Vieux Port where you can find the cheapest pastis (€1.50). Local suits and workers in overalls converge here during their lunch break to enjoy the view of the port and sip their drinks while munching on the free peanuts. Open for breakfast as well.

🍃 *Vieux Port bus stop.* 💲 *Pastis €1.50. Breakfast €2. Drinks €7.* 🕓 *Open daily 6am-midnight.*

YACHT CLUB SUR LES QUAIS
⚲♈♿ CLUB

46 quai François Mitterrand ☎04 42 08 14 14 ▣www.yclc.com

Giant warehouse club that explodes during the summer months. Two stories of dance floor with a massive iron ship marooned in the center, also serving as a dance platform. Only open from June to Sept, this place more than makes up for the closure during the rest of the year. Featuring jazz, salsa, world music, DJs, and even black tie events, this club makes up for the surprisingly low number of bars and clubs.

💲 *Cover varies on event.* 🕓 *M-Sa 10pm-3am. Open June-Sept.*

ESSENTIALS
🔋

Practicalities

- **TOURIST OFFICE:** Offers free maps, free hotel bookings, and information on restaurants, sights and hotels. *(bld. Anatole France* ☎04 42 08 61 32 ▣www.toursime-laciotat.com 🕓 Open Nov-May daily 9am-noon, 2-6pm; Jun-Sep M-Sa 9am-8pm, Su 10am-1pm.)*

- **MARINA:** Info on docking and boat rental. *(☎04 42 08 08 00)*

- **INTERNET:** Wi-Fi available at Bar l'Asphalte.

- **POST OFFICE: La Poste.** *(28 av. Theodore Aubanel* ☎04 42 83 80 65 🕓 *Open M-Tu 9:30am-noon and 1:30-4:30pm, Th-F 9:30am-noon and 1:30-4:30pm, Sa 9-11:45am.)*

Emergency!

- **POLICE: Hotel de Police.** *(square de Verdun* ☎04 42 83 83 40)*

- **HOSPITAL:** *(bld. Lamartine* ☎04 42 08 76 00)*

Getting There
🗺

Gare Routiere **buses** stop right in front of tourist office and go throughout the city. *(☎04 42 08 90 90 🕓 Buses run 6am-8pm.)* Gare SNCF **trains** go to Marseille and Toulon. *(☎36 35 0 891 70 3000).*

orange ☎0490

Orange may exude an attractive small town vibe, but that charm only lasts until about 4pm; by that point, you will have circled through its worthwhile sights about 8 times. All the same, Orange is one of the last strongholds of provincialism in Provence that remains untarnished by tourists. Its tiny street cafes and boulangeries are enough to entertain the locals, who live quiet lives, raise their kids, or enjoy their retirement in the shade of the Roman theater that dominates the town's skyline. Because of this unique demographic, there are few bars and fewer young people older than high school age left in the town. You can still find locals here who don't speak a word of English, but who are all too happy to try to communicate, a sense of generosity that has since been lost in other parts of France.

ORIENTATION
▣

The town is easily navigable by foot. The **train station** is a straight shot into the *centre-ville*, on **rue de la République**, where you find the city's shops. **Place de la République** is where you'll find your requisite cafes and brasseries; turn left from the place to reach the **theatre** and its **museum**. Behind the theatre is the **Parc Colline Saint Eutrope**, a hill that serves as the southern border to the town and the natural grade upon which the theater was built. The town's boutique hotels and small shops are situated between these two locations, along with a network of alleyways that make little sense. Don't worry though—if you get turned around, walking any direction for 5min. will bring you to the edge of town, and you can reorient yourself according to the **Parc.**

ACCOMMODATIONS

Most of the accommodations in Orange are boutique hotels in the old city, or camping sites and chain hotels in the outskirts. While the chain hotels are cheaper, it's worth it to stay within the walls of the old city especially if you're sharing a room—while these aren't exactly hostel prices, you'll find the most affordable petit hotels in all of France.

ST. FLORENT
♨(ᵗⁱᵖ)☒ HOTEL ❸

4 rue du Mazeau ☎04 90 34 18 53 ◾www.hotelsaintflorent.com

Small boutique hotel less than a block from the theatre. Features small and brightly colored blue, pink, and orange rooms. More like a small B and B, but without the insane prices.

⚐ *Facing the theatre, walk to the right half a block. Turn right on rue du Mazeau, hotel is on the right.* *i* TVs with cable. ⓢ *Singles €35; doubles and triples €77.*

L'HERBIER D'ORANGE
♨(ᵗⁱᵖ)☒ HOTEL ❸

8 pl. aux Herbes ☎04 90 34 09 23 ◾www.lherbierdorange.com

A modern chic hotel with all the comforts of a boutique, small rooms face an inner coutyard where breakfast is served. Nestled in the corner of the pl. aux Herbes, this is a quiet hotel bigger than the the usual small French establishment. Each room is scented with Provençal herbs and perfumes.

⚐ *From the theater, turn right and walk half a block to rue du Mazeau. Turn right and walk until in pl. aux Herbes, hotel on the right.* ⓢ *Singles from €37; doubles from €45-55.*

FORMULE 1
♨ᴊ(ᵗⁱᵖ) HOSTEL ❷

rue Agis Rigord. Le Jonquier sud. ☎08 91 70 53 45 ◾www.formule1.com

When you and your two friends don't want to spend any more than €8 each for a shared room, this is where you go. 10min walk from the *centre-ville,* and about a million miles away from boutique charm, this cut and dry hostel provides a bed to sleep in, clean, shared baths, and not much else. It's not a place to socialize or mingle. If you find anything cheaper, they will match the price. Don't worry though, you won't.

⚐ *From the tourist office, walk away from the city center, over the canal on Caderousse. Turn right on rue Agis Rigord. Hotel is on your right.* *i* Breakfast €3.70. TV with cable. ⓢ *Singles, doubles, and triples €24.*

LE JONQUIER CAMPING
♨ᴊ CAMPGROUND ❸

rue Alexis Carrel ☎04 90 34 49 48 ◾www.campinglejonquier.com

Not the cheapest camping, but it's there. 15min. from the city center, and equipped with a mini-golf course, pool and sauna. 70 plots for parking or single tenting.

⚐ *From the tourist office: walk away from the city center, over the canal on Caderousse. Turn right on rue Agis Rigord. Follow signs to Camping for another 15min. walk.* *i* Electricity not included. Playground, pool, and tennis court. ⓢ *Rooms €24.*

SIGHTS

THEATRE ANTIQUE AND MUSEUM
♨☒ HISTORICAL SITE

pl. des Freres Mounet ☎04 90 51 17 60 ◾www.theatre-antique.com

Orange's *theatre antique* is the best preserved Roman ampitheater in Western Europe, and the price of admission is worth the view of the city from the stadium's nosebleed sections alone. As the informative audio tour included in your ticket price will tell you, the theater originally hosted Roman productions of

Greek dramas, then devolved into a forum for pantomime, and eventually stage pornography. Rome fell, and today things are a little tamer: the statues that were once situated in the alcoves of the theatre are housed in the adjoining **Musée d'Art et Histoire** (admission is included in Theatre visit). It's a good thing that the museum is free, because its murals of the history of Orange might otherwise be a disappointment.

ℹ Audio tour included. $ €8, students €6. Ticket prices include Theatre and Museum. ⏰ Open M-Sa 11am-12am.

PARC COLLINE SAINT-EUTROPE — PARK

The park not only boasts the best view of Orange, but also houses some of the city's more innocuous sights, including an oak tree that was planted by Queen Julia of the Netherlands in 1952. As if a less-than-notable monarch planting a tree in a less-than-notable French city isn't exciting enough for you, you can also see a destroyed fortress that lasted no longer than 51 years (1622-1673). The castle was ordered to be destroyed by Louis XIV who centralized the power of the French monarchy. Keep in mind that this was also the monarch who moved all of his nobles to Versailles so he could play royal day care. Anyway, those ruins are in the parc too, as well as the usual trees and winding pathways.

➔ It's the large hill behind the theatre antique, a short walk around the theatre up either the Decendre des Princes des Baux, or the Montée des Princes d'Orange. ⏰ Essentially open all the time, but we don't advise checking it out at night.

ARC DE TRIOMPHE — MONUMENT

av. de l'Arc de Triomphe

When you feel compelled to see a less-famous replica of a famous Parisian sight, walk to the end of the street that bears its name and take two seconds to snap a picture of Orange's newly restored Arc. Built in commemoration of the Roman victory over the Gauls, the carvings on the Arc depict a series of captive Gauls in chains. Dates from the 1st century CE, as do all Roman things in Orange.

FOOD

AU PETIT PATIO — 🌿♿🍸 ROMANTIC [3]

58 cours Aristride Briand ☎04 90 29 69 27

Best (and probably only) gourmet meal for under €20. Outside patio area is covered in ivy and ringed by terra cotta roof tiles and whitewashed walls, making for an intimate dining experience that keeps out the riff raff. Four-course meal starts with sampling appetizers, followed by Provençal egg and salad, olive stuffed chicken and potatos, and coffee with rasberry mousse *(€24)*. If you splurge for the set menu *(€33)*, you have a choice of chocolate fondue for dessert.

$ 5 course lunch special €18, dinner specials €24-33. ⏰ Open M-Tu 12-2:30pm and 7-11:30pm, Th-Sa 12-2:30pm and 7-11:30pm.

ACADEMY OF BILLIARDS — ♿🍸📶 AMERICAN [1]

67 cours Pourtoules ☎04 32 81 17 90

See how the French interprete an "American diner" at this bar/diner/pool hall, complete with 9 billiard tables and a tournament every Monday night. Serves burgers and sandwiches, but finally gives into French culture with *croque monsieurs (€3.50)*.

ℹ Billiards use €12 per hour. $ Burgers and sandwiches €3-8. Pizza €6.60-7.80. Beer €2.40. ⏰ Open M-Sa 7am-1:30am.

ROSELIÈRE — ♿🍸 TRADITIONAL [2]

16 rue Ancien Hotel de Ville ☎04 90 34 50 42

This little restaurant resists any and all influence that is not specifically French and more specifically Provençal, going so far as to routinely violate anti-smoking laws on the grounds of maintaining French culture. We're not sure what the string of mannequins in underwear and accordions that hang from the ceiling says about Provençal tradition, but nevermind. Serves dishes as bold as its attitude, such as pigs feet, sardine salad, rillettes, and foie gras.

i In case you missed it, smoking is allowed. $ Dishes €7-11. ⏰

CHEZ DANIEL ITALIAN [2]

10 rue Segund Waber ☎04 90 34 63 48

Hidden in an alleyway off of pl. de la République, this Italian pizzeria is probably a better choice for cheap dessert, since the pizza isn't as budget friendly. Chocolate mousse and crêpes are some of the options available, but if you are dying for a slice, you'll have to get a small pie *(€8-10).*

$ €2.50-3 crêpes, €4-5 desserts, €8-10 pizzas. ⏰ Open M-Sa 12-10:30pm.

NIGHTLIFE

Orange does not have any outright bars, or many people between the ages of 20-30 (we suspect there's a causal relationship here). As a result, most local hangouts are simply cafes that stay open late, like the **Academy of Billiards**.

ESSENTIALS

Practicalities

- **TOURIST OFFICE:** Offers free maps, free hotel booking and guides on housing rentals and sights in Orange and surrounding areas. *(5 cours Aristride Briand ☎ 04 90 34 70 88 💻www.otorange.fr. ⏰Open M-Sa 10am-6pm, Su 10am-1:30pm.)*
- **BANKS:** ATMs are located along rue Voltaire, from the East old gate of the city.
- **POLICE MUNICIPAL:** *(427 bld. Daladier ☎04 90 51 55 55. ⏰ Open M-F 8am-noon, 1-5pm.)*
- **LAUNDROMAT:** **Laverie** *(5 cours Pourtoules ⏰ Open daily 7am-9pm.)*
- **HOSPITAL:** *(10 de l'abrian ☎04 90 11 21 53).*

Getting There

The easiest way to get to Orange is by **train.** The local train station *(☎04 90 11 88 03)* provides services to and from **Marseille** and **Toulon.** *($ €13. ⏰ 1½hr.)* High-speed **TVN** trains to **Paris**depart and arrive twice a day. *($ €85. ⏰ 3hr. 20min.)*

Getting Around

Orange is a very walkable city. If you're anti-exercise, there's Vaucluse runs a local bus system, which also connects it to neighboring small towns *(☎04 90 16 15 00 💻www.vaucluse.fr).* The train station is about 3km outside of the center of town, but is easily accessible by taxi *(€10).*

arles ☎0490

Combine ancient Rome with French culture and a psychotic Dutch artist, and you get the eccentric historical cocktail that is Arles. Every street in this town seems to end in a Roman ruin, a cafe that inspired a Van Gogh painting, or both. This historical legacy has transformed Arles into a hotspot for busloads of French tourists. If you can stand the crowds, the old city does have its classical charm, not to mention its Roman ruins; bullfights are still held in the town's ancient amphitheatre. Arles is the destination for those who want to experience a Provencal small town without actually having to stand the slower pace of neighboring areas. Local tortured artists and musicians cultivate a small but active bar and concert scene here; the hype peaks around July during the local photography festival.

ORIENTATION

Getting into Arles is fairly easy from the **train station.** Follow the signs to one of the northern gate of the city. **Rue Voltaire** leads right up to the **Amphitheatre,** and is cluttered with ATMs and cheap hotels. Behind the Ampitheatre is the **Theatre Antique,** which is on **rue de la République.** This main road goes by all the museums and the nun cloister. Cafes and brasseries within the city congregate around the **pl. de la Forum,** as well as **pl. de la République.** Further south is the edge of the old city, **bld. George Clemenceau,** where the bars and more modern restaurants and concert venues are. This bld. turns into **Des Lices,** where you find the **tourist office,** right next to the carousel.

ACCOMMODATIONS

AUBERGE DE JEUNESSE ♿ (Wi-Fi) 🍸 HOSTEL ❷

20 av. Maréchal Foch ☎04 90 96 18 25 💻www.fuaj.org

Standardized as always, the local branch of this regional chain of hostels is situated 10min. from tourist office. While Auberge de Jeunesse has the expected seating area, bar and clean rooms, the catch here is that there is a midnight curfew and lockout from 10am-5pm. So you forgot your camera? Or your Epipen? Bummer for you.

 # Take bus #3 to the tourist office from the train station (last bus at 7:15pm). Behind the tourists office is Émile Zola. Walk straight and follow the road as it turns to the left over the train tracks. Auberje de Jeunesse signs point for you to turn left onto Maréchal Foch. i Free breakfast. $ Dorms €17. 🕐 Reception open from 7-10am, and 5-11pm (midnight July-Aug). Auberge is closed 10am-5pm daily.

HOTEL DE LA MUETTE 🚭 🍸 (Wi-Fi) HOTEL ❸

15 rue des Suisse ☎04 90 96 15 39 💻www.hotel-muette.com

Be careful not to call this establishment Spanish within earshot of its owners: the pictures of bullfighters that line la Muette's walls and the bull's head mounted above the reception are both very much Provençal. Quiet hotel right in the middle of the city and miraculously sequestered from tourists. Large rooms with quilted beds and tile floors. 1-5 person rooms available.

 # Facing the arena on rue Voltaire, walk around the arena to the right until getting to rue des Arenes. Make your second right onto rue Robert Doisneau. Hotel will be on your left in the place. i Breakfast €8. $ Singles €48-60; doubles €54-65; triples, quads, and quints €75-90.

HOTEL VOLTAIRE 🍸 (Wi-Fi) ♿ HOTEL ❷

1 pl. Voltaire ☎04 90 96 49 18

Budget hotel close to the amphitheater and above restuarant and bar. A little overboard with the bullfighting theme, but we guess that's allowed. Rooms are simple (bed and that's it) and showers are extra.

 # From the north gate, walk straight down the street past the fountain (tile mosaic thing) until you get to pl. Voltaire. Hotel on your left. $ Rooms with sink €30, with showers €35, with shower and TV €40.

LE CALENDAL (Wi-Fi) 🍸 ♿ HOTEL ❹

5 rue Porte de Laure ☎04 90 96 11 89 💻www.lecalendal.com

This posh hotel and spa sits right next the Amphitheater; you can see it from the lobby. Garden dining area and classy bullfighting pics decorating this Provençal hotel.

 # Get to the amphitheatre. Behind it is the pl. de Bornier. The hotel is across from the crêpes restaurant. i Spa? Oh yeah. Free Wi-Fi. 2 rooms are handicapped accessible. Parking upon reservation. Breakfast €12. $ Singles €69-159; doubles €79-159; triples €119-159; quads €159.

SIGHTS

👁

The Passport liberte *(€9; students €7)* offers entrance to a total of 5 sights, and is valid for 1 month. The Roman Pass offers entrance to just the Antique sites, but is worth the same as the Pssport Liberte, so go with that one for everything.

LES ARÈNES
AMPHITHEATER

☎04 90 49 36 86 🖥www.arlestourisme.com

The giant amphitheater dates back to the first century AD, and still showcases bullfights and other spectacles. The arena used to hold 20,000 spectators; during gladiator tournaments, citizens mobbed the stadium and filled the ampitheater to capacity in under 10min. It took 25min. for the audience to filter out afterwards. You think the time difference says something about human violence? The small tower provides a pretty impressive view of Arles' tiled rooftops.

$ €6, students €4.50. ⏰ Open Nov-Feb 10am-5pm, Mar-Apr 9am-6pm, May-Sep 9am-7pm, Oct 9am-6pm.

MUSÉE DE L'ARLES ANTIQUE
MUSEUM

Presqu'il du Cirque Romain ☎04 90 18 88 80 🖥www.arlestourisme.com

Some of the best preserved archeological finds from Arles' Roman days are just outside of town. Ancient history buffs and tourists who are dying to get that SPQR tattoo should definitely check out this museum, which traces the Camargue from prehistoric times through the decline of the Western Roman empire in the 6th century AD. The collection features mosaics, *amphorrae* (ancient storage jars), statues and jewelry, as well as the second-largest collection of ancient sarcophagi in the world.

➜ Presqu'ile to Cirque Romaine. 10min. from the centre-ville. From tourist office, turn left, walk along George Clemenceau to the end and follow signs to the museum. Or take bus #1 (dir. Barriol) from bld. Georges Clemenceau to Salvador Allende. $ €6, students €4. During expo. €7.50, students €5.50. ⏰ Open M 10am-6pm, W-Su 10am-6pm.

ABBAYE DE MONTMAJOUR
ABBEY

☎04 90 54 64 17 🖥www.monuments-nationaux.fr

5km from the center of Arles, this medieval abbey has been greeting visitors ever since the Prosper Mérimée decided that it was about time to show off the place in the mid 19th-century. And it was quite a lot to brag about. Over the centuries, the abbey amassed a fortune in donations and unofficial payments for religious ceremonies and blessings; a pretty good deal for the monks, if you ask us. A UNESCO World Heritage Sight, the courtyard reveals the magnificent **Pons de l'Orme** tower, and the arched ceilings will keep you gazing up in awe. Be careful not to run into any of the scattered thick collumns.

➜ From Arles gare routiere, take #17 bus or 11. 10min, M-Sa 15 per day. Su 6 per day €1-2. $ Ages 18-26 €4.50, under 18 free. ⏰ Open July-Sep daily 10am-6:30pm. Oct-Mar Tu-Su 10am-5pm, Apr-Jun daily 9:30am-6pm. Last entry 45min. before close. July-Sep guided French tours by reservation.

THÉÂTRE ANTIQUE
THEATER

rue de la Calade ☎04 90 93 05 23

Especially when compared to the local amphitheater and gardens, Arles' theater is much less impressive than, say, the *théâtre antique* in Orange, or even your local theater back home. Nearly in ruins, the theater is only recognizable by its large seating area and two remaining columns, which are often hidden behind the scaffolding of modern productions that make use of the ruins' excellent acoustics. Tarrif included when you visit the amphitheater. If you didn't do that, you can get a solid (free) look around the theatre since the fence is low, but be prepared to beat back tourists to get the prime picture spot.

$ Tarrif included with visit to amphitheatre. Students €6. ⏰ Open Nov-Feb 10am-5pm, Mar-Apr 9am-6pm, May-Sep 9am-7pm, Oct 9am-6pm.

FOOD

FADOLI
SANDWICHES, SUSHI ❶

46 rue des Arènes ☎04 90 49 70 73

Hole-in-the-wall panini bar that also serves sushi (because the two go hand in hand, obviously). Creative panini names such as Aphrodite are less descriptive than the Vitamin E panini, which overflows with enough avocado to make a Californian hallucinate and see the Golden Gate Bridge.

Near the pl. de la Forum. $ Paninis €3-6, sushi €7. ⏰ Open Tu-Su noon-late.

LE TROPICAL
CRÊPERIE, BAR ❷

28 rue Porte de Laure ☎04 90 47 55 08

Crêperie and bar with creative indoor seating constructed to look like an outdoor garden. Serves elaborate ice cream creations that render a banana split the most simple choice on the menu. Skylights and ivy growth on the "patio" make it feel authentic, even though the A/C is welcomingly modern.

$ Salades and plates €8-12 Desserts and ice cream €3-8. Crêpes €2.50-4. Beer €2.50-3. ⏰ daily 10m-12:30am.

SOLEILIS
DESSERTS ❶

9 rue Docteur Fanton ☎04 90 93 30 76

Best ice cream ever. Features flavors previously unknown to the pallet, such as *fadoli*—an awesome mix of honey, almonds, and nectar of the Gods—and bitter almonds that really aren't bitter at all.

$ 1 scoop €1.40, sundae €7. ⏰ Open July-Aug M 2-6:30pm, Tu-Su 2:30-6:30pm and 8:30-10pm or later. Set-Oct and Mar-Jun daily 2-6:30pm.

DUNE
TRADITIONAL, NORTH AFRICAN ❸

8 rue Reattu ☎04 90 49 66 67

French *assiettes* with an Algerian twist, such as tomatoes, olives, lamb, and vegetarian. Look for the the bright pictures of sand dunes and camels in the front windows, which are as cheesy as the restaurant in unique.

i Vegetarian plates. $ Assiettes €7.50-13. Prix fixe €16 for ansiette, mint tea and pastry. ⏰ Open M-Sa 12-2pm and 7-9pm.

NIGHTLIFE

WALLABEER
BAR

7 rue Molière ☎06 67 42 84 84

Australian bar with dancing at night and a terrace overlooking the main road that's ideal for people-watching. Fun atmosphere with surfboards and mounted TVs on the walls featuring rugby and surfing.

i Entrance behind the main road. $ Beer €2.50-5. Bottles of liquor €50-60. ⏰ Open Oct.-May Tu-Su 10am-1am or later, Jun-Aug daily 10am-1am or later.

CARGO DE NUIT
CLUB, VENUE

7 av. Sadi-Carnot ☎04 90 49 55 99 💻www.cargodenuit.com

Arles' only concert venue and nightclub features a wide range of music, from jazz to rock to DJs. Due to its monopoly on clubbing, its very popular with young locals and travelers.

i Concerts scheduled online. $ Check online for varying prices. Tickets available at location and at fnac.com ⏰ Concerts open doors at 9pm for start at 9:30 or 10pm.

L'APOSTROPHE
BAR, CAFE

7 pl. du Forum ☎04 90 96 34 17 💻www.lapostroph-arles.com

Relaxed bar and cafe in the pl. du Forum, right next to where Van Gogh painted Cafe du Soir. Covered seating inside; hosts soirees in winter.

i Ben and Jerry's fridge. $ Beer 2.50-4. Mixed drinks €5. ⏰ Open M-Sa 8am-12:30am (or later), Su 9am-close.

COCO BONGO BAR

14 bld. des Lices ☎04 90 43 55 27 www.resto-bar-coc-bongo.fr

Cuban-themed tapas bar that serves customers long into the night. Fake barrels of rum scattered around the bar serve as tables. Salsa dancing every Wednesday.

$Tapas €3, beer €2, run drinks €3. ⏰ Open low season daily 9am-12am, high season daily 9am-1:30am.

ESSENTIALS

Practicalities

- **TOURIST OFFICES:** *(esplanade de Chares de Gaulle. From the train station, turn left and walk to pl. Lamartine, and left onto bld. Émilie Courbes. Walk all the way around the city, following the wall, and turn right at the interesction of the southeast old tower (where av. Victor Hugo turns into bld. des Lices) onto bld. des Lices. ☎04 90 18 41 20 www.arlestourisme.com i Will book hotels for €1. ⏰ Open daily Apr-Sept 9am-6:45pm; Oct-Mar 9am-4:45pm.)*
- **LUGGAGE STORAGE:** Hotel Acacias, *(2 rue de la Cavalerie ☎04 90 96 37 88 $ €5/day. ⏰ Open daily 7:30am-10pm.)*
- **LAUNDROMATS:** Laverie Miele, *(12 rue Portagnel $ Wash €3.50-7, dry €1 per 10 min. ⏰ Open daily 7am-9pm.)*
- **INTERNET ACCESS:** Cafe Taxiphone, *(31 pl. Voltaire. ☎04 90 18 87 40 $ €3/hr. ⏰ Open daily 9am-noon, 2:30-9pm.)*
- **POST OFFICE:** *(5 bld. des Lices, next to tourist office ☎04 90 18 41 15 i Currency exchange available. Open M 8:30am-6pm, Tu-W 8:30am-7pm, Th-F 8:30am-6pm, Sa 8:15am-12:30pm.)*
- **POSTAL CODE:** 13200.

Emergency!

- **POLICE:** *(corner of bld. des Lices and av. des Alyscamps ☎04 90 18 45 00).*
- **AMBULANCE:** SMUR *(☎04 90 49 29 22).*
- **HOSPITAL:** *(quartier Fourchon ☎04 90 49 29 29).*

Getting Around

- **PETIT TRAIN:** *(☎06 15 77 67 47).* Leaves from the main tourist office and Les Arenes every 40 min to your the old city. Apr-Oct only 10am-7pm. 30 min. €6.50.

aix-en-provence ☎04 42

In Aix-en-Provence—the city of Paul Cézanne, Victor Vasarely, and Émile Zola—nearly every golden facade or cafe has had a brush with creative genius. In keeping with such a high-art history, Aix continues to boast a flourishing cultural scene with a world-renowned music festival held every July and over 40,000 students who provide the fuel during the year. When it comes to the *vieille ville* (old city), it may very well feel as if there are more restaurants and shops per capita than anywhere else in France. In the summertime, tourists come in droves to take advantage. There's always the escape to nearby Mont Ste-Victoire, but no matter the crowds, Aix's loveliness remains unspoiled.

ORIENTATION

You're in Aix-en-Provence. So far so good. Now you need to find **pl. de la Rotonde,** a large, spritzing fountain and traffic circle that marks the entrance to the *vieille ville.* This is your homebase and the hub for Aix's public transportation. Thankfully, the **tourist office** is right next door, so you'll probably pick up a map and render this orientation useless. But just in case, here's the lowdown.

From pl. de la Rotonde, **av. des Belges** stretches downhill away from the old city and toward another traffic circle where it meets **av. de L'Europe.** The **Gare Routière** (bus station) is at this intersection, and the **Auberge de Jeunesse** is a 30min. walk straight along av. de l'Europe (or a 5min. bus ride on #4). Back at the fountain and your home-base (keep your eye on the ball), **cours Mirabeau** is a tree-lined boulevard with numerous cafes. This is your promenading ground for essential services, food, and partying at all hours. Any left turn on cours Mirabeau leads into the alleys of the old city with shops and restaurants galore. The best way to reach the heart of the old city, **pl. de l'Hotel de Ville,** is by using a map from the tourist office (sorry bud... those medieval streets are confusing.) Other awesome squares in the old city are **pl. des Cardeurs** to one side of pl. de l'Hotel de Ville and **pl. Richelme** just below it.

The remaining main street to know is **av. Bonaparte,** which exits from pl. de la Rotonde in the opposite direction of cours Mirabeau. The next main street av. Bonaparte hits is the perpendicular **cours Sextius,** which has nightlife hotspots. It forms one border of the old city. Moving in a circle around the old city from Cours Sextius, **bld. Jean Jaurès/bld. Aristide Briand** (same street, but the name changes), **cours Saint Louis/bld. Carnot** and **bld. du Roi René** form the other borders. Now that you're oriented, go eat a *trianon* cake at **Patissier Riederer.**

ACCOMMODATIONS

At Aix's most affordable accommodations—the friendly youth hostel and leafy campgrounds—you'll have to accept being at a slight remove from *centre ville.* Thankfully, the bus service is so excellent that you won't feel the difference. The price jumps €20 or more as you approach the middle of town, but the hotels tend to be well situated on the periphery of the old city, and most offer amenities and Provençal charm. Staying in town might be pricey, but you'll get to appreciate Aix from the heart.

AUBERGE DE JEUNESSE — YOUTH HOSTEL ❶

3 av. Marcel Pagnol ☎04 42 20 15 99 www.auberge-jeunesse-aix.fr

Aix's most affordable accommodation is a veritable institution that sleeps 140 people in long hallways of four-person dormitories. The uniform bunk beds are comfortable, and although the baths vary in quality—with the occasional absence of a mirror or toilet seat—the porcelain is spotless. Without a doubt, the hostel's best feature is the casual restaurant and lounge, which gets going at 7:30pm. You can eat beautifully *(€5)*, or grab a beer and listen to the music.

From pl. de la Rotonde or the Gare Routière, take bus #4 (dir: La Mayanelle) to the Vasarely stop, and the hostel gates are right there. Alternatively, walk away from the city center down av. de l'Europe. Pass through three traffic circles and follow well-marked signs. ℹ Breakfast included. Dinner €5. $ 4-bed dorms €19 with a HI card (€11). ⏰ Open daily 7am-2:30pm and 4:30pm-1am. Breakfast 7-9am. Vacate rooms by 10am for cleaning.

HOTEL PAUL — HOTEL ❷

10 av. Pasteur ☎04 42 23 23 90 hotel.paul@wanadoo.fr

A charming farmhouse converted into a no-frills hotel with simple rooms. In keeping with the homage to Cézanne in the lobby, there are dozens of flowers in the gorgeous garden. The rooms may not have A/C, and some lack showers, but they are equipped with fans, double beds, and miniature pastoral landscapes. Overall, the feel is lovely and the hotel is perfectly situated with respect to the *centre ville*. Reserve in advance and expect reception to be accommodating but strict about hotel rules.

⚑ *From pl. de l'Hotel de Ville, walk straight uphill on rue Gastan de Saporta until it exits the old city and becomes av. Pasteur. Continue straight, and the hotel is on your right. 10min. by foot.* ⓘ *Breakfast €5.* ⓢ *Singles €46-56; doubles €47-57; triples €69.* ⓩ *Reception opens at 7:15am.*

HOTEL DU GLOBE
⚑⬧❈ HOTEL ❸

74 cours Sextus ☎04 42 26 03 58 💻www.hotelduglobe.com

Between the powerful A/C and the sweet-smelling rooms in Provençal blue and white, this two-star hotel close to the heart of Aix is undeniably appealing. The sun-soaked terrace looks up at the cathedral steeple, there's a recently renovated breakfast salon in the lobby, and the amiable elevator speaks in a woman's voice as the doors are opening. Request a room on the higher floors with a balcony over cours Sextus.

⚑ *On Cours Sextus across from the Apple Store.* ⓘ *Breakfast €7.80.* ⓢ *May-Sept singles €46, with bath €62; doubles €78; triples €99. Oct-Apr singles €42, with bath €59; doubles €74; triples €96. Daily tax €0.85.*

CAMPING ARC-EN-CIEL
⚑((ᵠ)) CAMPGROUND ❶

50 av. Malacrida ☎04 42 26 14 28 💻www.campingarcenciel.com

The old legend is true: there is a pot of gold at the end of the rainbow, and it's Camping Arc-en-Ciel. A gorgeous campground run by the the Carlier-Berger family since 1950, the 50 campsites are usually filled up with happy campers in vans and tents. Each site has electricity, running water, and free Wi-Fi in addition to shared goods like the public pool, ping-pong table, and TV lounge. The bridge over the green river flowing through the campground is straight out of Monet.

⚑ *From the city center, take bus #3 down cours Gambetta until the Les 3 Sautets stop. Walk along av. Malacrida, and the campground is on your right. Signs point the way.* ⓢ *1 person €12.55. 2 people €19.20; €6.40 per person thereafter.* ⓩ *Open Apr-Sept. Gates open daily 8am-8pm. Otherwise, personal keys given upon request with a €10 deposit. Quiet hour 11pm.*

CAMPING CHANTICLEER
⚑((ᵠ)) CAMPGROUND ❶

41 av. du Val St. André ☎04 42 26 12 98 💻www.campingchanticleer.com

This complex of campsites has an on-site restaurant that stays open late, a sparkling pool, a beach volleyball court, and a view of the hills. The communal baths are immaculate, and the miniature cabins rented on a weekly basis make for especially economical accommodations in Aix if you're traveling as a big group. Nature-lovers won't mind being far from the city center, and there's an easy 10min. bus ride into town.

⚑ *From the city center, take bus #3 to the Val St-André stop. Walk straight uphill to the traffic circle and turn right. Follow the signs for the campground.* ⓢ *June-July tent sites €7.40; €6.60 per person; electricity €4.10; cabins €500-750. Aug-May tent sites €7.10; €6.20 per person; electricity €3.40; cabins €428-694.*

SIGHTS
◉

🖼 FONDATION VASARELY
⚑ MUSEUM

1 av. Marcel Pagnol ☎04 42 20 01 09 💻www.fondationvasarely.org

It's like nothing you've ever seen before; after all, the very act of seeing changes the dizzying shapes before your eyes. The father of optical-illusion art, the Hungarian-born French artist Vasarely wanted to bring about the "polychromatic city of happiness" with his massive creations of funky geometric forms in vibrant block colors, and the crazy shapes in this gallery can't help but make you happy in any of the museum's eight alcoves, each of which is its own colorful universe. *Gestalt Blue #164* in the "homage to the hexagon" room is an especially cool take on the möbius strip. In addition to the permanent collection, the gallery also holds exhibits of the most avant-garde art around.

provence

🚌 *Take bus #4 from pl. de la Rotonde to Vasarely. The museum is the very modern building next to the youth hostel, where you're most likely staying.* $ *€9, students €6.* 🕐 *Open T-Su 10am-1pm and 2-6pm.*

CHEMIN DE CÉZANNE/ L'ATELIER DE CÉZANNE — MUSEUM

9 av. Paul Cézanne ☎04 42 21 06 53 🖥www.atelier-cezanne.com

Golden markers trace the footsteps of the artist on a 2hr. walking tour of the old city. Lounge at Le Cafe Des Deux Garçons *(53 cours Mirabeau, #3 on the route)* or marvel at the stained glass of the Cathédrale St-Saveur *(#31)*. In fact, the tour is a good way to get to know Aix's old city in general, since there are few streets Cézanne didn't grace with his presence. Unfortunately, most sights along the tour are only the facades of private bulidings, so the real gem is the last stop: **L'Atelier de Cézanne,** the Impressionist's recreated studio. World-famous wrinkled fruit, a green jug, and a rum bottle sit where Cézanne painted them, and his beret still hangs in the far corner. Staff in the studio are there to answer all questions in fluent English, and the wild garden around the studio transforms in the summer into a performance space for hip music and theater.

🚌 *Pick up a walking tour from the tourist office to trace Cézanne's footsteps in Aix. For the Atelier, take rue Gaston de Saporta uphill from pl. L'Hotel de Ville until it leaves the old city and turns into av. Pasteur. Keep walking straight and take the right street when the road forks. Walk 10min. uphill on Av. Paul Cézanne and the studio is on your left. The path is well signed.* $ *€5.50, students €2.* 🕐 *Open July-Aug daily 10am-6pm; Oct-Mar daily 10am-noon and 2-5pm; Apr-June daily 10am-noon and 2-6pm.*

LA CITÉ DU LIVRE — HISTORIC MONUMENT

8-10 rue des Allumettes ☎04 42 91 98 88 🖥www.citedulivre-aix.com

The heart of Aix's literary life can be found in an industrial factory that once produced matches and now invites the likes of Salman Rushdie and Nobel Laureate V. S. Naipaul to give public readings and lectures. The building is also home to the *Méjanes* Library, named for the *Marquis de Méjanes*, a passionate bibliophile who bequeathed his collection to the public in 1790. Since then, the library's stock has only grown and now impressively includes a 40m tall copy of *Le Petit Prince* at the main entrance. In addition to the wonderful books, CDs, and DVDs on loan, the library has the official archives of Albert Camus, a permanent exhibit on Émile Zola, bimonthly festivals, and creative special events. Free internet and tons of study spaces mean the desks are full around exam time. Check the website to see if the festivals coincide with your visit.

🚌 *From pl. de la Rotonde, walk downhill on av. des Belges until the traffic circle. Turn right onto av. L'Europe and at the next traffic circle turn right again. La Cité du Livre is immediately on the left.* 🕐 *Open Tu noon-6pm, W 10am-6pm, Th-F noon-6pm, Sa 10am-6pm. Additional hours for festivals and readings. Centre Albert Camus open Tu-Sa 2-6pm.*

MUSÉE GRANET — MUSEUM

pl. St-Jean de Malte ☎04 52 52 88 32 🖥www.muséegranet-aixenprovence.fr

The large and excellent permanent collection includes nearly 600 works of art, with an emphasis on the French school from the 17th to the 19th centuries. There are rooms with titanic oil paintings of Roman gods and the picturesque pastoral landscapes that typically come to mind when you imagine French art. The room of oil paintings by Aix's favorite native son, Paul Cézanne, is exciting, but you'll beg for more; nine paintings really isn't enough. Temporary exhibits fill the other half of the museum, change annually, and are guaranteed to display someone important.

🚌 *From pl. de la Rotonde, walk up cours Mirabeau until the end. Turn right onto rue d'Italie and follow the signs for the the museum 2 blocks ahead and to the right.* ℹ *Exhibits change year to year, but permanent exhibits are grouped thematically.* $ *€6, students, handicapped, and under 25 €4. Audio tour €3, students €1.* 🕐 *Open Tu-W 10am-7pm, Th noon-10pm, F-Su 10am-7pm.*

CATHÉDRALE SAINT-SAVEUR
pl. de l'Université

CHURCH

Because construction happened over the course of an entire millenium, there are multiple stylistic elements fused into this mega-church. Begun in the fifth century, the cathedral received its clock in 1430, its Gothic facade in the 1500s, and the Baroque chapel in the 16th century. Through the wooden doors, you'll find a dark, cavernous, and awe-inspiring interior with a famous triptych painted by Nicholas Fromant called *Brusson Ardent*. There's a room of Roman sculptures by the door as well as the oldest baptistry that still functions in all of France.
⚑ On rue Gaston de Saporta, uphill from pl. de l'Hotel de Ville. ⌚ Open daily 8am-noon and 2-6pm. Mass M-Sa 8am, Su 10:30am and 7pm.

FOOD

Aix's *centre-ville* is practically all restaurants, which means the city boasts an intensely comprehensive selection of international and Provençal cuisines. The food may be good, but the desserts are even better. The city's staple *bonbon* is the *calisson d'Aix*, an iced almond-and-candied-melon treat. Other specialties include *merveilles de Provence*, which are pralines with kirsch and chocolate available only at Christmastime, and any number of magnificent pastries, notably the decadent *trianon*, at the 200-year-old **Pâtissier Riederer** *(67 cours Mirabeau ☎04 42 66 90 91 ⑤ €3.80.)* At dinnertime, tables crowd **pl. Ramus** and **pl. des Cardeurs**. For a place to see and be seen, nothing is better than one of the cafes or restaurants on **cours Mirabeau. Fruit and vegetable markets** are at **pl. de l'Hôtel de Ville, pl. Richelme** *(⌚ Open daily 7am-1pm)* and **pl. de la Mairie** *(⌚ Open Tu 7am-1pm, Th 7am-1pm, Sa 7am-1pm.)* Three **Petit Casinos** serve all your supermarket needs: 5 rue Gaston de Saporta *(⌚ Open M-Sa 8am-8pm)*, 16 rue d'Italia *(⌚ Open Tu-Su 8am-9pm)* and 3 cours d'Orbitelle. *(⌚ Open M-F 8am-1pm and 4-8pm, Sa 8am-1pm and 4-:7:30pm.)*

▨ BRUNCH
4 rue Portalis

◉ PROVENÇAL ❷
☎06 98 36 00 76

Five tables, a glass counter of fresh food, and two women. That's all it takes to produce beautiful Provençal cuisine in this tiny lunch place. The salads are a meal in themselves, with tuna, chicken, goat cheese, or avocado resting on top of a deep bowl of grated carrots, cabbage, onion, lettuce, and potato. For a heartier meal, order a *quiche* or the perfectly priced *plat du jour*, which is usually a meat dish. And if you only have €2.50 to spend for the day, skip right to dessert, since the strawberries in *crème anglaise* are too good to eat in public. The nursery-rhyme paintings contribute to the joyful ambience, but most of the joy radiates from the grandmotherly woman bustling about to serve your food.
⚑ Follow rue d'Italie all the way to pl. des Pecheurs. Turn right onto rue Portalis and look for the grandmotherly figure bustling in the window. ⑤ Lunch €4-7.50. Dessert €2.50. ⌚ Open M-F 10am-7:30pm, Sa 10am-5pm.

PASTA COSY
5 rue D'Entrecasteaux

◆⌓ PASTA ❸
☎04 42 38 02 28

Pasta, pasta everywhere, and all of it to eat. This chic restaurant makes good on its promise of *toutes les pâtes du monde*. Homemade pastas like *fiochetti* (purses) are cooked in woks with eclectic ingredients borrowed from kitchens of the world, but the hunk of reggiano grated freshly onto your noodles still says old-fashioned Italian. A tapas menu also offers tasting portions of dill *crème brulée*, risotto, samosas, and other fusion dishes.
⚑ From pl. de la Rotone, walk up rue des Espariat until a left turn onto rue des Tanneurs. Walk straight and take your 3rd left onto what looks like a mostly residential street. The restaurant is on your left. ⑤ Pastas €14-19. ⌚ Open daily 7pm-midnight.

VITAMFRUITS
🍴 CRÊPES, SMOOTHIES [1]

8 rue Gaston de Saporta ☎04 42 26 61 69 💻www.vitamfruits.fr

Three concession stands distributed throughout Aix's *vieille ville* that refreshing smoothies made from your favorite fruits and cook up crêpes for a great mid-afternoon snack (nutella) or a light meal on the go (egg, cheese, and ham). Try the peach-raspberry-lemon smoothie, blended before your eyes.

➡ Gaston de Saporta: just above pl. L'Hôtel de Ville. Bédarride: at the corner of rue Espariate and rue Bédarride. ℹ Other locations at 2 rue Bédarride and 11 Cours Mirabeau. Ⓢ Crêpes €2-2.50. Smoothies €3.50. ⏰ Open daily 9am-8pm with some variations between franchises.

AUX DÉLICES DU LEBAN
🍴 LEBANESE [3]

33 rue Lieutaud ☎04 42 26 79 91

This little restaurant serves delicious and well-priced Lebanese basics, including hummus, *baba ganoush*, and plates of meaty *brochettes*. Much of the food is cooked on a decades-old baker's oven in the back of the kitchen. In the warm weather, head straight to the terrace seating area.

➡ At the very bottom of pl. des Cardeurs once it hits rue Lieutaud. Ⓢ Mezzes appetizers €6-6.50. Plates 12-13.50. ⏰ Open daily noon-2pm and 7-11pm.

NIKOLAUS
🍴🍸 GREEK [3]

5 rue Chabrier ☎04 42 21 69 92

A big fat Greek prepared-food shop with beloved standards like moussaka, tzatziki, and baklava on tantalizing display in the restaurant's long glass counter, making it an ideal place for buffet takeout with friends. The hitch is that you probably won't understand the names of anything you're eating. For a more thorough education, sit down at lunchtime beside a blown-up photo of the Mediterranean and order the bargain *menu dégustation* (€12.50) that comes with *mezes* (three dips), salad, an entree, and dessert. The *aubergine* is so tasty!

➡ Just off pl. Richelme on rue Chabrier. Ⓢ Salads €9.50. Dips (3) €8.50. Plates €10. Desserts €3.50. Lunch special (mezes, plate, dessert) €12.50. ⏰ Open M-F 9am-3pm and 4:30-7:30pm, Sa 9:30am-7:30pm, Su 10am-1pm. Open for sit down lunch M-Sa noon-2:30pm.

JACQUOU LE CROQUANT
🍴 PROVENÇAL [3]

2 rue de L'Aumone Vielle ☎04 42 27 37 19

If the French take their dining very seriously, then family-run Jacquou Le Croquant tries to out-French them all with an introduction to their menu that waxes philosophical on *le plaisir de manger* (the pleasure of eating) and *le plaisir de diner* (the pleasure of dining.) The restaurateurs insist on both pleasures, with an abundance of tender game meats like duck and goose in creamy sauces that are served at casual tables in the backyard of an apartment building. The *plat du jour* has the best price tag, but ordering a la carte guarantees a dinner right out of the oven.

➡ Left turn into pl. Ramus of rue Bédarride. Follow the road right, then left. Le Croquant is past the group of restaurants on the right. Ⓢ Salads €9-14. Plates €14-17. Plat du jour €10. ⏰ Open daily noon-3pm and 7-11pm.

NIGHTLIFE

Crowds of students during the year and festival-goers in the summer make partying a year-round pastime in Aix. The nightlife picks up on Tuesday and rocks on until Saturday. Locals and visitors can be found in cafes and bars until closing time at 2am, when the party moves to Aix's clubs. On any given summer weekend, it feels like every seat is taken in the cafes and bars in **pl. de la Richelme, pl. des Cardeurs,** and, of course, along the central **cours Mirabeau.** As the bars close, student clubs open their doors. Unfortunately, the only option for gay travelers in Aix is **Mediterranean Boy** *(5 rue de la Paix. Turn left on rue Vanloo at the top of cours Sextius and make your next left onto rue de la Paix ☎04 42 27 21 47 ⏰ Open 10pm-late.)* Since most gay travelers head to Marseille for nightlife, the bar doesn't see too much action.

LE MISTRAL

3 rue Frédéric Mistral   ☎04 42 38 16 49 🖳www.mistraclub.fr

▬ CLUB

Your nightly literary and geography lessons: Frédéric Mistral was a Nobel-Prize winning poet whose last name refers to a characteristic west wind that has blown through Provence for millennia. What does that have to do with Aix's most popular nightclub? Not much. Other than the fact that you'll beg for a breeze when the dancing hot bodies around you get too hot. Plus, this super chic club has hosted DJs like Bob Sinclair and and Carl Cox, modern-day poets on the club circuit. Everyday DJs Nikko and Moussa spin house, R and B, and hip hop for the crowds. Themes like '80s and '90s, electro, and ladies' night. Dress to impress.

✄ *Immediately off cours Mirabeau on rue Frédéric Mistral.* **i** *Ladies' Night Tu. Check website for other theme nights.* Ⓢ *Cover for guys €20; girls usually get in free. Gender equality hasn't reached Le Mistral just yet. Drinks €10. Bottles €125.* ☼ *Open nightly midnight-6am.*

LE SEXTIUS BAR

▬ BAR, CAFE

61 cours Sextius

A modern-day Batman in bar format, Le Sextius is an unassuming cafe by day and a life-saving student bar by night. The bartenders might not be superheroes, but the combo of frothy beer and live musicians on weekends will rescue your night from the grip of evil Dr. Banality. Regrettably, the Roman philosopher Sextius, a Stoic and the bar's namesake, would probably disapprove of the frolicking crowds that spread up and down the street in summer time.

✄ *From pl. de la Rotonde, walk along av. Bonaparte and turn right onto Cours Sextius. The bar is ahead on your right.* Ⓢ *Beer €2.20-5. Cocktails €7.* ☼ *Open daily 9pm-2am.*

LE CUBA LIBRE

▬ CLUB

4 bld. Carnot   ☎04 42 63 05 21 🖳www.cuba-libre-aix.com

Le Cuba Libre used to be a taste of island life with cigars and tropical beverages. Used to be, that is, until the manager gave the place a full makeover, turning former communist fun into a sleek and silvery bar that's meant for casual dancing to the live DJ and blue lights. Castro hasn't left the building just yet, since Monday, Tuesday, and Wednesday are salsa nights *(9pm.)* Tell the gregarious bartender, Yass, that he's the best in Aix and you'll make his night. Maybe he'll return the favor with a free drink?

✄*From pl. de la Rotonde take av. Victor Hugo until a left turn on bld. du Roi René. Le Cuba Libre is a 10min walk straight ahead.* **i** *Salsa night M-W 9pm.* Ⓢ *Beer €4.50. Cocktails €9. Liquor €2.50-7.50. Bottles €72-90.* ☼ *Open M-F 5pm-2am, Sa-Su 1pm-2am.*

IPN

▬ BAR, CLUB

23 cours Sextius

A haven for students—especially Americans, Brits, and Swedes. In fact, the Italian owner has been listening to Miley Cyrus so devotedly that twice a month there really is a party in the USA when the club gets decked out in flags like it's the Fourth of July. Dress the part to make it past the bouncers and into the cave down the stairs, and if you're a student in Aix who likes to party, ask the manager about working part-time.

✄ *Take av. Bonaparte from pl. de la Rotonde and turn right onto cours Sextius. The red bar is an inconspicuous entrance on the right.* Ⓢ *Cover €5. Shots €2. Beer €6-6.50.* ☼ *Open midnight-5am.*

ARTS AND CULTURE 🎵

Travelers visiting Aix in July will face the rather lucky predicament of having too many world-class concerts and too little time (and money) to attend them all. To navigate the wealth of culture, visit the tourist office or the **Bureau Information Culture** *(19 rue Gaston du Saporta* ☎*04 42 91 99 19* ☼ *Open Tu-Sa 10-6:30pm.)*

LE FESTIVAL D'AIX-EN-PROVENCE 🎫♿ CITYWIDE

28 pl. des Martyrs de la Résistance ☎04 42 17 34 00 🖥www.festival-aix.com

Every July, Aix-en-Provence attracts a mass of orchestras, musicians, and performing artists from every nook and cranny of the Western world. After listening to Mozart's *Don Giovanni*, pick up your violin and attend one of the many master classes or catch a show of modern dance.

$ Concerts €10, operas €15. ⏰ July. 2011 dates to be announced.

LE GRAND THÉATRE DE PROVENCE 🎫♿ CITYWIDE

av. A Lunel ☎04 42 91 69 69 🖥www.legrandtheatre.net

Aix-en-Provence's venerated theater explodes with opera, dance, symphonies, jazz, and even circus performances year round.

$ Tickets €8-50, under 28 €8-25.

CINEMA MAZARIN 🎫♿ CINEMA

6 rue Laroque. ☎04 42 26 85 12.

The most exceptional of the movie theaters in Aix's *centre ville*, Cinema Mazarin is dedicated entirely to *art et essai* films, which translates into independent (read: not Harry Potter) films from around the world, screened in their original versions with French subtitles. Mazarin holds regular festivals, including gay, hispanic and class film festivals.

 # Down rue Laroque off of cours Mirabeau. $ €8.70-9.30, students €7.50-7.70. ⏰ Last showings are around 10pm.

ESSENTIALS [i]

Practicalities

- **TOURIST OFFICE:** Offers a huge number of services, including maps, walking tours, pamphlets on art and culture, a **city guide** for university students, apartment listings, and an entire desk dedicated to helping with accommodations searching. *(2 pl. du Général de Gaulle ☎04 42 16 11 61 🖥www.aixenprovencetourism.com)* **Daily tours** are organized to Marseille *(€49)*, the lavender fields of Luberon *(€59)*, and Van Gogh heritage sights in Arles *(€69)*. The **Aix Pass** gets discounts at museums, concerts, and sights *(€2.)* **Public bus passes** are sold here as well *(☎04 42 26 37 28 🖥www.aixenbus.com ⏰ Open M-Sa 8:30am-7pm, Su 10am-1pm and 2-6pm.)* The office also houses **Ticket Sales** for Aix's concerts *(☎04 42 161 170 ⏰ Open M-Sa 9am-noon and 2-6pm.)*
- **CURRENCY EXCHANGE: Change de l'Agence.** Accepts traveler's checks. *(15 cours Mirabeau ☎04 42 26 84 77 ⏰ Open M-F 9am-noon and 2-6:30pm, Sa 9am-noon and 2-5pm.)*
- **LOST PROPERTY: SOS Voyageurs.** *(☎04 91 62 12 80)*
- **INTERNET ACCESS: Point Com** *(6 rue Gaston de Saporta $€6 per hr. ⏰ Open M-F 10am-1pm and 2-6:30pm, Sa 10am-1pm.)*
- **POST OFFICE: Place Hotel de Ville.** Poste restante and Western Union inside. *(⏰ Open M 8:30am-4pm, Tu 8:30am-12:15pm and 1:30-6pm, W-F 8:30am-4pm, Sa 8:30am-12:30pm.)* The Principal Post Office is at the corner of rue Lapierre and av. des Belges one block south of pl. de la Rotonde.

Emergency!

- **POLICE: Police Municipale.** *(2 cours des Minimes ☎04 42 91 91 11, or the general number ☎17.)*
- **HOSPITAL: Centre Hospitalier Du Pays D'Aix.** *(av. des Tamaris. A 10min. walk north of the old city center on av. Pasteur. Emergency line ☎04 42 33 90 28.)*

- **AMBULANCE:** ☎15. **SOS Medecins.** *(☎04 42 26 24 00.)* Doctors on-call for home visits.
- **PHARMACY:** There are pharmacies every 2 blocks along cours Mirabeau and a collection of 3 at pl. des chapeliers. Among them is **Pharmacie du Cours Mirabeau** *(17 cours Mirabeau ☎04 42 93 63 60 ⏰ Open M-F 8:30am-7:30pm.)* For night service, call the **Commissariat** *(☎04 42 93 97 00)* and they will contact the *pharmacie de garde* (24hr. pharmacy) for that night. For weekend service, check the list of rotating *pharmacies de garde (open 9am-2pm)* posted outside all pharmacies in Aix. Otherwise, call the *Commissariat*.

Getting There

By Train

The **Gare SNCF** train station is located at at pl. Gustave des Places, and services regional trains *(☎36 35. ⏰Automatic ticketing window open daily 7am-7pm. Reservation and info offices open M-Sa 9am-6pm.)* To: **Marseille** *($€5.30-7.⏰40min., 27 per day);* **Cannes** *($€31. ⏰3½hr., 25 per day.);* **Nice.** *($€34.40. ⏰3-4 hr., 25 per day.)* Note that train numbers decrease substantially on weekends. The **Gare d'Aix-en-Provence TGV** is located 20min. outside of the city, and connects travelers to major cities throughout France via the TGB. To **Paris Charles de Gaulle** *($€80-110.⏰3-5 hr. depending on whether you go direct, 18 per day).* The Gare TGV can be reached by **shuttles** from the bus stations *($€5. ⏰20min., every 10min.)*

By Bus

Gare Routière *(av. de l'Europe. ☎08 91 02 40 25.⏰Info desk open M-F 7:30am-7:30-m, Sa 7:30am-12:30pm and 1:30-6pm.)* To: **Marseille** *(💻www.navetteaixmarseille.com. $€5. ⏰30 min., the Navette Rapideruns from 6:10am-8:10pm roughly every 10min. Less frequent early morning service from 5:45am and night service until 11:30pm);* **Nice** *($€30. ⏰ 2½hr., 9am, 10:55am, 1:20pm, 2:30pm and 6pm);* **Avignon** *($€14.70. ⏰ 1¼hr., run daily 8:30am, M-F 7am, 8:30am, 11:30am, 1pm, 5pm, and 6:45pm);* **Arles** *(⏰ 1hr.; runs daily 10am, 2pm, and 6:15pm, M-F 6am, 6:50am, 7:55am, 4:35pm, 5:20pm).* A Youth Card for €15 per month permits a 50% reduction in fares.

Getting Around

Aix-en-Bus is *the* way to get around Aix, with fantastically frequent service *(☎04 42 26 37 28. $ Tickets €1. 3-day pass 5€. 10 rides €7.)* Complete table of bus schedules and routes, bus passes and maps available at the Tourist Office. The **Association Des Taxis Radio Aixois** is also available *(☎04 42 27 71 11.)*

NICE AND MONACO

When that rich friend of yours utters the words "Côte d'Azur" you immediately think of these twin cities of fame and fortune. Ok, one is a country, but it's no bigger than a city. Linked by a 20min. rail trip, these millionaire Meccas have even the most well-funded backpackers cowering in in the hills that line the PACA region. While undoubtedly adorable, they can get tame and repetitive, which is when you double-dog-dare your wallet to venture into the coastal region. After the initial shock of yachts, gambling, and real-life celebs, you'll start to see the grittier side of Nice that's full of bars, backpackers and cheap finger foods. And about the grittier side of Monaco... does a used Ferrari dealership count?

Despite umbrella rental prices that make Disneyland seem affordable, the cheapest and most reliable activity is the beach and sun. After all, if you're going to travel somewhere to sunbathe for free, you might as well do it in the most expensive place possible—the story you tell after will be that much better. The appeal of the sun is what brought Americans to the southern shores in the 1920s and it's still what keeps tourists and backpackers from all over the globe coming here year after year. When the sun goes down, these two cities are famous for the even glitzier nightlife. Despite the commonplace €10 cocktail, finding a cheap beer is no further than the closest British or Irish pub which always seems to be a couple blocks away.

greatest hits

- **FROM RUSSIA WITH LOVE:** Not really, but Matisse was famously obsessed with a Russian girl, who inspired an impressive percentage of his artwork. Check it out at the Musée Matisse (p. 283).
- **DRIVERS WITH DEATH WISHES:** Monaco's most famous drag race pits Mercedes-McLauren against Ferrari every June and sends Formula 1 racers careening through Monaco's historic streets (p. 302).
- **VATICAN-APPROVED T AND A:** France might bill itself as a proudly secular country, but when it comes to church-condoned feathers, falsies, and masquerade balls, Nice conveniently becomes a Catholic stronghold again (p. 290).

You saved all semester for your trip to the Riviera and you're not looking to blow it all in Monaco (that is unless you gamble). Lucky for you, there's **Menton** to keep you frugal. Just 11 minutes by train from Monaco, Menton promises the beauty of the French Riviera but with a price tag well within a student budget. Try **Hotel de Belgique**; save your stay at the **Hotel de Paris** in Monaco for when you win the lottery or go into I-Banking (when that becomes a viable profession again).

nice ☎04

Nice has been on the backpacker must-see list since the youth of the world discovered its beaches and cheap wine. Combining a wealthy reputation with an affordable underbelly, Nice neatly condenses everything amazing about the Côte d'Azur into one sizzling metropolis. While those of you who'd like to escape the tourists will groan when you see the busloads of cruise-shipping retirees and loudmouthed anglophones in the Vieille Ville, you'll cheer when you see the rock-bottom happy hour prices at the local bars, and grin when you interact with the well-established youth culture that goes out of its way to make travelers feel welcome (a rarity in France). Daytime activities revolve around the rocky beaches and immense seaside promenade; extensive shopping opportunities and an unparalleled array of museums are available for those of you who can't just lie around all day. The city just about explodes at night, with live music in almost every bar and club and non-stop parties that make it hard to keep from dropping dead with exhaustion.

ORIENTATION

Vieux Nice

Vieux Nice is bounded by **bld. Jean Juares** to the north, the **château** to the east, and the **Jardin Albert I** to the west. Its winding steets are sometimes confusing for the tourists that invade the area around lunchtime and after sunset. The **cours Saleya** hosts local markets during the day that give way to cafes at night. Some of the largest crowds gather around the **Église St. Jeaques** and the **Palais du Justice** for street preformers. This is also where you'll find most of Nice's nightlife, backpackers, and cruise ship tourists. Small shops selling liqueurs, oils, and soaps are interspersed amongst the small boutique restaurants and hookah lounges.

Massena

Bounded by the **train station** to the north, the **Jardin Albert 1er** to the southwest, and the **bus station** and **old city** to the east, Massena is one of the busiest areas for any commerce that extends beyond tourism in Nice. The **tram** runs right through the middle of the neighborhood along **Jean Medecin,** and stops in front of the **main square,** the **shopping center,** and the **train station.** The closer you get to the train station, the higher the frequency of sex shops and neon lights. On the plus side, the hotels around here are cheaper. Closer to the old city, you can find row upon row of cheap clothing outlets (or at least cheap compared to other towns on the Riviera). Massena also hosts most of the city's metropolitan **museums;** almost all of them are free, though a couple of the private musuems, such as the **Musée National Mesage Biblique Marc Chagall,** are not. The local restaurants and bars mostly cater to residents, and you'll be hard pressed to find fellow tourists.

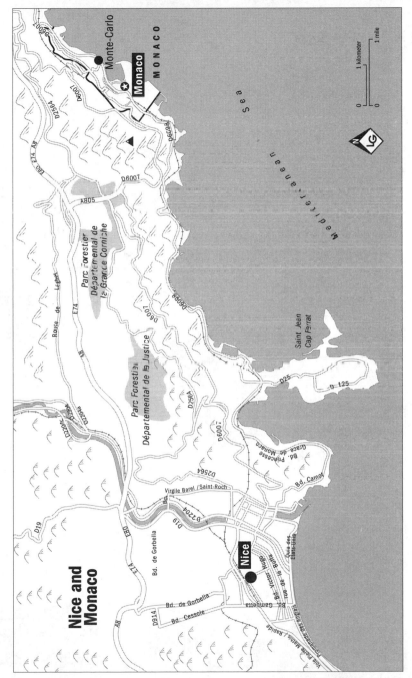

Nice and Monaco

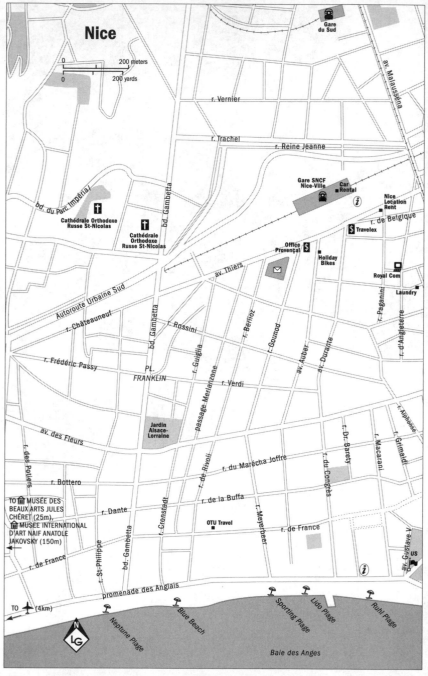

Nice

0 ———— 200 meters
0 ———— 200 yards

r. Vernier

r. Trachel
r. Reine Jeanne

Gare
du Sud

av. Malausséna

Gare SNCF
Nice-Ville
Car
Rental

Nice
Location
Rent

r. de Belgique

Travelex

bd. du Parc Impérial

Cathédrale Orthodoxe
Russe St-Nicolas

Cathédrale
Orthodoxe
Russe St-Nicolas

bd. Gambetta

av. Thiers

Office
Provençal

Holiday
Bikes

Royal Com

Laundry

Autoroute Urbaine Sud

r. Châteauneuf

r. Rossini

bd. Gambetta

r. Berlioz

r. Gounod

av. Auber

av. Duranie

r. Paganini

r. d'Angleterre

r. Frédéric Passy

PL.
FRANKLIN

r. Guiglia

Passage Merlanzone

r. Verdi

r. Alphonse

av. des Fleurs

Jardin
Alsace-
Lorraine

r. de Rivoli

r. du Maréchal Joffre

r. Dr. Barety

r. Macarani

r. Grimaldi

r. Bottero

r. des Potiers

TO MUSÉE DES
BEAUX ARTS JULES
CHÉRET (25m),
MUSÉE INTERNATIONAL
D'ART NAIF ANATOLE
JAKOVSKY (150m)

r. Dante

Cronstadt

r. de la Buffa

r. du Congrès

OTU Travel

r. Meyerbeer

r. de France

av. Gustave V

US

r. France

r. St-Philippe

bd. Gambetta

promenade des Anglais

TO ✈ (4km)

N

Neptune Plage

Blue Beach

Sporting Plage

Lido Plage

Ruhl Plage

Baie des Anges

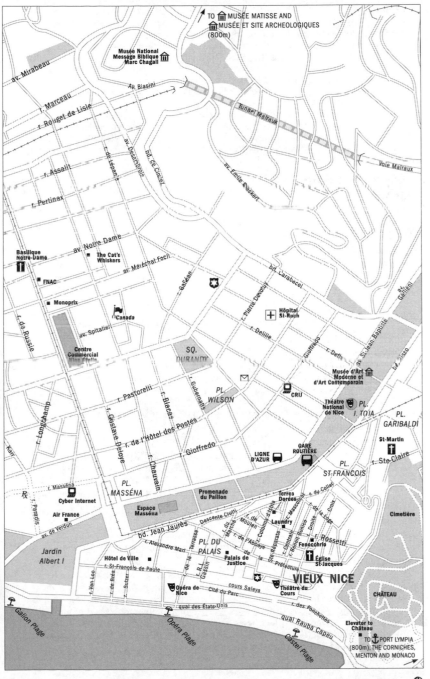

Sea Front

The Sea Front is the easiest part of Nice to navigate. Step one: face ocean. Step two: walk either left or right. Boom, you have just oriented yourself along the only axis of this neighborhood. Dotted with the Massena Museum and the Opera, with the Hotel Negresco standing in the middle, the Sea Front is the least budget-friendly place to be in Nice. The hotels are pricey, the restaurants are formal, and the beaches are private. If you walk along any of the streets that run perpendicular to the ocean, you can find cheap food stands and two-star hotels. By doing so, you will have to give up the ocean view, unless you want to kink your neck in a manner befitting a circus performer to get a whiff of the salt air. A block up from the ocean runs streets parallel to the ocean, where you find more laid-back bars and cafes, as well as some affordable shopping. For those who want to escape the tourist-infested Vieux Nice at night, this is the perfect area to wander the boulevards in search of a more undiscovered Nice, one without the unattractive fanny packs and unwashed backpacks.

ACCOMMODATIONS

Vieux Nice

You'll pay more for a smaller room in the Vieux Nice, but you can't get any closer to the action than these hotels. It might be worth the credit card bill to keep from relying on Nice's tram to get you from where you want to be to where you want to pass out.

👍 **HOTEL VILLA LA TOUR** 💳♿🍸❄⛅ BOUTIQUE HOTEL [4]

4 rue de la Tour ☎04 93 80 08 15 💻www.villa-la-tour.com

An adorable boutique hotel in a former 18th-century monastery, La Villa de la Tour is a classier place for travelers who don't mind paying a little extra for convenience and luxury. Check out the rooftop terrace for an intimate view of Vieux Nice.

➔ Take the Tram (dir. Pont Michel) to Catedral Vieille Ville. Walk in same direction as tram for 2-3 blocks and turn right onto rue de la Tour. $ Singles €49-129; doubles €52-139; triples €150.

AU PICARDY HOTEL 💳♿❄⛅ HOTEL [2]

10 bld. Jean Juares ☎02 93 85 75 51

This budget traveler's favorite is easy to find and centrally located in the Vieux Nice. The family-run hotel offers simple rooms and a shared terrace that connects all the rooms to each other.

➔ Take the tram (dir. Pont Michel) to Catedral Vieille Ville. Walk in same direction as tram for 1 block. Hotel on your right. $ Singles and doubles €25-38; triples and quads €40-54.

HOTEL DE LA MER 💳♿📶🍸❄⛅ HOTEL [4]

4 pl. Massena, 1st fl. ☎04 93 92 09 10

A slightly more expensive, traditional hotel on the border of Massena and Vieux Nice. With exceptional views of the place Massena and the fountain, l'Hotel de la Mer is for those who want proximity to shopping and the beach, and don't mind the added cost.

➔ Take the tram (dir. Pont Michel) to Massena. Walk around the fountain and toward the ocean. Hotel is on the right. $ Singles and doubles €65-95; triples €90-129; quads €110-159.

Massena

While the sex shops and neon lights might be a turnoff, Massena hosts the cheapest hotels in Nice. Don't worry: the hotels we've included here don't rent by the hour.

👍 **VILLA SAINT EXUPERY** 💳♿📶🍸⛅ HOSTEL [2]

22 av. Gravier ☎08 00 30 74 09 💻www.vsaint.com

One of Europe's coolest hostels, Villa Saint Exupery boasts one of the most extensive lists of organized activities we've ever seen, including sailing trips to St-Tropez and "Anything But Clothes" parties in its newly renovated monastery-turned-social-space. The place used to be one of the farthest hostels from the Vieille Ville, but all that changed in 2010 with the opening of its sister hostel in the pl. Massena. Family-run with English-speaking staff.

➔ From the Comte de Falicon tram stop, walk toward the post office and walk up av. du Ray.

Continue straight as the road turns into av. Gravier. Walk 2 blocks and make a sharp left turn up the steep hill to the hostel on your left. $ *Prices change frequently depending on occupancy. Dorms €16-30; doubles €54-90.* ⏰ *Reception open 8am-noon and 6pm-2am.*

HOTEL BELLE MEUNIERE — HOSTEL ❶

21 av. Durant ☎04 93 88 66 15 💻www.bellemeuniere.com

This manor-turned-hostel is a backpacker's dream. Forget about the kitsch and the coin-operated soap dispensers; this place is unapologetically simple in its design and home-makeover feel. The rooms are all different and packed with loud social youth, who are attracted by the hostel's ideal location and "Backpacker special." New apartments with kitchenettes are also available for weekly rent not far from hostel.

⇞ *From the train station, walk across the street and down the stairs to av. Durant. Walk half a block and hostel is on your right.* ℹ *Backpacker Special: Breakfast, linen, and shower €18.* $ *Doubles €49-52; triples €45-60; quads €80.* ⏰ *Reception until midnight.*

PETIT LOUVRE — HOTEL ❸

10 rue Emma et Phillip Tiranty ☎04 93 80 15 54

Hidden on a side street off the main drag, this hotel is centrally located and one of the best budget options for a long-term stay. The small but clean rooms offer baths, beds, and kitchenettes equipped with pots, pans, and silverware. While it may look like an Ikea catalogue, the prices are much more budget friendly.

⇞ *From the tram stop Thiers, walk away from the train station down av. Jean Medecibout 4 blocks past the Notre Dame cathedral. Turn left onto rue Emma et Phillip Tiranty. Hotel is on your left.* ℹ *Kitchenettes available.* $ *Singles €45-51, weekly €288; doubles €57/369; triples €68.50/440.*

HOTEL CRILLON — HOTEL ❸

44 rue Pastorelli ☎04 93 85 43 59 💻www.crillon-hotel-nice.com

This old hotel has certainly been around the block a couple of times. While the halls smell of the good old days when smoking indoors was kosher, the newly renovated clean rooms are a nice surprise, and the steel cage of an elevator completes the archaic vibe.

⇞ *From the tram stop Medecin, continue along av. Jean Medecin 2 blocks and make a left onto rue Pastorelli. Hotel is on your left.* $ *Singles €49-60; doubles €60-80; triples €70-90.*

HOTEL INTERLAKEN — HOTEL ❸

26 rue Durant ☎04 93 88 30 15 💻www.hotelinterlaken.fr

Once upon a time, Picasso and Andy Warhol had a love child. That love child was then asked to decorate a hostel in Nice. This is that hostel. Seemingly random stripes, colors, mismatched kitschy chandeliers, and shiny objects are scattered among the brightly colored and spacious rooms. Just to make everything groovier, the hotel comes with a bar.

⇞ *Opposite the train station.* $ *Singles €44-55; doubles €49-62; triples €69-81; quads €84-104.*

Sea Front

Not to burst your bubble, but the hotels along the Sea Front are, well, expensive. Who would have thought that such a pristine location right next to the beaches in southern France would be expensive? Surely not us.

HOTEL CRONSTADT — HOTEL ❺

3 rue Cronstadt ☎04 93 02 00 30 💻www.hotelcronstadt.com

One of the most down-to-earth hotels on the seafront, this establishment is run by an old lady who apparently still decorates like it's 1873. Old pictures, chandeliers, quilted bedspreads, and eerie silence add to the feel that this place might be haunted. The only question is if you see Casper, who ya gonna call?

⇞ *Bus #8, 11, 52, 60, 62 to Gambetta/Promenade. From the bus stop, along the promenade des Anglais, walk towards the Hotel Negresco and turn left onto rue de Cronstadt. Hotel is on your left.* ℹ *Wi-Fi available.* $ *Singles €70-75; doubles 90-95; triples €110.*

HOTEL ALBERT 1ER HOTEL [4]

4 av. des Phoceans ☎04 93 85 74 01 🖳www.hotel-albert-1er.com

Your basic example of what an pricey, chain hotel will look like in the neighborhood. Nicely decorated and air-conditioned, this hotel will give you the buffet breakfast and comfy beds, so long as you're willing to put up with the demanding French and German families at the front desk.

Next to the Jardin Albert 1er, the side closest to the old city. i Wi-Fi available. $ Singles €69-89. €10 extra per person.

HOTEL CANADA HOTEL [4]

8 rue Halevy ☎04 93 87 98 94

A welcomed two-star hotel in this expensive neighborhood. Decorated with replicas of Fernand Leger paintings, this colorful and laid-back hotel has clean rooms and a calm breakfast terrace. If you can stand the heat without A/C, you can live the Niçois lifestyle here.

Bus #8, 11, 52, 59, 60, 62 to Gustave V. Facing direction of bus, walk across and down the street to the left of Le Meridien. Continue 1 block; hotel is on your right. $ Singles €52-60; doubles €65-85; triples €89-100.

SIGHTS

Vieux Nice

MUSÉE D'ART MODERNE ET D'ART COMTEMPORAIN MUSEUM

Promenade des Arts ☎04 93 62 61 62 🖳www.mamac-nice.org

Located just blocks from the Vieux Nice, Nice's massive Museum of Modern and Contemporary Art offers minimalist galleries that pay homage to the French new Realists, as well as American pop artists like Warhol. Rotating contemporary exhibits showcase artists from around the world. Don't miss the collection of statues by Niki St-Phalle, which routinely frighten even the most hardcore hallucinogen users.

Promenade des Arts. Take the tram to Catedrale - Vieille Ville. $ Free. Tours €3, students €1.50. ⏰ Open Tu-Su 10am-6pm.

CHÂTEAU CASTLE HILL FORTRESS

☎04 93 85 62 33

The remains of an 11th-century fort located on the hill overlooking Vieux Nice, this château is the oldest spot in the city. Celto-Ligurians claimed the sight until the Romans decided it would make a good spot for a fort in 154 CE. Centuries later, Provençal nobles built a castle and cathedral on the hill as a symbol of their authority. During King Louis XIV's great centralization of France, the fortress was destroyed. Today, all that remains is the large park and waterfall that were made from the ruins. The climb may be tiresome, but the view is well worth it, and offers 360 degree views of Nice and the Med.

$ Free. ⏰ Open June-Aug daily 9am-8pm; Sept 10am-7pm; Oct-Mar 8am-6pm; Apr-May 8am-7pm. Info booth open July-Aug Tu-F 9:30am-12:30pm and 1:30-6pm.

COURS SALEYA SQUARE, MARKET

cours Saleya

Built on the ramparts in the 18th century, the cours Saleya is now a bustling hub of activity ideally situated between Nice Vieille Ville and the beach. Nice's open-air market is located here by day, and a collection of hip cafes set out tables at night. The square is also home to the famous *Marché aux Fleurs*, where you can buy opulent bouquets of local flora. A perfect spot to wander through Nice's winding alleyways.

⏰ Market daily 7:30am-1pm.

WAR MEMORIAL MEMORIAL

place Guynemer

At the foot of the castle hill, this enormous WWI memorial stands in honor of the 4000 Niçois who died in the line of duty between 1914 and 1919. Over 50m tall, this monument was erected in 1924, and cut directly into the old quarries. Some

of the most spectacular views of the Mediterranean are along this promenade, which links the port to the Vieille Ville. Although there are signs that warn against it, don't be surprised to see local kids skateboarding on the memorial steps.
$ Free.

CATEDRALE ST. RÉPARATE — CATHEDRAL
pl. Rossetti
Nice's largest and most opulent cathedral was inspired by early Baroque architectural models from Rome. It is not an accident that the design is a miniature version of the larger and more famous St. Peter's in Rome, complete with a triple nave and a transept.
⏰ Open daily 7am-6pm. Closed for visits during services.

ADAM AND EVE HOUSE — HISTORIC SIGHT
rue de la Poissonerie
You'll walk right by this one if you're not careful. The Adam and Eve house, as it's called locally, is one of the last examples in Vieux Nice of the detailed facades that historically decorated the homes here. The house's bas-relief dates back to 1584, and depicts Adam and Eve, naked in the Garden of Eden, threatening each other with clubs. Apparently this WWE version of the Bible never made into the mainstream in English-language trasnlation.

PLACE GARIBALDI — SQUARE
pl. Garibaldi
On the eastern end of the Vieille Ville, the large open space of *place* Garibaldi is lined by elegant, red buildings with green shutters and vaulted porticos. You can see the perfectly integrated Chappelle St-Sepulcre nestled amongst the buildings surrounding the statue and fountain of Garibaldi.

Massena

👍 MUSÉE MATISSE — ♿ MUSEUM
164 rue des Arenes ☎04 93 81 08 08 💻www.musée-matisse-nice.org
This expertly renovated Genoese villa displays decades of art by one of France's most elusive artists. The permanent collection includes Matisse's early sketches, as well as gouache 3D cardboard cut-outs... er... sorry... "*tableaux.*" If you can't make it up to Vence to see Matisse's whimsical *Chapelle du Rosaire de Vence* for yourself, check out the museum's model of the chapel, and the exhibit that examines his creative process, including the artist's initial attempts to depict the stations of the cross in black and white finger paint. Temporary exhibits generally display more oblique aspects of Matisse's life and work, such as his decades-long artistic obsession for a Russian girl (he drew her and only her for 10 years) named Lydia.
🚶 Take bus #15, 17, 20, 22 or 25 to Arenes. Free shuttle between Chagall and Matisse museums. ℹ Tours in English by reservation. $ Free. ⏰ Open M 10am-6pm, W-Su 10am-6pm.

MUSÉE NATIONAL MESAGE BIBLIQUE MARC CHAGALL — 👍 MUSEUM
av. Dr. Menard ☎04 93 53 87 20 💻www.musée-chagall.fr
The museum showcases Chagall's interpretation of the Hebrew Bible, comprised of 12 massive canvases that the artist chose to arrange by color rather than chonologically. The adjacent rooms display his "creative" blending of the Bible and the Russian Revolution (because when you say Lenin, we think Crucifixion). The museum also includes an auditorium that hosts concerts and other events, with stained-glass panels by the artist depicting the story of creation.
🚶 Walk 15min. northeast from the train station or take bus #22 (dir. Rimez to Musée Chagall). $ €9.50 under 26. Art students and EU citizens free. ⏰ Open May-Oct M 10am-6pm, W-Su 10am-6pm; Nov-Mar M 10am-5pm, W-Su 10am-5pm. Last entry 30min. before close.

MONESTERE CIMIEZ — ♿ MONASTERY, MUSEUM
av. du Monestere
The monastery was a Franciscan hideout before it was confiscated by the Revolu-

tion. When the Revolution collapse, Monestere Cimiez was returned to the church, and the monks expanded its gardens; they now overlook the port, and stretch to the cemetery where Matisse is buried. Inside the church is a nearly 6m tall marble cross, accompanied by small statues that portray figures from St. Francis' visions.

Take bus #15, 17, 20, 22 or 25 to Arenes. Walk across the park to the Monastery. $ Free. ⏰ Open M-Tu 10am-5pm, Th-Sa 10am-5pm. Closed on Su during service.

SAINTE JEANNE D'ARC CHURCH ♿ CHURCH

11 rue Grammont

A modern wonder in its day, this church was built in the 1930s entirely out of concrete, then painted white to resemble some blend of sci-fi and Middle Eastern architecture. The domed Byzantine ceiling is laden with symbolism: pat yourself on the back if you can figure out the numerical significance of the seven mini domes supporting the church's three larger domes. Alright, well it has to do with a certain number of virtues supporting a trinity. The church is named after the small chapel to the side, which is dedicated to France's favorite 17-year-old saint (or witch, if you ask the English).

Take the T37 or bus 22 to Église Jean d'Arc. ⏰ Open 8am-4:30pm.

MONT ALBAN FORT ♿ FORT

av. du Mont-Alban

Once a 16th-century fort, this massive and now defunct hilltop bastion boasts a stunning view of Nice, the nearby Cap d'Ail, and even Antibes. The brochure says that on a clear day you can see Corsica, but we sadly didn't. If you're yearning for a long uphill hike in hot weather, this fort's for you. Nice plans to convert the fort into a contemporary art museum in the near future, but for now you'll have to settle for a stroll around the battlements, as visitors are not allowed inside.

Take bus #14 to chemin du Fort and walk downhill to the fort. Also a footpath exists near the bus stop Escalliers de Verre (bus #81 and 100)

PLACE MASSENA ♿ SQUARE

pl. Massena

One of the main centers of the city, this large town square is patterned like a checkerboard, and unlike many areas of Nice, remained relatively untouched during both world wars. The most recent renovations incorporated the tramway into the area, in addition to seven meditating statues perched atop a collection of large poles, designed by Spanish artist Juame Plensa (they supposedly represent each of the seven continents). These figures are joined by breakdancers and street performers during the day and a grittier crowd at night.(Read: take the tram at night.)

Sea Front

The sights that line the Sea Front are largely architectural, with the exception of the villas and estates that have been converted into pretty impressive museums.

MASSENA MUSEUM ♿ MUSEUM

65 rue de France and 35 promenade des Anglais ☎04 93 91 19 10

Once home to (you guessed it!) the prominent Massena family, this giant seaside estate was donated to the city at the turn of the century by Andre Massena, much to the chagrin of the eldest son who had hoped to inherit it. Exhibits include paintings and photographs of Nice's old carnival pier and other neighborhoods, as well as a collection of elaborate dresses that would make Barbie blush. The ornate estate proves that France retained a nobility long after the Revolution.

⏰ Open M 10am-6pm, W-Su 10am-6pm. $ Free.

MUSÉE BEAUX ARTS ♿ MUSEUM

33 av. des Baumettes ☎04 92 15 28 28 🖥www.musée-beaux-arts-nice.org

When you first see its inconvenient location in the far corner of the city, you'll be tempted to blow it off (we almost did). For art lovers, that would be a terrible mistake. This villa turned museum holds works by both Picasso and Rodin. One of the most maccabre collections is a gallery by Niçois artist Gustav-Adolf Mossa, whose work includes the most nightmarish, surrealist paintings imaginable,

including clowns with bloody knives and harpies on the piles of dead bodies.
🕐 *Open M 10am-6pm, W-Su 10am-6pm.* Ⓢ *Free.*

PROMENADE DES ANGLAIS
                                              ⤴ PROMENADE
promenade des Anglais
Once a six-feet-wide dirt path, this main artery of Nice was expanded in 1820 by a wealthy Englishman, then inaugurated in 1931 by the Duke of Connaught, one of Queen Victoria's sons. Today it runs along the beach and connects the Sea Front to the Vieille Ville, and provides an easy footpath between private beaches.

BEACHES
                                                ⤴ BEACH
promenade des Anglais
The public and private ▰beaches alternate along the Baie des Anges from Vieux Nice as far as the Sea Front goes. Expect to pay for the umbrellas and chairs at the private beaches, bring multiple towels for padding, or buy a cheap beach mat—the beaches here are pretty rugged, and you don't want to end up sunbathing on jagged rocks. We recommend that you give up the search for sand and just go swimming.

HOTEL NEGRESCO
                                 ⤴ HOTEL, HISTORIC BUILDING
37 promenade des Anglais
There's a reason we didn't list Hotel Negresco under the accommodations—this place is over €400 a night. The classic Niçois architecture is pretty spectacular, though. The hotel has been clasified as a historical building since 2003, ensuring that its bright white walls and pink dome will be in postcards well in the future.

FOOD

Vieux Nice
Food is plentiful and cheap in this part of town. You'll be able to find the expensive restaurants easily enough, but the charm of Vieux Nice lies in its small snack shacks, markets, and hole-in-the-wall *socca* joints. While heavy on the tourists, Vieux Nice still offers thriving local markets in the Marché aux Fleurs and the cours Saleya *(daily 7am-1pm)*, where flowers are sold at slashed prices alongside candied fruits, fresh produce, olives, and Italian cannolis. There are two large **Monoprix** supermarkets located in on av. Jean Medecin *(🕐 open M-Sa 8:30am-8pm)* and in pl. Garibaldi *(🕐 open M-Sa 8:30am-8pm).*

▨ LA FERME SALEYA
                                ➪⤴♈ TRADITIONAL ❸
8 rue Jules Gilly   ☎06 71 84 07 32
This traditional French restaurant will make you think that you're in the rural countryside of Bretagne or Angers. Cute pottery farm animals hint at the largely carnivorous meal that you're about to eat. Call ahead for a group, and the chef will prepare a personalized menu at prices that are comparable to the house *formule.*
Ⓢ *Formule €15-22.* 🕐 *Open Tu-Su 12-2:30pm and 7-10pm.*

FENOCCHIO
                                       ➪⤴♘ ICE CREAM ❶
2 pl. Rossetti   ☎04 93 80 72 52
Serving the best ice cream in France, Fenocchio offers 96 flavors of Italian gelatto, including more eccentric flavors such as beer, avocado, and rose. Traditional flavors like vanilla and pistachio are delicious here too. *Let's Go* recommends one of their decadent sundaes for €10-20.
Ⓢ *1 scoop €2, 2 scoops €3.50.* 🕐 *Open daily 10am-midnight.*

RENE SOCCA
                                       ➪⤴♈♘ SOCCA ❶
2 rue Miralheti   ☎04 93 92 05 73
Forget the tourist-frequented *socca* joints—this is the only authentic one you'll find. The lines around the block indicate that this place serves some of the best quality fried Niçois dishes in whole city. Terrace seating with one drink minimum under signs that strongly advise against the use of silverware.
Ⓢ *Socca €2.50. Plats €5-10.* 🕐 *Open daily noon-9pm.*

FLORIAN
CANDY SHOP ❷

14 quai Papacino ☎04 93 55 43 50 ◙www.confiserieflorian.com

Every sweet tooth's dream come true, this confectionery offers tours of its factory, where you learn how to make candied fruit, crystalized flowers, and candied orange peels. While the tour might make your mouth water, remain in control of you wallet, since you'll want to splurge (understandably so) in the pricey yet delicious boutique after being teased with samples. *In the New Port.* **i** *Tours of factory on demand with video in English or French.* Ⓢ *Candied flowers €6. Candied fruit assortment €36.* Ⓩ *Open M-Sa 11am-8pm.*

SNACK LA BANANE
CRÊPERIE, PANINI ❶

6 rue de la Poissonnerie ☎04 93 79 07 54

Simple snack shack taken to the extreme with kitschy, banana-themed decor. Provocative signs and pop art paintings make this a hip place for smoothies, paninis, or crêpes. Ⓢ *Panini €3.50-4. Crêpes €7.* Ⓩ *Open daily 8am-midnight.*

L'ÉCURIE
TRADITIONAL ❷

4 rue du Marché ☎04 93 62 32 62

A classic farm-themed French restaurant, this establishment serves traditional meat dishes (or wood-fired pizza for the less ambitious) in four different dining rooms; each one is decorated according to a different theme, ranging from beach cottage to countryside stable. Ⓢ *Plats €12-17. Menu €22.* Ⓩ *Open daily 9am-midnight. Kitchen open noon-11pm.*

LA MERANDA
PROVENÇAL ❷

4 rue de la Terrasse ☎08 92 68 06 89

A small 12-table gem on the edge of Vieux Nice, Le Meranda's chef Dominique le Stanc produces an outstanding menu that changes daily based on the local market fare. Ratatouille and pizza are regularly served here, in addition to traditional Provençal dishes. Ⓢ *Plats €9-13.* **i** *Reserve in person for lunch and dinner.* Ⓩ *Open M-F noon-1:30pm and 7-9pm.*

Massena

Massena might not offer the backpacker staples of *socca* and cheap fast food, but if you have a little extra to spend on one night out, this is where you want to go. Classy, local, and cheap(er than Vieille Ville), Massena is not as infested with tourists as the rest of the city, and has the traditional cuisine you came to France for.

◪ MANGEZ-MOI
FRENCH ❸

9 rue Blacas ☎04 93 87 54 71 ◙www.restaurantmangezmoi.com

Adorable French/seafood blend restaurant that has all the kitschy decorations octegenarians go crazy for. Cozy garden seating on ivy-covered terrace. Come for the taster menu of changing daily specials. Ⓢ *€15 menu. €25 3-course.* Ⓩ *Open Tu-Th 9am-8:30pm, F-Sa 8:30-10pm.*

◪ SPEAKEASY
VEGAN ❷

7 rue Lamartine ☎04 93 85 59 50

A throwback to the Haight-Ashbury circa 1967, this vegan restaurant is run by a friendly American expat hippie. Strangers share the small tables when it gets crowded. The menu changes frequently; cross your fingers and hope that Jane whips up her vegan pie. Ⓢ *€14 2-course menu. Specials €9-11.* **i** *Open M-F noon-2:15pm and 7-9:15pm, Sa noon-2:15pm.*

LE NOLITA
CRÊPERIE ❷

8 av. Durant ☎06 23 74 66 67

The small, New York-themed crêpe cafe serves lunch and breakfast specials on the small outdoor patio. Pasta specials accompany dessert *du jour* such as *Mousse au Chocolat* and sweet crêpes. Ⓢ *Midi menu €11. Crêpes €7-8.* Ⓩ *Open daily 8am-8pm.*

COSY CAFE
✦ ♿ ⚲ ♨ CRÊPERIE ❷

5 rue Clemenceau **☎04 93 88 92 99**

If you're tired of the French but not their food, come to this popular hangout for English med students (thanks to the hospital across the street), who come in droves for the €10 crêpe specials; each special includes a free glass of cider.

Ⓢ *Panini €4. Crêpes €2.50-7. Prix-fixe menu €10.* Ⓩ *Open daily 7:30am-6pm.*

GRAND CAFE DE LYON
✦ ♿ ⚲ ♨ BRASSERIE ❷

33 av. Jean Medecin **☎04 93 88 13 17 ▣www.cafedelyon.fr**

One of the oldest brasseries in Nice, this centrally located giant of a bar dominates the shopping area, and is a must for those craving the most elaborate sundae or people-watching combos. Crowds escape the heat by lounging in wicker chairs under rotating fans.

Ⓢ *Ice cream €5-11. Cocktails €5.30-7.70.* Ⓩ *Open daily 7am-11pm.*

LUNA ROSSA
✦ ♿ ⚲ ♨ ITALIAN ❷

3 rue Chauvain **☎04 93 85 55 66 ▣www.lulunurossu.com**

While not the cheapest place for pizza or Italian food, this place is definitely worth a visit, if only for the murals of street art that decorates its walls. Luna Rossa closes early in the evening (by Niçois standards anyway), so up your BAC here at the chic wine bar before officially starting your night.

Ⓢ *Plats €9.50-15. Salads €9.50-11.* Ⓩ *Open Tu-F noon-2pm and 7:30-10:30pm, Sa 7:30-10:30pm.*

Sea Front

Most of the restaurants in this neighborhood are small cafes or more upscale brasseries. While eating out here along the promenade might be out of your reach, any of the small alleys that run perpendicular to the beach have cheap gyro stands and pizza places that sell by the slice. If you do happen to sit down at one of the pricey bistros, go for any of the fruit/ice cream cocktails that are frequently served up.

🖼 CAFE DE LA PROMENADE
✦ ♿ ⚲ ♨ BRASSERIE ❶

3 promenade des Anglais **☎04 93 82 54 55**

If you're aching for a real American or English breakfast (as real as France can provide, anyway), come to this cabana-esque diner, which features the plush vinyl booths of your local Denny's and the calorie intake to match.

Ⓢ *Sandwiches and salads €7-12. Sundaes €7.70-9.70. American breakfast €13.50.* Ⓩ *Open daily 7:30am-2am.*

LA CANNE A SUCRE
✦ ♿ ♨ BRASSERIE ❸

11 promenade des Anglais **☎04 93 87 19 35**

This vaguely tropical cafe serves cool ice cream crêpes, cocktails, and smoothies. The palm trees, fake fruit, and a certain Barry Manilow soundtrack are excessive enough to embarrass Chiquita Banana.

Ⓢ *Pizza €9-14. Salads €6-15.* Ⓩ *Open daily 11am-11pm.*

LE DOLCE MOMENTO
✦ ♿ ⚲ ♨ BRASSERIE ❶

25 promenade des Anglais **☎04 93 80 90 18**

This small brasserie/cafe by the sea serves an American-ish breakfast and traditional French food. The peaceful and informal setting is perfect for a quick bite after an exhausting day of sunbathing.

Ⓢ *Breakfast €2.50-7.70. Plats €10.* Ⓩ *Open Tu-Su 8am-10pm.*

NISS'TANBUL
◉ ♿ ⚲ ♨ GREEK ❶

4 bld. Gambetta **☎06 23 12 66 32**

A budget traveler's dream. Renowned for its cheap gyros and Turkish fast food, Niss'tanbul whips up hot kebabs and baklava and pours out cheap Greek and Turkish wine.

Ⓢ *Gyro €5. Plats €9-10.* Ⓩ *Open daily 11am-midnight.*

POMODORISSIMO
◉ ♿ ♨ PIZZA ❶

2 rue Gambetta **☎04 93 02 43 67**

Enabling the beach bums of the world one slice at a time, this hole-in-the-wall

nice • food

fast-food joint is ideally located for sunbathers. There's also a small seating area, if you aren't in a hurry to get back to the sand.
Ⓢ *Pizza slice €2.50.* Ⓞ *Open daily 11am-8:30pm.*

NIGHTLIFE

Vieux Nice

BULLDOG PUB POMPEII   ◆⊗Ⓨ☺ BAR, LIVE MUSIC
14, 16 rue de l'Abbaye   ☎04 93 85 04 06 ▣www.bulldogpub.com
One of Nice's best-kept secrets for locals and intrepid backpackers, this '60s and '70s rock-themed pub hosts live music every night. The house is regularly packed with young people, who resort to barstools and tablestops for standing room.
i Live music, smoking lounge upstairs. Ⓢ *Beer €6. Cocktails €8. 6 shots €18.* Ⓞ *Open daily 8am-4am. Live music starts at 10pm.*

WAYNE'S BAR   ◆♿Ⓨ☺ PUB
15 rue de la Prefecture   ☎04 93 13 46 99
Wayne's is a late-night institution in Nice, with an English-speaking staff that caters to rowdy, spitting crowds of unwashed backpackers. Huge crowds at night gather for pop-rock music and drunk, travel story swapping (sounds like a *Let's Go* office party).
i Tourist bookings for bungee jumping, sailing, day trips to towns. Happy hour pints €3.90. Ⓢ *Beer €6.20. Cocktails €7.50.* Ⓞ *Open daily noon-2am. Kitchen open noon-11pm. Happy hour 5-8pm.*

MA NOLANS   ◆♿Ⓨ☺ PUB
2 rue François   ☎04 93 81 46 90
Upscale and fun Irish pub that offers karaoke and trivia (with prizes for the winners). House speciality here is pear cider, if you happeneed to be debating a splurge on a pint or whiskey cocktail.
i Trivia night on M 8pm. Karaoke F 10pm-close. Ⓢ *Beer €3.90. Cocktails €7.50.* Ⓞ *Open M-Sa noon-2am. Happy hour 5-8pm.*

LE SIX   ◆♿Ⓨ☺▼ GAY BAR
6 rue Raoul Bosio   ☎04 93 62 66 64
One of the most opulent and creative gay bars in the Riviera. The large space dates back to the Belle Époque, with a room displaying the shower for its nightly shower show. Telephones scattered throughout bar randomly connect to each other for secret chatting with anonymous patrons.
Ⓢ *Beer €7. Cocktails €10.* Ⓞ *Open daily 10pm-5am.*

3 DIABLES   ◆♿Ⓨ☺ BAR
2 cours Saleya   ☎04 93 62 47 00 ▣www.les3diables.com
This bar has become a hopping youth hangout thanks to its Thursday night student prices; just flash your student ID for a dramatic reduction in prices. The two-story bar regularly serves both locals and backpackers. After midnight, DJs turn the bar upstairs into more of a club.
i Karaoke W night. Student night Th, pints €4.. Ⓢ *Liquor €3.50. Pints €6.80. Cocktails €8.* Ⓞ *Open daily 5pm-3am. Happy hour 5-9pm.*

PADDY'S PUB   ♿⁽ᵗⁿ⁾Ⓨ☺ PUB
40 rue Droite   ☎04 93 80 06 75
Your typical Irish pub, Paddy's is a welcoming haven for backpackers and expats; take a seat on the rough and beaten bar stools. The large TV screens show sporting events, and the bar features 9 rotating beer on tap. Live music on the weekends.
i Happy hour drinks €4.50. Ⓢ *Beer €6. Cocktails €7.50.* Ⓞ *Open daily 3pm-2am. Happy hour 6-8:30pm.*

NOCY-BÈ   ◆⊗ HOOKAH
4,6 rue Jules Gilly   ☎04 93 16 93 20
Traditional Maghreb hookah bar with low lighting, low couches, and no alcohol

consumption. Bright cushions, Moroccan lamps, and arched doorways allow you to take a trip across the Mediterranean without the 24hr boat ride.

i No alcohol served. 1-drink min. (as in soda or tea). $ Hookah €10. Tea €4. ⏰ Open M-Sa 3:30pm-12:30am.

PUB OXFORD PUB

4 rue Mascoïnat ☎04 93 92 24 54

The cheapest booze in town is served at this new English pub in the center of the old city. Walk through the red telephone booth in the doorway and enjoy the delightfully tacky atmosphere and good company.

i Happy hour shooters €1.50; cocktails €4; pints €3. $ Liquor €6.40. Beer €6.50. ⏰ Open daily 7pm-5am. Happy hour 7-11pm.

HANIBAL LOUNGE HOOKAH, BAR

2 pl. Vieille ☎04 93 80 18 08

In the basement of a local bar, this social hookah joint encourages friend-making in its large cushioned booths. Designed to imitate the interior of a Roman bath, this lounge is decorated with mosaic tiles and offers a Western-friendly drink menu (read: booze).

$ Hookah €10.50. Cocktails €6. Tea €3.50. ⏰ Open M-Sa 7pm-midnight.

THE PLEASURE BAR, SEX SHOP

27 rue Benoît Bunico ☎06 83 81 61 63

For the truly adventurous or hedonistic, this sex shop/bar should take you well past your limits, with its pink feathery decor and extensive drink list of suggestive cocktails such as "Sensual" and "Desire." Friendly owner has experience calming down visibly uncomfortable customers, and regularly reassures patrons that this is a "normal bar."

$ Cocktails €6-10. ⏰ Open Tu-Su 6pm-12:30am.

LES DISTILLERIES BAR

24 rue de la Prefecture ☎04 93 62 10 66

Classy bar reminiscent of a turn-of-the-century *brasserie*. Belt-driven fans and antiquated radios complement the veteran adjoining brewery, reminding us that the Niçois have always drank like sailors, even in the classy Belle Époche.

$ Shots €3. Beer €7. Cocktails €7.50. ⏰ Open M-Sa noon-2am. Happy hour 6-8pm.

BLAST AMERICAN BAR BAR

8 pl. Charles Felix ☎04 93 80 00 50

For homesick Americans looking for a comfy outdoor lounge, come to Blast in the *cours Saleya* for some good old-fashioned American breakfast, which is served until 3pm. Come back after sunset for a laid-back beer with the likes of Uncle Sam and the Mount Rushmore presidents.

$ Beer €4. Cocktails €9. Breakfast €6.50-8. ⏰ Open daily 10am-2am. Kitchen open until midnight.

BLUE WHALES PUB

1 rue Mascoïnat ☎04 93 62 90 94

One of the cheaper pubs in the city, Blue Whales offers live music and a lengthy happy hour in an authentic bar scene reserved for budget backpackers and locals.

$ Beer €2. Shooters €3-4. 2 shooters for €10. ⏰ Open daily 6:30pm-4:30am. Happy hour 6:30pm-midnight. Live music 11pm-4am.

Massena

Massena might not be the backpacker's first choice for nightlife, but it might tickle your fancy if you're in town for longer than a week and in need of some serious cultural immersion. Few internationals venture beyond the realms of the Vieille Ville and the comfort of Wayne's, after all.

LA BODEGUITA DEL HAVANA BAR

14 rue Chauvain ☎04 93 92 67 24

Papered with Che pics and with rum barrels as tables, this Cuban salsa bar and disco has the feel of a run-down bar in Havana. Serves up Cuban dishes and an extensive list of mojitos *(€10.50)*.

ℹ Salsa dancing W-Th 7:30pm. Ⓢ Beer €3. Cocktails €10.50. ⏰ Open Tu-Su 8pm-2am.

LE TONO 💳♿🍸⛱ TAPAS, WINE BAR

18 rue Clemenceau ☎04 93 87 84 17

This laid-back wine bar was repeatedly recommended by locals, and serves tapas at an impressively reasonable €6. The menu is mostly vegetarian, but carnivores can find something to eat here too. The outdoor seating and relaxed jazzy vibe lure customers in for late lunches and drinks long after the sun sets.

Ⓢ Wine glasses €3-4. Beer €5. Vegetarian tapas €6. ⏰ Open Tu-Su 3pm-midnight.

LE TRENTE 7 💳♿🍸 CAFE, BAR

37 rue Pastorelli ☎04 93 85 27 21

This somewhat typical bar is centrally located in the middle of an up-and-coming neighborhood. Extensively decorated with neon orange (in a good way), Le Trente 7 manages to be chic without raising its prices to match. It's not particularly popular with tourists or backpackers, so be prepared for some French immersion.

Ⓢ Beer €2.70-5. Cocktails €7-9.50. ⏰ Open M noon-3pm, Tu-Sa noon-3pm and 6pm-late.

LE ROMAGNA 💳♿🍸 JAZZ BAR

22 rue d'Angleterre ☎04 93 87 91 55

La Romagna recently changed owners, and is now open infrequently. The dusty bar has the cheapest liqueur in town, and plays a diverse set list from the extensive collection of jazz records that line the shelves.

Ⓢ Beer €2.50. Shots €3. ⏰ Open Sa 7-9pm.

ARTS AND CULTURE ♫

Festivals and Carnivals

Nice is known for its summer music festivals, particularly the Fête de la Music that occurs on the summer solstice. The bacchanalian Carnival takes place in February or March.

👍 **FÊTE DE LA MUSIQUE** ♿⛱ CITYWIDE

This citywide festival is as unofficial as it is awesome. A treasured Niçois tradition since the mid-'80s, this celebration gets every bar, disco, and restaurant in the city puts on free live music in the streets, cafes and alleyways of the city on the summer solstice. Nice comes alive with everything from pop rock to DJ party music. The crowds get particularly rowdy in the *vieille ville*, so make sure to watch out for pickpockets and those who wish to ruin the fun, drunken times. Apart from that minor setback, this is Nice at its best; many of the bars open early and stay open well after 3 or 4am, and the fast food joints take advantage of the partiers and offer *socca* and pizza in the early morning as well. Head to the area around Wayne's and the cours Saleya for the best and most international bands.

⏰ Summer Solstice (June).

👍 **CARNIVAL** SEA FRONT

💻www.nicecarnaval.com

France might take pride in its secular society, but this annual excuse to get really drunk and dance around owes its existence to the Catholic culture of Nice. The promenade des Anglais and the quai des Etats-Unis host two weeks of parades, fireworks, and concerts, while confetti falls like rain in Seattle. Flower processions, masked balls, and endless partying make this the liveliest time in Nice's winter.

Ⓢ Tickets €10-30.

NICE JAZZ FESTIVAL 💳 CIMIEZ

Arenes et Jardins de Cimiez ☎08 20 80 04 00 💻www.nicejazzfestival.fr

Every July, the quiet area of Cimiez and gardens outside of the Matisse Museum swell with over 55,000 spectators, who flock to the city for the eight-day festival, featuring 75 concerts and over 500 individual musicians.

i Free shuttle from the pl. Massena during concerts. $ €29-49 per night, students €22-36; 3-day passes €96-105; 8-day €185. ⏰ Concerts 7pm-midnight.

Cinema, Opera, and Theater

CINEMATHEQUE DE NICE — MASSENA

3 espalande de Kennedy ☎04 92 04 06 66 💻 www.cinematheque-nice.com

The historic theater screens old black-and-white films, documentaries, and art-house staples. The prices here are an absolute steal, but don't expect box office hits or convenient show times. Schedule changes weekly, and is available at the tourism office and local museums.

$ Tickets €2. ⏰ Showings between 11am-8:15pm.

RIALTO CINEMA — SEA FRONT

4 rue de Rivoli ☎08 92 68 00 41

Rialto shows box office hits in their original (read: English) language. During the week-long *Fête du Cinema* in late June, movie tickets are only €3 if you've already paid full admission to a movie at one of the festival's participating theaters.

$ €9, students €6. ⏰ Showings 2-10pm.

OPÉRA DE NICE — SEA FRONT

4-6 rue St-François de Paule ☎04 92 17 40 79

Produces stage performances September-May, and hosts visiting orchestras and individual soloists year round. Ballet and Opéra schedule changes and is available at the tourist office.

$ €7-40. ⏰ Box office open M-F 8:30am-4:30pm.

THEATRE NATIONAL DE NICE — SEA FRONT

Promenade des Arts ☎04 93 13 90 90 💻www.tnn.fr

Puts on concerts and plays. Check website for changing annual schedule.

$ €10-30, students €7.50-28. ⏰ Box office open June-July Tu-Sa 1-7pm; Aug-May Tu-Sa 2-7pm. Su at 1pm for same-day entrance only.

ESSENTIALS

Practicalities

- **TOURIST OFFICE: Branch on av. Thiers** has hotel reservations, restaurant and sights guides as well as a city map and practical guide (*Next to the train station. ☎08 92 70 74 07 💻www.nicetourisme.com ⏰ Open Jun-Sept M-Sa 8am-8pm, Su 9am-7pm; Oct-May M-Sa 8am-7pm, Su 10am-5pm.*) **Branches at 5 promenade des Anglais.** (*☎08 92 70 74 07 ⏰ Open Jun-Sept M-Sa 8am-8pm, Su 9am-6pm; Oct-May M-Sa 9am-6pm.*) **Airport Location.** (*Terminal 1 ☎08 92 70 74 07 ⏰ Open Jun-Sept daily 8am-9pm; Oct-May M-Sa 8am-9pm.*)
- **CONSULATES: Canada.** *(10 rue Lamartine ☎04 93 92 93 22 ⏰ Open M-F 9am-noon.)* **UK.** *(Embassy in Monaco, 33 bld. Princesss Charlotte ☎377 93 50 99 54)* **US.** *(7 av. Gustave V ☎04 93 88 89 55 ⏰ Open M-F 9-11:30am and 1:30-4:30pm.)*
- **YOUTH CENTER: Centre Regional d'Information Jeaunesse (CRIJ)** Posts summer jobs for students and provides info on long term housing, sudy, and recreation.*(19 rue Gioffredo, near the Museum of Contemproary Art. ☎04 93 80 93 93 💻www.crijca.fr i Free itnernet access with Student ID. ⏰ Open M-F 10am-6pm.)*
- **LAUNDROMATS:** These are plentiful in Nice, so check to make sure you're not around the corner from one already before going to. *(7 rue d'Italie ☎04 93 85 88 14 $ Wash €3.50, dry €1 per 18min.) (11 rue de Pont Vieux ☎04 93 85 88 14 $ Wash €2.50-6.50. dry €.50 per 8 min. ⏰ Open Daily 7am-9pm.)*
- **INTERNET ACCESS:** Internet access is available on almost every street corner in Nice, usually marked by neon signs in Arabic. Free internet at the CRIJ and Wi-Fi at

selected cafes and bars. Closest Internet from the train station is on av. Theirs across from the Thiers tram stop.

- **POST OFFICE:** *(23 av. Thiers ☎04 93 82 65 22 💻www.lapost.fr ⏰ Open M-F 8am-7pm. Sa 8am-noon.)* Additional branches everywhere in the city.
- **POSTAL CODE:** 06033.

Emergency!

- **POLICE:** *(1 ave. amrechal Foch ☎04 92 17 22 22)*
- **LATE-NIGHT PHARMACY:** Check Nice Matin for rotating Pharmacie de Garde (24 hour pharmacy). Late-night service available by phone. *(7 rue Massena ☎04 93 87 78 94).*
- **HOSPITAL:** *(5 rue Pierre Devoluy ☎04 92 03 33 75).*

Getting There

By Plane

Aeroport Nice-Côte d'Azur (*NCE; ☎08 20 42 33 33*). Municipal Ligne d'Azur Buses leave ever 30 min for the airport from the train station *(#98 direct bus; 8am-9pm, €4).* Before 8am, bus #23 (*every 15-25min. €1*) Makes several stops, including train station. EasyJet flies to London, Vueling to Barcelona and Air France to Paris and other domestic and international destinations.

By Train

There are two train stations in Nice, although the SNCF is far more useful and centrally located.

Gare SNCF Nice-Ville: av. Thiers *(☎04 93 14 82 12 💻www.sncf.com)* Cannes *(40min., every 20min. 5:15am-12am, €6)*; Marseille *(2.5hr., 15 per day, €29-70)*; Monaco *(15min., every 20min. €3.30)*; Paris *(5hr. 6 per day, €94)*.

Gare de Nice CP. *(☎04 97 03 80 80 💻www.trainprovence.com)*, is located at 4bis rue Alfred Binet, 800 m from Nice-Ville. Chemins de Fer de Provence runs to Digne-les-Bains *(3.5hr., 5 per day, 6:25am-6:15pm, €18)* and Plan du Var *(40min., 10 per day, 6:07am-6:15pm. €3.40)*.

By Bus

Gare Routiere: 5 bld. Jean Juares. *(☎04 92 00 42 93)*. Buses to national and international destinations. Info booth open M-F 8:30am-5:30pm, Sa 9am-4pm. Bus #100 runs between Nice and Menton via Monaco. Leaves to Monaco every 10-30min. 6am-8pm, Su every 20min. 1hr., puchrchase tickets onbaord for €1. Leaves for Cannes *(40min., every 20min. €1)*.

By Ferry

Corsica Ferries *(☎04 92 00 42 93 💻www.corsicaferries.com)* and **SNCM** *(☎04 93 13 66 66)* send high-speed ferries from the new port. Reduced rates for those under 25 and over 60. Take bus #1 or 2 to the port. To Corsica (*5-6hr., €15-45; bikes €10; small cars €45-75.)* The two terminals are on opposite sides of the port, so check schedule ahead of time.

Getting Around

By Bus and Tram

Ligne d'Azur, 3 pl. Massena *(☎04 93 13 53 13 💻www.ligneazur.com)*, is the public bus company in Nice. Office open M-F 7:45am-6:30pm. Sa 8:30am-6pm. Buses operate daily 6am-9pm. Tourist office gives out bus schedule and posted times are on bus stops. *($ Individual passes €1, day pass €4, week-long pass €15. ⏰ Night bus runs 9:10pm-1:10am. Tram line runs through Jean Medecin and pl. Massena. Stops every 5 min, 6am-2am along its 9 km route.)*

By Taxi

Central Taxi Riviera *(☎04 93 13 78 78)* company runs throughout the city *($ €20-40 from the airport to the center-ville)* Be sure to ask for the price before boarding and make sure the meter is turned on. Night fares charged from 7pm-7am.

By Bike

Velo Blue (*www.velobleu.org)* is Nice's bike rental company. They require that you call or have a French credit card to rent the bike from bike stands. Stands are located all around the city. (Ⓢ *30min. free, €1 per hr.)*

monaco ☎+377

Not every country's synonymous with flashy cars, yachts, gambling, and income taxes; Monaco's a pretty special place. Evading taxes turned out to be such a popular idea that the mega-rich flocked here for centuries, hoping to partake in material excess without being pestered by the IRS. While Monaco's fiscal policies have changed recently, the allure of this tiny principality still revolves around its unparalleled and shameless sense of wealth. Every year, the world stops spinning for the Monaco Grand Prix, where automotive companies and drivers compete to win the world's most difficult course, then party it up in the glamorous clubs near the first place finish. One step off of the train, and you'll realize why Grace Kelly was so quick to ditch US citizenship for a life of luxury in this oasis of old world royalty, jammed in the middle of a modern and jetsetting life.

ORIENTATION

Monaco-Ville

Monaco-Ville sits atop the **rocher de Monaco,** which François Grimaldi climbed and conquered while dressed as a monk (or *monaco,* in Italian) in 1297. Today, it overlooks the **Port of Hercules,** and houses the **Royal Palace** and everything else royal within the city limits. The principality's royal aquarium, palace, car collection, and church are all located atop this neighborhood, which is barely larger than 5x9 blocks. There's a reason that this is the area of Monaco that's most densely packed with tourists. Take some pics, see the sights, then hurry back down the mountain before you feel the need to push past that old lady with a walker who's keeping that extremely slow cruise ship group from moving on.

comment t'appeles tu?

Determining how to refer to the 🔲city/🔲country/🔲territory of Monaco and its administrative areas is sometimes (read: almost always) confusing. Here are a few clarifications on what the heck this place is, and what it isn't.

Like Andorra and Liechtenstein, Monaco is an independent principality ruled by a prince (neither Fresh nor Purple), and it answers to no other government.

People often refer to Monte Carlo as the capital city, but it's a district. There is no capital city of Monaco, because it's a city-state with the entire country confined in the city limits.

It has no standing army, but France is willing to provide them with military protection—a provision which strangely comforts them.

Monte Carlo

OK, we've all heard of this place. Centered around the **Carre d'Or** and the **Monte Carlo Casino,** Monte Carlo boasts the fanciest cars, fastest women, and opulent clubs in Monaco. It might cost you a fortune just to step foot in this part of town, but if you don't mind being Monte Carlo's token pleibian you should put on your best and go people watch. Who knows—you might even find a rich sugar daddy. Keep going past the casino and you'll reach the only **beach** in the principality, as well as the **Forum** and **Sporting Complex.**

La Condamine

This neighborhood boasts the cheapest shops, bars, and general cost of living in Monaco. It's also refreshingly clear of tourists during the day, who are off on excursions to the rocher; at night, it hosts a series of laid-back bars that are seriously lacking in the other parts of Monaco. Located below Monaco-Ville, La Condamine is also where the port's affordable hotels are, but keep in mind that "affordable" in Monaco requires a slight price adjustment, even from the already expensive Riviera.

Fotvieille

This neighborhood is the quiet western side of Monaco. Home to private apartments and yacht clubs, the parties here happen behind close doors, and there isn't much left for the common folk, unless you're looking for a job in the industrial sector. The area is also home to a large **shopping complex** and Monaco's **soccer stadium,** in case you were planning to see the home team.

ACCOMMODATIONS

Oddly enough, the cheapest place to stay in Monaco is in France; the best deals in the area are located in **Beausoleil,** a small town that overlooks Monte Carlo. If you're a purist and want to stay within the principality, **La Condamine** is your best bet for hotels under €100.

Monaco-Ville

There aren't any. Sorry. The Royal Palace and the private apartments of the uber-rich are located here, and they don't want anyone renting a room with a sniper rifle and getting a shot at the prince (thats *Let's Go's* guess, anyway).

Monte Carlo

Actually, these hotels aren't even in Monaco. They're in France, but don't worry about it—Monaco's literally right across the street.

HOTEL VILLA BOERI — BUDGET HOTEL [4]

29 bld. Leclerc ☎04 93 78 38 10 www.www.hotelboeri.com

It may look sketchy and overgrown from the outside, and the decorative mirrors may date back to the '70s, but this hotel is clean, simple, and cheap for the area. Small rooms with large beds and bath.

Take either the #4 or #1 bus to Église St. Charles. With the church on your left, walk along bld. des Moulins until coming to a stairwell on your left. Walk up the stairwell and turn right. Walk another 60m. Hotel is on your left. i Free Wi-Fi and computer. $ Singles and doubles €58-81; 3rd person €8; 4th person €12.

HOTEL DIANA — HOTEL [4]

17 bld. Leclerc ☎04 93 78 47 58 www.monte-carlo.mc/hotel-diana-beausoleil

Large comfortable rooms in a classy hotel overlooking the Église St. Charles.

Take either the #4 or #1 bus to Église St. Charles. With the church on your left, walk along bld. des Moulins until coming to a stairwell on your left. Walk up the stairwell and turn left. Hotel is on your right. i Parking and free Wi-Fi. $ Singles €45-60, doubles €45-72. Prices vary with inside/port view.

HOTEL OLYMPIA — HOTEL [5]

17 bld. Leclerc ☎04 93 78 12 20 www.olympiahotel.fr

More opulent boutique hotel, but because it's one street over from Monaco, it's *almost* within budget range by Monaco standards. Balcony suites and multiple-balcony suites (yep, you can have two) overlook port as well as mountains behind Monaco.

Take either the #4 or #1 bus to Église St. Charles. With the church on your left, walk along bld. des Moulins until coming to a stairwell on your left. Walk up the stairwell and turn right. Hotel is on your immediate left. i Free Wi-Fi. $ Singles and doubles with internal view €85-130, with port view €95-135.

La Condamine

HOTEL DE FRANCE HOTEL [5]

6 rue de la Turbie ☎93 30 24 64 www.monte-carlo.mc/france

Simple Monaco-budget hotel in the heart of the shopping district of the Condamine. Clean rooms with bathrooms and A/C.

Follow direction "Fontvieille-Monaco Ville"; through tunnel with moving walkway. At the exit, make a left to cross rue Prince Pierre and take stairs down to rue de la Turbie. Hotel is on your left. $ Singles €75-94; doubles €85-116; triples €105-140.

NI HOTEL HOTEL [5]

1 rue Grimaldi ☎97 97 51 51 www.nihotel.com

This zany hotel is a cross between a fun house and a madhouse. Crooked bright orange walls and oddly placed mirrors make Ni Hotel a challenge for the epileptic or criminally insane. Suites and apartments available.

From the train station, exit to La Condamine, making a right as you exit the tunnel rue Grimaldi. Continue while the road curves to the left. Hotel on your right. $ Singles €90-140; doubles from €170.

HOTEL DE VERSIALLES HOTEL [5]

4 av. Prince Pierre ☎93 50 79 34 www.monte-carlo.mc/versailles

Closest hotel to the Grimaldi palace, as well as the train station. At these prices, you'd think you were staying at the real Versailles...

From the train station, exit to La Condamine and turn right on rue Grimaldi. Walk as the road turns to the left, and turn right on av. Prince Pierre. Hotel on immediate right. $ Singles €90-110; doubles from €140.

Fotviellle

HOTEL COLUMBUS HOTEL [5]

23 av. des Papalins ☎92 05 90 00 www.columbusmonaco.com

Only a stones throw from Monaco's heliport, this unparalleled chic hotel provides views of the Princess Grace Rose Garden, as well as three auditoriums for business or private cocktail parties.

If you arrive by helicopter, its across the street (duh). $ Singles €240; doubles €275. Breakfast €25.

SIGHTS

Monaco-Ville

THE PRINCE'S PALACE PALACE

Monaco-Ville ☎93 25 18 31 www.palais.mc

The lavish palace is open to tourists when the flag is lowered and the prince is away, which, it turns out, is quite often. The free audio tour is offered in 11 languages, and will walk you past the silk tapestries, Royal Courtyard, and chambers that combine the opulence of Versailles with the shock of knowing that a monarch still lives here. Judging by the crowds, you could easily mistake the official portrait of Princess Grace as nothing short of the Madonna, herself.

i Access not available for travelers with disabilities. $ €8, students €3.50. Open Apr 2-Oct 31 daily 10am-6:15pm.

MUSÉE OCÉANGRAPHIQUE AQUARIUM

av. St. Martin, Monaco-Ville ☎93 15 36 00 www.oceano.mc

Originally a hobby of Prince Albert I, the monarchy's extensive collection of exotic Mediterranean fish is publicly displayed in a palatial, five-story aquarium. The aquarium's main attraction is the shark lagoon and naturalized marine mammals, both alive and stuffed as models. The permanent exhibit on the poles has an impressive section dedicated to global climate change, and each of the aquarium's 90 tanks manages to recycle 100% of the 250,000 gallons of water that the institution funnels from the marina every day; considering the 80ft. cliff that

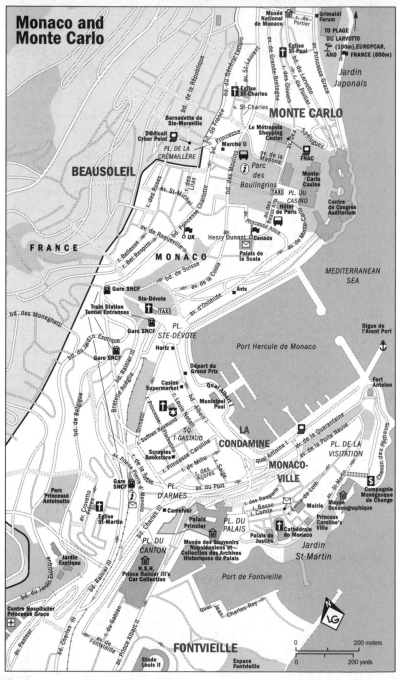

Monaco and Monte Carlo

Musée
National
de Monaco

Grimaldi
Forum

r. du
Portier

TO PLAGE
DU LARVOTTO
(100m), EUROPCAR,
AND FRANCE (800m)

Église
St-Paul

r. des Oliviers

r. du Portier

Jardin
Japonais

Bernadette de
Ste-Moreville

Église
St-Charles

v. St-Charles

MONTE CARLO

Dødicall
Cyber Point

PL. DE LA
CRÉMAILLÈRE

Marché U

Le Métropole
Shopping
Center

av. de la
Madone

FNAC

BEAUSOLEIL

Parc
des
Boulingrins

Monte-
Carlo
Casino

TAXI PL. DU
CASINO

Centre
de Congrès
Auditorium

av. de Roqueville

UK

Hôtel
de Paris

Henry Dunant

Canada

FRANCE

MONACO

bd. de Suisse

Palais de
la Scala

MEDITERRANEAN
SEA

av. de la Costa

av. d'Ostende

Avis

Gare SNCF

Ste-Dévote

TAXI

Train Station
Tunnel Entrances

Gare SNCF

PL.
STE-DÉVOTE

Port Hercule de Monaco

Digue de
l'Avant Port

bd. des Moneghetti

Gare SNCF

Hertz

Départ du
Grand Prix

Fort
Antoine

Casino
Supermarket

Municipal
Pool

LA
CONDAMINE

av. de la Quarantaine

PL. DE LA
VISITATION

SQ.
T-GASTAUD

av. de la Porte-Neuve

Scruples
Bookstore

MONACO-
VILLE

Gare SNCF

PL.
D'ARMES

Compagnie
Monégasque
de Change

Parc
Princesse
Antoinette

Église
St-Martin

Carrefour

Palais
Princier

PL. DU
PALAIS

Musée
Océanographique

Mairie

Princess
Caroline's
Villa

Cathédrale
de Monaco

Palais
de
Justice

Jardin
Exotique

PL. DU
CANTON

Musée des Souvenirs
Napoléoniens et
Collection des Archives
Historiques du Palais

Jardin
St-Martin

H.S.H.
Prince Rainier III's
Car Collection

Centre Hospitalier
Princesse Grace

Port de Fontvieille

quai Jean Charles-Rey

VG

0   200 meters

0   200 yards

FONTVIEILLE

Stade
Louis II

Espace
Fontvieille

houses the museum and its restaurant, it's quite a feat of engineering.

Ⓢ *Adults €13, students €6.50.* Ⓞ *Open Apr-Jun daily 9:30am-7pm, July-Aug daily 9:30am-7:30pm, Sept daily 9:30am-7pm, Oct-Mar daily 10am-6pm.*

NAPOLEONIC HISTORY MUSEUM ⊗ MUSEUM

place du Palais ☎93 25 18 31 ▣www.palais.mc

Containing over 1,000 items from France's First Empire, this museum was a gift to Albert II from his grandfather. Exhibits display letters of correspondence written by the megalomaniacal general concerning his conquest of Europe and even after his imprisonment on St. Helena. Not straying too far from Monegasque history, the museum also contains the charter granting Monaco's independence by Louis XII.

Ⓢ*Adults €4, students €2.* Ⓞ*Open Jan-Apr 1 (no joke) daily 10:30am-5pm, Apr 2-Oct 10am-6:15pm, Dec daily 10:30am-5pm.*

Monte Carlo

Let's be honest: you came to Monte Carlo for the casino, and we don't blame you. Let's Go won't advise you on how to play, but we can tell you that citizens of Monaco are banned from gambling—why take money from the rich?

CASINO MONTE CARLO ૬ ¥ CASINO

☎92 16 20 00 ▣www.casinomontecarlo.com

The renowned gambling house was infamous well before it was Ian Flemming's inspiration for the first book in the ▣James Bond series, Casino Royale, and continues to this day to conjure up images of Charles Wells breaking the bank at the turn of the century. While the well-dressed and optimistic can try their luck at any of the casino's table games or slot machines, the less intrepid can get a drink and hang out in the **Atrium du Casino** and marvel at the casino's opulence, which rivals the Royal Palace. Dress code is not in effect until 8pm, but jeans, sneakers, and T-shirts are frowned upon. 18+ gambling is strictly enforced. bring photo ID.

Ⓢ *€10 cover.* Ⓞ *Slots open July-Aug daily from noon, Sept-Jun from 2pm, Sa-Su from noon. Roulette daily from noon.*

JARDIN EXOTIQUE ⊗ GARDEN

62 bld. du Jardin Exotique ☎93 15 29 80 ▣www.jardin-exotique.mc

This garden of rare plant species from around the world has been growing since the 16th century, when New World explorers brought over cacti and rainforest plants. Accompanying the garden are the Observatory Caves and the prehistory museum, which takes visitors through a series of underground passageways and grottos through the local limerich cave system. Forget which ones are stalagmites and stalagtites? So do we.

Ⓢ *Adults €7, students €3.70.* Ⓞ *Open May 15-Sep 15 9am-7pm, Sept 16-May 14 9am-6pm (or until nightfall).*

La Condamine

PORT OF HERCULES ૬ PORT

La Condamine

Home to more money floating on water than a Kevin Costner flop, this port is the main service center for the mega yachts that visit the area. Surrounding the port is the famous stretch of the **Monaco Grand Prix,** as well as a series of cafes and bars ideal for escaping the sun.

Fontvieille

HSH PRINCE RAINIER III'S CAR COLLECTION ૬ MUSEUM

Terrasses de Fontvieille ☎92 05 28 56 ▣www.palais.mc

If you thought that the cars parked in front of the casino were impressive, think again—Prince Ranier III's antique car collection puts them all to shame. Highlights include the Cintroen Torpedo that crossed Asia for the Yellow Expedition race in the 1930's, and the sexy '56 Rolls Royce Silver Cloud that carried the prince and Grace Kelly on their wedding day. Don't miss the oldest specimen, the 1903 De Dion Bouton, one of the first widely manufactured steam engine cars. Ⓢ*Adults €6, students €3.* Ⓩ*Open daily 10am-6pm.*

LOUIS II STADIUM
                                                   ὅ ♈ SPORTS FACILITY
3 av. des Castelans   ☎92 05 40 11
One of the best-funded sports facilities in the world, the stadium is the home feild of AS Monaco, as well as an Olympic swimming pool and multisports hall surrounded by a world class althetic track. Ⓢ*Adults €4, students €2.* Ⓩ*Tours M, Tu, Th, and F 10:30am,11:30am, 2:30pm, and 4pm. W 10:30am and 11:30am.*

MONACO ZOO
                                                          ὅ ZOO
Terrasse de Fontvieille   ☎93 50 40 30 ▣www.palais.mc
Home to 250 animals and 50 different species, this zoo was once the private animal collection of Prince Ranier III before he opened up the grounds to the public in 1954. Ⓢ*Adults €4, students €2..* Ⓩ*Open Oct-Feb 10am-noon, 2-5pm, Mar-May 10am-noon, 2-6pm, Jun-Sep 9am-noon, 2-7pm.*

BEACHES   🔒

PLAGE DU LARVOTTO
                                                    ὅ BEACH
av. Princess Grace
Well, it's the best and worst beach in Monaco, since it's also the only one. Comprised of two man-made lagoons separated by a divider, this convenient sandy beach does not require a long hike or a daring leap over jagged rocks or cliffs to get to. Larvotto is also one of Monaco's few great equalizers, since everyone in the country who wishes to sunbathe must either come here or, you know, stick to their private yachts' sunbeds. *i Lifeguard, toilets and handicapped access.*

FOOD   🔗
Monaco-Ville

CHOCOLATERIE DE MONACO
                                      🍴ὅ⊿ CHOCOLATIER ❶
pl. de la Visitation   ☎97 97 88 88
Chocolatier specializing in Monaco-themed chocolates and a Viennese chocolate drink that is richer than the Prince himself. Ⓢ *Average of €1/10g of chocolate. €4.10 chocolate drinks.* Ⓩ *Open Daily 9am-6:30pm.*

U'CAVAGNATU
                                      🍴ὅ♈⊿ MONEGASQUE ❸
12 Comte Felix Gastaldi   ☎97 89 20 40
Traditional *monegasque* cuisine that blends both French and Italian influences into a fusion of Mediterranean styles. Obscure foods include fried zuccini, and olive and onion omelets. Ⓢ *Lunch plates €12.50-15, €25.50 fixed menu.* Ⓩ *Open Daily 12-5pm, 7-1pm.*

COSTA MONACO
                                    🍴ὅ♈ CAFE, CRÊPERIE ❷
8-10 rue Basse   ☎93 50 60 85
Small and relaxed cafe with low, blue couches in a low ceilinged room. Serves tarts, crêpes and drinks. Ⓢ *Crêpes €3-3.60, Pizza €5.40, Sandwiches €2-5.70.* Ⓩ *Open Daily 6am-8pm.*

RESTAURANT L'AURORE
                                🍴ὅ♈ MONEGASQUE, ITALIAN ❷
6,8 rue Princess Marie de Lorraine   ☎93 30 37 75
Monegasque/Italian restaurant open to large groups by reservation. The menu

breaking the bank

If you feel the need to throw your hard-earned euro at one of the richest institutions in the world, do yourself a favor and go for the Roulette wheel. Several resourceful (read: cheating) men have made out quite successfully, including **Joseph Jagger** (distant cousin to Mick) in 1873.

Joseph discovered a slight advantage—one particular wheel landed on 7, 8, 9, 17, 18, 19, 22, 28 and 29 more often than on the other numbers. After placing 7 bets, he quickly made over $1 million on the first day. The casino figured out the flaw and quickly moved tables to throw Jagger off. He was able to find the wheel again in the sea of tables by identifying a chip in the wheel, continued winning, and left with over two million francs, or $5 million in 2005 USD.

Con man **Charles Wells** worked a similar steal, again on the Roulette wheel, in 1891. Wells ⌘**broke the bank** (winning more than the chips on the table) 12 times, winning $2.5 million in 11 hours. In one particularly absurd run, he bet the number 5 for five consecutive turns, and won each time. Despite hiring private detectives to investigate, the casino never found out his system. Wells chalked it up to ⌘**"luck."**

is a little seafood heavy, so if you're not into fish you might want to try eating elsewhere. Reserve in advance because the restaurant is packed at night.
Ⓢ €13 plat du jour, €21 menu. Ⓣ Open Daily 12-2:30pm, 6:30pm-close.

Monte Carlo

SAKURA ⌘Ⓑ♈ SUSHI ❸
1 av. Henri Dunant ☎93 50 87 33
Sushi restaurant and bar in the Carre d'Or or Monte Carlo. All white interior serves a specialty of fatty tuna and a variety of California rolls. You'll want to dress up to go anywhere near the Carre d'Or, and this chic sushi bar is no exception. Dress to impress.
Ⓢ €13 rolls, €5 pieces of sashimi. Ⓣ Open Daily 12-2pm, 7-10:30pm.

IL TERRAZZINO ⌘Ⓑ♈ ITALIAN ❸
2 rue d'Iris ☎93 50 24 27
Highly praised restaurant known for its festive interior, which is designed to look like an outdoor market. Enjoy fine Italian cuisine while taking in a great view of the casino.
Ⓢ€45 prix-fixe, €12 plat du jour. ⓉOpen M-Sa 12-2:30pm, 7:30-11pm.

LA MAISON DU CAVIAR ⌘♿♈♨ FRENCH, TRADITIONAL ❹
1 av. St. Charles ☎93 30 80 06
Think your pallette is refined enough for caviar? There's no better place to try it in Monaco than at this classy French restaurant and wine bar, which specializes in its namesake, as well as other traditional French dishes. If fish eggs aren't for you, don't worry. the 4-course meal comes with *amuse bouche*, *fois gras*, an entrée or soup or salad, and beef tartar or and dessert. You certainly won't leave hungry, and for what you're getting the €28 price tag isn't too bad. For a meal this classy though, you'll want to look the part.
Ⓢ €28 4-course meal. Dishes €18-35. Ⓣ Open M-F 12-2:30pm, 7-10pm, Sa 7-10pm.

LA TAVERNE ⌘♿♈♨ TRADITIONAL, BRASSERIE ❷
10 bld. de la République ☎04 93 35 07 87
Located in Beausoleil, this French bistro and brasserie has cheaper French op-

monaco . food

tions with a lunch menu for €15. Local and casual.

$ Lunch menu €15, plates €9-16. ⏰ Open Tu-Su 12-2:30pm, 5-11pm.

La Condamine

LA PROVENCE
💳♿🍸⛅ PROVENÇAL [3]

22 rue Grimaldi ☎97 98 37 81

Upscale Provençal restaurant in the Condamine. Enjoy specialties like beef tartare in a classy atmosphere. You'll dine at wrought iron tables that give La Provence a mix of traditional flair and modern architecture. Don't worry about getting too dressed up, but make sure you look "nice."

$ Lunch menu €16, plates from €9-18. ⏰ Open Daily 12-3pm, 7-10pm.

PLACE DU MARCHE
💳♿ SANDWICH [1]

3 pl. d'Armes ☎97 77 73 40

If there was a French version Quiznos, it would probably be something like this sandwich shop, which specializes in typical French combinations of goat cheese and ham. The varying menu also features salads named after American cities, although the city's theme doesn't always hold true. Let's Go gives them an A for effort (and an A+ for price).

$€5.80-9 sandwiches, €6-7 salads. ⏰ Open Daily 11am-7pm.

Fotvieille

ALDEN T
💳♿🍸⛅ PASTA BAR [2]

rue de la Lüjerneta ☎97 98 57 57

Trendy pasta bar in the industrial section of Monaco. Open for breakfast and lunch.

$ Pasta €6.50, drink+pasta+dessert €9. ⏰Open Daily 7am-6pm.

NIGHTLIFE

Monaco-Ville

Do you really want to be the backpacker that woke up the royal family? Didn't think so. Monaco-Ville is the sleepy side of town, with no bars or clubs to note.

Monte Carlo

This neighborhood hosts some of the glitziest parties and expensive bars and clubs in all of Monaco, not to mention the world. If you're not dressed like a count, be prepared to be turned away at the door (especially if you are a guy or group of guys). While the glam of the **casino** seems to rub off on the surrounding clubs and bars, there are some holdout low-key establishments here that still accept jeans and T-shirts; if it's a **pub,** you're probably in the clear. The **beach** is lined with lounges, and the **av. Princesse Grace** boasts some of Monaco's mot expensive bars. The more laidback pubs and wine bars run along **rue Portier.**

MCCARTHY'S
💳♿🍸⛅ IRISH PUB

7 rue du Portier ☎93 50 88 10 💻www.mcpam.com

The last bastion of normalcy in the ritziest area of Monaco. This laidback Irish pub serves Irish cocktails (read: whiskey and bailys inspired) and some staple Kilkenny and Guiness in a welcoming atmosphere filled. Whiskey barrels are used for tables, and the walls are covered with Irish road signs.

$ €6 beer, €9-12 cocktails. Happy hour prices up to 30% off. ⏰ Open Daily 5pm-5am. Happy hour M-F 5-8pm.

COSMOPOLITAN
💳♿🍸⛅ WINE BAR

5 rue Portier ☎93 25 78 60 💻www.cosmopolitan.com

Upscale wine bar where elite patrons blow the bank on €600 bottles of Bordeaux, and backpackers like us sit around and look classy with a €4 glass. Quiet outdoor seating provides an ideal space for a casual conversation and a laidback start to a wild night.

$ €10-14 cocktails, €4-5 glass of wine. ⏰ Open Daily 12:30-2pm, 6-11pm.

LA NOTE BLEUE PIANO, JAZZ BAR

Plage du Larvotto ☎93 50 05 02 🖥www.lanotebleue.mc

For those who as a general rule don't leave the beach if you can help it, this classy jazz and piano bar is spitting distance from the water. The whitewashed walls and low couches make for a comfy place to sip your "Pure Happiness" (vodka, peach) or "Pure Pleasure" (vodka, strawberry, champgane) cocktails.

$ €12 cocktails, €7 beer. ⏰ Open Daily 6:30pm-3am. Wed-Sat concerts from 6:30pm-12am.

FLASHMAN CAFE BAR AND DISCO

7 av. de la Princesse Alice ☎93 30 09 03

Closest to the casino, this tiny disco bar's music changes slowly from jazz to club jams as the night goes on. The long dance hall in the back almost doubles the size of the bar, and the strategic happy hour and uncommonly late closing time ensures that people routinely start and end their nights here.

$ €5 beer, €10 cocktails. ⏰ Open W-M 9am-5am.

KARE(MENT) CLUB

10 av. Princess Grace ☎99 99 20 20 🖥www.karement.com

Located in the Grimaldy Forum, this enormous homage to debauchery is comprised of 3 bars and a dance floor, and hovers 100ft over the water. The views of the ocean from the third bar are particularly dramatic, and the nightly live DJs keep the party hopping. Thursdays are "Salsa Ladies Night"—and features heavily discounted drinks—until 11pm, when the theme changes abruptly to "'80s Night." Think those two themes fit well? Neither do we.

$ Prices. ⏰ Open summer everyday 8am-5am, Winter M-F 8:30am-5am, Sa 6pm-5am.

THE LIVING ROOM PIANO BAR, CLUB

7 rue Speluges ☎93 50 80 31

Old school piano bar and throwback to the 1920's and '30s, with a particularly casual patio deck. DJ music gradually incorporates modern music into the bar's repetoire as the night goes on, and expertly syncs modern mixes with the jazz piano.

$ €10 beer, €15 cocktails. ⏰ Open M-Sa 11pm-5am.

CAFE SASS LOUNGE, BAR

11 av. Princess Grace ☎93 25 52 10 🖥www.sasscafe.com

The name says it all. This sassy bar has all the attitude of the glitzy bars, minus the stuffy pretention. While still pricey, this bar teaches the other half how to have fun in the adjoining restaurant/bar, which hosts private parties and mixers for the snazzily dressed.

$€8 beer, €18 cocktails ⏰Open 8pm-5am (food served until 1am in summer).

ZELO'S RESTAURANT, LOUNGE

Grimaldi Forum ☎99 99 25 50 🖥www.zelosworld.com

Stuffy top floor bar of the Grimaldi Forum that is redeemed by the stunning views of the ocean and Monaco Ville. The Terrace seating and lounge area are the perfect place to consider ordering a drink, so long as its before 11pm, when the prices nearly double.

$Before 11pm: €6 beer, €5 shooter, €9 cocktail. After 11pm: €10 beer, €10 shooter, €15 cocktail. ⏰Open Daily 6:30pm-2:30am.

La Condamine

The slacker hub of Monaco, La Condamine doesn't require you to dress up completely, though a collared shirt or heels would be nice. Most of the ex-pat bars are located in this area, as well as some of the best happy hour deals.

■ SLAMMERS

♦&♀☆ BRITISH PUB

6 rue Saffren
☎97 70 36 56

The name says it all. British-run and Morrocan-designed pub with an open mike jam session every Sunday. Low couches on outdoor patio are packed with disaffected youth. Owner encourages ordering takeout for delivery to the bar from neighboring restaurants.

⑤€4 beer, €10.50 alcohols. Happy hours almost half price. ⚅Open M-F 5pm-1am, Sa-Su 1pm-1am. Happy hours 5-8pm.

■ STARS AND BARS

♦&⑴♀☆ BAR

6 quai Antoine 1er
☎97 97 95 95 ▨www.starsnbars.com

The ideal guy hangout, Stars and Bars boasts an awesome collection of auto sports memorabilia, a collection of fooseball tables, and crowds that regularly overflow onto the port. The bar serves killer beer cocktails—we recommend the "Exotic," a combo of light beer, pineapple and Malibu rum that will knock you on your ass.

⑤€8 beer cocktails, €5 beer. Half priced Happy hour. ⚅Open Daily 5:30pm-3 am. Happu Hour from opening to 7:30pm.

RASCASSE

♦&♀☆▼ BAR, CLUB

Antoine 1er
☎93 25 56 90 ▨www.larascasse.mc

One of the most upscale bars and clubs in this neighborhood, the Rascasse is well known for its 5hr happy hour and nightly DJs. The bar is located on the famous turn of the Grand Prix, and remains a sure bet for those who want some class in their evening without feeling intimidated or ripped-off.

i Happy hour half-priced drinks. ⑤ Beer €6. Cocktails €10. ⚅ Open daily noon-5am. Happy hour M-F 6-11pm. Music F-Sa (Th Jul-Aug) 11:30pm to close.

BRASSERIE DE MONACO

♦♀☆▼ BAR

36 route de la Piscine
☎93 30 09 09

Young, fun hangout for travellers and locals. Right on the port, this bar and pseudo-club has all the traits of a strip club, from the dancing girls to the flatscreen TVs playing looped taps of models' photoshoots. Don't worry; it isn't. The fun crowd gathers around long cafeteria style tables for easy conversation and making friends.

⑤ Beer €6. Cocktails €15. ⚅ Open daily 11am-3am.

Fotvieille

The only popular bar here is in the **Columbus Hotel,** but it's for stiffs and rich people, and probably not your idea of a good time. As multiple Bond movies suggest, the Columbus serves wicket martinis, but you need to dress up for it and be prepared to leave and catch a bus back to the fun side of town.

GRAND PRIX

There are two **Grand Prix** in Monaco every year, despite what you have heard. The first is the granddaddy of all that is fast and expensive, known in the racing world as the **Formula 1 Grand Prix.** Flashy cars tear up the streets of Monaco during a three day weekend in May every year, as the country plays host to ridiculous yacht parties and mind-blowing hotel prices. Expect to shell out €600 for the good seats (€125 for nosebleed section) to watch Mercedes-McLauren or Ferrari battle it out for the title with their Formula 1 racers. Be aware that prices all the way to Cannes almost triple during this weekend, and transport becomes almost impossible by car. The best plan is to stay in France and commute to Monaco for raceday; to reduce the cost further, forego the finals on Sunday and attent the trials days on Friday or Saturday instead, when the cost it almost halved.

The second of these Grand Prix is the **Historic Grand Prix,** which occurs exactly 2 weeks before the Formula 1 Grand Prix. This race takes place on the same track and involves the same car manufacturers, but the rides themselves are all shout outs to years past. Cars made from the 1930's to the late 1980's that have ever particpated in the Grand Prix are bracketed and raced; unsurprisingly, tickets to this event are much more affordable. In 2011. the racing dates for the Formula 1 Grand Prix are May 26-29. The Historic Grand Prix is 2 weeks prior.

a day at the races

The **Formula One** race in Monaco may be the epitome of monetary excess, but it is possible to get by without spending thousands on gambling, drinking and jacuzzi parties with some self-control and clever budgeting.

- **WHEN TO GO:** The races are held over a three-day period in May. The upcoming dates are May 26-29, 2011 and May 24-27, 2012.
- **WHERE TO STAY:** No, not huddled on a park bench begging for a sniff of a champagne cork, but most reliably (and cheaply) in **Menton or Nice**. You can try and swing it at the Monte Carlo, but as of 2010, there are very few availabilities in 2011 (and you probably don't want to pay their rates anyway). Your best bet is to stay in Nice and take one of the frequent trains to Monaco. For those with a little pocket change, it is possible to rent the terraces of apartments that face the course for €3500 per week (jacuzzi not included).
- **TICKETS AND SEATING:** The official ticketing agency sells them online at www.monaco-grand-prix.com/en/TICKETS, but like the cars, they go fast. Keep in mind the best seating is in sections A1, A4, V, Z1 and Z2. Sections A and V cost €600-700 for the finals on Sunday, and Z sections cost around €150. Preliminary days are substantially cheaper (€200-300 for Saturday A sections, €106 for Thursday).
- **THE PRIX IS RIGHT:** Note the difference between the Grand Prix Historique vs. the Grand Prix F1. The F1 is the famous one, with the Formula One race cars featuring Mercedes-McLaren and Ferrari. In the Prix Historique, old race cars from before 1940 to current Formula Three cars tear through the town. It takes place 2 weeks before the Formula 1, races the same course as the big one, but the two-day package tickets only costs €88.

ESSENTIALS

Practicalities

- **TOURIST OFFICE:** 2A bld. des Moulins *(☎92 16 61 16)*, uphill from the casino. English speaking staff provides city maps, extensive pocket guides for restuarants, hotels, nightlife, and attractions, rendering *Let's Go* almost obsolete. Open M-Sa-9am-7pm, Su 11am-1pm. Annexes in the train station at the av. Prince Pierre exit, in the chemin des Pecheurs parking garage, in the port and outside the Jardin Exotique (open mid-Jun to Aug).
- **EMBASSIES AND CONSULATES: Canada.** *(1 av. Henry Durant ☎97 70 62 42);* **France.** *(1 chemin du Tenao ☎92 16 54 60);* **UK.** *(33 bld. de la Princess Charlotte ☎93 50 99 54).* Nearest **US** embassy is in Nice *(☎04 93 88 89 55).*
- **CURRENCY EXCHANGE:** Bureau de Change, in Compagnie Monegasque de Change, in the chemins des Pecheurs parking garage. *(Av. de la Quarantine ☎93 25 02 50* $ Cash advances €50 min. ⏰ *Open M-Sa 9:30am-5:30pm.)*

- **INTERNET ACCESS: FNAC,** 17 av. des Speluges *(☎93 10 81 81)* in Le Metropole Shopping Center. *(ℹ Frequent lines. $ 20min. free. ⏰ Open M-Sa 10am-5:30pm.)* **D@dicall Cyber Point,** 1 impasse General Leclerc (Beausoleil), has Wi-Fi. *(☎04 93 57 42 14 $ Internet €4 per hr. ⏰ Open daily 10:30am-8pm.)*
- **POST OFFICE:** 23 av. Albert II *(☎98 98 41 41 ⏰ Open M-F 9am-7pm, Sa 8am-noon.)* All mail posted in the principality must bear Monegasque stamps. Annex at av. Prince Pierre train station exit. 4 additional branches.
- **POSTAL CODE:** MC 98000 Monaco.

Emergency!

- **EMERGENCY NUMBERS: Ambulance:** ☎93 25 33 25.
- **POLICE:** *(3 rue Louis Notari ☎93 15 30 15).* 5 other stations in Monaco.
- **HOSPITAL: Centre Hospitalier Princesse Grace,** Av. Pasteur *(☎97 98 99 00).* Accessible by bus #5 (dir. Hospital).

Getting There

By Train

Gare SNCF has 4 main access points: galerie Prince Pierre, pl. St-Devote, bld. de Belgique, and bld. de la Princesse Charlotte. *(⏰ Open daily 4am-1am. Info desk and ticket window open M-F 5:50am-8:30pm, Sa-Su 5:50am-8:10pm.)* Trains run to: **Antibes** *(1 hr., every 30 min, €6.30);* **Nice** *(25 min, every 30 min., €2.70);* **Cannes** *(1 hr. 10 min., every 30 min., €7.50);* **Menton** *(11min., every 30 min., €1.70).*

By Bus

Buses leave from the bld. des Moulins and av. Princesse Grace, near the tourist office. **TAM** and **RCA** *(☎93 85 64 44).* To Nice *(45 min)* and Menton *(25 min).* Cap d'Ail, St-Jean-Cap-Ferrat and the -sur Mer's via route to Nice. There is also a direct line from the Nice Airport (RCA) via the A8 motorway *(45 min., every hour between 9am-9:15pm, €16.10, under 26 €11.50, return €26).*

By Helicopter

Hey, you never know. It is Monaco, after all.**Heli Air Monaco** lands in Fontvielle at the Monaco Heliport. *($ €7 min. €120 per 30min.)*

Getting Around

The **bus** system in Monaco is a godsend from its hilly terrain built onto the side of a steep shoreline. The six lines run pretty much to wherever from wherever. *($ Individual ticket €1, 24hr. pass €3. ⏰ M-F every 10min., Sa-Su every 20-30min.)* Buy tickets on board. **Taxis** *(☎93 15 01 01 $ €10 min.)* run 24hr. and wait at 11 taxi stands throughout the city, including the casino, pl. des Moulins, and the train station. If you like control of your own wheels, you can also rent a **scooter** from Auto-Moto Garage, 7 rue de Milo. *(☎93 50 10 80 ℹ Credit cards accepted. $ 50cc scooter €40 per day, €45 per 24hr., €260 per week. €1000 credit security charge. ⏰ Open M-F 8am-noon and 2-7pm, Sa 8am-noon.)*

villefranche sur mer ☎04 93

This small fishing village 10min. from Gare Nice is a haven for those trying to escape the noise and fellow backpackers of Nice. The much appreciated sandy beach (in a region generally devoid of sand beaches) right off of the train tracks makes this village an ideal location for a daytrip—dig your toes into the sand and swim around without the crowds from neighboring towns. While the town itself is small, the sights are mostly free and feature local heroes and famous artists known only in this region.

Be prepared for steep hills and make your way through winding alleyways of Villefranche's old town. Our advice: stalk up on fruit and sandwiches in the old town and head for the harbor or beach for a day's picnic in this peaceful escape.

ACCOMMODATIONS

Villefranche-sur-Mer has ample accommodations for the budget traveler, but you can find cheaper and more backpacker friendly locations in neighboring Nice (and a better nightlife, btw). The budget hotels are towards the top of the city's hill near the tourist office, while the quai boasts expensive waterfront properties crawling with older crowds looking to get away from loud noises and fun things in general.

LA REGENCE — 📶🍸 HOTEL [3]

2 av. Marechal Foch — ☎04 93 01 70 91

Simple hotel rooms with a prime location on top of the city's hill, near the Citadel and the Tourist office. The balconies overlook the port, and there's a lovely restaurant and bar on the ground floor. Simplicity is the name of the game here: think bare walls, white bedspreads. Color is only a distraction anyway.

➡ Across the street from the tourist office. $ Singles €58; doubles and triples €72. Breakfast €6.50.

HOTEL PROVENÇAL — ♿📶🍸 HOTEL [1]

av. Marechal Joffre — ☎04 93 76 53 53 🖥 www.hotelProvençal.com

This clean hotel two blocks down from the tourist office hosts a classy restaurant and brightly colored rooms with air-conditioning. Balcony and window views of the port and the citadel.

➡ With your back to the tourist office, walk to the intersection and turn right. Hotel is down the street two blocks on the right. $ Doubles €59-90; triples €69-120. Breakfast €10. Prices higher in summer season.

SIGHTS

Villefranche is a small village whose sights don't exactly put it on the tourist map, even within the scope of Southern France. While its citadel is impressive enough, and its St. Peter's chapel is cute and historical, the town boasts what could be considered the holy grail to sun and surf travelers: a sand beach devoid of private clubs or development in an area that is full of rocky beaches.

PLAGE DES MARINIERS — ♿ BEACH

quai l'Admiral Ponchardier

Located steps from the train station, this long stretch of **sand** beach is exactly what the purists are dreaming about when they step foot on any of the rocky beaches in Nice or Cagnes. Devoid of private clubs or development, it's well worth the trip from Nice just to dig your toes into the warm, welcoming sand and swim in the calm, natural *baie La Rade*.

LA CITADELLE — FORTRESS

Fosses de la Citadelle, entrance at Place Philibert

The imposing fortress was built in 1557 by the cunning military strategist Emmanuel Philibert, who's Machiavellian list of accomplishments included regaining Turin from the Spanish and French by exploiting a regional squabble. Today, the citadel houses the town's numerous free museums, including a recreation of the town in the Middle Ages, the Volti Museum, and the museum of Goetz-Boumeeter, a French American surrealist painter whose little black book includes Picasso and Miro.

$ Free entry. ⏰ Museums open Oct-May 10am-noon, 2-5:30pm; Jun-Sep 10am-noon, 2:30-6:30pm. Closed Sunday mornings and November.

CHAPELLE SAINT-PIERRE PAR JEAN COCTEAU — CHURCH

quai de l'Admiral Courbert, at the end of rue Gabetta

Romanesque Chapel designed and painted by French Rennasissance Man

Jean Cocteau. This avant garde poet, artist, playwright, director and lover (his girlfriends include Edith Piaf and Coco Chanel) organized the town's craftsmen Wikipedia-style—everyone pitched in and added a bit of their own style to its construction and decoration. The interior was painted by Cocteau, and the ceramics and boats were built by local craftsmen and dedicated to local fisherman.

$ *Admission €2.50* ⏰ *Open Tu-Su 10am-noon, 2-6pm (3-7pm in summer). Closed from mid-November to mid-December.*

FOOD

Food in Villefranche can be cheap, if you know where to look. The small alleyways in the old city harbor the cutest eats and best deals for a sit down meal, while the *quai* has a more picturesque setting on the boardwalk (and higher prices). Picnics on the docks seem to be a popular choice; stop by the local Casino market *(1 rue Poilu, Open M-Sa 9am-noon, 2-7pm)* and then head towards the water, or stocking up on fruit in Nice before you leave for this small town.

L'ESCALE
💳🚫🍸☀ CRÊPES, BURGERS, TAPAS ❶

2 rue de l'Église ☎04 93 55 35 27

Cute cafe and tapas restaurant located on a large patio at the bottom of an alleyway's narrow stairs. The menu is comprised of pretty basic fare, including kebab, burgers, and sandwiches.

$ *Sandwiches €6.50. Plat du jour €13. Salads €8-11. Burgers €6.* ⏰ *Open Daily 10am-2am.*

LES GARCONS
💳♿🍸☀ PROVENÇAL ❷

18 rue Poilu ☎04 95 76 62 40

A modern Provençal restaurant with hints of rustic charm. The modern lighting contrasts with the earth tone walls and the rust colored, wooden tables. The outdoor seating is in a quiet plaza near the cathedral. The vibe manages to be relaxed and chic at the same time.

$ *Plats €13-15, lunch menu (entree+plat+dessert) €15.* ⏰ *Open M-Sa 12-2pm, 7-10pm.*

LA SERRE
💳🚫🍸☀ PIZZERIA, SANDWICHES ❶

rue de la May ☎04 93 76 79 91

This hole in the wall pizzeria serves pizzas named after American States. Try the Texan or the Californian, but be warned that the theme doesn't really hold at all. When was the last time you had tuna and anchovies in either of the Dakotas?

$ *Pizzas €5-6. Pasta €8.* ⏰ *Open Tu-Sa 11am-2pm, 5-10pm.*

LE ROXY
⊛♿🍸☀ PIZZERIA ❶

2 av. Grand-Bretagne ☎04 93 76 71 80

Pizzeria and cafe at the top of the city's hill that offers views of the port and Citadel. Cheap pasta and pizzas to go (and take to beach, hint hint).

$ *Pasta €5. Pizza and drink €13.* ⏰ *Open Daily 12:30-4pm, 6:30-11pm. Cash only.*

NIGHTLIFE

There's a reason you don't need to go to this town for nightlife—Villefranche is smashed right between Nice and Monaco. If you want to get leisurely a beer after chilling all day in the sun, this one bar is the best place in town:

LOMBARDO'S BAR
⊛♿🍸☀ BAR

5 rue du Poilu ☎04 93 01 94 74

A local, laidback sports bar with walls covered in soccor jerseys and scarfs from teams all over France. Lombardo's is the perfect place to chat up Olympique Marseille's win in 2010 and the prospects of Paris Saint-Germain in the coming seasons.

$ *€1.50 demi, €5 pints, €5 alcohol.* ⏰ *Open Daily 11am-1:30am (or later). Cash only.*

Practicalities

- **TOURIST OFFICE: Jardin Fraonçois Binon.** At the highest point in the city. Keep following signs going uphill, no matter if you think its pointing downhill. (*☎04 93 01 73 68* Ⓓ *Open M-Sa 9am-noon, 2-6pm. July and August 7 days a week.)*

- **TOURS:** Guided tour of the old town and Citadel organized by **tourist office** (Ⓢ*€5, under 12 free).* The May-Sep "Citadel Mornings" tour includes light breakfast in Volti Museum courtyard and guided tour of old town and Citadel (Ⓢ *€8 per person.* Ⓓ *every F 9am).*

- **BANK: BNP Paribas.** ATM available *(1 av. Albert I.* ☎*04 93 76 34 83).*

- **LAUNDROMAT: Laverie Automoatique** *(9 av. Sadi Carnot* ☎*06 09 16 25 53.* Ⓓ*Open Daily 7am-9pm).*

- **TELEPHONE CENTER: Duquesne Telecom.** Recharge of prepaid phone cards or 5 sur 5 and Orange *(10 av. Foch* ☎*04 93 76 90 00).*

- **POST OFFICE:** Av. Alber I and Sadi Carnot. *(*☎*04 93 76 30 80.* Ⓓ*Open M-F 9am-noon, 2-5:15pm, Sa 9am-noon.)*

Emergency!

- **POLICE: Police Municipale.** (☎*04 93 76 33 42)*

- **PHARMACY: Marchal Foch.** *(av. Laurent* ☎*04 93 01 70 10.* Ⓓ *Open M-Sa 8:45am-12:15pm and 2:30-7:15pm).*

Getting There

By Train

The **Gare SNCF** services the area. Automatic ticket dispensers for those with European bank cards. *(av. Georges Clemenceau* ☎*36 35* Ⓓ *Trains run 5am-9pm. Ticket office open 6am-noon and 1-7pm).* Trains run to **Nice** (Ⓢ *€2.30.* Ⓓ *10min., every 30min.)* and **Monaco** (Ⓢ *€5.* Ⓓ *15min., every 30min.)*

By Bus

#81 runs regularly to Villefranche from Nice *(dir. Saint Jean Cap Ferrat.* Ⓢ *€5.* Ⓓ *20min., every 15min.).* The **TAM #100 bus** that connects Nice to Menton also stops in Villefranche.

menton   ☎04 93

Often called the Secret Riviera, Menton offers the chance to bask in Côte d'Azur sunshine and wander through quaint alleyways without the gouging prices and snobby club scene thats pervades the coastline between Monaco and St-Tropez. Reminiscent of a time before discotheques, Menton is a quiet town with a slow pace of life; we don't think it's a coincidence that the city feels more Italian than French. With the Italian border just a couple of minutes away, you definitely feel the culture seeping in, with *gelaterias* and Italian cuisine frequently mixed with French menus and seafood. The town is still a popular destination for French and Italian tourists, so don't expect undiscovered bliss. Still, Menton's hybrid culture with an Italian twang is more than worth a trip—any town that features pizza and gelato on the average *menu du jour* is a friend of ours.

ORIENTATION

Menton is neatly divided into three parts: the **Old Town,** the **New Town,** and the **beach** or **port.** While the beach is practically the only sight that is not in the Old Town, and the port de Garavan is mostly local and devoid of tourists, the **new port** on the border of the old city prominently features the **Bastion fort.** Head towards the **chapel tower** from the Bastion to enter the old city. The **pl. du Cap** with its slew of small restaurants is at its heart, while the **pl. St. Michel** is the oldest part of town in front of the church. The two main walkways that snake through the old town and towards the new town are the **rue St. Michel** and the **rue de la République,** which pass by the **Hôtel de Ville.**In the new city, the **av. de Verdun** is the main road that clearly separates the new and old cities, and leads right to the doors of the casino and nightclub, passing by the **Palais de l'Europe** and the **Tourism Office.** Follow that road up and turn left to reach the **train** and **bus stations.**

ACCOMMODATIONS

HOTEL DE BELGIQUE

BUDGET HOTEL ❸

1 av. de la Gare ☎04 93 35 72 66

Located close to the train station, this budget hotel offers 20 simple rooms with A/C and phones. The balconies provide great views of the new part of town.

Exit train station and walk straight. Hotel is on your right. $ Singles and doubles €34-49; triples and quads €65-90. Book well ahead of time in summer. Reception open 7am-2:30pm, 5:30-10pm.

AUBERGE DE JEUNESSE

HOSTEL ❶

pl. St. Michel ☎04 93 35 93 www.fuaj.org

Basic and backpacker friendly, this local branch of France's most reliable chain of hostels comes complete with a full bar and cheap drinks, as well as clean bathrooms and sturdy bunks in the single sex dorms. Be warned: walking here can be a challenge, and the area feels abandoned at night.

Take bus #6 (8:30am, 11:10am, 2 and 5pm, €1). $ €17.50 per bed.

L'AUBERGE PROVENÇAL

HOTEL, RESTAURANT ❸

11 rue Trenca ☎04 93 35 77 29

Basic hotel in the heart of the old city. Located right off of rue St. Michel, the hotel offers free Wi-Fi, a bar, and A/C in 12 simple rooms.

Between rue St. Michel and rue de la République. i Restaurant, parking, and phones available. $ Singles and doubles €39-55.

RICHELIEU

HOTEL ❹

26 rue Partouneaux ☎04 93 35 74 71 www.richelieu-menton.com

Simple hotel behind the Palais de l'Europe, removed from the main drag of nearby shopping stores. If you gamble, you'll appreciate its proximity to the casino, but hopefully you're a good gambler—if you're paying the rates to stay here, you can't afford to lose much more.

From the Palais de l'Europe, walk behind it onto rue Partouneaux. Hotel on the left $ Singles €40-55, doubles €57-90, triples €80-115.

CAMPING SAINT MICHEL

CAMPING ❶

route des Ciappes ☎04 93 35 81 23 www.tourisme-menton.fr

Nearby campsite with tent spots and caravans for rent. Close to the Auberge de Jeunesse and shaded by rows of olive trees. Awesome views overlooking Menton and the ocean. On-site restaurant offers pizzas *(€9)* and pastas *(€9-16).* Fooseball tables and pool as well.

Take bus #6 (8:30am, 11:10am, 2 and 5pm, €1) $ Tents €4.45. Caravan €21.30. Electricity €2.80. Car €13. Reception open M-Sa 8:30am-noon, 3-7pm, Su 8:30am--12:30pm, 5-6:30pm.

SIGHTS

SERRE DE LA MADONE — GARDEN

74 route de Gorbio ☎04 93 57 73 90 🖳www.serredelamadone.com

One of the most spectacular gardens in a garden-packed city, the Serre de la Madone manages to be "Heaven on Earth" by organizing its repetoire of flowers so that there is always a flower bed in bloom. The pathways designed by American Lawrence Johnson take you past quiet pools and mazes of hedgerow, as well as the enormous **dragon tree** imported from the Canary Islands (though we didn't think it looked anything like a **dragon**).

Serre de la Madone stop on bus #7 (10 min., €1) $ €8 adults, €4 under 18 and students. ⏰ Open Tu-Su Apr-Oct 10am-6pm, Dec-Mar 10am-5pm. Guided tours 3pm.

MUSÉE JEAN COCTEAU — MUSEUM

quai Napoleon ☎04 93 57 72 30

Located inside the Bastion, the museum's building is as much of an artistic triumph as the paintings it holds. In addition to his other work, Cocteau was known for applying his avant garde aesthetic to decrepid historical buildings, and spent years revamping this abandoned fortress, which was originally built by the Prince of Monaco in 1616. The artist died before he could complete the renovations, but not before he could replace the windows with wrought iron, mosaic the hallways, scatter zoomorphic statues throughout the rooms.

$ €3 adults, €1.50 students. ⏰ Open M and W-Su 10am-noon, 2-6pm, free first Sunday of the month.

MONASTERE ANNONCIADE — MONASTERY

2135 corniche André Tardieu ☎04 93 35 76 92

A symbol of Menton, this monastery is perched 225m above the harbor and old city. The Virgin of the Annonciade allegedly cured Princess Isabella of Monaco's leprosy here, and the hike up is now peppered with 15 mini-chapels, each dedicated to one of the stations of the cross. You might never be this preoccupied with the Stations of the Cross ever again (unless you're Catholic, in which case you run through them every Friday in Lent); each chapel brings you closer to the awesome views from the top of the city below.

Take #4 bus from the Gare Routière at 8:30am, 11:40am, 2:30pm, and 6:35pm. ⏰ Open Daily 8am-noon, 2-6pm. Mass Jul-Aug M-Sa 7:30am, Su 10am; Sep-Jun M-Sa 11:15am, Su 10am.

BASILLIQUE SAINT MICHEL — BASILICA

Parvis Saint Michel

The tower over the old city serves as a convenient landmark for tourists, and it should not be hard to locate the Baroque Chapel. The sheer grandeur of the church's glass chandaliers and suspended gold crown is somewhat undermineed by its history; Menton didn't have any cemeteries until 1850, so poor locals were buried in a mass grave under the cathedral.

From rue St. Michel, turn left onto rue des Logettes, then go up the steps of the rue des Ecole Pie. ⏰ Open M-F and Su 10am-noon, 2-6:15pm. Sept May 10am-noon, 3-5:15pm. Mass Su 10:30am.

FOOD

Known for its markets, Menton's whole "my town is a garden" slogan is onto something. Numerous open-air markets line the ave. Sospel, including the bustling Marché Carei *(Open Daily 7am-1pm)*. The Marché du Bastion offers a seaside shopping for produce on quai Napoleon III. Restaurants are packed in the old town along rue St. Michel and rue de la République. Local supermarkets line the rue de la République closer to the new city.

CAFE MENTONNAIS — MENTON CUISINE [3]

5 rue deu Vieux College ☎04 93 35 43 08

A small cafe tucked away off of rue St. Michel, the Cafe Mentonnais serves a

traditional fusion of Italian and French dishes with a heavy seafood influence from the sea. The walls are covered in sketches of the city and colorful modern art.
Ⓢ *Formule €16. Lunch menu €13.* Ⓓ *Open Tu-Su 12-11pm.*

MAISON HERBIN ET SON ARCHE DES CONFITURES 🍴♿🍷 SPECIALTY MARKET ❷
2 rue Vieux College   ☎04 93 57 20 29 🖥www.confitures-herbin.com
The Maison Herbin is stacked wall-to-wall, floor-to-ceiling with jams, sauces, and honeys produced daily in the kitchen out back. Menton citruses are used to make the tangy jams, as well as the Liqueur de Menton (*€11.75*), a French version of Limoncella. Flavors such as "lavender honey" or "dark chocolate orange jam" will run you more than the traditional flavors, but are worth the splurge.
Ⓢ *Honey €4.30-7.70. Jams €4-6.* ⓘ *Free guided tours with free tastes M,W,and F 10:30am.* Ⓓ *Open Jun-Aug daily 9am-12:30pm, 3:15-7:30pm. May-Sep closed Sundays.*

THE LAST BEACH 🍴♿🍷🍨 FAST FOOD, ITALIAN, ICE CREAM ❷
1563 promendade du Soleil   ☎04 93 86 99 73
With seating right on the beach, this cheap fast food cafe serves pretty much any kind of (Mediterranean) food you'll ever want, from ice cream to lasagna (*€11*). A gluten free menu is available, in additon to a wide array of salads and tarts for dessert.
ⓘ *Italian speaking.* Ⓢ *Plat du jour €11. Paninis €4. Ice cream €2.* Ⓓ *Open daily 9am-8pm. Winter closes at 5pm.*

LE GAMBAS ROUGE 🍴♿🍷🍨 SEAFOOD ❷
rue de la Marne   ☎04 93 28 54 75
Resembling a Louisiana shrimp house, this culinary blend of Italian and French cuisine serves a cheap *plat du jour* (*€10*) in an almost entirely outdoor seating area. Look for the large picture of a friendly-looking shrimp on the sign hanging over the tattered doors and windows.
Ⓢ *€10 plat du jour.* Ⓓ *Open daily 12-2:30pm, 7-10pm.*

PETIT TRAITEUR 🍴♿🍨 ROTISSERIE ❶
3 rue Trenca   ☎04 93 57 29 86
This hole-in-the-wall French fast food place specializes in rotisserie chicken, and also sells quiche, roastbeef and bottles of port wine. While nothing fancy, the eatery is right next to the beach and serves as a one stop shop for a high class picnic at dirt cheap prices.
Ⓢ *Whole chickens €3.50, quiche and meats €2. Port wine €9.* Ⓓ *Open daily 10am-6pm.*

YOGURTLANDIA 🍴♿🍨 FROZEN YOGURT ❶
9 rue St. Michel   ☎04 93 45 82 33
Tiny frozen yogurt cafe serves crêpes, cheap sandwiches and, of course, its namesake. Yogurt cups come with a choice of two toppings, which ranging from raspberry to nutella to mint syrup. The colorful and fun interior is decorated with kindergarten colors and fake flowers that lighten the mood.
Ⓢ *Small yogurt €2.50, medium €3.50, large €4.50. Sandwiches €3-4. Crêpes €3.* Ⓓ *Open daily 12-8pm.*

NIGHTLIFE

LE TERRASSE 🍴🚫🍷🍨 BAR, LOUNGE
av. Felix Faure   ☎04 92 10 16 16
The patio lounge and bar attached to the casino. The neon couches look out over the ocean and foster a pretty laidback atmosphere, considering that most of the customers are here to get rich or die trying next door.
ⓘ *Drink prices double after midnight. 18+ only, bring photo ID.* Ⓢ *Drinks before midnight €3-7.* Ⓓ *Open M-Sa 7pm-4am.*

LE BRUMMELL 🍴🍷 CLUB
av. Felix Faure   ☎04 92 10 16 16
The nightclub attached to the casino. The large open dance floor is surrounded

by low couches and leftover decorations from soirees past. The bright lights generate a clubby atmosphere that's less intimidating than the occasional elitism of neighboring Monaco or the seedy clubs of Nice.

i Soirees including 70s Night and White Party. $ Cover €15, includes free drink. Free for women before 1am. ⏰ Open 11pm-4am (or later).

CAFE DU MUSÉE

BAR

25 quai Monleon ☎04 93 35 46 38

Seaside cafe and bar that is covered with old posters of Monaco's Grand Prix and Nice's celebs. Specialty drinks incude the Italian Mojitos made with Italian sparkling white wine. The bar's closing hours are uncertain—it technically closes at midnight, but can stay open for hours afterwards until everyone leaves. The party really gets going on Fridays, when the DJ starts mixing popular music.

$ Beer €4. Cocktails €7-8. ⏰ Open Daily 8am-12am. Friday DJ starts at 8:30pm.

LE BRAZZA

BRASSERIE

2 pl. Clemenceau ☎04 93 35 73 12

Laidback brasserie in the heart of the old town. The classic outdoor setting with TVs playing sports matches. The cheap beer and drinks make for an easy night out after a long day at the beach.

$ Beer €2.60. Cocktails €4.90-7.50. ⏰ Open Daily 11am-midnight.

FESTIVALS

FESTIVAL DE MUSIQUE

☎04 92 41 76 76 🖥www.musique-menton.fr

Citywide music festival taking place in Menton's gardens, chapels and cathedrals. Starting in late July and running until mid-August, the festival allows visitors to appreciate the blooming gardens and charming town with a soothing soundtrack of classical music, opera, and chamber music.

$ Ticket prices vary with seating, students and under 25 up to 25% off. Packages of 3, 6 and 9 concerts €25-110, €50-205 and €60-205. Individual concerts ranging between €10-60.

FETE DU CITRON

☎04 92 41 76 76 🖥www.feteducitron.com

Festival from mid-Feb to early March celebrating all things citrus, this Mentonnais party features parades with floats built from oranges, grapefruits, and lemons. Think Rose Bowl with lemons. Escape scurvy with copious amounts of the town's famous lemon liqueur and enjoy the percussion bands and fire dancers in this sour Mardi-gras-esque revelry.

$€9-23 depending on event. Students up to 25% off. ticket available online. ⏰ From mid-Feb to early March.

ESSENTIALS

Practicalities

- **TOURIST OFFICE:** Located inside the Palais de l'Europe. English speaking staff offers free maps and restaurant and hotel guides, as well as festival information. *(8 av. Boyer ☎04 92 41 76 76 🖥www.villedementon.com. ⏰ Open Jun-Sept M-Sa 8:30am-7pm, Su 9am-7pm; Oct-May M-Sa 8:30am-12:30pm and 2-6pm, Su 9am-12:30pm.)*
- **TOURS: Petit Train** covers major sights in the city with multilingual listening guides *(departs from the promenade du Soliel, near the Bastion. $ Adults €7, under 9 €3. ⏰ 40min., every 40min. Operates Sept-June 10am-noon and 2:15-5pm; July-Aug 10am-noon, 2:15-5pm, and 7-11pm.)*
- **INTERNET ACCESS:** Le Cafe des Arts, 16 rue de la République. *(☎04 93 35 78 67*

🖳www.cafedesarts.com. i Credit card €10 min. $ €6 per hr. ⏰ Open M-Sa 7:30am-8pm. Internet 7:30am-11am and 2:30-8pm.)

- **POST OFFICE:** cours George V. Currency exchange available. Postal Code 06500. *(☎04 93 28 64 87 ⏰ Open M-W 8am-6:30pm, Th 8am-6pm, F 8am-6:30pm, Sa 8:30am-noon.)*

Emergency!

- **POLICE:** rue de la République. *(☎04 92 10 50 50).*
- **HOSPITAL:** La Palmosa, rue Peglion. *(☎04 93 28 77 77, emergencies ☎04 93 28 72 40).*

Getting There

Gare SNCF, in pl. de la Gare, runs **trains** to **Monaco** *($ €1.70. ⏰ 11 min.)* and **Nice** *($ €4.20. ⏰ 35min.)* promenade du Marechal Leclerc has **buses** *(☎04 93 35 93 60 ⏰ Open M-F 8:30am-noon and 1:30-6pm, Sa 10am-noon.)* TAM bus #100 connects Menton to **Nice** through **Monaco.** *($ €1. ⏰ Every 15min. 6:30am-7:30pm.)*

Getting Around

Menton is very pedestrian-friendly; most of the main roads are either entirely pedestrian or have ample sidewalk space. From the train station, walking straight and making your first right at the major intersection, and continue for a kilometer to reach the center of town.

Compagnie des Transports de la Riviera **buses** serve Menton and neighborhoods with 10 lines. *($ €1, 10 trips €7.50, day pass €3.)* Most buses link the Marché to the Gare Routière. **Taxis** pick up from five stands in the city *(☎04 92 10 47 02 i Reserve by phone in off-hours. ⏰ Available daily 6:30am-7pm.)* You can also rent **bikes** at 4 esplanade G. Pompidou. *(☎04 92 10 99 98 $ Bikes from €15 per day, €60/week. Scooters €40 per day with €500 deposit. ⏰ Open M-F 9:30am-12:30pm and 3-6:30pm, Sa 9:30am-noon and 5-6:30pm.)*

CÔTE D'AZUR

OK, we'll admit it: our expectations were pretty high for the Riviera, and after 50 years in this business, we didn't think we could still be surprised. Talk about getting schooled. During four weeks of caffeinated hostel-hopping, we got (wo)man-handled at Drag Nights, passed out on the yachts/couches/floors of strangers, and may or may not have stolen a rental scooter. Once a humble Greco-Roman commercial base, this rambling stretch of sun-drenched beaches and aquamarine waters has been an oasis of luxury and lust since Hercules swung by for a little R and R. You're just as likely to find a Mediterranean god or goddess sipping absinthe here today as you were way back then.

Hedonism aside, the Riviera also boasts a cultural richness and vibrancy that give other French regions a run for their money. The Côte d'Azur has been the inspiration of artists from F. Scott Fitzgerald to Picasso, as well as the chosen resort of celebrities ranging from Brigitte Bardot to Bono. Many of the smaller towns that dot the coast feature a chapel, room, or wall decorated by artists like Cocteau, Chagall, or Matisse. The idyllic villas that overlook plunging cliffs are reminders that the Riviera is a mecca of international wealth. Each May, high society makes its yearly pilgrimage to the Cannes Film Festival and the Monte-Carlo Grand Prix, while Nice's raucous Carnival in February and summer jazz festivals—less exclusive and more budget-friendly—draw a diverse crowd. Despite the Côte d'Azur's reputation for glitz and glamor, penny-pinchers can soak up the spectacle and their share of sun, sea, and sand.

greatest hits

- **BEND THAT GENDER:** Soak up the vibrant gay nightlife in Cannes (p. 340).
- **BEST BLOW:** By which we mean glass-blowing. Head to Biot (p. 327).
- **CLOTHING OPTIONAL:** Funny story. A certain Let's Go researcher went to St-Tropez and discovered its high concentration of topless beaches. Then he missed his ferry home (p. 353).

student life

Party like a (French) rockstar. Sure you'll hit the beach, you'll try some food but let's face is you're here to get your drink on. You're probably not cool enough to get into the film festival (sorry to break it to you) but **Cannes** still has plenty to offer in terms of nightlife. If you're self-conscious about your karaoke skills, you won't be after knocking back a few brews at 👍**The Station Tavern**. For a *fabulous* time be sure to check out some of the GLBT nightlife like **Le Must** or **Tsar**.

antibes ☎04 93

Antibes has the largest port on the Mediterranean, attracting sailors and scallywags of all varieties from around the world. A strange island of English-speaking visitors and residents, Antibes has its fair share of rugged British and Irish pubs, with very little of the hopping club scene found in Juan-les-Pins or Cannes. People are either here to drift or to look for work, so the crowd can range from drunk and entertaining to sketchy and intimidating. Antibes has the free beaches that you've been searching for, as well as some good SCUBA diving spots and snorkeling off of the Cap d'Antibes. While the museums, with the exception of the Picasso Museum, might be a tad on the dull side, the real attraction is the laid-back people and easygoing atmosphere, only 10min. from one of the craziest party cities on the Riviera.

ORIENTATION

Antibes is easy to navigate between the **port** and the ***vieux ville,*** even though the streets can be poorly labeled and the helpful tourist arrows can sometimes lead you into a wall. The easiest way to orient yourself is along the town's main streets: **rue de la République** and **bld. d'Aguillon.** Both lead you right into the *vieux ville*, while offering totally different attractions along the way. Rue de la République is where you'll find upscale restaurants and shopping, while the sleezy port crowd will hang out at the laid-back pubs that line bld. d'Aguillon. Unfortunately the **Cap,**where you'll find secluded beaches and nicer hotels, is either a 20min. walk or a bus ride away. The **#2 bus** goes along the coast. Within the *vieux ville*, no matter where you turn you'll almost always end up back at the **Marché Provençale,** a central sqaure that sells fruits and vegetables during the day and turns into a flea market at night.

ACCOMMODATIONS

These are the cheapest ones in town. To find any hotels that are actually budget, you'll have to go to Juan-les-Pins or take a hike up the highway. These places get above €100 in the high season, and its over €200 for rooms of three to four. We don't want to subject our readers to such financial pain and suffering. Please go to Juan-les-Pins. If you're a trust fund baby, don't mind credit card debt, or absolutely must stay in Antibes for some reason, these are the best deals in town:

THE CREW HOUSE 💳♿📶🍸☀ HOSTEL [2]

1 av. St. Roch ☎04 92 90 49 39

Not the most luxurious place to stay, even by hostel standards, but definitely a fun experience for those willing to take a leap outside of their comfort zone and bunk with the rugged sailors and drifters who frequent this predominantly Anglophone hostel. For those used to the cramped living conditions and limited personal space of boats (or for those looking to give it a try).

➤ From the train station, walk straight on down av. de la Libération, take 2nd right on the round about, hostel on your right. $ Apr-Oct dorms €25; Nov-Mar €20. ⏰ No lockout.

côte d'azur

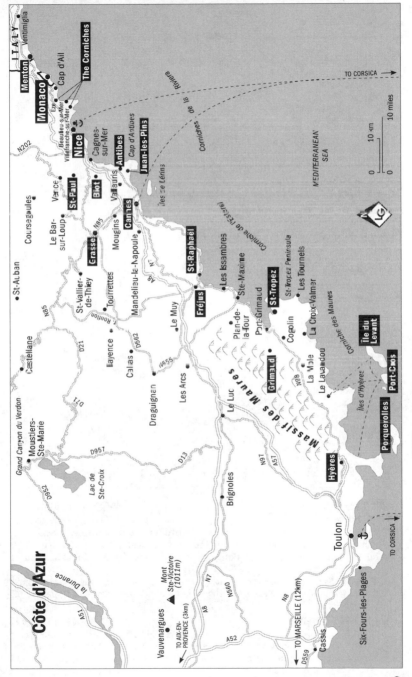

Côte d'Azur

antibes ∙ accommodations

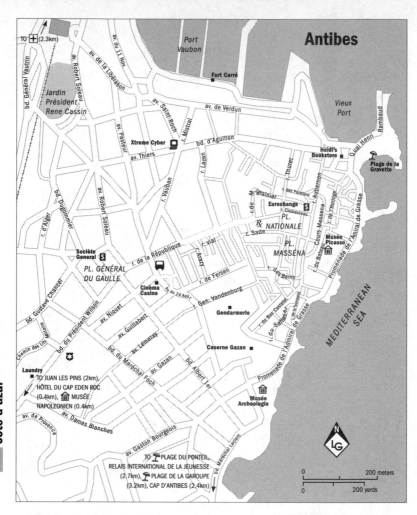

Antibes

RELAIS INTERNATIONAL DE LA JEUNESSE

⬦⊘(ᵖ)⌇☂ HOSTEL ❶

272 bld. de la Garoupe ☎04 93 61 34 40 🖳www.clajsud.fr

Closer to Juan-les-Pins than Antibes, Relais International provides guests with clean rooms and an escape from the busy city center. Located next to the beach on the Cap, this English-speaking hostel also provides free breakfast and a youthful atmosphere.

⚑ *Take bus #4 to the Telais de Jeunesse stop or the #2 to the Garoupe stop. Facing the water, walk to your right for 10min.* ⓘ *Breakfast included. Free bar and outdoor seating.* ⓢ *Dorms €18.* ☒ *Open Apr-Sep.*

HOTEL PETIT RESERVE

⬦⊘ BUDGET HOTEL ❸

20 bld. James Wyllie ☎04 93 61 55 86 🖳www.petitreserve.com

Seven-room hotel on the Cap with ocean views. They've tried to liven up the simple rooms with mismatched colors and patterns (like light green and red

côte d'azur

plaid). While the decor might suggest color blindness, staff are very attentive to service detail, which calms the nerves of a predominantly German clientele.

From the train station, walk left onto Robert Soleau for 200m until you get to Place du Général de Gaulle. Walk across the place onto bld. Albert 1er and follow it until you get to the beach (7 blocks). Turn right at the beach and walk for 700m. Hotel on your right. i Traveler's checks accepted. $ Singles €31-51; doubles €48-98; suite 3-4-person suites) €94-155.

HOTEL LE RELAIS DU POSTILLON — HOTEL [4]

8 rue Championnet ☎04 93 34 20 77 www.relaisdupostillon.com

Luxurious rooms with fancy bed curtains and antique painted furniture. Close to the center of town, but still separate from the bars and loud restaurants. Honeymoon level-rooms for cheap.

From the train station, walk straight on down av. de la Libération, take 1st right on the round-about onto av. Mirabeau for 300m. Turn right onto rue Vauban, and take a left onto rue Championnet. $ Singles €49-96; doubles €67-96.

HOTEL L'AUBERGE PROVENÇALE — BOUTIQUE HOTEL [4]

61 rue de la République ☎04 93 34 13 24 www.aubergeprovencale.com

It really says something that the cheapest room in Hotel l'Auberge Provençale comes with a four-poster double bed. This classy boutique hotel boasts a royal red theme wherever you go, from the drapes, to the bedspreads, to the place settings at breakfast.

From the train station, walk right down av. Robert Soleau until the pl. de Gaulle. Turn left onto rue de la République. Hotel is in the place Nationale. i Restaurant on ground floor. Dinner €20. $ Singles and doubles from €65-120. Prices spike during the Monaco Grand Prix and Film Festival. ⏰ Reception 8:30am-1:30pm and 5:30pm-midnight.

HOTEL LE PONTEIL — HOTEL [4]

11 impasse Jean Mensier ☎04 93 34 67 02 www.leponteil.com

Tucked away at the end of a cul-de-sac under the trees, this quiet hotel will have you itching to leave for the nearby beach, where there is more life and color than in this *hébergement*. The prices really make the establishment's bland character worth it.

From the train station, turn left onto Robert Soleau and walk 200m until you get to place du Général de Gaulle. Walk across the place onto bld. Albert 1er until one block before the beach (6 blocks). Turn right onto av. du Général Maizière (keeping to the left at the intersection) and walk 200m. Turn left onto impasse Jean Mensier. Hotel is at the end. i Parking. $ Singles €58-87; doubles €58-105.

SIGHTS

MUSÉE PICASSO — MUSEUM

pl. Mariejol ☎04 92 90 54 20 www.musee-picasso.fr

Displays the artist's lesser-known paintings from the 1940s and video clips of him at work on sketches and paintings.

$ €8.50, students €6, under 18 free. ⏰ Open June 15-Sep 15 M 10am-6pm, W-Su 10am-6pm; Sep 15-June 14 M 10am-noon and 2-6pm, W-Su 10am-noon and 2-6pm.

FORT CARRÉ — HISTORIC SIGHT

Sentier du Fort Carré ☎06 14 89 17 45

Once an important fortress guarding the port Vauban, the largest private marina in the Mediterranean, this fortress now serves as a showcase for swords and a statue of Napoleon on a horse. Yeah, it still doesn't compensate for his height. Maybe one of those 2400 yachts in the harbor, appropriately dubbed "Millionaire's Row," that would have eased his—well—Napoleon complex.

i Only by guided English or French tour. $ €3, under 18 free. ⏰ Open June 15-Sept 15 Tu-Su 10am-6pm; Sept 15-June 14 Tu-Su 10am-4:30pm.

MUSÉE D'ARCHÉOLOGIE

MUSEUM

On the waterfront in Bastion St-Andre-sur-les-Ramparts   ☎04 95 34 00 39

If you thought the pottery museum in Biot was a hoot, you'll love the ancient Greek and Roman ceramics in this one. The temporary exhibits might be a little more interesting. Past exhibits included present-day objects aged 2000 years to look like archaeological finds from the future.

Ⓢ *Students €3. Under 18 free.* ⌚ *Open June 15-Sept 15 M 10am-noon and 2-6pm, W-Su 10am-noon and 2-6pm; Sept 15-June 14 M 10am-1pm and 2-5pm, W-Su 10am-1pm and 2-5pm.*

MUSÉE PEYNET

MUSEUM

pl. Nationale

Features the drawings of the Lovers of Peynet. For those confused like us, Peynet was an illustrator for a Parisian newpaper who became famous for drawing the same two fictional lovers over and over again in different situations. His work went on to become a French symbol of love and humor in the 1950s.

Ⓢ *Students €3, under 18 free.* ⌚ *Open June 15-Sept 15 M 10am-noon and 2-6pm, W-Su 10am-noon and 2-6pm. Sept 15-June 14 W-M 10am-1pm and 2-5pm.*

MARCHÉ PROVENÇALE

rue Aubernon

A market during the day, this covered area turns into a flea market during the evenings, and at seemingly random times during the summer months. Cafes line the market, so the area at the very least makes for good peoplewatching in the shade.

⌚ *Open June-Aug Tu-Sa mornings, afternoon and evenings in Jun-Aug; Sept-May Tu-Sa mornings.*

BEACHES

PLAGE DU PONTEIL

BEACH

Antibes's largest public beach. The long stretch of sand is lined with street vendors and snack stands. It gets very crowded in summer during peak hours of the day.

⚡ *Turn right from the vieux ville; walk along coast.*

PLAGE DE LA SALIS

BEACH

Small public beach that's closer to the port, and the sunbathing hotspot that's closest to the *vieux ville*. The breakwater forms an almost enclosed cove for swimming in the calm, manmade lagoon.

⚡ *Towards Port Vauban, right from vieux ville.*

CAP D'ANTIBES

BEACH

A rocky beach surrounds the Cap, with crystal clear water that's perfect for snorkeling. Isolated and far from the crowds on the main public beaches.

⚡ *Take the #2 bus from the bus station to Tour Gandolphe (M-Sa, every 40 min 6:50am-7:30pm). Follow av. Monseigneurs-Lt. Beaumont to the end. Turn left onto pedestrian road, then right when a small door appears in the surrounding walls; take dirt path to the isolated beach cove.*

PLAGE GAROUPE

BEACH

On the Cap. Sandy beach that was frequented by celebs such as F. Scott Fitzgerald, Picasso, and Cole Porter in the 1920s.

⚡ *Cap d'Antibes.*

FOOD

🔖 KEY WEST

COMFORT FOOD ❷

30 bld. d'Aguillon   ☎04 93 34 58 20 📧www.lecapdantibes.com

This laid-back restaurant is your go-to place for comfort food like waffles and anything that you could possibly have a craving for. Sailing theme reminiscent of the Florida Keys, with whales and Hemingway featuring prominently on the

côte d'azur

lime green walls.

$ *Breakfast food €1.80-6.50. Waffles €2.90-4.90. Cheesecake, salads, sanwiches €3-9.* ⏰ *Open Mar-Dec daily 7:30am-7:30pm (until 2am Jul-Aug).*

BRULOT 💳♿🍸⛱ WOOD FIRED [3]

3 rue Federic Isnard ☎04 93 34 17 76

Wood-fired cuisine in this tavern-like restaurant. Farm implements hang from the ceiling, reminding you where your meat and fish dishes (€12) came from. Three-course *prix-fixe* (€19) features shrimp au pastis and creme brulee to top it off.

$ *Plats €12-17. Lunch €14. Dinner €19.* ⏰ *Open daily 7pm-12am.*

LE CRÊME BRÛLÉE 💳♿🍸⛱ PROVENCAL, FAMILY [2]

21 rue Thuret ☎04 93 34 56 58

Farm-themed Provençal restaurant serves up crêpes, sandwiches, and *plats*, as well as its dessert namesake. Inside walls are painted to look as though cows are looking in on you while you eat. If that doesn't confuse/frighten you enough, check out the pots hanging from the ceiling that serve as lights.

$ *Sandwiches €5.50. Crêpes €4-8. Plats €12-15.* ⏰ *Open daily 9am-11pm.*

LE VILLAGE 💳🍸 PROVENCAL [3]

31 rue James Close ☎04 93 34 19 66

This classy joint serves up local mussels, roast duck, and escargots in a traditionally decoarated Provençal establishment. Though the decor isn't remarkable, with whitewash plaster walls, the food is quite good. On a tight budget? Go for lunch to get the gourmet taste for almost half the price of the dinner menu. .

$ *Lunch €15. Dinner €28. Kids menu €11.50.* ⏰ *Open M-Tu noon-2pm and 7-10pm, Th-Su noon-2pm and 7-10pm.*

CASA DEL PANINO 🥡♿ PANINI [1]

20 pl. Nationale

Colorful panini bar serves up 15 types of cheap, fast, and giant paninis.

$ *€4 for everything.* ⏰ *Open M 7am-7:30pm, W-Su 7am-7:30pm.*

LE KASHMIR 💳♿🍸⛱ INDIAN [3]

22 rue Thuret ☎04 92 94 00 03

Indian breads (€2) for incredibly cheap, although the elephants and camels painted on the wall are a bit tacky. Sit outside if it really bothers you.

$ *Lamb €13-14. Dinner menu €19. Nan and bread €2.* ⏰ *Open M-Sa noon-9pm.*

MAISON ROLAR ♿🍸 MARKET [1]

pl. Nationale

Old-school market with fresh veggies and fruit next to the town butcher.

⏰ *Open M-Sa 7am-7:30pm, Su 8:30am-1pm.*

NIGHTLIFE

LA BALADE ♿🍸 ABSINTHE BAR

25B cours Massena ☎04 93 34 93 00

One of the world's few absinthe bars, La Balade is a famed subterranean hotspot that exclusively serves that one special drink. Don't look naive and ask if you haullucinate. You don't. Thanks to its 140+ proof, you'll be lucky if you see anything at all. Posters and bowler hats cover the walls in tribute to the 19th-centruy avant-garde, who guzzled the drink with a side of laudanum.

⏰ *Open daily 9am-midnight.*

THE HOP STORE 💳♿🍸⛱ BAR

38 bld. d'Aguillon ☎04 93 34 04 06

Antibes's largest pub. With a giant patio that's almost always packed with a young crowd, this two-room bar hosts local rock bands and other live music performances every Wednesday, Friday, and Saturday. Although technically classified as an Irish pub, The Hop Store is the most international spot in all of Antibes.

Ⓢ *Beer €2.50. Cocktails €7.* Ⓧ *Open in summer 9am-12:30am, in winter 3pm-12:30am.*

THE BLUE LADY   ✇ & (ᵗᵖ) ♉ ᵭ PUB
Galerie du Port   ☎04 93 34 41 00

Laid-back pub done up to look like the interior of a steamship in the American South. The wood and brass bar is decorated with entertaining signs referring to gamblers and loose women. Outdoor seating and live bands every other Friday. Don't miss out on their homemade pub grub, like hand-rolled sausage (€3.50).

Ⓢ *Beer €3.40-5.50. Cocktails €6.80-9.20.* Ⓧ *Open 7:30am-midnight. Kitchen open until 3:30pm.*

THE COLONIAL   ✇ & ♉ ᵭ BAR
36 bld. d'Aguillon   ☎04 93 34 83 53

African colonial-themed bar complete with safari lounge upstairs (by reservation only) and elephant tusks and pictures of the "Big 5" (elephant, lion, rhino, jaguar, and the 🐃cape buffalo) on the walls. The outdoor seating is packed with wooden bar tables and stools, occupied by Anglophones.

Ⓢ *Beer €4. Cocktails €8.* Ⓧ *Open daily 7pm-2:30am.*

ESSENTIALS   ⓰

Practicalities

- **TOURIST OFFICE:** Free maps, info on hotels, restaurants, and festivals. Help with hotel reservations *(11 pl. de Gaulle ☎04 97 23 11 11* ▣*www.antibesjuanlespins. com.* Ⓧ *Open July-Aug daily 9am-7pm; Sept-Jun M-F 9am-noon and 1:30-6pm, Sa 9am-noon and 2-6pm, Su 10am-noon and 2:30-5pm.)*

- **TOURS:** The **Petit Train** covers both Antibes and Juan-les-Pins sights. *(Departure from pl. de la Poste ☎06 15 77 67 47.* Ⓢ *€7.* Ⓧ *July-Aug 10am-10pm; Mar-Oct 10am-6pm.)*

- **INTERNET ACCESS: Xtreme Cyber.** *(8 bld. d'Aguillon in Galerie du Port ☎04 89 89 93 88* Ⓢ *€5 per hr.* Ⓧ *Open M-F 10am-8pm, Sa 10am-4pm.)*

- **POST OFFICE:** pl. des Martyrs de la Resistance *(☎04 92 90 61 00* Ⓧ *Open M-F 8am-7pm, Sa 8am-noon.)*

- **POSTAL CODE:** 06600.

Emergency!

- **POLICE:** 33 bld. President Wilson *(☎04 92 90 78 00 or 92 90 53 12).*

- **PHARMACY:** Consult Nice Matin newspaper for rotating hours of Pharmacie de Garde *(63 pl. Nationale ☎04 93 34 01 63).*

- **HOSPITAL: Chemin des Quatres Chemins** *(☎04 92 91 77 77).*

Getting There   ⊠

By Train

Gare SNCF *(pl. Pierre Semard.* Ⓧ *Ticket desk open daily 5:45am-10:45pm. Info desk open daily 9am-8pm. Station open 5:25am-12:10am.)* runs trains to **Cannes** *(*Ⓢ *€2.20.* Ⓧ *15min, every 30min.);* **Nice** *(*Ⓢ *€3.40.* Ⓧ *15min, every 30min.),* **Monaco** *(*Ⓢ *€6.* Ⓧ *1hr, 5 per day.);* **Marseille.** *(*Ⓢ *€24.* Ⓧ *2hr, every hr.)*

côte d'azur

By Bus

RCA *(☎04 93 39 11 39)* buses run from pl. de Gaulle to **Cannes** *($ €1. ⏰ 20min., every 20-40min.)*, **Nice** *($ €1. ⏰ 1hr., every 20-40min.)*, and **Nice Airport** *($ €1.⏰ 30min., every 20-40min.)*

Getting Around

Walking is the easiest way to get around in the *vieux ville*.From the **train station,** turn left and walk for 5min., and you'll eventually hit the main drag of **rue de la République**, which takes you all the way to the port. To get anywhere farther away, such as the Cap, **buses** *(#2 to the Cap)* leave from the **pl. Guynemer** *(☎04 93 34 37 60 $ €1, day pass €4, week pass €10. ⏰ M-Sa every 40min. 6:50am-7:30pm)*. The **free mini bus** connects the city to the beaches, train station and bus station. **Taxis** are also available from the train station *(☎04 93 67 67 67 $ €18 to Juan-les-Pins. ⏰ 24hr.)*

cagnes-sur-mer ☎04 93

Cagnes-sur-Mer is the halfway point between Nice and Cannes, and it provides access to all the provincial towns and medieval villages in between. It also features a medieval village of its own and the illustrious Grimaldi Castle, as well as a lively city center and beachfront fishing community. You can find more spectacular palaces and cuter fishing boats than those in Canges-sur-Mer, but you'll be hard pressed to find all of those qualities in one city. If you're facing a time crunch, a stay here will ensure that you'll see all the major highlights of the region, even if you aren't seeing the best of the best. The cheap eats and hotels are a big draw for young travelers; just be warned that many establishments lower their prices at the expense of regional charm.

ACCOMMODATIONS

TURF HOTEL
💳 HOTEL [3]

9 rue des Capucines ☎04 93 20 64 0

Budget hotel near the beach. Simple rooms ranging from terrace suites to prison-cell-sized singles.

➥ Located along the Port de Cros-des-Cagnes in between av. de la Serre and av. Leclerc. ℹ Parking available. $ Singles and doubles €40-82; triples €62-87.

VAL DUCHESSE
💳🚭📶🍸🏊 HOTEL [4]

11 rue de Paris ☎04 92 13 40 00 ✉val.duchesse@wanadoo.fr

Beautifully tiled guesthouse that offers single rooms and apartments for rent. The modern decor is accented by bright traditional colors and furniture; facilities include a pool in case the 50m walk to the beach is too far for you.

➥ Located along the Port de Cros-des-Cagnes in between av. de la Serre and bld. JFK. $ Studio €56-78; apartments €77-106. Prices change depending on season, getting more expensive in the summer months. 10% discount for a week's stay. 20% discount for two weeks' stay between Oct-Apr.

LE MAS D'AZUR
💳♿📶🍸 HOTEL [3]

42 av. de Nice ☎04 93 20 19 19

Provençal house run by a local family. The rooms are small but elegant, and the lobby nails that "homey" vibe with fireplaces and comfy couches. The furniture has an antique shop feel to it, which is fitting: the building dates back to the mid-18th century.

➥ Located along the Port de Cros-des-Cagnes in between av. de la Serre and rue de la Pinede. Right as the highway divides. $ Singles and doubles €41-63; triples and quads €61-76.

LE COLOMBIER
☻❣ HOTEL ❶
35 chemin de Sainte-Colombe   ☎04 93 73 12 77

Family-oriented campground, which includes 33 shady plots with concrete risers for tents.

🏕 *1.5km from the train sation on the route de Vence.* **i** *Bar, pool, electricity, and washer/dryer.* Ⓢ *Jul-Aug singles €14; doubles €16.20. Sep-Jun singles €11.80; doubles €14.20.*

SIGHTS   👁

GRIMALDI CASTLE
✏ CASTLE
Huat-des-Cagnes   ☎04 92 02 47 30

Built by a distant relative of Monaco's royal family in 1300, the Grimaldi Castle now serves as the city's municipal museum and houses The Olive Tree museum, the Soldier Donation, and the local Modern Art museum. Additional rooms have been authentically restored to appear as they were in the Baroque era of Louis XIII. Swing by the top of the tower to see the stunning 360 degree view of Canges and the beach.

Ⓢ *€4 for 2 students, under 18 free. Double ticket for Renoir Museum and Castle €6.* 🕐 *Open July-Aug 10am-noon and 2-6pm; Sept-June Tu-Su 10am-noon and 2-5pm.*

RENOIR MUSEUM
✏ MUSEUM
Chemin des Collettes   ☎04 93 20 61 07

The museum harbors 11 original paintings, sculptures, and sketchings by the town's most famous resident. Hoping that some ocean air would help with his arthritis, Renoir retreated to Cagnes-sur-Mer towards the end of his life. He immortalized the beauty of the coastline in paintings until 1919 when he died. Renoir's estate is still preserved to this day with rooms containing his wheelchair and easel as they would have been.

Ⓢ *€4 for 2 students, under 18 free. Double ticket for Renoir Museum and Castle €6.* 🕐 *Open July-Aug Tu-Su 10am-noon and 2-6pm; Sept-June Tu-Su 10am-noon and 2-5pm.*

FOOD   📷

L'ILOT
✏&♿🍴 PANINI, SALADS ❶
rue du Captitaine de Fregate Henri Vial   ☎04 93 31 80 97

Cheap panini stand right on the ocean. Sick view of the water and rock beach below.

Ⓢ *Paninis €4. Salads €5.* 🕐 *Open M-Sa 11am-10pm.*

AUBERGE DU PORT
✏&♿❣🍴 MEDITERRANEAN ❸
95 bld. de la Plage   ☎04 93 07 25 28

Conveniently located right on the bord du Mer, this restaurant specializes in fish and Mediterranean dishes. A nice place to eat well without breaking the bank; the outdoor seating overlooks the promenade.

i *If fish grosses you out, this probably isn't the place for you.* Ⓢ *Lunch menu €15; 3-course dinner menu €24-31.* 🕐 *Open M-Sa noon-11pm.*

LE PROVENÇAL
✏&♿❣🍴 PROVENÇAL, BURGERS ❸
4 pl. du Château   ☎04 93 20 08 86

Outdoor cafe in the shadow of the Grimaldi Castle. Specializes in Provençal cuisine, but also an impressive range of burgers. It might take a French palate to tell, but each type of burger is prepared with specific types of beef; some of the patties are even made with *foie gras*. Try ordering that at Burger King.

Ⓢ *Burgers €8-18.* 🕐 *Open M-Sa 11am-11:30pm.*

BRASSERIE DES HALLES
✏&♿❣🍴 BAR, TAPAS ❷
8 rue J. Raimond Giacosa   ☎04 92 02 77 29

Brasserie in the pedestrian center of town. Ages range from the young and pierced to the old and walker-bound. Sandwiches, tapas and 12 different beer on tap.

$ Plat du jour €10. Menus €12-14.90. ⏰ Open Tu-Sa 11:30am-11:45pm.

ESSENTIALS

Practicalities

- **TOURIST OFFICE:** Offers free bus schedules, maps, restaurant, and hotel guides *(6 bld. Marechal Juin ☎04 93 20 61 64 💻www.cagnes-tourisme.com ⏰ Open Jul-Aug M-Sa 9am-12:30pm and 2-6pm; Sept-Jun M-F 9am-noon and 2-6pm, Sa 9am-noon.)* Other locations are on the beach at 99 promenade de la Plage *(☎04 93 07 67 08)*, and on Huat-des-Cagnes in pl. Docteur Maurel *(☎04 92 02 85 05)*.
- **YOUTH CENTER:** Beach sports center including beach volleyball, windsurfing, kayaking, and sailing. *(bld. de la Plage ☎04 93 07 33 04 ⏰ Open Jul-Aug daily 9:30am-6pm)*.

Emergency!

- **POLICE: Police Municipale** 21 sq. des Grands Plans *(☎04 93 22 19 22)*.
- **HOSPITAL: Clinique Saint Jean** *(92 av. du Dr. Maurice Donat ☎04 92 13 53 33)*.
- **PHARMACY: Pharmacie Centrale** 4 av. Auguste Renoir *(☎04 93 20 61 08)*.

Getting There

By Train

Gare SNCF is located on the corner of Cros-des-Cagnes and bord de mer. *(☎04 92 35 35 35)*. To **Cannes** *($ €6. ⏰ Every 30min.)*, **Nice** *($ €3.20. ⏰ Every 30min.)*, and **Marseille** via Cannes *($ €25)*.

By Bus

TAM line #200 *(€1)* runs between Cannes and Nice stops at the Cagnes-sur-Mer train station, Gare Routière. From **Nice** *(⏰ 35min., every 15min. between 6:30am-6pm, every 30min. between 6-8pm.)* from **Cannes** *(⏰ 1hr. 15min., every 15min. 6:15am-6pm, every 30min. 6-8pm.)*

Getting Around

Free **shuttle bus** *(#44)* runs between gare routière and Haut-des-Cagnes *(daily 7am-8pm)*.

vence ☎04 93

A mid-sized medieval village in the hills above Cagnes-sur-Mer, this peaceful haven is most famous for the healing properties of its drinking water; laugh all you want, but its powers were "proven" when it healed Nero's wife, Poppaea, and preserved the life of Henri Matisse, who designed and painted the nearby Chapelle du Rosaire. While the sights here might not be much of a draw for young travelers, it's certainly worth visiting this town to deliberately do nothing and relax in its small peaceful squares, or sample one of the ubiquitous open air markets. Make a mental note to come back here when you're old and feeble, because something about the city is incredibly calming, even with its lively underbelly and riotous, month-long music festival.

ACCOMMODATIONS

LA LUBIANE HOTEL [3]

10 av. Marechal Joffre ☎04 93 58 01 10

A cheap guesthouse run by a little old lady. The rooms all have similar flowery wallpaper, which will repeatedly remind you that someone over 70 did the decorating for the whole hotel. If you can get past that, though, this is a great option for a quiet stay in Vence. Since it's a former restaurant, La Lubiane has a large dining area and an awesome terrace view of the valley.

From the tourist office, walk towards the city entrance, taking the first right onto av. Elise. Turn left onto av. des Poilus and continue past the intersection. The hotel is on the right. $ Singles €36.60-41; doubles €51-62.20; triples and quads €70-77.40.

LA CLOSERIE DES GENETS — HOTEL 3

4 impasse Macellin Maruel ☎04 93 58 35 18 www.closeriedesgenets.com

Hotel and restaurant with 10 rooms for rent. The funky modern art made from household metal scraps hangs throughout the hallways, and the simple rooms are painted sherbert-y hues that range from aqua to pink.

From the tourist office, turn left and walk towards the old city. Walk three blocks on Marcellin Maurcel and make a right onto impasse Marcellin Marucel. i Bar and Wi-Fi. $ Singles €40; doubles €80; triples €95; quads €110.

LA COLOMBE DE VENCE — BED AND BREAKFAST 4

1458 chemin de Saint Colombe ☎06 25 61 52 47

B and B run by old lady who might not know what the internet is and speaks no English. The garden terrace overlooks an amazing view of the valley, though. Have the tourist office check availabilty and book your room here for you; the B and B is this woman's house, and she is not kind to strangers just showing up without prior notice. Seriously though.

From the tourist office, walk around the old city until you reach chemin St. Colombe. Walk about 1km to 1458. Will be on your right. i Breakfast included. Three nights minimum. $ Rooms €49. ⏰ 3-night min. stay.

DOMAINE DE BERGERIE — CAMPGROUND 4

route de la Sine ☎04 93 58 09 36 www.domainelabergerie.fr

Camping grounds in the middle of the forest. Complete with small waterpark and mobile homes for rent.

From gare routière, take the #46 bus to Bergerie. i Pool, electricity, parking, and grocery store. $ Low-season site for 1-2 people with electricity €18.90; high-season €39.

SIGHTS

CHAPELLE DU ROSAIRE — CHURCH

466 av. Henri Mattisse ☎04 93 58 03 26

Small chapel run by Dominican nuns who look like they'll break your fingers if you attempt to take a picture—and we can understand why they're so protective: these are Matisse originals. They may just look like black-and-white stick figure drawings, but these are the famous artist's Stations of the Cross. Nod politely when the 146-year-old nun talks about each interpretation and try not to look confused.

$ Admission €3.20. ⏰ Open M 2-5:30pm, Tu 10-11:30am, W 2-5:30pm, Th 10-11:30am, Sa 2-5:30pm.

CATHEDRALE — CATHEDRAL

Cité Historique

Impressive cathedral in the center of town that was built in the fourth century AD; the site was previously occupied by a pagan Roman temple. Contains "Moses saved from the Nile," a baptistry mosaic by Marc Chagall.

$ Free. ⏰ Open daily 9am-6pm, except during religious services.

PEYRA GATE FOUNTAIN — FOUNTAIN

Cité Historique

The current quadrafoil fountain was erected in 1822, on the site of a fountain dating back to 1578. The Fontaine de Peyra was one of only three sources of drinking water in Vence until the city was piped in 1886, and remains drinkable today. If you're looking for a Biblical miracle, this is (allegedly) the place to go—the waters of the Foux have very low sodium content, and as a result may be particularly good for you. They became famous for their healing properties when Nero sent his fragile wife Poppea to drink from the waters of Vence. She left the town in good health. Our personal theory is that she just needed a little time off from Nero.

FOOD

LA TAVERNE SAINT VERAN

PIZZERIA [1]

9 pl. Surian ☎04 93 24 00 98

Pizzeria in the heart of the old city. The wooden outdoor furniture and large stucco painting of Vence as it once was in the Middle Ages make it seem like they've been cooking pizza here since before the revolution.

$ Pizza €11. ⏰ Open T-Sa 11am-2pm and 5-10pm.

CRÊPERIE BRETONNE

CRÊPERIE [1]

6 pl. Surian ☎04 93 24 08 20

A charming little traditional crêperie with a classic menu; try the classic ham, cheese, and egg over easy. Also serves its own brewed cider. The indoor seating area can get a little stuffy, so take your crêpes outside to bask in the sunlight.

$ Crepes €3-9. Menu €10.90. ⏰ Open Tu-Sa noon-11pm.

LE CRAB ENRAGÉ

SEAFOOD [2]

4 impasse Marcellin Maurel ☎04 93 58 35 18

Seafood restaurant in the hotel Closeirc des Genets. Covered terrace or garden seating. Wednesday is "Mussel Day," when fresh mussels go for €12.50 per plate. Weird art made from scrap metal is scattered throughout the restaurant.

$ Prix-fixe €15. ⏰ Open Tu-Sa noon-2pm and 5-10pm.

BAR DE L'ETOILE

CAFE, BAR, FAST FOOD [1]

204 av. des Poilus ☎04 93 58 25 81

More of a bar than a restaurant, this place serves up traditional Provençal dishes as well as the occasional burger. Cheap plates and a deal-of-a-three-course menu is what makes this place attractive; l'Etoile's curb appeal doesn't do much for it.

$ Plates €6.50-9.50. Menus €13-15. ⏰ Open daily 11am-2:30am.

ARTS AND CULTURE

Festivals

NUITS DU SUD

Vence

World music festival that takes place every summer, and stretches from the beginning of July to the beginning of August. The music is usually more Latin influenced. If you don't want to pay, you can sit at any cafe along the place and be an eavesdropping freeloader.

$ €10-18. Some performances free. ⏰ July-Aug.

ESSENTIALS

Practicalities

- **TOURIST OFFICE:** Provides maps, restaurant and hotel guides as well as makes same day hotel and B&B reservations for free. *(8 pl. de Grand Jardin ☎04 93 58 06 38. ⏰ Open M-Sa 9:30am-6pm, Su 10am-2:30pm.)*

- **BANK: BNP Paribas.** ATM available *(pl. du Grand Jardin ☎08 20 82 00 01 ⏰ Open M-F 9:30am-noon, 2-7pm, Sa 10am-noon.)*
- **INTERNET: SOS Informatique** *(147 ave. des Polius ☎04 93 24 37 97)* has Wi-Fi.
- **POST OFFICE:** av. Tuby *(☎04 93 58 44 00).*

Emergency!

- **POLICE MUNICIPAL:** pl. Marechal Juin *(☎04 93 58 03 20).*
- **PHARMACY: Pharmacie du Frene.** *(1 pl. du Frêne ☎04 93 58 03 04).*

Getting There ✈

TAM **bus** line #400 goes between Nice and Vence, stopping at the Cagnes SNCF train station *($ €1. ⏰ 22min., runs every 30-40min. M-F 7:23am-3:10pm, Sa 8:20am-2:40pm, Su 8:30am-8:57pm.)*

îles des lérins ☎04 92

Ever wonder what it would be like to be stranded on a desert island? The Îles des Lérins are about as close as you'll want to get (and you probably won't want to stay long). A 15-20min. boat ride from Cannes, the two small islands, Sainte-Maguerite and Saint-Honorat, have no accommodations; they quite literally close at night, so bring a tent if you don't think you'll make the last boat back. If you're having flashbacks to Jurassic Park or nightmares about **dragons,** we feel you. We really, really do.

SIGHTS 👁

Sainte-Marguerite

FORT ROYAL

An impressive old fort that now serves as museum of underwater archaeology, the Fort Royal is most famous for its stint as a prison—the man in the Iron Mask was held here for 11 years. No, he's not just a fictional character played by Leonardo DiCaprio. To this day, no one knows the identity of the nameless man jailed by Louis XIV, whose face remained covered by a velvet cloth for the duration of his imprisonment (sorry, the iron mask is only a legend, introduced by Dumas' swashbuckling fictions). Over 60 names have been proposed, including everyone from a Richard Cromwell (son of Oliver Cromwell of England) to Louis XIV's half brother. Our guess? It was Colonel Mustard in the Library with the candlestick. The **mysterious man** was later moved to the Bastille in Paris, where he died in 1703.

i Admission includes guided tour that runs Jun-Sep at 11am, 2pm, and 3:30pm. $ €3.20, under 26 free. ⏰ Open June-Sept 10am-5:45pm; Oct-May 10:30am-1:15pm and 2:15-5:45pm. Tours June-Sept 11am, 2pm, 3:30pm.

LA MONESTÈRE FORTIFIÉ

Saint-Honorat

The monastery has been in continuous use since the year 400 AD, in spite of small interruptions like the invasion of the Saracens and WWII. While the modern monastery is closed to visitors, the abbey is open to the public, though modest dress is required for entry. The adjoining shop sells wine produced by the monks on the island's vineyards.

$ Free. ⏰ Open daily 8am-6pm.

FOOD 🍴

Sainte-Maguerite and Saint Honorat each host a few food stands, in addition to several restaurants. The stands are the better deal, and serve sandwiches, ice cream, and other types of fast food.

LA GUERITE SEAFOOD, PROVENÇAL [5]

Sainte-Marguerite

Pricey and picturesque, La Guerite is only accessible by private dock or by a trek in the woods. The restaurant is broken into a cafe and beachfront dining area, in the shadow of Fort Royal. This luxurious setting comes at a hefty price though—the grilled lobster special will set you back €60. The restaurant stays open late for those who docked their yachts off the coast of the island.

$ Plats €30-60. Prix-fixe menu €55. ⏰ Open daily 11am-8pm.

L'ESCALE PIZZERIA [3]

Sainte-Marguerite

The cheaper of the two prominent restaurants on the island. It's easy to get to from the dock, and serves pizza and melon *assiettes* on a covered patio overlooking the sea.

$ Pizzas €13-14. ⏰ Open daily noon-6pm.

LA TONNELLE PROVENÇAL [4]

Saint-Honorat

Restaurant and snack shack open only for lunch. Serves traditional Provençal cuisine, as well as extensive seafood grill.

$ Plats €19-30. ⏰ Open Mar 10-Nov daily noon-4pm.

ESSENTIALS

Getting There

To get to St-Marguerite, take the **Trans Côte d'Azure** from **Cannes** (*☎04 92 98 71 30 🖳www.trans-côte-azur.com. $ €11.50, students €9.50. ⏰ 15min., every 30min. 9am-5:30pm. Last departure from island 6pm Sep-Jun, 7pm Jul-Aug.*) **Planeria** runs ferries from **Cannesto Saint-Honorat** (*☎04 92 98 71 38 🖳www.cannes-ilesdeslerins.com $ €11. ⏰ 20min. Departures May-Sep every hr. 8am-3pm, 4:30-5:30pm; return trips every hr. 8:30am-3:30pm, 5-6pm. Departures Oct-May every hour between 8am-4:30pm; return trips every hr. 8:30am-3:30pm, 5pm. Ticket booth open Sept-May M-Sa 9:30am-5pm, Su 8:30am-5pm, June-Aug M-Sa 9:30am-6pm, Su 8:30am-5pm.*)

biot ☎04 93

Biot is the glassblowing capital of France. While it has some less than interesting museums on pottery, the real attractions are the modern day artisans, who mold molten glass with the same tools used centuries ago. The town itself hasn't changed much since the 1400s, and the townspeople have clung to the old Provençal architecture of whitewashed walls and tiled floors, making every hotel, restaurant, and cafe the most adorable place you've ever seen. While at first you might be met with suspicion by locals who are highly aware that you're a foreigner, they are more than eager to open up, especially the many restauranteurs and artisans. Getting around in the city is pretty easy, since the town is no more than a couple hundred meters across. Because you could walk Biot in under 30min., it's best to explore the town slowly, wander through some shops, and enjoy the long lunches.

ACCOMMODATIONS

HOTEL DES ARCADES HOTEL [3]

16 pl. des Arcades ☎04 93 65 01 04 🖳www.hotel-restaurant-les-arcades.com

Located in the heart of the old city, this charming hotel and restaurant feels more like a warm guesthouse than a hotel. The large rooms with whitewashed walls and painted antique furniture will make you think this place costs a fortune, but it's actually the only affordable place in the city.

From the entrance of town, walk until the rue de la Calade and turn right. Hotel is in the place on

your left. ℹ *Restaurant on ground floor.* $ *Singles and doubles €55-100.*

L'AUBERGE DE LA VALLÉE VERT — HOTEL 3

3400 route de Valbonne ☎04 93 65 10 93 ✉nicodex@wanadoo.fr

A converted farmhouse in the hills above the city. The small rooms are part of a large house with a huge dining area, designed for banquets and wedding receptions. A little far from the old city, but the peace and quiet is well worth it, especially by the pool in summer.

➔ *From the town center, take the #7 or 10 bus to chemin des Soulières. Hotel is across the street.* $ *Singles and doubles €60-70; triples and quads €80; quints €90.*

LE CAMPING L'EDEN — CAMPGROUND 2

63 chemin du Val de Pôme ☎04 93 65 63 70 ✉www.campingleden.fr

"Camping" is a relative term when the campsite comes with a full bar and pool complex that resembles a waterpark. Eden indeed. The campground also offers a restaurant, grocery store, and mobile homes for rent. Avoid the place in July and August, when prices more than double.

➔ *Next to the Verrerie du Val de Pôme. From the train station, take the #10 bus to chemin Pres. Walk in the direction of the bus line until chemin du Val de Pôme. Turn right and walk 300 m. Camping on your left.* ℹ *Wi-Fi €5 per 30min., €8 per hr.* $ *Tent sites June-Aug €32-45; Sept €20; Apr €20. Each additional person €4-7.* ⏰ *Open Apr 1-Oct 30.*

SIGHTS

VERRERIE DE BIOT — GLASSBLOWER

chemin des Combes ☎04 93 65 03 00 ✉www.verreriebiot.com

Oldest and most impressive of all the glassblowers. This is the place that created the bubble glass effect, now endlessly replicated by plastic knock-offs at Crate and Barrel. A large open pathway ushers tourists into the factory, as well as a glassblowing museum that will tempt you to buy everything at the gift shop, so long as it doesn't break in your backpack.

$ *Free.* ⏰ *Workshop open daily June-Aug 9:30am-8pm; Sept-May 9:30am-6pm.*

MUSÉE NATIONAL FERNAND LÉGER — MUSEUM

chemin Val du Pome ☎04 92 91 50 30 ✉www.musée-fernandleger.fr

Museum featuring the work of Ferdinand Léger. We guarantee that you saw his stuff in an art history book. He's the one with the curvy black and white images of women with random swaths of bright color that seem to be random... er... artisically brilliant.

$ *€2, ages 26 and under free. Free first Su every month. Free audio tour available in English.* ⏰ *Open May-Oct. M 10am-6pm, W-Su 10am-6pm; Nov-Apr M 10am-5pm, W-Su 10am-5pm.*

ARTISIANS OF BIOT — SHOPPING DISTRICT

Biot is a condensed artisan capital, packed with jewelers, glassblowers, painters, and sculptors. They all have their own stores, which are treasure troves of art for tourists, ranging from your average sculpture to Moroccan leatherwork to plaster-of-Paris figurines. Stop by the tourist office for a large brochure on where to find all of them.

⏰ *Generally open M-Sa 10am-7pm. Times may differ.*

MUSÉE D'HISTOIRE ET DE CÉRAMIQUE BIOTESSE — MUSEUM

9 rue St. Sebastien ☎04 93 65 54 54

Museum of the ceramic history of Biot (really). It's exactly as interesting as it sounds. Entire rooms are reconstructed to show visitors how pottery was fired way back when. Exhibits feature large pots and iron works that look like ancient torture devices. Or they fall under the "art" catagory.

$ *€2.* ⏰ *Open daily June-Aug W-Su 11am-7pm; Sept-May 2-6pm.*

FOOD

LA CRÊPERIE DU VIEUX VILLAGE
🌿♿📶🍸⛱ CRÊPERIE [2]

2 rue Saint Sebastien ☎04 93 65 72 73

Cottage-like crêperie with flowers laidout on the tables and painted on the walls, and a cute reading nook by the window. The *menu classique (€12.50)* includes ham and cheese crêpe, salad, and dessert crêpe, as well as a big kiss and hug from the cheery owner. The neighborhood favorite will be changing locations in mid-2011 and moving to 29 rue St. Sebastien; the new premises will feature a terrace and shiny new alcohol license.

$ Crêpes €8-10. Sweet crêpes €3-5. ⏰ Open July-Aug W 9am-10pm, F-Su 9am-10pm; Sept-May W 9am-6pm, F-Su 9am-6pm.

LA GALERIE DES ARCADES
💳🍸📶⛱ PROVENÇAL [3]

16 pl. des Arcades ☎04 93 65 01 04

Cheap, traditional Provençal menu under the shade of an ivy covered terrace, on the bottom floor of an adorable hotel that you cannot afford. Modern art covers walls and jives well with the traditional architecture.

$ Plates €15. 3-course menu €32. ⏰ Open July-Aug Tu-Su 11am-10pm; Sept M 11am-2:30pm, Tu-Sa 11am-10pm.

PIZZERIA DU SOLEIL
💳♿ PIZZERIA [2]

9 passage de la Bourgade ☎04 93 65 74 74

Tiny, really tiny pizzeria hidden away from the main street. If you have no need for personal space, this restaurant and its 4 tables will suite your needs well. Cramped? Try standing next to the bar and scarfing down your oven-fired pizza.

$ Pizzas €7.50-9. Plat and entree €9. ⏰ Open M 11:30am-10pm, Tu 11:30am-3pm, W-Sa 11:30am-10pm.

LA CAFE DE LA POSTE
💳♿🍸⛱ CAFE [3]

24 rue St. Sebastien ☎04 93 65 19 32

La Poste's huge banquet-hall-sized seating area and bar make the term "cafe" something of a misnomer here. There's relaxing outside seating in the middle of the square, but the interior's tiled tables and cozy feel will drag you inside for at least a look.

$ Mussels €12.50. Plats €13. Prix-fixe menu €30. ⏰ Open in high-season daily 10am-midnight; low-season M-Th noon-3pm, F-Sa 5pm-midnight, Su noon-3pm.

NIGHTLIFE

CAFE BRUN
💳♿🍸⛱ BAR, CAFE, VEGETARIAN

44 impasse St. Sebastien ☎04 93 65 04 83

Welcoming bar with the jerseys of different sports teams hanging on the walls. The shiny brass bar and wooden tables are a throwback to another century, and exude some good old small town charm. And if you don't particularly like sports, small towns, or other centuries, you'll probably end up drinking here anyway; this is the only bar in town.

$ Beer €3. Cocktails €6. Vegetarian dishes €12. Plats from €10. ⏰ Open M-Th 11am-7pm, F-Sa 11am-12:30am. Happy hour 6-8pm.

ESSENTIALS

Practicalities

- **TOURIST OFFICE:** Offers maps, brochures and advice on glassblowers and walking routes depending on interests *(46 rue Saint Sebastien ☎04 93 65 78 00 💻www.biot.fr ⏰ Open daily 9am-6pm.)*

- **BANK: Caisse d'Espargne.** ATM available *(1 chemin Neuf ☎04 93 65 11 78.)*

Emergency!

- **POLICE MUNICIPALE:** 7 calade des Bachettes *(☎04 93 65 06 66).*
- **PHARMACY:** 1 chemin Neuf *(☎04 93 65 00 16 ⏰ Open daily 10am-7pm.)*
- **HOSPITAL: Centre Medical,** chemin des Bachettes *(☎04 93 65 00 23).*
- **POST OFFICE:** rue Sainte Sebastien, next to tourist office *(☎04 93 65 11 49 ⏰ Open M 9am-noon and 2-5:15pm, Tu 9am-noon, W-F 9am-noon and 2-5:15pm, Sa 9am-noon.)*
- **POSTAL CODE:** 06018.

Getting There

Gare SNCF trains run to **Biot train station (TER)** *(⏰ Open 6am-11pm.)* Trains to **Cannes** *(⏰ 15min., every 30min. $€3);* **Antibes** *(⏰ 9min., every 30min. $€1.20);* **Nice** *(⏰ 25min., every 30min. $ €3.40);* **Marseille** via Cannes *($€28.30).* From the train station, **bus** lines #7 and 10 go to city center *($€1 ⏰last return at 7:39pm).*

TAM line #200 (€1) that runs between Cannes and Nice stops at the Biot train station. From **Nice** *(⏰ 45min., every 15min. 6:30am-6pm, every 30min. 6-8pm.)* from **Cannes** *(⏰ 1hr. 25min., every 15min. 5am-6pm, every 30min. 6-8pm.)* Arrives at Gare SNCF. Take bus #7 or #10 to town center.

Taxis: For **taxis**, call Biot Taxi *(☎06 09 65 96 48).*

Getting Around

Within the town, walk any direction for 3min. and you'll have left town. To get to the *verreries* (glassblowing workshops), there are frequent buses (#7 and 10, €1). Consult tourist office for exact timetables. As a general rule, buses run every 10-15min. 7am-8pm.

juan-les-pins ☎04

Whenever Cannes outprices the Riviera's Spring Break crowd (think Film Festival), Juan-les-Pins subs in as the life of the party. In July and August, the clubs stay open until breakfast—or lunch—and the warm beach welcomes the excessively tan and hungover back into the relaxed rhythm of town life. Situated on the east side of the Cape of Antibes, Juan-les-Pins differs from its historic sister city in that there is little to do other than party, soak in the sun, and play in the water. You'll find actual young people on the beach here, and a very vibrant nightlife that isn't choked by glitz and exploit (cough, Cannes, cough). Be sure to still dress up when you go out—despite the sun and fun, the people here dress to impress, especially during the summer months.

ORIENTATION

Juan-les-Pins is pretty easy to get around; any street from the **train station** leads directly to the beach. A walk down **av. Docteur Favre** takes you right into the middle of the *bar du nuits* and clubs, with the casino conveniently nearby. Walking straight out of the train station down **av. Marechal Joffre** leads you to the main beach and **tourist office,** while **av. l'Esterel** takes you to the budget hotels and cheaper restaurants before hitting the beach on the other side of the train tracks.

ACCOMMODATIONS

HOTEL DE LA PINÈDE HOTEL [3]

7 av. Georges Gallice ☎0648 29 52 74 www.hotel-pinede.com

This classy but funky boutique hotel is a stone's throw from Juan-les-Pins's party district. Don't worry about shut-eye; the windows are soundproof. We're not sure what to make of the paintings of the New York skyline or the Buddha statues, but with a breakfast terrace that's this prime for sunbathing, we don't mind the non sequiturs.

 # From the train station, walk down on av. du Doctueur Fabre. When you reach bld. de la Pinede, make a right. When you reach a 5-point intersection, make a slight right onto av. George Gallice. Hotel is on your immediate right. i Breakfast €5.50. Soundproof windows. $ Singles €45-50; doubles €60-90; triples €90-120. Prices are higher in summer season.

HOTEL CECIL
HOTEL ❶

rue Jonnard BP 51 ☎04 93 61 05 12 www.hotelcecil-France.com

Tucked away on the opposite side of town, this quiet Belle Époque hotel will have you thinking about putting some pink furniture in your own house.

 # From the train station, turn right and walk down av. de Esterel 3 blocks. Turn right onto rue Jonnard. Hotel is halfway down the street on your left. i Breakfast €6.50. Prices increase in summer months. $ Singles €55-76; doubles €58-89; triples €105.

PARISIANA
HOTEL ❷

16 av. de l'Esterel ☎04 93 61 03 hotelparisiana@wanadoo.fr

This budget hotel is close to the train station, and has a breakfast terrace and skylights in the central stairwell. The small rooms make for a cozy experience, especially in the triple room.

 # Take a right out of the train station down the street 2-3 blocks. Hotel on your right. $ Singles €32-48; doubles €45-62; triples €57-74; quads €67-82. Prices increase in summer. ⏰ Reception 8am-10pm.

TRIANON HOTEL
HOTEL ❷

14 av. de l'Esterel ☎04 93 61 18 11

This budget hotel's rooms are a pleasant surprise, considering the ridiculously low prices. The yellow and lavender paintings of flowers add a domestic touch. If it didn't face away from the beach, the bright breakfast terrace would be perfect, but at least it's close to the train station.

 # From the train station, turn right onto rue l'Esterel. Hotel is 2-3 blocks down on your right. i Breakfast €5. $ Singles €30-43; doubles €40-62; triples €64-74; quad €73-82. ⏰ Quiet hours from 10:30pm-8:30am.

BEACHES

The beaches are ordered from east to west.

PLAGE D'ANTIBES-LES-PINS
bld. du Littoral

The furthest from the city center (it's almost closer to St-Raphaël), Plage d'Antibes-les-Pins is less crowded than its sister beaches. This is particularly noticeable during the summer months, when it's usually impossible to see any sand in Juan-les-Pins because the umbrellas are so packed together.

PLAGE DU PONT DULYS
bld. Charles Guillaumont

One of the most youth-centric beaches in town. It's far enough from the city's center to keep out the elderly and children, but not quite out of the reach for lazy teenagers.

PLAGE LA GALLICE
bld. Edouard Baudoin

The closest beach to the town, La Gallice is right next to the port, so you can watch the boats sailing in and out of the harbor. You can also get some good people watching in, since this beach is also the most crowded.

PLAGE EPI HOLLYWOOD

bld. Edouard Baudoin

Just out of reach of the city, this beach is where you'll most likely find skinny dippers around 5am who've just been kicked out of the nearby clubs. During the day it's pretty quiet and provides some escape from town.

PLAGE DES ONDES

bld. Maréchal Juin

In Juan-les-Pins, less sand equals lighter crowds, but it also means less comfortable sunbathing. Some of the coastline at Ondes is more like loose gravel, and no part of the beach is quite like the picturesque white sands that line the coast.

FOOD

LE SWEET CAFFE
DINER ❷

16 bld. Edouard Baudoin ☎04 93 67 82 12

This relaxing cafe and diner lies on the edge of Juan-les-Pins's party district. Come here after leaving the party early to munch on everything any other restaurant in Juan les Pins has to offer, but at lower prices. The outside patio is lively at night.

Ⓢ *Pizzas €8.40-11. Crepes €3.30-9. Salads €7-13. Cocktails €8. Ice cream cocktails €8.* Ⓒ *Open May-Sept 8am-2am or later; Nov-Apr 8am-7pm.*

LE RUBAN BLEU
BRASSERIE ❸

promenade du soleil ☎04 93 61 31 02 ✉plage.rubanbleu@wanadoo.fr

Beachfront brasserie and restaurant that is ideal for watching the young and the fabulous strut their stuff down the boardwalk. You'll pay for the awesome view, unfortunately; the prices here get pretty high. An outdoor seating area opens up on the beach as the night wears on.

Ⓢ *Plates €19-25. Crêpes €3.50-5.* Ⓒ *Open M-Sa noon-3pm, Su noon-4pm. Beach restaurant open F-Sa 7:30-10:30pm.*

LA BAMBA
PIZZERIA ❸

18/20 av. Docteur Datheville ☎04 93 61 32 64

Upscale pizzeria and restaurant a block away from the shopping and party center of Juan-les-Pins. Open air restaurant where you can still feel the heat from the woodfired stoves in the back.

Ⓢ *Dishes €13-15. Pizza €7.80-14. 3-course prix-fixe menu €17.50.* Ⓒ *Open daily noon-10:30pm.*

LA PÂTE À CRÊPES
CRÊPERIE ❷

24 av. de l'Esterel ☎04 93 61 33 14

If crêpes were ever a classy dining option, this place would collect Michelin stars like no other. Chic blue lighting and metal tables add to the modern experience without hurting the wallet.

Ⓢ *Prix fixe galette, crêpe, and carafe of wine €12.50. Crêpes €2.50-3.50.* Ⓒ *Open July-Aug Tu-Su 12-10:30pm; Sept-June Tu-Su 11:45am-2:30pm and 6:30-10:30pm.*

L'HORIZON
SEAFOOD ❸

37 bld. Charles Guillaumont ☎04 93 67 23 11 ✉www.horizon-restaurant.com

This unassuming, quiet restaurant serves seafood right on the beach. Tucked in between a beach shop and smaller restaurant, this marina-themed establishment serves up whatever the local fishermen caught fresh that day, including lobsters and shellfish on occasion.

Ⓢ *Plates €18-28. Plat du jour €12.* Ⓒ *Open Jan-Nov 23 M-Tu 11:45am-2pm and 6-10:30pm, Th-Su 11:45am-2pm and 6-10:30pm.*

côte d'azur

NIGHTLIFE

PAM PAM
♿🍸⛅ BAR

137 bld. du Président Wilson ☎04 93 61 11 05 💻www.pampam.fr

Brazilian bar that serves drinks out of tiki statues. Bright-colored and life-sized tiki gods take the stage with festively dressed dancers at 10pm. Outdoor seating allows some escape from the bongo drums.

$ Apértifs €5. Cocktails €8-12. ⏰ Open daily 3pm-3am.

L'IDEM
🚭🍸▼ BAR, LOUNGE

6 bld. de la Pinede ☎06 09 53 02 49 💻www.lidem06.unblog.fr

There's 24/7 salsa dancing at this lounge and bar, a block away from the crazy clubs and parties. Skills range from beginner to the pros, who are all too happy to take a greenhorn onto the floor. Lessons are available, and include a night with your instructor or partner on the floor every Thursday night *(€12-22).*

$ Beer €6. Liqueur €5-10. Cocktails €9. ⏰ Open M-Th 7pm-1am (or later), F-Sa 7pm-4am (or later), Su 7pm-1am (or later).

HEMINGWAY COCKTAILS AND CIGARS
♿🍸⛅▼ BAR

carrefour de la Nouvelle Orléans

Formerly known as the Che Cafe, this *bar du nuit* kept the Cuban decor, added some Hemingway books, and renamed itself. Two stories of Cuban maps and pictures of the famous author make their rum specials seem slightly more authentic.

ℹ Cigar cave. $ Beer €4. Mixed rum drinks €9-15. ⏰ Open Apr-Sept daily 3pm-5am.

LE CRISTAL
💳♿🍸⛅▼ BAR

av. Georges Gallice ☎04 93 61 62 51

A chill crowd gathers on the terrace to watch local clubbers strut by, or they surround the bar to watch the barmen (literally) juggle bottles as they mix their special ice cream cocktails *(€10).*

$ Ice cream cocktails €10. ⏰ Open daily 8:30am-2:30am.

ZAPATA
🚭🍸⛅ BAR

av. du Docteur Dautheville 💻www.juanbynight.com

Think you'll only see someone order 10 shots for himself in Mexico? Think again. We saw it at this Mexican bar, which specializes in shots of "fuego" (gin, run, vodka, spices and lime). Walls covered in old pre-Revolution photos of Zapata and Hidalgo.

$ Tequila shots €6. Beer €7. ⏰ Open daily 7pm-3am.

LE VILLAGE
♿🍸 DISCOTHÈQUE

1 bld. de la Pinede ☎04 92 93 90 00

Crowds line up early and stretch across the street for this Cuban-themed discothèque and *bar du nuit.* Anticipation for nightly DJ mixes and live performances throughout July and August keeps the city buzzing all year.

$ Cover €13. Drinks €9. ⏰ Open July-Aug daily midnight-5am; Sept-June F-Sa midnight-5am.

MILK
♿🍸 DISCOTHÈQUE

av. George Gallice ☎04 93 67 22 74

Swanky bar and discothèque entirely decorated in white. Dress up if you think you'll be let in, and get here early to avoid the long lines at the doors, especially on weekends.

$ Cover €16; includes 1 drink. Drinks €12-18. ⏰ Open July-Aug daily noon-6am; Sept-June F-Sa noon-6am.

EDEN CASINO
💳🍸 CASINO

bld. Edouard Baudoin ☎04 92 93 71 71 💻www.casinojuanlespins.com

Underground casino made to look like a literal cave. The fake plants and colorful lighting add to the Vegas factor, while the prices remind you that you're still in Europe. Blackjack (€5 min.), roulette (€5 min.) and poker are played regularly, as well as slot machines (no craps, unfortunately). Present passport for entry. Must be 18+ and well-dressed for table games (for the Apatow-esque out there, that means no sneakers, jeans, or T-shirts).

i *18+ for table games.* Ⓢ *Beer €4. Cocktails €8.* Ⓓ *Open noon-4am.*

FESTIVALS

FESTIVAL DE JAZZ A JUAN

☎04 97 23 11 19 ▣www.antibesjuanlespins.com/html/htm_vie.asp?htmlD=162 Ten-day jazz festival where the town population triples as beatniks and old timers alike flood the streets to jam. Oh yeah, and it's the longest-running jazz festival in Europe. The jam fest is usually held in mid to late July, but its dates, the location of its concerts throughout town, and each concert's admission prices vary each year depending on who's performing. As of this writing, Juan-les-Pins has yet to set its 2011 program; check the city's website for more information.

Ⓢ *A good percentage of the performances are free; check website for more information.* Ⓓ *Expected 2011 dates July 14-25.*

ESSENTIALS

Practicalities

- **TOURIST OFFICE:** 51 bld. Charles Guillaumont. From the train station, walk down av. Maréchal Joffre and turn right when you hit the beach. Tourist office is 2min. away on the right, at the intersection of av. de l'Admiral Courbet and av. Charles Guillaumont. (☎*04 97 23 11 10* ▣*www.antibes-juanlespins.com.* Ⓓ *Open M-Sa 9am-noon and 2-6pm, Su 10am-5pm.*)

- **LAUNDROMAT:** On the corner of av. de l'Esterel and av. du Docteur Fabre. (☎*04 93 61 52 04* Ⓢ*Wash €3.90, dry €.050 per 15min.* Ⓓ*Open daily 7am-10:30pm.*)

- **INTERNET:** **Mediterr@net,** 3 av. du Docteur Fabre. (☎*04 93 61 04 03*Ⓢ *€3 per hr.* Ⓓ*Open M-Sa 9am-10pm, Su 10am-9pm.*)

- **POST OFFICE:** Av. de Maréchal Joffre. (☎*04 92 93 75 50*Ⓓ *Open M-F 8am-noon and 2-5:45pm, Sa 8:30am-noon.*) ATM available on opposite side (ave. Doctuer Fabre).

- **POSTAL CODE:** 06160.

Emergency!

- **POLICE:** ☎04 97 21 75 60.

- **PHARMACY:** 1 av. de l'Admiral Courbet. (☎*04 93 61 12 96.* Ⓓ *Open daily 8am-12:30pm and 2-6:30pm.*)

Getting There

To get to Juan-les-Pins by **train,** go to the Gare SNCF station (*av. de l'Esterel.* Ⓓ*Open daily 6:30am-8:55pm. Ticket window open 8:50am-noon and 1:30-5pm.*) To **Antibes** (Ⓢ*€1.25.* Ⓓ*5min., 25 per day.*), **Cannes** (Ⓢ*€1.75.* Ⓓ*10min., 25 per day.*); **Monaco** (Ⓢ*€6.80.* Ⓓ*1hr., 10 per day.*); **Nice** (Ⓢ*€4.10.* Ⓓ*30min., 25 per day.*). You can also get to Juan-les-Pins by **bus** (☎*04 93 34 37 60.*) **Bus #1** (Ⓢ*€1.* Ⓓ*10min., every 20min. 7am-8pm*) runs from Sillages to pl. Guynemer in Antibes, where you can transfer to the Gare Routiere (regional buses). Night bus #1 between pl. de Gaulle in Antibes and Juan-les-Pins in summer only (Ⓓ *Jul-Aug 8pm-12:30am*). **Taxis** (☎*04 92 93 07 07 or 08 25 56 07 07.*) At the Jardin de la Pinede and outside the train station. The bus from Juan-les-Pins to Antibes is €14-16.

côte d'azur

Getting Around

Most of Juan-les-Pins is very walkable; the only problem that we suspect will arise is deciding which beach you should settle on before you start breaking a sweat. If you are completely averse to exercise, the **tourist train** is more than happy to shuttle you around to see the surrounding sights, in case you don't want to walk there yourself. (☎06 15 77 67 47 *i* Runs from bld. Edouard Baudoin to Antibes, then the vieille ville, and back again to Juan-les-Pins. ⏰ 30min.; Mar-Oct Mo-Su every hr. 10:30am-6:30pm, Jul-Aug runs every hr. 7:30-11:30pm).

cannes ☎0493

This star-studded, glitzy city on the water definitely has its pricey side, especially during the film festival. If you plan your trip carefully, though, Cannes is probably one of the cheapest places for backpackers to go on the French Riviera. Defined by a distinctly laid back atmosphere for 10 months out of the year (July and August see massive swells in millionaires and their paparazzi, of course), Cannes harbors some of the best that Côte d'Azur has to offer in shopping and beaches, not to mention the fresh shellfish at any of its open air markets. The club scene can be a little intimidating at first, but dressing up just a little bit will go a long way when it comes to getting past the bouncers. In fact, dressing up in general is a good idea here, if only to fit in. Between the hours of 7 and 8pm, locals and tourists magically go from topless and nude (always in vogue here) to full makeup or sports jackets. Don't get caught on the wrong side of this unspoken dress code.

Everyone knows about the Cannes Film Festival, and the city's residents benefit from it; local movie theaters here are able to show Palme d'Or winners before anywhere else in the world. The Palais des Festivals hosts additional expos and concerts throughout the year, which puts Cannes in the party mood almost all the time. You might have to splurge on accommodations a centrally located place in the city and near the beach is worth the price. Hostels have yet to find their way to the pricey coast of southern France.

ORIENTATION

Cannes is a very easy city to get around; it's a lot smaller than you imagined it was in that last dream of yours where you won Palme d'Or and exchanged room keys with 🎬**Matt Damon.** The town can be easily divided into two areas—the expensive part of town and the normal part, where the actual residents live. To the **East of the Palais des Festivals,** the hotels, prices, and breast augmentations get bigger. With names like Dior and Chanel scattered around the private beaches, it's easy to get overwhelmed. If the bling is too much for you, head back towards **the Castre**—the large castle on hill to the West—back to the **Suquet,** where the restaurants are intimate, the prices are lower and people in general are a little more mellow. The nightlife thrives around **rue Doctuer Gerard Monod,** but residents generally stick to the cafes and brasseries that line **rue Felix Fauvre.** The best (and free) bacchanalias are further West past the **Vieux Port,** where you'll find the local population of the young and the restless partying it up almost year round.

ACCOMMODATIONS

HOTEL ALNEA
✦⊛⟨ᵗⁱ⟩✦ HOTEL ❹

20 rue Jean de Riouffe   ☎04 93 68 72 77 🖵www.hotel-alnea.com

Upscale hotel with walls covered in paintings reminiscent of Gauguin's Tahiti phase. Bright colors make this place come alive, and the beach theme will soon have you dying to go to work on your tanline. Large, clean rooms are each

cannes • accommodations

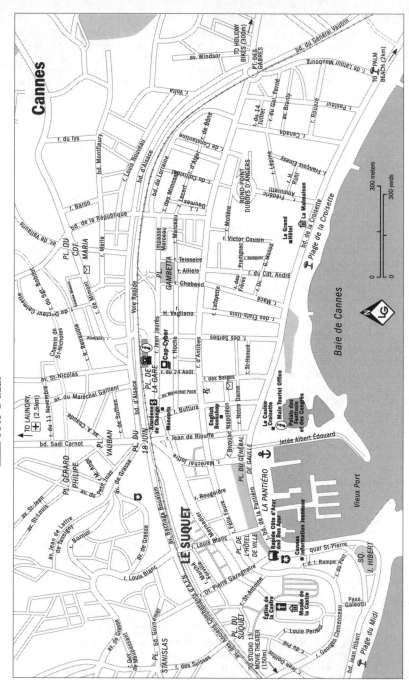

Cannes

côte d'azur

themed according to a famous tropical island or locale.

⚑ *From the train station, turn right and walk to the MonoPrix. At the intersection, keep going straight one block to rue. Jean de Riouffe. Turn left. Hotel is on your immediate left.* ℹ *Breakfast €7.50.* Ⓢ *Singles €60; doubles €70; twin €80.* ⌚ *Check-In 2pm, Checkout 11am. Reception 8am-8pm.*

HOTEL 7
⚑♿(p) HOTEL ❹

23 rue Maréchal Joffre
☎04 93 68 66 66

This star-studded hotel opened in January 2010 and still has that new car smell. Pictures of old movies and movie stars are framed on the silver, chic walls. The minimalist decor in the rooms make them feel less small. Handicapped room on ground floor is opened up into a TV lounge when not occupied.

⚑ *From the train station, turn right and walk until the highway entrance. Walk up the sidewalk to the highway and make a left onto Maréchal Joffre. Hotel will have movie posters on the side facing the train station.* ℹ *Breakfast €6. Handicapped room on ground floor.* Ⓢ *Singles €60; doubles €70-80. Family room (4 person) €90.*

HOTEL PLM
⚑♿(p) HOTEL ❹

3 rue Hoche
☎04 93 38 31 19 🖳www.hotel-plm.com

Boutique hotel with deals if you stay for a while. Clean, nice smelling rooms with purple bathtubs make this simple hotel worth the extra euros, if only to avoid the local dumps.

⚑ *From the train station, walk right down Juan Juares. Turn left at rue de 24 Aout. Walk for one block until at rue Hoche. Turn right and walk one block. Hotel on right.* ℹ *3rd night 25% off. 6th night is 50% off. Breakfast €8.* Ⓢ *Singles €46-71; doubles €54-79; superior doubles €59-85.*

HOTEL MIMONT
⚑Ⓧ(p) HOTEL ❷

39 rue Mimont
☎04 93 39 51 64 🖳www.canneshotelmimont.com

Still the best budget option in town. Large, clean rooms for relatively cheap, and special *petit chambres* with bed, sink, shared toilet, and shower upon request. On the other side of the train tracks, but still 5min from town. The incredibly hospitable hosts speak English and are very welcoming to Let's Go readers and Americans, who seem to be the majority of their clients.

⚑ *From the train station, turn left and take the underpass next to the tourist office to rue Mimont. Turn right, and walk for 3 blocks past the post office. Hotel is on your left.* ℹ *Breakfast €6.20.* Ⓢ *Petit chambre €30; singles €37-43; doubles €42; triples €58.*

LA VILLA TOSCA
⚑(p) HOTEL ❺

11 rue Hoche
☎04 93 38 34 40 🖳www.villa-tosca.com

Amazing, spacious, and centrally located, but prohibitively expensive for most students. Lavish boutique hotel that is probably the best quality for what you pay in all of Cannes. Huge rooms with armoires and couches, and a breakfast area that looks like something Louis XIV would approve of.

⚑ *From the train station, walk right on Juan Juares. Turn left on rue de 24 Aout and walk for one block. Turn left on rue Hoche, hotel is on your left.* ℹ *Free Wi-Fi.* Ⓢ *Singles €61-98; doubles €82-125; triples €109-161; quads €131-183.*

HOTEL ASCOTT
⚑Ⓧ(p) HOTEL ❸

27 rue des Serbes
☎04 93 99 18 24 🖳www.canneshotel.com

Budget hotel that's a little pricey for what you get. Decor is from the early '90s (read: lingering '80s vibe), and the metal panels that cover the windows from the outside make the rooms dark and dreary, but at least the bathroom is clean.

⚑ *From the train station walk left half a block and turn right down rue des Serbes. Hotel is 2-3 blocks down on your right.* Ⓢ *Singles €46-61; doubles €51-72; triples €68-90.*

HOTEL L'ESTEREL
⚑♿(p) HOTEL ❹

15 rue de 24 Aout
☎04 93 38 82 82 🖳reservations@hotellesterel.com

Boutique hotel that's easy to find and close to the market and train station. The large, well-lit rooms are standard, but what sets this place apart is the rooftop terrace, which provides a breakfast with a view of all of Cannes.

☕ *From the train station, turn right and walk half a block until rue de 24 Aout. Turn left and walk 1 block down the street. Hotel is on your right.* **i** *Breakfast €8.* ⑤ *Singles €50-80; doubles €63-80; double deluxe €74-90.*

MODERN WAIKIKI HOTEL
11 rue des Serbes

⛵⊗🐱((𝑖)) HOTEL ❹
☎04 93 39 09 87

Funky hotel with bright pinks, zany lavender shapes, and pictures of celebrities covering the walls. Chic rooms with dark bedspreads and carpet each come with private bathrooms, and a shower with 9 shower heads.

☕ *From the train station, walk left half a block until rue des Serbes. Turn right and walk 4 blocks, past rue d'Anitbes to the hotel on your right.* ⑤ *Singles €50-60; doubles €65-85; triples €75-95.*

SIGHTS
🎯

L'ÉGLISE DE LA CASTRE
CHURCH

Towering over the old city and Vieux Port, this church provides crystal clear views of Cannes all the way to Palm Beach on a clear day. The local landmark nearly bankrupted the city, which had to constantly fundraise for 80 years to complete the stucture and commission its glass and crystal chandeliers, not to mention the neo-Gothic organ that puts Notre Dame's to shame.

⑤ *Free.* 🕐 *Open daily June-Aug 9am-noon and 3:15-7pm; Sept-May 9am-noon and 2:15-6pm.*

MUSÉE DE LA CASTRE
MUSEUM
☎04 93 38 55 26

Formerly the private castle of the monks of Lérins, this museum houses a permanent collection of ancient relics from the Americas, as well as a display of musical instruments from around the world. The only thing relevant to Cannes is its Provençal art collection from the late 19th and early 20th centuries, which feature depictions of day-to-day life in the city.

⑤ *€3, students €2.* 🕐 *Open Tu-Su July-Aug 10am-7pm; Sept and Apr-June 10am-1pm and 2-6pm; Oct-Mar 10am-1pm and 2-5pm.*

CENTRE D'ART/MALMAISON
MUSEUM
47 bld. de la Croisette
☎04 97 06 44 90

Hosts multiple temporary exhibits that change depending on what's politically popular at the time. Issues like green living and globalization are popular.

⑤ *€4, under 25 €2.* 🕐 *Open June-Sep M-Th and Sa-Su 11am-8pm, F 11am-10pm; Oct-Nov Tu-Su 10am-1pm and 2-6pm.*

CASINO CRIOSETTE
CASINO
1 espace Lucien Barrière
☎04 92 98 78 00

The most accessible casino in the area, Criosette features slot machines, blackjack, craps and roulette, as well as a series of fake statues of Greek gods. Kinda like Vegas, only less sleezy. Wait, nevermind: a bunch of guys with slicked hair and their shirts unbuttoned to their belly button just walked in.

i *No dress code for slots. No jeans, sneakers, or T-shirts for table games* 🕐 *Slots open at 10am, tables open 8pm-4am.*

PLAGE DE LA CROISETTE
BEACH
Between Vieux Port and the Port Canto

A series of private beaches where you will have to shell out €20 for a beach umbrella or beach chair. Pure heresy, in our opinion. The beaches are lined with even pricier restaurants, so you don't need to wander far from your towel to give away even more money.

PLAGES DU MIDI   BEACH

East of the Croisette.

Beautiful sandy beach that's free to the public. Packed in the summertime, this is where you go to meet locals and brush up on some volleyball skills, assuming you know how to say "serve" in French.

FOOD

BELLIARD   ♠ & BAKERY ❷

1 rue Chabaud   ☎04 93 39 42 72

The 75-year-old *boulangerie* has maintained its humility in one of the priciest areas of Cannes. The neighborhood institution sells an array of charming and affordable *assiettes (€9.50)* as well as tarts, cakes, and a rum raisin ice cream that will put hair on your chest.

Ⓢ *Assiette du Jour €9.50.Tarts and cakes €2-3.50.* Ⓒ *Open daily 7am-8pm.*

AKWABAMO EXOTICK   ♠ & AFRICAN ❷

36 rue Mimont   ☎04 93 99 89 10

This awesome Côte d'Ivoire restaurant specializes in West African cuisine of chicken and beef *brochettes (€10)*. Pick from 6 unpronounceable sauces or endulge in the fish dish with rice *(€13)*. Down it with homemade pineapple and coconut rum. Baskets and crafts cover the walls of this simple establishment.

Ⓢ *Dishes €9-18.* Ⓒ *Open Tu-F 11am-10pm, Sa-Su 11am-midnight.*

LE FREATE   ♠ & ♨ ITALIAN ❸

26 rue Jean Hibert.   ☎04 93 39 45 39

In business since '47, this Cannes staple sates its clients with grilled meats and pizza, and provides its patrons with that perfect opportunity to escape the hussle in the glitzy part of Cannes for some laidback cafe action near the beach.

Ⓔ *Plates €7.50-15.* Ⓒ *Open Jun-Sep 6:30am-2am, Oct-May 6:30am-1pm.*

LES MAREYEURS DU SUB-EST   ☺☒ MARKET ❶

rue Docteur Pierre   ☎04 96 39 39 23

Just cause you're on a budget doesn't mean you can't get lobster. You'll just have to cook it yourself, since this market specializes in live blue lobsters from the daily catch. Make sure you get a fighter, they have the most meat.

Ⓢ *€15 per kg.* Ⓒ *Open daily 8am-noon.*

MARCHÉ FORVILLE   ☺☒ MARKET ❶

rue Marché Forville

This large, covered market sells everything from fruit to eels to flowers to dairy products. Get up early, since the best products go fast.

Ⓒ *Open Tu-Su 7am-1pm.*

LA CRÊPERIE   ♠ & ♨ CRÊPERIE ❷

66 rue Maynadier

A small crêpe place in the heart of the cheap stores on rue Maynadier, its outdoor seating provides the opportunity for judging passerby based on which fake brands they bought.

Ⓢ*Crêpes €2.80-8.70.* Ⓒ*Open Tu-Su 1pm-8pm.*

CARREFOUR   ♠ & MARKET ❶

Intersection of rue Maynadier and rue Docteur Pierre

The Costco of France, come here for cheap everything, especially liquor and wine in the back of the store.

Ⓢ *Varying.* Ⓒ *Open daily 9am-8pm.*

LAETITIA PASTA   ♠ ☒ ♨ ITALIAN ❷

18 av. Maréchal Joffre   ☎04 93 39 52 79

Incredibly cheap pasta and salads for students and budget travelers alike, as

the student menu gets you a pasta and drink for ridiculously reasonable prices
(€6.50). The simple interior decor matches the simplicity of its menu, while the
small stand outside proudly boasts its main dish of the day.
Ⓢ *Students menu €6.50, Normal menu €8 for pasta and drink. Salads €5.90, pastas €5.50-
7.10.* Ⓩ *Open M-Sa 8:30am-7:30pm.*

NIGHTLIFE

THE STATION TAVERN
⚓👤♿♀☕ BAR

18 rue Juan Juares
☎04 93 38 34 91

A godsend for young budget travelers, since cheap beer and karaoke is all you
need to fill a small lounge with every under-25 in Cannes. The karaoke nights *(Th-
Sa at 9pm)* are completely unpretentious, and totally awesome in its cheesiness.
i Karaoke Th-Sa 9pm. Ⓢ *Beer €3.50, 10 beer for €16, 10 shots for €16.* Ⓩ *Open M-Sa 6pm-2am.*

MORRISON'S
♀ BAR

10 rue Teisseire
☎04 92 98 16 17 🖥www.morrisonspub.com

This laid-back pub gets mobbed early in the evening and stays packed until closing. The walls are covered with the quotes from Irish playwrights, as well as the
drunken musings of local patrons. Irish and British staff breathe a sigh of relief
when they get to converse in English.
*i Live music W-Th and Su at 9:30pm. Ladies night on Su, unlimited beer and wine for women
€8.* Ⓢ *Happy hour €4 pints, normal hours €6 pints. Whiskey €8.* Ⓩ *Happy hour 5-8pm, Open
daily 5pm-2am.*

BROWN SUGAR
⚓♀☕▼ BAR, RESTAURANT

17 rue des Frères Pradignac
☎04 93 39 70 10

Cooky Holland-themed bar goes all out with bicycle wheels, accordions, skis,
pots and sleds hanging from ceiling. Noticeable family clientele that tapers off as
the night goes on. Come before 9:30pm and you get a free tapa with the purchase
of a drink. How come you taste so good?
Ⓢ *Beer €4-7, shooters €5, cocktails €8.* Ⓩ *Open daily 6pm-2:30am.*

CARRE D'OR
⚓👤♀☕ BAR

16 rue des Frères Pradignac
☎04 93 38 91 70

The club's walls of mirrors makes it seem bigger than it is. Center bar is an island
in the middle of the dance floor, but you won't see this upscale crowd anywhere
up there before 1am, or before going through a €700 bottle of Absolut.
Ⓢ *Cocktails €10, beer €7.* Ⓩ *Open 7pm-2:30am.*

SPARKLING AND 4U
⚓👤♀☕▼ NIGHTCLUB

6/8 rue des Frères Pradignac
☎04 93 39 71 21

And sparkle it does. This joint bar and club is what a club looks like in everyone's
wildest dream. Multiple rooms, colors, and textures are enough to keep even the
most ADD child interested and focused on this club for the night. A large circular
bar (4U bar) sits in the center of the main room, and additional bars are scattered throughout the establishment. Thursday is theme-night. First Thursday of
the month is GLBT night.
Ⓢ *Shooters €4, cocktails €12.* Ⓩ *Open M-Sa 6pm-5am.*

ZANZIBAR
⚓♀☕▼ BAR

85 rue Felix Fauvre
☎04 93 39 30 75 🖥www.lezanzibar.com

Europe's oldest official gay bar, Zanzibar showcases a classic sailor theme. A
small, barrel-like room is covered in images depicting jolly young men drinking
and singing on the waterfront. The bar attracts a somewhat older crowd early on
in the night, but beckons Americans and youth after midnight.
i GLBT info at 🖥www.hexagonegay.com. Ⓢ *Beer €4.50, cocktails €9-10.* Ⓩ *Open daily 7pm-
5am (or later).*

côte d'azur

LE 7

7 rue Rouguière

CABARET, NIGHTCLUB

☎04 93 39 10 36 ☐www.discotheque-le7.com

Get prepared for a raunchy all-nighter: this local legend's outrageous drag shows start at 2am, and the drinks and fabulously dressed preformers continue until 5am. Cannes' most famous caberet club, Le 7 caters to all genders and sexual orientations.

Ⓢ *Cover Fri-Sa €12, includes one free drink. Drinks €9.50, shooters €7.* ☼ *Open Th-Su 11:30pm-5am.*

VOGUE

20 rue du Suquet

BAR

☎04 93 39 99 18

Prepare to be (wo)man-handled. This Hollywood/*fabulous* GLBT bar in the heart of the Suquet compensates for its small size with sparkling mirrors, images of red carpet divas, and a soundtrack fit to accompany your strut down the runway. Come here to play guess-what-gender, then be told very proudly that gender is a construct.

Ⓢ *Cocktails €8.* ☼ *Open daily 8:30pm-2:30am.*

SOON

3 rue Commandant André

BAR

☎06 23 59 98 12 ☐www.lesoon.fr

If the giant champagne bottles don't get you thinking that you've made it in life, maybe the light-up bar or silver faux alligator cushions will. If you find that's too much for you to handle, the outside seating provides a slight escape from pretentiousness.

Ⓢ *Beer €5-8, mixed drinks €13.* ☼ *Open M-Sa 7pm-2:30am.*

LE MUST

14 rue du Batéguier

BAR, CLUB

☎06 68 14 27 40

Like a scene out of a 1970s porn flick, this *bar du nuit* has chic, glittery plastic barstools, private alcoves in dimly lit areas, and a giant picture of Marilyn Monroe. Outside seating has low couches and a hookah water pipe when you reach sparkley overload. Theme nights include a Russia Night where vodka is discounted.

Ⓢ *Shooters €5, beer €6-8, cocktails €10.* ☼ *Open Mar-Oct daily 7pm-2:30am, Nov-Feb F-Sa 7pm-2:30am.*

PEOPLE BAR

6 rue des Frères Pradignac

BAR

☎04 93 68 65 66 ☐www.lepeople-bar.fr.

Small and simple, classy bar is completely silver, right down to the large picture of Marilyn Monroe (she's a favorite in Cannes, apparently).

Ⓢ *Shooters €5, cocktails €10.* ☼ *Open M-Sa 6pm-2:30am.*

SOF: SPIRIT OF FOOD

4 pl. Gambetta

RESTAURANT, BAR

☎04 93 38 38 10

More of a restaurant that's just open really late than an actual bar, this hip establishment refuses to be pinned down. American, Italian, Chinese, French... whatever kind of cuisine you're craving, they probably have it. That goes for the international beer selection too. Laidback crowd and family atmosphere, or people who just want a break between clubs. Come before 9:30pm and get a pint and tapas (*€12*). Live music on the weekends.

Ⓢ *Beer €3.50, cocktails €8.50.* ☼ *Open daily 6am-2:30pm and 6pm-2:30am.*

AU BUREAU

49 rue Felix Fauvre

BAR

☎04 93 39 06 32

Beachy bar complete with sand covering the floor. 11 different kinds of Mojitos will drain your wallet and lift your spirits (*€11*). This is where the swanky crowd comes to pretend that they're laid back.

Ⓢ *Mojitos €10, cocktails €11.* ☼ *Open daily noon-2:30am.*

ESSENTIALS

Practicalities

- **TOURIST OFFICE:** In the Palais des Festivals. Booking tickets for events and provides free maps of the city.*(1 bld. de la Croisette ☎ 04 92 99 84 22 ▪www.cannes. fr. ✆ Open Jul-Aug 9am-8pm, Sep-Jun 9am-7pm).* Also a branch next to the train station *(☎04 93 99 19 77 ✆ Open M-Sa 9am-7pm.)*

- **CURRENCY EXCHANGE: Trevelex.** €80 min cash advance. *(8 rue d'Antibes ☎04 93 37 41 45 ✆Open M-Tu 9am-6pm, W 9:45am-6pm, Th-F 8:50am-6pm, Sa 9:45am-6pm.)*

- **AMBULANCE:** *(☎04 92 97 90 21.)*

- **YOUTH CENTER: Cannes Information Jeuenesse.** Info on jobs and housing. *(5 quai St-Pierre ☎04 97 06 46 25 ▪lekiosque@ville-cannes.fr. ✆Open M-Th 8:30am-12:30pm and 1:30-6pm, F 8:30am-12:30pm and 1:30-5pm.)*

- **INTERNET: Cyber Atlas** *(Corner of Juan Juares and Helene Vagliano ☎04 93 69 42 86. ⑤€3 per hr. ✆ Open Jul-Aug 10am-11pm, Sep-Jun 10am-10pm).*

- **POST OFFICE:** 22 rue de Bivouac Napoleon *(☎04 93 06 26 50 ✆ Open M-F 9am-7pm, Sa 9am-noon).* Branch at 34 rue Mimont *(☎04 93 06 27 00 ✆ Open M-F 8:30am-noon, 1:30-5pm, Sa 8:30am-noon).*

- **POSTAL CODE:** 06400.

Emergency!

- **PHARMACY: Pharmacie des Allees.** Staff speaks Russian, Italian, German, English and French. *(2 av. Felix Fauvre ☎04 93 39 00 18 ✆Open Sept-June M-Sa 9:30am-7:30pm, Jul-Aug 9:30am-9pm.)*

- **POLICE:** 1 av. de Grasse *(☎04 93 06 22 22)* and 2 quai St-Pierre *(☎08 00 11 71 18).*

- **HOSPITAL: Hopital des Broussailles** *(13 av. des Broussailles☎04 93 69 70 00).*

Getting There

Trains leave from 1 rue Juan Juares. Automatic ticket booths if you have a European card. *(✆Station open 5:20am-1:10am. Ticket office open daily 5:30am-10:30pm. Info desk open M-Sa 8:30am-5:30pm.)* To **Antibes** *(✆ 15min. ⑤ €2.75.);* **Grasse** *(✆ 25min. ⑤€3.30.);* **Marseille** *(✆2hr. ⑤€27.40.);* **Monaco** *(✆1hr. ⑤ €11);* **Nice** *(✆ 45min. ⑤ €6.20);* **St-Raphaël** *(✆ 25min. ⑤ €6.30);* **TGV to Paris via Marseille** *(✆ 5hr. ⑤ €80-100).*

The principal bus company is **Rapide Côte d'Azur,** *(pl. Hotel de Ville ☎04 93 48 70 30).* To **Nice** *(✆ 1hr., every 20min. ⑤ €6.)* and **Nice Airport** *(✆ 1hr., every 30min. Runs M-Sa 7am-7pm, Su 8:30am-7pm ⑤ €15.).* Buses to **Grasse** *(✆ 50min., every 45min. ⑤ €1.50.)* leave from the train station.The closest airport is **Nice-Côte d'Azur** *(NCE ☎08 20 42 33 33).*

Getting Around

Walking is the easiest option in Cannes, since you'll find that its a much smaller city than in your Hollywood dreams and is incredibly manageable by foot. If you have to make it further than local campgrounds, take the **bus** *(€1)* in front of the train station. The Gare Routiere is in front of the Hotel de Ville, and is valid for one hour. The local **train station** leads to any city within reach. There are no subways or tram lines.

côte d'azur

grasse   ☎04

If your French hookup in Nice kind of smelled, you'd better thank Grasse. The perfume capital of France, Grasse is so famous for its fragrances that regional kings used to maneuver and fight for control over the rose fields back in the day. Blessed with the perfect climate, soil, and local species of rose, this is where they figured out that you could distill floral scents and apply it instead of bathing. While bathing has gained in popularity since the plague, the prevalence of perfume in France hasn't waned, and Grasse has supplied it for nearly 300 years. You'd think that the city might be a little more active due to the large influx of tourists, but Grasse maintains a colorful small-town vibe; the *perfumeries* are about the only things here that consistently stay in business, and the resulting cheap land and foreclosed buildings have recently provided opportunities to a large influx of immigrants in the tiny town. Situated on top of the hills overlooking the valley to Cannes, you can find a stunning sight at the edge of any street or balcony in Grasse. Come, smell, and leave, because after the last bus leaves town, Grasse goes to sleep, with the exception of a couple of local bars and clubs that remain open on the weekends. You won't find many tourists except during museum hours, but you'll struggle to find cheap accommodations that haven't already been booked up by old people in touring companies.

ORIENTATION

We're sorry. Orientation is hard in Grasse. One wrong left turn down the wrong alleyway could mean that you have to trek back uphill, only to find that the restaurant you wanted was at the bottom of the hill anyway. As far as basics go, the maps are hard to follow, since the numerous alleys and steps are not well marked, and may not qualify enough as streets to show up on a map. Asking for directions was never more utilized by our writers than here. Thankfully, the worthwhile museums are all centrally located, and the **bus station** will take you to the far away museums and **parfumeries.** The main areas that you must concern yourself with include the **pl. aux Aires,** where you'll find you cafes and a weekend market of olive oils, dried fruits, and wine. The town's nicer restaurants are located in offshoots of this place. The **bld. du Jeu de Ballon** has all of your bars and small cafes, as well as a theater and cinema. Hotels are located around the city, particularly around the **pl. de Patti** and in the **pl. des Cours.** The single most important place you must know is the **bus station,** at the top of the bld. du Jeu de Ballon, which will take you to the **Gare SNCF,** as well as Cannes, and all the campgrounds and *perfumeries* along the way.

ACCOMMODATIONS

Grasse is not very budget-friendly for hotelgoers. It seems that the only hotels that last are chains, since the ones that start up either fizzle out due to either the difficult location or poor tourist attendance. The hotels that do last are in the center of the city, and they've used that as an excuse to jack up prices, let quality slide, or both. There's one hotel that we recommend, but it's a short walk from the center, and only recommended for groups of travelers. Otherwise, getting to and from camping locations will take you longer (and be more expensive) than just staying in Cannes and taking the train in for day trips.

◼ MANDARINA   ✦♿(ツ)♉♨ HOTEL ❺

39 rue Yves-Emmanuel Baudoin   ☎04 93 36 10 29 ▤www.mandarinahotel.com

Out of the way, but the views and cleanliness are worth staying uphill from the old town. Modern hotel with the comforts of lavender perfume (you are in Grasse, after all), comfy couches, and a terrace view of the valley that will take your breath away. Seriously, awesome view.

✦ *From the Gare Routiere, go up the steps toward the Odalys hotel and turn left. Walk up the street*

200m; hotel is on your left. $ *Singles €80-85; doubles €85-95; triples €90-95; quads €95-100.*

HOTEL DU PATTI HOTEL [4]

pl. du Patti ☎04 93 36 01 00 www.hotelpatti.com

Romantic (read: expensive) boutique hotel in the center of town. You pay for the convenient location, but are compensated with blue tile bathrooms and pink suites. Book ahead of time, since it's almost always booked by some group of septuagenarians touring the countryside before they die.

From the Gare Routiere, walk toward the road and turn left, going down the narrow alley next to the bus station to pl. des Faineants. Continue walking downhill until you get the pl. du Patti. Hotel on your left. ℹ *Breakfast €9.* $ *Singles and doubles €69-125; triples €105.*

CAMPING DE LA PAOUTE CAMPING [2]

160 route de Cannes ☎04 93 09 11 42 www.campinglapaoute.com

Camping option that is about three quarters of the way to Grasse from Cannes, or one quarter of the way to Cannes from Grasse, depending on whether you're a glass half full or empty type. Has ample space for parking and mobile homes for rent, for those who plan to "camp" like they do in Deliverance.

From the Gare Routiere, take the #600 bus to Cannes. Tell the driver you want to get off at Paoute for the camp site. Bus runs M-Sa every 30min., Su every hr. ℹ *10% discount when you stay longer than 8 nights. Hot shower and pool use included.* $ *1 person €12-17; 2 people €16-21. Electricity €4 per day.*

ODALYS: HOTEL DES PARFUMS HOTEL [5]

rue Eugene Charabot ☎04 92 42 35 35 www.hoteldesparfums.com

Chain hotel up the street from the Gare Routiere. Offers a pool, and mountain or valley views from the balcony rooms. Nice, but expensive.

From the Gare Routiere, look up the hill. You will see it. Walk up the steps to it. ℹ *Offers discounts on purchases at Galimard and golfing passes.* $ *Singles €88-104; doubles €115-147; triples €152-185; quads €178-214. Prices vary depending on season and moutain/valley view.*

HOTEL PANORAMA HOTEL [5]

2 pl. du Cours ☎04 93 36 80 80

Not the most spectacular of hotels for this price, but conveniently next to the tourist office, with balcony views (for a price) of the valley below. Don't expect luxury, or even boutique cuteness, and be willing to settle for budget hotel quality without the budget.

From the tourist office, 100m up the hill. ℹ *Breakfast €8.* $ *Singles and doubles €70-80.*

SIGHTS

MOLINARD PARFUMERIE

60 rue Victor Hugo ☎04 92 42 33 11 www.molinard.com

While not the most tourist-friendly place in the city, the 2km walk and lighter crowds that result from it is worth the extra attention. The free tour of this *parfumerie* will give you insight into the four famous flowers of Grasse, and how they have been combined at this factory, built by Gustav Eiffel, to make some of the most famous scents since the 1700s. You can make your own perfume here by reservation for 30min, 1 hr. 30 min or 2hr. session.

ℹ *Reservations required for workshops, held M-F 9:30am-4pm.* $ *Free. Workshops €27-96. Free tours in English available.* ⏰ *Open July-Aug daily 9am-7pm; Sept daily 9am-6:30pm; Oct-Mar M-F 9am-12:30pm and 2-6pm, Sa 9am-noon 2-6pm; Apr-June daily 9am-6:30pm. Tours July 9:30am-6pm; Aug-June 9:30am-noon and 2-5:30pm.*

FRAGONARD PARFUMERIE

20 bld. Fragonard ☎04 93 36 44 65 www.fragonard.com

Though perhaps less luxurious than Molinard, this *parfumerie* is accessible, and conveniently located in the heart of the museums and tourist office. Free tours are available of the exquisitely preserved, nearly 230-year-old factory. The top floor is a free museum on the history of perfume, where you can find international perfume bottles ranging from ancient Egypt and China to Chanel No. 5. Display of the old, retired distilling vats fill up an entire room.

$ Free tours in English. ⏰ Open daily 9am-6:30pm.

GALIMARD — PARFUMERIE

73 routes a Cannes ☎04 93 09 20 00 💻www.galimard,com

Opened in 1747, this was Louis XIV's royal source for perfume, located right next to the Grasse rose fields. Learn that not all roses are the same, and only the Grasse variety are used in high-class perfumes today. The factory offers 2hr. sessions with a professional nose, who will help you create your own perfume from a variety of base notes, heart notes and head notes. Ask your "nose" what that means.

From the Gare Routiere, take the #600 bus to Cannes. Ask the driver to drop you off right in front of the parfumerie, also next door to a Quick burger place. ℹ Reservation required for perfume workshop. $ Free tours. Perfume creation €40. ⏰ Open daily June-Sept 9am-6:30pm; Oct-May 9am-noon and 2-6pm.

MUSÉE INTERNATIONAL DE LA PARFUMERIE — MUSEUM

8 pl. des Cours ☎04 97 05 58 00

Shows large displays of how perfume is made all around the world, from soaking things in animal fat to soak up the scent to boiling them in large vats to distill the smell. Apparently it's not just for good smells either, as evidenced by the 3000-year-old mummy's hand that has been preserved entirely by perfume.

$ €3, students €1.50, under 18 free. ⏰ Open May-Sept M-F 10am-7pm, Sa 10am-9pm, Su 10am-7pm; Oct-May M 10am-12:30pm and 2-5:30pm, W-Su 10am-12:30pm and 2-5:30pm.

MUSÉE D'ART ET D'HISTOIRE DE PROVENCE — MUSEUM

2 rue Mirabelle ☎04 93 36 01 61

Free museum that you wouldn't visit if it wasn't. It was a noble's residence from the 1600s until the Revolution, and now showcases a series of paintings and daily articles that would be interesting if they were in your great-grandparent's house, but that don't really deserve their own museum. Hey, it's free.

⏰ Open May-Sept daily 10am-7pm; Oct-Apr M 11am-6pm, W-Su 11am-6pm.

MUSÉE JEAN HONORÉ FRAGONARD — MUSEUM

23 bld. Fragonard ☎04 93 36 01 61

Another free museum where you can see what an old house looked like a long time ago. Large paintings dominate the residence of this Grasse artist, whose name the *parfumerie* adopted in 1923.

⏰ Open daily May-Sept 10am-7pm; Oct-Apr 11am-6pm.

FOOD

EL TAPAS — TAPAS BAR, PIZZERIA ❸

2 av. Chiris ☎04 93 36 33 19 💻eltapas@orange.fr

Tapas bar and pizzeria down the hill from the old city. The covered patio makes you feel like you're in Pamplona, waiting for the running of the bulls. It's impressive that at least one place in town has the "huevos" to offer cheap pizzas *(€5 each)*. Provençal theme mixed with some Spanish flair; just don't call it Spanish.

$ Pizzas €5. Tapas plate €8. ⏰ Open daily 8pm-3am.

LA CRÊPERIE — CRÊPERIE ❷

pl. aux Aires ☎04 93 11 23 84

Cheapest place in the pl. aux Aires. Sit outside and enjoy your cheap crêpes *(€3-8.50)* or go all out with an entree, *plat du jour,* and dessert *(€14.50.)* Casual and laid-back, no need to worry about what you're wearing.

Plats €5-12. Specials €14.50. 🕙 *Open Tu-Su 11:30am-7pm.*

SPAGHETTERIA   ♿ CAFE ❶
9 rue Jean Ossola   ☎06 23 59 10 96

Cheap sandwiches and crêpes from this quick eatery. Croque monsiers and baguette sandwiches on-the-go from a jolly old man that gives Santa a run for his money.

Crêpes €2-4.50. Sandwiches €5. 🕙 *Open M-Sa 10am-6pm.*

LE PECHÉ GOURMANT   BOULANGERIE ❸
6 rue de l'Oratoire   ☎06 62 69 61 57

Le Peché serves up its own dishes of Provençal cuisine, along with its macaroons and *galettes*. This small, jazzy place also scoops 90 different kinds of ice cream.

Plates and pastries €12. Cakes €1-5. 🕙 *Open W-Su 10am-7:30pm.*

LOU CALENDON   TRADITIONAL ❹
5 rue des Fabreries   ☎04 93 60 04 49

Completely unrecognizable as a Michelin-rated rastaurant, turn down an alley and through a back door to dine at this cozy upscale joint. The menu changes every three weeks according to what's in season.

✠ *Pl. aux Aires.* *Plat du jour, glass of wine, and coffee €19. Plats from €20.* 🕙 *Open Tu-Su noon-2:30pm and 5-10pm.*

ANGEL ICE   CAFE, GLACERIE ❷
6 rue Jean Ossola

The weird totem pole signs will catch your attention, as well as the curious menu items that almost seem American. Hot dogs and milkshakes are served alongside *croque monsieurs* and crêpes. Totally off the wall and purely gimmicky, but definitely cheap.

Hotdogs €3.50. Milkshakes €4. 2 scoops of ice cream €3. 🕙 *Open daily 10am-7pm.*

CAFE DES MUSÉES   CAFE ❸
1 rue Ossola   ☎04 92 60 99 00

This small cafe catches all the tourists coming out of the museums; you can infer that even from its name. Nonetheless, the place is pretty cute, with its shaded patio and barreled arch ceiling, and has reasonably priced formules (*€12*).

Formule plat and dessert €12. Dessert du jour €4.50. 🕙 *Open M-Sa 9am-6:30pm, Su noon-6:30pm.*

NIGHTLIFE

MANNEKEN PIS PUB   BAR
37 bld. du Jeu de Ballon   ☎04 93 40 03 72

An awesome little cave of a bar (literally; it's decorated like a cave). The central theme of this Belgian brewhouse is its namesake, a tiny peeing statue and replica of a famous Brussels' landmark. Drink cheap beer and watch rugby and soccer on their two giant screens.

Drinks €5-7. 🕙 *Open Tu-Su 5pm-2am.*

ZIG ZAG BAR   BAR, CLUB
13 bld. du Jeu de Ballon   ☎06 58 41 01 06 🖳www.zigzagbar.com

Trendy, two-story bar and club covered in zebra stripes with soirees every Friday and Saturday night.

Beer €4. Cocktails €7. 🕙 *Open noon-2am.*

B.O. CAFE   BAR, CLUB
2 pl. de la Foux   ☎04 93 40 07 18

An unfortunately named bar with a central location and large terrace seating. The funky decor reminds us of what the future looked like in 1959—but add a little glitter to a B-list movie and you've got B.O. Cafe. Sports on TVs and cheap beer almost don't go with the bar's decor, but it's appreciated by budget travelers.

i Happy hour cocktails €5. $ Beer €2.70. ⏰ Open M-Th noon-8:30pm, F-Sa noon-late, Su noon-8:30pm. Happy hour 5-7pm.

CAFE DES NEGOTIANTS ♿🍸 BAR

33 bld. du Jeu de Ballon ☎04 93 36 01 54

Local bar that's popular with Grasse's elderly population and budget travelers. Decorated like an old diner, with walls that are covered in Coke ads from the'50s and an old pinball machine that you'll be shocked still works.

$ Beer €3. Other drinks €6. ⏰ Open M-Sa 2:30pm-1:30am.

ARTS AND CULTURE

THÈÂTRE DE GRASSE THEATER

☎04 93 40 53 00 🖥www.theatredegrasse.com

Everything from drama to the circus shows on Grasse's stage. Musical performances, dances and the occasional Hitchcock classic are also popular. Check website for rotating schedule.

i 3 spectacle pass €33. $ Student prices €14-25, depending on the celebrity status of the actors, and popularity of performance.

CINEMA LE STUDIO CINEMA

15 bld. du Jeu de Ballon ☎08 92 68 27 45

Only cinema in town that shows movies dubbed in French.

$ Students €8. ⏰ Open M-Sa 10am-10pm.

FÊTE DU JASMIN FESTIVAL

☎04 97 05 57 92 🖥www.ville-grasse.com

Giant festival in early August that celebrates the city's famous fragrant flower, powering all three of their *perfumeries*. The town uses an average of 150,000 blossoms a year in decorations alone.

$ Free. ⏰ Starting the 1st weekend in August.

ESSENTIALS

Practicalities

- **TOURIST OFFICE: Cours Honoré Cresp,** next to the Palais des Congrès.*(☎04 93 36 66 66 🖥www.grasse.fr ⏰ Open June-Sept M-Sa 9am-7pm, Su 9am-1pm and 2-6pm; Oct-May M-Sa 9am-12:30pm and 2-6pm.)* Free maps in multiple languages, as well as suggested walking routes in the city. Provides hotel restaurant guides and 1hr. guided tours in English *($ €2. ⏰ July-Aug Sa at 2pm).* A petit train runs to *parfumeries* and museums *(☎06 07 7563 60. $ €6, students €3. ⏰ Every 45min.)*
- **INTERNET: Webphone,** 3 rue Fabreries *(☎04 93 77 78 62. $ €2 per hr. ⏰ Open daily 10am-10pm).*
- **POST OFFICE:** In garage under the Gare Routiere bus station *(☎04 92 42 31 11 ⏰ Open M-F 9am-noon and 2-5pm, Sa 9am-noon.)*
- **POSTAL CODE:** 06103.

Emergency!

- **POLICE:** 12 bld. Carnot *(☎04 93 40 31 60).*
- **PHARMACY:** 26 pl. aux Aires *(☎04 93 36 05 35).*
- **HOSPITAL:** chemin de Clavary *(☎04 93 36 05 35).*

Getting There

Traverse de la Gare runs trains through Grasse on a regular basis *(⏰Ticket window open M-Sa 6:15am-8:55pm, Su 9:30am-noon and 1-5pm.)* Trains run to **Antibes** *(€5.50)*, **Cannes** *(€3.50)*, and **Nice** *(€8.20)*. From the train station, there is a **free shuttle** that runs every 15min. to the *centre-ville*. You can also take the #1, 2, 3, or 4 bus to the Palais des Congrès *(€1.)* You can also get to Grasse by the **RCA** bus, pl. Notre Dame des Fleurs *(☎04 93 36 08 43. ⏰ Open M-Th 7:30am-1:30pm and 2-5pm, F 7:30am-1:30pm and 2-4pm.)* Services to **Cannes** *($ €1. ⏰ 50min.; M-Sa every 30min. 6am-8:15pm, Su every hr. 7:30am-7:30pm)*, and **Nice** *($ €1. ⏰ 1hr.; July-Aug 15 per day, Sept-Jun 20 per day.)* **Taxis** can be reached at ☎04 93 36 37 07.

Getting Around

No matter where you are in Grasse, it's always an uphill battle to get to your destination. Literally. Remember when your grandpa told you that in the old country he walked uphill both ways to get from home to school? Well, he grew up in Grasse. Unfortunately, the streets are so small that cars and buses cannot go through, so walking will have to do. To get anywhere outside the city, the **Gare Routière** is around the corner from the theater and easy to find, and will take you along the routes to Cannes or Nice. The buses can also take you to the *perfumeries*. The easiest way honestly is the **Petit Train.** Save yourself the walking or bus-confusing; you don't want to get turned around and be heading the wrong direction, since it's uphill all the way back to the start.

st-raphaël ☎04

St-Raphaël has all of the beaches, bikinis, and ensuing debauchery of its more popular neighbors, but at budget prices—by Riviera standards, anyway; the town's still not the rock-bottom deal you're probably looking for, but when you consider that Cannes and St-Tropez cater to counts, Clooney, and women who want Clooney, St-Raphaël starts to look like a steal. Midway through summer, the town boardwalk turns into a carnival in the evenings, and becomes packed with gaming booths and flirty teenagers. If you need to escape the crowds, the secluded beaches along the coast provide the perfect spot to avoid the crazy excesses of the Côte d'Azur. If nothing else, use this place as a launch point for a trip to St-Tropez—the ferry is definitely affordable and accessible from this point.

ORIENTATION

St-Raphaël is centered at its port and the **pl. Pierre Coullet,** where cute cafes and mom-and-pops rub elbows with big hotels and businesses. The **old city** lies between the train tracks and the water, while the newer part of the city (where you find lower prices) is on the other side of the tracks. The city gets confusing when it comes to addresses—two roads go by multiple names. **Cours Jean Bart** and **promenade Guilbaud** are the same thoroughfare, and businesses use either street name. The street is located on the **port,** closer to **Frejus.** The other main street in St-Raphaël runs along the **plage de Veillat,** and goes by one of three names: **promenade Rene Coty, bld. de la Liberation,** or **promenade de Lattre de Tassigny.** Within the old port, the streets are neatly laid out in a grid, but lose their uniformity once you get into the newer part of the city.

ACCOMMODATIONS

St-Raphaël's choices are limited in terms of hostels. What would buy you a room in a nice hostel elsewhere gets you a low quality (read: run-down) hostel in this town. There are more budget options the closer you get to Frejus, just up the beach from St-Raphaël.

LES PYRAMIDES
🚭📶🍸☕ HOTEL [3]

77 av. Paul Doumer ☎04 98 11 10 10

Conveniently close to the beach and one of the cheapest places in St-Raphaël. There's a large covered patio for breakfast, and tiki masks on the wall that contribute to the hotel's vague island theme.

➜ From the train station, turn left and walk to the end of the street. Turn right onto av. Henri Vadon and walk toward the beach. Make next immediate left and walk up 50m. Hotel is on the left. $ Singles €35-40; doubles €48-70; triples €70-75; quads €80-85.

HOTEL BELLEVUE
💳🚭☕ HOTEL [3]

22 bld. Felix Martin ☎04 94 18 90 10

Another beach-themed hotel in the middle of the old town, close to the beach and the pl. Coullet.

➜ From the train station, turn right and walk down rue Rousseau. Turn left onto bld. Felix Martin. Hotel is on your right 3 blocks down. ℹ Breakfast €6. $ Singles and doubles €40-55; triples €55-90; quads €60-110; quints €70-140.

HOTEL D'EUROPE - GARE TERMINUS
💳📶 HOTEL [4]

358 pl. Pierre Coullet ☎04 94 95 42 91

Right across the street from the train station (hence the name). The clean rooms come with balconies that look over the pl. Coullet, if you're willing to shell out the extra cash.

➜ Walk out of train station; the hotel is across the street to your right. ℹ Breakfast €6. $ Singles €50-60; doubles €55-70; triples €75.

HOTEL PROVENÇAL
💳♿ HOTEL [4]

195 rue de la Garome ☎04 98 11 85 00 💻www.hotel-provencal.com

Motel-esque hotel where you can rent by the week as well as by night. Simple rooms with weird patterned bedspreads and clean, private bathrooms.

➜ From the train station, turn right and walk 2 blocks. Turn right onto rue Basso, walk to pl. Victor Hugo. Turn left onto rue de la Garome. Follow signs to the hotel on your left. ℹ Breakfast €8. $ Singles and doubles €55-80. Weekly apartment rental €600.

LES PALMIERS
💳♿📶☕ HOTEL [4]

109 bld. de la Liberation ☎04 94 51 18 72

Upscale hotel right on the water. Yes, you'll pay through the nose for a room here, but the balconies, faux finish walls, and blue tile floors make Les Palmiers a refreshing change from the skeezy hostels you're probably used to staying in.

➜ Closer to Frejus than St-Raphaël. Walk along beach for 20min. toward Frejus until arriving at hotel. ℹ Half board available. $ Singles and doubles €55-100. Half board €18 per day.

NOUVEL HOTEL
💳🚭📶 HOTEL [4]

66 av. Henri Vadon ☎04 94 95 23 30 💻www.nouvelhotel.com

A hole-in-the-wall hotel next to a gyro and shawarma stand, Nouvel is also close to the train station and beach. The rooms come with flowers and bright reds and blues, which attempt to offset the hotel's lack of curb appeal.

➜ From the train station, turn left and walk one block. Turn right onto Henri Vadon. Hotel on your right. ℹ Breakfast €6.50. $ Singles €49-60; doubles €54-69; triples €69-90. Half-board €25 per day.

SIGHTS 👁

BASILIQUE NOTRE DAME DE LA VICTOIRE

bld. Felix Martin ☎04 94 83 26 98

The basilica was built to commemorate the battle of Lepante in 1571, even though the church was built in 1883. The architecture is an odd synthesis of Roman and Belle Époque style, and features an impressive mosaic floor and 35m high ceilings.

⏰ Open daily 7am-9pm.

LA PYRAMIDE DE NAPOLEON

av. Guilbaud

Easy to miss in a crowd due to its small size—like its namesake—this pyramid commemorates Napoleon's landing in St-Raphaël before beginning his second attempt to become France's emperor and generally conquer the world. It's located at the major crossroads of the Port, so you won't have to go out of your way to see it.

MUSÉE DE PRÉHISTOIRE ET D'ARCHÉOLOGIE SOUS-MARINE

pl. de la Vieille Église ☎04 94 19 25 75

The museum showcases a collection of artifacts and professional analyses that examine the day-to-day life of ancient Roman settlers, including ancient fishing techniques. The lesson on harpoon work could come in handy if you're low on cash, but otherwise the museum is as exciting as ancient fishing sounds.

$ Free. ⏰ Open Dec-Oct Tu-Sa 9am-noon and 2-6pm.

ÎLE D'OR

Originally bought by a naval sergeant in 1897 for 280 francs, this private island off of the coast of St-Raphaël was subsequently lost to a doctor in a card game. That doctor built the tower you see here today in 1912. He then changed his name to Augustus I, crowned himself king of Île d'Or, and printed stamps and minted coins with his picture on them, and celebrated with a feast. We're serious. Apart from a temporary occupation by Allied forces using the beach to storm Provence in 1944, the island is still inhabited to this day; the "royal" family still lives in the tower and raises its flag whenever they're home. Because it's a private island, visitors are not welcome, but you can see the dramatic tower from St-Raphaël's coast.

JARDIN NAPOLEON

quai Admiral Nomy

A public garden commemorating the man himself. Taking up over 20,000 sq. m on the old port, this area serves the purpose of open space for childrens' games, which is just what Napoleon would have wanted.

⏰ Open dawn-dusk.

BEACHES

The area's picturesque and secluded beaches are the main draw to both St-Raphaël and its neighboring twin city Frejus. While the coastline features a mix of sand and less accommodating rocks, you won't have any problems finding the water.

PLAGE DU VEILLAT ♿

Centre ville

The closest and easiest beach to get to, Veillat is also the most crowded. It's little wonder why; the coast is lined with a dense concentration of restaurants, and is the only prominent beach in the area with a lifeguard in July and August.

🚏 Walk toward Frejus; it's the large sandy beach expanse in front of you.

PLAGE DE LA TORTUE

Town of Valescure

A half-rock, half-sand beach that's popular with swimmers because of its protected bay.

🚏 Either bus #5, which leaves from St-Raphaël-Valescure SNCF, or the train station at Valescure.

PLAGE DE LA GARDE VIEILLE

Boulouris

Small, sand beach with absolutely no reminders of human life. Bring water and food.

🚏 Either bus #8, which leaves from St-Raphaël-Valescure SNCF, or the train station at Boulouris.

PLAGE DU CAMP LONG

Dramont

A small, sand beach with a small, sandy restaurant. It's right around the corner from plage de Debarquement, where the Allies landed on the beaches of France in 1944. That beach is a little more crowded, though.

Either bus #8, which leaves from St-Raphaël-Valescure SNCF, or the train station at Dramont.

PLAGE D'AGAY

Agay

Large stretch of beach with swimming, restaurants, and on-duty life guards. Popular with local families.

Either bus #8, which leaves from St-Raphaël-Valescure SNCF, or the train station at Agay.

FOOD

CITIZEN — PASTA BAR ❷

rue Vadon, right across from the train station ☎04 94 19 46 90 citizen.ctzn@live.fr

You'll want to perform your civic duty after visiting this godsend of cheap eating and drinking for budget travelers. Serves up pasta and pizza in a youthful atomosphere. TVs, lime green chairs and a weird backwards logo advertise its quirky attitude. Top top it all off, it's one of the few establishments in town with free Wi-Fi.

$ Pizza €7. Pasta €5. Beer €1.60. Open M-Sa 10am-3pm and 6-10pm.

LE GRILLARDIN — PIZZERIA ❸

42 rue Thiers ☎04 94 17 11 41

Classy pizza joint that serves up decent three-course *prix-fixe* menus or express lunches (pizza and coffee). Stone walls and wooden tables make you feel like you're in a cave.

$ Pizza €7.90-14.80. 3-course set menu €14.50. Open M-Sa noon-3pm and 7-11pm.

LATIONS — CAFE, ICE CREAM ❶

70 cours de Guilbaud

One of many ice cream shops in St-Raphaël with a line that stretches around the block, but the only one that serves unique flavors like Red Bull (in slushie form too) and Bailey's. The free Wi-Fi and cheap crêpes complete the French budget traveler's three main food groups: ice cream, crêpes, and free internet.

$ 2 scoops €3. Smoothies €2.50. Crêpes €3. Open M-Sa noon-10pm.

CRÊPERIE VIEUX PORT — CRÊPERIE ❷

20 cours Guilbaud ☎04 94 19 44 88

Let this crêperie brighten your day with pretty (though synthetic) sunflowers on every table. Cool off with the signature ice cream crêpes. The outdoor seating is shaded by a giant, magical-looking tree; we suspect this is where the local elves churn the ice cream.

$ Salads €5-7. Crêpes €7-8. Open M-Sa noon-11pm.

CALDERON — CHOCOLATIER ❶

89 pl. de la Mairie ☎04 94 83 68 08

Old, famous chocolaterie that specializes in macaroons and fruit-flavored chocolates, including flavors like orange or strawberry.

$ Macaroons €1. Chocolates €69 per kg. Open Tu-Sa 9am-12:30pm and 2:30-7pm, Su 9am-12:30pm.

HALLES RAPHAELOISE — OPEN MARKET ❶

rue Charles Hatral

Large open-air market for fruits and vegetables. Cheap and local.

$ Market prices. Open M-Th 6am-12:30pm and 3:30-7:30pm, F-Sa 6am-7:30pm, Su 6am-12:30pm.

NIGHTLIFE

ALBARIÑO
BAR, LOUNGE

105 bld. Gen. de Gaulle ☎04 94 45 48 16

You'll think you're in the riotous medinas of Fez at this outrageous Morrocan and Spanish tapas bar, right across from the beach. Lounge on the bright red and orange carpets or the collection of low couches while indulging in chocolate fondue *(€9)* or, if you come on Tuesday's Zen soiree, a free massage.

$ Tapas €8-12. Fondue €9. Cocktails €8-10. ⏰ Open Sept-May Tu-Su 8:30am-1am; June-Aug Tu-Su 8:30am-3am.

BLUE BAR
BAR

133 rue Jules Barbier ☎04 94 95 48 16

A St-Raphaël institution, the large maritime *bar du nuit* specializes in blond beer, but serves beer from around the world, a selling point that they hammer home with the old world maps that paper the tables.

$ Beer €2.40, L of beer €9. Giraffes €24. Cocktails €7.50-8. ⏰ Open daily Sept-Oct 7am-3am; June-Aug 7am-4am.

LOCH NESS BAR
PUB

15 av. Valescure ☎04 94 95 49 49

Rugby jerseys, photos of hazy nights on the moors, and other Scottish paraphernalia cover the walls of this standard pub. Perfect for a laid-back night of aggressive drinking.

$ Beer €3-6. Giraffes €35. Cocktails €8. ⏰ Open daily noon-2am.

LA FACTORY
CAFE, BAR

3 quai Albert 1er ☎04 94 95 12 59

New York themed, despite the misleading name. Relaxed outdoor seating allows for the usual people watching ops. A retractable canvas awning is used for shade.

$ Beer €3-5. Cocktails €7.50. ⏰ Open Tu-Sa noon-1:30am.

ESSENTIALS

Practicalities

- **TOURIST OFFICE:** Located in the new port. Ignore signs that point to old tourist office. Free internet. *(99 quai Albert 1er ☎04 94 19 52 52 💻www.saint-raphael.com. ⏰ Open July-Aug daily 9am-7pm; Sept-June M-Sa 9am-12:30pm and 2-6:30pm.)*
- **BANKS:** Societe Generale *(bld. Felix Martin ☎04 94 19 57 00 ⏰ Open M-F 8:30am-noon and 1:45-5:30pm.)*
- **YOUTH CENTER:** Free condoms, job info, and CV counciling. *(21 pl. Gallienei ☎04 98 11 89 75 ⏰ Open M-Th -8am-noon and 1:30-5pm, F 8am-noon and 1:30-4:30pm.)*
- **POST OFFICE:** Av. Victor Hugo, behind station. *(☎04 94 19 52 00 ⏰ Open M-F 8am-6:30pm, Sa 8am-noon.)*
- **POSTAL CODE:** 83700.

Emergency!

- **POLICE:** rue de Châteaudun *(☎04 94 95 24 24).*
- **PHARMACY:** 46 pl. Pierre Coullet. English spoken. *(☎04 94 95 04 05 ⏰ Open daily 8:30am-7:30pm.)*

Getting There

St-Raphaël's **train station** is located at pl. de la Gare (🎫 *Ticket booth open daily 6:30am-9pm.*) To **Cannes** (💲 *€6.30.* 🕐 *25min., every 30min.*), **Marseille** (💲 *€23.* 🕐 *2hr., 6 per day.*), **Nice** (💲 *€12.* 🕐 *1hr., every 30min.*) **TER** also runs trains to Cannes that stop at Boulouris, Le Dramont, Agay, Antheor, and Le Trayas for beach access. **Buses** run from Navette to the **Nice Airport** (☎04 94 76 02 29). The bus service **Esterel Cars** run to to **Frejus** (💲 *€1.* 🕐 *25min., every hr., 7:30am-6:40pm);* the bus service **Sodetrav** runs to **St-Tropez** (💲 *€2.* 🕐 *1½hr., every hr. 6am-9pm);* and the bus service **Beltram** runs to **Cannes** via Trayas(💲 *€7.* 🕐 *1 hr., 8 per day)* and to the airport in **Nice** (💲 *€22.* 🕐 *1 hr., 4 per day). Buses run later Jul-Aug,* but are infrequent during the year. Ferries depart from Les Bateaux de St-Raphaël to St-Tropez in the summer (☎04 94 95 17 46. 💲 *€13, €22 roundtrip.* 🕐 *2 per day.*)

Getting Around

Again, tiny towns don't require (or provide) a lot of public transportation apart from walking. The old port pretty much has everything you could ever need within walking distance. To get to the further away beaches, use the **buses** at **Gare SNCF** (*#5 and 8, dir. Trayas.* 💲 *€1.*), rent a **scooter** (*Patrick Moto, 199 av. Gen Leclerc* ☎04 94 53 65 99 💲 *€30 per day, €172 per week.* 🕐 *Open M 9am-noon and 2:30-6pm, Tu 2:30-6pm, W-Sa 9am-noon and 2:30-6pm.*), or hire a **taxi** (☎04 94 83 24 24).

st-tropez ☎04 94

St-Tropez is the excess capital of the world. You'd be stunned at the prices, if you weren't distracted by the beautiful yachts and beautiful people. Independent wealth thrives here, as evidenced by the numerous boats flying the flags of blacklisted tax havens. In a town where the tip to the dockmaster can run you as much as €5000, it can be hard to find deals. Apparently rich people just like spending money as a way to keep out the petty-folk. The real attraction here are the party beaches, which light up at night and continue until day break. Unfortunately, these parties are exclusive and hard to access without a yacht or some serious nighttime espionage. Beyond the money, St-Tropez is an incredibly beautiful town, and unlike any other on the Riviera in terms of architecture and layout of the town. Villas and small alleys make up the heart of the town, and it vaguely resembles a seaside village in Spain or Italy with its terra-cotta rooftops and colored tiles. It's easy to see why Hollywood and the mega wealthy fell in love with it, but that means making a serious dent in your wallet to enjoy it yourself.

ORIENTATION

Its wealth per square kilometer might outdo the Vatican, but St-Tropez is a very tiny town. Walking is the easiest way to get around here between the **old and new ports.** Unfortunately, the **beaches** are far away from the town center, requiring **shuttles** or a **scooter rental** (a good option for those who want freedom from tedious timetables) to get there. The most affordable restaurants, hotels, and shops are on the outskirts of town. The closer you are to the port or the quais, the higher the prices. From the **bus station** or **new port,** turn left and walk right into town. The **pl. des Lices** is the main square that is the most normal, local part of St-Tropez, with small stands for food, and banks and the market surrounding it. Most of the main roads lead to pl. des Lices. To get to the beaches, either walk around the **citadel** past the cemetery on **chemin des Graniers,** or take the main road at the entrance of the town **(route des Plages)** where turning left at any intersection will take you to the beaches.

ACCOMMODATIONS ⚡

There are lots of places to stay in St-Tropez, so long as you have lots of money. The cheaper places are located in St. Maxime, the next town over, or just on the outskirts of St-Tropez. The hotels we listed are in the actual town, easy to get to, and under €100.

❏ LE COLOMBIER   ⊗⁽ᵠ⁾♈⌂ HOTEL ❺
impasse des Conquettes   ☎04 94 97 05 31

Beautiful, small hotel just on the edge of the old city. Small rooms, but a private breakfast available in the garden. Cheapest place in St-Tropez, but miraculously still very chic.

❧ *From the pl. des Lices (center of town), walk away from the citadel. Take the most left street (bld. Louis Blanc) from the sq. J. Moulin. Walk 1-2 blocks, turn left onto av. Paul Roussel. Turn left again onto imapsse des Conquettes. Hotel is at the end of street.* ℹ *Cheapest rooms have no A/C and shared bath.* ⓢ *Singles and doubles €63-110.*

LES PALMIERS   ⊗⁽ᵠ⁾♈⌂ HOTEL ❺
24 bld. Lavoir Vasserot   ☎04 94 97 01 61

Small, boutique hotel in the style of a Tropezienne villa. The orange walls and low, plastered ceilings make this affordable hotel even more attractive. Clean rooms and old-fashioned bar. The entry garden is overgrown, so it's an adventure just to find the reception. The villas overlook the garden.

❧ *From the pl. les Lices, walk away from the hill and rue joseph Quaranta on your slight right. Hotel is on your left.* ℹ *Breakfast €11.* ⓢ *Singles and doubles €89-189.*

HOTEL MEDITERRANÉE   ♿⁽ᵠ⁾♈⌂ HOTEL ❺
21 bld. Louis-Blanc   ☎04 94 97 00 44

Old-school hotel with small singles and doubles and a 1940s vibe. The old Provençal-style wooden doors and furniture hint at the history of St-Tropez before Hollywood discovered it.

❧ *From the pl. Croix de Fer, head toward to the citadel, keeping to the right for 30m and then keeping to the left, onto bld. Louis-Blanc. Hotel is on your right.* ℹ *Last minute deals sometimes available in low season.* ⓢ *Singles €82-101; doubles €102-144.*

FOOD 🄲

Food in St-Tropez is—surprise!—very expensive, especially for sit-down meals. There are some cheaper prix-fixe menus in the old city up near the Citadel, as well as closer to the new port (sailors gotta eat too). All over the pl. des Lices, you'll find cheap food options in the form of stands, and there is a local **Monoprix** (🕑 *Open daily 9am-6pm*) right as you walk into town from the new port.

CRÊPERIE BRETONNE   ♿♈⌂ CRÊPERIE ❷
quai Frederic Mistral   ☎04 94 97 48 53

Authentic Breton crêperie that serves its own cider. Not your typical crêpes, though—these babies are crispy, folded halfway and left partially open, like they do it up north. Right on the port so you can feel like you're rich while you're dining on the patio. Old sailing paraphernalia cover the walls.

ⓢ *Crêpes €3.50-8. Cider €5.* 🕑 *Open daily noon-8pm.*

L'OLIVE   ⊗♈⌂ TRADITIONAL ❸
9 rue de l'Aire du Chemin   ☎04 94 97 09 21

Finally, a three-course meal in St-Tropez that doesn't cost a fortune. Serves Provencal dishes near the citadel on a patio under a canopy of jasmin.

ⓢ *Prix fixe 3 course meals €18.* 🕑 *Open M-Sa 7-10pm.*

LA TANNELLE   ⊗♈⌂ PIZZERIA ❸
passage Gambetta   ☎04 94 54 82 02

Rooftop pizzeria that has a view of the old port. The pizza is cheap, and the ivy growth on the patio provides ample shade. A warning though: the sign out front explicitly states that they don't accept €500 bills. Sorry, Richie Rich.

⑨ *Pizza €11.50-13. Order for takeout €10.* ⏰ *Open daily noon-9pm.*

MIJO CRÊPES
          ᴥᴥ   CRÊPERIE ❶
Marché Couvert, pl. des Lices
In the pl. des Lices, there's a covered market with permanent stands of cheap crêpes, which serve the cheapest and the sweetest in town.

⑨ *Crêpes €2.50-5.* ⏰ *Open daily July-Aug 9am-10:30pm; Sept-June 10am-7pm.*

ROTISSERIE TROPZIENNE
        ᴥ   CHICKEN ❶
Marché Couvert, pl. des Lices
           ☎04 94 54 85 04
Serves half or whole rotisserie chickens. A random Thai influence brings noodles and peanut sauce into the mix for some dishes.

⑨ *Whole chicken €8.50, half €4.50. Thai chicken salad €3.50. Beer €2.50* ⏰ *Open Sept-June daily 10am-1:30pm and 5-7pm; July-Aug daily 10am 1:30pm and 5-9pm.*

PAUSE-DOUCEUR
         ⊗ CHOCOLATIER ❷
11 rue Allard
           ☎04 94 57 27 58
Searving Provençal syrup and *galettes* since the 1800s, this chocolatier is here to stay for a while, even if the owner decides to work whenever she wants, making the store's hours difficult to track. We suggest you stop by in the morning, when the proprietess is most likely to be there.

⑨ *Chocolate €2-4. Galettes €5.* ⏰ *Open M-Sa 9am-late (or whenever the owner wants).*

LA FRÉGATE
        ᴥ ⅄ᴥ   PIZZERIA ❸
52 rue Allard
           ☎04 94 97 07 08
Small pizzeria with a small patio, but the real attraction is the cozy air-conditioned dining room, with wooden chairs and tables under St-Tropez's traditional low ceilings. Serves 14 kinds of pizza.

⑨ *Pizzas €10.50.* ⏰ *Open daily noon-2:30pm and 5-10pm.*

NIGHTLIFE

▨ LE QUAI
        ⅄ᴥ▼   BAR
22 quai Jean Juares
           ☎04 94 97 04 07
Less pretentious lounge and bar that turns into a madhouse of packed bodies and pumping music. When the patrons start to climb onto the furniture, you're not sure if they are drunk or just trying to get out of the mosh pit. Expect absolutely debacherous behavior.

⑨ *Beer €5. Cocktails €13.* ⏰ *Open Mar-Oct noon-4am.*

▨ CABANITO
        ᴥ ⅄ᴥ   BAR
16 quai de l'Epi
           ☎05 14 12 28 60
Pound back shots underneath Che posters to the sounds of Cuban music and reggaeton. The super chill crowd gathers for latin salsa, killer mojitos, and €4 beer. Soirees on Tuesday nights.

⑨ *Beer €4. Cocktails €8.* ⏰ *Open daily 5pm-3am.*

KELLY'S IRISH PUB
       ⌀ᴥ ⅄ᴥ   PUB
port du St-Tropez
           ☎04 94 54 89 11
The only real laid-back bar in town. Unpretentious and unapologetic, Kelly's is the last stronghold of working locals and musicians that play classic American rock on the weekends. If barstools could talk...

⑨ *Pints €6. Jagerbombs and shooters €6.* ⏰ *Open daily midnight-3am.*

PAPAGAYO
        ⌀⅄ᴥ▼   CLUB
Résidence du Port
           ☎04 94 97 95 95
One of St-Tropez's most famous clubs, where bottles of booze cost more than

your starting salary. If you can dress up and get past the bouncer, get ready for a packed house that vibrates with the bass, and keep your eyes out for what color a €500 bill is (hint: it matches the walls). Lounge seating by reservation only. If you forget, the large bouncer will remind you.

$ Cocktails €19. ⏰ Open May-June F-Sa 12:30am-6am; July-Aug daily 12:30am-6am; Sept F-Sa 12:30am-6am.

MICASA SUSHI 💳🍸⛅ SUSHI, BAR
1 pl. Alphonse Celli ☎04 94 97 04 32
All-white interior sushi bar where everyone sits outside to enjoy the live rock music on the weekends. The older crowd jams and young crowd cases the lines at the exclusive clubs.

$ Beer €4. Cocktails €13. ⏰ Open daily 6pm-2am (or later).

CHEZ MAGGIE 💳♿🍸▼ BAR
7 rue Sibille ☎04 94 97 16 12
Clubby atmosphere without the stress of not getting in '70s decor and disco hits make this a popular location for soirees and a slightly older crowd.

$ Cocktails €12. ⏰ Open daily 8:30pm-3am.

TSAR 💳🍸⛅▼ BAR
1 quai de l'Epi ☎06 11 95 76 43
Gay bar that is frequented by all genders and sexualities for the use of its hookahs. Pink, sparkly, and "fabulously" laid-back (think Claire's, only gay-er), this is the best place for a middle ground thats less than a club and more than a bar.

$ Beer €8. Cocktails €15. Hookah €20. ⏰ Open daily 6pm-3am.

CHEZ LES GARÇONS 🚫🍸⛅▼ GAY BAR
11-13 rue de Crepoun ☎04 94 43 68 70 💻www.chezlesgarcons.com
If the name didn't give it away, the small bar packed with older men will—this is one of the most popular gay bars in St-Tropez, and unlike the Tsar caters almost exclusively to gay men. Outside seating doubles the bar's size. Inside is a DJ and pink and blue arched ceiling.

$ Cocktails €12. ⏰ Open Jun-Aug daily 7pm-3am, Sept-Dec Th-Su 7pm-3am; Feb-May Th-Su 7pm-3am.

ARTS AND CULTURE 🎵

PALAIS DES FESTIVALS ET DES CONGRÈS LA CROISETTE
bld. de la Croisette ☎04 93 39 01 01 💻www.palaisdesfestivals.com
Large venue that hosts every festival or expo that comes through Cannes. Everything from dance, to arts, to concerts to the film festival in May.

$ Prices vary, call director. ⏰ Open M-Sa 9am-noon and 2-6pm.

ESPACE MIRAMAR LA CROISETTE
Angle bld. de La Croisette ☎04 93 43 86 26 💻www.cannes.com
Smaller venue that hosts dances, art shows and small plays.

⏰ Open Nov-Feb 1-6pm, Mar-Sep 2-7pm.

ARCADE THEATRE CENTRE-VILLE
77 rue Félix Faure ☎ 08 92 68 00 39
Shows English-language movies in their original version (English), and is right in the middle of the city, closer to the Suquet.

$ €8, students €6. Wed special €6 for everyone. Sa and Su 10:30am show €4.50. ⏰ Depending on show times.

FESTIVAL DE PLAISSANCE CENTRE-VILLE
Vieux Port ☎01 46 04 08 62 💻www.salonnautiquecannes.com
In case you wanted to feel worse about yourself for not having giggles of money,

check out this aptly named boat show where the entire Vieux Port is filled with multimillion dollar yachts and megayachts during this week long festival in September.
ⓢ €15 entrance for the whole week.

STUDIO 13 ◆ LE SUQUET
23 av. du Docteur Picaud ☎04 93 06 29 90 🖳www.mjcpicaud.com
A little mini Cannes film festival that reoccurs every night in this theatre 0.5km from town. All films shown in their original version.
ⓢ €6, students €4. 🕙 Showings Sep-Jun M-Th and Sa at 6 and 8:30pm, F 2:30, 6, and 8:30pm.

FESTIVAL INTERNATIONALE DU FILM CANNES
Palais des Festivals 🖳www.festival-cannes.com
Whats Cannes without its fiml festival? Well sorry for you, but you can't go unless you're famous or connected, either way you need an invitation. At least you can gawk at the celebrities and prices during this week long festival in May.
ⓢ Too much for you. 🕙 Doesn't matter. You're not invited.

SHOPPING
Real talk: shopping in St-Tropez is great. So is having a lot of money. Unfortunately, without a lot of money, there aren't any shopping options for you here. Really.

ESSENTIALS
Practicalities

- **TOURIST OFFICE:** On the corner of quai Jean Jaures and rue Victor Laugier. English spoken, free maps, and events guide. (☎04 94 97 45 21 🖳www.saint-tropez.st ⓢ €1 bus schedules. 🕙Open daily from late June to early Sept 9:30am-8pm; from mid-Sept to early Oct and from late Mar to mid-June 9:30am-12:30pm and 2-7pm; from mid-Oct to mid-Mar 9:30am-12:30pm and 2-6pm.)

- **CURRENCY EXCHANGE: Societe Generale,** pl. des Lices. (☎04 94 12 81 40 🕙 Open M-F 8:15am-12.15pm and 2-5.30pm, Sa 8.15am-12.25pm.)

- **INTERNET: Kreatik Cafe.** (19 av. Gen. Leclerc ☎04 94 97 40 61 🖳www.kreatik.com ⓢ €2 per 10min., €4 per 30min., €7 per hr. 🕙 Open M-Sa 9:30am-noon, Su 2-10pm.)

- **POST OFFICE:** pl. Alphonse Celli, between old and new ports. (☎04 94 55 96 50 🕙 Open M-F 8:30am-noon and 2-5pm, Sa 8:30am-noon.)

- **POSTAL CODE:** 83990.

Emergency!

- **POLICE MUNICIPAL:** Av. Gen. Leclerc (☎04 94 54 86 65).

- **AMBULANCE:** ☎04 94 56 60 64.

- **PHARMACY: Pharmacie du Port.** (9 quai Suffren ☎04 94 97 00 06 🕙 Open M-Sa 8:30am-8:30pm.)

Getting There

St-Tropez is far from any train line, but there is a regular **ferry service** from **Les Bateaux de St-Raphaël** (☎04 94 95 17 46 🖳www.tmr-saintraphael.com ⓢ One-way €13, round-trip €23. 🕙 1hr.; twice daily at -9:30am and -2:30pm, return at -10:30am and -5:15pm.) There is also a **bus ride** from the **St Raphaël SNCF Gare** (bus line #7601. ⓢ €2. 🕙 1½hr., Sept-June arrivals every hr. 6am-8:15pm, return trips every hr. 6am-8:20pm; July-Aug arrivals every hr. 6am-8:15pm, return trips every hr. 6am-9pm.)

st-tropez . essentials

Getting Around

This is a very easy city to walk. To get to the beaches, take the **shuttle service,** whose schedule you can pick up at the tourist office. You can also take a **taxi** (☎04 94 97 05 27), or rent a **scooter** *(Espcae 83, across the street from Cafe Kreatik* ☎04 94 55 80 00 ✪ *Open M-Sa 9am-noon and 2-6pm.)*

ESSENTIALS

You don't have to be a rocket scientist to plan a good trip. (It might help, but it's not required.) You do, however, need to be well prepared, and that's what we can do for you. Essentials is the chapter that gives you all the nitty-gritty you need to know for your trip: the hard information gleaned from 50 years of collective wisdom (and that phone call to France the other day that put us on hold for an hour). Planning your trip? Check. Staying safe and healthy? Check. The dirt on transportation? Check. We've also thrown in communications info, meteorological charts, and a **phrasebook**, just for good measure. Plus, for overall trip-planning advice from what to pack (money and as little underwear as possible) to how to take a good passport photo (it's physically impossible; consider airbrushing), you can also check out the Essentials section of www.letsgo.com.

We're not going to lie—this chapter is tough for us to write, and you might not find it as fun of a read as 101 or Discover. But please, for the love of all that is good, read it! It's super helpful, and, most importantly, it means we didn't compile all this technical info and put it in one place for you (yes YOU) for nothing.

greatest hits

- **GET A VISA.** Put it on your spring-cleaning list, since you'll need to apply six to eight weeks in advance (p. 360).

- **DOLLAR DOLLAR BILLS Y'ALL.** Need them? We all do. Need them from across the ocean? Get them the easiest way possible (p. 362).

- **SHIP SOUVENIRS HOME BY SURFACE MAIL.** Our scintillating "By Snail Mail" section will tell you how. You'll laugh, you'll cry (p. 369).

- **FRENCH IS FOR LOVERS.** And travelers to France; our phrasebook will have you professing love and stomach pains in no time (p. 371).

planning your trip

entrance requirements

- **PASSPORT:** Required for citizens of all countries.
- **VISA:** Required for citizens of any country for stays longer than 90 days .
- **WORK PERMIT:** Required for all non-EU citizens planning to work in France.

DOCUMENTS AND FORMALITIES

You've got your visa, your invitation, and your work permit, just like Let's Go told you to, and then you realize you've forgotten the most important thing: your passport. Well, we're not going to let that happen. **Don't forget your passport!**

Visas

EU citizens do not need a visa to globetrot through France. Citizens of Australia, Canada, New Zealand, and the US do not need a visa for stays of up to 90 days, but this three-month period begins upon entry into any of the countries that belong to the EU's **freedom of movement** zone. For more information, see **One Europe**. Those staying longer than 90 days may purchase a visa at a French consulate. A visa costs €99 and allows the holder to spend up to 90 days within a six month period in any Schengen countries.

one europe

The EU's policy of freedom of movement means that most border controls have been abolished and visa policies harmonized. Under this treaty, formally known as the Schengen Agreement, you're still required to carry a passport (or government-issued ID card for EU citizens) when crossing an internal border, but, once you've been admitted into one country, you're free to travel to other participating states. Most EU states are already members of Schengen (excluding Cyprus), as are Iceland and Norway. For more consequences of the EU for travelers, see **The Euro** feature later in this chapter.

Double-check entrance requirements at the nearest embassy or consulate of France (listed on the next page) for up-to-date information before departure. US citizens can also consult ▉http://travel.state.gov.

Entering France to study requires a special visa. For more information, see the **Beyond Tourism** chapter.

Work Permits

Admittance to a country as a traveler does not include the right to work, which is authorized only by a work permit. For more information, see the **Beyond Tourism** chapter.

TIME DIFFERENCES

 France is 1hr. ahead of Greenwich Mean Time (GMT) and observes Daylight Saving Time. This means that it is 6hr. ahead of New York City, 9hr. ahead of Los Angeles, 1hr. ahead of the British Isles, 8hr. behind Sydney, and 10hr. behind New Zealand.

essentials

french embassies abroad

- **FRENCH CONSULAR SERVICES IN AUSTRALIA: Consulate.** *(Level 26, St-Martins Tower, 31 Market St., Sydney NSW 2000* ☎*02 9268 2400* ▪️*www.ambafrance-au.org* 🕐 *Open M-F 9am-1pm.)*
- **FRENCH CONSULAR SERVICES IN CANADA: Consulate.** *(1 pl. Ville Marie Montréal, QC H3B 4S3, Canada* ☎*514 878 3485* ▪️*www.consulfrance-montreal.org* 🕐 *Open M-F 9:30am-4:30pm.)*
- **FRENCH CONSULAR SERVICES IN IRELAND: Embassy.** *(36 Ailesbury Road, Dublin 4, Ireland* ☎*+353 1 277 5000* ▪️*www.ambafrance.ie* 🕐 *Open M-F 9:30am-noon.)*
- **FRENCH CONSULAR SERVICES IN NEW ZEALAND: Embassy.** *(34-42 Manners Str PO Box 11-343 Wellington, New Zealand* ☎*43 04 25 55* ▪️*www.ambafrance-nz.org* 🕐 *Open M-Th 9am-6pm, F 9am-4pm.)*
- **FRENCH CONSULAR SERVICES IN UNITED KINGDOM: Consulate.** *(21 Cromwell Rd., London SW2 2EN* ☎*020 7073 1250* ▪️*www.ambafrance-uk.org* 🕐 *Open M-Th 8:45am-noon, F 8:45am-11:30am.)*
- **FRENCH CONSULAR SERVICES IN UNITED STATES: Consulate.** *(4101 Reservoir Rd. Northwest, Washington, DC 20007-2151* ☎*202 944 6000* ▪️*www.ambafrance-us.org* 🕐 *Open M-F 8:45am-12:45pm.)*

embassies in france

- **AUSTRALIAN CONSULAR SERVICES IN PARIS: Embassy.** *4 rue Jean Rey, 75015 Paris, France* ☎*+01 40 59 33 06* ▪️*www.france.embassy.gov.au* 🕐 *Open M-F 9am-5pm.)*
- **CANADIAN CONSULAR SERVICES IN PARIS: Embassy.** *(35 av. Montaigne, 75008 Paris, France* ☎*01 44 43 29 00* ▪️*www.france.gc.ca* 🕐 *Open M-F 9am-noon and 2-5pm.*
- **IRISH CONSULAR SERVICES IN PARIS: Embassy.** *(4 rue Rude, 75116 Paris, France* ☎*01 44 17 67 00* ▪️*www.embassyofireland.fr* 🕐 *Open M-F 9:30am-noon.)*
- **NEW ZEALAND CONSULAR SERVICES IN PARIS: Embassy.** *(7ter rue Léonard da Vinci, 75116 Paris, France* ☎*01 45 01 43 43* ▪️*www.nzembassy.com/france* 🕐 *Open July-Aug M-Th 9am-1pm and 2-4:30pm, F 9am-2pm; Sept-June M-Th 9am-1pm and 2-5:30pm, F 9am-1pm and 2-4pm.)*
- **UNITED KINGDOM CONSULAR SERVICES IN PARIS: Embassy.** *(2 av. Gabriel 75382 Paris, France* ☎*01 43 12 22 22* ▪️*ukinfrance.fco.gov.uk/en* 🕐 *Open M-F 9:30am-1pm and 2:30-6pm.)*
- **UNITED STATES CONSULAR SERVICES IN PARIS: Embassy.** *(35 rue du Faubourg St Honoré, 75363 Paris, France* ☎*01 44 51 31 00* ▪️*french.france.usembassy.gov* 🕐 *Open M-F 9:30am-1pm and 2:30-6pm.)*

planning your trip . time differences

money

GETTING MONEY FROM HOME

Stuff happens. When stuff happens, you might need some money. When you need some money, the easiest and cheapest solution is to have someone back home make a deposit to your bank account. Otherwise, consider one of the following options.

Wiring Money

Arranging a **bank money transfer** means asking a bank back home to wire money to a bank in France. This is the cheapest way to transfer cash, but it's also the slowest and most agonizing, usually taking several days or more. Note that some banks may only release your funds in local currency, potentially sticking you with a poor exchange rate; inquire about this in advance. In France, bank transfers can be performed at post office banks. Banque de France has some of the most competitve rates for international transfers in France. Money transfer services like **Western Union** are faster and more convenient than bank transfers—but also much pricier. Western Union has many locations worldwide. To find one, visit ✪www.westernunion.com or call the appropriate number: in Australia ☎1800 173 833, in Canada and the US ☎800-325-6000, in the UK ☎0800 735 1815, or in France ☎+33 1 48 26 64 91. To wire money using a credit card in Canada and the US, call ☎800-CALL-CASH; in the UK, ☎0800 833 833. Money transfer services are also available to **American Express** cardholders and at selected **Thomas Cook** offices.

US State Department (US Citizens only)

In serious emergencies only, the US State Department will forward money within hours to the nearest consular office, which will then disburse it according to instructions for a US$30 fee. If you wish to use this service, you must contact the Overseas Citizens Services division of the US State Department. *(☎+1-202-501-4444, from ☎US 888-407-4747)*

pins and atms

To use a debit or credit card to withdraw money from a cash machine (ATM) in Europe, you must have a four-digit Personal Identification Number (PIN). If your PIN is longer than four digits, ask your bank whether you can just use the first four or whether you'll need a new one. Credit cards don't usually come with PINs, so if you intend to hit up ATMs in Europe with a credit card to get cash advances, call your credit card company before leaving to request one.

Travelers with alphabetic rather than numeric PINs may also be thrown off by the absence of letters on European cash machines. Here are the corresponding numbers to use: 1 = QZ; 2 = ABC; 3 = DEF; 4 = GHI; 5 = JKL; 6 = MNO; 7 = PRS; 8 = TUV; 9 = WXY. Note that if you mistakenly punch the wrong code into the machine multiple (often three) times, it can swallow (gulp!) your card for good.

TIPPING AND BARGAINING

By law in France, service is added to bills in bars and restaurants, called *"service compris."* Most people do, however, leave some change (up to €2) for drinks and food, and in nicer restaurants, it is not uncommon to leave 5% of the bill. For other services, like taxis and haircuts, 10-15% tip is acceptable.

TAXES

As a member of the EU, France requires a value added tax (VAT) of 19.6%, which is applied to a variety of goods and services (e.g. food, accommodations), though it is less for food (5.5%). Non-European Economic Community visitors to France who are taking these goods home may be refunded this tax for purchases totaling over

essentials

the euro

Despite what many dollar-possessing Americans might want to hear, the official currency of 16 members of the European Union—Austria, Belgium, Cyprus, Finland, France, Germany, Greece, Ireland, Italy, Luxembourg, Malta, the Netherlands, Portugal, Slovakia, Slovenia, and Spain—is the euro.

Still, the currency has some important—and positive—consequences for travelers hitting more than one eurozone country. For one thing, money changers across the eurozone are obliged to exchange money at the official, fixed rate (below) and at no commission (though they may still charge a small service fee). Second, euro-denominated traveler's checks allow you to pay for goods and services across the eurozone, again at the official rate and commission-free. For more info, check a currency converter (such as ▩www.xe.com) or ▩www.europa.eu.int.

€175 per store. When making purchases, request a VAT form, and present them at the *détaxe* booth at the airport. These goods must be carried at all times while traveling, and refunds must be claimed within 6 months.

safety and health

GENERAL ADVICE

In any type of crisis, the most important thing to do is **stay calm.** Your country's embassy abroad is usually your best resource in an emergency; registering with that embassy upon arrival in the country is a good idea. The government offices listed in the **Travel Advisories** feature at the end of this section can provide information on the services they offer their citizens in case of emergencies abroad.

Local Laws and Police

La Police Nationale is the branch of French law enforcement that is most often seen in urban areas. To reach the French police, call ☎17.

Drugs and Alcohol

There is no drinking age in France, but to purchase alcohol one must be at least 18 years old. The legal blood-alcohol level for driving in France is .05%, which is less than it is in countries like the US, UK, New Zealand, and Ireland, so exercise appropriate caution when driving in France.

Specific Concerns

Demonstrations and Political Gatherings

The French Revolution may have been in 1789, but the spirit of the revolution certainly hasn't died. Protests and strikes are frequent in France, but violence does not often occur. You may find yourself in Grenoble on the day of a transit strike (as one Let's Go researcher did) but who hasn't always wanted to see France by Vespa?

PRE-DEPARTURE HEALTH

Matching a prescription to a foreign equivalent is not always easy, safe, or possible, so if you take **prescription drugs,** carry up-to-date prescriptions or a statement from your doctor stating the medications' trade names, manufacturers, chemical names, and dosages. Be sure to keep all medication with you in your carry-on luggage.

The names in France for common drugs are: *aspirine* (aspirin), *acétaminophène* (acetaminophen), *ibuprofène* (ibuprofen), *antihistaminiques* (antihistamines), and *pénicilline* (penicillin).

travel advisories

The following government offices provide travel information and advisories by telephone, by fax, or via the web:

- **AUSTRALIA: Department of Foreign Affairs and Trade.** *(☎+61 2 6261 1111 🖳www.dfat.gov.au/index.html)*
- **CANADA: Department of Foreign Affairs and International Trade (DFAIT).** Call or visit the website for the free booklet *Bon Voyage...But.* *(☎+1-800 267-8376 🖳www.dfait-maeci.gc.ca)*
- **NEW ZEALAND: Ministry of Foreign Affairs.** *(☎+64 4 439 8000 🖳www.mfat.govt.nz)*
- **UK: Foreign and Commonwealth Office.** *(☎+44 20 7008 1500 🖳www.fco.gov.uk)*
- **US: Department of State.** *(☎888-407-4747 from the US, +1-202-501-4444 elsewhere 🖳http://travel.state.gov)*

Immunizations and Precautions

Travelers over two years old should make sure that the following vaccines are up to date: MMR (for measles, mumps, and rubella); DTaP or Td (for diphtheria, tetanus, and pertussis); IPV (for polio); Hib (for *Haemophilus influenzae* B); and HepB (for Hepatitis B). For recommendations on immunizations and prophylaxis, check with a doctor and consult the **Centers for Disease Control and Prevention (CDC)** in the US or the equivalent in your home country. *(☎+1-800-CDC-INFO/232-4636 🖳www.cdc.gov/travel)*

STAYING HEALTHY

Medical Care

Most towns in France have a hospital, and non-French-speaking travelers will be pleased to find that often the staff will speak English. While treatment can be expensive, French health care is more than adequate.

getting around

For information on how to get to France and save a bundle while doing so, check out the Essentials section of **🖳www.letsgo.com.** (In case you can't tell, we think our website's the bomb.)

BY PLANE

Commercial Airlines

For small-scale travel on the continent, *Let's Go* suggests **🖳budget airlines** for budget travelers, but more traditional carriers have made efforts to keep up with the revolution. The **Star Alliance Europe Airpass** offers low economy-class fares for travel within Europe to 220 destinations in 45 countries. The pass is available to non-European passengers on Star Alliance carriers, including Lufthansa, bmi, Spanair, and TAP Portugal *(🖳www.staralliance.com)*. **EuropebyAir's** snazzy FlightPass also allows you to hop between hundreds of cities in Europe and North Africa. *(☎+1-888-321-4737 🖳www.europebyair.com $ Most flights US$99.)*

In addition, a number of European airlines offer discount coupon packets. Most are only available as tack-ons for transatlantic passengers, but some are standalone offers. Most must be purchased before departure, so research in advance. For example, **oneworld,** a coalition of 10 major international airlines, offers deals and cheap connections all over the world, including within Europe. *(🖳www.oneworld.com)*

budget airlines

The recent emergence of no-frills airlines has made hopscotching around Europe by air increasingly affordable. Though these flights often feature inconvenient hours or serve less popular regional airports, with ticket prices often dipping into single digits, it's never been faster or easier to jet across the continent. The following resources will be useful not only for crisscrossing France but also for those ever-popular weekend trips to nearby international destinations.

- **BMIBABY:** Departures from multiple cities in the UK to Paris, Nice, and other cities in France. *(☎0871 224 0224 for the UK, +44 870 126 6726 elsewhere 🖥www.bmibaby.com)*
- **EASYJET:** London to Bordeaux and other cities in France. *(☎+44 871 244 2366, 10p per min. 🖥www.easyjet.com $ UK£50-150.)*
- **RYANAIR:** From Dublin, Glasgow, Liverpool, London, and Shannon to destinations in France. *(☎0818 30 30 30 for Ireland, 0871 246 0000 for the UK 🖥www.ryanair.com)*
- **SKYEUROPE:** Forty destinations in 19 countries around Europe. *(☎0905 722 2747 for the UK, +421 2 3301 7301 elsewhere 🖥www.skyeurope.com)*
- **STERLING:** The first Scandinavian-based budget airline connects Denmark, Norway, and Sweden to 47 European destinations, including Montpellier, Nice, and Paris. *(☎70 10 84 84 for Denmark, 0870 787 8038 for the UK 🖥www.sterling.dk)*
- **TRANSAVIA:** Short hops from Krakow to Paris. *(☎020 7365 4997 for the UK 🖥www.transavia.com $ From €49 one-way.)*
- **WIZZ AIR:** Paris from Budapest, Krakow, and Warsaw. *(☎0904 475 9500 for the UK, 65p per min. 🖥www.wizzair.com)*

BY TRAIN

Trains in France are generally comfortable, convenient, and reasonably swift. Second-class compartments, which seat from two to six people, are great places to meet fellow travelers. Make sure you are on the correct car, as trains sometimes split at crossroads. Towns listed in parentheses on European train schedules require a train switch at the town listed immediately before the parentheses.

You can either buy a **railpass,** which allows you unlimited travel within a particular region for a given period of time, or rely on buying individual **point-to-point** tickets as you go. Almost all countries give students or youths (under 26, usually) direct discounts on regular domestic rail tickets, and many also sell a student or youth card that provides 20-50% off all fares for up to a year.

BY BUS

Though European trains and railpasses are extremely popular, in some cases buses prove a better option. In France however, bus travel is often a hassle. Travelers generally opt for bus travel only for short trips between destinations that are not served by trains. However, often cheaper than railpasses, **international bus passes** allow unlimited travel on a hop-on, hop-off basis between major European cities. **Busabout,** for instance, offers three interconnecting bus circuits covering 29 of Europe's best bus hubs. *(☎+44 8450 267 514 🖥www.busabout.com $ 1 circuit in high season starts at US$579, students US$549.)* **Eurolines,** meanwhile, is the largest operator of Europe-wide coach services. We get misty-eyed just thinking about their unlimited 15- and 30-day passes

- **WWW.RAILEUROPE.COM:** Info on rail travel and railpasses.
- **POINT-TO-POINT FARES AND SCHEDULES:** ▧www.raileurope.com/us/ rail/fares_schedules/index.htm allows you to calculate whether buying a railpass would save you money.
- **WWW.RAILSAVER.COM:** Uses your itinerary to calculate the best railpass for your trip.
- **WWW.RAILFANEUROPE.NET:** Links to rail servers throughout Europe.
- **WWW.LETSGO.COM:** Check out the Essentials section for more details.

to 11 major European cities. (☎0 892 89 90 91, €0.34 per min, ▧www.eurolines.com ③ High season 15-day pass €345, 30-day pass €455; under 26 €290/375. Mid-season €240/330; under 26 €205/270. Low season €205/310; under 26 €176/240.)

BY BOAT

Most European ferries are quite comfortable; the cheapest ticket typically still includes a reclining chair or couchette. Fares jump sharply in July and August. Ask for discounts; ISIC and Eurail Pass holders get many reductions and free trips. You'll occasionally have to pay a port tax *(under US$10)*. Ferries are a great budget option for travel in the south of France. **Corsica Ferries** runs from Nice and Toulon to Corsica. For the traveler with a little more money to burn, there are also ferries to St-Tropez from St-Raphaël. They run more frequently during July and August, check ▧*www. bateauxsaintraphael.com* for more information.

BY BICYCLE

Some youth hostels rent bicycles for low prices, and in some cities in France, it is possible to rent bikes from street locations that often allow you to drop them off elsewhere. In addition to **panniers** *(US$40-150)* to hold your luggage, you'll need a good **helmet** *(US$10-40)* and a sturdy **lock** *(from US$30)*. For more country-specific books on biking through France, try **Mountaineers Books.** *(1001 SW Klickitat Way, Ste. 201, Seattle, WA 98134, USA ☎+1-206-223-6303 ▧www.mountaineersbooks.org)*

keeping in touch

BY EMAIL AND INTERNET

Hello and welcome to the 21st century, where you can check your email in most major European cities, though sometimes you'll have to pay a few bucks or buy a drink for internet access. Although in some places it's possible to forge a remote link with your home server, in most cases this is a much slower (and thus more expensive) option than taking advantage of free **web-based email accounts** (e.g., ▧**www. gmail.com**). **Internet cafes** and the occasional free internet terminal at a public library or university are listed in the **Practicalities** sections of cities that we cover. For lists of additional cybercafes in France, check out specific websites—examples include ▧www.cybercaptive.com and www.netcafeguide.com.

Wireless hot spots make internet access possible in public and remote places. Unfortunately, they also pose security risks. Hot spots are public, open networks that use unencrypted, unsecured connections. They are susceptible to hacks and "packet sniffing"— the theft of passwords and other private information. To prevent problems, disable "ad hoc" mode, turn off file sharing and network discovery, encrypt your email, turn on your firewall, beware of phony networks, and watch for over-the-shoulder creeps.

BY TELEPHONE

Calling Home from France

Prepaid phone cards are a common and relatively inexpensive means of calling abroad. Each one comes with a Personal Identification Number (PIN) and a toll-free access number. You call the access number and then follow the directions for dialing your PIN. To purchase prepaid phone cards, check online for the best rates; ■www.callingcards.com is a good place to start. Online providers generally send your access number and PIN via email, with no actual "card" involved. You can also call home with prepaid phone cards purchased in France.

If you have internet access, your best—i.e., cheapest, most convenient, and most tech-savvy—bet is probably our good friend **Skype**. (■www.skype.com) You can even videochat if you have one of those new-fangled webcams. Calls to other Skype users are free; calls to landlines and mobiles worldwide start at US$0.021 per minute, depending on where you're calling.

Another option is a **calling card,** linked to a major national telecommunications service in your home country. Calls are billed collect or to your account. Cards generally come with instructions for dialing both domestically and internationally.

Placing a collect call through an international operator can be expensive but may be necessary in case of an emergency. You can frequently call collect without even possessing a company's calling card just by calling its access number and following the instructions.

Cellular Phones

The international standard for cell phones is **Global System for Mobile Communication (GSM).** To make and receive calls in France, you will need a GSM-compatible phone and a **SIM (Subscriber Identity Module) card,** a country-specific, thumbnail-size chip that gives you a local phone number and plugs you into the local network. Many SIM cards are prepaid, and incoming calls are frequently free. You can buy additional cards or vouchers (usually available at convenience stores) to "top up" your phone. For more information on GSM phones, check out ■www.telestial.com. Companies like **Cellular Abroad** (■www.cellularabroad.com) and **OneSimCard** (■www.onesimcard.com) rent cell phones and SIM cards that work in a variety of destinations around the world. In France, **Orange** is a great cell phone option for travelers, offering affordable phones *(approx. €35)* that come pre-loaded with minutes and can be recharged at most supermarkets and tobacco shops (■www.orange.co.uk).

---

international calls

To call France from home or to call home from France, dial:

- **1. THE INTERNATIONAL DIALING PREFIX.** To call from Australia, dial ☎0011; Canada or the US, ☎011; Ireland, New Zealand, France, or the UK, ☎00.

- **2. THE COUNTRY CODE OF THE COUNTRY YOU WANT TO CALL.** To call Australia, dial ☎61; Canada or the US, ☎1; Ireland, ☎353; New Zealand, ☎64; the UK, ☎44; France, ☎33.

- **3. THE CITY/AREA CODE.** *Let's Go* lists the city/area codes for cities and towns in France, opposite the city or town name, next to a ☎, as well as in every phone number. If the first digit is a zero (e.g., ☎01 for Paris), omit the zero when calling from abroad (e.g., dial ☎1 from Canada to reach Paris).

- **4. THE LOCAL NUMBER.**

essentials

BY SNAIL MAIL

Sending Mail Home from France

Airmail is the best way to send mail home from France. **Aerogrammes,** printed sheets that fold into envelopes and travel via airmail, are available at post offices. Write "airmail" or *"par avion,"* on the front. Most post offices will charge exorbitant fees or simply refuse to send aerogrammes with enclosures. Surface mail is by far the cheapest and slowest way to send mail. It takes one to two months to cross the Atlantic and one to three to cross the Pacific—good for heavy items you won't need for a while, like souvenirs that you've acquired along the way.

Sending Mail to France

In addition to the standard postage system whose rates are listed below, **Federal Express** handles express mail services from most countries to France. (☎+1-800-463-3339 🖳www.fedex.com) Sending a postcard within France costs €0.56, while sending letters (up to 20g) domestically requires €0.56.

There are several ways to arrange pickup of letters sent to you while you are abroad. In France, you can request that a FedEx package be held for pickup at the FedEx office, rather than having it sent to an address. Mail can also be sent via **Poste Restante** (General Delivery) to almost any city or town in France with a post office, but it is not very reliable. Address Poste Restante letters like so:

Napoleon BONAPARTE
Poste Restante
Paris, France

The mail will go to a special desk in the central post office, unless you specify a post office by street address or postal code. It's best to use the largest post office, since mail may be sent there regardless. It is usually safer and quicker, though more expensive, to send mail express or registered. Bring your passport (or other photo ID) for pickup; there may be a small fee. If the clerks insist that there is nothing for you, ask them to check under your first name as well.

American Express has travel offices throughout the world that offer a free **Client Letter Service** (mail held up to 30 days and forwarded upon request) for cardholders who contact them in advance. Some offices provide these services to non-cardholders (especially AmEx Travelers Cheque holders), but call ahead to make sure. For a complete list of AmEx locations, call ☎1-800-528-4800 or visit 🖳www.americanexpress.com/travel.

climate

France's climate, much like its women, is rather unpredictable. Overall a temperate country, it is colder in the winter and warmer in summer. However, the climate in the northern France is similar to weather found in the UK (though women here are said to be pleasant and warm). Central France has generally more extreme seasonal changes, and you'll find more Mediterranean climates near...the Mediterranean. Southern France features the mildest winters in the country and the warmest sunniest summers—perfect for tanning though you'll probably want to arrive with a solid base tan. Note: if you blush easily, you'll definitely want to read up on beaches before you set out...

AVG. TEMP. (LOW/ HIGH), PRECIP.	JANUARY			APRIL			JULY			OCTOBER		
	°C	°F	mm	°C	°F	mm	°C	°F	mm	°C	°F	mm
Cherbourg	4/8	39/46	109	7/12	45/54	49	14/19	57/66	55	10/15	50/59	99
Paris	1/6	34/43	56	6/16	46/61	42	15/25	59/77	59	8/16	46/61	50
Lyon	-1/5	30/41	52	6/16	46/61	56	15/27	59/81	56	7/16	45/61	77
Marseille	2/10	36/50	43	8/18	46/64	42	17/29	63/84	11	10/20	50/68	76

BACKPACKING
by the numbers:
117 photos snapped
41 gelato flavors (3 lbs gained)
23 miles walked (in the *right* direction)
6 buses missed
4 benches napped on
2½ hostel romances
1 Let's Go Travel Guide
0 REGRETS.
LET'S GO
www.letsgo.com
we'd rather be traveling, too.

To convert from degrees Fahrenheit to degrees Celsius, subtract 32 and multiply by 5/9. To convert from Celsius to Fahrenheit, multiply by 9/5 and add 32.

°CELSIUS	-5	0	5	10	15	20	25	30	35	40
°FAHRENHEIT	23	32	41	50	59	68	77	86	95	104

measurements

Like the rest of the rational world, France uses the metric system. The basic unit of length is the meter (m), which is divided into 100 centimeters (cm) or 1000 millimeters (mm). One thousand meters make up one kilometer (km). Fluids are measured in liters (L), each divided into 1000 milliliters (mL). A liter of pure water weighs one kilogram (kg), the unit of mass that is divided into 1000 grams (g). One metric ton is 1000kg.

MEASUREMENT CONVERSIONS	
1 inch (in.) = 25.4mm	1 millimeter (mm) = 0.039 in.
1 foot (ft.) = 0.305m	1 meter (m) = 3.28 ft.
1 yard (yd.) = 0.914m	1 meter (m) = 1.094 yd.
1 mile (mi.) = 1.609km	1 kilometer (km) = 0.621 mi.
1 ounce (oz.) = 28.35g	1 gram (g) = 0.035 oz.
1 pound (lb.) = 0.454kg	1 kilogram (kg) = 2.205 lb.
1 fluid ounce (fl. oz.) = 29.57mL	1 milliliter (mL) = 0.034 fl. oz.
1 gallon (gal.) = 3.785L	1 liter (l) = 0.264 gal.

language

You'll be surprised to learn that the official language in France is French. Really (we promise). English speakers will be happy to note that English is the most commonly taught foreign language in France, followed by Spanish and German. As you move closer to certain borders (e.g. the Spanish-French border in the south, the German-French border in the east), you're more likely to find bi- and tri-lingual speakers, as well as some regional languages, like Catalan, Corsican, and Breton.

PRONUNCIATION

What you've heard is true: the French resent tourists who don't speak their language. They are quite good at turning their noses up at you (centuries of snootiness can do that). However, what you probably don't know is that the French people are more than happy to help if you at least attempt French. Reading French can be tricky, but the table below should help you out.

PHONETIC UNIT	PRONUNCIATION	PHONETIC UNIT	PRONUNCIATION
au	o, as in "go"	ch	sh, as in "shoe"
oi	ua, as in "guava"	ou	oo, as in "igloo"
ai	ay, as in "lay"	â	ah, as in "menorah"

PHRASEBOOK

ENGLISH	FRENCH	PRONUNCIATION
Hello!/Hi!	Bonjour!	bohn-jhoor
Goodbye!	Au revoir!	oh ruh-vwah
Yes.	Oui.	wee
No.	Non.	nohn
Sorry!	Désolé!	day-zoh-lay

EMERGENCY		
Go away!	Allez-vous en!	ah-lay vooz on
Help!	Au secours!	oh sek-oor
Call the police!	Appelez les flics!	apple-ay lay fleeks
Get a doctor!	Va chercher un médecin!	vah share-shay un mayd-sin
Police station	Poste de Police	Exactly like you'd think.
Hospital	Hôpital	Ho-pee-tal
Liquor Store	Magasin d'alcool	Maga-zin dal-cool

FOOD		
Waiter/waitress	Serveur/Serveuse	server/servers
I'd like...	Je voudrais...	Je voo-dray
Thank you!	Merci!	mare-see
Check please!	La facture, s'il-vous-plait!	La fact-tour, seal-voo-play
Where is...?	Où est...?	Oo ay...?

ENGLISH	FRENCH	ENGLISH	FRENCH
I am from (the US/ Europe).	Je suis des Etats-Unis/de l'Europe.	What's the problem, sir/ madam?	Quelle est la problème, monsieur/madame?
I have a visa/ID.	J'ai un visa/de l'identification.	I lost my passport/ luggage.	J'ai perdu mon passeport/ baggage.
I will be here for less than six months.	Je serai ici pour moins de six mois.	I have nothing to declare.	Je n'ai rien à déclarer.
You are the woman of my dreams.	Vous êtes la femme de mes rêves.	Perhaps I can help you with that?	Puis-je vous aider avec ça?
Your hostel, or mine?	Votre hôtel, ou le mien?	Do you have protection?	Avez-vous un préservatif?
I would like a round-trip ticket.	Je voudrais un billet aller-retour.	Where is the train sta- tion?	Où est la gare?
Can I see a double room?	Puis-je voir un chambre pour deux?	How much does this cost?	Combien ça coûte?
Where is the bathroom?	Où est la salle de bain?	Is there a bar near here?	Est-ce qu'il y a un bar près d'ici?
What time is the next train?	A quelle heure est la prochaine train?	Do you have this baithing suit in another size?	Avez-vous cette maillot de bain dans une autre taille?
Can I have another drink please?	Puis-je prendre un autre boisson s'il vous-plait?	Please don't arrest me!	S'il vous plait, ne m'arretez pas!
I'm in a committed relationship.	Je suis dans une relation engagée.	You talkin' to me?	Vous me parlez?
It was like this when I got here.	C'était comme ça quand je suis arrivé(e).	I don't speak much French.	Je ne parle pas beaucoup de Français.
I feel sick.	Je me sent malade.	Leave me alone!	Laissez-moi tranquille!
What time does reception close?	A quelle heure est-ce que la réception ferme?	I don't understand.	Je ne comprends pas.
Actually, I'm from Canada.	Actuellement, je suis Canadien(ne).	I didn't vote for him, I swear.	Je n'ai pas voté pour lui, je el jure.

essentials

let's go online

Plan your next trip on our spiffy website, ▪www.letsgo.com. It features full book content, the latest travel info on your favorite destinations, and tons of interactive features: make your own itinerary, read blogs from our trusty Researcher-Writers, browse our photo library, watch exclusive videos, check out our newsletter, find travel deals, follow us on Facebook, and buy new guides. Plus, if this Essentials wasn't enough for you, we've got even more online. We're always updating and adding new features, so check back often!

FRANCE 101

Let's Go is sure you've heard tell of that infamous French snobbiness—how they think Americans are ignorant, English speakers are inferior, and foreigners in general are pretty sub-par. But they're really not as scary as all that. They've just grown up in the land of Monet and Molière, of Bonaparte and the Bastille, a country that's produced 49 Nobel Prize winners and 31 UNESCO World Heritage Sites, been the seat of three empires and the source of countless artistic movements. It's no wonder they're so proud to be French—and it's also no wonder that they don't think it's cute when you can't tell a Gaul from de Gaulle. So if you don't really like being that kid (who does?), dive into this chapter and read up on the history, art, literature, and customs of France. We'll take you from the first hundred years of the Roman Empire to the Hundred Years' War, from religious repression to artistic expression, and, most importantly, from an oh-you-silly-American Stone Age to an educated Enlightenment. We promise this will be more entertaining and informative than the in-flight movie. (Unless, of course, that movie happens to be *A Witty and Irreverent Introduction to France*. But we doubt you'll get that lucky.)

facts and figures

- **NUMBER OF FRENCH NOBEL LAUREATES:** 49.
- **LITERS OF WINE CONSUMED PER PERSON ANNUALLY:** 47.
- **LIKELIHOOD THE PREVIOUS TWO FACTS ARE RELATED:** 93.7%.
- **NUMBER OF MISTRESSES KEPT SIMULTANEOUSLY BY SARTRE:** 9.
- **NUMBER OF PEOPLE LIBERATED FROM THE BASTILLE IN 1789:** 7.
- **NUMBER OF YOUTH ARRESTED ON NOVEMBER 14TH DURING RIOTS OF 2005:** 71.

28,000 BCE
Neanderthals die
and Homo Sapiens
take over. Go us!

ECCENTRICS OF YORE

Modern humans originally journeyed to France 50,000 years ago in search of a mild climate. A haven for the creatively neurotic even in Paleolithic times, angsty prehistoric Frenchmen culturally eclipsed their **Neanderthal** neighbors with whimsical cave paintings of wild game, on view today in **Lascaux** and **Gargas**. Critics at the time dismissed their work as "pedestrian," citing its "lack of breadth and imagination."

51 BCE
Julius Caesar shows
the Gaul who's boss.

SUCH GAUL!

A smorgasbord of Celtic and Belgae tribes gradually invaded the area between 1500 and 500 BCE, and persuaded the locals via broadsword to exchange their free-love fertility goddess for a militarized social hierarchy. This assortment of Druids and headhunters were collectively christened **"Gauls"** by the **Romans**, whose imperial superiority complex didn't jive well with Gaulish military culture. Centuries of conflict were ignited in 393 BCE, when a Gaulish band of miscreants led by **Brennus** invaded Rome. After laughing hysterically, the Roman army swiftly obliterated them, then conquered most of Gaul in 58 BC under the leadership of one **Julius Caesar.** Druid necklaces of human heads were exchanged for aqueducts and amphitheaters as Gaul underwent a cultural makeover. Several centuries later, the Carthaginian general **Hannibal** (sans Lector) recruited the Gauls in a second invasion of Rome. War elephants and the Alps proved to be mutually exclusive, and the campaign was very unsuccessful. Centuries of struggle later, neither the Romans nor the Gauls were ultimately able to control the region. After a flurry of **Barbarian invasions** in the fifth century CE, Gaul was carved up into **Visigoth**, **Burgundian,** and **Frankish** territory.

732 CE
Charles Martel prays
to God. God answers.

886
Paris is attacked by
Vikings. Shockingly,
they don't surrender
immediately.

FRANKLY MY DEAR...

For the next five centuries or so, France was subjected to routine invasions and coups as a motley crew of monarchs attempted to control the region. In 486 CE, **Clovis I** defeated the last of any Roman influence in the area, crowned himself king of the Franks, and set about uniting the country. The **Merovingian Dynasty** that Clovis instated defeated the Visigoths, cemented Catholicism's hold in the region, but was ultimately short-lived; upon his death, France was divided amongst his heirs into four different kingdoms. Descendents of the original rulers increasingly delegated power to their *majordomos.* These medieval men behind the curtain officially rose to power when majordomo **Charles Martel** took the initiative and defeated invading Muslim forces at the **Battle of Tours** in 732, then used his ensuing popularity to lay the groundwork for an empire of his own. The **Carolingian Dynasty** that followed reached the pinnacle of its power when Martel's grandson, **Charlemagne,** was crowned the Emperor of the Romans by **Pope Leo III** for beating back the Moors as far as Barcelona. Like all

1254
Sorbonne is
founded, giving
American college
students a place
to study for their
"life changing" year
abroad.

MAY 30, 1431
Joan of Arc prays to
God. God doesn't
answer.

france 101

good things though, this Empire did not last. **Vikings** raided the Frankish kingdom and cut the French territory down to a small area around Paris. Some less-than-consensual sex occurred between Viking raiders and Frankish maidens at this point, resulting in the population of **Normans** in the North of Europe.

Taking advantage of increased infighting at court, **Hugh Capet** successfully unseated the Carolingians in 987. After several centuries of an extensive royal game of Risk, the **Capetians** expanded and consolidated their kingdom beyond their stronghold in Paris, but were never quite able to get a handle on their nobles. As a case in point, the renegade conquest of England by the bastard duke **William the Conqueror** occurred completely outside the crown's authority. Capetian international influence reached its own peak when **Saint Louis IX** became king in 1226. Though he lost every crusade he participated in, Saint Louis received kudos points from Rome for trying and was awarded an additional gold star by the Papacy for channeling his inner Jesus and kicking the Jews out of France. So great was the Papacy's approval that for seven Popes, the Papacy resided in **Avignon** during a period known as the **Babylonian Captivity**.

UNICORNS AND BALLOONS (KIDDING, DEATH AND PLAGUE)

As if the **Black Death** wasn't cheerful enough, a succession crisis over the French crown catalyzed the **Hundred Years' War** between England and France, which lasted 16 years longer than its name suggests. The English **longbow** made its first appearance on the continent in this period, wiping out the French at the **Battle of Agincourt** in 1415. England seized Paris five years later. Despite the valiant antics of a teenage girl and possible schizophrenic named **Joan de Arc**, who led a failed siege of the city in 1429, the occupation held until **Charles VII** finally recaptured the city in 1436, and officially booted the English out. Taking advantage of the chaos, **Louis XI, The Spider King** managed to consolidate all the regions of modern-day France under the French monarchy. Aside from his Mexican wrestling ability, the name "Spider King" refers to Louis's talent for weaving webs of deceit and trickery in order to obtain lands for the crown.

OUT OF THE DARK... SORT OF

The French monarchy expanded in both size and power during the 300 years preceding the Revolution. The French had the uncanny ability to win wars in Burgundy (1493), Brittany (1532), and other areas in their immediate vicinity, but they ran into trouble when the weak **Valois King Francis I** tried to fight Holy Roman Emperor and Spanish monarch **Charles V**. Charles forced Francis to sign over major Italian lands previously under French control. Following this halted period of land acquisition, France vaulted itself into the **Wars of Religion**, a conflict between Roman Catholics and Protestant Huguenots which resulted in a series of genocidal massacres that

1437
The Hundred Years' War officially goes over budget.

1584-1598
The War of Three Henrys leads the the predictable win of King Henry.

1648
The Thirty Years' War ends on its 30th year of fighting. Take that Hundred Years' War.

1682
The Palace of Versailles smells like a mix of perfume and body odor, as the popularity of bathing decreases and perfume increases.

1789
The French totally plagiarize the Declaration of Independence with the Declaration of the Rights of Man and Citizen.

history · out of the dark... sort of

took place over the course of 30 years. Out of the chaos rose the gallant **Henry IV**, who guaranteed the Huguenots' religious freedom through the **Edict of Nantes** in 1598. Henry IV converted to Catholicism to appease the people, but had trouble appeasing the psychotic contingent of his new religion and was knifed by a deranged Jesuit in 1610. In the spirit of brotherly love, a Parisian mob executed his assassin by scalding and then quartering him.

BOURBON ON THE ROCKS

Henry was succeeded by the Bourbon monarchy and a long line of Louis's, the first being his son, nine-year-old **Louis XIII**. Despite a nasty stutter, little Louis did an adequate job in maintaining France's reputation as an economic and artistic stronghold, but the monarchy's approval ratings plummeted when his successor, **Louis XIV**, came along. After major discontent between the nobility and bourgeoisie generated a series of civil wars called the **Fronde**, the self-proclaimed "Sun King" tightened his grip by conveniently introducing the concept of absolute monarchy. In addition to his sociopathic tendencies, Louis XIV was also a wuss, and fled to **Versailles** in fear of his citizens in 1682. During the reign of the following two Louis's (XV and XVI), France spent billions in today's money on foreign conflicts, including a near world war over territories in the Americas known as the **Seven Years' War**. France lost badly, even by French standards, and was forced to give up almost all North American territory. Seeking revenge against the British, **Louis XVI** heavily funded a colonial insurgency against the British in 1776. Britain, willing to negotiate with terrorists engaged in guerilla warfare, agreed to acknowledge the **United States of America**. The conflict led to huge debts and, coupled with **Marie Antoinette**'s expensive taste in cakes, left France inconveniently bankrupt in a period of increasing civil unrest. Oh yeah, the two famines didn't help the situation either.

TALKIN' ABOUT A REVOLUTION

The **French Revolution** was initially catalyzed by a flawed attempt at land reform and tax increases. Nobles refused to pay taxes, which irritated the people of France to such an extent that the **Third Estate** (the Estate of the People) broke away from the Estates General and interrupted some poor fellows playing a game of tennis on June 20, 1789. This new **National Assembly** vowed to always meet and "never to separate" until a constitution was granted. Under the threat of **Royalist** attack on the Assembly, Paris began to riot, making the French riots in the summer of 2005 look like a cultural peace parade. The armory and symbol of monarchial oppression, the **Bastille**, was stormed on July 14, 1789 liberating the thousands of innocent civilians (read: seven people) from prison.

The Revolution took a more radical turn with the rise of the **Jacobins**, who demanded that **Louis XVI** be executed for his refusal to sign the constitution of the National Assembly. The Sun King was tried by a "fair and balanced" military tribunal, and executed by guillotine in 1793. Led by **Maximilien**

1793
Committee of Public Safety becomes ironic and kills 18,000 civilians.

1804
Someone calls Napoleon "shorty pants" one too many times; vertically-challenged Corsican takes over France.

1814
Russians burn down their own capital to defeat Napoleon. Hah! Take that, Napoleon.

1851
"Fool me once, shame on you. Fool me twice... dammit why did we put another Napoleon in power?"

1940
Amory dealer's sign reads, "Used French Rifle: Never fired and dropped once."

france 101

Robespierre and **Jean-Paul Marat**, the Jacobins advanced their **"Reign of Terror"** by executing nearly 18,000 monarchists and counter revolutionaries over the course of following year. Not everyone was cool with this return to murderous despotism, and in 1794, the **Thermadorian Reaction** arrested Robespierre and executed him with own favorite revolutionary symbol. A bureaucracy called the **Directory** was established in Paris. Coups were all the rage back then, however, and a diminutive Corsican named **Napoleon Bonaparte** took over several years later in 1804.

TAKE TWO (OR THREE)

After establishing the French Empire in 1804, Napoleon attempted to exorcise his hangups about height by invading other countries. France crushed Austria and Prussia and expanded throughout the Continent, extending as far north as Norway. In what would become a habit among European megalomaniacs throughout the ages (see: Hitler), Napoleon's military cunning did not anticipate Russia's damn cold winters, and he blithely marched his coalition into the snow in 1812. Armed with an excess of vodka, the Russians waited it out and watched Napoleon's troops freeze. Napoleon abdicated and was sent to exile in Elba in 1814, but came back for more in 1815 for his famous **100 Days**. European Royalists ultimately defeated him at **Waterloo**; France restored their monarchy, and established Louis XVIII as the head of state.

About 30 years later, the people of France were due for a riot and erupted in 1848, leading to the establishment of the **Second Republic**. Unaware that repeating the same actions and expecting different results is a casebook definition of insanity, France elected **Napoleon III** as its president. To everyone's surprise, he declared France an Empire in 1851 and ruled for the next 20 years. French revolutions are revolutions in a literal sense; the proletariat riots, the intelligentsia pontificates, and the country does a social 360, ending up right back where it started. Wait 10 years. Repeat. In 1870, France's swift surrender to the invading Prussians marked the final end of the empire. Culturally, the **Third Republic** ushered in an era fondly known as the **Belle Époque,** a period characterized by flourishing modern art, entertainment, fashion, and an epic Worlds Fair.

THE WAR YEARS

France suffered considerably during WWI and the interwar period, but was too immersed in an inebriated cultural revolution to notice. The unofficial mothership of the world's expatriates, Paris generated **Surrealism**, **Expressionism**, and other major artistic and philosophical movements in this period, in spite of the dismal economy. An abundance of wine and Prohibition-fleeing Americans probably had something to do with it. Boozin' and floozin' were put on hold with the onset of WWII, which subjected the country to a terrorizing **Nazi occupation** from 1940-1944. France valiantly resisted the German invasion for 5 whole weeks; in their defense, the

1954
France leaves Vietnam after the Battle of Dien Bien Phu. The US thinks it can do better.

1999
The Euro is adopted throughout the continent. No one ever thinks that Germany and Greece will budget differently.

2009
France demands worldwide financial regulation. Goldman Sachs laughs.

2010
Goldman isn't laughing anymore.

summer months were coming up, and the war conflicted with their family vacation plans. The French-German armistice that followed divided the country into a Nazi-occupied zone to the North and a "free," French-governed zone to the South, which was in reality controlled by the collaborationist **Vichy regime.** A resistance movement led by **General Charles de Gaulle** helped liberate Paris after the Allied forces landed in Normandy in 1944. Most of France's historical buildings and monuments were spared from the destruction of the war. Over half a million French citizens were not so lucky.

ANY ROYALISTS LEFT? OH WELL, WE'LL RAISE HELL ANYWAY

Catching its breath after the Nazis, France saw little action until the global **acid trip** that was the 1960s. In 1961, a peaceful demonstration by **North Africans** protesting the Algerian War turned into a bloody massacre, with over 100 activists killed by police and dumped into the Seine River. In **1968**, nine million workers staged strikes to protest big business, and that same year demonstrations by students against university policy pushed Paris to the brink of anarchy. De Gaulle took on the Nazis, but he couldn't handle angry hippie kids. He retired, and **Georges Pompidou** became president in 1969.

AIN'T SO CHILLY NO MORE

The end of the **Cold War** brought about huge changes in the political and economic influence of France. After France gradually patched up its relationship with Germany, the two countries became the driving forces of the European economy, spearheading the **Treaty of Maastricht** in 1992 and establishing the European Union. France was also able to turn all its nuclear capacity from bombs into energy plants, and has since produced 80% of its supply domestically using nuclear power. Today, the French continue to drive towards a more centralized Europe, adopting the **euro** in 1999 and involving itself in Airbus, Eurocorps and the Galileo positioning system. Despite the country's leaps and bounds in economic development, France's progressivism continues to be undermined by racial tensions between the ethnic French and North Africans. In 2005, **violent riots** broke out in the Parisian streets and chaos soon spread around the country as rioters, mostly the frustrated children of North African immigrants, razed the streets and attacked police. Tensions between these two groups were most recently manifested in the French ban on **full facial covers on women** in 2010.

customs and etiquette

FIRST IMPRESSIONS

The first time you meet in France, shaking hands is expected, although friends will greet one another with a kiss on the cheek. Women are expected to kiss twice. If you're planning on eating in a restaurant or heading out clubbing, dress it up— the easiest way to stand out as a tourist is to wear shorts and a T-shirt out to dinner. Don't expect to be let into the club wearring sneakers. At restaurants, the tip is included in the bill, but feel free to leave a 5-10% tip for exceptional service.

WHAT NOT TO SAY

In French culture, never discuss money in private or public company. Doing so is seen as tasteless. In restaurants, arguing over who had what when the bill comes up is even more shameless. The host usually is expected to pay; among friends it is more common to split the bill by the number in your party. In addition to money, talking about business is also considered boring.

DEMAIN

If you're invited to dinner at someone's house, you'll find them unprepared if you show up "on time." Try aiming to be 15 to 30 min. late. The attitude of "do it later/ tomorrow" is one that France, and Southern Europe generally, embraces. While a German meeting might work differently, a cafe rendezvous typically never starts punctually.

WE'RE CLOSED

In France, restaurants, cafes, and other serves that usually stay open on Sundays are closed on Mondays instead. If you're planning a hot date on a Monday, make sure to reschedule for later in the week. Besides, who goes on dates on Monday night?

USE YOUR CRAPPY FRENCH

When entering any sort of establishment, remember that it is the patron's (your) job to initiate conversation. Using French is crucial; it's a sign that you're trying to adapt to the culture and that you're willing to embarrass yourself to do so. French appreciate the struggle and, as most know a few words of English themselves, will often bail you out and start talking in English.

the arts

LITERATURE AND PHILOSOPHY

Not so Enlightened

An oasis for egotistical visionaries, ennui-ridden madmen, and their ensuing authority issues, France has been an intellectual epicenter since its more sensitive cavemen discovered rock drawing. Due to the French predisposition towards joining mobs and executing monarchs, however, it took a few centuries for the country to stop trying to kill off its own proteges. After immersing himself in **Humanism** at the University of Paris, **John Calvin** was forced to flee the city and its Wars of Religion in 1533. In 1588, famed essayist **Michel de Montaigne** was imprisoned twice in the same brief trip to Paris by the League of Protestants, and was almost prevented from publishing a revised edition of his *Essais*.

Guillotines? Cut the Crap

Conditions for individual thought improved in the 17th and 18th centuries when the city played host to the **Enlightenment**, an intellectual movement which championed human reason over dogmatism. Inspired in part by Parisian *libertine* intellectuals, **Rene Descartes** proved his own existence through his much-parodied deduction, "I think, therefore I am" in 1638. As a young man in the 18th century, **Voltaire** spent most of his time in Paris pretending to go to law school, getting locked in the Bastille, and promoting social reform through satire. The theories of **Jean-Jacques Rousseau** only fanned the flames of social unrest. In 1792, the Enlightenment's political theories catalyzed the **French Revolution**, and Jacobins expressed their commitment to rational discourse via guillotine.

Realists vs. Romantics

Nineteenth-century France was defined by crosscurrents of **Realism**, **Romanticism**, and perpetual social upheaval. Referring to Paris as his "dear old hell," **Honore de Balzac** gregariously slept his way through the city while writing his *Comedie Humaine*. The work established the novel as the pre-eminent literary medium of the age, a position which **Victor Hugo**'s wildly popular *The Hunchback of Notre Dame* confirmed. Though immediately acclaimed, Romantics and Realists often ran afoul of French censorship laws. **Gustave Flaubert** was prosecuted for immorality in 1858 due to the detailed descriptions of the adulterous *Madame Bovary*.

Alcoholics Not so Anonymous

20th-century France was characterized by an intensive rebellion against the "rationalism" of prior centuries. Attracted the country's intellectualism (read: jazz and liquor), alienated ex-pats from around the world flocked to Paris throughout the 1920s and '30s. **F. Scott Fitzgerald**, **Ernest Hemingway**, **Gertrude Stein** and other writers of the **"Lost Generation"** produced groundbreaking works of American literature at a safe distance from the country they criticized.

"No Exit" to Postmodernism

When they weren't busy sleeping with each other, **Jean-Paul Sartre** and **Simone de Beauvoir** spent their time dominating Parisian academic circles with theories of **Existentialism** and **Second Wave Feminism**, respectively. **Postmodernists** of the 1970s such as **Michel Foucault** and **Jacques Derrida** revolutionized academic thought and brought the transparency of philosophical writing to new lows.

FINE ARTS AND ARCHITECTURE

Church vs. Nudists

Exchanging the ▇**homoerotic nudes** of the Classical age for excessive portrayals of hellfire, religion maintained a stranglehold on the art world throughout the Middle Ages. **Saint-Denis Basilica,** considered the first Gothic building ever built, was finished in 1144 in what is now a suburb of Paris. The **Notre Dame,** sans hunchback, followed soon after, as did the wondrous **Sainte-Chapelle.** By the 15th century, Gothic art and architecture morphed into an Italian-influenced **Renaissance** style, which recovered both realistic linear perspective and an appreciation for very naked people.

Baroque and Rococo

Drawing on the raw emotion of Italian artwork, a unique French Baroque style emerged under the reign of Louis XIII. The artform reached its height with Louis XIV's flamboyant renovations of **Versailles,** an exorbitant spectacle which the prols of Paris were rumored to have issues with. By the 1720s, the light-hearted and asymmetrical **Rococo** style of interior design began to supersede Baroque style and was much preferred by Louis XV. Paintings of bestial fetes and ▇**naughty shepardesses** abounded.

Old-School Classics

After the Revolution and the rise of Napoleon I, Neoclassicism emerged as a reaction to the aristocratic Baroque and Rococo styles. Ancient Greek and Roman forms were once again depicted on canvas and in sculpture, and landmarks such as the **Arc de Triomphe** and the **Pantheon** were erected as odes to ancient architecture. Napoleon, in his infinite modesty, hired period artist **Jacques-Louis David** to paint gigantic portraits of him, idolizing the emperor as hero and god.

Make a Good Impression

After marrying his father's mistress, Parisian **Édouard Manet** started experimenting with color, texture, and nudity in ways that had never been dreamed of. The seeds of **Impressionism** were thus sown. The miraculous works of **Claude Monet, Pierre-Auguste Renoir,** and **Edgar Degas** soon graced Paris, capturing and focusing on light and color in ways that have yet to be surpassed. **Post-Impressionists** took their techniques to a new level: **Vincent van Gogh** (actually a Dutchman, but give him credit for living in Paris) delved into emotional **expressionism, Georges Seurat's** bold **Pointilist** style rocked the art world in 1884, and **Paul Cézanne** experimented with dimension.

Romantics Unite

The vivid and sometimes shocking scenes depicted by **Eugène Delacroix** and **Jean-Auguste-Dominique Ingres**, both of whose ceiling paintings you can crane your neck to admire in Hotel de Villes and the Louvre repectively, captured the raw passion of the Romanticism that characterized the late 19th century. In **Saint-Jean-Cap-Ferrat**, you can see a perfect example of the beginning of the **Belle Époque** in the **Villa Ephrussi de Rothschild**. In Nice, the **Hotel Negresco** is another example of the Belle Époque. Built in 1912 by then-famous architect **Eiffel**, the hotel has every extravagant feature you can hope for to attract wealthy clients, including the 16,309 crystal chandelier commissioned by **Czar Nicholas II**. He did not get to deliver it due to the **October Revolution**.

Hip to be a Square

The rise of Cubism in Paris was marked by exalted Cubist **Pablo Picasso's** painting *Les Demoiselles d'Avignon*, which he painted in Paris in 1907. Using pure, brilliant color and strong expression, Picasso's rival, **Henri Matisse**, whose collection can be found in **Cimlez**, squeezed his paint from the tube directly onto the canvas in a bid against Cubism; critics found his style offensively wild and brutish, and disdainfully called it **Fauvism** (from *fauves*, or wild animals).

Contemporary Art

After WWII, French artist diverged into **Abstract Expressionsim, pop art,** and other innovative movements. Today, the Centre Pompidou in Paris houses the **Musée National d'Art Moderne**, the largest collection of modern art in Europe. The building itself is an ode to modern architecture with all the stuff usually hidden by walls—electrical lines, piping, etc.—exposed on the outside of the building in brightly colored tubes.

food and drink

A French **breakfast** typically consists of lighter fare— a quick stop for coffee and a *croissant* at the nearest cafe, or a few *tartines* (slices) of bread with jelly. Stop at a *boulangerie* to pick up a pastry or a baguette that was made mere minutes before the shop opened. **Lunch** is a longer affair, but it is becoming less leisurely as even Parisians adjust to the busybody workday of a globalized world. Simple yet savory lunch chow found in cafes and brasseries includes salads, quiche, and tasty croque monsieur, otherwise known as a grilled ham and cheese. Eating out for lunch can be more intimidating for non-French speakers, but it's just a matter of having some cojones and testing out your throaty *s'il vous plait*, no matter how big the waiter's scowl is.

The same goes for **dinner,** where tourists subject themselves to confusion and anxiety as an intimidating *maître'd* recites the menu in rapid-fire French. Stay strong; the food's worth it. A traditional French meal consists of five courses: hors d'oeuvres, soup, a main course, salad, cheese, and dessert, each paired with a wine. Except for the most extravagant five-star establishments, however, a restaurant meal is typically two or three courses depending on your appetite and budget. Some economical travelers may opt to skip the food and just indulge in the wine, but we suggest you do both. Most restaurants open around 7:30pm or 8pm and take orders until 11pm; keep a look out for classic French dishes such as *cassoulet*, a meat stew, or *coq au vin*, wine-cooked chicken. It is law for restaurants to have a *prix-fixe* menu, so if they aren't showing you one but you're interested in the potentially cheaper option, do not hesitate to inquire.

NORTH

Nord Pas-de-Calais, Brittany and Normandy rely heavily on the crustations and bass at the North Sea. Brittany is especially famous for its crêpes, as well as *galettes*, which are made from the buckwheat that grows in the region. Many of the dishes are also paired with cider from northern apple trees, for those who are alcoholically inclined.

SOUTH

You'll never get tired of citrus and fruits— unless you go the South of France. This area is one of Europe's main suppliers of herbs (no, not in a Humboldt County sense). Honey is a staple and prized ingredient in this region, as well as goat cheese, sausages, and lamb. Making use of the sea as well, there are also many dishes that include garlic anchovies. Try drinking **pastis**, a yellow anise flavored alcoholic drink. Hemmingway coined the colorful phrase "Death in the Afternoon" to refer to a mix of pastis and Champagne, reminding all of us how much a hangover sucks at 5pm.

WEST

The Basque cuisine has definitely made its way into this region's food. Even though Bordeaux is known for its wine, it's also famous for its dried meats, including lamb. The region is also France's largest producers of *foie gras*, or fattened goose liver. The food is also heavily influenced by tomatoes, red pepper, wheat products and Arbequina olive oils.

WEST AND CENTRAL

The Loire Valley is rich in fruits, as well as the more famous liqueurs that come from those fruits. Most of the meat in this region isd wild game, Charolais cattle, and guinea fowl, while the region is especially famous for its goat cheeses. Go a little to the west and run into Champagne country, which is also famous for its German influenced cakes and beer.

BEYOND TOURISM

If you are reading this, then you are a member of an elite group—and we don't mean "the literate." You're a student preparing for a semester abroad. You're taking a gap year to save the trees, the whales, or the dates. You're an 80-year-old woman who has devoted her life to egg-laying platypuses and figuring out what the hell is up with that. In short, you're a traveler, not a tourist; like any good spy, you don't observe your surroundings—you become an active part of them.

Your mission, should you choose to accept it, is to study, volunteer, or work in France as laid out in the dossier—er, chapter—below. More general wisdom, including international organizations with a presence in many destinations and tips on how to pick the right program, is also accessible by logging onto the Beyond Tourism section of ◻www.letsgo.com. We leave the rest (when to go, whom to bring, and how many changes of underwear to pack) in your hands. This message will ▓**self-destruct** in five seconds. Good luck.

greatest hits

- **FOSTER YOUR FOODIE SIDE** at the planet's most prestigious culinary school in the world's most culinary city at the Cordon Bleu Paris Culinary Arts Institute (p. 387).
- **GET TO KNOW DELACROIX BETTER THAN HIS MOTHER DID** with some art history classes at L'ecole du Louvre (p. 387).
- **INDULGE YOUR INNER ARISTOCRAT** while paying tribute to the proleteriat by restoring castles and learning medieval masonry with the Club du Vieux Manoir (p. 389).

studying

We know, we know, it's become a cliché: the American college student heading off to France to discover Proust, Parisian men, and the perfect croissant. But there's a reason more than 15,000 students study abroad in France each year. Paris, obviously the most popular destination, provides a Mecca for the art and architecture-inclined with its world-famous cultural landmarks, while smaller cities make it easy to meet local students and practice your French. Dijon, Strasbourg, Nice, Aix-en-Provence, Grenoble, Tours, and Bordeaux are all fun university towns home to major universities. If you speak decent French, don't be afraid to enroll directly in the French university system. Navigating the bureaucracy of course enrollment can be a nightmare, and that first exposé oral may be terrifying, but there's no better way to immerse yourself in French life. Otherwise, there are dozens of American-run study-abroad programs, so you can make your fautes and faux-pas in the company of fellow foreigners.

visa information

If you're lucky enough to have an EU passport, stop reading and count your blessing. Non-EU citizens hoping to study abroad in France, on the other hand, must obtain a special student visa from the French consulate. The process of applying for and obtaining a visa can take time, so give yourself at least two and a half months. Short-stay visas are good for up to 90 days, but if you're studying abroad, chances are you'll be there at least a semester, in which case you'll need one of two long-stay visas. Prospective long-term travelers must fill out two to four applications—depending on the consulate—for the appropriate visa and provide a passport valid for at least three months after the student's last day in France, plus two extra passport photos. Additionally, students must give proof of enrollment in or admission to a French learning institute, a letter from the home university or institution certifying current registration as a student, a financial guarantee with a monthly allowance of US$600 per month during the intended stay, and proof of medical insurance. Finally, there is a visa application fee of €60 for short-stay visas and €99 for long-stay. When in France, students with long-stay visas must obtain a carte de séjour (residency permit) from the local Préfecture de Police; students should file to obtain the card as soon as possible upon arrival. They will be required to undergo a medical examination (including x-rays) in addition to providing proof of residency (if your name's not on the electicity/gas bill, the bill of your host family or landlord and a copy of their French identity card will do). You'll also need to bring two passport photos, proof of financial resources and €55, which is the cost of the carte de séjour.

UNIVERSITIES

The French higher education system operates very differently from the American system. Unlike in the States, where high school seniors agonize over SATs and college applications, any French student who has obtained their Baccalaureat is eligible to enroll in university. (The weeding-out process doesn't happen until later, when students who don't pass their final exams are forced to redo the previous year or just drop out.) Given that education is heavily subsidized (one year at the prestigious Sorbonne costs a mere €400) and that most students live at home rent-free throughout their college years, it's no surprise that almost everyone at least starts university.

International Programs

- **AMERICAN INSTITUTE FOR FOREIGN STUDY (AIFS):** With programs in 17 different countries and over 50,000 participants each year, AIFS is one of the oldest and largest cultural exchange organizations out there. In France, AIFS offers semester, year-long, and summer programs in Paris, Cannes, and Grenoble (term-time only) in both French and English. *(☎800-727-2437 🖳www.aifs.com $ Semester $13,695-16,495; summer $6495-8495.)*
- **COUNCIL ON INTERNATIONAL EDUCATIONAL EXCHANGE (CIEE):** With programs in Paris and Rennes, CIEE offers students a range of options in terms of length of stay (semester, year long, and summer programs), housing arrangements, and expected language experience. *(☎800-407-8839 🖳www.ciee.org $ Semester $13,800-16,800; three-week summer $3375, six-week $6550.)*
- **SCHOOL FOR INTERNATIONAL TRAINING (SIT) STUDY ABROAD:** Priding itself on its experiential, field-based approach, SIT offers a program based in Toulouse that encourages students to think about social issues in France and post-colonial relationships with the Francophone world. Students live with local host families and take courses in French at the Institut Catholique de Toulouse. The program also requires students to take a seminar on Community and Social Change and to complete a Community Service Program. Open to students with advanced-beginner and intermediate level French ability. *(☎888-272-7881 🖳www.sit.edu/studyabroad $ Semester $20,705.)*
- **ARCADIA UNIVERSITY:** Arcadia's semester study abroad program in France is based around an interdisciplinary seminar entitled "History, Politics, and Diplomacy of France and Europe" in which students are expected to develop an individual research project. The six-week summer program has a similar focus on "Intensive French and Politics: Economics, Diplomacy, and the European Union." Students are housed in residence dorms in Paris. *(☎866-927-2234 or 215-572-2901 🖳www.arcadia.edu/abroad $ Semester $16,990. Estimate does not include meals.)*
- **INSTITUTE FOR THE INTERNATIONAL EDUCATION OF STUDENTS:** IES offers a summer program in Arles, a semester or academic year program in Nantes, and summer, semester, and academic year programs in Paris. Business students can earn a Certificate in International Management by enrolling in a full-time master's program with French and international students. Otherwise, students take some of their classes on-site at the IES Abroad Center but are encouraged to take one or two courses at one of the French IES partner institutions. *(☎800-995-1750 or312-994-1750 🖳www.iesabroad.org $Semester $16,700-18,215; summer $6500-6675.)*
- **EXPERIMENTAL LEARNING INTERNATIONAL:** ELI's semester-long study and internship program, based in Paris, involves academic coursework, an internship where students work alongside French professionals, and a final research project. The goal is to help students begin to build a professional network in France in their area of interest. *(☎303-321-8278 🖳www.eliabroad.org $ Semester €6500.)*
- **CULTURAL EXPERIENCES ABROAD (CEA):** CEA offers summer, semester, trimester, short-term, or academic-year programs in Paris, Aix-en-Provence, Grenoble (in the French Alps), and the French Riviera. Most students live in shared apartments, but there is the option to "upgrade" to a homestay or independent living arrangement.*(☎800-266-4441 🖳www.gowithcea.com $ Fees range from $4395 for a 4-week session to $25,995 for an academic year.)*

- **CCIS STUDY ABROAD (CEA):** The College Consortium for International Studies (CCIS) is a partnership of colleges and universities that sponsors a number of study-abroad programs around the world. In France, students can choose between Aix-en-Provence (which offers an intensive studio art option), Avignon, Chambéry and Annecy (in the French alps), Nice, Paris, and Angers (summer only). *(☎800-453-6956 or 202-223-0330 🖳www.ccisabroad.org [$] Semester $6490-10,861; summer $2617-5484. Estimates do not include room and board and vary depending on length and location of program.)*

French Programs

- **CENTER FOR UNIVERSITY PROGRAMS ABROAD (CUPA):** CUPA specializes in study abroad exclusively in Paris. The program is geared toward those very comfortable in French; after a three-week orientation, students are enrolled directly in French universities and expected to do the same work as their Parisian peers. *(☎413-549-6960 🖳www.cupa-paris.org [$] Semester $16,950; academic year $23,250. Optional host family housing and meals $6450 per semester or $11,700/year.)*
- **MIDDLEBURY SCHOOLS ABROAD:** Open to students from all universities, Middlebury Schools Abroad are known for their rigorous immersion experience; all students take courses at one of Middlebury's partner universities and are required to sign a language pledge attesting that they will only speak French with one another. Independent housing is not permitted; students either live with local families or in French residence halls. Semester and year-long programs are offered in Bordeaux, Poitiers, and Paris. *(☎802-443-5745 🖳www.middlebury.edu/sa [$] Semester $11,200. Estimate does not include room and board.)*
- **COLUMBIA-PENN PROGRAM IN PARIS AT REID HALL:** The Columbia-Penn Program at Reid Hall offers students the choice of taking courses in French in-house at Reid Hall or in the French university system (including Sciences Po). All participants are required to take a course on French academic writing in the humanities and social sciences. *(☎212-854-2559 🖳www.columbia.edu/cu/ogp/index.html [$] Semester $16,300. Estimate does not include room and board.)*
- **VASSAR-WESLEYAN PROGRAM IN PARIS (VWPP):** Heavily populated by Vassar and Wesleyan folk (read: leggings and scarves a must), the Vassar-Wesleyan program is neverthertheless open to students from all colleges and universities for semester or full-year study abroad. Students stay with host families and take most of their courses in-house at the Reid Hall facility, but are encouraged to take at least one course at one of the French partner universities. Fall semester begins with a two-week intensive language program in Bordeaux, while spring semester orientation takes place in Paris.*(☎860-685-2550 🖳www.wesleyan.edu/ois/programs/paris/intro.html [$] Semester $23,800. Fee includes most meals.)*

LANGUAGE SCHOOLS

As renowned novelist Gustave Flaubert once said, "Language is a cracked kettle on which we beat out tunes for bears to dance to." While we at Let's Go have absolutely no clue what he was talking about, we do know that the following are good resources for learning French.

- **ALLIANCE FRANÇAISE:** The Alliance Française offers classes for all levels, from beginner to advanced, as well as evening workshops on topics like pronunciation or written French and professional courses on Business French, Legal French, Tourism French, and Medical French for those looking to work in France long-term. Private and group lessons and self-guided learning courses using the Multimedia Resource Center are also available. *(101 bl. Raspail ☎+33 1 42 84 90 00 🖳www.ccfs-sorbonne.fr)*

- **COURS DE CIVILISATION FRANÇAISE DE LA SORBONNE:** A popular option for Americans looking for an excuse to be eligible for a student visa, the Cours de Civilisation Française de la Sorbonne offers sessions ranging in length from three to 12 weeks. Regular language and civilization classes meet 12hr. per week, intensive courses meet 25hr. per week. (☎+33 1 44 10 77 00 ▣www.ccfs-sorbonne.fr)
- **EUROCENTRES:** With sites in Paris, La Rochelle, and Amboise, Eurocentres offers French classes mostly in the mornings, with an option for Business French. The schools all provide recreation rooms and free internet access, and organize a variety of outings and social activities.(☎+41 1 44 85 50 40 ▣www.eurocentres.com)

CULINARY SCHOOLS

CORDON BLEU PARIS CULINARY ARTS INSTITUTE

8 rue Léon Delhomme, Paris ☎+33 1 53 68 22 50 ▣www.cordonbleu.edu

There's no more prestigious training academy for the serious aspiring chef than the original Paris branch of the Cordon Bleu. Certificate and degree programs available. More tourist-friendly options include two- to four-hour workshops and short courses that range in length from two days to one week. Price of a one-day taste of Provence workshop? €175. Bragging rights? Priceless.

PROMENADES GOURMANDES

187 rue du Temple, Paris ☎+33 1 48 04 56 84 ▣www.fmeunier.com

If the corporate Cordon Bleu is too impersonal for you, Paule Caillat's cooking classes and market tours are just the opposite. Capped at eight students, classes are scheduled on request and take place in a home kitchen in the Marais in either French or English. Every class includes a three-course lunch that you will have prepared and a cheese tasting.

ⓈHalf-day cooking classes €270 per person.

ART SCHOOLS AND COURSES

L'ÉCOLE DU LOUVRE

Palais du Louvre, porte Jaujard, Paris ☎+33 1 55 35 18 35 ▣www.ecoledulouvre.fr

Installed in the Louvre in 1882, the École du Louvre, dedicated to "making the Louvre into a living center of study," offers degree-granting undergraduate, graduate, and post-graduate classes in art history and museum studies, as well as evening and summer classes and an art auctioneer training program. Looking for less of a commitment? Every Monday, Tuesday, and Thursday from 6:30-7:45pm, the École organizes free lectures by academics, curators, and other museum professionals.

MUSÉE DES ARTS DÉCORATIFS

111 rue de Rivoli, Paris ☎+33 1 44 55 59 02 ▣www.lesartsdecoratifs.fr

The Musée des Arts décoratifs offers year-long day and evening classes and intensive holiday workshops in studio art. Topics range from the conventional (oil painting, sculpture, figure drawing) to the more esoteric (trompe l'oeil painting, engraving, and comic book-making).

FONDATION CARTIER POUR L'ART CONTEMPORAIN

261 boulevard Raspail, Paris ☎+33 1 42 18 56 67 ▣www.fondation.cartier.fr

The Fondation Cartier, housed in a unique Jean Nouvel building, offers a variety of different courses designed to initiate students in modern and contemporary art. Classes take place on Tuesdays from 7:30-9pm, and are organized into eight-week sessions. Students can choose between 13 different sessions on topics such as architecture, photography, fashion, design, and gardening.

volunteering

"When good Americans die, they go to Paris," Oscar Wilde once famously said. Well, we're here to help you earn your place in French heaven by being a "good" American tourist and leaving the country in better shape than you found it.

Despite being the fifth-richest country in the world by GDP, France nonetheless faces a variety of social issues, and so there is no shortage of aid organizations looking for volunteers. Whether you want to devote yourself to wildlife conservation, raise awareness about AIDS among urban youth, or take part in archaeological restoration, France abounds with organizations and volunteer opportunities to suit every interest and commitment level.

If you're interested in part-time or relatively short-term volunteer work, get in touch with one of the volunteer centers listed below. For travelers looking for a much longer or more immersive volunteer experience, volunteer companies are often the way to go, especially for younger or less-experienced travelers looking for community and support. These parent organizations will charge a fee in most cases, but in exchange they will usually take care of all the logistical details, arrange your airfare, room, and board if necessary, and provide you with a group environment. Of these, the **International Volunteer Program** *(www.ivpsf.org)*, which places volunteers in French non-profits for six weeks during the summer, and **Volunteers for Peace** *(www.vfp.org)*, which runs International Voluntary Service projects ranging from historic preservation work to AIDS/HIV education are among the best. Websites like www.transitionsabroad.com, www.volunteerabroad.com, www.volunteer international.org, and www.idealist.org are also great places to start your search for jobs, internships, or volunteer opportunities abroad.

ENVIRONMENTAL WORK

- **CENTRES PERMANENTS D'INITIATIVES POUR L'ENVIRONNEMENT (CPIE):** With 80 offices throughout France as well as in Corsica, Guadeloupe, Guyana, Martinique, and Réunion, CPIE works on environmental education for sustainable development. *(26 rue Beaubourg, Paris ☎+33 1 44 61 75 35 🖳www.cpie.fr)*
- **ORGANISATION MONDIALE DE PROTECTION DE L'ENVIRONNEMENT:** The French branch of the World Wildlife Fund, the Organisation Mondiale de Protection de l'Environnement offers a variety of volunteer opportunities on environmental issues like climate change and the protection of endangered species. *(1 Carrefour de Longchamp, Paris ☎+33 1 55 25 84 84 🖳www.wwf.fr)*
- **WORLDWIDE OPPORTUNITIES ON ORGANIC FARMS (WWOOF) FRANCE:** "WWOOFING" has become increasingly popular in recent years for budget travelers. Volunteers work on the farm in exchange for free food, accommodation, and opportunities to learn first-hand about sustainable agriculture and organic farming techniques. In order to WWOOF in France, you must join the French WWOOF organization. Subscription requires purchase of a booklet listing the over 300 host farms. *(🖳www.wwoof.fr [$]Booklet €15 in electronic format, €25 printed.)*

beyond tourism

YOUTH AND COMMUNITY

GROUPEMENT ÉTUDIANT NATIONAL D'ENSEIGNEMENT AUX PERSONNES INCARCERÉES (GENEPI)

12 rue Charles Fourier, Paris ☎+33 1 45 88 37 00 🖳www.genepi.fr

Founded by students after the violent riots over the prison system in the early 70s, GENEPI pairs student volunteers with inmates in French prisons to promote social rehabilitation.

SECOURS POPULAIRE FRANÇAIS

9-11 rue Froissart, Paris   ☎+33 1 44 78 21 00 📧www.secourspopulaire.asso.fr

A humanitarian organization created in 1945, Secours Populaire Français helps to combat poverty by providing food, clothing, health care, and temporary housing and organizing sporting and cultural activities for poor children and families.

CONSERVATION AND ARCHAEOLOGY

CLUB DU VIEUX MANOIR

Ancienne Abbaye du Moncel, Pontpoint   ☎+33 44 72 33 98
📧www.clubduvieuxmanoir.asso.fr

Club du Vieux Manoir arranges projects of various lengths to restore castles and churches and teach young people about the importance of protecting the *patrimoine national*.

i   *Most programs 14+* Ⓢ *Membership and insurance fee €16 per year. Program fee €14 per day, includes food and lodging.*

LA SABRANENQUE RESTORATION PROJECTS

rue de la Tour de l'Oume, St. Victor la Coste   ☎+33 1 46 88 37 00
📧www.sabranenque.com

Volunteers live in a small town in Provence and participate in the preservation of Mediterranean architecture, learning techniques such as stone masonry, stone cutting, and drystone walling. Afternoons often include hikes in the countryside or visits to nearby towns.

i   *One-week "visit" sessions and two-week extended sessions.*

MINISTRY OF CULTURE, SOUS-DIRECTION DE L'ARCHÉOLOGIE

3 rue de Valois, Paris Cedex   ☎01 +33 1 40 15 77 01 📧www.oulturo.gouv.fr

This government department that oversees archaeological digs on French soil publishes a list of summer excavations that accept volunteers in May.

REMPART

1, rue des Guillemites, Paris   ☎+33 1 42 71 96 55 www.rempart.com

A union of nearly 170 nonprofit organizations throughout France that accept volunteers for restoring historic sites and monuments, including military heritage sites, religious heritage sites, civic heritage sites, industrial heritage sites, and natural heritage sites.

i   *18+. Basic French knowledge recommended.* Ⓢ *Room and board vary by camp. Registration fee covers accident insurance.*

working

If you're looking to stay in France for longer than just a vacation, you'll probably need to find a way to *gagne de l'argent*. As with volunteering, work opportunities tend to fall into two categories. Some travelers want long-term jobs that allow them to integrate into a community, while others seek out short-term jobs to finance the next leg of their travels. With France's 7.4% unemployment rate, long-term jobs are currently hard to come by. Travelers without EU citizenship face a particular challenge when searching for a job in France: only employers who cannot find qualified workers in the EU may petition to bring in a long-term worker who is not an EU citizen. If you're undeterred by the less-than-welcoming attitude toward foreign workers, you may want to try a job that requires English-language skills, as bilingual candidates have a better chance of finding work. Working as an au pair or teaching English are both popular long-term employment options. If you're in the market for a short-term stint, be on the lookout for a service or agricultural job.

Classified advertisements in newspapers and online are good resources for international job-seekers. Agence Nationale pour l'Emploi (⊠*www.anpe.fr*) has listings for many skilled and unskilled jobs alike, while Agence pour l'Emploi de Cadres (⊠*www.apec.fr*) catalogues professional job listings. Michael Page (⊠*www.michaelpage.fr*) is another job recruiting agency with offices in major French cities as well as international locations. The American Chamber of Commerce (⊠*www.amchamfrance.org*), located in Paris, fosters Franco-American business relations, and is currently generating an online job and internship directory. Note that working abroad often requires a special work visa.

more visa info

EU citizens have the right to work in France without a visa, and can easily obtain a carte de séjour (residency permit) by presenting a passport, proof of employment, and other identification documents. Visit www.infomobil.org for a complete list of requirements. Non-EU citizens hoping to work in France for less than 90 days must apply for an Autorisation Provisoire de Travail at a local branch of Direction Départementale du Travail, de l'Emploi et de la Formation Professionnelle (D.D.T.E.F.P.). A passport and proof of short-term employment are necessary to secure authorization; a short-term, or Schengen visa *(US$82)* is also sometimes required. Non-EU citizens wishing to work in France for more than 90 days must have an offer of employment authorized by the French Ministry of Labor (www.travail.gouv.fr/) before applying for a long-stay visa *(US$136)* through their local French consulate. Within 8 days of arrival in France, holders of long-stay visas must apply for a carte de séjour. International students hoping to secure a job must possess a carte de séjour d'étudiant (student residency card) and apply for an Autorisation Provisoire de Travail at a D.D.T.E.F.P. office. Students in France are permitted to work up to 19½hr. per week during the academic year, and full time during summer and holidays. Special rules apply for au pairs and teaching assistants; see www.consulfrance-washington.org for more info.

LONG-TERM WORK

As we mentioned, it can be tricky finding long-term work in France. American firms, however, are a more likely bet. A listing of American firms in France is available for purchase American Chamber of Commerce in France. Go to www.amchamfrance.org or e-mail amchamfrance@amchamfrance.org for more information.

Teaching English

Teaching in French public schools and universities is largely restricted to French citizens. One of the only exceptions is the French government's foreign language assistants program, coordinated by the French embassy in your home country. Teaching assistants commit to teaching for 7-9 months in public schools throughout metropolitan France, as well as overseas in Guadeloupe, Martinique, French Guiana, and Reunion. Assistants work 12 hours per week in an elementary school (ages 8-11) or secondary school (ages 11-18). The salary is approximately €780 per month, which includes mandatory health insurance and French social security. No prior teaching experience necessary, but some background in French language is required. Applicants must be 20-29 years of age and have completed a bachelor's degree. Interested American citizens and permanent residents should contact the embassy in Washington at least six months prior to the start of the academic year.

For more information, visit www.ambafrance-us.org.

It is also sometimes possible to find jobs independently, but in most cases you'll need a Teaching English as a Foreign Language (TEFL) certificate. ESL Base (✉www. eslbase.com) posts notices for schools seeking native English speakers as teachers, then you contact the school directly. Full-time and part-time opportunities.

University fellowship programs can be a great way to find a teaching job. Some people have also found jobs by contacting schools directly. If you want to try your luck, the best time to do so is several weeks before the start of the academic year.

Au Pair Work

Au pairs in France are typically paid between €50 and €75 per week. Much of the au pair experience depends on the family with which you are placed. The agencies below are a good starting point for looking for employment. There is also a database for au pair agencies at www.europa-pages.com/au_pair/france.html.

- **ACCUEIL INTERNATIONAL SERVICES** (☎+33 1 39 73 04 98 ✉www.accueil-international.com)
- **AGENCE AU PAIR FLY** (☎+33 3 34 37 65 70 83 ✉www.aupairfly.com)
- **INTEREXCHANGE** (☎1-212-924-0446 ✉www.interexchange.org).
- **CHILDCARE INTERNATIONAL** (☎+44 20 89 06 31 16 ✉www.childint.co.uk)
- **INTERNATIONAL AU PAIR ASSOCIATION** (☎+31 20 421 2800 ✉www.iapa.org)

SHORT-TERM WORK

Scouting the flyers at famed Parisian English-language bookstore Shakespeare and Co. can be a great way for English speakers to find short-term jobs like tutoring or babysitting. Websites like www.craigslist.com and www.franglo.com are good virtual equivalents.

- **EASY EXPAT**: Easy-to-navigate with summer, seasonal, and short-term jobs as well as volunteer opportunities and internships. Options range from teaching ski lessons to working at Disneyland Paris. (✉www.easyexpat.com/paris_en.htm)
- **FÉDÉRATION UNIE DES AUBERGES DE JEUNESSE:** Offers short-term work in member youth hostels, from catering to reception. Submit application to individual hostels. (☎+33 1 40 15 77 81 ✉www.fuaj.org)au pair sites

tell the world

If your friends are tired of hearring about that time you saved a baby orangutan in Indonesia, there's clearly only one thing to do: get new friends. Find them at our website, www.letsgo.com, where you can post your study-, volunteer-, or work-abroad stories for other, more appreciative community members to read.

working · short-term work

INDEX

a

airlines 365
Aix-en-Provence 266
  accommodations 267
  arts and culture 272
  essentials 273
  food 270
  nightlife 271
  orientation 267
  sights 268
ampitheater 264
Antibes 314
  accommodations 314
  beaches 318
  essentials 320
  food 318
  nightlife 319
  orientation 314
  shopping 320
  sights 317
Arcachon 210
  accommodations 210
  essentials 211
  food 211
  orientation 210
  sights 211
Arc de Triomphe 44
Arles 262
  accommodations 263
  essentials 266
  food 265
  nightlife 265
  orientation 263
  sights 264
art schools and courses 387
Avignon 250
  accommodations 250
  essentials 252
  food 251
  nightlife 252
  orientation 250
  sights 251

b

Basilique Saint Sernin 217
Bastille Prison 48

Bayeux 144
  accommodations 144
  essentials 146
  food 146
  orientation 144
  sights 145
Bayeux Tapestry 145
beaches
  Antibes 318
  Cassis 254
  Dune du Pyla 211
  Juan-les-Pins 331
  Marseille 241
  Monaco 298
  Nice 285
  Saint-Raphaël 350
Belle Époque 377
Beyond Tourism 383
Biarritz 204
  accommodations 205
  essentials 208
  food 206
  nightlife 207
  orientation 204
  sights 205
Bibliotheque Nationale 50
Biot 327
  accommodations 327
  essentials 329
  food 329
  nightlife 329
  sights 328
Blois 102
  accommodations 102
  châteaux 104
  essentials 106
  food 105
  nightlife 106
  orientation 102
  sights 103
Bordeaux 192
  accommodations 192
  arts and culture 198
  essentials 198
  food 196
  nightlife 197
  orientation 192
  sights 194

Bordeaux and Wine Country 191
Brittany and Normandy 121

c

cabaret 79
Caen 139
  accommodations 139
  essentials 143
  food 142
  nightlife 143
  orientation 139
  sights 140
Cagnes-sur-Mer 321
  accommodations 321
  essentials 323
  food 322
  sights 322
Cannes 335
  accommodations 335
  essentials 342
  food 339
  nightlife 340
  orientation 335
  sights 338
Cassis 253
  accommodations 253
  beaches 254
  essentials 255
  food 254
  nightlife 255
  orientation 253
catacombs 51
cell phones 368
Centre Pompidou 38
Cézanne, Paul 269, 380
Champs de Mars 42
Champs-Élysées 45
Charlemagne 374
châteaux
  Amboise 105
  Âzay-le-rideau 113
  Chambord 104
  Château de blois 104
  Chenonceau 112
  Cheverny 104

index

Germingy-des-Prés (Germingy)
98
Langeais 115
Sully-Sur-Loire 98
Ussé 114
Villandry 113
Cimetière du Père Lachaise
55
climate 369
consulates 361
Côte d'Azur 313
culinary schools 387
customs and etiquette 378

d

D-Day Beaches 146
Arromanches 140
Gold Beach 149
Juno Beach 148
Omaha Beach 148
Pointe du Hoc 147
de Gaulle, Charles 378

e

Edict of Nantes 376
Eiffel Tower 42
Enlightenment, the 379

f

Fitzgerald, F. Scott 380
Flaubert, Gustave 379
food and drink 381
French history 373
French Revolution 376

g

Gaul 374
Grasse 343
accommodations 343
arts and culture 347
essentials 347
food 345
nightlife 346
orientation 343
sights 344
Graves 204
Grenoble 181

accommodations 181
arts and culture 188
essentials 189
food 185
nightlife 187
orientation 181
sights 183
the great outdoors 184
guignol 81

h

Hemingway, Ernest 380
Hugo, Victor 379
Hundred Year's War 375

i

Îles des Lérins 326
essentials 327
food 326
sights 326
Impressionism 380

j

Jardin du Luxembourg 41
Jim Morrison 20
Juan-les-Pins 330
accommodations 330
beaches 331
essentials 334
festivals 334
food 332
nightlife 333
orientation 330

l

La Ciotat 256
accommodations 256
essentials 259
food 258
nightlife 258
orientation 256
sights 257
language pronunciation 371
language schools 386
Loire Valley 91
Louis XIV 376
Louvre 34
Lyon 164

accommodations 165
arts and culture 178
essentials 179
food 172
nightlife 176
orientation 164
sights 169

m

Marie Antoinette 376
Marseille 234
accommodations 235
arts and culture 246
essentials 248
food 242
great outdoors 241
nightlife 244
orientation 234
shopping 246
sights 239
Matisse, Henri 381
measurements 371
Médoc 204
Menton 307
accommodations 308
essentials 311
festivals 311
food 309
nightlife 310
orientation 308
sights 309
Monaco 293
accommodations 294
beaches 298
essentials 303
food 298
grand prix 302
nightlife 300
orientation 293
sights 295
Mona Lisa 35
Monet, Claude 380
Mont St. Michel 136
accommodations 137
essentials 138
food 138
orientation 137
sights 137
Monte Carlo (casino) 297
Montpellier 223
accommodations 224

index

arts and culture 230
essentials 231
food 227
nightlife 229
orientation 223
shopping 230
sights 226
Musée d'Orsay 43
Musée Fabre 226

n

Napoleon Bonaparte 377
Napoleon III 377
Nazi occupation 377
Nice 276
accommodations 280
arts and culture 290
essentials 291
food 285
nightlife 288
orientation 276
sights 282
Normandy (Brittany and
Normandy) 121
Normans 375
Notre Dame 30

o

obelisk 46
opera 80
Grand Théâtre Bordeaux 198
Orange 259
accommodations 260
essentials 262
food 261
nightlife 262
orientatin 259
sights 260
Orléans 92
accommodations 94
arts and culture 101
châteaux 98
essentials 101
food 98
nightlife 100
orientation 92
sights 96

p

Paris 13
accommodations 21
arts and culture 79
essentials 84
excursions 88
food 57
nightlife 68
orientation 14
shopping 81
sights 30
phone cards 368
phrasebook 371
Picasso, Pablo 381
Place de la Concorde 46
plague 375
Pompidou, Georges 378
Provence 233

r

rail pass 366
Realism 379
Reign of Terror 377
Renaissance 380
Rennes 122
accommodations 122
arts and culture 128
essentials 129
food 125
nightlife 127
orientation 122
shopping 129
sights 124
Renoir, Pierre-Auguste 380
Rhône-Alpes 163
Robespierre, Maximillien 377
Roman Empire 374
Roman ruins
Arles 264
Romanticism 379
Rouen 130
accommodations 131
essentials 135
food 134
nightlife 135
orientation 131
sights 132

s

Sacré-Coeur 53
safety and health 363
Saint-Émilion 200
accommodations 200
essentials 203
food 201
orientation 200
sights 201
vineyards 203
Saint Louis IX 375
St-Raphaël 348
accommodations 348
beaches 350
essentials 352
food 351
nightlife 352
orientation 348
sights 349
St-Tropez 353
accommodations 354
arts and culture 356
essentials 357
food 354
nightlife 355
orientation 353
shopping 357
Sartre, Jean-Paul 380
Strasbourg 151
accommodations 152
arts and culture 160
essentials 161
food 154
nightlife 158
orientation 152
shopping 161
sights 154
student visa 384
study abroad 384
French programs 386
international programs 385
Sun King 376
Surrealism 377

t

taxes 362
theater 79
Toulouse 214
accommodations 214

arts and culture 220
essentials 222
food 218
nightlife 219
orientation 214
shopping 221
sights 217
Toulouse and Montpellier 213
Tours 107
accommodations 107
arts and culture 119
châteaux 112
essentials 120
food 115
nightlife 118
orientation 107
sights 110
trains 366
train stations
Aix-en-Provence 274
Marseille 249
Rennes 130
Rouen 136
Tuileries 36

V

Vence 323
accommodations 323
arts and culture 325
essentials 325
food 325
sights 324
Venus de Milo 35
Versailles 88
Vichy France 378
Villefranche-sur-Mer 304
accommodations 305
essentials 307
food 306
nightlife 306
sights 305
vineyards
Château Villemaurine Cardinal 203
visas 360
Voltaire 379
volunteer opportunities 388

W

Wars of Religion 375
Waterloo 377
Wi-Fi 367
William the Conqueror 375
wine country 191
wiring money 362
work abroad 389
work permits 360
work visa 390
World War I 377
World War II 377

index

MAP INDEX

map index

Antibes	316
Bordeaux	193
Cannes	336
Côte d'Azur	315
Grenoble	182
Loire Valley	93
Lyon	166-167
Marseille	236-237
Monaco and Monte Carlo	296
Montpellier	224
Nice	278-279
Nice and Monaco	277
Normandy	132
Paris Neighborhoods	16-17
Provence	235
Toulouse	215
Wine Country	202

MAP LEGEND

▪	Sight/Service	🏰	Castle	💻	Internet Cafe	♣	Police
✈	Airport	⛪	Church	📗	Library	✉	Post Office
⌂	Arch/Gate	🚩	Consulate/Embassy	Ⓜ Ⓜ	Metro Station	🎿	Skiing
$	Bank	✝	Convent/Monastery	⛰	Mountain	✡	Synagogue
🏖	Beach	⚓	Ferry Landing	🕌	Mosque	☎	Telephone Office
🚌	Bus Station	(347)	Highway Sign	🏛	Museum	🎭	Theater
✪	Capital City	✚	Hospital	℞	Pharmacy	ⓘ	Tourist Office
						🚂	Train Station

The Let's Go compass always points NORTH.

········· Pedestrian Zone
▩▩▩▩▩ Stairs

Park   Water   Beach

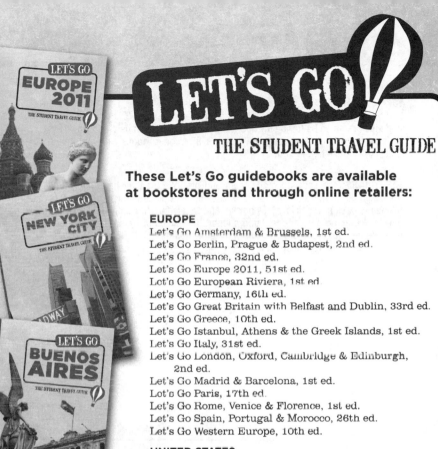

LET'S GO!

THE STUDENT TRAVEL GUIDE

These Let's Go guidebooks are available at bookstores and through online retailers:

EUROPE
Let's Go Amsterdam & Brussels, 1st ed.
Let's Go Berlin, Prague & Budapest, 2nd ed.
Let's Go France, 32nd ed.
Let's Go Europe 2011, 51st ed.
Let's Go European Riviera, 1st ed.
Let's Go Germany, 16th ed.
Let's Go Great Britain with Belfast and Dublin, 33rd ed.
Let's Go Greece, 10th ed.
Let's Go Istanbul, Athens & the Greek Islands, 1st ed.
Let's Go Italy, 31st ed.
Let's Go London, Oxford, Cambridge & Edinburgh, 2nd ed.
Let's Go Madrid & Barcelona, 1st ed.
Let's Go Paris, 17th ed.
Let's Go Rome, Venice & Florence, 1st ed.
Let's Go Spain, Portugal & Morocco, 26th ed.
Let's Go Western Europe, 10th ed.

UNITED STATES
Let's Go Boston, 6th ed.
Let's Go New York City, 19th ed.
Let's Go Roadtripping USA, 4th ed.

MEXICO, CENTRAL & SOUTH AMERICA
Let's Go Buenos Aires, 2nd ed.
Let's Go Central America, 10th ed.
Let's Go Costa Rica, 5th ed.
Let's Go Costa Rica, Nicaragua & Panama, 1st ed.
Let's Go Guatemala & Belize, 1st ed.
Let's Go Yucatán Peninsula, 1st ed.

ASIA & THE MIDDLE EAST
Let's Go Israel, 5th ed.
Let's Go Thailand, 5th ed.

ACKNOWLEDGMENTS

TERESA THANKS: Veggie Planet pizzas and Petsi Pies coffee, Liza Flum's kitchen and bootleg TV and the rickety machines at the Central Square Y. I thank Joe Gaspard and my pod-mates for having my back, and my parents, bad music, and David Foster Wallace for getting me through. My uncle's 80s comic books and my grandpa's Chicago sundaes helped too.

JOE THANKS: the Let's Go office team and his RWs for their hard work. Special thanks go out to the Starbucks staff for keeping me well caffeinated, to Bolt Bus for taking me back to Dix Hills, to my brother and sisters for always being down to party, and to my mother for her continued support. The ladies of Harem Pod never failed to make me laugh, even when I was pulling my hair out. Lady Gaga should also be thanked for her part in keeping me happy; we could definitely have a bad romance.

DIRECTOR OF PUBLISHING   Ashley R. Laporte
EXECUTIVE EDITOR   Nathaniel Rakich
PRODUCTION AND DESIGN DIRECTOR   Sara Plana
PUBLICITY AND MARKETING DIRECTOR   Joseph Molimock
MANAGING EDITORS   Charlotte Alter, Daniel C. Barbero, Marykate Jasper, Iya Megre
TECHNOLOGY PROJECT MANAGERS   Daniel J. Choi, C. Alexander Tremblay
PRODUCTION ASSOCIATES   Rebecca Cooper, Melissa Niu
FINANCIAL ASSOCIATE   Louis Caputo

DIRECTOR OF IT   Yasha Iravantchi
PRESIDENT   Meagan Hill
GENERAL MANAGER   Jim McKellar

ABOUT LET'S GO

THE STUDENT TRAVEL GUIDE

Let's Go publishes the world's favorite student travel guides, written entirely by Harvard students. Armed with pens, notebooks, and a few changes of clothes stuffed into their backpacks, our student researchers go across continents, through time zones, and above expectations to seek out invaluable travel experiences for our readers. Because we are a completely student-run company, we have a unique perspective on how students travel, where they want to go, and what they're looking to do when they get there. If your dream is to grab a machete and forge through the jungles of Costa Rica, we can take you there. If you'd rather bask in the Riviera sun at a beachside cafe, we'll set you a table. In short, we write for readers who know that there's more to travel than tour buses. To keep up, visit our website, www.letsgo. com, where you can sign up to blog, post photos from your trips, and connect with the Let's Go community.

TRAVELING BEYOND TOURISM

We're on a mission to provide our readers with sharp, fresh coverage packed with socially responsible opportunities to go beyond tourism. Each guide's Beyond Tourism chapter shares ideas about responsible travel, study abroad, and how to give back to the places you visit while on the road. To help you gain a deeper connection with the places you travel, our fearless researchers scour the globe to give you the heads-up on both world-renowned and off-the-beaten-track opportunities. We've also opened our pages to respected writers and scholars to hear their takes on the countries and regions we cover, and asked travelers who have worked, studied, or volunteered abroad to contribute first-person accounts of their experiences.

FIFTY-ONE YEARS OF WISDOM

Let's Go has been on the road for 51 years and counting. We've grown a lot since publishing our first 20-page pamphlet to Europe in 1960, but five decades and 60 titles later, our witty, candid guides are still researched and written entirely by students on shoestring budgets who know that train strikes, stolen luggage, food poisoning, and marriage proposals are all part of a day's work. Meanwhile, we're still bringing readers fresh new features, such as a student-life section with advice on how and where to meet students from around the world; a revamped, user-friendly layout for our listings; and greater emphasis on the experiences that make travel abroad a rite of passage for readers of all ages. And, of course, this year's 16 titles—including five brand-new guides—are still brimming with editorial honesty, a commitment to students, and our irreverent style.

THE LET'S GO COMMUNITY

More than just a travel guide company, Let's Go is a community that reaches from our headquarters in Cambridge, MA, all across the globe. Our small staff of dedicated student editors, writers, and tech nerds comes together because of our shared passion for travel and our desire to help other travelers get the most out of their experience. We love it when our readers become part of the Let's Go community as well—when you travel, drop us a postcard (67 Mt. Auburn St., Cambridge, MA 02138, USA), send us an email (feedback@letsgo.com), or sign up on our website (www. letsgo.com) to tell us about your adventures and discoveries.

For more information, updated travel coverage, and news from our researcher team, visit us online at www.letsgo.com.

THANKS TO OUR SPONSOR

- **HOTEL DU LION D'OR.** 5 rue de la Sourdiere, 75001 Paris. ☎33(0)1 42 60 79 04. ✉www.hotelduliondor.com.

HELPING LET'S GO. If you want to share your discoveries, suggestions, or corrections, please drop us a line. We appreciate every piece of correspondence, whether a postcard, a 10-page email, or a coconut. Visit Let's Go at **www.letsgo.com** or send an email to:

feedback@letsgo.com, subject: "Let's Go France"

Address mail to:

Let's Go France, 67 Mount Auburn St., Cambridge, MA 02138, USA

In addition to the invaluable travel advice our readers share with us, many are kind enough to offer their services as researchers or editors. Unfortunately, our charter enables us to employ only currently enrolled Harvard students.

Maps © Let's Go and Avalon Travel
Design Support by Jane Musser, Sarah Juckniess, Tim McGrath

Distributed by Publishers Group West.
Printed in Canada by Friesens Corp.

ISBN-13: 978-1-59880-703-5

Thirty-second edition
10 9 8 7 6 5 4 3 2 1

Let's Go France is written by Let's Go Publications, 67 Mt. Auburn St., Cambridge, MA 02138, USA.

Let's Go® and the LG logo are trademarks of Let's Go, Inc.

quick reference

YOUR GUIDE TO LET'S GO ICONS

☎	Phone numbers	⊘	Not wheelchair-accessible	❄	Has A/C
▣	Websites	((ụ))	Has internet access	⚛	Directions
💳	Takes credit cards	☂	Has outdoor seating	*i*	Other hard info
🚫	Cash only	▼	Is GLBT or GLBT-friendly	Ⓢ	Prices
♿	Wheelchair-accessible	🍸	Serves alcohol	🕐	Hours

PRICE RANGES

Let's Go includes price ranges, marked by icons ❶ through ❺, in accommodations and food listings. For an expanded explanation, see the chart in How To Use This Book.

FRANCE	❶	❷	❸	❹	❺
ACCOMMODATIONS	up to €25	€25-€40	€40-€60	€60-€80	€80 or above
FOOD	up to €15	€15-€25	€25-€35	€35-€45	€45 or above

IMPORTANT PHONE NUMBERS

EMERGENCY: POLICE ☎17, FIRE ☎18, MEDICAL EMERGENCY ☎15			
European emergency	☎112	Directory assistance	☎118 218
English-language crisis line	☎01 47 23 80 80	SNCF train reservations and information	☎08 92 30 83 08

To call France from home or to call home from France, dial the international dialing prefix (from Australia ☎0011; Canada or the US ☎011; New Zealand, France, or other European countries ☎00) + country code for the country you're calling (Australia 61; Canada or the US 1; Ireland 353; the UK 44; France 33) + area code (omit initial zeroes if calling from abroad) + local number.

USEFUL FRENCH PHRASES

ENGLISH	FRENCH	PRONUNCIATION
Hello!/Hi!	Bonjour!	bohn-jhoor
Do you speak English?	Parlez-vous anglais?	par-lay voo ong-lay
Yes.	Oui	wee
No.	Non	nohn
Help!	Au secours!	oh sek-oor
I'm lost	Je suis perdu(e)	jh'swee perh-doo
I don't understand	Je ne comprends pas	jh'ne kom-prahn pa

TEMPERATURE CONVERSIONS

°CELSIUS	-5	0	5	10	15	20	25	30	35	40
°FAHRENHEIT	23	32	41	50	59	68	77	86	95	104

MEASUREMENT CONVERSIONS

1 inch (in.) = 25.4mm	1 millimeter (mm) = 0.039 in.
1 foot (ft.) = 0.305m	1 meter (m) = 3.28 ft.
1 mile (mi.) = 1.609km	1 kilometer (km) = 0.621 mi.
1 pound (lb.) = 0.454kg	1 kilogram (kg) = 2.205 lb.
1 gallon (gal.) = 3.785L	1 liter (L) = 0.264 gal.